STUDIES AND ESSAYS IN HONOR OF
ABRAHAM A. NEUMAN

STUDIES AND ESSAYS

IN HONOR OF

ABRAHAM A. NEUMAN

PRESIDENT, DROPSIE COLLEGE FOR HEBREW AND
COGNATE LEARNING, PHILADELPHIA

EDITED BY

MEIR BEN-HORIN
BERNARD D. WEINRYB
SOLOMON ZEITLIN

E. J. BRILL, LEIDEN
FOR THE DROPSIE COLLEGE, PHILADELPHIA
1962

PRINTED IN THE NETHERLANDS BY E. J. BRILL LEIDEN

CONTENTS

v

vi CONTENTS

INTRODUCTION

By Solomon Zeitlin

THE GOVERNORS and the faculty of Dropsie College present this Jubilee Volume as a tribute to Doctor Abraham A. Neuman in recognition of his distinguished service during the two decades of his presidency and in observance of his seventieth birthday. Thirty-three scholars, Jews and Christians, from different countries and continents, have contributed essays and studies dealing with all periods of Jewish history. Some of the authors are his colleagues; others are former pupils who have risen to prominent positions in the scholarly world. The enthusiastic response of the contributors bespeaks the position of honor and esteem which Doctor Neuman holds both as President of Dropsie College and as a scholar.

Doctor Neuman's book on *The Jews in Spain*, published in two volumes in 1942, is a monumental work in which, for the first time in America, Jewish historiography emerges as a science. The old school of history writing was based on the German *jüdische Wissenschaft*. Hitherto Jewish historiography consisted of chronicles relating important events in Jewish life, persecutions, pogroms or edicts issued against them by popes and kings and lesser authorities. This type of history was written to impress the readers ideologically or to play upon their emotions. Ancient Greek historians set an example for it and were taken to task by Polybius (208-123 BCE) who observed that "an historical author should not write to thrill his readers by such exaggerated pictures, nor should he, like a tragic poet, try to imagine the probable utterances of his characters." Polybius maintained that an historian should "simply record what really happened and what really was said" (Book II, 56). Clearly, Polybius really refers to a chronographer, not to an historian.

Facts alone set forth in an historical work are meaningless, and require explanation. Events recited as facts do not occur in a vacuum. There must be causes which led to these events. On the other hand, events influence the future. Hence, it is the function of the historian no only to explain but also to give the causes of events and to trace their influence on subsequent events.

It has often been debated whether history is a science or an art, *i.e.*, literature. In fact, it is both. An historian must be well versed in the sources in order to evaluate the facts, yet he must also have vision, foresight. The latter alone would create literary fiction, but wide knowledge of the sources without vision would produce more of the chronographic class of literature than of historiography.

Doctor Neuman possesses both knowledge of the sources and the vision of their meaning. These qualifications are writ large in his main work, *The Jews in Spain*, and in all his writings. He demonstrates sovereign mastery of his sources and keen sensitivity to historical facts. The rabbinic responsa, with which he is concerned, are court decisions in epistolary form, formulated by eminent rabbis or leaders of the academies of learning in reply to written questions from colleagues, rabbinical judges, communal authorities or individual Jews. These questions and answers cover the entire field of Jewish daily life in Spain. The customs of the community, the ceremonies in synagogue and home, social manners, moral and spiritual values of the high and of the humble, as well as their demoralization, are dealt with. These dry responsa give a vivid picture of the rise and fall of Spanish Jewry, from the time of the reconquest of the Iberian peninsula by the Christians, down to the expulsion of the Jews from Spain. Doctor Neuman has drawn upon these responsa to the fullest extent.

Many of the responsa deal with halakot or legal decisions, which are mainly of rabbinic and academic value. Other responsa deal with the practical life of the people and hence are of considerable historical value. To distinguish between the academic and the practical requires precisely that deep knowledge, acumen, and ingenuity, which Doctor Neuman applies to his research. His book is a masterpiece revealing the two chief qualities of the historian—knowledge and vision.

The essays and monographs of Doctor Neuman present a distinct contribution to Jewish history. His opuscule, *Judaism*, is a comprehensive portrayal of the interdependence of Judaism and the Jewish people. The presentation, without avoiding even the hidden and obscure bypaths, enters adroitly into Jewish theology, dwelling on its problems and describing in detail the religious institutions of Judaism. This constitutes a full, scholarly and objective interpretation of the ideologies of the religious groups in American Jewry of today: orthodox, conservative, reform and emergent reconstructionism.

Doctor Neuman reveals his gift of interpretation in all his historical essays. One notes this in his treatment of the two sixteenth-century historians, Solomon ibn Verga, author of *Shebet Yehudah*, and Samuel Usque, a Marrano who escaped from Portugal and composed in his native Portuguese the *Consolation for the Tribulations of Israel*. Doctor Neuman clarifies the different approaches of these two historians to the problems and causes of Jewish persecutions. He shows how ibn Verga depicted the sufferings of the Jews against the social, economic and historical background of the times and how, on the other hand, Usque saw the sorrows of his people as a thread in the divine tapestry of history, which would change to brighter hues and culminate in great happiness. Doctor Neuman brilliantly demonstrates that these books are as valid for our time as they were when they were written.

Doctor Neuman has now completed his twentieth year as President of Dropsie College. This college bears the name of its founder, Moses Aaron Dropsie, who conceived the idea of a college to be devoted to all branches of Jewish and cognate learning. In his will, Dropsie left funds for the establishment of a college in Philadelphia, stipulating that it should be non-sectarian and non-theological, and that it should be open to all regardless of creed, race or sex. The College was founded two years after his death in 1907. The first president and architect of the college was Doctor Cyrus Adler. The chief purpose of the College was and is to train scholars and equip them for service in institutions of higher learning. It is the only Jewish institution of its kind in America. It seeks to achieve its goal by instruction and research in basic Jewish and cognate disciplines in an objective, non-partisan spirit of true scholarship.

When I came to Dropsie College in 1915, there were two professors on the faculty: Max L. Margolis, in Biblical Philology, and Henry Malter, in Rabbinics. In addition, there were three instructors: Benzion Halper, in Arabic, Jacob Hoschander, in Assyriology and Abraham A. Neuman, in History. When I first became acquainted with Doctor Neuman, he was young and full of enthusiasm about the teaching of history. Even then, as later in his books, he brought a new approach to the subject. History had been taught as chronography, presenting the facts just as they had occurred, and as chronology, setting forth the dates when the events occurred. Gifted as Doctor Neuman is in the writing of history, so is he in his classroom lectures. He presents the facts to the students, vividly bringing out the background of the events and elucidating the sequences which follow. He enchants the students with his eloquence and fervor, and his ingenious interpretation of history, making it a science as well as an part.

After the death of Doctor Cyrus Adler in 1940, Doctor Abraham A. Neuman became President of the College. He has adhered to the principles of academic freedom which were followed by his predecessor, and the College has not interfered with the views of the professors as long as they were based on scholarly research. On assuming the presidency, Doctor Neuman was not satisfied with the status quo of the College. He appointed new professors and added new departments—the School of Education and the Institute for Israel and the Middle East. He recognized the need of a Jewish graduate school of education on American soil. Since American Jewry is the largest Jewish community in the world, it was necessary that the discipline of Jewish educators rise to the highest academic level. Doctor Neuman perceived the deep need for a school of higher education, irrespective of their adherence to either orthodox, conservative or reform Judaism. The school was organized under the direction of the eminent Jewish educator, Doctor Leo L. Honor. Under his guidance, the school became a bastion of higher Jewish education in America.

The Middle East Institute was established in 1948. It was the first complete unit of Middle East studies in any American university, embracing history, anthropology, economics, religious, social and political institutions in the countries of the Middle East, with parallel courses relating to Israel.

With the addition of new departments and the enlargement of the faculty, the student body grew in numbers. As the saying went, "There is one post-graduate college in the United States which has more professors than students." This is no longer the case, for under the administration of Doctor Neuman, the enrollment of Jews, Christians and Moslems has greatly increased.

Graduates of Dropsie College serve as professors and administrative leaders in all the Jewish seminaries, in Christian seminaries, and in many universities throughout the United States and abroad. They hold positions as editors and leading educators, and have published many valuable works under the auspices of the College and otherwise.

Responsibility for the *Jewish Quarterly Review*, originally published in London, was accepted by Doctor Cyrus Adler, President of the College, in 1910. After his death, Doctor Neuman and I joined as editors. As a silent co-editor, I had been associated with the journal for many years before Doctor Adler's death.

On Wednesday, February 7th, 1940, when I came to the College to conduct my classes, I found a message from Mrs.

Adler asking that I telephone her. She informed me at that time that Doctor Adler, who was very ill, wished to see me that afternoon on an urgent matter. When I visited him that afternoon, he told me that he had decided to discontinue the *Jewish Quarterly Review*. He said that the forthcoming April 1940 issue would be the last, terminating its thirtieth year as a Dropsie College publication. I pleaded with him and sought to impress upon him the fact that the discontinuation would be a great loss to the College and to scholarship in general, since it was the only scientific quarterly left after the destruction of the Jewish centers of learning in Europe. He answered that the *Quarterly* had a great deficit, and that, in view of his illness, he could see no way of obtaining necessary funds. Later Doctor Adler spoke to Doctor Neuman, too, about his intention to end the publication of the *Jewish Quarterly Review* with the forthcoming April issue, "which will round out thirty years of publication under the aegis of the Dropsie College and twenty years in London under the editorship of Claude J. Montefiore and Israel Abrahams." Doctor Neuman was as shocked as I had been and pleaded for its continuation. Again Doctor Adler in his weak state of health complained of the deficit. Finally he said, "Talk to your colleague, Doctor Zeitlin, and let the two of you join forces and carry on." I may add that I had previously suggested the name of another scholar whom I thought Doctor Adler would like to become associated with the *Quarterly*. When his response was in the negative, I suggested another name but the answer again was "No." It was Adler's express wish that Doctor Neuman and the present writer edit the *Quarterly*, and since July 1940, the *Jewish Quarterly Review* has in fact been published under the editorship of Doctor Neuman and the present writer.

A number of works has been published by Dropsie College during the presidency of Doctor Neuman. One of these has been a highly significant undertaking in the annals of Jewish scholarship, namely the edition of the Jewish Apocryphal Literature. These products of the genius of the Jewish people had been rejected for some reason by the sages of the first century of our era, but have now been reclaimed. Hitherto this literature was translated and edited by Christian scholars. It is for the first time in Jewish history that this literature, which is fundamental for a proper understanding of the history and development of Judaism in all its phases, has been scientifically edited and translated anew by a group of Jewish scholars, working under the auspices of Dropsie College. Seven books of the Jewish Apocryphal Literature have already been published. Doctor Neuman is Chairman of Editorial Board and the present writer is the Editor-in-Chief.

In 1952 the Board of Governors, the faculty and the alumni of Dropsie College celebrated Doctor Neuman's decennial as President of the College. On this occasion a collection of his writing was published under the title of *Landmarks and Goals*. In the Foreword I wrote: "In his addresses Doctor Neuman reveals not only the knowledge of the historian but also the fervor of the prophet. Against the background of Jewish history he analyzes the present trends in Jewish life, often raising his voice to sound a warning to Jewish leaders and to point out the danger signals in contemporary Jewish life."

As a colleague and friend for over forty-five years and as the senior member of the faculty and the oldest alumnus of the College, I speak for the faculty, the alumni, as well as the editors and contributors of the volume in wishing Doctor Neuman many fruitful years to come as President, as teacher, and as scholar. May he be granted health and vigor of body and of spirit to continue his career as one of the foremost intellectual leaders that have arisen in American Jewry.

THE ORAL TRADITIONS OF PRE-CRUSADE ASHKENAZIC JEWRY

By Irving A. Agus

Yeshiva University

In the past century and a half modern Jewish scholars studied diligently the biographical and literary history of the renowned leaders of German and French Jewry of the pre-crusade period. [1] Names of rabbinic authorities were catalogued, relationships of students to teachers were traced, dates and places of births and deaths were investigated, and the literary productions were gathered, edited, and described. [2] Little attention was paid, however, to the social and cultural implications of the fact that a tiny group of people (in the last quarter of the eleventh century the Jews of northern France and Germany numbered about thirty thousand souls, [3] while at the beginning of the tenth century they were probably fewer than ten thousand) was able to preserve a vast body of oral learning and to transmit it from generation to generation.

The tremendous implications of that fact, as an historical phenomenon, were overlooked mainly for two reasons. First,

[1] See the bibliography in Irving A. Agus, *Rabbi Meir of Rothenburg* (Philadelphia 1947), vol. ii, pp. 703-19.

[2] See S. L. Rappaport, ספר יריעות שלמה (Warsaw 1903); his introduction to תשובות גאונים קדמונים, (Berlin 1848); J. H. Weiss דור דור ודורשיו, (Vilna 1904) vol. iv; Abraham Epstein's introduction to ספר מעשי הגאונים (Berlin 1909); Solomon Buber's introductions to ס׳ תרומת הדשן (Lemberg 1905); to סידור רש״י (Berlin 1911); ספר האורה (Vilna 1886); Henri Gross, *Gallia Judaica* (Paris 1897); M. Brann, A. Freimann and H. Tykocinsky, *Germania Judaica* (Frankfurt a.M. 1917); H. J. Michael אור החיים, (Frankfurt a.M. 1891); Victor Aptowitzer מבוא לספר ראבי״ה (Jerusalem 1938).

[3] The victims of the first crusade, who numbered about six to eight thousand souls, probably constituted one fourth to one third of the Jewish population of Germany and northern France.

modern historians had little sympathy with students of the
Talmud and very little appreciation of the zeal, the energy,
and the enormous labor expended by these students in master-
ing their subject. [1] They, therefore, failed to consider the
significance of the tremendous social forces and social
pressures that compelled a large proportion of the numerically small population, while living in a barbarous and
brutal environment, to devote most of their time and energy
to purely cultural pursuits. [2] It was taken for granted that
religion was the sole compelling force, and the popular
devotion of Ashkenazic Jewry to talmudic studies was taken
as another indication of the religious meticulousness of that
Jewry. It is highly doubtful, however, whether religious
devotion alone ever produced widespread scholarship of a
high order. [3] Second, the enormity of the labor expended by
a Talmud student in the tenth and the eleventh centuries
was not fully appreciated. The modern scholar who has at
his disposal a printed text of the entire Talmud, numerous
commentaries, supercommentaries, codes and responsa—
mostly poorly indexed, but provided with good cross-
references—could hardly visualize the enormous difficulties
of a tenth-century student who had before him a bare manuscript of a text whose soundness could not be relied on.
Eight centuries of use of Rashi's commentary and five
centuries of printed texts have obliterated any trace of the

[1] *Cf.* H. Graetz, *Geschichte der Juden*, (Magdeburg 1860), vol. v,
pp. 401-5; even Weiss, *op. cit.* p. 277, had a condescending attitude
toward the scholarship of Ashkenazic Jewry. The quest for practical
decisions was extolled by him as a great good, while a purely cultural
preoccupation with talmudic literature was deprecated.

[2] The attitude of the modern historian is reflected not so much
in his positive statement, but rather in his failing to appreciate the
tremendous effort that was involved in keeping alive an enormously
complex body of learning during the extremely difficult times of the
early middle ages.

[3] The fact that in the past millenium practically every Jewish
male received a comparatively high degree of education, led many to
overlook the previous two millenia of enormous effort and concentration until this state of universal literacy was brought about.

method of learning employed in the High Middle Ages. We failed to see the social and cultural implications of the vast erudition displayed by many Ashkenazic scholars of the pre-Rashi period. [1]

In order to understand the character of the people who became the forefathers of Ashkenazic Jewry (*i.e.*, the Jews of Germany and France of the ninth, tenth, and eleventh centuries), [2] in order to correctly evaluate the social and cultural forces that moulded their lives, the values and ideals that were dear to them, the scholarly pursuits to which they were willing to devote their greatest efforts, and the achievements for which they reserved the highest honors—we must re-examine the oral traditions of that Jewry as evidenced by their literary remains. For, during the first millenium of our era, the forefathers of Ashkenazic Jewry preserved and transmitted a rich oral tradition. They preserved an elaborate form of community organization and inter-community cooperation, based on a highly developed system of public law such as

---

[1] We must emphasize here that in a social milieu the degree of true culture attained by a particular group is not as important as the total number of hours spent by a typical member of that group throughout his lifetime.

[2] Here I must take issue with Prof. Salo W. Baron (*The Social and Religious History of the Jews*, second edition, Philadelphia 1957, vol. iv, p. 86; and especially p. 90) who claims that "masses of Jews" settled in the western lands during the twelfth century. This has no foundation in the sources. There is not a single mention of a clash of custom between native and immigrant Jews, in the rabbinic literature of the twelfth and thirteenth centuries—which would have been inevitable had Baron's statement been true. The fact that occasionally a few Jews of Spanish origin are mentioned among the martyrs of a German town (Sinzig, 1266; *cf.* Siegmund Salfeld, *Martyrologium*, p. 16), does not prove anything, since there were always rare individuals forced by circumstances to do the unusual. But there were no "masses of Jews who settled in ever increasing numbers" in Germany and France. The Jews of these countries of the thirteenth century were almost all descendants from the very few families that lived in these same countries in the pre-Crusade period. The large increase in population in the abovementioned century was due to natural increase only. The few individual exceptions made very little difference in the social structure of Ashkenazic Jewry.

was barely echoed in the Talmud. In the rabbinic literature of the twelfth and thirteenth centuries the complex details of that law—and its application in organizing, administering and guiding countless communities with a fine sense of justice and with remarkable efficiency—are already clearly described [1]. However, this complex law, no doubt, was not developed in the middle ages, nor was it modified in any way through contact with the Germanic peoples or with Roman law, but every one of its numerous details was transmitted orally from the days of the Second Temple.

Jewish public law recognizes three distinct types of community legislation. First, in order to protect his private rights, an individual could demand that the community leaders legislate on his behalf. [2] For such legislative acts the consent of the members of the community was not required. Second, all legislative acts designed to strengthen the community or to enhance religious observance, could be enacted by a vote of the majority of the members of the community. Third, all other legislation required the unanimous consent of all the members of the community. [3] The Jews who had lived in the Hellenistic cities before and during the period of Roman domination were well acquainted with the principle of majority rule. But motivated by a lofty sense of justice towards the rights of the individual, [4] they set a limit to this principle and insisted that certain acts of legislation required unanimous agreement of all the members of the community before they became binding on these members. This limitation upon the power of the majority was the most significant, as well as the the most characteristic, feature of Jewish public law.

[1]　*See* my *R. Meir of Rothenburg*, vol. i, pp. 54-124.
[2]　*Cf.* Joel Mueller **תשובות חכמי צרפת ולותיר** (Vienna 1881), the last part of no. 88; no. 97.
[3]　*See* my *R. Meir of Rothenburg*, vol. i, p. 119 f.
[4]　*See* my "The Rights and Immunities of the Minority," *JQR*, vol. xlv (1954), 120-9.

The fact that legislation was divided into three distinct categories made the administration of community law very cumbersome and very complicated, requiring at all times a high degree of legal training on the part of several members of the community. Hence, the preservation and the transmission of a workable knowledge of Jewish public law were not a simple matter. It was largely forgotten during the fourteenth century. [1] Yet it was fully preserved, though only by the forefathers of Ashkenazic Jewry, for more than a thousand years.

As has been shown elsewhere, the *Tosefta* clearly delineated the last two types of legislation. [2] We may, however, have additional proof of the fact that the principle of unanimity was an indigenous part of Jewish public law even in the period of the Second Temple. Josephus quotes the speech of Joshua, "the eldest of the high priests next to Ananus", delivered to the Idumeans before they attacked Jerusalem (in the war with the Romans) : "But further, whether do they pretend that we, who are the rulers of the people, have sent thus privately to the Romans, or hath it been done by the common suffrages of the people? . . . But if they lay this charge against the people, this must have been done at a public consultation, and not one of the people must have dissented from the rest of the Assembly." [3] It seems that in

---

[1]   Thus most of the serious controversies of Ashkenazic scholars, involving the use of *herem*, of the fifteenth and sixteenth centuries (*cf*. M. Frank קהלות אשכנז ובתי דיניהם, Tel Aviv, 1938, p. 109 f.; Alexander Marx, *Studies in Jewish History and Booklore*, New York 1944, pp. 107-154), were due to the fact that in the large-scale destruction of Jewish life and of scholarship, of 1298, 1336-8, and 1348-9, the knowledge of many of the details of Jewish public law was lost. *Cf*. R. Moses Isserles, in his note to *Shulhan Aruch, Hoshen Mishpat*, 2, 1, where he lists the two types of legislation (b and c of our text) as a mere difference of opinion among scholars.

[2]   *JQR*, vol. xlv (1954), 126-8.

[3]   *Bel. Jud.* IV, 4, 3. The expression used is οὐδεὶς ἀπεστάτει. H. St. J. Thackery, ("Loeb Classics") translated it: "was not absent". This rendering, however, makes no sense in this connection, since whether or not a person was absent from the assembly, could not so

the revolt of the Jews against the Romans indigenous Jewish
public law was revived—note the frequent meetings of
courts of seventy men [1]—and with it the requirement that
"at a public consultation" not one of the people must dissent
from the rest of the assembly before that assembly could
pass a resolution. This was probably a revival of an earlier
practice. During the Hasmonean revolt Jewish public law,
heretofore taught theoretically by the *Soferim* to a few
outstanding students, was temporarily adopted in actual
practice; [2] and both Jonathan the Hasmonean and his
brother Simon passed important legislative acts, even
affecting sacrosanct law of Temple-ritual, through what
appears to be a unanimous vote of the people. [3] Apparently,
therefore, this exceedingly important principle was part of
the teachings of original Judaism; it was taught by the sages,
or *Soferim*, to their advanced students only (in great secrecy,
since these were explosive ideas), [4] and became known to the

easily be ascertained; nor could it have any legal significance. In this
connection, therefore, the verb, ἀποστατέω was probably used in the
sense of active disapproval, and protestingly standing aloof from the
opinion expressed by the assembly. It was because of this active
meaning of the verb, that the religious rebel was later called an
apostate by the Church.

[1] I *Maccabees*, 14, 46; *Bel. Jud.* IV, 5, 4; *Vita* 14; *ibid.* 66. It is
possible, however, that Josephus merely interpreted the Hasmonean
period in the light of the practice of his day.

[2] *Cf.* Josephus, *Ant.* XIII, 16, 2: "Alexandra ... also restored
again those practices which the Pharisees had introduced, according
to the traditions of their forefathers, and which her father-in-law,
Hyrcanus, had abrogated." Thus the *Soferim* occasionally succeeded
in introducing many elements of the "oral law" into the actual political and legal life of the people, while many other elements of that law
were being taught by them as mere theoretical ideas, while they
waited for an opportunity to force their adoption into actual practice.

[3] *Cf. Ant.* XIII, 5, 11; 6, 4, and 7.

[4] The principle that certain legislative acts required unanimity,
was based on the idea that man is free and that forcing him to do
something against his will, is a grave sin. This idea, that freedom is
a religious requirement, was the main cause of the revolts against
Rome. Linking the "right to freedom" with the Jewish religion and
stating that Judaism abhored foreign rule, was extremely dangerous;

public when temporarily adopted on a national scale, but
more lastingly in local communities, in the days of the
Hasmonean revolt. This principle was revived in the days of
the Great Revolt when the ideas of democracy, no taxation
by outside rulers, freedom of man, no rule of man over man
—fundamental principles of Jewish religion—became the
rallying cries of the revolutionaries. [1] It was probably
adopted in the local communities of Palestine and Syria
after the destruction of the Temple; [2] was carried to Italy
by the revolutionaries who were taken there as prisoners of
war, and was preserved by the descendants of these prisoners
until it reached full florescence in the communities of Germany
and France during the middle ages. Thus the forefathers of
Ashkenazic Jewry preserved and transmitted orally a highly
developed body of law, which became part and substance of
its organized community life.

In addition to the organizational part of their life, every
other detail of their activity and conduct was fully based on

and Josephus tried very hard to camouflage these claims of the
revolutionaries. He tried to ascribe to the latter a Greek type of
freedom-loving, rather than a typically Jewish one, based on religious
considerations. There is no doubt, however, that the revolt of the
Jews against Rome, as their revolt against Antiochus Epiphanes,
was motivated mainly by religious considerations, and that the main
argument of the revolutionaries was that obeying a tyrant is strictly
forbidden in Jewish law—a very dangerous idea for the Roman
world.

[1]   *Bel. Jud.* II, 17, 9; V, 11, 2; VI, 3, 4; and especially Book II,
chapter 8.

[2]   There is abundant evidence of the fact that, after the destruction
of the Temple especially, local self-government of towns and villages
predominated in Palestine and Syria. See Gedaljahu Alon תולדות
היהודים בא״י בתקופת המשנה והתלמוד (Tel-Aviv 1952) I, pp. 92-113,
139, 155, 206, 210, and 306 f. That the system of organization of these
local governments was based on Jewish public law, and was therefore
similar to that of the medieval communities, we learn from the fact
that a Mishnaic section was devoted to their courts ((*Sanhedrin* III, 1).
R. Yohanan asserted that this section refers to the courts of the local
communities of Syria. See *Sanh.* 23a: אמר ר׳ יוחנן בערכאות שבסוריא שנו;
thus in the court-system too the Ashkenazic communities continued
the early practices of the Palestinian towns.

Jewish law. This fact involves as a necessary antecedent
condition a very intimate and detailed knowledge of that
law on the part of a large portion of the population. Since
very few and meagre custumals and codes were available in
the eighth, ninth, and tenth centuries, the great majority of
this vast body of knowledge had to be transmitted orally.
The scholars of the eleventh and twelfth centuries had great
respect for the legal and ritual knowledge of the *Kadmonim*,
the original settlers of Germany and France. [1] The former
were convinced that the latter possessed greater, more
accurate, and more authoritative, knowledge of Jewish law
than their own. This was not mere romanticism. Near in
time to these generations, they had accurate information
about the degree of their knowledge and the quality of their
scholarship. The fact that the early communities did not
develop a professional rabbinate again proves that learning
was widely diffused and scholarship of a high caliber was
quite common. [2]

It is true that the major part of the legal and ritual knowledge, so accurately possessed by these *Kadmonim*, was
clearly discussed in the Talmud and thus did not have to
depend entirely on oral transmission. But the very understanding of the Talmud depended so overwhelmingly on
oral transmission. Scholars have often wondered at the fact
that scarcely any books came down to us from European

[1] *Cf.* S. Assaf, חליפת שו״ת בין ספרד ובין צרפת ואשכנז, *Tarbitz*, vol.
viii (1937), 169-70; ספר מעשי הגאונים p. 55; Rashi, *Responsa*, no. 258;
Tosephot to *Nazir*, 30a, s.v. ה״ג; *ibid.* s.v. האיש; R. Eliezer b. Nathan
ס׳ ראב״ן nos. 10, 17, 20, 24, 60, 79, 214, 303, 308-11, 315; and especially p. 70, b and c.
[2] *See* my תשובות בעלי התוספות, pp. 18-20. Ordinary merchants
often display superior knowledge of Jewish law. *Cf.* Müller, תשו׳ גאו׳
מזרח ומערב, (Berlin 1888), no. 34 (these תלמידים were merchants and
not students on the way to Babylonian Yeshivot); טעם זקנים, pp. 54 f;
תמים דעים, no. 119; תשובות גאונים קדמונים no. 150 (B was well
acquainted with the law of *asmakhta*, Prof. Ginzberg to the contrary
notwithstanding: *Cf.* Louis Ginzberg, *Ginzei Schechter*, vol. ii, p. 198);
Müller תשובות חכמי צרפת ולותיר (Vienna 1881), no. 101.

scholars of the eighth, ninth, and tenth centuries. [1] This is
especially true of books dealing with legal and ritual matters.
Some scholars were content with one or two meagre compositions that they had assigned to this period, and thought
that they had solved the problem. [2] Others assumed that
many books were composed and used in this period, but that
few were preserved. [3] The difficulty with the latter view is
the fact that the literary compositions of the eleventh century
do not quote any such earlier sources. [4] The only answer to
this problem lies in the very character of rabbinic scholarship.
For from its very inception this scholarship relied mainly on
oral transmission. Every so-called flowering of literary composition was not the result of a great upsurge in cultural
activity but rather the aftermath of a great tragedy. The
Mishne, the *Tosefta*, and the tannaitic *Midrashim* came after
the great slaughter of rabbinic scholars during the Bar
Kochba revolt and the Hadrianic persecutions that followed
it. The Palestinian Talmud was composed because of the
persecutions of schools and scholars in Palestine, following
the Christianization of the Roman empire. The Babylonian
Talmud was put to writing because the Yeshivoth were
closed and the scholars martyred in the great religious
upheavals during the rule of Khavad I. The literary compositions of the school of Rashi and of the Tosaphists were
similarly due to the destruction of the great centers of
talmudic learning in 1096. The motivation for both the act
of composing books and their preservation was always the
same: to save from oblivion any remnant of rabbinic learning
that had been studied orally by hundreds of teachers and
students immediately before catastrophe struck.

[1] *Cf.* H. Vogelstein and P. Rieger, *Geschichte der Juden in Rom*
(Berlin 1895), p. 179; Weiss, *op. cit.*, vol. iv, p. 306; I. Halevy דורות
הראשונים (Berlin 1920), vol. iii, p. 149.

[2] Mordecai Margulies הלכות קצובות (Jerusalem 1942) p. 7.

[3] Weiss, *op. cit.*

[4] *See* introduction to ס׳ מעשי הגאונים pp. X-XXIV; Solomon
Buber, ed., ספר האורה, pp. 10-23; 52-60; 73-85; and 94-120; Alexander
Kohut, ס׳ הערוך השלם, vol. i, pp. X-XXI.

With the destruction of Mayence, Worms, and Cologne in 1096, a radical change took place in the method of studying the Talmud. Rather than relying completely on the ear, learners would henceforth derive a great deal of information through the eye—from written commentaries, collections of responsa, and elaborate custumals. Formerly, in the pre-crusade period, a student had before him only the bare text of the Talmud and studied it laboriously, phrase by phrase, with the help of an oral explanation he "heard from the mouth of his teacher". An ambitious student who wanted to master all the thirty-six tractates of the Talmud that possessed Amoraic elaboration (Gemara) and the other twenty-seven that did not, had to study every page of every treatise "from the mouth of his teacher". For such learning from a teacher consisted of three distinct parts. First, one had to learn the exact wording of the text. The manuscript in front of the student could not be relied on to contain accurately the exact wording of the traditionally accepted text. A few scribal errors, a few slight changes, due to ignorance, carelessness or human limitation, would radically change the meaning of the text. Rabbinic students, before printing was invented, were well acquainted with textual criticism and with all the pitfalls of a written text. [1] An outstanding scholar especially could not rely on a manuscript, but had to commit to memory the exact wording of each phrase. The expression *haka garsinan*, meaning "thus we repeat by rote," was probably meant literally in the pre-crusade period. The scholars of this period, therefore, could rely implicitly on the Babylonian Talmud, since they possessed a very accurate text whose exact wording was not only attested to by written manuscripts but also by an uninterrupted tradition of oral

---

[1] Note the many differances between the explanations of Rashi and those of R. Tam, based on different readings of the talmud, in every tractate. See especially *Rashi* to *Shebuot* 3b, s.v. ‏קשיא:‏ ‏הך דאלו הן הלוקין כו׳ לא גרסינן; ותלמיד טועה שהוקשה לו כתבה בגליון ספרו: "קשיא לי הך דאלו הן הלוקין"/, וכתבוה סופרים בגמרא; · · · והתלמיד טועה, שאינה קשיא‏

transmission and a well cultivated memory. The Palestinian
Talmud, on the other hand, was not so reliable, merely
because it lacked that uninterrupted oral testimony.

Secondly, the student learned the meaning of each word
and phrase. In the course of the centuries a large part of this
oral explanation became highly standardized and solidified,
since it was repeated verbatim by the student while he
committed it to memory, and in later years, when he became
a teacher, he so repeated it to his students. The study of the
Talmud, every page and every tractate, thus came to be
accompanied by a rigid oral commentary, often elaborated on
and explained by the teacher; its bare minimum was laboriously committed to memory and almost became a part of the
text itself. [1] A young student learnt his first tractates from
a local teacher and continued his advanced study in a
renowned Yeshivah under an outstanding teacher. But
every tractate he had to learn from the mouth of some
teacher, [2] and whatever he did so learn, he had to repeat
many times, and to review systematically at frequent intervals
in later years, in order not to forget it. [3] The third part of his
study consisted of a thorough analysis of the contents of
these tractates, a discussion of the legal principles involved,
and the elaboration of a method of deriving final decis-

---

[1] *Cf.* Rashi's explanation of the Talmudic statement (A. Z 19a):
לעולם ילמד אדם תורה ואחר כך יהגה
Rashi writes: ילמד אדם מרבו עד שתהא גירסת התלמוד ופירושו שגורה
לו בפיו: ואח״כ יהגה. יעיין בתלמודו לדמות מילתא למילתא, להקשות ולתרץ;
ובראשונה לא יעשה כן, שמא יבטל, והרב לא ימצא לו כל שעה
The fact that Rashi added the words "and its commentary" (not
mentioned in the Talmud), proves that he was describing the method
of study of his day.

[2] In his commentary to the Talmud Rashi often informs us that
he received his information "from the mouth of his teacher". *Cf.*
Gittin, 82a; *Pesahim,* 111b; *Erekin,* 12b; B.K. 9a; and numerous
other places.

[3] *Cf.* A.Z. 19a, s.v. כל מי שלומד וגורס מעט :ורב ששת אמר
מעט ומחזר עליו פעמים הרבה עד ששגור בפיו, אח״כ חזור ולומד, תלמודו
מתקיים.

ions in law and ritual. This form of learning is still carried on today in Yeshivoth. The exact methods used are,
therefore, well known and need no further elaboration here.

Everything a scholar knew, he had derived orally from the
mouth of his teachers. In his commentary Rashi uses the
phrase "I heard" only when he records conflicting interpretations. Whenever he did not hear an explanation, but
derived it from his teacher's notes or from the notes of his
fellow students, he always informs us of that fact. The
implication is that all the other explanations he did indeed
"hear" from his teachers. [1] If, however, a person failed to
learn a particular tractate from one of his teachers, he simply
did not know that tractate and could not remove that
deficiency through his own efforts. R. Eliezer the Great
(first half of eleventh century) did not study the tractate
Abodah Zarah with his teachers and, therefore, never mastered
it to the extent that he could derive correct halakic decisions
from its rulings and discussions. [2] The entire mass of the
talmudic text was wholly unusable without an accompanying
traditional commentary orally transmitted from generation
to generation.

It is a peculiar characteristic of an oral complex of learning
that it cannot withstand interruption even for a single
generation and that it requires a whole group of extremely
dedicated men to devote the major part of their waking
hours to its perpetuation. To function properly, such a group
cannot live in isolation and apart from a warmly sympathetic
atmosphere of likeminded men. Two questions arise at this
point. What kind of pressures caused a considerable portion

---

[1] See especially *Rashi* to *Gittin* 82a; to *Rosh Hashanah* 32a;
B.K. 9a, and 20a.

[2] See *Sefer haPardes* (Warsaw 1870), no. 238: אבל רבינו אליעזר
הגדול לא למד מסכת ע״ז, ומשום דלא איפשיט ליה החמיר עליו•••
R. Eliezer lived in Mayence where a number of texts of the tractate
Abodah Zarah were available. The only reason that he did not master
this tractate was that he never learned it from his teacher.

of the tiny Jewish population in the early middle ages to devote most of its time and energy to the mastery and transmission of a body of learning of gigantic proportions? Where did this stupendous body of learning come from?

The source of this knowledge was usually ascribed to the Babylonian Geonim. [1] This simple answer is untenable, however, for a number of reasons. The enormous bulk of the oral traditions sustained by the pre-crusade scholars and the wide diffusion of the knowledge of these oral traditions, [2] make it inconceivable that it was all generated by a few individuals who transplanted a presumably foreign culture among a widely scattered people, while that people was in the throes of an unprecedented struggle for existence. Jewish public law, which constituted a very significant part of these oral traditions, was not known at all to the scholars of Babylonia; [3] hence, this knowledge could not have been learned from them. Moreover, the practical application of that law can only take place in a group fully imbued with a thorough knowledge of the entire field of Jewish private law as well. The independent existence of the former, therefore,

---

[1]   Responsum no. 29 of R. Solomon Luria states that R. Gershon was a student of R. Hai; cf. Azulai שם הגדולים (Vienna 1864), III, 13; H. J. Michael אור החיים (Frankfurt 1891) no. 677, who blindly follows that statement. Graetz, op. cit., p. 403, claims that Nathan the Babylonian was the teacher of Rabbi Leontin (R. Judah b. Meir haCohen), the acknowledged teacher of R. Gershom. Weiss was more cautious, but still stressed the influence of the Babylonian Yeshivot; cf. op. cit. p. 278. Cf. also Baron, op. cit., vol. vi, pp. 48, 53, and 55. One simply cannot accept Baron's statement (p. 48): "Western Europe's Jewish exegetical tradition started in the days of Yehudah bar Meir ha-Kohen . . . ."

[2]   Thus Rabbi Leontin, the teacher of Rabbenu Gershom, assumes (ס' כל בו no. 142) that the majority of the members of the community of Troyes, are talmudic scholars. Rashi's teacher, R. Isaac haLevi had a high respect for the scholarship of the general public of his day; see *Responsa of Rashi*, p. 66. Cf. also *Tarbitz*, vol. viii (1937), 169.

[3]   The subject of community legislation is rarely discussed in the geonic literature. For the hundreds of communities that lived under the jurisdiction of the geonim, had an aristocratic form of government—the exact opposite of the form of Ashkenazic communities. Cf. A. Harkavy, *Responsen der Geonim*, (Berlin 1885) nos. 180, and 214.

presupposes the independent existence of the latter. We find
no traces of any considerable influence by the Babylonian
Geonim on the scholars of the tenth or the eleventh century. [1]
If the bulk of the latter's talmudic knowledge had come from
the former, the connection between the two would have
extended to these centuries also. The traditional oral commentary on the Talmud described above was probably composed in Hebrew, and Ashkenazic scholars, therefore, studied
Talmud in Hebrew. This would explain the numerous simi-
larities between the *Aruk* of R. Nathan b. Yehiel and the
commentary of Rashi, especially in the explanation of
single words (since in the translation of words oral traditions
are extremely tenacious). [2] It would explain why after the
First Crusade the commentary of Rashi was usually com-

---

[1] R. Meshullam b. Kalonymus sent a list of questions to R.
Sherira Goan (Ginzberg, *Geonica* II, p. 57), but this was an isolated
case. Moreover, in their Responsa R. Meshullam, his father, R.
Gershom, R. Joseph Tob-Elem, and R. Judah haCohen, quote the
geonim but rarely.

[2] See Alexander Kohut's introduction to ערוך השלם (Vienna
1926), vol. i, p. XXII f.; a check on the parallelisms listed by Kohut
shows that in the translation of single words the similarity is striking.
Kohut's view, however, that Rashi saw the *Aruk*, is untenable. That
the text of the Talmud was studied with a Hebrew commentary, and
the discussions among the students were in Hebrew, may perhaps be
learned from a Responsum of R. Saadiah Gaon, probably sent to a
Central European community (thus it is contained in שו״ת שערי צדק,
Salonici 1792, p. 18b, a collection that was compiled in Germany or
France). The well preserved question described a betrothal ceremony
that took place in a synagogue. The groom gave *kiddushin* to a father
of two daughters, but failed to say explicitly for which daughter the
kiddushin was intended: והיו התלמידים בני ר' נתן ז״ל יושבין בצדן
פתח שמעון ואמר: ,,תהא בתך מקודשת לי בטבעת זו׳׳· ואמרו לו בלשון
הקדש: ,,פרש פרש׳׳, כמו ארבעה וחמשה פעמים·
Thus in a very tense situation the scholars ejaculated in Hebrew.
The fact that the groom used a Hebrew sentence, associated in the
minds of talmudic students with legalistic discussions, and in a
situation highly charged with legalistic niceties, reverted the scholars
to the school atmosphere. Therefore they automatically used the
language of the school. Under similar circumstances a nineteenth
century talmudic student would have resorted to Yiddish.

mitted to memory, as evidenced by the verbatim reproduct-
ions by Isaiah di Trani and R. Nissin Girundi who wove
Rashi's comments into their own with an ease and perfection
that preclude the copying from a written text. It would also
explain how R. Asher b. Yehiel (born in Germany about 1250)
could at the age of fifty or more become a teacher of Talmud
to Spanish-speaking students. Apparently the tradition of
teaching the Talmud in the language of the sages [1] (*i.e.*,
Hebrew), lasted well into the fourteenth century. [2] This
manner of studying the Talmud could not have originated
in Babylonia. [3]

  We are, therefore, forced to conclude that the forefathers of Ashkenazic Jewry were, in the main, a remnant of
that particular segment of Jewish society in the western
Roman Empire which was extremely devoted to talmudic
studies. In the first centuries of the common era a very tiny
proportion of the Jews of the Roman empire were fully
dedicated to these studies. But it was this very group that
resisted most successfully the tremendous pressure exerted
by the Church, from the fifth through the seventh centuries,
to convert the Jews. The few who survived these pressures
as well as the enormous slaughter and destruction wrought

  [1] See the expostulations of R. Judah b. Jehezkel, *Kiddushin* 70a;
which prove that at the end of the third century rabbinic scholars
still spoke Hebrew.
  [2] This would also explain the fundamental difference between
the Jews of the Moslem world, and those of the Christian world, in
respect to the use of the vernacular. The scholars of the former Jews
often wrote Responsa, codes and commentaries in Arabic, while the
scholars of the latter wrote exclusively in Hebrew.
  [3] In Babylon the Aramaic of the Talmud was well understood in
rabbinic circles, and the Aramaic expressions of the Talmud required
no Hebrew translation. If such a translation were necessary, it would
have been supplied in Arabic. In Babylonia too an oral tradition was
laboriously transmitted from generation to generation, but there the
scholars used the talmudic vernacular. *See* A. Harkavy, *Responsen
der Geonim* (Berlin 1887), no. 214: משמא דרבואתא וסדירן בפומא דרבנן
ראשונים דמן בתר סאבורא כי היכין דסדיר גמרא אילין מילי כלשון הזה:
מנא'/זגמן (?) היכי דאמי כגון דקני מן בעלי דינין וכך Cf. also S. Albeck,
Sefer hasEhkol (Jerusalem, 1938), II, p. 76.

by the various waves of invasions and wars and were still living as Jews in the ninth century—were mainly the descendants of that group, and they continued the traditions of their scholarly forefathers well into the late middle ages. The immense body of oral learning possessed by the Ashkenazic Jews of the pre-crusade period, most of which was eventually written down by the schools of Rashi and of the Tosaphists, was the result of a continuous process of oral transmission, from generation to generation, by an extremely dedicated and highly cultured group of Jews in the western Roman Empire who had survived the eroding forces of the fourth through the eighth centuries, mainly because of that very dedication and culture. This extraordinary group became the forefathers of Ashkenazic Jewry.

MEDIEVAL NATIONALISM AND JEWISH SERFDOM

By Salo W. Baron
Columbia University

MUCH HAS BEEN written over the last century about the institution of "Jewish serfdom" in the Middle Ages. Scholars have been particularly intrigued by the origin of the term, *servi camerae*, which in the 1230s makes its formal appearance in both a Sicilian and a German decree issued by Frederick II, the last recognized Hohenstaufen emperor of Germany and king of Sicily. However, practically all research has hitherto been concentrated on the evolution of that concept in the Holy Roman Empire, whereas the parallel developments in the other western countries have been paid but scant attention.

Even the German "chamber serfdom" and its connection with the ancient Church doctrine of the Jewish subjection to the Christian world are far from fully clarified. In fact, the present author hopes to have contributed something to that clarification in a recent Hebrew essay on "'Plenitude of Apostolic Powers' and Medieval 'Jewish Serfdom'", [1] in which the gradual unfolding of the divergent papal and imperial interpretations of the origin and extent of the Christian overlordship over Jews is shown against the background of the ever sharpening conflict between the Papacy and the Empire from Gregory VII to Innocent IV and from

[1] In *Sefer Yobel le Yiṣḥaq Baer* (Yitzhak F. Baer Jubilee Volume), (Jerusalem 1960), pp. 102-24. In that essay are reproduced many of the principal sources relating to the conflict between the Papacy and the Empire and its bearing on Jewish serfdom; they need not be repeated here. Nor do we have to revert again in this presentation to the numerous moot problems in the story of Jewish serfdom mentioned in that Hebrew article.

Emperor Henry IV to Frederick II. Jurists on both sides adduced a variety of legal and historical arguments to support the claims of either the Church or the Empire to supremacy over the Jewish communities not only within the areas of their respective political controls, but through all of Christendom, if not all over the world.

Not surprisingly, the monarchs ruling over the other western lands were far from ready meekly to accept such authority over their Jews by these outside powers. Before long they insisted upon their own, wholly independent mastery over their Jewish subjects. But these rationales likewise require further elucidation; doubly so, as they were both reactions to and derivatives of the papal and, to a lesser extent, the imperial doctrines. In the present essay an effort will be made to show how the rise of the national consciousness among the western nations—a consciousness which, despite its obvious religious overtones, was secular in nature—affected also the position of the Jewish "serfs."

In essence all these theories went back to the ancient concept, shared by Jews and Christians, that after the loss of their national independence the Jews had become subject to foreign domination. Jews equated their "exile" with such foreign domination (shi'abud malkhioth) which had come as a result of their forefathers' sins and which, they expected, would disappear after the advent of their Messiah. The Christians agreed, except that they identified those sins committed by the ancestors of the Jews with their repudiation of Christ and, for the most part, taught that this Jewish subjection would end with the second coming of Christ. There was no question, therefore, that Jewish serfdom was but a temporary, if long-lasting, punishment and that the date of its termination depended on the grace divine. But for the duration of the Exile the Church claimed that the elder faith was to be subject to the younger religion, that is the Church as such, in accordance with the ancient prediction that "the elder shall serve the younger" (Gen 25: 23). At the height of their conflict with the popes, however, the emperors and their juristic advisers underscored rather the secular origin of Jewish serfdom, namely in Titus' conquest of Jerusalem, since which time Jews had become tributary to the ancient Roman emperors and their successors on the throne of Germany. The kings could not invoke that *translatio imperii* [1] and had to fall back on the general subjection of the Jews to Christians rule. But they interpreted such rule as that of effective dominion by all God-appointed monarchs.

Medieval Nationalism

Such Jewish allegiance to all rulers was only part of the general evolution of medieval nationalism. For a long time the leading thinkers of Christendom, largely recruited from among theologians and jurists, insisted upon the supremacy of the universal powers of the Papacy and Empire over all Christian states. Whatever they thought about the mutual relations between these two universal institutions, they had no doubt that the various kingdoms were but provinces of the same body of Christianity entrusted to the leadership of pope and emperor. Such leading glossators as Bartolus and his pupil, Baldus, agreed that, to quote the former, "he who says that the Lord Emperor is not the lord and king of the whole world is a heretic, for he says it against the decision of the Church and against the testimony of the Holy Gospel." Baldus called such a contention an outright "sacrilege." [2]

---

[1] *See* especially the comprehensive analysis by Werner Goez, *Translatio imperii: ein Beitrag zur Geschichte des Geschichtsdenkens und der politischen Theorien des Mittelalters und in der frühen Neuzeit* (Tübingen 1958). Goez also quotes some of the enormous literature on this subject, supplementing in part our references given in the aforementioned Hebrew essay.

[2] Bartolus de Saxoferrato in his *Commentary* on the *Corpus iuris civilis*, Dig. xlix.15, 24: "*Si quis diceret dominum imperatorem non esse dominum et monarcham totius orbis, esset hereticus, quid diceret contra determinationem ecclesiae, contra testimonium S. Evangelii . . .*" (with reference to Luke 2); Petrus Baldus de Ubaldis in his *Consilia*, III, cons. ccxviii: "*Quia imperator est dominus universalis . . . Nam in*

The emperor's universal power naturally extended over the Jews as well. Another leading jurist, Johannes Teutonicus, made it explicit when he summarized the prevailing view: "The emperor is placed above all kings... and all nations are under him... the Jews, too, are under him." [1]

However, partly as a result of the weakening of the Empire in the course of its struggle with the Papacy from the eleventh to the thirteenth centuries the western nations and their rulers became ever more self-assertive. In England and Spain, where geographic distance made the imperial claims somewhat academic, national independence arose gradually without entering into direct conflict with the demands of Empire. In fact, some Castilian kings started arrogating to themselves the title emperor and finally Alphonso the Wise entertained serious pretensions to the very imperial throne of Germany. [2]

dubio omnis temporalis jurisdictio sua est ... et contrarium dicere est sacrilegium" (edition Venice 1609, III, fol. 62a). The meaning of these extreme statements within the general political theories of these outstanding jurists will become clearer in the light of the recent analyses by Walter Ullmann, "The Development of the Medieval Idea of Sovereignty", *English Historical Review*, vol. lxiv (1949), 1-33; and Francesco Calasso, *I Glossatori e la teoria de la sovranità; studio di diritto comune pubblico*, 2nd ed. (Milan 1951). Ullmann subsequently restated his views in his comprehensive analysis of *The Growth of Papal Government in the Middle Ages: A Study in the Ideological Relation of Clerical to Lay Power* (New York 1953). His general theories, which are also pertinent to our subject, have stood the test of various criticisms, such as voiced by another well-informed student, Friedrich Kempf. *See* the latter's "Die päpstliche Gewalt in der mittelalterlichen Welt. Eine Auseinandersetzung mit Walter Ullmann," in *Saggi storici intorno al Papato* (Rome 1959), (Miscellanea historiae pontificiae, XXI), pp. 117-69.

[1] Johannes Teutonicus in his *Apparatus* to Compilation III: "*Est autem imperator super omnes reges ... et omnes naciones sub eo sunt .... Etiam iudei sub eo sunt .... Neque aliquis regum potuit eximi ab imperio quia illud esset acefalum."* *See* the improved version, cited from MSS by Gaines Post in his "Two Notes on Nationalism in the Middle Ages", *Traditio*, vol. ix (1953), 281-320, especially, p. 299 n. 10. Such absence of a single "head" of all Christendom appeared, indeed, as utterly unnatural to many legists, as well as canonists.

[2] One of the clearest equations of royal and imperial power and, by intimation, also an assertion of the independence of kings from

Similarly, England's Henry III, after discarding King John's submission to the Papacy, threw covetous eyes on the heritage left behind by the declining Hohenstaufen. He tried to place his brother Richard of Cornwall on the throne of the Holy Roman Empire, just as he sought for his son Edmund the Sicilian crown.

Not surprisingly, therefore, even Johannes Teutonicus extolled Spain as being "wealthy in horses, celebrated for food, and shining with gold; steadfast and wise, the envy of all; skilled in the law, and standing high on sublime pillars." Understandably, this pro-imperial jurist, at least according to some manuscript versions, made the following characteristic reservation: "Thus the world government, with the exception of the Spanish government, has been handed over to the Teutons." [1] In England John of Salisbury emphasized, in his *Policraticus* written in 1159, the position of the *princeps* as against the emperor, an idea which was

emperors, is found in the famous Castilian code, *Las Siete Partidas*, ii.1, 1 and 5, edited by Gregorio Lopez, new impression, 5 vols., Paris, 1847, II, 3 ff., 11. Here Alphonso X stated succinctly: "*Vicarios de Dios son los reyes, cada uno en su regno, puestos sobre las gentes para mantenerlas en justicia et en verdad quanto en lo temporal, bien asi como el emperador en su imperio.*" It is to be noted that Alphonso VII had been crowned in Leon in 1135 under the title of "Emperor of Spain and King of the men of the two religions", that is of Christians and Muslims. One of his successors, Ferdinand III (1217-52), went further. Despite his Christian piety, which earned him later the designation Saint, he styled himself "King of the three religions", that is of Jews as well as of Christians and Muslims. On the Spanish quest for empire see Ramón Menéndez Pidal, *El imperio hispánico y los cincos reinos. Dos épocas en la estructura política de España*, Madrid, 1950, esp. pp. 155 ff.; and Hermann J. Hüffer, "Die mittelalterliche spanische Kaiseridee und ihre Probleme", *Saeculum*, vol. iii (1952), 425-43. *See also* my *A Social and Religious History of the Jews*, 2d ed., vol. iv, pp. 28, 245 f., n. 30.

[1] The passage *excepto regimine hyspanie* is missing in many MSS and may be but a later insertion. Yet it is fully in line with Johannes Teutonicus' glorification of Spain. *See* G. Post's observations in *Traditio*, vol. ix, pp. 299, 307

expanded by the subsequent English political thinkers, particularly Bracton. [1]

Somewhat more slowly this idea gained ground also in France which, by geographic proximity as well as by traditions of the Carolingian age, was more closely linked to the destinies of the Holy Roman Empire. The absence of a unitary monarchical rule extending over the whole country likewise militated against the full self-assertion of the Capetian kings, at least until the rise of the French Crown under Louis IX and his successors. But in the days of Philip the Fair, with the Empire humiliated by the Papacy, France took up the cudgels against the supremacy of Rome as well. The papal claims to universal power also in temporal matters, culminating in Boniface VIII's well-known bull *Unam sanctam* of 1302, exploded, so to say, in the pope's face. Within a few years France forced the popes to take up their residence in formerly French Avignon, reducing the supreme pontiffs, some of them Frenchmen by nationality, to mere appendages of French rule. These transformations found their theoretical counterpart in the political writings of such contemporaries as Pierre Dubois. [2] Some people began interpreting the term *francus* as being etymologically derived from free, that is free from imperial overlordship. [3] In short, the growingly accepted view now was that the king of France "has no superior" and that, more broadly, every "king is an emperor in his country."

---

[1] That John of Salisbury exerted considerable influence on the thinking of jurists even in Italy was shown by the extensive data assembled by Walter Ullmann in "The Influence of John of Salisbury on Medieval Italian Jurists," *English Historical Review*, vol. lix (1944), pp. 384-92. The political ideas of Bracton have likewise frequently been studied. *See* especially Fritz Schulz, "Bracton on Kingship," *ibid.*, vol. lx (1945), pp. 136-76. In view of Bracton's importance for the royal doctrine of medieval Jewish serfdom, his political theories will have to be briefly mentioned again, *infra*, n. 38.

[2] *See* Hellmut Kämpf, *Pierre Dubois und die geistigen Grundlagen des französichen Nationalbewusstseins um* 1300 (Leipzig 1935).

[3] Ullmann, in *English Historical Review*, vol. lxiv, p. 12.

Connected with this progressive emancipation of the western kings from papal and imperial tutelage was also their increasing self-assertion within their respective realms. While the Empire progressively declined also in its internal controls and soon had to concede increased independence to the territorial princes, both lay and ecclesiastical, the English, French, and Iberian crowns succeeded in controlling ever more effectively the destinies of their countries. Only the English kings suffered some reversals through the Magna Carta and the rise of the parliamentary system. But they retained the essential unitarian controls over their possessions on both the British Isles and the Continent. The French and Spanish kings, on the other hand, increasingly overcame the resistance of feudal barons, and toward the end of the Middle Ages France and Spain tended to live under a concentrated, almost absolute, royal power. [1] The formerly debated question as to whether the old Roman crime of *laesa maiestas* applied

[1] Perhaps the clearest expression of the French monarchy's self-assertion may be found in Philip the Fair's sharp repudiation of the order given him by Boniface VIII to suspend hostilities with both the emperor and the king of England. We are told that he "ordered and commanded . . . that such protests as the following be made: namely, that the government of the temporality of his realm belongs to him alone, as king, and to no one else, and that he recognizes no superior in it, and that he is not obliged and does not intend, in matters pertaining to the temporal government of the realm, to submit or subject himself in any way to any living man; but he rather intends to do justice over his fiefs, to defend his kingdom continually, and, with his subjects, his allies, and his warriors, to further the right of his kingdom in every way."

See Pierre Dupuy, *Histoire du différend d'entre le Pape Boniface VIII et Philippe le Bel Roy de France* (Paris 1655), pp. 27 f.; cited here in the English translation by Ewart Lewis in his *Medieval Political Ideas*, 2 vols. (New York 1954), vol. ii, p. 529. *See also* other recent literature reviewed by Alfonso M. Stickler in his "Sacerdozio e regno nelle nuove ricerche attorno ai secoli XII e XIII nei decretisti e decretalisti fino alle decretali di Gregorio IX," in *Sacerdozio e regno da Gregorio VII a Bonifacio VIII* [edited by Friedrich Kempf] (Rome 1954), (Miscellanea historiae pontificiae, XVIII), pp. 1-26.

only to the emperor or also to the kings, was now answered in favor of the latter by all competent jurists. [1]

On a more popular level, too, nationalism was gaining ground. At the growing universities, in particular, such as those of Bologna, Paris and Oxford, which attracted pupils from many lands, the student bodies formed separate *nationes*.[2] Even the universal church councils which, by their very nature, were intended to underscore the unity of Christendom, increasingly resembled a modern United Nations with voting blocs of representatives of various states and nationalities. Ultimately, at the famous Council of Constance (1414-18) it was agreed to establish four geographic regions, called *nationes*, voting as single units. [3] In short, "from the beginning of the twelfth century, European nationalism has [had] a continuous history." [4]

All this unavoidably affected the Jewish status as well. In another context I have tried to explain how deeply the rise of the medieval national state, as well as the persistence of some multi-national states, had influenced their whole attitude toward the Jewish minority. [5] Here we need concern

---

[1] An interesting illustration was furnished in 1259, when a French baron was condemned by the royal court for the crime of *lèse-majesté*. See Count Beugnot, *Les Olim, ou registres des arrêts rendus par la cour du roi, sous les règnes de St. Louis, de Philippe le Hardi, de Philippe le Bel, Louis le Hutin et Philippe le Long*, 3 vols. (Paris 1839-48), vol. i, p. 460, no. iv.

[2] Pearl Kibre, *The Nations in the Mediaeval Universities* (Cambridge, Mass., 1948), (Publications of the Mediaeval Academy, XLIX).

[3] George C. Powers, *Nationalism at the Council of Constance* (1414-1418) (Washington D.C., 1927) (Diss. Catholic University of America); and Heinrich Finke, "Die Nation in den spätmittelalterlichen allgemeinen Konzilien," *Historisches Jahrbuch*, vol. lvii (1937), pp. 323-38.

[4] Halvdan Koht, "The Dawn of Nationalism in Europe," *American Historical Review*, vol. lii (1947), p. 279.

[5] *See* my "Nationalism and Intolerance", *Menorah Journal*, vol. xvi (1929), 405-15; vol. xvii (1929), pp. 148-58 (also reprint); and, more generally, my *Modern Nationalism and Religion* (New York 1947), (The Rauschenbusch Lectures for 1944, Colgate-Rochester Divinity School); 2d impression (New York 1960).

ourselves only with the impact of that growing national self-assertion upon the development of Jewish serfdom as applied in the various western kingdoms in contradistinction to the teachings expounded by the canonists and the imperial jurists.

Spain and Portugal

The incipient transition from the ecclesiastical doctrine of Jewish serfdom as subjection to the Church, to the royal concept of Jews being serfs of the Christian kings, occurred in Visigothic Spain. There the church councils of Toledo combined ecclesiastical with secular functions and actually sat as parliaments of the realm. Presided over by the kings, they passed resolutions which became canons of the Church and, subject to royal approval, also laws of the land. It was in the Seventeenth Council of Toledo of 694 that the memorable phrase of Jewry being *perpetuae servituti subacta* was used to justify regulations which cut across the lines of state and Church. [1] This canon was frequently quoted thereafter in the ecclesiastical literature and, by being repeated also in the Gregorian *Decretales*, became part and parcel of universal canon law. [2] At the same time it could be used by legists to justify also royal supremacy over Jews, inasmuch as the *Lex Visigothorum* remained the fountainhead of all civil law in

[1]   J. D. Mansi, ed., *Sacrorum conciliorum nova et amplissima collectio*, 53 vols., Paris, 1901-27, vol. xii, p. 102, canon 8. On the background of this phrase *see* my *A Social and Religious History*, vol. iii, pp. 42 f.

[2]   For one example, in his letter to the Archbishop of Sens and the Bishop of Paris of July 15, 1205 Innocent III used the phrase, *"ne cervicem perpetue servitutis jugo submissam presumant erigere."* Solomon Grayzel, *The Church and the Jews in the XIIIth Century* (Philadelphia 1933), pp. 114 ff., no. 18. Like many other statements by that powerful pope, this epistle was taken over into the *Decretales*, v. 6, 13 in the *Corpus iuris canonici*, ed. by Emil Friedberg, vol. ii, pp. 775 f. It may be noted, however, that in the earlier compilation, the *Decretum Gratiani*, some of the most extreme resolutions of the Toledan Councils, including that here cited, were omitted. *See* my *History*, vol. iv, p. 241, n. 19.

the few remaining Christian provinces of the Peninsula not overrun by the Moors. It also greatly influenced the autonomous life of the Mozarab population in the Muslim parts of Spain. With the reconquest of the Peninsula by the Christian Crusaders many old Visigothic principles reasserted themselves and profoundly colored the whole legal structure of the newer kingdoms of Castile, Aragon, and Portugal. [1]

It was not surprising that the Spanish kingdoms early arrogated to themselves independent authority over their Jews. Even the pro-imperial Jacobus de Albenga had admitted that "the French, the Spaniards, and some other provinces, though *de jure* they should be subject to the Empire... yet *de facto* are not so subjected." [2] Of course, the Spanish kings, especially the Castilian emperors of the twelfth and thirteenth centuries, cast away such restraints. Their view was clearly expressed in the thirteenth-century *Libro de los Fueros de Castilla*, a distinguished collection of local Castilian custumals approved by the king. The pertinent passage read: "The Jews are the king's. No matter whether they live under the authority of all the dignitaries, the nobles, or others, or under that of monasteries, all of them belong to the king, live under his tutelage and for his service." [3] In another local custumal,

---

[1] To be sure, the later Spanish *Fueros* often diverged from the Visigothic law. But this was owing in part to the ever-present conflict between the local customs and the royal laws in Spain. For the Visigothic period *see* especially Theofil Melicher, *Der Kampf zwischen Gesetzes- und Gewohnheitsrecht im Westgotenreich* (Weimar 1930). Nevertheless, the persistence of Visigothic tradition has long been recognized. In fact, a good case has been made for the assumption that medieval Spanish nationalism had its roots in the doctrines of Isidore of Seville of the Visigothic age. *See* José Antonio Maravall, "Sobre el concepto de monarquía en la edad media española", *Estudios dedicados a Menéndez Pidal*, 7 vols. (Madrid 1950-57), vol. v, pp. 401-17, especially pp. 406 f., 410; and, more generally, W. Reinhart, "La Tradición visigoda en el nacimiento de Castilla", *ibid.*, vol. i, pp. 535-54.

[2] Jacobus de Albenga in his *Apparatus* to Compilation V (Decretales of Honorius III), cited from a British Museum MS by Post in *Traditio*, vol. ix, p. 302.

[3] *Libro de los Fueros de Castilla*, Art. 107: "*Esto es por fuero: que*

the *Fuero* of Salamanca (about 1170), King Ferdinand II of Leon reached an agreement with the Jews and the city authorities in which he stated: "And the king places them [the Jews] in the hands of the Salamanca council so that they have no other master but the king. And the Salamanca council [promises] that it will govern them with justice." On the other hand, in the *Fuero* of Ledesma, another Leonese community, probably likewise issued by Ferdinand II, the king agreed to share his authority with the municipal organs by stating that "all the Jews shall be in the power of the king and the council." [1]

It was because of this particular relationship that the kings felt entitled to utilize their Jewish "serfs" in important administrative posts. The Jews could be trusted with safeguarding the interests of the Crown over those of the nobles, clergy, and burghers in that strenuous period of the country's reconstruction during the progressive *Reconquista*. This exten-

---

los judios son del rey; maguer que sean so poder de ricos omnes o con sus cavalleros o con otros omnes o so poder de monesterios, todos deven ser del rey en su goarda e para su servycio." Cited from Galo Sanchez's edition, Barcelona, 1924, by Fritz Baer in *Die Juden im christlichen Spanien*, 2 vols. (Berlin 1929-36), vol. ii, p. 36, no. 60. The translation here given of *ricos omnes* by dignitaries, rather than rich men, follows the etymology of the *ricos* as derived from a root similar to the German *Reich*.

[1]   *Fuero of Salamanca*, Art. 341: "*Esto faz conceyo de Salamanca con los iodios, alcaldes e iusticias e iurados, por manos del rey don Fernando. E metelos el rey en manos del conceyo de Salamanca que non ayan otro senor se non el Rey. E el conceyo de Salamanca quelos ampare con derecho.*" *Fuero of Ledesma*, Art. 399: "*Todos elos iudios seyan en poder del rey e del conceyo.*" Both in the *Fueros Leoneses de Zamora, Salamanca, Ledesma y Alba de Tormes*, ed. by Américo Castro and Federico de Onís (Madrid 1916), pp. 201 f., 286; and Baer, *Die Juden*, vol. ii, pp. 30 ff. Nos. 57-58. Such a division of authority between the king and municipal council or baron was not unusual in medieval Spain and other countries. Of interest may also be Nilda Guglielmi's Buenos Aires dissertation, *La Administración regia en León y Castilla de Fernando I a Alfonso X*. Unfortunately, the brief summary published in the *Revista* of the University of Buenos Aires, II (1957), pp. 141-43, does not give a sufficient inkling of the author's treatment of the royal administration of Castilian Jewish affairs.

sive employment of Jewish officials in high posts called down
upon the kings the censure of many powerful popes, including
Honorius III. [1] But the need for Jewish assistance was so
great that the papal bulls were simply disregarded. Only
much later, after the consolidation of the royal power, could
the assistance of Jewish administrators, if not also of fiscal
advisers, be more readily dispensed with. The Jews reciprocated and actually enjoyed their status under royal protection.
In a remarkable report about the long-lasting controversies
between the burghers and the abbot of Sahagun, an anonymous chronicler mentions the argument presented in 1255
by the local Jews "that they in no way belonged to the jurisdiction of the Abbot, for they are serfs of the Lord King and
are obliged to serve the royal power in all matters. They also
claimed that the lord Abbot had in many ways aggrieved them
without reason." [2]

This nexus between the kings and the Jews continued

---

[1] *See* especially Honorius' circular letters, addressed on March 20,
1220 to the Spanish kings and bishops and relating to the employment
of Jewish diplomats. An earlier protest had been dispatched by
Innocent III to Alphonso VIII of Castile (May 5, 1205). Here the pope
contrasted several forms of favoritism extended by the king to Jews
while the clergy was being oppressed, the result being *"ut synagoga
crescente, decrescat ecclesia, et libere preponatur ancilla."* Grayzel,
The Church, pp. 112 ff., 158 ff., nos. 17, 45-46. *See also* Demetrio
Mansilla Resyo, "Inocencio III y los reinos hispanos," *Anthologica
annua*, vol. ii (1954), pp. 9-50. On the extensive employment of Jewish
officials by medieval Spanish kings, *see* the data assembled by Abraham A. Neuman in *The Jews in Spain: Their Social, Political and
Cultural Life during the Middle Ages*, 2 vols. (Philadelphia 1948),
vol. ii, pp. 221 ff.; and by Yitzhak Baer, in his *Toledoth ha-Yehudim
bi-Sefarad ha-noṣrith* (A History of the Jews in Christian Spain),
2d ed. (Tel-Aviv 1959), *passim*. See also *infra*, p. 14 n. 1.

[2] The anonymous monk of Sahagun in his *Chronicle*, edited by
Julio Puyol y Alonso in "Las Crónicas anónimas di Sahagun", *Boletín*
of the Academia de la historia, vol. lxxvii (1920), 151-92, especially
pp. 181 f: the Jews *"afirmavan que en ninguna manera pertenescian a
la jurisdición del abad, ca siervos eran del senyor rey e eran tenudos en
todas las cosas de servir al poderio real. Decian aun quel señor abad los
agraviaba a sin raçon en muchas maneras"*. See also the comments
thereon by Fritz Baer in *Die Juden*, vol. ii, pp. 56, no. 70.

through the following centuries, the former often unabashedly admitting their pre-eminently fiscal interests in this matter. During Ferrand Martinez' rabble-rousing propaganda in Seville, John II enjoined him from pursuing his hostile preaching. "You should know," wrote the king, "that it is Our will and grace that the said Jews be protected, defended, and maintained as Our and Our Chamber's property." [1]

Without any imperial aspirations Aragon nonetheless followed suit. In fact, we find in its area one of the earliest formulations of royal authority over Jews. As early as 1176, the important *Fuero* of Teruel unequivocally assigned to the king the *wergeld* due for an assault on a Jew. Evidently brooking no contradiction, the author of that custumal wrote: "Be it known that the Jew has no part in the fine paid for an assault or homicide on him, but that it all belongs to the Lord King. For the Jews are serfs of the king and always belong to the Royal Treasury [*nam iudei servi regis sunt et semper fisco regio deputati*]." [2] The kings upheld that principle particularly after James I threw off the Church supremacy recognized by his father. Defying all the fulminations of local and Roman ecclesiastics, he extensively employed Jewish bailiffs in the service of the Crown. He considered Jewish leaders like Jahuda de Cavalleria and several members of the house of Ravaya as the most effective agents

---

[1]   John I's letter to Ferrand Martinez of March 3, 1382, published from a Toledo MS by Baer, *ibid.*, pp. 214 f., no. 221. The crucial passage reads: "*E sabed que nuestra voluntad e merced es que los dichos judios sean guardados e defendidos e mantenidos como cosa nuestra e de la nuestra camera.*"

[2]   Fuero of Teruel (*Forum Turolii*), Art. 425, reproduced from Francisco Aznar Navarro's edition by Baer in *Die Juden*, vol. i, 1043; in the Romance trans., edited by Max Gorosch (Stockholm 1950), (Leges hispanicae medii aevi, I), p. 320, no. 568. Although this *Fuero* was extremely influential and widely imitated in other local custumals, this text is by no means necessarily original. None of the extant MSS antedates the late thirteenth century and especially the phrase *fiscus regius* (*real bolsa*) may have been a subsequent interpolation. *See* Gorosch's intro., pp. 11 ff.

in cementing the unity of his widely scattered possessions. [1]
Not being able, however, to counterpose an imperial claim
similar to that advanced by his contemporary Frederick II,
he could only invoke the general principle that all Christian
sovereigns enjoyed full authority over the Jews. In a remarkable order, addressed to the municipality of Montpellier in
1252, he opposed the attempt of the municipal council to
impose local taxes upon Jews. He declared that such taxation
then and at any future occasion would run counter to the
royal jurisdiction and honor, "for the Jews in almost all
lands are subject to the serfdom of Christian princes [*fere in
terris omnibus Christianorum principum subiacent servituti*]." [2]

This point of view was maintained throughout the Jewish
settlement in Aragon. Using a somewhat different terminology,
the author of the *Fueros de Āragon* declared that "all the
Jews... shall be... under the special protection of the Lord
King." [3] As late as 1481, but eleven years before their decree
of expulsion of the Jews from Spain, Ferdinand and Isabella
severely lectured the prior of the Cathedral of Saragossa who
had issued an unauthorized public appeal seeking to confine
the Jews in a quarter of their own. "It appertains to none,"
the king declared, "but Ourselves and Our own person to
provide and ordain in matters relating to Jews, who are Our
chests and Our patrimony." [4]

[1]   *See* the data assembled by Jerome Lee Shneidman in "Jews as
Royal Bailiffs in Thirteenth-Century Aragon," *Historia Judaica*,
vol. xix (1957), 55-66; and *supra*, p. 28 [12] n. 1.
[2]   Salomon Kahn, "Documents inédits sur les Juifs de Montpellier,"
REJ, vol. xix (1889), 259-81, especially p. 261, n. 2. *See also* the other
sources cited by Baer in *Studien zur Geschichte der Juden im Königreich
Aragonien während des 13. und 14. Jahrhunderts* (Berlin 1913),
(Historische Studien, CVI), pp. 11 ff.
[3]   Jesus Bergna Canon, "Fueros de Aragon de 1265 a 1381,"
Anuario de derecho aragonès, V, 455: "*Que todos los judios ... sean ...
en especial guarda del senyor rey*," cited by Shneidman in *Historia
Judaica*, vol. xix, p. 66, n. 72.
[4]   Ferdinand the Catholic's letter to the Prior of the Cathedral
of Saragossa of August 17, 1481: "*Mandamiento de cessar y sobresseer
en ellos, y ninguno no deve tener audacia tan temeraria de fazer nin*

In Portugal, too, the kings made excellent use of Jewish officials because of their greater reliability. Or, as Queen Leonore observed concerning her deceased husband, Ferdinand, in 1383, because he had "trusted them [the Jews] more than the Christians." In this sense, being "serfs" of the king—a term used in Portugal far less frequently than elsewhere—established a mutuality of interests and responsibility which for a long time accrued to the benefit of both. At times, to be sure, his high position at court misled one or another Jewish official into participating in court intrigues and political conflicts which might have adversely reflected on the whole community. Yet even in the crucial transition of the regime to John 1 in 1383-85, the danger passed rather quickly, and other Jews continued "serving" the Portuguese kings in various capacities. [1]

England

Nearly total dependence of Jews on the royal power was most evident in England. From the outset the English kings enjoyed considerable authority within and outside their country. As early as *ca.* 1100 an unnamed York monk contended that both the state and the Church ought to pay allegiance to the king enthroned by God. This doctrine was too radical, however, even for his English contemporaries and

proveer tales actos sino con consentimiento nuestro expresso, specialmente que proveer y ordenar sobre los judios, que son cofres nuestros y de nuestro patrimonio, no pertenesce a ninguno sino a nos e a nuestra propria persona". Baer, *Die Juden,* vol i, p. 898, no. 554. It is noteworthy that in this connection the Catholic monarchs did not use the traditional term "serfs" but the more modern circumlocution of chests and patrimony, essentially meaning the same thing.

[1] Ferñao Lopes, *Chronica d'el rey D. Fernando,* in the *Collecçao de livros inéditos de historia portuguesa,* vol. iv, pp. 121-525, especially pp. 502 ff.; quoted here in the English translation by E. Prestage in the *Chronicles of Fernao Lopes and Gomes Eannes de Zurara,* pp. 41 f.; and, more generally, Meyer Kayserling, *Geschichte der Juden in Portugal* (Leipzig 1867), pp. 23 ff. On the general evolution of Portuguese nationalism, *see* Albin Eduard Beau, *Die Entwicklung des portugiesischen Nationalbewusstseins* (Hamburg 1944); and the more recent Portuguese essays collected in his *Estudos,* vol. i (Coimbra 1959).

was left dormant in a manuscript. It was later discovered and published by John Wyclif when independence from the Papacy became a major battle cry of the Reformers. However, the York doctrine was symptomatic of both the rising English nationalism and the quest for concentrated royal power. [1]

Under these circumstances, it was perfectly natural to attribute also the exclusive supremacy over Jews to the kings. Characteristically, it was during the midtwelfth century when Edward the Confessor was canonized, a step generally recognized today as an important phase in the progress of English national self-realization, that a contemporary jurist attributed to this revered pre-Norman king a statute which stated bluntly,

> It shall be known that all Jews, wheresoever in the realm they be, ought to be under the guard and protection of the king's liege. Nor ought any of them place himself under any mighty man without the king's license. For the Jews and all theirs belong to the king. And if any detain anything of theirs, let the king ask their money back as if it were his own. [2]

[1] *See* especially the York Anonymus' fourth tractate *De Conservatione Pontificum et Regum* in *Libelle de Lite*, in the excerpt translated into English by Ewart Lewis in *Medieval Political Ideas*, vol. ii, pp. 562 ff. *See also* Albert Brackmann, "Die Ursachen der geistigen und politischen Wandlung Europas im 11. und 12. Jahrhundert," *Historische Zeitschrift*, vol. cxlix (1934), pp. 229-39; and *idem*, "Der mittelalterliche Ursprung der Nationalstaaten," *Sitzungsberichte* der Preussischen Akademie der Wissenschaften, Phil.-hist. Klasse, 1936, pp. 128-42, especially pp. 131 f.

[2] Pseudo-Edward the Confessor's *Leges Ecclesiasticae e saecularibus suis depromptae*, xxi, in Migne's *Patrologia Latina*, vol. cli, pp. 1193 f.: "*Sciendum quoque quod omnes Judaei, ubicunque in regno sunt, sub tutela et defensione regis debent esse nec quilibet eorum alicui diviti se potest subdere sine regis licentia. Judaei enim, et omnia sua, regis sunt*". Cited in the text from Joseph Jacobs's English translation in *The Jews of Angevin England*, p. 68. It has long been recognized that this passage was not enacted by Edward himself nor by any of his contemporaries, but rather dated from the period of Roger Howden's *Chronica*, where it was first reported (*ca.* 1180). It was entirely in line with Henry II's declaration at the Diet of Clarendon of 1161 about the Crown's supremacy over the English Church. *See* Brackmann in the aforementioned *Sitzungsberichte*, p. 136.

This did not mean that the property of the Jews could be readily expropriated by the king except for cause. In fact, the Charter of 1201, whose provisions went back to those enacted by Henry I, expressly stated that "when a Jew dies, his body shall not be detained above earth, but his heirs shall have his money and his debts." [1]

In the course of the thirteenth century the status of English Jewry greatly deteriorated. Yet the principle remained the same. Despite his numerous inconsistencies, even John Lackland upheld it. His attitude toward Jews varied much less than, for instance, that toward the Papacy, to which he first submitted as a vassal, but from whose tutelage he subsequently extricated himself more or less successfully. He so angered the domineering Innocent III that the pope excommunicated him, although he did not depose him, as is often asserted. While squeezing out of his Jewish subjects as much money as he could, John in his own self-interest endeavored to safeguard their commercial activities. In his aforementioned Charter of 1201 he provided, therefore,

> And wherever Jews be, be it lawful for them to go wheresoever they will with all their chattels, as our proper goods [*sicut res nostrae propriae*], and be it unlawful for any to delay or forbid them. And We ordain, that throughout the whole of England and Normandy they be quit of all customs and tolls and prisage of wine, as our proper chattel [*sicut nostrum proprium catallum*]. And We com-

[1] John I's Charter of 1201, Art. iii, in *The Rotuli chartarum*, ed. for The Record Commission by T. D. Hardy, London, 1837, vol. i, p. 93 (in Jacobs's English translation, p. 212). Of course, in theory, the king, as the Jews' overlord, could freely inherit all their property. Under exceptional circumstances he did expropriate an entire estate, such as that of Aaron of Lincoln, the incompleted liquidation of which took the royal bureaucracy sixteen years. But, as a rule, the Treasury was satisfied with a moderate estate tax. In essence, this held true also of the estates of practically the entire baronage of England, where an estate tax in practice substituted for the exercise by the king of his theoretical eminent domain. *See* my *A Social and Religious History of the Jews*, 2d ed., vol. iv, pp. 79, 278, n. 103.

mand you and ordain, that you have them in ward and guard and countenance. [1]

While generally adhering to these principles, Henry III found himself so frequently in financial straits that he began exploiting his Jewish resource with unprecedented severity. In 1255 he plaintively replied to a Jewish delegation which asked him for mercy in his tax assessment, "It is no wonder that I covet money, for it is dreadful to think of the debts in which I am involved.... I am a mutilated and diminished king....I am, therefore, under the necessity of living on money obtained in all quarters, from whomsoever and in what manner so ever I can acquire it." [2] Finally, he had to pawn his Jews for a loan of £ 5,000 to his brother, Richard of Cornwall. Having surrounded himself, moreover, with a number of Continental advisers, whose ruthless exploitation antagonized all classes of society and greatly contributed to the unrest which ultimately resulted in the "Barons'

[1] John's decree loc. cit. The king's purported deposition by Innocent III, which might have spelled a temporary end to England's national independence, has rightly been denied by C. R. Chenney in "The Alleged Deposition of King John," Studies in Medieval History Presented to F. M. Powicke (London 1948), pp. 100-116. In fact, John's submission and following excommunication, as well as his subsequent enactment of the Magna Carta and its futile denunciation by the Pope—all high-lighted the growth of national sovereignty of the English monarchy. See also Marcel David, La Souveraineté et les limites juridiques du pouvoir monarchique du XIe au XVe siècle (Paris 1954), (Annales de la Faculté de droit et des sciences politiques de Strasbourg, I), especially pp. 212 ff.

[2] Matthew Paris, Chronica majora, edited by Henry Richard Luard, 7 vols. (London 1872-73), especially vol. v, pp. 487 f.; in the partial English translation by J. A. Giles entitled English History from the Year 1235 to 1273, 3 vols. (London 1852-54), vol. iii, p. 114. Modern scholars have compiled a number of lists of Jewish taxes during Henry III's regime. Some of the fullest are those presented by Peter Elman in "The Economic Causes of the Expulsion of the Jews in 1290," Economic History Review, vol. vii (1936-37), pp. 145-54, especially pp. 153 f.; and by Cecil Roth in A History of the Jews in England (Oxford 1941), pp. 270 f. These lists require a "drastic reduction", however, according to Frederick M. Powicke in his King Henry III and the Lord Edward, 2 vols. (London 1947), vol. i, p. 311.

Revolt," he used some of these officials also in administering all Jewish fiscal affairs. As early as June 28, 1232, he granted Peter de Rivaux (Rivallis) "the custody of the king's Jewry of England, so that all the Jews of England shall be intendant and accountable to him of all things belonging to the king." A month later he extended Peter's authority over the Jews of Ireland "for life." [1] Finally, Henry came to the sweeping conclusion that "no Jew remain in England unless he do the King's service, and from the hour of birth every Jew whether male or female serve Us in some way." This statement, included in Henry III's mandate to the Justices of the Jews in 1253, reflected both the growing dependence of Jews on the Crown and the latter's increasing reciprocal dependence on the Jewish revenue. [2]

It was out of this atmosphere of overassertion of the royal power, partly intended to counteract the growingly rebellious trends among the nobles, that the distinguished English jurist, Henry de Bracton, overemphasized also the royal authority over Jews. As a student of Roman law, this jurist was generally inclined to attribute to the kings of England some of the *auctoritas* of the ancient Roman emperors. Perhaps with unconscious humor he observed, therefore, that "a Jew cannot have anything of his own, because whatever he acquires, he acquires not for himself but for the king; because they [the Jews] do live not for themselves but for others, and so they acquire for others and not for themselves." [3]

[1]   Henry's grants to Peter de Rivaux are reproduced in the *Calendar of the Charter Rolls*, I, p. 163, 166 f.

[2]   Henry III's *Mandatum* of 1253 began by stating: "*Quod nullus Judeus maneat in Anglia nisi servicium Regis faciat; et quam cito aliquis Judeus natus fuerit, sive sit masculus sive femina, serviat Nobis in aliquo.*" This *Mandatum* is reproduced in Latin and in English translation in J. M. Rigg, ed., *Select Pleas, Starrs, and Other Records from the Rolls of the Exchequer of the Jews A.D.* 1220-1284 (London 1902), pp. xlviii f.

[3]   Henry de Bracton, *De legibus et consuetudinibus Angliae*, v. 6, 6, edited by Travers Twiss, VI, 50 f.: "*Judaeus vero nihil proprium habere potest, quia quicquid acquirit non sibi acquirit sed regi, quia*

This assertion, written in the 1250s, has led many modern scholars to view the status of medieval English Jewry in terms of total inferiority and "rightlessness." Even such eminent students of medieval English law as Frederick Pollock and Frederick William Maitland, who admitted that they had not found the actual term *servus* applied to Jews in any medieval text, nevertheless stated unequivocally that "the Jews' relation to the king is very much like the villein's relation to his lord." [1]

non vivunt sibi ipsis sed aliis, et sic aliis acquirunt et non sibi ipsis." This statement of the famous English jurist, made in connection with the law of warranty and comparing the Jew with a landless Christian, neither of whom owned land subject to foreclosure, has often been quoted in Jewish historical literature, but without reference to Bracton's very complicated juridical and historical theories. As a student of the Italian glossators of Roman law, Bracton tried to assimilate the status of the English king to that of the ancient Roman emperor, as reflected in the Roman law codes. Hence, his theory of kingship, including the king's power over Jews, resembled in many ways the imperial doctrine of Jewish serfdom as defined in the contemporary German law books; of course, without the latter's direct reference to the Holy Roman emperors' succession to the ancient caesars and their mastery over the descendants of "captives" vanquished by Titus. It must also be borne in mind that the extant texts of Bracton's treatises leave much to be desired and that, generally, "Bracton's doctrine is a web artificially woven with threads of various kinds and various provenance." *See* Schulz's "Conclusion," in *English Historical Review*, vol. lx, 175; Charles H. McIlwain, "The Present Status of the Problem of the Bracton Text," *Harvard Law Review*, vol. lvii (1943), 220-40; and, more generally, his *Constitutionalism, Ancient and Modern*, 2d ed. (Ithaca 1947); and the searching chapter devoted to Bracton by Ernst H. Kantorowicz in *The King's Two Bodies: A Study in Mediaeval Political Theology* (Princeton 1957), pp. 143 ff. In contrast to his namesake H. Kantorowicz, this author accepts the more widely held assumption that Bracton's *De Legibus* was completed around 1259. *Ibid.*, p. 145, n. 173. See also *supra*, p. 6 n. 1.

[1]   Frederick Pollock and Frederick William Maitland, *The History of English Law Before the Time of Edward I*, 2d ed. (Cambridge 1903-23), vol. i, pp. 471 ff. This view of the distinguished historians of English law still represents the regnant opinion among Jewish historians as well. Frank I. Schechter, especially, went all out in trying to prove "The Rightlessness of Medieval English Jewry," *JQR*, n.s., vol. iv (1913-14), 121-51. Scholars were too prone to overlook the very serious reservations against this view expressed by Cyril M.

Such exaggerations have, to some extent, been rectified in more recent research. But the mere fact that Jews appeared to the public as pawns of royal power sufficed to bring down upon them the wrath of the nobles, as well as of the competitive burghers. Among the complaints voiced by the gentry before the "Barons' War" was that there was "collusion" between the Jews and the king, inasmuch as, through their loans to the much-indebted nobility, Jews had often foreclosed the latter's landed estates and thus indirectly transferred them to the royal domain. For other reasons the burghers likewise resented the alliance between the royal power and Jewry and often insisted that the kings grant their particular cities the right of not tolerating Jews at all. Ultimately, the Crown in the person of Edward I yielded to these ever-accumulating pressures and in 1290 agreed to expel the Jews from the country. [1]

Picciotto in his stimulating analysis of "The Legal Position of the Jews in Pre-Expulsion England, as Shown by the Plea Rolls of the Jewish Exchequer," *Transactions of the Jewish Historical Society of England*, vol. ix (1922), pp. 67-84. In all these discussions, however, there is no reference to the incipient nationalism and, connected with it also, the growing secularization of English life. On the latter, *see* especially J. R. Strayer, "The Laicization of French and English Society in the Thirteenth Century," *Speculum*, vol. xv (1940), pp. 76-86; and Georges de Lagarde, *La Naissance de l'esprit laïque au déclin du moyen âge*, I: Bilan du XIIIe siècle, 3d ed. (Louvain 1956).

[1]   While refraining from specifically naming the king, the barons clearly had him in mind when they spoke of the "powerful personages" who had conspired with the Jews in expropriating some of the large estates for the benefit of the Crown. *See* the data cited by Rigg in his *Select Pleas*, pp. xxxvii f.; and, more generally, R. F. Treharne, *The Baronial Plan of Reform, 1258-1263* (Manchester 1932), (Publications of the University of Manchester, Historical Series, LXII). On the expulsion of the Jews from England, by virtue of which the king gave up a substantial, if declining, revenue from his Jewish "serfs" in return for a financial contribution voted by Parliament, *see* the older, but still highly informative study by B. L. Abrahams, "The Expulsion of the Jews from England in 1290," *JQR*, vol. vii (1894-95), pp. 75-100, 236-58, 428-58.

France

Across the Channel the situation was much more complicated. In those large sections of France which during the
thirteenth century were under the suzerainty of the English
Crown, the kings tried to establish the royal supremacy over
Jews along the English lines. But the rest of the country
was deeply divided. Some of the vassals of the Capetian
kings—even the kings of England in their capacity as dukes
of Normandy formally were such vassals of the French
dynasty—were to all intents and purposes independent kings,
more or less equal in power with their nominal overlords.
Certainly the Counts of Champagne or Toulouse could not be
dictated to from Paris. But slowly and imperceptibly the
royal family concentrated more and more power in its hands
and before long transformed France into an even more unitarian
monarchy than those of its Spanish and English neighbors.

This accomplishment came about only after a protracted
three-cornered struggle against papal supremacy, the pretensions of the Holy Roman Empire, and the self-assertive
French princes and nobles. In the case of Jews, it was relatively
easy for the French kings to affirm that in all temporal matters
relating to the taxation of Jews and their judicial administration, the pope should exercise no direct authority. St. Louis
and his successors were ready to go along with the papal
demands in such spiritual matters as the defense of the Christian faith against the alleged "blasphemies" contained in the
Talmud. If Gregory IX's assault on that Jewish classic was
to some extent influenced by his critical struggle with Emperor
Frederick II, [1] the French king was the only one among the
European monarchs appealed to by the pope to respond
quickly and effectively. The result was the well-known burning
of the Talmud in 1244. Louis also actively promoted Jewish
conversions to Christianity, although each conversion involved
the loss of a taxpayer. In time, however, even in spiritual

---

[1] *See* the article mentioned *supra*, p. 17 [1] n. 1.

matters such as the relapse of a convert, or sexual relations between a Jew and a Christian woman, royal officials, acting upon the king's orders, often prevented the ecclesiastical Inquisitors from exercising what they considered their legitimate jurisdiction. [1]

In its struggle with the Empire the French Crown had to overcome not only the imperial claims to universal overlordship but also certain specific rights enjoyed by the emperors within French territory. Not only was Burgundy a more or less permanent bone of contention between the two countries, but Frederick I Barbarossa held direct seniorates in southern France which affected Jews as well. In 1177, for instance, he issued a privilege in favor of Archbishop Raymond de Bollène of Arles which read in part:

We generously add as a gift of Our benevolence the extension of his and his successor's power over the Jews residing in the city of Arles who belong to Our Chamber. We firmly state that no one shall dare for any reason whatever to impose upon them his rule through any exactions without his [the Archbishop's] consent and counsel. Anyone running counter to this statute and order of Our Majesty should know that he will without any doubt fall under Our ban, be peremptorily excluded from Our grace, and be subject to a fine of forty pounds of gold of the best alloy, of which one half shall be paid to Our Treasury, and the other half to the offended Archbishop.

[1]   Charles V. Langlois, "Formulaires et lettres du XIIe, du XIIIe et du XIVe siècle", *Notices et extraits des manuscrits de la Bibliothèque Nationale et autres bibliothèques*, vol. xxxiv, Part 1 (1891), pp. 19 f., n. 14; Robert Anchel, *Les Juifs de France*, (Paris 1946), pp. 116 f. These measures contrasted sharply with the judicial principle enunciated by the Paris Parlement, as late as 1319, in its order to the bailiff of Meaux. Here the royal official was told to remove certain Jewish defendants from the jurisdiction of the episcopal court, unless their crimes *"talia sint, quod fidem catholicam tangent"*. See the *Actes du Parlement de Paris*, ed. by Edgar Boutaric, 1st ser. II, Paris, 1867, p. 291 No. 5848. This decision was more in keeping with the general order issued by Philip the Fair and reproduced by Langlois, *loc. cit.*

This privilege placed the ancient community of Arles on a par with those of many other feudal possessions of the kingdom. [1] Gradually the doctrine prevailed that "the king of France is the first [*princeps*] in his kingdom" (this phrase was used by William Durand who otherwise still considered the emperor "lord of the world"). Yet there still was sufficient lack of clarity concerning the ultimate dependence of French Jewry in the early fourteenth century for an Austrian chronicler to explain the expulsion of Jews from France in 1306 by the French king's refusal to keep within his territory serfs of the imperial Chamber, that is, subjects of a foreign, often hostile power. [2] But these were ideological exaggerations which by that time hardly had any tangible impact on reality.

More serious were the difficulties encountered by the kings outside the Ile de France. In the twelfth century the monarchy was still weak enough for Philip Augustus to try to resolve them by mutual agreement. Prompted by greed, he ousted the Jews from the royal possessions in 1182, but he soon realized that his financial gain was short-lived and that the expulsion really accrued to the benefit of his vassals. For

[1] J. L. A. Huillard-Bréholles, *Historia diplomatica Friderici Secundi sive constitutiones, privilegia, mandata, instrumenta quae supersunt istius imperatoris et filiorum ejus*, 7 vols. (Paris 1851-61), vol. ii, Part 1, pp. 473 ff. (this is Frederick II's confirmation, in 1225, of Frederick I's earlier privilege).

[2] Ottokar von Horneck, *Österreichische Reimchronik*, vv. 91239-775, especially 91276-78, edited by Joseph Saemüller, 2 parts (Hanover 1893), (*Monumenta Germaniae Historica*, Deutsche Chroniken, V), vol. ii, pp. 1186 ff. This tale by the Austrian chronicler need not be taken at its face value. Yet it is symptomatic of what contemporaries considered probable. Otherwise, Philip IV's France was reaching a stage of national consciousness which far exceeded anything known in the earlier generations. *See* Laetita Boehm, "Gedanken zum Frankreich-Bewusstsein im frühen 12. Jahrhundert," *Historisches Jahrbuch*, vol. lxxiv (1954), pp. 681-87; Mario delle Piane, "Saggio sull'ideologia nazionale nella Francia di Filippo il Bello," *Studi senesi*, vols. lxvi-lxvii (1954-55), 65-96. In the light of these newly understood nationalist trends, the expulsions of the Jews from France in 1306 and thereafter, will likewise have to be re-evaluated. *See* for the time being Isidore Loeb, "Les Expulsions des Juifs de France au XIV⁺ siècle", *Jubelschrift ... H. Grätz* (Breslau 1887), pp. 39-56.

this reason he not only recalled the Jews in 1198, and made other efforts to attract them to his domains, but he also concluded remarkable treaties with Count Thibaut of Champagne and, somewhat later, with the counts of St. Paul and Nevers (1198-1210). The counts promised to restore to the king not only the Jews who had left France after the expulsion but also all future Jewish settlers from the royal domain. Reciprocally, the king promised to "extradite" Jews hailing from the other provinces. This policy of holding on to the royal serfs was pursued also by Philip II's successors, Louis VIII and Louis IX. These agreements culminated in the convention of Melun of 1230, in which Louis IX and a very large number of French lords mutually pledged themselves not to raid one another's Jewries. In contrast to the earlier agreements, this Convention was specifically extended to all the barons of the realm and provided that "no one in the entire kingdom shall be able to retain a Jew of another lord. Wherever a master shall find his Jew, he may freely seize him like his own serf, no matter how long the Jew might have dwelled under the dominion of another lord, or in another kingdom." [1] This extreme type of allegiance involved, of course, particularly the lord's control over the Jews' property. It is not surprising, therefore, to find Count Thibaut requesting Louis VIII for a seven-year extension in the repayment of a substantial loan of 10,500 livres which he owed to three royal Jews. [2]

---

[1]   E. J. de Laurière, et al., eds., Ordonnances des roys de France de la troisième race, 21 vols. (Paris 1723-1849), vol. i, pp. 47, 53; vol. iii, p. 475, Art. 3. Of course, there remained many equivocal situations. Typical of the medieval ambiguity was, for example, the complaint of the bishop of Nîmes to Philip the Fair about the seizure of his Jews. Philip recognized in 1295 the bishop's mastery over the Jews, but simultaneously insisted that these Jews were also the king's. He ordered their recapture from various barons. See the text reproduced by Léon Ménard in his Histoire civile, ecclésiastique et littéraire de la ville de Nismes, 7 vols. (Paris 1750-55), vol. i pp. 125 f., no. xciii (Preuves). On the earlier agreements, see my History, vol. iv, pp. 62 f., 269 f., n. 81.

Ulysse Robert, "Catalogue d'actes relatifs aux Juifs pendant le moyen âge," REJ, vol. iii (1881), pp. 211-24, especially 212 f.; and

All this was but a stopgap measure, however. With the growth of the royal authority no further agreements were needed, particularly after the expulsion of the Jews from France in 1306 and their readmission in 1315. Philip the Fair and his successors fought off not only the papal and imperial supremacy, but also effectively consolidated the power of the Crown over all of France. In the few decades still allowed to the French Jews before their final expulsion of 1394, royal control extended over ever larger parts of France and no one contested the king's authority over the Jews of that growing domain. Only a few vassal duchies remained on the periphery of royal France, such as the Provence, Savoy and Burgundy, where the Jews flourished during the fifteenth century. But the theory that the Jews remained subjects of their respective sovereigns remained uncontested.

Meaning of Serfdom

This is not the place to analyze in any detail the range of the various doctrines of Jewish serfdom and their manifold legal ramifications. Understandably, modern scholars reading in medieval texts the term *servitus Judaeorum* readily conjured in their minds the picture of Jews being treated as members of an unfree class, more or less on a par with the medieval villeins. This picture was imbued with much color and vitality from the indubitable facts of the great Jewish insecurity, the frequent persecutions and expulsions. It was further reinforced by the long-accepted "lachrymose concep-

Israel Lévi, "Louis VIII et les Juifs," *ibid.*, vol. xxx (1895), pp. 284-88. Not surprisingly, French courts had frequent occasions to decide in controversies concerning the mastery over Jews. For instance, in 1260 a soldier, Philippe de Chauvry, secured a decision in his favour after proving that a particular Jew had been *"cubans et levans"* on his property, but he had to promise *"quod non tractaret turpiter ipsum judeum."* Courts were called upon to decide even in a major conflict over the possession of a single Jew, Abraham, between the king of France and the duke of Burgundy. They finally decided in favor of the royal claim (1270). *See* Beugnot, *Les Olim*, vol. i, p. 122, no. xiii, 364 f.

tion of Jewish history" which saw in the entire period of Exile an unending succession of unmitigated sufferings.

However, the attentive reader of the documents here cited will have noted that the term "serfdom" has, for the most part, been employed by the medieval rulers when they wished to protect the Jews. True, they never clearly defined the meaning of that term. It was to the best interest of the monarchs and their juristic advisers to refrain from defining the terms too clearly, since obscurity in legal terminology could only play into their hands. They could use, even abuse, the existing regulations to suit their own needs. But on the whole they sought to safeguard at least the economic well-being of that major fiscal preserve. Hence the kings found it necessary not only to intervene in behalf of their Jews threatened by outside forces but, on occasion, also to stem some internal disorders within the Jewish community. For one example, Infante John of Aragon consented in 1380 and 1384 to the enlargement of the Jewish communal council of Perpignan to twenty-three members because, as he contended, the Jews, being his and the king's "treasure," he was forced to take action "for the public good of that community and its preservation." [1]

Moreover, the medieval legislators as well as the Jews were perfectly aware of the distinction between Jewish "serfdom" and real slavery. The latter was actually threatened as a sanction for various transgressions committed by Jews such as attempted illegal emigration. For instance, the crime of illicit circumcision of Moorish or Tartar slaves in Spain, or an attempt to leave the country without specific royal authorization were punishable by the confiscation of the transgressor's property and his real loss of personal freedom which he had therefore fully enjoyed. [2] This characteristic distinction

---

[1]   Baer, *Die Juden*, vol. i, pp. 487 ff., no. 330, 565 ff., no. 371.

[2]   *See*, for instance, the decree of John I of Castile dated September 3, 1380. Here the king threatened the Jews circumcizing Moorish slaves in the Jewish way "*qual quier o quales quier judios que lo fizieren,*"

appears clearly also in the privilege enacted by the German king William in favor of the city of Goslar in 1252. The king promised: "The city's Jews shall suffer no undue molestation or *captivity* from Us, and We shall protect them amicably and benevolently as *special serfs* or Our Chamber; but as it is proper, they shall serve Us as their lord and Roman king." [1] With reference to the conditions in the Spanish kingdoms, the fourteenth century jurist, Martin Didaci d'Aux, observed:

A Saracen or a Jew cannot oblige himself by contract or loan to become anybody's slave. They must not do it even on account of hunger, for their persons belong to the king. Not even the king can sell them except in the case of a crime. Neither do they really deserve to be called captives or serfs in the sense that they may be sold, because according to law they have the liberty to move about [*liberum habent volatum juxta forum*], but they may be given away. [2]

que ellos mesmos seyan nuestros cativos. E eso mesmo aquellas personas, a quien asi fizieren tornar de otra ley a la suya, para que mandemos fazer dellos lo que la nuestra merced fuere." See Baer, *ibid.*, vol. ii, p. 222, no. 227. Similarly, in the sharp decree of January 2, 1412, John II of Castile put the same sanction on the unauthorized Jewish emigration from Castile: "*e ellos sean mis cativos para syenpre.*" *Ibid.*, p. 270, no. 275, Art. 23. It may be noted that this entire law was repeated with some important modifications by Ferdinand I of Aragon. *See* the excerpts in Catalan cited by Baer, *ibid.*, I, 790 f. no. 485.

[1] William's Goslar privilege of April 3, 1252 is conveniently excerpted from the Goslar statutes by Julius Aronius, *et. al.* in *Regesten zur Geschichte der Juden im Fränkischen und Deutschen Reiche bis zum Jahre 1273* (Berlin 1902), p. 249, no. 585. The crucial statement "*Ad hec nullam indebitam molestiam sive captivitatem Iudei civitatis sustinebunt a nobis, et defendemus ipsos amicabiliter et benigne tamquam speciales camerae servos: sed sicut debitum est servient nobis tamquam domino suo et Romanorum regi,*" is cited here, notwithstanding our main concern with West-European, rather than German conditions, because it sheds an interesting light on the contrast between serfdom and slavery even in Germany, the center of the *servitus camerae*.

[2] Martin Didaci d'Aux, *Observantiae consuetudinesque scriptae regni Aragonum in usum communiter habitae*, fol. xxix r., cited by Baer in his *Studien*, p. 14, n. 12, where one may find additional illustrations.

Even the right to give the Jews away or else pawn them as security for a loan, occurrences frequently recorded in the medieval sources, were really not transactions between private owners, but rather arrangements between lords in public law. In this connection one must also bear in mind that whatever the king's theoretical prerogatives may have been, in practice they were severely circumscribed by custom and the generally prevailing sense of equity. As C. M. Picciotto has pointed out, even today "the King is the ultimate overlord of every yard of land in England. . . [he] can in law do innumerable things which he never does, such as attending Parliament, refusing his assent to a bill, or sitting in the Court of the King's bench. King Charles I lost his head for much less." [1] It was, indeed, this power of custom that the distinguished Tosafist, Isaac ben Samuel of Dampierre (Rashi's great grandson), invoked when he discussed the civil effects of Philip II's decree of expulsion. "For we have seen in the countries around us," R. Isaac declared, "that Jews have had the right to reside wherever they wished like the nobles, . . . therefore, if there is a regime which tries to alter the law and make a new law unto itself, this is not to be considered the 'law of the kingdom' for this is not a proper law at all." [2]

[1] C. M. Picciotto in *Transactions of the Jewish Historical Society of England*, vol. ix, p. 82.

[2] Isaac b. Samuel of Dampierre cited in *Tosafot* on Baba Qamma 58a, *s.v.* אי נמי; later quoted with approval also by the Spaniard, Moses b. Naḥman in his *Responsa* No. 46, edited by Simhah Assaf in his ספרן של ראשונים, Jerusalem, 1935 (Publications of the Mekize Nirdamim), p. 88. A similar position was taken by a number of later Spanish scholars in connection with an *affaire célèbre* concerning a controversy affecting the Jewish community of Perpignan after 1346. One of the scholars replying to the pertinent inquiry of Cresques Elias asserted bluntly: ומוסכם הוא מקדם בחצרות המלכים ומרגלא בפומיהו... שהיהודים בני חורין ואין ביד המלכים למחות בידם להעתיק דירתם אל אשר יהיה שמה הרוח ללכת. Another rabbi quoted verbatim R. Isaac's statement: כי דין היהודים כדין הפרשים להיות חפשים ללכת בכל מקום. *See* these answers, excerpted from a Bodleian MS by Baer in *Die Juden*, vol. i, p. 315, no. 224a, Replies 2-3. These rabbinic statements can give us merely an inkling of the Jews' interpretation of the nature

The very term *servitus* and the underlying conception of
lack of freedom have an entirely different meaning in the
medieval theological and juristic terminology than they have
today. Quite frequently *servitus* is used merely as the equivalent of our English word "service." For example, Bishop
Hexilo of Hildesheim wrote to Emperor Henry IV in June
1075, reiteratedly reassuring him of his faithful services
(*fidelis* or *fidelissima servitus*). [1] At times, the popes looked
with jaundiced eye on those monarchs or clergymen who
arrogated to themselves the use of the papal formula and
signed *servi servorum Dei*. More relevantly, as Otto Stobbe
has already pointed out, the term *servi* was often employed
in official documents with reference to the *ministeriales*, at
a time when these officials enjoyed not only a social but also
a legal position high above that of the free burghers and
peasants. [2]

Nor must we lose sight of the fact that the concept of
liberty in the Middle Ages presupposed a certain measure of

of the "serfdom" of their community, but we cannot expatiate here
on this aspect.

    [1] *Briefsammlungen der Zeit Heinrichs IV*, edited by Carl Erdmann
and Norbert Fickermann, Weimar, 1950 (*Monumenta Germaniae
Historica*, Die Briefe der deutschen Kaiserzeit, V), pp. 31 f., no. 13.
On the various uses of the term *servitus* in the Middle Ages *see also*
Charles de Fresne du Cange, *Glossarium mediae et infimae latinitatis*,
new edition by Léopold Favre, 10 vols. (Graz 1954-55), vol. vi, pp.
454-58. It is noteworthy that we hardly ever find the designation of
an individual Jew as *servus*, a designation which incidentally dis-
appears also in many documents relating to villeins. *See*, for instance,
the careful examination of that terminology in two French districts
by George Duby in his "Géographie ou chronologie du servage?
Note sur les 'servi' en Forez et en Mâconnais du Xe au XIIe siècle,"
Hommage à Lucien Febvre (Paris 1953), vol. i, pp. 147-49.

    [2] Otto Stobbe, *Die Juden in Deutschland während des Mittelalters
in politischer, socialer und rechtlicher Beziehung*, 3d ed. (Berlin 1923),
pp. 13 f.; Karl Bosl, *Die Reichsministerialität der Salier und Staufer*,
2 parts (Stuttgart 1950-51), (Schriften der *Monumenta Germaniae
Historica*, X). In this careful examination of the numerous documents,
extant particularly in Oppenheim, the author shows the gradual
transition from a purely mercenary to a vassal-noble relationship
between the *Ministeriales* and their kingly overlords.

dependence. We need not accept such extreme formulations as that advanced in 1939 by Adolf Waas that "liberty exists [in the Middle Ages] only under dominion, whereas the nineteenth century saw liberty only in the absence of dominion." Yet the whole medieval outlook on life was colored by the ecclesiastical doctrine of liberty which, until today, has never been able to grant to the individual full freedom of deciding about the truth of a religious tradition unequivocally stated in the revealed sources. Discussing the views of Gregory VII, A. Nitschke declared, "Under liberty Gregory understands not the freedom of human decision, but on the contrary man's freedom from purely human decisions by his full submission to the will divine." [1] Not surprisingly, therefore, the medieval jurists, according to Eberhard Otto, defined the free man as "a protected individual.... Originally anyone who was not unprotected or rightless was called free.... The very idea of freedom necessarily presupposes a master who protects and safeguards." [2] It was, indeed, in this widely accepted legal meaning of living as free men under royal protection that the Jews and most of their masters conceived their status as royal "serfs."

The full implications of these doctrines and their practical

[1] Adolf Waas, *Die alte deutsche Freiheit, ihr Wesen und ihre Geschichte* (Munich 1939), p. 29; A. Nitschke, "Die Wirksamkeit Gottes in der Welt Gregors VII," *Studi Gregoriani*, vol. v (1956), pp. 115-219, especially pp. 169 ff.

[2] Eberhard Otto, *Adel und Freiheit im deutschen Staat des frühen Mittelalters. Studien über Nobiles und Ministerialen* (Berlin 1937), (Neue deutsche Forschungen, CCCXXX), p. 37. In many of these writings, to be sure, one senses the impact of the Nazi ideology and its disparagement of liberty which dominated German thinking in the 1930s. But they do furnish some new insights into the medieval concepts of liberty which differed so greatly from those of our modern libertarian democracy. For a more balanced judgment *see* Herbert Grundmann's recent analysis of "Freiheit als religiöses, politisches und persönliches Postulat im Mittelalter", *Historische Zeitschrift*, vol. clxxxiii (1957), 23-53. This vast subject, too, and its impact on medieval Jewish status, will have to be discussed more fully in another context.

applications can become manifest only from a detailed analysis of the complicated status of medieval Jewry in western Europe. I hope to present it within the given spatial limitations in the continuation of *A Social and Religious History of the Jews*, Volumes IX-X.

CIVILIZATION OF "THE RELIGIOUS"
A Study in Contemporary Interpretations of Judaism

By Meir Ben-Horin
Dropsie College

"A vision is not a scene but it can enable us to construct scenes which would not exist without it." [1] Applied to definition, this observation permits a practical import beyond the academic penchant to become visible: a definition is not so much a description of reality as it is a programmatic announcement. Presenting itself as a culmination of inquiry or reflection, it signifies a momentary pause, a regrouping of forces, a readjusting of tactics. A definition signalizes a plan for the resumption of more fruitful activity.

Like more elaborate claims, like ideas, hypotheses, truths, definitions are judged by their consequences in action. These consequencas may be events reliably reported and confirmed in chronicles of the past; they may be anticipations based on commonly experienced recurrences; or they may be intuitions of events without precedent. Essentially, definitions are projective acts captured in concise statement, awaiting release in application.

It follows that to define Judaism is to deal in plans, programs, future acts. What is seemingly an academic exercise, amounts in effect to a declaration of policy. To define government as a nightwatchman is one example. To define man as a praying animal is another. To define God as One is a third.

To say what Judaism is, is to say what Judaism is to be. For "all things that *are* have potentialities." [2] This states the dimensions of the problem and, at the same time, its limita.

---

[1] John Dewey, *Logic: The Theory of Inquiry* (New York 1938), p. 304.
[2] *Ibid.*

tions. For estimates of future fullfilment and declarations
of desirabilities are essentially elements of faith in search of
validation. It is only to some that their pre-validated status
would recommend them. They will not readily command
unanimity of acceptance until shown to have been as nearly
accurate as they professed to be. Newer definitions seem to
both wax and wane on subjectivity.

What is Judaism?

Efforts to arrive at an acceptable answer to the question
"What is Judaism?" often are obstructed by the ambiguity
of the word "is" in the question itself. "Is," being, existence,
reality, readily dissolve in mystery beyond intelligent discourse as reality preceding, succeeding and/or enveloping,
overwhelming, absorbing the realm of human experience.
When all existence is mystery, when inquiry is an affair of
establishing the place of individual existences within an
hierarchy of mysterious grades and shades, speculation about
the nature of Judaism is reduced to verbalizations on the
theme, "all things are equally mysterious, only some are
more so than others." Judaism is then classified with all the
other mysteries of existence and "understood" as enjoying
the status of a particularly mysterious kind of mystery,
of—metamystery. It belongs to the aristocracy, as it were,
of an otherwise democratic universe of awesome riddles
wrapped in enigma.

Contrary to this manner of reasoning, the present paper
will assume that an existence, whether its distinctive properties are of the mathematical-mechanical plane or of the
psycho-physical plane of plants and animals or of the psychical
or mental plane of human beings [1]—an existence, any existence at all, anything that *is*, is what it is in action or in

---

[1] See *id.*, *Experience and Nature* (Chicago 1925), ch. vii; John L.
Childs, *American Pragmatism and Education* (New York 1956), ch.
4; John H. Randall, Jr., *Nature and Historical Experience* (New York
1958), pp. 205 ff.

interaction. A thing is the aggregate of its doings, its dones, and its to-be-dones—to the extent that the latter affect the former. Existence, being, "is", is an affair or an event [1] in the realm of experience, the universe or that "totality of conditions with which the self is connected," [2] that dynamic, temporal, spatial, and pluralistic thick of doings and under-goings, "at once spiritual and material, complex and simple, intellectual and emotional." [3] Jewish life, existence, and being will be viewed as belonging to this realm of thisworldly interaction, transaction, and involvement. Judaism not only is *in* the dimension of geography, history, and society; it is also *of* it.

In his book *Israel and Palestine* (1952), Martin Buber, in a polemic against Theodor Herzl's thisworldly conception of the "promised land," urges us to believe that "it is of crucial importance to know that what is planned for the people and the land [of Israel] stems not from reflection but from a destiny embedded in the origins of time." [4] Now

[1]   Alfred N. Whitehead, *Science and the Modern World* (New York 1949 [1925]), p. 105: "We must start with the event as the ultimate unit of natural occurrence. An event has to do with all there is, and in particular with all other events." On p. 74: "...nature is a structure of evolving processes. The reality is the process.... The realities of nature are... the events in nature." *Cf.* Bertrand Russell, *A History of Western Philosophy* (New York 1945, 11th printing), p. 832. Randall (*op. cit.*, pp. 150 ff.) rejects the term "events" in favor of "substance" or the existing world which "is encountered as 'activities' or 'operations' taking place in various determinate ways—as acting and interacting with us and with other activities, as cooperating with us and with each other, as doing things to us, as something to which we do things in return."

[2]   John Dewey, *A Common Faith* (New Haven 1934), p. 19.

[3]   Theodore Brameld, *Philosophies of Education in Cultural Perspective* (New York 1955), pp. 101-103.

[4]   Martin Buber, *Israel and Palestine: The History of an Idea* (London 1952), p. 125. — John Brown, in 1859 awaiting execution as a traitor for fomenting rebellion of slaves in Virginia, refused, like Socrates, to consider plans for escape. For what had happened had been "decreed to happen ages before the world was made." Quoted from Horace M. Kallen, *Secularism is the Will of God* (New York 1954), p. 27.

contemporary astronomy speaks of light reaching its instruments after travelling some two billion light years, a
light year being the distance traversed by light in a year
at the speed of 186,000 miles per second. Electronic devices
may permit a range extension from two to six billion light
years, *i.e.* to light which started on its journey from distant
galaxies some three billion years before the earth came into
being. These figures suggest that the age and size of the cosmos is a matter of incomprehensible blocks of space-time,
of timeless time and spaces beyond space. Against this background, Buber's postulate is less than imposing despite its
enigmatic "depth": "It is," he says, castigating Herzl's
blindness to mystery, "of crucial importance to know that
what is planned for the people and the land stems not from
reflection [or human intelligence] but from a destiny embedded in the origins of time." If these "origins" precede time
itself, it is clear that Buber counsels abdication of reflective
thought in planning for the people and the land of Israel, in
favor of self-abandonment to mysterious patterns embedded
not *in* time but "in the origins of time," in pre-time or in the
absurdity of a time which, billions of aeons ago, preceded
time and—*mirabile dictu*—at a point in time proceeded to
give birth to it, presumably in immaculate origination.

To invoke mystery is to call a halt to inquiry. The effort
to understand what Judaism is is not advanced by reference
to an *is* which was wondrously ordained untold billions of
years before the earth appeared on the cosmic horizon and
millions of years before the Neanderthal stalked the land and
uncounted millenia before Abraham and Moses and Herzl.
Not answers but questions are formulated by allusions to
Israel or Torah or plans for our people or any people whose
is is grounded in the dimension of absurdity.

The realm of answers, albeit hypothetical ones requiring
correction, is the realm of natural events. To naturalize
Judaism in this realm is not to deny in advance its individuality, its uniqueness, its extraordinariness. It is to deny its

inexplicability and essential mystery. It is to accept the validity of the pragmatic thesis that "the most *extraordinary* events are *ordinary* events, in the sense that we must seek to explain and understand them in terms of their operations—that is, in terms of the empirical conditions from which they arise and of the empirical consequences to which they lead." [1] In this sense, phenomena are either "ordinary" or capable of becoming ordinary and hence meaningful— or they are not at all.

Taking the nature-based pragmatic view of existences as being in essence the sum total of their functions or powers in action, our search for an answer to "What is Judaism?" may be expected to have reached its goal when a formula is found which encompasses the sum total of the functions of Judaism.

The following four propositions will be briefly examined in the context of recent writings and will be rejected as falling short of the anticipated goal. A fifth proposition will be defended.

(1) *Judaism is a form of racialism.* Even in the 1960s it is not entirely superfluous to consider the racial definition of Judaism. Racism has not been defeated with the defeat of the Nazi power which incorporated it in its ideology. References to the "Jewish race" continue to appear in print. L. J. Cheney writes of the Jews that "no other race has survived as they have done from remote antiquity.... Wherever they travelled and settled, whether in Alexandria or Rome or Athens, they remained a race apart, meeting for prayers and reading of the Scriptures..." The Jews rebuild the State of Israel "with the skill and zeal of a race that has endured two

---

[1]   John L. Childs, *Education and Morals* (New York 1950), p. 169.— Max Picard (*The World of Silence* [Chicago 1952], p. 229) wrote: "When the layer of silence [which is the world before creation] is missing, the extraordinary becomes connected with the ordinary, with the routine flow of things, and man reduces the extraordinary to a mere part of the ordinary, a mere part of the mechanical routine." However, there is no need to link ordinary events with routine occurrences when "ordinary" is intended to refer to the order of human experience and hence to cover affairs with or without precedent.

thousand years of persecution, and yet has kept its own traditions." [1] Arthur Koestler describes the Jewish religion not merely as a system of faith and worship but as implying "membership of a definite race and potential reaction.... To be a good Jew one must profess to belong to a chosen race.... If a Judaic religion is to survive outside Israel... it would have to be a system of faith and cosmopolitan ethics freed from all racial presumption and national exclusivity." [2] Lucien Price recorded this comment by Alfred North Whitehead on September 10, 1941: "The Jews as a race are probably the most able of any in existence. Now when a gifted person is charming and uses his exceptional ability generously, he is a paragon and people adore him; but in the same way, if a person with unusual ability is disagreeable, his ability makes him just so much more disagreeable, and thus the disagreeable individuals in that race are the more conspicuous." [3] Reverend A. Cohen, in his discussion of "Judaism in Jewish History," concludes that Jewish history teaches unmistakably the Jewish people "is unique because the common bond has always been Judaism. Religion is so interwoven

[1] L. J. Cheney, *A History of the Western World* (New York 1959), pp. 56, 288.—Professor Karl Stern in *The Pillar of Fire* (New York 1951), the story of his conversion from Jewish orthodoxy to Catholicism, observed: "The Jews maintained the idea of racial integrity at a time when it had lost its transcendental meaning; for 'all was fulfilled' in Christ. If death, as Berdyaev expresses it, 'gives meaning to life,' here the ultimate death of a nation will give meaning to its life. But before that happens our people is condemned to live on as some sort of a ghost representing the idea of racism. It seems that in modern times the fate of the Jews becomes more and more intimately associated with the fate of the racist idea" (p. 184).—Professor Solomon Zeitlin has shown in an historical study on *The Jews: Race, Nation, or Religion* (Philadelphia 1936) that "by the time of the Second Commonwealth there was no longer a pure Hebrew race" and Jews were united by religion and culture. *See also* his "Who is Jew?" in *JQR*, vol. xlix, no. 4 (April 1954), 241-270.

[2] Arthur Koestler, *Promise and Fulfilment* (New York 1949), pp. 334 f.

[3] *Dialogues of Alfred North Whitehead*, L. Price, recorder (New York 1954), p. 147.

with race that they cannot be separated from one another. Eliminate the religion, and the race must fall to pieces." [1] Simone Weil charged in 1942: "The Hebrews took for their idol, not something made of metal or wood, but a race, a nation, something just as earthy. Their religion is essentially inseparable from idolatry, because of the notion of the 'chosen people'." [2] Finally, Professor William Barrett recently put it thus: "Biblical man, too, has his *knowledge*, though it is not the intellectual knowledge of the Greek....; he has it rather through body and blood, bones and bowels, through trust and anger and confusion and love and fear;... through living, not reasoning." [3]

But the case against the racialist definition remains airtight. Allport holds it "certainly wrong to think of Jews as a 'race'. They do not even constitute a 'type' within the Caucasoid stock. Such physical identifiablity as they have is due to the fact that in the region of the world where Judaism began an Armenoid type was common But this type included many peoples who were not Jews." [4] Kluckhohn

---

[1]   Leo Jung, editor, *The Jewish Library* (New York 1943), p. 51.
In an essay on "Race and Religion" (ca. 1910 - date and place of publication not given in the reprint available in the Dropsie College library) Prof. Israel Friedlaender suggested Jews were a "religious race" which made the interests of race subservient to those of religion.

[2]   Simone Weil, *Letter to a Priest* (New York 1954), p. 16. *Cf.* James Shotwell, *The Long Way to Freedom* (Indianapolis—New York 1960), pp. 64-68; 107.

[3]   William Barrett, "Hebraism and Hellenism," *Reconstructionist*, vol. xxiv, no. 16 (December 12, 1958).—Moshe Sharet, in an address before the Ideological Conference in Jerusalem, August 1957, asked: "What is the basic, worldwide Jewish concern? Clearly, it is the continued existence of the Jewish race and the preservation of Judaism." *Hazuth*, vol. 4 (Jerusalem 1958), p. 18 (in Hebrew). *Cf.* also Rav Zair, "Who is a Jew?" *Bizaron*, vol. xx, no. 3 (January 1959), 145 f. (in Hebrew [originally published in *Bizaron* in 1947]) and a letter from Sharet, *ibid.*, vol. xl, no. 7 (July 1959), 191; Zeev Jabotinsky, "The Race," *Diaspora and Assimilation* (Tel-Aviv 1936), pp. 288-296 (in Hebrew).

[4]   Gordon W. Allport, *The Nature of Prejudice* (New York 1958 [1954]), p. 117. *See also* Wilton M. Krogman, "The Concept of Race" in Ralph Linton, editor, *The Science of Man in the World Crisis* (New York 1947; fifth printing), p. 54.

dismisses racialism on the ground that "virtually all human beings are mongrels!... To speak of 'the Italian race' is nonsense, for there is every reason to assume that the Italians of Piedmont share more ancestors with persons who are French or Swiss than they share with their fellow Italians of Sicily. 'The Jewish race' is equally a misnomer because there is great diversity in physical type among those who practice or whose parents or grandparents have practiced the Jewish religion and because the physical stereotype which is popularly considered Jewish is actually common among all sorts of Levantine and Near Eastern peoples who are not and have never been Jewish in religion or in other aspects of culture." [1] Finally, a statement released by UNESCO's Committee of Experts on Race Problems on July 18, 1950, recommends that the term "race" be dropped altogether in favor of "ethnic groups," for

to most people, a race is any group of people whom they choose to describe as a race. Thus, many national, religious, geographic, linguistic or cultural groups have, in such loose usage, been called "races," when obviously Americans are not a race, nor are Englishmen, nor Frenchmen, nor any other national group. Catholics, Protestants, Moslems, and Jews are not races.... National, religious, geographic, linguistic, and cultural groups do not necessarily coincide with racial groups; and the cultural traits of such groups have no demonstrated genetic connection with racial traits. [2]

What plans and future acts are implied in the racialist definition of Judaism? External racialism requires discriminatory legislation (say, restrictions on immigration), separation from the body politic, and—under totalitarianism—physical destruction. Internal racialism advocates disengagement from the affairs of "the races," withdrawal into "chosenness," discriminatory legislation, higher and more

[1] Clyde Kluckhohn, *Mirror for Man* (New York 1949), pp. 110-112.
[2] The Scientific Basis for Human Unity," *The Phi Delta Kappan*, vol. xxxii no. 2 (October 1950), 34-36. *Cf.* Harry L. Shapiro, *The Jewish People* — A Biological History (Unesco 1960).

intricate barbed-wire fences around the "law," the "blood," and the spirit. [1]

(2) *Judaism is a form of nationalism.* Judaism, undoubtedly, has a share in evolving some of the ingredients of nationalism and in producing forms of nationalism that are peculiarly its own. Yet nationalism as such or the nationalism of the Jewish people is not coextensive with Judaism.

Three essential traits of nationalism, to follow Hans Kohn, originated with ancient Israel: the idea of the chosen people, the consciousness of national history, and both nationalistic and universalistic Messianism. [2] And "Jewish" nationalism became manifest in political, cultural, religious, and socialist Zionism, in culturalist autonomism, in culture-based federalism, in cultural pluralism or "orchestrationism." [3]

Man, as has been suggested, is imbued with a keen sensitiveness to "the call of the group." The state of mind of group solidarity "is in its strength and vigor an assertion of the group will to live, and is therefore as deep and mysterious and indeed as permanent as the eternal nisus of nature, the insistent push of everything that throbs with life and energy." [4] If so, it would be futile to assert that in Judaism the call of the Jewish group is not sounded and that the assertion of the group will to live is without strength and vigor. At the same time, however, it seems equally futile to reduce Judaism to the principle of nationalist homogeneity, consciousness, and cohesion.

[1] *Cf.* H. Loewe, "Introduction," *A Rabbinic Anthology* (New York ca. 1960 [1938], pp. lxxx-lxxxi.

[2] Hans Kohn, *The Idea of Nationalism* (New York 1944), pp. 36, 45; *id.*, *Nationalism: Its Meaning and History* (Princeton, N. J., 1955), ch. i. *See also* Koppel S. Pinson, "The National Theories of Simon Dubnow," *Jewish Social Studies*, vol. x, no. 4 (October 1948), 335-358; Chaim W. Reines, "Sources and Character of Modern Jewish Nationalism," *Yivo Bleter*, vol. xli (1957/58), 264-289; Simon Dubnow, *Nationalism and History*, edited by Koppel S. Pinson (Philadelphia 1958).

[3] Horace M. Kallen, *"Of Them Which Say They Are Jews"* (New York 1954), p. 83.

[4] Harry Elmer Barnes, "Nationalism," *The Encyclopedia Americana* (1953).

Liberty, as Kohn has pointed out, although often inseparable from nationalism, is different "in origin and substance,
in effect and duration.... Compared with it, nationalism is
only a passing form of integration, beneficial and vitalizing,
yet by its own exaggeration and dynamism easily destructive
of human liberty.... From Hebrew and Greek ideas the
age of nationalism drew many of its initial and fundamental
inspirations, but from Jerusalem and Athens shine also the
eternal guiding stars which lift the age of nationalism above
itself, pointing forward on the road to deeper liberty and to
higher forms of integration." [1]

The point is that while it would certainly be unwarranted
to identify Judaism with that malignant nationalism which
absolutizes the nation or its land and thereby transforms it
into a rapacious monster, [2] it is equally erroneous to conjugate
it with that fruitful and beneficent nationalism which strives
to restore to its people "the conditions of a creative culture—
pride of soil; a sense of historic continuity; deep roots in a
superbly aristocratic cultural tradition; and the special ex-
altation which attends a people in the great hours of its national
revival." [3]

For it is not that Judaism exists in one form of nationalism
or another; it is rather that a variety of nationalisms exist
in Judaism which, in itself, is an integration of a different
order.

In his essay on Jewish ethnicism, Professor Salo W. Baron
stressed the fact that religion and nationalism are for Jews
not conflicting categories "but an extraordinary organic
wholeness. In fact, one may legitimately doubt whether

---

[1] Kohn, *The Idea of Nationalism*, pp. 575 f. *See also* Moses Hess,
Rom und Jerusalem (Leipzig 1899; second edition), pp. 5, 15 and
Moses Hess Briefwechsel, edited by Edmund Silberner (The Hague
1959), pp. 397-405.

[2] *Cf.* John Dewey, "Nationalism and Its Fruits," *Intelligence in
the Modern World*, edited by Joseph Ratner (New York 1939), pp.
467-474; Christopher Dawson, *The Movement of World Revolution*
(New York 1959), pp. 152 ff.

[3] Abba Eban, *Voice of Israel* (New York 1957), p. 161.

these terms genuinely correspond to Jewish reality." Neither Bible nor Talmud have a word for "religion." *Dath* means something more akin to law and mores. "Judaism has indeed always been more a way of life than a system of beliefs and doctrines." Judaism

> must lean heavily on its religious heritage as the main positive basis for its unity. This heritage is reinforced by a certain community of physical descent which, far from being "racial" in the technical sense— even ancient Israel already was a racial mixture of ethnic groups speaking a variety of Semitic and non-Semitic dialects—has nevertheless helped maintain the historic links with a hundred earlier generations. This extraordinary combination of substantial physical and cultural continuity amidst great territorial diversity, of religious particularism and universalism, of obvious national insufficiency and high messianic aspiration has often defied classification under the usual categories of thinking. [1]

What plans and future acts are implied in the nationalist definition of Judaism? Its chief function is to make permanent and effective the alliance of the Jewish communities throughout the world with the State of Israel and to help defend Jewish communities in distress. The activities involved come, in the main, under the categories of financial aid, political démarches, diplomatic interventions, mass meetings, journalistic efforts—all aiming at the removal of the clear and present danger and the restoration of the *status quo ante*.

The chief weakness of the nationalist definition of Judaism derives from the fact that nationalism as such is not concerned with religio-philosophical reconstruction. It may create conditions requisite for such reconstructions, but the *use* of these conditions is beyond its province. [2]

It is worth noting that, externally, the nationalist definition serves the purpose of both excluding Jews from certain rights and including them in others. Schopenhauer, for example,

---

[1] Salo W. Baron, *Modern Nationalism and Religion* (New York 1947 [1960]), pp. 248-49.
[2] *Cf.* Nathan Rotenstreich, "Trends in Modern Jewish Nationalism," *Judaism*, vol. 7, no. 2 (Spring 1958), 138-146; Baron, *op. cit.*, pp. 217 ff.

concerned to block the emancipation of the Jews from pro-
gressing so far as to admit them to participation "in the
administration and government of Christian lands," pointed
out that historically the peculiar Jewish patriotism *sine
patria* proved more inspiring than any other: "The Jew's
fatherland is all the other Jews.... Their religion ... is
chiefly the bond which holds them together, the *point de
ralliement* and the field insignia by which they recognize
each other." Consequently he branded "a highly superficial
and false opinion" the view of Jews as constituting merely
a religious sect or the designation of Judaism as *Juedische
Konfession* or Jewish denomination: *"Vielmehr ist 'Juedische
Nation' das Richtige"* (rather is "Jewish Nation" the correct
definition). [1]

Early political Zionists, on the other hand, regarded the
adoption of the national definition by government authorities
as a political gain of the first order. In connection with the
British Government's East Africa offer, Leopold Greenberg,
Herzl's assistant in England, reported to the Zionist president
on June 7, 1903:

> It seems to me that intrinsically there is not great value in East
> Africa. It will not form a great attraction to our people for it has no
> moral or historical claim. But the value of the proposal of Chamberlain
> is politically immense.... it will for the first time since the Diaspora
> almost be a recognition of the necessity for aiding our people as a
> whole—not as a mere local section as was the case in the Berlin Treaty
> for instance—and hence will be the first recognition of our people as
> a Nation.... Everything after that will have to start from that point—
> the point of recognition of us as a Nation. [2]

Definitions, indeed, like "natural rights" and "natural laws,"
are declarations of policy rather than formulae expressing
the reality of things.

---

[1] Arthur, Schopenhauer, *Parerga und Paralipomena*, par. 132;
also Adolf Hitler, *Mein Kampf* (Munich 1939 [1925]), pp. 334-337;
Solomon M. Schwarz, *The Jews in the Soviet Union* (Syracuse University Press 1951), chs. 2, 14.
[2] Oskar K. Rabinowicz, *Herzl, Architect of the Balfour Declaration*
(New York 1958), p. 50.

(3) *Judaism is a reflection of cosmic mystery.* "Judaism is a link to eternity, kinship with ultimate reality.... Judaism is *the art of surpassing civilization*, sanctification of time, sanctification of history." [1]

In these formulations Judaism is divested of identity and dissolves in generality. Judaism may, indeed, be *a* link to eternity but it can hardly claim to be anything but one among many such links. Any other religion is such a link, [2] any culture, any philosophy, art, science. Love is such a link; thought, faith, goodness, truth, beauty are man's bridges "from here to eternity." To establish Judaism as *the* link par excellence is either to drown Judaism in the cosmic sea or to shrink eternity to a partiality or particularity.

Similarly, "kinship with ultimate reality" is probably enjoyed by all of reality, not by only certain segments. An *ultimate* reality that exhibits such partialities seems lacking in ultimacy; a more ultimate reality is likely to transcend it. [3] At any rate, a definition of Judaism would require a statement as to the particular *kind* of link to eternity, the unique nature of kinship with ultimate reality which identifies Judaism among the innumerable links and kinships with ultimate reality. And there is the additional difficulty of identifying eternity and ultimate reality.

As for "the art of surpassing civilization," Judaism is not its only practitioner. This art is a function of human intel-

---

[1]   Abraham J. Heschel, *God in Search of Man* (New York 1955), pp. 422, 418.

[2]   *Cf*. Christopher Dawson, *Dynamics of World History* (New York 1956), pp. 167 ff., 261. Joseph M. Kitagawa, "The History of Religions in America," *The History of Religions—Essays in Methodology*, edited by Mircea Eliade and Joseph M. Kitagawa (University of Chicago Press 1960), suggests that "any religion is man's experience of, response and commitment to, Ultimate Reality in a specific historic situation. No religion, however regional and ethnocentric, can be interpreted without reference to universal human themes, such as birth, death, love, marriage, frustration, meaninglessness, and beatific vision" (pp. 28 f.).

[3]   *Cf*. Meir Ben-Horin, "A Note on Faith," *The Reconstructionist*, vol. xxv, no. 11 (October 2, 1959).

ligence and human compassion, of the sciences, the philosophies, the arts, the systems of education, the religions. [1]
To the extent that a civilization is a civilization, it has the capacity for self-correction, self-improvement, self-transcendence. Such capacity is particularly characteristic of science-oriented cultures which refuse to be bound by assumptions of "ultimate reality" and boldly proceed to give "eternity" and "ultimacy" ever wider dimensions. [2] The art of surpassing civilization may be one of the arts of Judaism but Judaism, once again, is another kind of integration.

Nor does the idea that Judaism is sanctification of time remain tenable upon closer inspection. Time is an elusive term. Bertrand Russell saw what is important to the philosopher in the theory of relativity in "the substitution of space-time for space and time." [3] Space is neither a substance (Newton) nor an adjective of extended bodies (Descartes) but a system of relations (Leibnitz). "Since Einstein, distance is between *events*, not between *things*, and involves time as well as space." [4] In recent years, physicists "bear in mind the possibility that experiments may well prove that small-

---

[1] "...every day of a man's life represents a small bit of the evolution of our species, which is still in full swing. It is true that a single day of one's life, nay even an individual life as a whole, is but a minute blow of the chisel at the ever unfinished statue. But the whole enormous evolution we have gone through in the past, it too has been brought about by myriads of such minute chisel blows.... At every step...something of the shape that we possessed until then has to change, to be overcome, to be deleted and replaced by something new." Erwin Schroedinger, *Mind and Matter* (Cambridge At The University Press 1958), p. 11.

[2] "The immense discoveries of the recent past made it impossible to hold the view that all that was really worth knowing had long been known." J. Robert Oppenheimer, *Science and the Common Understanding* (New York 1954), p. 15. "It is a peculiar and revealing paradox that those who dream of total escape from the temporal perspectives of history end by turning local and temporary conditions into eternal verities." Charles Frankel, *The Case for Modern Man* (New York 1956), p. 77.

[3] Russell, *op. cit.*, p. 832.

[4] *Ibid.*, p. 71.

scale space-time processes may run in reverse to the causal sequence." [1] Speaking of Einstein and others, Professor Erwin Schroedinger indicates their discoveries made such a great stir among the general public and among philosophers because they meant "the dethronement of time as a rigid tyrant imposed on us from outside, a liberation from the unbreakable rule of 'before and after'." [2] Viscount Samuel went as far as to assert that "the real universe knows nothing of Space. And nothing of Time either. The same must follow of their combination of Spacetime." [3] They are mental devices or figments of men's minds, used to lay hold upon natural events. But these events do not happen *in* space or *in* time: "happening in" is not a fact but a form of speech.

Sanctification of time as constrasted with space is nothing but another figure of speech. Nor is there much substance in the notion of Judaism as sanctification of historical time. Which history? Is Judaism conceivable as sanctification of Chinese history, American, Russian, German, African history? It is not even meaningful to regard it as sanctification of Jewish history for this would imply a dichotomy of Judaism and Jewish history, the former being an extraneous force acting upon the latter and both being personifications of processes which actually center in human beings, namely the Jewish people.

Perhaps the principal weakness of the mystical definition of Judaism is its failure to make sufficient allowance in the meaning of Judaism for the Jewish people and for the variety of Jewish experience and expression. [4]

What plans and future acts are implied in the neo-mystical definition of Judaism? Influential Christian writers who

[1] Werner Heisenberg, *The Physicist's Conception of Nature* (New York 1958 [1955]), pp. 49 f.

[2] Schroedinger, *op. cit.*, p. 82.

[3] Viscount Samuel, *In Search of Reality* (New York 1957), pp. 41-44.

[4] *Cf.* Meir Ben-Horin, "Via Mystica," *JQR*, vol. xlv, no. 3 (January, 1955).

propose mystical definitions follow through with the recommendation that Judaism be permitted to attain its consummation in Christianity. Maritain, for example, in *A Christian Looks at the Jewish Question*, quotes Paul (11 Rom. 15, 25, 26, 28-32) and writes: "Thus from the first Israel appears to us a mystery; of the same order as the mystery of the World and the mystery of the Church. Like them it is a mystery lying at the very core of redemption. And we must say that, if St. Paul be right, what is called the *Jewish problem* is an *insoluble problem*, that is, one without *definitive* solution until the great reconciliation foretold by the apostle, which will resemble a resurrection from among the dead." [1] Like the Church which considers itself a mysterious body, so is Israel a *corpus mysticum* bound together not merely by ethico-historical bonds but by "a sacred and suprahistorical bond,... one of promise and yearning rather than of possession." [2] Reconciliation of Church and Synagogue is the condition of a solution. [3] Paul Tillich introduces the Jewish nation as "the nation of time in a sense which cannot be said of any other nation.... It has a tragic fate when considered as a nation of space like every other nation, but as the nation of time, it is beyond tragedy." [4] However, "Judaism has made a decision for space, namely for its national law," and therefore Christianity has separated from it. But "Synagogue and Church should be united in our age, in the struggle for the God of time against the gods of space." [5] What is the Church with which the Synagogue is to be united? It "is the place where the New Being is real, and the place where we can go to introduce the New Being into reality." [6] And the New Being or New Reality is "eternity conquering temporality.

[1]   Jacques Maritain, *A Christian Looks at the Jewish Question* (New York 1939), p. 25.
[2]   *Ibid.*, p. 26.
[3]   *Ibid.*, p. 33.
[4]   Paul Tillich, *Theology of Culture* (New York 1959), p. 38.
[5]   *Ibid.*, p. 39.
[6]   *Ibid.*, p. 212.

It is grace conquering sin. It is ultimate reality conquering doubt." [1] It is Christ.

Internal mysticism, allying itself with revelationism maintained by orthodox, conservative, and reform versions of Judaism, counsels piety as "unconditional loyalty to the holy." [2] But "the demands of piety are a mystery before which man is reduced to reverence and silence." [3] Its observances do not serve "hygiene, happiness or the vitality of man" but rather "add holiness to hygiene, grandeur to happiness, spirit to vitality." [4] It is characteristic of Jewish piety not to be mindful of the reasons for the *mizvoth* "but to forget all reasons and to make place in the mind for the awareness of God. . . . What reason could compete with the claim: This is the will of God?" [5]

Neo-mysticism, retreating from reason as incapable "to compete" with traditional authority, would discourage the growth of democratic trends in Judaism, the call for consent of the governed, the efforts to make manifest Judaism's relevance to modern man through the application of critical and inventive intelligence to its ways of thinking and doing. Instead, it encourages the reestablishment of a rabbinocratic or zaddikocratic order in Jewish life, especially the life of the Jewish spirit, the rule of "the sages" [6] and of the "pious men" who are committed to "higher incomprehension," to "wonder or radical amazement, the state of maladjustment

---

[1]   *Ibid.*, p. 213. *See also* his *The New Being* (New York 1955), pp. 17-18.

[2]   Heschel, *op. cit.*, p. 346.

[3]   *Ibid.*, p. 349. For an entirely different view of piety *see* "The Sane Piety" by Professor Sing-nan Fen in *The Review of Religion*, vol. xxii, nos. 1-2 (November 1957), 7-13.

[4]   Heschel, *op. cit.*, p. 351.

[5]   Heschel, *Man's Quest for God* (New York 1954), p. 137. *See also* his *God in Search of Man*, p.232.—The young Franz Rosenzweig thought of Italian art: "It is absolute music. . .it is something so incomprehensible that one could found a religion on it." Quoted from Jacob B. Agus, *Modern Philosophies of Judaism* (New York 1941), p. 133.

[6]   Heschel, *God in Search of Man*, p. 299.

to words and notions" [1] and to the subordination of philosophy, reason [2] and science to "spirit" which tells us "what to
do with science" [3] and to a neo-Biblicism which takes its
cue from a legendary Moses who when beholding the martyr-
dom of Rabbi Akiba asked his question and was told, "Be
silent, for such is My decree." [4] This neo-mystical scriptura-
lism is consistent when it deplores earnest study of philosophy:
In the seminaries "it is not the Psalmist, Rabbi Jehudah
Halevi, Rabbi Isaiah Horovitz or Rabbi Nahman of Bratslav;
it is Hegel, Freud, or Dewey who have become the guides in
matters of Jewish prayer and God." [5]

Attempting to spearhead a Jewish counterenlightenment
and counterreconstruction, neo-mysticism teaches a fanatical
absolutism which is not defensive toward free inquiry but
which goes forth from its sites to attack and to silence it.

As neo-mysticism is suspicious and disdainful toward
intelligence and democracy, so is it wary of Zionism, Judasm's
most dramatic return from revelationism and mystical ecstasy
to the world of intelligence and democratic association. Behind
its definition of Judaism lurks a medievalist program for
education, community organization, and "foreign relations",
a program which the voluminous vacuities of its recent versions cannot conceal. [6]

---

[1]   *Ibid.*, p. 46.
[2]   *Ibid.*, pp. 8, 20, 65.
[3]   *Ibid.*, p. 19.
[4]   *Ibid.*, pp. 68-70.
[5]   Heschel, *Man's Quest for God*, p. 60.
[6]   The following passages from Franz Rosenzweig's *Star of Redemption*, quoted from *Franz Rosenzweig: His Life and Thought*, presented
by Nahum N. Glatzer (Philadelphia 1933), pp. 339, 301, are as unsatisfactory: The Jewish soul, "replete with the vistas afforded by
hope, grows numb to the concerns, the doing and the struggling of
the world. The consecration poured over it as over a priestly people
renders its life 'unproductive'. Its holiness hinders it from devoting
its soul to a still unhallowed world... This people must deny itself
active and full participation in the life of this world.... In order to
keep unharmed the vision of the ultimate community it must deny
itself the satisfaction the peoples of the world constantly enjoy in

(4) *Judaism is the religion or the God-ordained way of life of the Jewish people*. This definition unites orthodox as well as varieties of conservative and reform versions of Jewish religion. It is also adduced for a variety of external purposes.

To orthodoxy, Judaism is the Torah way of life, and Torah, revealed by God, must regulate every moment of life alike of the individual and the Jewish people as a whole. "The essence of traditional Judaism," President Samuel Belkin of Yeshiva University wrote, "is the undisputable fact that the Torah, the revealed word of God, is not a mere constitution or code, but... represents divine authority and contains the highest wisdom and loftiest truths, and that as such, the divine law is sufficient for all time and should control and guide the entire life and destiny of our people." [1]

Obviously, the Torah requires clarification and application to specific instances. Hence, in the language of Rabbi Leo Jung, "interpretation, consistent with the basic principles of revelation, has ever been a characteristic of Judaism.... Through interpretation and re-interpretation, progressive revelation of the will of God and His guidance of man has been maintained.... Not how we find God, but the fact of reaching Him is essential. [Hence our] rare liberalism in interpretation." [2] Rabbi Rackman, President of the orthodox

the functioning of their state.... So far as God's people is concerned, eternity has already come—even in the midst of time." The Jewish people, he felt, "is denied a life in time for the sake of life in eternity.... It is not alive in the sense the nations are alive: in a national life manifest on this earth, in a national language giving voice to the soul of the people, in national territory, solidly based and staked out on the soil. It is alive only in that which guarantees it will endure beyond time, in that which pledges it everlastingness, in drawing its own eternity from the sources of the blood."

[1] Samuel Belkin, *Essays in Traditional Jewish Thought* (New York 1956), p. 36.

[2] Leo Jung, "Major Aspects of Judaism," *Judaism in a Changing World* (New York 1939), pp. 3-4.—The term "rare liberalism" itself is open to both liberal and illiberal interpretation. An example of the latter is the response by Rabbi Joseph B. Soloveitchik (*Conservative*

Rabbinical Council of America, suggested that Judaism should not be conceived of as a religion or a faith but rather "as a legal order,... an international legal order for Jews," with God's Revelation or Torah its basic norm. The three basic dogmas of Jewish theology are: "First, God is personal—He intervenes in the lives of individuals and nations. Second, He chose a particular people. Third, He and this people are forever bound by the provisions of the Torah." Through the process of interpretation Torah is kept viable, even progressive and liberal. [1] Or in the words of Rabbi Isidore Epstein, Principal of Jews' College in London: "The authority of all the affirmations of Judaism rests on the fact that it is a revealed religion." But while the experience of revelation remains a mystery, revelation "by no means denotes an interference in the natural course of things. Given a mind at the living heart of existence, all creation is but a revelation of the creative activity of the Mind of the Universe; and all the activities of the human spirit, as expressed in science, art or

Judaism, vol. xi, no. 1 [Fall, 1956], pp. 50 f.) to the question of mixed seating arrangements in a Cincinnati Synagogue: "The separation of the sexes in the synagogue is a basic tenet in our faith. It dates back to the very dawn of our religious halachic community and constitutes a Pentateuchal injunction (*issur de-oraitha*)which can never be abandoned by any legislative act on the part of a rabbinic or lay body regardless of its numeric strength or social prominence. What was decreed by God can never be undone by human hand.... A transcendental tenet is binding regardless of its unpopularity with the multitudes. Was the commandment against murder declared null and void while the Nazi hordes were practicing genocide?"—An example of the former interpretation is a response by Professor Louis Ginzberg (*ibid.*, p. 39): "If...conditions of a congregation are such that continued separation of family units during services presents a great danger to its spiritual welfare, the minority ought to yield to the spiritual needs of the majority." Going back to Jewish opposition to pagan immorality, this practice was not always observed even in the Temple in Jerusalem.

[1] Emanuel Rackman, "What is Orthodox Judaism?" in *Jewish Heritage*, vol. 2, no. 3 (Winter 1959-1960), 5-12. An important statement is the essay by Rabbi Shelomo Goren, Chief of Chaplains in the Israeli army, "Halakic Definitions of a Jew," *Or Hamizrach*, vol. vii, no. 1 (New York, December 1959), 8-11.

literature, are in a sense a revelation of that Supreme Mind."
The Torah given to Israel must be accepted, for through
Israel's testimony to God by means of the Torah, "there is
to be effected the moralization of all humanity, the hearts of
all mankind turning to the worship of the One and Only
God in purity and in truth, and to each other as brothers
with one Heavenly Father." [1]

The orthodox formulations, aside from their implications
for practice, are quite similar to basic tenets of reform Judaism
which, in its "Guiding Principles" adopted at Columbus,
Ohio, on May 27, 1937, defined Judaism as "the historical
religious experience of the Jewish people" and as "the soul
of which Israel [meaning the Jewish people] is the body."
Rabbi Julian Morgenstern, President Emeritus of the Hebrew
Union College, thus summarized the reform position in 1949:

We are returning, as it were, to the concept of revelation and of
religion which was held by the prophets; we are interpreting all our
history, from its beginning unto the present day, in the same spirit
as they interpreted it; we are conscious of the God of our fathers
revealing Himself to us still today, and to all mankind throughout
eternity, as He did to Israel of old. We, too, like the prophets, may
feel His spirit upon us, His voice speaking through us, and His message
of the ages upon our tongues. God in history, in the history of the
present and the future, as well as of the past; God eternally revealing
Himself and His purpose unto mankind; and we the agents of His
revelation...—this is the true message of Judaism.... In this spirit
of truth, progress, continuous revelation and historic evolution... we
must study and interpret our Bible for ourselves and for the Jewish
people at large; and not only our Bible, but all our vast literature and
all our unique, wonderful and inspiring history.... We of the Reform
wing conceive of Israel as a people, endowed from very birth with a
genius for seeing God in every aspect of existence and of interpreting
all of life, nature and history from the standpoint of the one, eternal
God and of His purpose and will for His universe and His creatures.
Israel... is chosen by God to be... the bearers... of His way of life
for mankind unto all nations and peoples and throughout all time....

[1]   Isidore Epstein, *The Faith of Judaism* (London 1954), pp. 119-
121; 290. *See also* his *Judaism—A Historical Presentation* (Penguin
Books 1959), ch. 3; Jacob B. Agus *Guideposts in Modern Judaism*
(New York 1954), pp. 292 ff.

Actually, modern Reform Judaism is the truest conservative Judaism, since its sole purpose is to conserve the ancient and eternal values in Judaism, while at the same time enlarging and enriching their content through new cultural contacts and contributions. [1]

While the most outright—and often scandalously malicious—self-dislodgment from the nationalist ingredient is advocated by reform rabbis identified with the American Council for Judaism, [2] conservative Judaism, at least in some of its formulations, assigns to Jewish nationhood a place of near equality with religion. Rabbi Robert Gordis, for example, warns that "conceiving of Jewish life either as merely a 'religion' or as a brand of 'nationalism' in the usual meaning of the terms means borrowing non-Jewish concepts which fail to do justice to the reality and the complexity of

---

[1]   Julian Morgenstern, *As A Mighty Stream* (Philadelphia 1949), pp. 34 f. *Selected Writings of Isaac M. Wise*, edited by David Philipson and Louis Grossman (Cincinnati 1900), pp. 260 ff. A reform rabbi, writing in 1959, hopes for the day when Jews decide to "reaffirm the ancient duty of Jewish survival. This will be possible only if the Jew has remembered, and accepted as authentic, the ancient encounter of his people with the living God. He will then accept himself as part of a people constituted by an encounter with the Nameless, and still extant as a people only because it continues to be committed to that encounter." Emil L. Fackenheim, "Jewish Existence and the Living God," *A People and Its Faith*, edited by Albert Rose (University of Toronto Press 1959), pp. 117-118. *Cf.* also Jakob J. Petuchowski, "The Concept of Revelation in Reform Judaism," *Year Book*, vol. lxix, Central Conference of American Rabbis (1959), pp. 212-239.

[2]   *Cf.* Morris S. Lazaron, *Bridges Not Walls* (New York 1959) who urges "American Jews can confidently reject Jewish nationalism and folkist basis for Jewish life, and at the same time believe in Judaism as a universal religion and the comradeship of world Jewry as a religious community" (p. 130). Lazaron ceases to be consistent when he condemns Jewish nationalism because, in part, "it was alien to the Jewish mind until recent times" (p. 121), but embraces Deweyan pragmatism as well as liberalism and reform.—For a discussion of "The Impact of Israel on American Jewish Ideologies," including the outlook of the American Council for Judaism, *see* Ben Halpern's essay under this title in *Jewish Social Studies*, vol. xxi, no. 1 (January 1959), 62-81.

the situation." [1] He, therefore, suggests that "if we insist
upon a modern sociological term, the Jews may be described
as a religio-cultural-ethnic group." But he immediately proceeds to explain that "the link which binds them together
is not political, but religio-cultural in essence, and the Jews'
most sacred concept is the Torah, which is both their law
and their lore, their culture and their code of practice, their
way of life and their world view, even if only in the sense
that it is the center from which they have diverged!" [2] The
priority of religion over nationhood appears with greater
clarity in a study entitled "Towards a Philosophy of Jewish
Law" by Professor Boaz Cohen of the Jewish Theological
Seminary of America. The first of the seven principles which
he believes were envisaged by the founders of conservative
or historical Judaism and "should be acceptable to most of
us today" is "the divine origin of the Law." The Mosaic
law—the second principle—is immutable and "not subject
to abrogation." From the time of Moses down to the Shulhan
Arukh—principle three—historical Judaism has undergone
an evolution without, however, "altering its original essence
or nature, or modifying its pristine principles and purposes."
Basic to conservative thinking—principle four—is the doctrine of *Kenesset Israel* which, despite the literal meaning
of the community of Israel, means "that the Jewish people
must be regarded as one community with respect to the
essential principles of Jewish Law and observance." Principle
five provides for a return to the Talmud "to reinforce our
flagging spirits. It is imperative now more than ever, to
recapture the spirit and significance of the Talmud with its
uncanny insights and precious intuitions, its homespun
philosophy, as well as the courage, independence and resour-
cefulness of its teachers." What is the ultimate authority for
Jewish ritual and civil practice? According to principle six

[1]   Robert Gordis, *Judaism for the Modern Age* (New York 1955),
p. 32.
[2]   *Ibid.*, pp. 47-48.

it is "the Biblical Law as interpreted by the rabbis and elaborated by the successive legal writers." Interpretation of the law can be entrusted "only to a body of men who combine expert knowledge of the Halakah, a special aptitude for applying theoretical rules to practical situations, a sense of the realities of the present, and a great devotion to the study of the law in all its aspects." The principle of interpretation—seventh—is "due process of Jewish law." [1]

The most telling summation of the conservative position on the nature of Judaism remains this passage from Solomon Schechter:

It is not the mere revealed Bible that is of first importance to the Jew, but the Bible as it repeats itself in history, in other words, as it is interpreted by Tradition... Since... the interpretation of Scripture or the Secondary Meaning is mainly a product of changing historical influences,... some *living body*... is best able to determine the nature of the Secondary Meaning. This living body, however, is not represented by any section of the nation, or any corporate priesthood, or Rabbihood, but by the collective conscience of Catholic Israel as embodied in the Universal Synagogue.... This Synagogue, the only true witness to the past, and forming in all ages the sublimest expression of Israel's religious life, must also retain its authority as the sole true guide for the present and the future. [2]

In the language of Rabbi Louis Finkelstein, chancellor of the Jewish Theological Seminary of America, this means that "any decision regarding the Jewish religion must be based on the Talmud, as the final résumé of the teachings of [the central living authorities] when they existed. The right of an individual to decide questions of religious Law depends entirely on his knowledge of the Bible, the Talmud, and the later manuals based on them, and upon his fidelity to their teachings. Those who acquired this knowledge are called *rabbis*." [3] In this sense, "Judaism is a way of life that

[1] Boaz Cohen, *Law and Tradition in Judaism* (New York 1959), pp. 1-38.
[2] Solomon Schechter, *Studies in Judaism* (Philadelphia 1911 [1896]), pp. xvii-xviii.
[3] Louis Finkelstein "The Jewish Religion: Its Beliefs and Practices" in *The Jews, Their History, Cultura, and Religion* (Philadelphia 1949), p. 1332.

endeavors to transform virtually every human action into a means of communion with God." [1]

What direction of future development is embedded in the religion-first definitions and understandings of Judaism? What are their chief implications for the life of Jewry?

In the first place, there is the obvious failure to encompass the varieties of Jewish experience. Whether revelation be conveived as "an intrusion from above," [2] as an enlightenment of the Universal Synagogue, or as endowment from birth "with a genius for seeing God in every aspect of existence"— the formula of Judaism as mysteriously or historically revealed religion falls short of embracing the multiversality of Judaism. It excludes (a) those versions of Jewish religion which reject revelation and ordained mission from a realm beyond the totality of natural events and (b) those versions of Judaism which regard religion as one element among several constituting the reality which is Judaism and which therefore reject the conjugation of Jewish religion with the totality of Jewishness. In his discussion of trends in Jewish life, Professor Eli Ginzberg pointed out that "too little weight has been ascribed to the collapse of the religious foundation of Judaism. Starting in the early nineteenth century and rapidly gaining momentum, the belief in revelation—the basic foundation of Western religion—became undermined. The full impact of this radical change is difficult to assess because it represents a phenomenon unique in Western civilization." [3] There was little basis for assuming any reversal of this trend: "It is impossible to contemplate a large-scale revival of orthodoxy in which the majority of American Jews could again recognize the overriding authority of the Bible and tradition." [4] For the Jew who finds little meaning in prayer and ceremonialism the

[1] *Ibid.*, p. 1327.
[2] Epstein, *The Faith of Judaism*, p. 107.
[3] Eli Ginzberg, *Agenda for American Jews* (New York 1950), p. 11.
[4] *Ibid.*, pp. 11 f.—For Israel *see* Aryeh Tartakower, "The Sociology of Political Life in Israel," *Jewish Social Studies*, vol. xxii, no. 2 (April 1960), 83-96.

synagogue is not likely to be life's primary institution. "The extent of change can be demonstrated by the fact that while previously most Jews attended services three times daily, the majority today do not attend three times yearly." [1] What has been called "religious revival," "the upsurge we are witnessing today may not be a completely unqualified revival of religion. It is, rather, a quest for the meaning of human existence... The number of Jews who are searching for values which can give meaning to their lives as Jews appears greater today than it has been in the past four decades of American Jewish life." [2]

The point is that neither enlightenment [3] nor nationalism nor socialism nor Zionism nor liberalism nor scientism, which have been answers to modern Jews' quest for values conferring meaning to their lives as Jews, culminated in the definition of Judaism as a God-ordained way of life. And unless these answers are to be condemned as "un-Jewish" and beyond the confines of Judaism, their emergence within the fold postulated an advance beyond the religious formulation, to the extent that they were incompatible with the notion of a God-ordained way of life. Indeed, they required the liberalization of even that intra-religious pluralism which consents to view Judaism as a "trifaith"—reform, conservative, orthodox [4]—version of the broader "trifaith" of Judaism,

---

[1]   Eli Ginzberg, *op. cit.*, p. 32. *Cf.* also Morris R. Cohen, *Reflections of a Wondering Jew* (Boston 1950), pp. 14 f.: "It is the strength of the Zionist movement that it recognizes that the primary reality is the Jewish people rather than any *ism*."

[2]   Albert I. Gordon, *Jews in Suburbia* (Boston 1959), p. 166. *See also* Arthur Hertzberg, "Religion," *American Jewish Year Book* 1958, pp. 113 ff.

[3]   Horace M. Kallen, "The Bearing of Emancipation on Jewish Survival," *Yivo Annual of Jewish Social Science*, vol xii (1958/1959), pp. 9-35, argues that with the *haskalah*, "Emancipation became far less emancipation from, far more emancipation for, the survival of the Jewish ethos in its diverse formations."

[4]   *Cf.* Solomon B. Freehof, "Directions for Reform Judaism," *CCAR Journal*, no. 19 (October 1957), 8-12, 18.

Catholicism, and Protestantism [1] or the still broader Judaism, Christianity, and Islam. [2] They called for a greater pluralism within and without the religious confines.

The effect, then, of the "God-ordained" definition of Judaism is, on the one hand, the restriction of the current Jewish quest for meaning to the problems, directions, and solutions already available to the defining authorities. On the other hand, its import is the restoration of social, economic, educational, and political (external relations) power to the hands of the religious establishment. Stated differently, in the struggle for the definition of Judaism or the projection of programs for Jewish continuity and reconstruction the issue of authority, *i.e.*, of directive power, is central. It seems to be the core meaning of the "religion first" definitions that the "Law," the "Universal Synagogue," or the reinterpreted words of the prophets, through ordained rabbis and allied laymen, must take charge of the destinies of the Jewish people, both in the State of Israel and in the lands of the dispersion. The search for definition, thus, is a moral undertaking in that it involves choice among significant life alternatives of the Jewish people.

It is instructive in this context to recall what Chaim Weizmann had to say on the subject of religion in Israel. He wrote: "I think it is our duty to make it clear... from the very beginning that whereas the State will treat with the highest respect the true religious feelings of the community, it cannot

---

[1] *Cf.* Will Herberg, *Protestant-Catholic-Jew* (New York 1955); *id.*, "The Making of a Pluralistic Society—A Jewish View," *Religion and the State University*, edited by Erich A. Walter (Ann Arbor, Mich., 1958), pp. 27-41. For a critique of Herberg's thesis *see* William K. Frankena, "A Point of View for the Future," *ibid.*, pp. 294-309; also Morris Kertzer, "Religions in a Democratic Society," *Reconstructionist*, vol. xxv, no. 1 (February 20, 1959), 3-8.

[2] Gandhi told Louis Fischer (*This is Our World* [New York 1956], p. 119) in 1942: "I am a Christian and a Hindu and a Moslim and a Jew." *See also* Friedrich Heiler, "The History of Religions as a Preparation for the Co-operation of Religions," Eliade and Kitagawa, *op. cit.*, pp. 132-160.

put the clock back by making religion the cardinal principle
in the conduct of the State. Religion should be relegated to
the synagogue and the homes of those families that want
it; it should occupy a special position in the schools; but it
shall not control the ministries of the State." [1] This hardly
means that the first President of Israel sought to remove
Judaism as "the cardinal principle in the conduct of the
State." It does mean that he regarded Judaism as having
a religion, not being one.

The consequences of viewing Judaism as a religion from
an outside vantage-ground often are the failure to recognize
the legitimacy and desirability of Jewish attitudes and efforts
in fields other than religion as well as the failure to perceive
the reality of growth and genuine novelty in Jewish religion
since the rise of Christianity and Islam. An example of the
first of these failures is the bewilderment of students and
observers upon first discovering that modern Judaism is
concerned with developing distinctive forms of education,
art, law, philosophy, science, associations, government, and
economics along with international and intercultural relations—all in addition to its religious concerns. [2] An example

---

[1]   Chaim Weizmann, *Trial and Error* (New York 1949), p. 464.
[2]   Crane Brinton, (*A History of Western Morals* [New York 1959],
pp. 340 f., observes: "To many Jews, the Zionist movement, even—
indeed, above all—in its partial success in Israel, has been an immoral
betrayal of the mission for which God long ago chose the Jews. For
them, Zion is no hill on this earth, and certainly no nation-state with
flag and army and a seat in the United Nations. To others, Israel is
truly the earthly Zion, without which no heavenly one, without which,
indeed, no chosen people. I do not think the mere historian can chose
here, for them or for us." In a note on p. 471 he suggests that the
"naturalistic-historical theology" of modern Christian thinkers is no
longer Christian and God as reformulated by the Jewish reconstruc-
tionists Kaplan and Cohen "certainly... is no longer even an heir of
Jehovah?"—This view contrasts sharply with that of Harry M.
Orlinsky, who wrote (*Ancient Israel* [Cornell University Press], pp.
29 f.) that "the fundamentally questioning and antidogmatic character
and outlook of ancient Israel" struck root in the patriarchal period.
God, conceived as theoretically omnipotent, was "actually subject
to considerable questioning." In fact, "the Hebrew mind expressed

of the second failure may be found in Toynbee's interpretation of Judaism as a form of "Man-worship." With Yohanan ben Zakkai, the British historian holds, Judaism took the road of non-violent archaism: "Yet is is an untoward achievement to have kept up, by this *tour de force* [of ritual worship], a form of Man-worship that has been found to be a bad religion by the general experience of Mankind; and, in any religion, a concentration of attention and effort on formalities is spiritually sterilizing....If non-violent Archaism has thus proved to be a blind alley, the acceptance of Suffering as the price of following the promptings of Pity and Love has proved to open up an approach towards Absolute Reality." [1]

its deepest self in its opposition to the absolute rule of any one man or tribe, be it kinsman or alien. This attitude extended even to the rule of God."

[1] Arnold Toynbee, *An Historian's Approach to Religion* (New York 1956), p. 85.— It is not more than a softening, not a reversal of view that a careful reading of—rather than into—a more recent statement by Toynbee would disclose. According to *World Jewry*, vol. ii, no. 2 (April 1959) he stated in part: "I would say that the future of Judaism is to convert the world... It is really something almost comic that outsiders [Christianity and Islam] should have seized on some of the essential truths of Judaism and have put them in what Jews must think a very garbled form.... Does not the real future of the Jews and Judaism lie in spreading Judaism in its authentic form, rather than in its Christian or Muslim form, over the whole world? After all, the Jews must have a more authentic form of Jewish monotheism than the Christians or the Muslims have. Is not this the Jews' future gift to the world? And is not this going to be the ultimate solution of the relation between the Jews and the rest of the world?" The decisive words seem to be "what Jews must think." Toynbee merely restated what some Jews have thought in the past and think now. In the volume just cited (pp. 298 f.) he rather suggested that the mission of the higher religions is not competitive but complementary and that "we can love [our own religion] without having to feel that it is the sole means of salvation." Elsewhere (*Civilization on Trial* [New York 1948], p. 90) he said the future world be would neither Western nor non-Western but would inherit "all the cultures which we Westerners have now brewed together in a single crucible." With all this vacillating between religio-civilizational co-existence and fusion, Zionism (*A Study of History*, Abridgement of Volumes VII-X by D. C. Somervell [New York and London 1957], pp. 178, 177) remained a "demonic effort" bringing to mind that of Nazism, inspired

The reduction of Judaism to its religious component, then, issues in attempts at various degrees of restriction for Judaism's "life-space" in both conception and action. [1] At the same time, it places Judaism within a category of association which is increasingly subject to massive challenge. As a religion, Judaism assumes a common uniqueness. "Let us be like all the nations" is transposed into "Let us be like all religions." But neither religions as such nor nations as such, many will agree, seem to be evolution's most successful formations. Strictly speaking, they have not been able to advance beyond the pre-historic, the pre-scientific, the pre-[fully]-human conditions of the twentieth century or the preceding forty or fifty centuries on written record. What has been hailed as "New Being" either is not new or simply is not. [2]

Judaism, in sum, is neither a form of racialism nor of rationalism. It is neither a reflection of cosmic mystery nor the religion or the God-ordained way of life of the Jewish people. Nor is it a mere combination of these elements.

The late Professor Louis Ginzberg's admonition to "the diametrically opposed theologians" applies: "What you say is so profoundly true and so utterly false! You are profoundly right in what you tell about the beliefs and doctrines of this rabbi or that apocalyptic author, but you are utterly wrong in your attempts to stamp as an expression of the Jewish soul what is only an individual opinion or a transitory fancy." [3]

The very fact of these varieties of interpretation argues,

"neither from the Law nor from the Prophets but from the narratives in the Books of Exodus and Joshua."

[1] Notable exceptions are Reinhold Niebuhr ("The Relations of Christians and Jews in Western Civilization," *CCAR Journal* [no. 21, April 1958], 18-32) and James W. Parkes (*ibid.* [no. 28, January 1960], 11-17). *Cf.* also James Parkes, *God at Work* (New York 1952), ch. 4 and his *The Foundations of Judaism and Christianity* (Chicago 1960).

[2] *Cf.* Meir Ben-Horin, "Toward the Dawn of History," *Essays on Jewish Life and Thought*, edited by Joseph L. Blau *et al.* (New York 1959), pp. 39-54.

[3] Louis Ginzberg, *Students, Scholars, and Saints* (Philadelphia 1928), p. 117.

on the one hand, that it is hazardous and even foolhardy to seek a formulation that, while transcending earlier ones, preserves what is valid in them and thus commands universal acceptance. Moreover, the principle of self-determination of peoples implies that the Jewish people, through appropriate structural devices for representation, should formulate what it regards as its own nature or self. For if Israel is our state, Judaism is our estate or our status. Finally, Ginzberg's warning is too compelling and encompassing to be arbitrarily restricted to some "individual opinion" and not to others.

On the other hand, the fact of these and other varieties call for a renewal of effort in the direction of their transcendence, however tentative and hypothetical. If ultimacy and finality is unattainable, the pursuit of correction—moderate but warranted—is continuous with the life of reason as it involves itself in the passing clusters of events. Within Judaism and about it, we will go on—to say it with Kallen— to "employ concepts to harness up diversification and multitude, to order and drive them according to our need or desire, to impel them upon a gradient of our preference to a goal of our choice. The concept is our postulate of prophecy and prediction." For "conception and understanding are the tactics, the strategy and the logistics of our struggle to go on struggling." [1] It is in this spirit that the fifth proposition or series of propositions is now set forth as more adequately expressing the nature of Judaism in the twentieth-century world.

(5) *Judaism is the Jewish people's civilization of "the religious."* In intent, this is identical with the definition of Judaism as the *dynamic religious civilization and the dynamic civilizing religion of the Jewish people*. It seems, however, more clearly inclusive of those versions of Judaism which stand beyond the pale of revelation-centered interpretations of religion. While fully compatible with revelationism, "the religious,"

[1] Horace M. Kallen, *Cultural Pluralism and the American Idea* (Philadelphia 1956), pp. 171, 173. *See also* Salo W. Baron, "Who Is a Jew?", *Midstream*, vol. vi, no. 2 (spring 1960), 5-16.

as will be shown presently, is equally hospitable to non-revelationist or secularist faith.

"Judaism," wrote Chief Rabbi Joseph H. Hertz of Great Britain in 1930, "cannot be reduced to a few theological and metaphysical principles, because it is the sum total of all the manifestations of the distinctively Jewish spirit. It is far more than a creed or a theology; it is greater than a denomination or a Church. Judaism is a *religious civilization* with its own language, its own literature, its own history, its own customs, and its own social institutions.... This Jewish civilization, aglow with a passion for righteousness, has resisted all tyrannies, overthrown all idols, and turned the course of history." [1] As a religious civilization, Judaism—in the language of Professor Mordecai M. Kaplan—"is the ensemble of the following organically interrelated elements of culture: a feeling of belonging to a historic and indivisible people, [2] rootage in a common land, a continuing history, a living language and literature, and common mores, laws and arts, with religion as the integrating and soul-giving factor of all those elements." [3]

As contrasted with brutalizing and de-humanizing religions of past and present, Judaism is both a religious civilization

[1] "Fundamental Ideals and Proclamations of Judaism," *The Jewish Library*, edited by Leo Jung (New York 1930), p. 54.

[2] Beryl D. Cohen writes in *Judaism in Theory and Practice* (New York 1948), pp. 54 f., the primary fact in Jewish life is "the peoplehood of Israel" and Judaism "basically is the historic religious experience of the Jewish people functioning today." Abba Hillel Silver, *Where Judaism Differed* (Philadelphia 1957), pp. 6 f., describes Judaism as "the emergent spiritual way of life of a historic people." It possesses the unity "not of a system but of a symphony." *See also* Huston Smith, *The Religions of Man* (New York 1959), p. 270.

[3] Mordecai M. Kaplan, *The Future of the American Jew* (New York 1948), pp. 35 f.—Leo Jung's distinction between civilization and culture, the latter being revealed—"Suddenly—a tremendous call!"—(*Living Judaism* [New York 1927, second edition], pp. 263-266) seems arbitrary. *Cf.* Ralph Marcus, "Notes on Civilizaton in Historical Perspective" in *Freedom and Reason*, edited by Salo W. Baron, Ernest Nagel, and Koppel S. Pinson (Glencoe, Ill., 1951), pp. 184-200.

and a civilizing religion. As such it is, on the one hand, an ethnicized socio-religious revolt against the imposition, from within or without, of an absolute, mystery-shrouded, untouchable and unchangeable pattern of living, believing, and knowing. In so revolting it expresses and embodies what Hegel in *The Philosophy of History* called the freedom of the spirit which "consists not in being at rest but in a constant negation of that which threatens to abrogate freedom." Couched in biblical style, this spirit seems to proclaim: "Thou shalt not make unto thee an Absolute, nor any manner of Ultimate, of anything that is in heaven above, or that is on earth beneath, or that is idea in the minds of intelligent beings wherever they may be. Thou shalt not bow down to them nor serve them, for I am a compassionate God, showing mercy to the soul erring in good faith and love to the creative spirits in all generations." [1]

On the positive side, Judaism as a civilizing religion or civilization of "the religious" is an ethnicized socio-religious *élan constructif*, a constructive energy of an historic-modern people's mind, heart, and might—directed and applied to the fulfilment of what it perceives to be the promise of individual men and women, of human societies, of the whole realm of human experience. Judaism as the Jewish people's civilization of "the religious" is grounded in faith in the reality of the promise of reality. "The religious" signifies attitude and conduct unified and franchised in selfless, inspired, and enduring dedication to the implementation of the ideal possibilities embedded in actuality. Or, in John Dewey's formulation, "the religious," if one prefers quite independent of the supernatural, denotes "the unification of the self through allegiance to inclusive ideal ends." [2] Possibility, potentiality, promise are as much aspects of reality as are denial, frustration,

[1]   Meir Ben-Horin, "Of New Space and Faith," *Judaism*, vol. 8, no. 1 (Winter 1959), 32.
[2]   Dewey, *Common Faith*, pp. 66, 33.

failure. Jewish civilization and religion *know* defeat and disaster. They are not so much battle-tested as they are cata-
strophe-tested. Yet Jewish religion and civilization *believe* in
the *possibility* of overcoming defeat through appropriate
works. They *have faith* in the promise of reality and in the
reality of the promise. In Judaism as a civilizing religion
God is felt and understood to reside in the promise of the
universe, that totality of events, processes, conditions which
sustain the awareness of the promise and transform it into
actuality or manifest reality. The hidden deity is not mystery
but promise, that aspect, configuration, or *Gestalt* of the
cosmos that constitutes the promise of ideal fulfilment or
salvation. God is what the cosmos does with its potentiality
for redemption. God is the "character" or the "personality"
of the cosmic processes through which ideal possibility—"the
promise of existence"—becomes practical actuality. "He"
signalizes universal events acting on the level of redemptive
potentiality. Revelation is awareness of the reality, presence,
nearness of the existential promise. Prayer is renewal of
faith in the reality of the promise, expression of this faith
and the "request" or renewed quest, the re-quest, for the
fuller meaning of the promise. Repentance, *teshubah*, is
return to the quest, to *tefilah*. *Zedakah*, charity, is contribution
to promise, making real part of the promise. Morality is the
continuous reorientation of conduct toward the promise and
toward the obligation to make it manifest in new fulfilment.
The categorial imperative of this faith reads: Regard reality
always under the aspect of the promise inherent therein and
orient your life toward its tranformation into new reality.
View reality always as "promising," never as final and "done."

   Zion, in this interpretation, is the promise actualized in
socio-political structure. *Geulah* is the actualization of the
promise, not through apocalyptic suspension of history but
through the redirection of history by mind and love. The
vision of the burning bush and of Mount Sinai ablaze with
the Presence is a mythical or poetic expression of the idea

that a physical object, that matter itself, that the world of human experience, may be seen as burning with promise, a burning which bespeaks the promise, a burning which may be seen, heard, sensed, dreamt, and thought.

As a civilization of "the religious," the commitment to faith in the promise, even in the face of catastrophe, even though "He will slay me," [1] Judaism has a religion, science, philosophy, art, education. Its religion is the consecration of human life to the pursuit of the promise and to its progressive realization. Its science is the experimental pursuit, its philosophy the intellectual pursuit of the promise of existence. Its art is the continuous realization of awareness of the promise through imaginative reorganization of portions of reality in stone, color, tone, word, movement, celebration of the memorable. Its education is the pursuit of the promise through continuous reorganization of individual and collective human capacities so as to attain to an ever fuller manifestation of humanity. In this sense "the religious" is "the integrating and soul-giving factor" of all the elements of Jewish civilization.

The familiar term *kelal yisrael* refers to both the whole complex of a people and its characteristic ways of doing called Jewish religious civilization and the whole complex of a people's characteristic beliefs and concomitant rituals called Jewish civilizing religion. *Kelal* means both community and principle. To belong to *kelal yisrael* as a human community is to belong to a community of fate, past, present, and future, known as world Jewry. To believe in *kalal yisrael* or the principle of Israel is to be committed to *bitahon*, faith in the promise of reality; [2] faith in the worthwhileness of life which is the effort spanning promise and fulfilment; faith in the supreme preciousness of human beings, the centers

[1] Job 13: 15. *See* the interpretation by Horace M. Kallen in his *The Book of Job as a Greek Tragedy* (New York 1959 [1918]), pp. 76 ff.; 109.
[2] *Cf.* Felix Eckstein, "Judaism—The Traditional, Existentialist and Humanist Approach," *Judaism*, vol. ii, no. 2 (April 1953), 148-159.

of creative thought and creative love, the instrumentalities of redemption; and faith in God as the "personality" of the cosmic processes through which ideal possibility—"the promise of existence"—becomes realized fulfilment.

Israel in his youth yearned for the Promised Land. Israel in his manhood yearns and strives for the Promised Earth, the Promised Humanity, the Promised Universe.

Judaism as the Jewish people's civilization of "the religious" or as the religious civilizations and civilizing religion of the Jewish people is at the same time a reality and an ideal projection which is to guide Jews and Jewish communities. It is partial fulfilment and anticipation of fuller realization of a "new being," a new stage in human evolution—the fusion of a people's significant life expressions with the awareness that everything given in experience is held in the embrace of the promise of existence.

What programs and policies are embedded in this generalist, "orchestrationist" and synoptic rather than exclusivist definition?

It implies that Jewish life, to rise to the challenge of its own promise, should flow through the following channels:

First, the channel of education. Jewish education is not only education for Judaism but no less significantly education of Judaism. It is Jewish civilization's chief instrument for making manifest the promise that inheres in the Jewish people. As such, its responsibility is to make catholic Israel aware of this internal challenge of which the external counterpart is the challenge to demonstrate Judaism's relevance to the human condition of the present and the foreseeable future. As such, its responsibility, in the second place, is to re-enroll the Jewish people as a whole in concentrated inquiry into its sources and resources, its triumphs and frustrations, its enduring commitments, its methods and modes of meeting life—all for the purpose of arriving at comprehensive formulations of what Judaism is and ought to be. Through the channel of education Jews should pursue fulfilment of their personalities and, at the same time, the attainment of "transpersonal personsalities." The schools of Judaism should be the institutions in which our people search for answers to the question of what reconstructions in thought and regimen of conduct may be required for Judaism to reveal its redemptive promise and power.

Second, the channel of Zionism. Zionism essentially is the striving for the transformation of reality into a "home," the effort to end man's cosmic "homelessness." It functions on the levels of individuals and families struggling to build homes for themselves; of peoples and nations; of mankind on earth; and of the human mind in the universe. For Jewry, Zionism in this, its universal sense, means the building of homes on all levels which embody the *kelal yisrael*, the principle of Israel, or the Jewish sense of "the religious." In particular it means the full development of its congregational existence and, simultaneously, the evolving of a congregationalism which is self-transcendent,—a transcongregational congregationalism. By the same token, it means fulfilment of our nationhood and its transcendence in the constitution of Jewry as a transnational nation. [1]

Third, the channel of civilization. Civilization is what man does to enhance his humanity, what mankind does with the promise of existence. "Religion," in Whitehead's famous phrase, "is what the individual does with his solitariness."[2]

[1]   Judaism is "a combination of non-cosmopolitan universalism and non-exclusive particularism." James Parkes, *Judaism and Christianity* (Chicago 1948), pp. 164-200.

[2]   Alfred N. Whitehead, *Religion in the Making* (New York 1926), p. 16.— Heschel (*Man Quest for God*, p. xiv) rejects Whitehead's dictum and substitutes for it "Religion is what man does with the presence of God." "True," he goes on to say, "God is hiding His face in our time, but He is hiding because we are evading him." This emendation of Whitehead is not too successful. It amounts to saying that in our time religion is what man does with the absence of God in the presence of his, man's, own absence. The implication is that man should disregard the Absence and cease being truant. The neo-mystical formulation fails to make clear that what man does *with* either the Presence or the Absence is inevitably what he does *in*

Civilization, then, is what man does with his humanity, enhancing it, bringing it to fuller fruition. [1] Hence, Judaism as a religious civilization is what man as Jew does with his segment of humanity and how he relates it to the rest. In Kaplan's words, "Judaism is what the Jewish People does with the land in which it arose, with Hebrew, with the Bible and the Talmud, with its religion, its social institutions, its customs and folkways." [2] This is what we do with our group-solitariness. But Judaism is also, it may be suggested, what the Jewish people does with the many lands in which it lives, with the languages it speaks, with the cultures that interact with its own, with the customs and folkways in which it participates. This is what we do with our humanity. Thus civilization is religious when it establishes solitariness, personhood, humanhood as an end, as ultimate, as holy. And religion civilizes when it transforms personal and social solitariness into personal and social solidarity.

Civilization is intercivilizational and transcivilization. A parochial civilization is a contradiction in terms. So is a civilization that is inhospitable to invention and impervious to correction. A civilization is man's declaration of creative and corrective independence and of cooperative, communicative interdependence. [3] It is his shelter and his adventure

His presence or absence, and this doing is what man does with his humanity, individually, inwardly, solitarily, as well as collectively, institutionally, communally.

[1] Frank Kingdom, "Faith as Experience" in *Faith for Today—Five Faiths Look at the World* (Garden City, N.Y., 1941), p. 70, also taking issue with Whitehead on this point, advances this revision: "Religion is what a man does with the sum of all his relationships."

[2] Mordecai M. Kaplan, *Questions Jews Ask: Reconstructionist Answers* (New York 1956), p. 472.

[3] *Cf.* David Ben-Gurion, "The State of Israel and the Future of the Jewish People," *Hazuth*, p. 40 (in Hebrew). —Kurt Lewin, *Resolving Social Conflicts* (New York 1948), p. 184, wrote a group "is best defined as a dynamic whole based on interdependence rather than on similarity." The main criterion of belongingness, to him, was "interdependence of fate." Hence, "young American Jews may abhor Jewish national mysticism; they may not be willing to suffer for

in the world of experience which ranges from Flood to Eden.

Through the channel of civilization, then, Judaism may achieve both self-preservation and self-transcendence. As President Neuman stated it,

> Judaism does not... merely seek vindication of its historic teachings. It looks to greater spiritual fruition in the future. The restoration of the Jews to their ancestral home in our day and the rebuilding in Palestine of a national home for the genius of the Jewish people may usher in a new epoch of prophetic creation comparable to that of the Second Commonwealth that saved Judaism and ended by giving birth to Christianity. [1]
>
> Never was there greater need for prophetic vision and utterance than in the present-day world of political confusion and moral frustration... Neither the church, synagogue or mosque, as at present constituted, possesses the dynamics for a new revelation. Nor can mankind look for this inspiration to the Council of the United Nations or NATO. Zion reborn may, as in days of yore, become the citadel of a new faith.... [It is] conceivable that the State of Israel which was born in suffering and tragedy will in time become a symbol of peace and healing for the world through the renewal of prophetic vision under the skies that once crashed with the lightning of divine inspiration. [2]

Through the sum total of acts constituting a civilization of "the religious" and making for continuity and transcendence, Judaism in orchestration with other civilizations may rise to new heights of relevance and be permitted to hear the voice that speaks not alone out of the whirlwind or ultimate silence but out of the promise of existence.

cultural or religious values which they do not fully understand, or perhaps even dislike; but they must be sufficiently fact-minded to see clearly their interdependence of fate with the rest of American Jews and indeed with the Jews all over the world." I suggest, however, that *inter-fatalism* is not enough. Jewish belonging also implies an interdependence of faith. *See also* Meir Ben-Horin, "Jewishness and the Jew," *The Reconstructionist*, vol. xxvi, no. 3 (March 18), 1960, 9-14. *Cf.* David M. Eichhorn, "Who is a Jew?" *Year Book*, vol. lxix, Central Conference of American Rabbis (1959), pp. 240-247.

[1] Abraham A. Neuman, "Judaism," *The Great Religions of the Modern World*, edited by Edward J. Jurji (Princeton University Press 1947), p. 282.

[2] *Idem*, "Our Historic Horizons, " JQR, vol. xlv, no. 4 (Tercentenary Issue, April 1955), 313, 314.

THE ETYMOLOGY OF ARABIC *MA'TAM* "MOURNING ASSEMBLY"

By Meïr M. Bravmann

Dropsie College

We quote the following poem from the *Dīwān* of 'Āmir b. aṭ-Ṭufail (No. 24): [1] (1) *la'amruka mā tanfakku 'annī malāmatan Banū Ğa'farin mā haiyağa ḍ-ḍiğnu Ğa'farā* (2) *iḏā qultu hāḏā ḥīnu/a rāğa'a wudduhā abā ḥiqduhā fī ṣ-ṣadri illā taḏakkurā* (3) *limahlaki afrāsin uṣibna warubbamā aṣābū bihā amṭālahā ṯumma akṯarā* (4) *mina l-arḍi ahlan ba'da mālin wağīratin wa'abqat lahum minnī ma'ātima ḥussarā.* Lyall translates it as follows: "(1) By thy life! the sons of Ja'far cease not to revile me, as often as hatreds stir up men's minds in Ja'far. (2) When I said—'Now is the time when their love will return,' the hatred that was in their breasts refused to do aught but harp upon old memories (of quarrel) (3) for the death of horses that have been slain; and ofttimes did they too slay in requital for them the like number, yea and many more— (4) people of the land, in addition to camels won, and clients. They (our horsemen), with me as their captain, rendered continuous to them (our foes) the meetings of mourning women, bare of head." [2]

---

[1] *The dīwāns of 'Abīd ibn al-Abraṣ . . . and 'Āmir ibn aṭ-Ṭufail,* edited by Sir Charles Lyall (Leiden and London 1913).

[2] The poem should be compared with another passage by 'Āmir (no. 34), to which Lyall (in a note to our poem) has drawn attention. But both of these passages of 'Āmir (especially the second one) are in content and form related to the following passage from a poem in which a contemporary of 'Āmir, that is, al-Ḥārit b. Ẓālim of Murrah (*ca.* 570-580 A.D.), boasts of having killed a half-grown son of his old adversary, king an-Nu'mān b. al-Munḍir, of Ḥīrah, in revenge of the confiscation by an-Nu'mān of certain property (camels and their attendants) belonging to certain women-clients of al-Ḥārit (*Mufaḍḍalīyāt,* no. 88, 4-5): (4) *fa'in taku aḏwādun uṣibna waṣibyatun fahāḏā bnu Salmā ra'suhū mutafāqimu* (5) *'alautu biḏī l-ḥaiyāti*

88

We touch here on only a few of the difficulties which the little poem offers. *Mā haiyaǧa...* (in v. 1) we would prefer to consider as a main clause, to mean: "How much has hatred stirred up the (Banū) Ǧaʿfar!" However one may interpret *mina ṭ-arḍi* (in v. 4), *ahl(an)* can—in opposition to Lyall's interpretation ("people of the land")—have no closer connection to the prepositional phrase immediately preceding it than have the nouns *māl* and *ǧīrat-* which follow. *Ahl* is the "property of men" which belongs to a man; it occurs very frequently in conjunction with *māl*, "property of cattle" (occasionally also "property of fields" or "pasture grounds"). In *abqat* (in v. 4; Lyall: "rendered continuous...") the idea of continuity is not implied. It merely means, "they left (caused) to them..." (*cf.* Ḥassān b. Ṯābit, no. 117,9, quoted below; further ʿĀmir b. aṭ-Ṭufail, no. 36, 1).

Ḥussar (in v. 4) "bare (pl.) of head" seems peculiar when used as an attribute to a noun which means *"meetings* of mourning women." The phrase *maʾātimu ḥussurum* makes satisfactory sense only, it we consider the plural *maʾātimu* not as a plural of the singular *maʾtam*, "meeting, or group, of mourning women" (the usual interpretation), but as a plural to a singular which refers to an individual, "mourning woman." The phrase then comes to mean simply "mourning women bare of head."

Maʾātim has exactly the same meaning ("mourning women") in a verse of Ḥassān b. Ṯābit [1] (no. 117,9) which is very similar to the line (4b) of the poem by ʿĀmir b. aṭ-

---

mafriqa raʾsihī ..." (4) And if there be a few parcels of camels seized, and a few boys—here is the son of Salmā! his head is a notable thing, not to be made light of. (5) I assailed with my serpent-sword the top of his head ..." (Lyall's translation). The phrase *raʾsuhū mutafāqimun*, rendered by Lyall (in agreement with the scholion) by "his head is a notable thing, not to be made light of" (Bevan, in the glossary to *Mufaḍḍal.*, explains *mutafāqimun*—with reference to our passage—by "a serious matter)", should be interpreted: "His head is gaping (cleft)."

[1] The *dīwān of Ḥassān b. Thābit*, edited by Hartwig Hirschfeld (Leiden and London 1910).

Ṭufail discussed here: *alam natruk ma'ātima mu'wilātin lahunna 'alā sarātikumū ranīnu,* "Have we not left (behind) wailing women mourners who lament over your slain chiefs?" Cf. also A'šā [1] (no. 9, 23): *fa'uqsimu billāhi lladī ana 'abduhū lataṣṭafiqan yauman 'alaika l-ma'ātimu,* "I swear by God whose servant I am: Some day women mourners shall clasp their hands over you!" And *ibid.*, no. 15,57: *ka'anna naḥīla š-šaṭṭi ġibba ḥarīqihī ma'ātimu sūdun sallabat 'inda ma'tami,* "The palm-trees on the bank of river resembled, after they had been set on fire, women mourners who, veiled in black dresses, and bare (of their trinkets), [2] stand there at the lamentation for the dead." We also refer to the following passage (in the scholion of the *Dīwān* of 'Āmir b. aṭ Ṭufail, p. 121,12) in which the formal singular *ma'tam* (see below) denotes a plural, "mourning women" (not "mourning gathering"): *'ašīyata qāma n-nā'iḥātu wašuqqiqat ḥudūdun bi'aidī ma'tamin aiyi ma'tami* "on the evening when there stood the wailing women, and cheeks were lacerated by the hands of 'women mourners' (*ma'tam*)—what a mourning gathering!"

As the singular form of the plural *ma'ātim* "women mourners," which occurs in the above-quoted passages, we identify the form *mu'timat-, mūtimat-,* the feminine form of the active participle of *aitama,* the causative of *yatima,* "to be orphaned" (to *yatīm* "orphan"). As the original meaning of this *mūtimat-* we may assume "woman whose children are orphaned" (by the fact that their father was slain).

---

[1] *Gedichte von 'Abû Baṣîr Maimûn ibn Qais al-'A'šâ . . ., arabisch herausgegeben von Rudolf Geyer* (London 1928).

[2] *Cf.* for the concept of *sallabat:* 'Antarah no. 4,2; *Sīrat Ibn Hišām,* p. 627,2; Aḫṭal p. 188,4; p. 289,7; and Labīd no. 53,22: *mutasallabātin fī musūḥi š-ša'ri abkāran wa'ūnā,* "die in härenen Gewändern ihre Gatten beweinen, Jungfrauen und Weiber mittleren Alters" (Huber-Brockelmann's translation). *Sallabat* (fem.) "to be stripped (of trinkets)" seems to be identical with "to be dressed in black, or in hairy dresses" (*silāb* "mourning garb"), *cf.* also Kumait, *Hāšimīyāt,* ed. J. Horovitz (Leiden 1904), no. 2,120 and scholion.

The participle *mūtimat-*, from an original root primae *y*, could, by virtue of a phonetic or merely orthographic process which is not infrequent, appear as *mu'timat-*, and thus could give the impression as if it belonged to an original root primae *alif*. The formation of a "broken" plural after the pattern *fa'ālil* had, in the instance at hand, necessarily to produce a form with *alif*: *ma-ātimu*, with so-called *hamzah baina baina* (collision of two vowels not separated by a glide or a glottal stop, in German terminology: "leiser Übergang"), which could develop into *ma'ātim*, with glottal stop between the two vowels; the *alif* which thus originated could then naturally also penetrate into the singular, *mu'timat-*, instead of the original *mūtimat-*. From the genuine ("broken") plural *ma'ā-tim* ("wailing women") of whose derivation from a root primae *y* linguistic consciousness was no longer aware, a singular form with "collective" meaning (that is, a singular which had the same or a similar meaning as the plural *ma'ātim*) could be formed: *ma'tam*; this form was used in a sense which was identical with that of the (plural) form from which it was derived ("wailing women," v. the above-quoted passages), or functioned as a singular with collective meaning: "a group," or "a meeting of mourning women." On the other hand, the form *ma'ātim* could also function as the plural of this singular with collective meaning: "groups," or "meetings, of mourning women."

The form *mūtimat-*, *mu'timat-* which we consider as the original singular form of the plural *ma'ātim*, "mourning women," is not merely inferred by us. This singular actually occurs in old-Arabic literature. We find it in a poem which refers to the conquest of Mecca by the Muslims and represents a speech which Ḥimās b. Qais b. Ḫālid, of the Banū Bakr, is said to have addressed to his wife when she rebuked him because of his flight from battle. The poem is extant in Ibn Hišām's *Sīrat Rasūl Allāh* (ed. Wüstenfeld, Göttingen 1860, p. 818, 6 ff) (and in the parallel report in aṭ-Ṭabarī's *Ta' rīḫ*), also in the *Dīwān* of the Huḏailites (under no. 183; ed. Well-

hausen, 31), [1] where the poet is designated by the name of
Abū r-Ra''ās aṣ-Ṣāhilī. (1) *Innaki lau šahidti yauma i-Ḥan-
damah* (2) *iḏ farra Ṣafwānu wafarra 'Ikrimah* (3) *wĀbū Yazīda
qā'imun kal-mu'timah...* (8) *lam tanṭiqī fī l-laumi adnā
kalimah.* We quote A. Guillaume's translation of the passage
from his translation of the *Sīrah* [2] (p 550): "If you had witnessed the battle of Khandama when Ṣafwān and 'Ikrima
fled and Abū Yazīd was standing like a pillar..., you would
not have uttered the least word of blame." Guillaume's interpretation of *mu'timat-* as "pillar," in which he follows an old
Arab philologist, is, without foundation, simply inferred from
the context. Only the derivation of the word (*i.e., mūtimat-*)
from the root *ytm* and its interpretation as "woman whose
children have lost their father," which is tantamount to
"mourning woman," is tenable [3]

The indigenous Arab philologists considered *ma'tam* as a
quasi-infinitive noun of a root *atama*, with the meaning "he
brought together," or "united two things" (*see* Lane, s. v.).
This derivation is also generally accepted by modern philologists. [4] Rhodokanakis compares North-Arabic *ma'tam* (interpreted by him as "gathering" in general, not "gathering of
mourning women" in particular) with the South-Arabic
m'tmt, ,,Zusammenkunft behufs Beratung und Beschluss-
fassung," *'tmt,* ,,Ergebniss der Übereinkunft, Beschluss," and
with the associated finite verbs of South-Arabic *'tm,* ,,ein

---

[1]　*Skizzen und Vorarbeiten,* 1. Heft (Berlin 1884).
[2]　*The life of Muḥammad; a translation of [Ibn] Isḥāq's Sīrat Rasūl
Allāh* ... by A. Guillaume (Oxford 1955).
[3]　Wellhausen's translation of the word in *Lieder der Hudhailiten*
(*Skizzen und Vorarbeiten,* 1. Heft [Berlin 1884]), Übersetzung, p. 137,
as "eine Mutter, die ihre Kinder verloren hat", does not seem to be
probable to us. For another instance of *mūtimat-* "woman with children who has become a widow" see, *e.g.,* Buḫārī, ed. L. Krehl (Leiden
1864), II, 396, 15 (here again spelled *mu'timat-*).
[4]　*See,* e.g., Rhodokanakis, *Ḳatabanische Texte zur Bodenwirtschaft,
I* (SBWA 194, 2; Vienna 1919), p. 95, and *Wiener Zeitschr. f. d.
Kunde des Morgenl.,* vol. xxxi 1924, p. 40, n. 5; *cf.* also *Ḳataban.
Texte* ..., II (SBWA 198, 2; Vienna 1922), p. 27.

Übereinkommen treffen," '*ttm*, „sich dem Übereinkommen
fügen." He also refers to the North-Arabic anatomical term
atūm (*al-mar'atu llatī ṣāra maslakāhā wāḥidan*, but also used
of the water-skin, see Lane, s. v.) which is also derived from
a verb *atama*, "to bring together, unite," by the Arab philologists (*see below*).

We on our part completely separate the North-Arabic
ma'tam (an expression which has the form of a singular, but
the meaning and function of a plural) "mourning women,"
or (secondarily) "group, or gathering of mourning women,"
and *mu'timat-*, *mūtimat-* from the South-Arabic etymon
compared with it. However, we maintain the assocation of
the South-Arabic words with North-Arabic *atūm*. We deal
here with a distinct root '*tm* which has nothing to do with
the root discussed above (from *ytm*). This root '*tm*, which
became especially productive in South-Arabic, must on its
part be considered a secondary variation of the root *t'm*,
which occurs in the common-Semitic term for "twins," *e.g.*,
Arabic *tau'am* and *tu'ām*. '*tm* originated from *t'm* through a
metathesis. The ideas of "agreement," "to make an agreement,"
"to keep an agreement" go very well with the idea of "twins."
A similar figurative usage of the root *t'm* (derived from the
noun *tᵉ'ōmīm*, *tō'ᵃmīm*, "twins") occurs, by the way, in later
Hebrew: *hit'īm*, "to fit, to correspond." Also the North-
Arabic anatomical term *atūm* can easily be derived from an
original meaning "duality occurring in oneness." A similar
derivation of a verb from the noun *tau'am* "twins," as is
present in the above-mentioned South-Arabic and Hebrew
words, is also present in the North-Arabic language itself in
the verb *wā'ama*, "to consent, to agree" (*e.g.*, in Ka'b b.
Zuhair, ed. Kowalski [Cracow 1950], no. 11,1; p. 72), also
"to imitate (v. *Mufaḍḍalīyāt*, Glossary, s.v.) and "to complete"
(v. the passages cited by Wellhausen, *Reste arabischen Hei-
dentumes*, [1] p. 85, n. 2).

[1]   *Skizzen und Vorarbeiten*, 3. Heft (Berlin 1887).

SOME HEBREW MANUSCRIPTS FROM SEVILLE

By Francisco Cantera Burgos

Instituto Arias Montano de
Estudios Hebraicos y Oriente Próximo, Madrid

It is well known that Spain, in spite of her strong Jewish tradition, cannot offer today a list of Hebrew manuscripts—in contrast to the Hebrew inscriptions which she possesses—comparable to the richer foreign libraries. Many factors must have contributed to this lack: the chief one, undoubtedly, seems to have been the fact that the Jews who emigrated from Spain in 1492, and at times before and after that year, took with them, as was to be expected, the most precious bibliographical treasures which they or their communities possessed. Many other manuscripts perished through carelessness or ignorance (some through theft) or disappeared in the course of our disturbed national existence along with so many others—in Spanish, Latin, Arabic, etc. However, we believe that in the libraries there still remains an appreciable quantity of material entirely forgotten or hardly explored, sometimes because of lack of interest difficult to understand or through misplaced zeal on the part of their owners.

So far we have been able to catalogue nearly four hundred Hebrew codices, manuscripts, fragments and documents in some thirty Spanish libraries. The outstanding among these are the National Historical Library and Archives of Madrid; monasteries like El Escorial and Montserrat; universities such as Madrid, Salamanca and Valladolid; secular academies such as the Royal Academy of History; cathedral chapters, such as those of Toledo, Barcelona, Calahorra, Gerona, León, Pamplona and Zaragoza; institutions such as the Library of the Royal Palace, the Lazaro Museum or the Biblical Institute Arias Montano and other libraries of lesser importance, including several private collections.

To the documents just referred to, surely of no little importance in themselves, we may add two more manuscripts located in Seville and not studied thus far. We shall describe them in this short study, which we are delighted to dedicate to Professor Abraham A. Neuman, president of The Dropsie College for Hebrew and Cognate Learning in Philadelphia and eminent historian, to whom the social, political and cultural history of Spanish Jewry in the Middle Ages owes so much.

1. Manuscript of Iarḥi in the Columbus Library

The noted Hebraist of Valenciano, Francisco Perez Bayer (1711-1794), whose achievements in the investigation of Spanish archaeology have so far not sufficiently been recognized, [1] informs us of two important Hebrew codices which he saw in Seville during a study tour through Andalusia and Portugal in the year 1782 when he was already 71 years old. [2]

Bayer notes that both codices are beautifully written on parchment and for good reason are treated with the greatest care. He describes one of them as a Hebrew Bible which King Alphonse the Wise presented or willed to the Holy Church of Seville and which is said to have been given to him by a brother of St. Louis of France. Unfortunately, we do not know its whereabouts at the present time; and we fear it may have disappeared from Spain.

About the other book, "a rabbinic book without points",

[1]   *Cf.* the magnificent monograph dedicated to him by our much lamented friend, Professor of the University of Salamanca, D. Leopoldo Juan Garcia, *Perez Bayer y Salamanca. Datos para la bio-bibliografia del hebraista valenciano* (Salamanca 1918).

[2]   He refers to it in his *Diario del viaje desde Valencia a Andalucia hecho por Don Francisco Perez Bayer en este año de 1782* and *Diario del viaje de Andalucia y Portugal*, 2 parts and folio, manuscript of the Madrid National Library, nos. 5953 and 5954 (*see* vol. ii, folios 153-156). *Cf.* the incomplete copy with illustrations in large quarto belonging to the Royal Historical Academy, "Extracto del Viaje Manuscrito del Iltmo. Sor. Bayer por lo perteneciente a las Antigüedades del Reyno de Sevilla", mss. 9-25-4-C77, fols. 181v to 183v of vol. ii.

Perez Bayer writes that "it contains the biblical commentary of R. Solomon *Iarchi*, that is, 'Luna' (because of his being born in Lunel in Lenguedoc, according to some authoities)." He is a twelfth-century scholar called *Rashi* (*R*abbi *S*olomon *I*arḥi). He is so highly thought of among his own people that they call him *The Interpreter of the Law*. This codex contains his gloss or running commentary on the whole Bible:

> The codex is written in a rabbinic hand, very perfect and remarkably even, one line looking just like another, and one page just like another and so the ink. At the end a leaf is missing on which at some time there must have appeared the name of the writer, the place and the year when it was written.
>
> On the title page beneath an oblong inscribed with Arabic [sic] letters and intertwined with a thousand flourishes of the pen and with the spaces between each line laboriously decorated, there are two circles ... inscribed in square Hebrew script without points, which I judge to be later than the fourteenth century A.D.

Our writer then includes the double inscription in seven lines (*see below*) and gives a not too happy interpretation of them. We can identify this codex with the one exhibited— the number is V-VI-S—in a showcase in the Columbus Library of Seville founded in the sixteenth century by Fernando Colon, son of the discoverer of America. Up to the present it has not been sufficiently studied, and therefore the numerous missing leaves have not been noticed. Nor has it been noticed that these are to be found together with the thirty-one folios of the Hebrew codex kept today in the Lazaro Museum of Madrid. We have recently described it for the first time. [1] Here a detailed account is offered of the manuscript from Seville, with an indication of its lacunae:

On folio lv we find the following:

תנו כבוד לרבינו שלמה אשר גבר עלי כל המפרשים ואם כלם
קדושים וחכמים כנגדם הוא כקדש הקדשים

(-ascribe glory to our Master Solomon who outshone all the

---

[1] *Cf.* our study ‥Nueva serie de manuscritos hebreos de Madrid", *Sefarad*, vol. xix (1959), 41 (p. 63 of the offprint).

commentators, and if they are holy and wise, compared with them he is the Holy of Holies").

There follow two notes: one, interestingly enough, relates to the person who gave the work to the Cathedral Chapter of Seville, the other concerns R. Solomon Iarḥi. They read as follows:

> La dio el Arcediano de Xerez segun acuerdo capitular / de 14 de Julio de 1480, y este se llamaba Dn. Juan de Gongora / como parece de la nomina de los que ganaron Misadas en / 1479, y como judío esta nombrado en el estatuto de limpicza / de 12 de Febrero de 1515, folio 170.
>
> Rabi Salomon Yarchi nacio en Troyes in Campana en / 1104, murio alli de 75 años en 1180. Escribió entre otras / cosas Comentarios sobre la Biblia como dice Dic- / cionario historico de Hombres grandes tomo I fol. 581 / edicion de Caen en 1786.

[Presented by the Archdeacon of Xerez, according to an agreement of the chapter of 14 July 1480. His name was Dn. Juan de Gongora, as it appears from the names of those who received monthly stipends in 1479. He is named as a Jew in the statute of racial purity of 12 February 1515, folio 170.

Rabbi Solomon Iarḥi was born in Troyes in 1104, died there in 1180 at the age of 75 years. Among other things he wrote commentaries on the Bible, as stated in the Historical Dictionary of Great Men, volume I, page 581, in the Caen edition of 1786.]

The first leaf of the folios in the Lazaro Museum would fit in perfectly here after this preliminary folio. It constitutes the actual frontispiece of the whole codex, although today it bears the number 67, and on its reverse side there begins *Genesis*, as may be seen in our study previously quoted and in the pictures which illustrate it. We do not know why or when it was given this numeration; but it is certain that this leaf is the first of the manuscript, since it is continued properly by folio 2r of Seville, which begins thus:

וברביעי צוה עליהן להתלות ברקיע וכן כל תולדות השמים
··· והארץ נבראו מיום ראשון

There follow the separate *parashiyyoth*, of which the first finishes on folio 4v, the end of which is indicated, as in each case thus: חֹסלת בראשׁית and in continuation there begins the second, indicated by a ב enclosed in a decorated eight-pointed star, opposite which is inscribed in a rectangle the title of the *parashah* נח אלה תולדות in dark gold letters on a red background. The former color is used for decoration, sometimes filled in with green.

After this there follow the *parashiyyoth* in this order: ג, ויאמר, fol. 6v; ד, וירא, folio 9r; ה, ויהיו חיי שרה (in red on green), folio 12r; ו, ואלה, (black on red), folio 13r; ז, ויצא, folio 14v; ח, וישלח, folio 17r; ט, וישב, folio 19r; י מקץ ויהי folio 20v; יא, ויגש, folio 22v; יב, ויהי, folio 23v; יג, ואלה שמות in black on red with green and gold ornamentation, making a very beautiful combination, folio 26r; יד, וידבר, folio 28r; טו, (after וארא חסלת) בא אל פרעה, folio 29v; יו, ויהי בשלח folio 32r; יז, וישמע (on a violet and red background, very beautiful), folio 35v; יח, ואלה המשפטים, folio 37v; יט, ויקחו לי תרומה, folio 41r; כ, ואתה תצוה, folio 451; כא, כי תשא, folio 47r; כב, ויקרא אל [sic], folio 51v; כג, אלה פקודי, folio 52r; כג ויקהל משה, (with very beautiful ornamentation on a gold and red background), folio 52v; כד, צו את אהרן, folio 54v; כה, ויהי ביום, folio 56r; כו, אשה כי תזריע, folio 57v; כז, השמיני, (in lilac) folio 58v; כח, אחרי, folio 59v; כט, קדושים תהיו, folio 61r; ל, אמור, folio 62v; לא, בהר סיני folio 64v; לב, אם בחקתי, folio 66r.

Here—as we have already noted—the folio which is no. 67v of the Lazaro Museum does not fit. Instead there belongs here no. 68r of the same museum, commencing the commentary of Rashi to Leviticus, as is shown on page 38 of our study of the Lazaro manuscript. There has no doubt been some confusion in the numeration of the folios here, since in the Seville codex, in which no. 67 is missing, there follows after 66 another 68, in whose recto after the חסלת במדבר marking the end of the first *parashah* of the biblical book וידבר, *i.e.* number לג, there comes לד or נשא.

It continues as follows:

ויקח, לח, בהעלותך, לה, folio 70r; לו, שלח לך, folio 73v; לח, folio 75r; לט, זאת חקת, folio 76v; מ, וירא בלק, folio 78v; מא, פינחס, folio 80v; מב, וידבד משה אל, folio 82v; מג, אלה מסעי, folio 83v. Here the Seville manuscript is without folios 84 to 95, which are in the Lazaro Museum and a description of which may be read in our study mentioned earlier. They correspond to the end of Leviticus, and to no. מד, חסלת אלה דברים, that is, the beginning of Deuteronomy (folio 85); מה (after the words אלה דברים, in a rectangle, indicating the end of this first *parasha* of Deuteronomy), ואתחנן, folio 87r; [1] והיה עקב, מו, folio 88r; מז, ראה, folio 89v; מח, שפטים (fourth *parashah* of Deuteronomy) folio 92r; מט, כי תצא, folio 93v; והיה כי תבא, נ, folio 95r. At this point the Columbus codex follows on folio 96r, after the indication חסלת כי תבא, with the *parashah* אתם נצבים corresponding to נא and then: נב, וילך משה in smaller letters and ornamentation, folio 96v; האזינו, נג, folio 97r; נד, וזאת הברכה, folio 99r; after which the Seville manuscript is without folios 100 to 103, which are to be found in the Lazaro Museum, and which continue the last *parashah* of Deuteronomy with beautiful ornamentation (*see* the illustration of folio 100v in our study) and the beginning of Joshua, which concludes at the end of the first column of 105r where, amid red ornamentation, we read חסלת ספר יהושע. In the second column begins the Book of Judges, the title of which, שופטים, appears in gold letters on a green and red background. Below, in a gold square with gold ornamentation there appear the words ויהי אחרי, the first of this biblical book, in black letters on a lilac background.

Between folio 108v and 109r something seems to be missing. On 109r, amid a variegated and not too delicate an ornamentation, we read סליק ספר שופטים which indicates the end of Judges, and then in large gold letters surrounded by ornamentation of the same color, the word שמואל, together

---

[1] According to our study, *ibid.*, p. 38, it is no. 86r. This is one of a few errors which occurred there and which we now correct.

with the beginning of that book ויהי איש אחד, in black letters on a green background.

In the Seville manuscript folio 119 is missing with its beautiful illumination,[1] which we have already mentioned in describing the folios of the manuscript in Lazaro Museum. The Books of Kings which begin on that folio finish on folio 130 of the Seville manuscript. In the letter we find the following texts enclosed in rectangles:

תהלה למלך המלכים בעזרת שוכן עליה	סליק ספר מלכים ואתחיל ספר ירמיה

On folio 131r, we find the first words of the book of Jeremiah דברי ירמיהו in gold letters with beautiful ornamentation. The book finishes on folio 141r, where these three lines appear within a large ornamental rectangle:

סליק ספר ירמיה

ואתחיל ספר ישעיה

חזון ישעיה בן

in gold letters.

In the same format, we find on folio 169r the end of Isaiah and the beginning of Ezekiel:

סליק ספר ישעיה

ואתחיל ספר

ויהי בשלשים

in gold.

On folio 185v, there is an illustration and on folio 188r a large final illustration relating to the temple. On folio 188v we find at the center of the top line the word ספר in gold and below it תרי עשר הושע.

This is what the rest of the codex contains:

Folio 193v, ספר יואל; 194r, דברי עמוס; 196v, חזון [עובדיה] in black on a red ornamentation; 197r, ויהי [דברי יונה]; 197v,

---

[1] The center part is in gold and the rest in black, red, green and grey.

מיכה ;199v, משא נינוה of Nahum; 200v, [חבקוק] המשא ;202r,
צפניה ;202v, חגי ;203r, זכריה ;207r, משא of Malachi.

On 208v we find:

נשלם פירוש התורה ופירוש שמונה נביאים: ועתה
אתחיל פירוש הכתובים והיו לך פירוש חמש מגלות
זו אחר זו

[—The commentary on the Torah is finished and the commentary on the eight Prophets, and now I shall begin the
commentary on the Writings and so you shall have a commentary on the five Scrolls one after the other].

There follows an ornamental square with bows in various
colors, similar to folio 284v at the Lazaro Museum which
we reproduced in our study.

On folio 209r we find in an ornamental square the words
ויהי בימי with which Esther begins. On the recto of the
following folio, after the words נשלם מגלת אסתר, there are
twenty-seven lines in an ornamental square which begin with
אחת דבר אלהים שתים and end with קץ אגדתיו והא לך שירתיו.

Below these there follows שיר השירים, the end of which is
indicated on folio 215v by נשלם שיר השירים. Below this we
read, in an ornamental square, the beginning of Ruth ויהי בימי.

On folio 215v begins איכה or Lamentations and in 218v
the [קהלת] דברי. On 226r there follow the Psalms, starting
with the words אשרי האיש beautifully ornamented. Each
Psalm carries its number in the margin (ב, ג, etc.) and in the
text, surrounded by a square, one or two of its initial words.
On folio 234r we find the title למנצח משכיל לבני קרח in an
ornamental square and on the margin the number מב corresponding to Psalm 42. On folio 242v an ornamental rectangle
contains the words תפלה למשה which are actually the title
of Psalm 90, although in the margin there appears פט—89.
On folio 249r, the words משלי שלמה (Proverbs) are enclosed
in an ornamental square. The commentary ends at the
bottom of the first column of folio 259r, as is indicated by the
words נשלם פירוש משלי which are enclosed in a decorative

rectangle. The second column begins with a beautiful ornamentation and the opening words איש היה of Job. This continues until folio 272r where the following lines appear amid
delicate ornamentation in green, red and lilac:

נשלם ספר איוב

ספר דניאל

בשנת

The Book of Daniel, thus begun, ends on folio 278r, where
the following lines appear

נשלם ספר דניאל

ספר עזרא

ובשנת

In certain places in the book of Ezra we find some words
in letters larger than the rest and surrounded by a small
square. In this way there appear the words דברי נחמיה on
folio 281r, column b.

Folios 282 to 293, missing in the Seville manuscript, may
be found in the Lazaro Museum. They contain the end of
Ezra with very beautiful ornamentation, as we have mentioned
in our study previously cited, and are followed by the commentary to Chronicles similarly illuminated.

The remaining folios, of the Columbus Library, contain
the rest of the commentary. The codex ends on folio 306,
the last line of which reads:

לא היה לאצר כסף וזהב· ואורות· אצטבלאות

There follow three blank folios.

The remaining details of the Seville codex are:
parchment, 27.8 × 21 centimeters, 47 lines, generally in
two columns; foliation was added later.

The manuscript probably belongs to the thirteenth
century. Its writing is cursive Franco-German, while the
ornamentation of the codex, in exquisite taste and often of
great richness and beauty, seems to have been executed in
Spain or by Sefardi artists, in mudejar style. The illustrations

which we published in our description of the Lazaro manuscript may be compared with illustration II used by Cecil
Roth in his most interesting study, "A Masterpiece of
Medieval Spanish-Jewish Art: The Kennicott Bible", *Sefarad*,
vol. xii (1952), 351-368.

The edges of the Seville codex are beautifully gilded, and
it has a beautiful binding in stamped leather. The clasps
which it must once have possessed are missing. This manuscript is then one of the most precious copies containing the
famous commentary of *Rashi* and is worthy to be put in line
with so many others of the National Library in Paris (numbers
154, 155, 156, 157, 158, 159, 160) and others in foreign
libraries.

2. *The Liber Radicum* of Bartolomé Valverde

The learned priest of Seville, Don Luis García Nieto, owns
another codex which we may include among the Hebrew
codices, and which up to the present has not been sufficiently
known. We hope to recive eventually the kind permission of
the owner to make a full study.

Until then, thanks to the kindness of Señor García Nieto,
we can present here some general characteristics of the
manuscript which we have been able to examine briefly.

The title page of the codex reads on folio 1r:

ספר השרשים   Hoc est
Liber Radicum seu Lexicon hebreum copiosissimum
ex triginta hebreorum autoribus et eorum
commentariis, et diversis targumis seu
sumo studio depromptum in quo vix
quidque desideres | q | ad sacra Bi
blia hebraica intelligenda
facere possit —: —

There follows a *Carmen Hebraicum in laudem libri et
favorem divinum petens*, in six lines which begin:

מגדל אל אשר כל הגדולות למול אחת גדולותיו נקלות

After this there follow these lines:

שלום רב לאוהבי תורתך
ולֹנצֹיה
אֹתֹקסה
ועתה אחל בעזרת המלמד לאדם דעת

[—Great peace to the lovers of his Law Valencia 1564-5/
and now I shall begin with the help of Him who teaches man
knowledge].

From here to folio 103 there follows an erudite dictionary
which shows unusual knowledge of Hebrew and Greek and
deserves a detailed study.

It ends on folio 102v in this manner:

קץ
בנֹלֹך
ואני ברטוֹ'/לומוש ולורדיוש שלמתי את מכתבו הספר הזה
פה ולֹנציה ביום הקדוש יוחנן שהוא אחרון של חודש דזאמרה
שנת אלף וחמש מאות וארבע וששים ל'וֹמֹנין ביאת ישוע גואלנו
שהו שנת בריאת העולם שכ"ד לפ"ק
ולֹנצֹיה

[—Finis—Blessed be he who gives strength to the weary—
and I, Bartolomeus Valverdius, concluded the writing of
this book here in Valencia on the day of St. John, that is
the last of the month of December [1] of the year 1564 of the
era of the coming of Jesus our Redeemer, which is the 324th
year of the creation of the world according to the lesser
computation. Valencia).

There follows on folio 103 a list of authors consulted which
concludes on the other side with these words:

Finis. τελος. סוף · סליק ·ונשלם תם and then nine verses of
six lines:

קחה מלים ברור דעת צרופים · · · ·

---

[1] The manuscript seems to read דיאמרה perhaps for דזאמרה or
דזיאמרה. The day of St. John the Evangelist is celebrated nowadays
on the 27th of the month and not on the 31st, which undoubtedly
was the former date.

and finally:

אׄ סׄ קׄ תׄ הׄ

חֲזֹק וְנַחֲזֹק

לֹ"א

יֹזק

Some day we shall dedicate a brief study to Bartolomé Valverde, erudite Hebraist of Gandía, worthy predecessor of Perez Bayer, Bachelor of Arts in the university of the city of Valencia. [1]

[1] This essay was translated from the Spanish by Alan D. Corré, minister of Congregation Mikveh Israel in Philadelphia.

THE GROWTH AND PROGRESS OF MODERN HEBREW

By WILLIAM CHOMSKY

Dropsie College

The Uniqueness of Hebrew

IN STUDYING a language historically it is customary to divide it into stages or periods. Each stage is marked off by certain distinguishing characteristics in its development. Thus the English language is divided chronologically into three major periods of development. They are: *Old English*, from about the eighth to the twelfth century, *Middle English*, from the twelfth to the fifteenth century, and *Modern English*, from then onwards. These periods are further subdivided into early and late stages, but these subdivisions need not concern us here.

The chronological stages may be defined as follows: *Old English* as the period of *full endings* (*mōna, sunu, stānas*), *Middle English* as the period of *levelled endings* (*mōne, sune, stōnes*), *Modern English* as the period of *lost endings* (*moon, son, stones*-stounz) [1].

In applying this phonetic analogy to the Hebrew language, the uniqueness of Hebrew is at once apparent. Biblical Hebrew, for example, extends over as long a period as that of the entire history of the English language. Yet biblical Hebrew, presumably, possesses not only a unitary pattern of phonology but also one of morphology and syntax.

This uniqueness is, however, more apparent than real. There is good reason to believe that the phonetic pattern of Hebrew during the period of Moses and Joshua differed in many respects from that of the period of Ezra. Indeed, documentary evidence, such as that of the Amarna letters,

[1] *See* Henry Sweet, *A Short History of English Grammar* (Oxford 1892), p. 1.

reveals that the "Hebrew" spoken in the fourteenth century B.C.E. possessed full vocalic endings, which were later discarded, even as in the case of English. Other phonetic variations are likewise in evidence. Furthermore, a careful examination will disclose some morphological and syntactic changes in the Hebrew of the early and the late biblical texts. It is quite obvious that Moses or Joshua would have found it extremely difficult to understand the Hebrew language spoken by the authors of Kohelet or Chronicles. They might even have regarded that language as vulgar or corrupt.

What, then, may account for the seeming unity of biblical Hebrew? Why is biblical Hebrew regarded as a single unitary stage in the evolutionary history of the Hebrew language?

Early Hebrew, doubtless, possessed, as was indicated above, vocalic endings, which were dropped at a later stage. This is clearly demonstrated by the Amarna letters, where the "Hebrew" glosses are written in the cuneiform script which employed a vowel-system. Thus we find in these glosses such spellings as *batnu* (= בֶּטֶן, belly), *hullu* (= עֹל, yoke), *kilubu* (= כְּלוּב, cage), *gitti rimmunima* (= גַּת רִמּוֹנִים, pomegranate press), *haparu* (= עָפָר, dust), and the like. [1]

The ancient Hebrew script, however, in which the Bible and other Hebrew documents were written, possessed no vowel system. Hence vocalic endings could not be recorded. When the vowel systems were established and adopted, the pronunciation recorded was not that of the respective biblical authors, but the one in vogue during the period in which the founders of the vowel systems flourished; namely, the seventh and eighth centuries. They, accordingly, treated all the texts alike, regardless of their respective antiquity, indicating a pronunciation which had become more or less

---

[1] In the cuneiform script, the ע is represented by *h*, and there is no sign indicating the *o* sound. Hence the *u* sign represented both the Hebrew *u* as well as *o* sound.

standardized during the talmudic age. Consequently, no phonetic differences may be noted in the language of the Song of Moses and in that of the books of Esther or Chronicles, about a millenium thereafter.

But the uniqueness in the evolution of the Hebrew language is remarkable also in the morphological and lexical areas. Taking again English as an illustration—and this applies generally to other languages as well—each stage in the development of the language displaced the preceding stage in its influence on the subsequent progress of the language. Thus, modern English, for example, is closer to Shakespearian English than it is to Chaucerean English, and the language of Chaucer is more directly related to modern English than is that of Alfred the Great.

This is not so in the case of Hebrew. The biblical Hebrew of 3,000 years ago still constitutes the hard core of modern Hebrew, and its influence on the modern revival of Hebrew far exceeds that of mishnaic and, certainly, of medieval Hebrew. The close to 8,000 basic words of the Bible are obviously far from adequate for modern needs. Indeed, the modern Hebrew dictionaries contain approximately 30,000 words, about 9,000 of which were introduced during the past several decades. But a partial analysis of the modern Hebrew classics (excluding ultra-modern Israeli writers) reveals that the proportion of biblical words employed in this literature ranges from about 70 per cent to over 90 per cent. Furthermore, the grammatical structure of biblical Hebrew remains basic in modern Hebrew, even in the Israeli vernacular.

To cite a few examples, a Hebrew-speaking visitor to Israel, who will use the biblical expression אני חפץ (I want) will immediately be identified as a "foreigner". In this instance the modern Israeli speaker prefers the mishnaic equivalent אני רוצה. Should this visitor then attempt to be consistent and say אני רוצה לילך לישב לידע, לישב, לידע (to go, to sit, to know), all of which are regular mishnaic infinitive forms, he will again be branded as an "alien", unfamiliar with the Israeli vernacular. These mishnaic forms of the infinitive have failed to gain vogue in modern Hebrew parlance, and the biblical equivalents of these forms are consistently preferred. Similarly, the biblical verb שוב (return) was replaced by the mishnaic חזר, but if someone will employ the expression אני אמתין עד שתחזור (I shall wait until you return), he will very likely be corrected and advised to say אני אחכה, which is the biblical equivalent of the mishnaic אני אמתין [1].

Modern Hebrew may, indeed, be designated as a synthesis of all the preceding stages of the language, with a predominance of the biblical stage in the areas of vocabulary and morphology, and with the prevalence of mishnaic Hebrew in the area of syntax. To illustrate, in the following lines by Saul Tchernichovsky לאחר שהורידהו מתוך העגלה, התעקש וגמר לנדוד, ואם ברגליו, והלך בשלג בצנה (כחם היום) all the words are biblical, but the syntax is mishnaic, while the biblical גמר is employed in the mishnaic meaning, and ואם is used in the medieval sense (even, though), under Arabic influence. Such examples could be multiplied.

Quite often biblical and mishnaic words are employed, side by side with the same meaning, e.g., פה and כאן (here), עץ and אילן (tree), איפה and היכן (where). More commonly, the biblical and mishnaic equivalents denote in modern Hebrew a difference in the shade of meaning. Thus the biblical אהב is synonymous with the mishnaic חבב, but in modern Hebrew the former signifies *loved* and the latter *liked*. Similarly, the biblical צחק and the mishnaic חייך both have the same meaning (laughed). In modern Hebrew, these two verbs are used in the sense of *laughed* and *smiled*, respectively. So also the biblical ילד and the mishnaic תינוק, both of which

[1]   As a matter of fact, a prominent Hebrew grammarian, the late Z. Har-Zahav, insisted, some sixty years ago, that modern Hebrew break loose from the shackles of biblical Hebrew and adopt, instead, the lexical and grammatical patterns of mishnaic Hebrew, wherever possible (*cf.* לשון דורנו Tel Aviv, 1930, pp. 26-31. The suggestion was originally offered in an article which appeared in 1891.) His advice was not, however, heeded, although he himself consistently followed in practice this theory.

have the same referent (a child), but are differentiated in modern Hebrew, where the biblical term refers to a child and the mishanic to an infant. In the case of the stem פסל, the mishnaic usage (to disqualify) is current in verbal forms, but the *nomen agentis* פסל is employed in the biblical sense (sculptor).

Change and Stability

The reason for the conservatism of the Hebrew language and for its dependence on literary sources, especially the Bible, is not far to seek. The Hebrew Bible has always occupied a central place in Jewish life, and every Jew, young and old, was steeped in its study. Biblical words and phrases were, accordingly, his daily diet, as it were. As a matter of fact, the Hebrew Bible still occupies a position of centrality in the Hebraic curriculum, wherever the language is seriously studied, whether in Israel or in the diaspora. Sources in mishnaic Hebrew were also studied but on higher levels and to a lesser degree. [1] Since the Hebrew language, up to the period of its revival as a modern vernacular, was limited to literary usage, its vocabulary and grammatical construction were predominatly influenced by the literary sources, especially the Bible.

At no time, however, in its long history, did the language remain static. No language can remain static and live. Change is inherent in all organic life, as well as in all social institutions, including language. The changes in the Hebrew language were accelerated, at a particularly rapid pace, since its revival as a vernacular, because of the exigencies of modern life for which the literary language proved inadequate.

But the normal and wholesome changes are not haphazard and random. "There is a divinity that shapes our ends, rough-hew them how we will." The pattern of life is governed

---

[1] To quote a talmudic source, only one hundred of every thousand starting the study of the Bible are initiated into the study of Mishna, and only ten into the study of Talmud (Gemara); *cf*. Kohelet Rabba 7.

by ceaseless change and creative novelty on the one hand and by symmetrical order and balanced stability on the other hand. Both change and stability are essential factors in human progress, complementing each other, and language, the symbolic guide to human progress and civilization, is subject, to the same factors.

Principles Underlying New Coinages and Changes

On examining the new coinages and changes in the language during the past several decades, certain principles emerge as basic. These principles were not newly invented; they have been in operation throughout the history of the language. They may be stated as follows:

1. *Direct Borrowing*. The Hebrew language, like the Hebrew people, has had a long history of exposure to foreign contacts and influences. Indeed foreign influences are evident in the culture and religion of the Jewish people, as well as in the Hebrew language, ever since the early beginnings down to modern times. But such influences, if properly digested and modified in consonance with the genius of the people, tend to enrich and enhance, instead of impair, its culture and language.

Even during the biblical period, we find linguistic injections stemming from Akkadian, Egyptian, Persian, even Greek, and principally, Aramaic. In the mishnaic period, Greek and Latin contributed a considerable number of new words and terms, while Aramaic, the *lingua franca* of the Near East during that period, served as the major source of influence. Similarly, the Arabic language left its imprint on Hebrew during the medieval period. In modern times, many new words and expressions are directly borrowed from the modern European languages, especially from Yiddish, the mother tongue of the majority of Israel's population who are responsible for the revival of Hebrew as a modern vernacular. Modern Arabic, likewise, owing to its geographic and family kinship with Hebrew, has left its deposits in the Israeli dialect. [1]

Some of the borrowed words were Hebraized by means of modifications in accordance with the Hebrew morphological pattern. Examples: טִלְגְרֵף-טֶלֶגְרָף (telegraphed), טִלְפֵּן-טֶלֶפוֹן (telephoned) אִרְגֵּן-אַרְגּוּן-אוֹרְגַּאנִי (organized), etc. This is a common phenomenon in all languages. Hence such anglicized forms as *sabbatical, paschal, jubilate,* which were borrowed, directly or indirectly, from the Hebrew; or the Hebraized mishnaic forms זוּג (paired, joined in wedlock), נתאכסן (lodged), הכריז (proclaimed), which stem from Greek nouns borrowed by mishnaic Hebrew. Similarly a Russian suffix *nik* indicating belongingness to a certain group, locality or party, is often employed in the modern Israeli vernacular; e.g.: *Mapamnik* (a member of the Mapam party), *kibbutznik* (a member of a *kibbutz*), etc. This foreign suffix is integrated with the Hebrew words and takes a normal Hebrew feminine suffix ־ית, or plural endings, both masculine and feminine; e.g. קבוצניקית- קבוצניקים- קבוצניקיות.

Even such modern classics as Mendele and Bialik did not hesitate to borrow Yiddish words and to put them in a morphological Hebrew garb. Thus the Yiddish interjection *beh,* which generally connotes the idea of "You are talking nonsense," is converted by Mendele into a Hebrew verb מבעבע. [2] Similarly, the Yiddish word *shnorer* (beggar) takes on both grammatical and idiomatic inflection of Hebrew in the expressions וכאשר שנוררתם תשנוררו (beggars you were, beggars you will be), in Bialik's famous poem *Be-Ir ha-Haregah* (In the City of Slaughter).

It is interesting to note, incidentally, that the borrowed words in modern Hebrew generally retain their original phonetic pattern, while submitting to the grammatical

[1] *See* examples quoted in my *Hebrew: The Eternal Language* (Philadelphia, 1957), pp. 198-200.

[2] *See* ספר הקבצנים. Additional examples of such borrowings by these two masters may be found in my book, *op. cit.*

structure of the Hebrew language. Hence, we carry on a *siha telephónit* (a telephone conversation) and not *tellepponit*, as would be required by the Hebrew phonetic pattern. For the same reason we generally say *tilphen* (telephoned) and *meballef* (bluffer) rather than *tilpen* and *mevallef* in keeping with the phonetic pattern of Hebrew. [1]

An interesting case of borrowing is the following: A familiar Hebrew word is employed, under the influence of a foreign word which bears a phonetic resemblance to it, in the sense of the foreign word, rather than in its original Hebrew meaning. For example, in such mishnaic expressions as אור לארבעה עשר (Pes. I, 1) the biblical word אור (light) is used in the sense of "night," under the influence of the Aramaic אורתא. For the same reason the term גר (biblical, "a stranger") took on the meaning of "a proselyte" in mishnaic Hebrew, because of its phonetic resemblance to the Aramaic גיורא, and אבר (biblical, "a wing") came to signify "a limb" (Aramaic איברא). Similarly, in medieval Hebrew the biblical word גיא (a valley) is used in the sense of "earth" under the influence of the Greek γῆ; while the biblical גשם (rain) is employed in the sense of "substance," "matter" under the influence of the Arabic *gismun*. [2]

In consonance with this principle, Mendele employed the mishnaic term בולבוסים (borrowed from Greek and referring to a bulbous root of an onion) in the sense of "potatoes," because it is used in this sense in Yiddish (probably under the influence of Polish). In like manner, the biblical גאון (pride, glory) assumed in medieval Hebrew the meaning of an honorary title (head of an academy) and in modern Hebrew

---

[1] An analogous situation may be found in Syriac, where borrowed Greek words are not subject to the rules of hardening and softening governing Syriac phonology, but retain instead their own phonetic pattern; *e.g.*, דפרצופא (Greek *prosopon* "face") "of the face," מן פיליפוס (from Philipos), instead of דפרצופא and פיליפוס as would be required in consonance with phonetic pattern of Syriac; *cf.* Noeldeke, *Syriac Grammar* (London, 1904), p. 19f.
[2] *Cf.* Binyamin Klar, מחקרים ועיונים (Tel Aviv 1954), p. 35f.

that of "genius," owing to phonetic resemblance. The same principle motivated the adoption, in modern Hebrew, of the biblical מכונה (base) to represent the term *machine* (*machina* in Latin and *mechane* in Greek). Another interesting example in modern Hebrew is the word נדנד, employed in the sense of the Yiddish *nood(j)en* (of Slavic origin, "to bore") in such expressions as הוא מנדנד לי על הנשמה, which is a direct translation of the Yiddish *er farnood(j)et mir di neshomo* (literally, "he bores my soul," but in the sense of "he bores me to death"). The original meaning of נדנד—of mishnaic origin—is "he rocked" or "shook."

The present trend to reduce the plethora of alien borrowings in the Israeli vernacular is also deserving of mention. The Hebrew Language Academy as well as the Hebrew press, radio broadcasters and authors, are endeavoring to check and control this alien intrusion, and these efforts are meeting with much success. Consequently, such foreign borrowings as ליקבידציה, דיקורציה, דימונסטרציה, גאראג׳, בודג׳ט טלגרמה, מימורנדום, ריאקציה, אינדיפרנטי, and the like, have been replaced, respectively, by the genuine Hebrew formations, תקציב, מברק, תזכיר, תגובה, אדיש, חיסול, תפאורה, הפגנה, מוסך.

2. *Loan Translation.* In this process a word which took on a secondary meaning is translated into Hebrew by a word corresponding to the original primary meaning of the borrowed word, thus lending the Hebrew word a meaning which it did not originally have. To illustrate, the English word *impression* is a direct borrowing from French. But the German *Eindruck* is a loan-translation from the French *impression*. The English word *conscience* was borrowed directly from the Latin *conscientia*, where it originally meant "knowledge," or "joint knowledge," and is still used in this sense in Early English, but later assumed the connotation of moral judgment and feeling applied to conduct in terms of right and wrong. When this Latin word, in its new connotation, was translated into German, which generally shuns direct borrowing, the term *Gewissen* (composed of *ge*, the equivalent of *con*, and

Wissen, "knowledge") was employed. On the same principle, the Arabic term *damir* (originally "hidden," but later "conscience") was rendered in medieval Hebrew by the biblical מצפון (hidden place) in the sense of "conscience."

In modern Hebrew many new words have been coined on this principle. Thus, the English word *convince,* originally meant *conquer, overcome* (Latin *convincere*), and is still used in this sense by Shakespeare. In translating this word, in its modern meaning, into Hebrew, the verb הכניע, the equivalent of the Latin or English, in its primary sense, would have to be used. But in order to avoid confusion, the equivalent grammatical form the *hiphil,* namely, the *shiphal* was employed, thus yielding the forms שכנע, alongside of הכניע (subdued), משוכנע (one who is convinced), נשתכנע (became convinced), etc. In the same manner evolved the forms שחזר (reconstructed, restored) alongside of החזיר (brought or gave back), שיקם (a translation of the German or Yiddish *wiederherstellen,* "rehabilitate") alongside of הקים (raised, established), as well as their respective nominal derivatives שחזור (reconstruction) and שיקום (rehabilitation), and the like.

In the same category may be included expressions in vogue in the Israeli vernacular, which are direct translations from the foreign languages with which the Israelis are in contact, especially English and Yiddish. Examples of such expressions are: היום עבדתי כמו כלום (I worked today like anything), הצטלבות דרכים (crossroads), הוא עושה לי את המות (literally, "he makes me the death," but in the sense of "he annoys me to death," in Yiddish), עשינו שָׂמֵחַ (literally, "we made happy," viz., in the Yiddish connotation, "We had a jolly time"). [1]

It should, however, be emphasized that whereas loan translations in words are a wholesome development in language, enriching it and rendering it more flexible and precise, the same process in expressions is negative in its effect on language growth. Such expressions tend to adulterate the language

---

[1] *See* further examples in my book, *op. cit.,* p. 194 ff.

and to jeopardize its pristine character and uniqueness. As a matter of fact, in the normal process of language growth, words coined by this process are generally incorporated into the language, while expressions have only an ephemeral existence. Thus terms coined during the medieval period by this process, like גדר (definition, translation of the Arabic *hadd*, "boundary" or "limit"), תנועה (physical movement, vowel, a translation of the Arabic *harakat* "movement"), and the like, are now an integral part of the language. Expressions or syntactic coinages borrowed from Arabic during that period failed to strike roots in the language and were discarded.

An outstanding example is the following: Under the influence of Arabic, verbs indicating motion, in the intransitive sense, when followed by the preposition ב, were transformed, in medieval Hebrew, into transitive verbs; e.g., בא ב··· (literally, came with) in the sense of הביא (brought), שב ב··· (literally, returned with) in the meaning of השיב (brought back), and the like. Some of the outstanding poets of that period employed such constructions. [1] Yet this usage failed to gain vogue, and it is now obsolete. Similar constructions in modern Hebrew will very likely meet the same fate.

3. *Popular Etymology* or *Analogical Extension*. The average speaker frequently fails to identify the stem of the word, and he uses analogy in coining new words, without regard to grammatical considerations. On this principle were coined in English such "erroneous" constructions as *witticism* on the analogy of *criticism*, *normalcy* on the analogy of *democracy* and *egotism* on the analogy of *despotism*. The fact that the *c* in both *criticism* and *democracy* and that the *t* in *despotism* are a part of the stem was disregarded, and the endings *cism* and *cy*

---

[1] *E.g.*, בנפשי כל אשר יבא בעזרה for יביא עזרה (Samuel ha-Nagid, Diwan, Haberman, III, p. 21). *See* other examples cited by Binyamin Klar, *op. cit.*, p. 36. Even Bialik, his keen sense of the Hebrew language notwithstanding, failed to grasp the meaning of the expression וירד בי למעמקי שאונים (for והוריד אותי) in Ibn Gabirol's poem. (*See* שירי שלמה בן יהודה, ed. Bialik-Ravnitzki, I, p. 51 and note *ad loc.*).

were envisaged as independent suffixes in constructing the new coinages. Similarly, we find in biblical Hebrew such "ungrammatical" forms as ונמלתם Gen 17: 11 and מִגַּן *ibid*. 14: 20, where the *nun* and *mem* are "erroneously" employed as the initial radicals of these two verbs, respectively.[1] In mishnaic Hebrew such coinages are plentiful; e.g., תרם, התחיל, התריע, and the like—all of which are derived from nouns (תרומה, תחלה, תרועה) in which the ת is a prefix and not a radical.

Modern Hebrew coins such forms freely, as need arises. Thus it evolved such verbs as התניע (from the noun תנועה, stem נוע) for "put into motion," "started a car," as well as "vocalized"; מיכן (from מכונה stem כן) "mechanized"; מינח (from מונח, stem נוח) "established a terminology"; תיעש (from תעשיה, stem עשה) "industrialized"; תמצת (from תמצית, stem מצה) "digested"; תרבת (from תרבות, stem רבה) "civilized," and the like.

4. *Blends*. Some new coinage in languages are apparently prompted by the motive of economy. Two words are fused into a unit which form a new word signifying the ideas represented by both words, as in the case of the English *smog* (*smoke* and *fog*), *chortle* (*chuckle* and *snort*) *electrocute* (*electric* and *execute*), *goodbye* (God be with you), *brunch* (*breakfast* and *lunch*). A large number of new words have been coined in modern Hebrew on this principle, such as בינאם (internationalized), מדחם (thermometer), כדורגל (football), רמזור (traffic light), תפוז (orange), מגדלור (lighthouse)—all of which are blends, respectively, of בין (between) and אם (nation), מדד (measured) and חם (heat), כדור (ball) and רגל (foot), רמז (wink, hint) and אור (light), תפוח (apple) and זהב (gold), מגדל (tower) and אור (light).

Especially interesting are such verbal blends as עדכן (brought up to date) composed of עד כאן (up to here) and מצוברח (moody) derived from מצב רוח (literally, state of

[1] *See* my article in *JQR*, vol. xlix, No. 3 (January 1959).

mind or mood). In these blends the fusion is so complete
that the identity of the component elements is almost entirely
ignored and the resulting units are treated as independent
quadriliteral verbs, subject to the normal verbal inflections.
Thus, for example, עדכן is capable of taking on all the inflections characteristic of *piel*, including the derivative conjugations *pual* and *nithpael*. A person possessing the latest information is designated as בן אדם מעודכן. ''The dictionary was
brought up to date'' would be rendered by המלון נתעדכן.

Similarly, in the case of מצוברח, the form is regarded as
a regular *pual* participle, in which the initial מ is viewed as
the normal participial preformative, rather than as an integral
element of מצב רוח, of which it is composed. As a matter
of fact, a quasi *hitphael* form מצטברח (getting into a bad
mood) is also recorded. [1]

Equally interesting are some nominal blends which have
shown a capacity for sprouting verbs, as well as new deverbal
nouns. To illustrate, the noun דוֹח is a blend of דין וחשבון
(report), which yielded the verbal form, דִוַּח (reported), as
well as the verbal noun דִוּוּחַ (reporting) and the occupational
noun דַוָּח (a reporter).

Normal Organic Developments

A large number of new coinages were evolved from the
normal organic structure of the language, and they are modelled on accepted patterns, which are already found in biblical
Hebrew, although, in some instances, to a very limited degree.
Included in this number are the following categories:

1. *Deverbal Nouns.* Each of the Hebrew conjugations with
the exceptions of the passive conjugations, *pual* and *hophal*,
are capable of yielding nominal forms which have evolved
from the regular gerund or infinitive forms of these respective conjugations. Thus the *kal* yields such forms
as בריאה (creation), אכילה (eating), etc. The *piel* gives rise

[1] *See* Y. Avineri, כבושי העברית בדורנו (Tel-Aviv 1946), p. 173.

to two formations, with slight differentiation in meaning, and so does the *hiphil*; e.g., קיבּול (receiving, acception) and קבּלה [1] (receipt, acceptance, tradition, traditional law) from קיבּל, הֶבְדֵל [2] (difference, distinction) and הבדלה [1] (separation, division) from הבדיל. In the *niphal* and *hithpael* conjugations these nominal forms are built by affixing the *ut*-ending, characteristic of the abstract nouns, to the regular infinitive forms; e.g., היבּדלות (differentiation, isolation) and התחברות (making an alliance). [3]

In biblical Hebrew, there are only scant and sporadic examples of these nominal forms. In mishnaic, medieval and, especially, modern Hebrew, such examples are too numerous to require citing. They are coined freely as the exigencies arise.

To mention only a few illustrations, the noun בקשה (request, wish), derived from the *piel*, is already found in the book of Esther and is used extensively in later Hebrew. But in modern times a term for "a demand" (of goods or merchandize) was required. The cognate form בּיקוש was accordingly coined for this purpose and is now widely in vogue. But the new needs required also the complementary antonym of "a demand" in the area of marketing; namely, "a supply." No such term could be found in the Hebrew literary sources. The biblical word הציע (spread out, unfolded, proposed)

[1]   These are regular infinitives of the *piel* and *hiphil*, respectively, in Aramaic. These formations in Hebrew are probably to be traced to Aramaic influence.

[2]   In biblical Hebrew this form is vocalized with *pathah* under the ה; *e.g.,* המשל Job 25: 2, השמד Isa 14: 23, הפצר I Sam 15: 23, הסתר Prov. 25: 2. But in later Hebrew this *pathah* was changed to segol, by the process of assimilation to the following *tzere*, its kindred vowel, with the result that in the פ"ן derivatives of this formation this vowel is generally represented in mishnaic Hebrew by a *yod*; *e.g.,* היקש, היזק, היתר, etc.

[3]   The *ut*-ending for building abstract nouns is another prolific source for new coinages in Hebrew. Both medieval and modern Hebrew have made considerable use of this formation to represent the numerous philosophical and general abstract concepts that have evolved. Incidentally, the construction of abstract concepts with this ending is already found in Akkadian.

suggested itself as an appropriate source for the coinage of
such a term. But one nominal derivative of this verb, namely
הצעה, had already gained wide vogue both in mishnaic and
modern Hebrew in different meanings. Hence, the cognate
derivative היצע (already coined by Maimonides [1] in the sense
of "formulation") has been introduced to signify "supply."
The Hebrew language is thus equipped with two new terms
for "supply" and "demand" in marketing; namely, היצע and
ביקוש, respectively.

Further extension in discrimination of shades of meaning
is made possible by a phonetic modification of the form *hak-
talah*; namely, *'aktalah*. [2] This modification is already in
evidence in mishnaic Hebrew (e.g., הגדה and אגדה), but it
is gaining extensive vogue in modern Hebrew. For example,
אבחנה (diagnosis) is an extension of the medieval coinage
הבחנה (discrimination), and אכזבה (disappointment) is an
outgrowth of הכזבה (denial, confutation). These nominal
extensions gave rise to the new verbs אבחן (diagnosed) and
אכזב (disappointed). Similarly, alongside of the medieval
הספקה (sufficiency, supplying) have been coined the modern
forms אספקה (supply, provision) and הספק (productive
capacity). We consequently say זהו מוסד להספקת סמי רפואה
(This is an institution for supplying drugs), הוא הביא את האספקה
הרפואית (He brought the medical supply), ההספק של הפועל
הזה רב הוא (The productive capacity of this worker is great).

2. *Occupational Nouns*. A special formation or nominal
pattern (*kattāl*) denotes a habitual occupation, trade, preoccupation or vocation. In biblical Hebrew, this formation
is represented by such nouns as טַבָּח (a cook), צַיָד (a hunter),
נַגָּח (an ox wont to gore), גַּנָּב (a thief), אִכָּר (peasant). This
formation is widely used in mishnaic Hebrew, and in modern
Hebrew it provides an inexhaustible source of new coinages;
e.g., רַשָּׁם (a draftsman, a registrar), פַּסָּל (a sculptor), כַּנָּר

---

[1] *Cf.* הלכות ברכות xi, 3.
[2] The interchange of א and ה is common in Hebrew.

(a violinist), נַוָּד (a nomad), נַהָג (a driver), and the like.

Other means of denoting occupational nouns in modern Hebrew are those of affixing the endings ־ָן, ־ָנִי or ־ַאי(־ַאי) to the noun signifying the area of occupation; e.g., מזרחָן (an orientalist), תעשׁיָן (an industrialist), חלבָּן (a milkman), כובעָן or כּובעָנִי (a hatter), תאותָן or תאותָנִי (passionate), רגשָׁן (excitable) and רגשָׁנִי (sentimental); [1] מכונאי (a machinist), מסאי (an essayist), טוראי (a private, a soldier of the ranks), ימאי (a seaman), חשמלאי (an electrician). These nouns are derived from the nouns מזרח (orient), תעשׂיה (industry), חלב (milk), כובע (hat), מכונה (machine), מסה (an essay), טור (row, rank), ים (sea), חשמל (electricity). [2]

3. *Instrumental Nouns.* A formation characterized by a preformative *mem*, namely, *maktel*, was employed in biblical Hebrew to signify instruments; e.g., מרצע (an awl), מסמר (a nail), מלבּן (a brickmold). Mishnaic and medieval Hebrew provide an additional list of such formations; e.g., מכבש (a vice, a press), מלגז (a pitchfork), מקדח (a drill), מטחן (a grinding mill), מחבט (a dusting stick), מזרק (a syringe). This formation is prolific of new coinages in modern Hebrew, serving to designate the new instruments that are constantly emerging; e.g., מצפּן (a compass), מצלמה (a camera), מבדד (an isolator or insulator), מתנע (a starter of car), מפצע (a nutcracker), מברג (a screwdriver), מפלג (a distributor in a car).

---

[1] The latter forms are analogous to the biblical רחמני (compassionate, Lam 4:10) and the mishnaic חנוני (storekeeper). On the relation of חנות to חנוה, which underlies the formation חנוני *see* my *Kimhi's Hebrew Grammar* (Mikhlol) (New York 1952), note 572.

[2] Both these endings, serving as occupational indications, are common in mishnaic Hebrew and are represented, to a limited degree, even in biblical Hebrew; *e.g.*, רחמן Lam 4:10, and אלמן Jer 51:5, כילי Isa 32:5.7, and אחרי Prov 28:23; *cf.* Ibn Janah, *Shor.* 23 and Joseph Kimhi, *Zik.* 12. The ending ־ָן may be an Aramaic equivalent of the Hebrew adjectival ending ־וֹן (*e.g.*, קיצון, חיצון, etc.), while the ־ִי ending may be related to the adjectival ending ־ִי (*e.g.*, עברי, חפשי, etc.).

4. *Medical Terms*. In biblical and mishnaic Hebrew physical defects or diseases are indicated by the nominal formation *kattelet*; e.g., שַׁחֶפֶת (wasting away, tuberculosis), דַּלֶּקֶת (inflammation), יַלֶּפֶת (a scab or scurf), קַדַּחַת (fever), צַלֶּקֶת (a scar), יַבֶּלֶת (a wart, an ulcer). This opens a new avenue in modern Hebrew for coinages designed to denote diseases for which no name may be found in the literary sources, or which are newly discovered; e.g., קַצֶּרֶת (asthma), קָרֶמֶת (diphteria), נַזֶּלֶת (head cold, catarrh), אַדֶּמֶת (measles), צַהֶבֶת (jaundice), שַׁעֶלֶת (whooping cough), שַׁפַּעַת (influenza), and the like.

5. *Formative Additions*. A considerable number of new nominal coinages have been constructed in modern Hebrew by affixing to the stem letters, or infixing in them, one or more of the formative letters וימנת. Such constructions are already common in the Bible and have been widely employed in later Hebrew. A particularly ingenious example of such coinages in modern Hebrew is that by Bialik for "import-export." Motivated by the phonetic likeness of these two terms, he coined the equivalent Hebrew terms יבוא – יצוא, where the former is modelled on the pattern of the biblical יקום (with prefixed *yod*), while the latter is built on the analogy of גבול (with infixed *waw*). [1] Other examples of new coinages in this category are מברק (a telegram), משׂכל (intelligence), מלון (dictionary), שעון (clock, watch), עתון (newspaper), אוירון (aeroplane), תקליט (gramophone record), תקדים (precedent), תסביך (complex), תזמרת (orchestra), תצרכת (needs, necessaries), תקבלת (parallelism), etc.

6. *Adjectival Forms Indicating Capability or Susceptibility*. Under the influence of the European languages a need was felt in modern Hebrew to coin a formation which would

---

[1] Incidentally, יקום is a unique formation in biblical Hebrew and no such formation is found in the literary sources until it was revived by Bialik.

represent adjectives designating capability or susceptibility, equivalent to adjectives with the suffix-*able* or *-ible* in English and *-bar* in German. For this purpose the form *katil* was selected, since this form is employed in biblical and mishnaic Hebrew to signify passive adjectives, which resemble in some manner the adjectives in the present category; e.g., שָׂכִיר (a hired laborer), משיח (an anointed one), שליח (messenger, one who is sent), and the like. On this analogy new coinages are emerging as need arises, such as גמיש (flexible), אכיל (edible), שביר (breakable), עביר (passable), שמיע (audible), etc. The difference in the two categories is that in the former case the subject is initially the recipient of the action, while thereafter he performs an active function. In the latter instance, however, the subject merely possesses the potentiality of being the recipient of the action.

7. *Semantic Metamorphosis.* When a new concept emerges for which no linguistic symbol is available, recourse is sometimes had to one of the old, perhaps obsolete or obscure, words, changing and adapting its meaning to represent the new concept. The word thus undergoes a metamorphosis in meaning. In Chaucerean English, for example, the word *clerk* meant "jurist" or "scholar." In modern English, it assumed an entirely different meaning.

The revolutionary change involved in converting Hebrew— a literary language for many centuries—into a modern vernacular necessitated the creation of many new words to represent the modern objects and concepts, and semantic metamorphosis was one of the devices employed to meet this need. Thus the noun חשמל which occurs in Ezek 1.4 is obscure and probably refers to a shining substance. The Septuagint translation of this word (*electron*—"amber," "an alloy of gold and silver") suggested to Judah L. Gordon, poet laureate of the Haskalah period, the idea of using this word in the modern sense of "electricity," and it has been used in this sense ever since, even giving rise to the verbal form חשמל (to electrify), מחושמל (one who is electrified), etc.

A number of obscure or archaic words were accordingly resuscitated, rejuvenated and reintroduced into the language. A new lease of life was given them by lending them new meanings in keeping with the modern exigencies. For example, words like מוסך (a *hapax legomenon* in 2 Kings 16: 18, probably "a covered structure"), משק (obscure in origin and in meaning, Gen 15: 2), מזח (Isa 23: 10, probably, belt, or girdle), מוקש (biblical, a lure, obstacle), מערכת (biblical, a row, a battle line), הפגין (mishnaic, cried out for help), סרט (mishnaic, an incision, a strip), מרץ (medieval, strength or rapidity), מען (medieval, a reply) and many others, were brought back to life and saved from oblivion by attaching to them the modern meanings, respectively, of "garage," "farm" or "household management," "pier," "mine," "editorial office" or "editorship," "demonstrated," "film," "energy," and "an address," (perhaps under the influence of the Arabic *unwān*).

8. *Syntactic Extension.* There has been considerable controversy among the Israeli grammarians and linguists over the widespread use, in the modern Hebrew vernacular, of the negative לא, instead of אין, with the present tense, or adjectival predicates, in such instances as אני לא רוצה (I do not want), אתה לא צריך (you don't need), היא לא יפה (she isn't pretty). This usage is undoubtedly due to the influence of the Indo-European languages, as well as perhaps to the tendency toward simplicity since, unlike לא, the use of אין may involve different inflections; e.g., אינני, אינך, etc., although the forms אין אני or אין אתה, etc. are also possible. In biblical Hebrew, as well as in mishnaic Hebrew לא is employed only with the verbal forms in the perfect and imperfect tenses, while אין is restricted, with few exceptions, [1] to nominal and adjectival, as well as to participial clauses.

The replacement of אין by לא in such instances is challenged by some Israeli grammarians as incorrect and contrary to

---

[1] *See* Ges-K. Sec. 152d and M. Z. Segal, דקדוק לשון המשנה (Tel-Aviv 1936), p. 134.

the genius of the Hebrew language. The present tense in Hebrew, these grammarians argue, is not verbal in the Hebrew sources but participial. It cannot, therefore, be placed on a par with the past and the future tenses where the use of לא is legitimate. [1]

The views of these grammarians notwithstanding, לא is now universally employed in the present tense, in the modern Israeli vernacular and is apparently deeply rooted. It can be justified on the principle of *syntactic extension*. The principle of *lexical extension* is familiar, according to which an old word is employed with extension of meaning to cover new concepts and meanings. Extension of syntactical constructions may be used in a similar manner. Thus, for example, the perfect and imperfect tenses in biblical Hebrew, as is well known, are qualitative rather than temporal. The tense-idea in classical Hebrew is related to the *kind*, rather than to the *time* of the action. The choice of tense is determined by whether the action, in the mind of the speaker, is completed or uncompleted. There are, strictly speaking, no "tenses" at all in Hebrew, as in the other Semitic languages. Instead, these languages distinguish only what may be called "aspect," that is, a state from an action, an activity (continuous) from an act (completed). In mishnaic Hebrew and, of course, in later Hebrew the use of these tenses was extended to cover temporal action in the same manner as in the Indo-European languages. Similarly, the participial form employed in biblical and mishnaic Hebrew may be extended in modern Hebrew to cover the present tense in the verbal sense pure and simple, even as it is employed generally in Indo-European languages.

An interesting case of syntactic extension is that of the prefixed particle ש in the constructions of the future tense. Hebrew, as is well known, does not possess auxiliary verbs denoting the future tense, as do German and Yiddish, as well as English (shall, should, will); or the jussive and optative, such as the English "let" and the German or Yiddish "zoll,"

---

[1]   *Cf.* לשוננו X, 2-3, Jerusalem.

in such an expression as "zoll er gehn," (let him go). Classical Hebrew has no specific or precise form for rendering the idea of such an expression. But in the modern Israeli vernacular this idea is signified by prefixing the particle שׁ to the future tense; namely, שׁילך, or in such constructions as ‏למה שלא אלך‎? (why shouldn't I go?), ‏למה שלא אדבר עברית‎? (why shouldn't I speak Hebrew?) ‏שיחשבו מה שהם רוצים‎ (let them think as they please). [1]

Incidentally, this construction is sometime employed to indicate also the imperative, especially in a commanding mood. Thus ‏שתלך‎ !, ‏שתגיד‎ ! in place of the classical ‏לך‎ (go), ‏הגד‎ (tell), although, perhaps more commonly, the future forms are used in place of the imperative; e.g., ‏תגיד‎, ‏תלך‎. This latter vernacular usage has its precedent in biblical Hebrew. [1]

Conclusions

The purpose of this article was to trace some of the principles by which the growth of modern Hebrew has been guided and to establish the legitimacy of these principles. There are, to be sure, in the modern Hebrew vernacular of Israel, a great many barbarisms and illicit injections from the foreign languages on which the immigrants from seventy different countries were reared. These alien injections threaten to jeopardize the normal growth of the language and to impair its identity. Particularly jarring are the stylistic and idiomatic adulterations, as well as the general impoverishment in regard to the unique Hebrew diction, which sometime characterize the present Hebrew vernacular in Israel.

It is, however, to be remembered that the present vernacular is still, probably, in a transitional stage, and there is reason to hope that the illicit expressions and usages will eventually

---

[1] Similar constructions may be found also in midrashic and medieval literature; see Avineri, op. cit., p. 161.

[1] Cf. Lev 19:3: ‏תשמרו‎ ••• ‏תיראו‎ Isa 18:3: ‏תשמעו‎ ••• ‏תראו‎ and numerous other examples.

be discarded. Many of the new immigrants are still illiterate or, at best, products of the *ulpanim*, lacking deep roots in the literary sources of the language. It may take a generation or longer before the vernacular takes on a definite Hebraic character. In the meantime the schools and the other educational agencies in Israel, especially the Hebrew Language Academy, are making every effort to guide and direct the growth of the language into channels of legitimate usage. These efforts, as the present outline of the growth of the language seems to indicate, are apparently meeting with a considerable measure of success.

PLURIMA MORTIS IMAGO

By Godfrey Rolles Driver
Oxford University

THE FOLLOWING REMARKS have arisen out of the new English translation of the Bible now being prepared by committees appointed by the various Churches in the United Kingdom; for the work on this undertaking, which is not a mere revision of existing versions but a completely new translation, has made a fresh examination of innumerable passages imperative.

I

The account of Absalom's death in the Old Testament is fraught with difficulties.

He is described in one passage as having a fine crop of hair; for "he weighed the hair of his head at two hundred shekels after the king's weight" (2 Sam 14: 26); and another passage says that "Absalom rode upon his mule, and the mule went under the thick boughs of a great oak (אֵלָה), and he was taken up (וַיֻּתַּן) between the heaven and the earth; and the mule that was under him went on" (2 Sam 18: 9, R.V.). The Old Testament lends no support to the view that the unfortunate man was caught by his hair in the oak and hung suspended from the tree until Joab and his men arrived. Josephus, [1] however, appears to be responsible for this form of the story by combining the two passages into one; for he says that "he [sc. Absalom] in fear of being captured by his enemies mounted his royal mule and fled. As he rode along at full speed, he was lifted up by the unsteady motion and

---

[1] Flavius Josephus, *Antiquities of the Jews*, Book VII, ch. x, 2, § 240.

his hair became entangled in a rugged tree with branches
extending far out, and in this strange fashion he remained
suspended. But his swiftly moving beast went on further
as though still carrying his master on his back, while Absalom
swung from the branches which held him" (Thackeray). This
composite account at once raises the question: how could
Absalom's hair, which would have been streaming behind
him as he was carried along by the mule, have become so
firmly entangled in the tree as to hold him fast?

The mystery deepens when the Old Testament goes on
to describe Absalom's death. It says that Joab, arriving on
the scene and finding the man who had come upon Absalom
suspended from the tree and had refrained from killing him,
after a brief conversation with him said "I may not tarry
thus (לא־כן אחילה) with thee. And he took three darts (שבטים)
and thrust them through the heart of Absalom, while he was
yet alive in the heart of the oak. And the young men that
had been Joab's armour-bearers compassed about and smote
Absalom, and slew him" (2 Sam 18: 14. R.V.). Josephus, [1]
who has again seen the difficulties, says "Joab thereupon
ordered him to show him where he had seen Absalom hanging
and shot an arrow into his heart and killed (τοξεύσας
κατὰ τῆς καρδίας ἀπέκτεινεν) him. Then Absalom's armour-
bearers surrounded the tree and pulled down the corpse
(κατασπῶσι τὸν νεκρὸν); and, casting it into a deep yawning
pit, they threw stones into this until it filled up and took on
the form and size of a tomb" (Thackeray).

Joab's statement to the man who had been telling him why
he had not killed Absalom, that "Not so shall I tarry," barely
makes sense in the context; for he had only just come and
showed no signs of delaying beyond asking the one question
and getting the answer. How too could "clubs" (not "darts", as
the Revisers mistranslate the word in order to obtain sense)
pierce a man's breast; for they were not a piercing weapon?

[1] *Ibid.*, §§ 241-242.

Further, even if the word meant 'darts', how could these be
driven deep into a man's body when it hung free; for it would
offer no resistance to the blows but would swing back when
struck even by a pointed weapon? And again, whether clubs
or darts, why were three required for the purpose; for, although a man stabbed in the heart might survive for several
hours if kept perfectly still, Absalom was not likely to have
hung motionless from the tree, like a patient in a hospital
bed, while three "darts" in succession were thrust into his
heart? Lastly, after having had his heart pierced by three
"darts" in succession, Absalom would beyond all doubt have
been dead; there would then have been no need for ten young
men to surround him and despatch him. Josephus simply
evades these difficulties by composing what is *au fond* a
different account, which is not history but fiction and may
therefore be disregarded.

Accordingly, if the account in the Old Testament is accepted,
Absalom was not caught by his hair in the tree and was not
killed by Joab as he hung there, as Klostermann saw long
ago. [1] That there is no basis for Klostermann's view, that
Joab merely released Absalom from the tree and that the
young men then despatched him on the ground, as Smith
claimed, [2] rests on a misunderstanding caused by the "emendation" of "clubs" (שבטים) into "darts" (שלחים) on the supposed
evidence of the LXX; [3] for they, like Josephus, had seen the
difficulty (or part of it) and sought in their own way to
eliminate it. At the same time, even though Klostermann's
explanation of Joab's action is accepted, his "emendation"
of the text (except on one small point) must be rejected; for
this can and therefore must be interpreted as it has been
transmitted.

[1]   In *Die Bücher Samuelis und Könige*, Kurzgefasster Kommentar
zu den heiligen Schriften A iii (Nordlingen 1887), p. 214.

[2]   Henry Preserved Smith, *Critical and Exegetical Commentary on
the Books of Samuel*, International Critical Commentary (Edinburgh
1912), p. 359.

[3]   Otto Thenius, *Die Bücher Samuelis*, Kurzgefasstes exegetisches
Handbuch zum Alten Testament, third edition (Leipzig 1898), p. 181.

The scene may now be explained as the original writer has described it, not as the modern scholar rewrites it.

Absalom, riding away on his mule in great haste late in the day, was carried under a great terebinth (rather than an oak), [1] "and his head was caught fast in the terebinth, and he was put set fixed between heaven and earth." The verb here translated "put set fixed" means literally "given"; but it is often used of putting a person or a thing into a certain position, e.g., a man into the stocks (Jer 20: 2; 29: 26) or his neck into a collar or yoke (Jer 27: 8, 11, 12), and wood on to an altar (1 Kings 18: 23, where נתן and שׂים have precisely the same sense). It is therefore quite properly used to describe how Absalom was put, set or fixed, between heaven and earth. The LXX's "he was hung" (וַיִּתָּל) therefore does not necessarily imply a different verb, however closely the two Hebrew verbs may superficially resemble one another; for, though supported by the other Versions, it may only be an interpretation, since it is found in no Hebrew manuscript and ought perhaps therefore to be rejected on the principle that *difficilior lectio potior* here as elsewhere. What happened then was presumably this: as Absalom rode under the tree, he was caught by the neck in the fork of two boughs which had been kept low down and held together by the surrounding branches; jolted by the impact of Absalom's weight, the fork became dislodged and its two arms closed round Absalom's neck as they sprang upwards, freed from entangling branches and carrying him with them. Somewhat similarly, Milon an athlete from Croton in the sixth century B.C., trying to escape from the tree which held him, was devoured alive by wolves.

Joab, reproaching the man who had found Absalom suspended from the tree, told him that he would have given him

---

[1] So Gen 35: 4 (Septuagint, Vulgate, Peshitta, Targum, Saadiah, Abu Said); *see also* Leo Anderlind in the *Zeitschrift des Deutschen Palästina-Vereins* (Leipzig 1890), vol. xiii, 233-234, and Friedrich Lundgren, *Die Benutzung der Pflanzenwelt in der alttestamentlichen Religion* (Giessen 1908), pp. 20-24.

a thousand shekels of silver if he had killed him on the spot;
but the man answered that that would have been "treachery"
(שֶׁקֶר) to the king, who had bidden anyone who found his
son to spare him and added "and if I were to take upon my
hands/handle ten thousand pieces of silver (for such a crime),
I would not put forth my hand against the king's son." The
word translated "treachery" presents no difficulty, as Smith
thinks when he says that "the killing of Absalom would not
be 'deceit' "; [1] for the word can surely import also treachery
or disloyalty. The verb in "if I were to take (שׁקל) upon my
hands" is commonly identified with that for "weighed"
(Ugar. *ṯql* = Hebr. *šāqal* = Aram. *t^eqal*), and "upon my
hands (כַּפָּי)" has been altered to "upon the pan of my scales
(כַּפֵּי)" to accord with this interpretation. [2] This "emendation"
is open to the two objections that it is not supported by the
ancient Vss. and that the pronominal "my" is otiose, if it
does not actually violate the natural sense. Also, it does not
get rid of the real difficulty, that it will be not the donor but
the recipient who weighs out the specified sum of money;
and this has brought other unsupported "emendations" in
its train. The easiest way out of the difficulty is to suppose
that the writer is employing a totally different verb, *i.e.* one
meaning "picked up, took away" (Ugar. *šql* = Aram.
š^eqal), which is supported by one Greek Version's "I should
take (λάβοιμι)"; [3] this immediately restores sense to the
passage. There is equally little reason to doubt the text when
the man goes on to report the king's *ipsissima verba*, namely
"beware that none touch the young man (שִׁמְרוּ־מִי בַנַּעַר)".
The Hebrew clause means literally "take care, who (ever you
are), in (the matter of) the young man" (as accented) or
"take care, who(ever of you is) by the young man" (which

---

[1]   *Ibid.*, p. 358.

[2]   Rudolf Kittel & Paul Kahle, *Biblia Hebraica*, third edition,
vol. i (Stuttgart 1937), p. 486.

[3]   Fridericus Field, *Origenis Hexapla quae supersunt*, vol. i (Oxford
c. 1875), p. 573 (18).

disregards the accentuation). This verb occasionally has
absolute force (*e.g.*, Judges 1: 24), but nowhere else apparently
is it followed by the preposition supposed in the first translation, so that the second interpretation may perhaps be
preferred; the preposition sometimes indicates proximity to
a person (*e.g.*, Isa 8: 16), and the form of the sentence will
then be comparable with that in "who (is) for the Lord,
(come) to me" (Ex 22: 26). Such colloquial expressions, partly
aposiopetic and partly exclamatory, are natural in direct
oration if obscure when read; and that the ancient translators,
followed by the copyists of some manuscripts, have altered
"who (מִי)?" into "for me (לִי)" is natural. Once again, the
principle of *difficilior lectio potior* may be invoked even
against their combined evidence.

Joab is then made to say to the man "I may not tarry thus
(לֹא־כֵן אֹחִילָה) with thee," which offers but a poor sense; consequently the LXX's alternative reading (Lucian) and that
of the Targum, namely "therefore I will begin (לָכֵן אָחֵלָה)
before thee" may be accepted. [1]

What Joab did must now be settled. The Hebrew text,
as ordinarily translated, says that "he took three clubs in
his hand and thrust them through the heart of Absalom,"
which is absurd, as said above. Absalom, held fast by the
neck in the fork of two boughs as by a vice, was suspended
out of reach of a man on the ground; Joab therefore picked
up some stout sticks, broken boughs lying as they had snapped
off or cut to shape for some purpose of husbandry, and prodded
Absalom in the chest with them in order to dislodge him from
the fork in which he was held. The same word serves for the
sticks used for beating cummin (Isa 28: 27); and another
form of the word for 'heart' (לֵב)' is used for the "chest (לֵבָב)'
in the case of the maidens mourning for Nineveh and "tabe-
ring upon their breasts" (Nahum 2: 7). The corresponding

[1] Karl Budde, *Die Bücher Samuelis*, Kurzer Handkommentar
zum Alten Testament, vol. viii (Tübingen und Leipzig 1902), pp.
283-284.

Assyrian word is similarly employed in "they came crawling on their bellies (*ina eli libbēšunu*.)" [1] Sense can thus be won without violence to the text. Thus dislodged from the tree, Absalom fell dazed and gasping for breath to the ground; there the young men surrounded him and did him to death, while Joab held back that his might not be the hand which struck the fatal blow.

The last problem is the number of Joab's armour-bearers. Here they are said to be ten; elsewhere the usual number is one, *e.g.*, in the cases of Jonathan (1 Sam 14: 1-14; 1 Chron 11: 39) and Saul (1 Sam 31: 4-6; 1 Chron 10: 4-5). Where Jonathan has two, the meaning of the text is in doubt (1 Sam 16: 2); and, when Saul takes David as such, the case is obviously exceptional (1 Sam 16: 21). Possibly therefore "armour-bearers" here stands loosely for Joab's body-guard rather than for armour-bearers in the restricted technical sense of the expression.

When Absalom's revolt collapsed, David pardoned Amasa, his commander-in-chief, and appointed him to command an army in place of Joab, who had been responsible for the victory. He then sent Amasa to rally the men of Judah in face of the threat from the fresh revolt which Sheba the Benjamite was raising; but Amasa for some unknown reason lingered over the task. Thereupon David, fearing the result of Sheba's activities if operations were delayed, sent Abishai, one of his most daring and devoted followers, in pursuit of the rebel, saying to him "take thou thy lord's servants and pursue after him, lest he get him fenced cities and escape out of our sight (וְהִצִּיל עֵינֵנוּ)." This last expression is still unexplained; and the verb as vocalized can only mean "(and) he will rescue" or "snatch away (our eyes)," as the Peshitta's "he will gouge out" shows. This translation, however, is nonsense. The LXX improve on the Massoretic pronunciation

---

[1] Maximilian Streck, *Assurbanipal*, vol. ii (Leipzig 1916), pp. 34-35 (26-27).

by translating the verb as "he will overshadow (σκιάσει, representing הַצַּל)." This is beyond doubt the correct vocalization [1] but equally so the wrong verb, which is not one meaning "overshadowed" (cf. Arab, 'aḍalla "was growing dark; obscured") but another and quite different one meaning "eluded" (cf. Arab. aḍalla "misled"); for the corresponding Arabic verb is met in a number of very similar expressions, such as "he missed (ḍalla 'an) his goal," "he missed (ḍalla) the way," 'perhaps I shall escape the notice of ('aḍallu) God" in the I theme and "such and such a thing eluded me ('aḍal-lani)" in the IV theme. [2] The Vulgate's ut effugiat nos confirms 'he will elude our gaze' as the time sense of the phrase.[3]

Amasa, however, as he came back, met Joab and Abishai "at the great stone which is in Gibeon," and Joab was seized with a fit of jealousy. According to the text, he was armed with a belt to which a sword in its scabbard was attached; and "as he went out (sc. to greet Amasa), it fell out. And Joab said to Amasa: Is it well with thee, my brother? And Joab took Amasa by the beard with his right hand to kiss him. But Amasa took no heed to the sword that was in Joab's hand; so he smote him therewith in the belly and shed out his bowels to the ground and struck him not again; and he died" (2 Sam 20: 4-10 R.V.). The difficulty in the biblical story is that in v. 8 Joab's sword is in its scabbard and then has fallen out on to the ground and immediately afterwards in v. 10, although he is not said to have picked it up, it is ready in his hand for the fatal blow. Josephus [4] therefore embroiders the story to eliminate the difficulty, saying that "as Amasa

---

[1] Cf. Heinrich Ewald, *Einleitung in die Geschichte des Volkes Israel*, third edition, vol. iii (Göttingen 1864-1868; 7 vols), p. 262, where this explanation of the verb is given; but the sense so obtained is not satisfactory.

[2] Edward William Lane, *An Arabic-English Lexicon* (London 1863-1893; 8 vols.), Bk. I, Part v, pp. 1796-1797.

[3] The Targum's יעיק לנא, "it will be distressing to us," seems to reflect the Arab. ṣalla "(a calamity) befell (a person)."

[4] *Antiquities*. Book VII, ch. xi, 7, §§ 283-284.

approached to greet him, he artfully contrived to have his
sword fall, as if by itself, out of its sheath. And he picked it
up from the ground and with his other hand seized Amasa,
who was now near him, to kiss him, and with an unforeseen
thrust in the belly killed him" (Thackeray). This reads far
too much into the text and is unnecessary. The words vocalized
to mean "and he had gone out, and it fell (וְהוּא יָצָא וַתִּפֹּל)"
may however be revocalized to mean "and he was going
out and behaving like a cad (וְהוּא יֹצֵא וְתָפֵל)" [1] after the
Targum's "he went and acted like a knave (אֲזִיל וּפֹסַע)." [2] His
unseemly or frivolous, even caddish, conduct showed itself
in approaching Amasa as a friend, grasping his beard with
one hand and kissing him, while he stabbed him with the
other; and such an action would not require Joab's sword to
fall out of the scabbard, whereby Amasa's suspicions might
easily have been roused. No objection can be brought against
reading this verb in the present passage, since both it and
the corresponding noun are found elsewhere in the Old Testament. So Jeremiah applies "frivolity" (תִּפֵל) to the words
of the Samaritan prophets (Jer 23: 13), and Job is said not
to charge God with it in allowing the Satan to try him (Job
1: 22), while "frivolity" (תִּפְלָה) is applied to various forms
of frivolous or unseemly conduct, especially idolatry, in post-
biblical literature; [3] further, the Aramaic verb from the same
root occurs in one version of one of the Psalms. [4]

Finally, Amasa is described as "wallowing (מִתְגֹּלֵל)" in
blood in the middle of the highway. This may well be the
true sense of the verb here; but it is translated by the LXX

[1] Cf. 1 Sam 18: 16 if participles are read. Or cf. 2 Sam 19: 10 and
1 Kings 2: 8 if perfect tenses are preferred.

[2] The Aram. פסע here corresponds to the Syr. psaʿ, 'the acted like
a knave" (Carolus Brockelmann, Lexicon Syriacum [Halle a.d. S.
1928], p. 582).

[3] Marcus Jastrow, A Dictionary of the Targumim, the Talmud
Babli and Yerushalmi, and the Midrashic Literature (London and
New York 1903 [1950]; 2 vols), vol. ii, p. 1686.

[4] 2 Sam 22: 27 (תִּתַּפָּל) = Ps 18: 27 (תִּתְפַּתָּל).

"soiled" (πεφυρμένος), which may sometimes be the sense, e.g., when applied to blood-stained garments (Isa 9: 4). The second sense easily arises out of the first, and which is meant can often hardly be said, especially when the word is used metaphorically of wallowing in or being soiled by sin (Ecclesiasticus 12: 14; Zadokite Documents [Rost] 5: 4; 9: 15A). The basic sense of the V *GLL* is that of rolling; and other words for soiling (גאל, גֹעל) may be expanded forms of the same root having the secondary sense. [1]

II

The writers, compilers or editors, of Israelite history, in recording the death of almost every king, say either that "he died" or that "he slept with his fathers"; and the problem is to discover what, if any, distinction between these two phrases can be detected.

Unqualified "he slept" (שׁכב) may refer either to sleeping in death, [2] i.e., being dead (Isa 43: 17; Job 14: 12; Ecclesiasticus 47: 23, where the Greek translator has ἀνεπαύσατο μετὰ τῶν πατέρων) or to lying in the grave (Isa 14: 18; Ps 88: 6; Job 21: 26). That the original meaning of "he slept with his fathers" was that the person concerned was buried in the ancestral grave or tomb, [3] is out of the question when the burial is subsequently described in different terms (Gen 47: 30) or when the person so described is known not to have been buried with his ancestors (Deut 31: 16; cf. 34: 6). The fate of Moses is fatal to this theory, and some other explanation of the expression must be sought.

The kings of whom the writers say simply that "he slept with his fathers" without any mention of the burial place are the following:

---

[1] *Cf.* Godfrey Rolles Driver in *Analecta Orientalia* (Rome 1953), vol. xii, p. 60.

[2] *Cf.* Ps 13: 4 (יִישַׁן).

[3] Alexander Heidel, *The Gilgamesh Epic and Old Testament Parallels* (Chicago 1946), p. 144.

Jeroboam I	(1 Kings 14: 20);
Ahab	(1 Kings 22: 40);
Jeroboam II	(2 Kings 14: 29);
Menahem	(2 Kings 15: 22);
Hezekiah	(2 Kings 20: 21);
Jehoiakim	(2 Kings 24: 6).

Another and different formula, that "he slept with his fathers, and they buried him" in such and such a place, is used in reference to the following kings:

Abijam or Abijah	(1 Kings 15: 8; 2 Chron 13: 22);
Jehu	(2 Kings 10: 25);
Jehoahaz of Israel	(2 Kings 13: 9);
Azariah or Uzziah	(2 Kings 15: 7; 2 Chron 26: 23).

The commonest formula, which is a merely verbal variation of this, is that "he slept with his fathers and was buried" in such and such a place; this is applied to the following kings:

David	(1 Kings 2: 10);
Solomon	(1 Kings 11: 43; 2 Chron 9: 31);
Rehoboam	(1 Kings 14: 31; 2 Chron 12: 16);
Asa	(1 Kings 15: 24; 2 Chron 16: 13);
Baasha	(1 Kings 16: 6);
Omri	(1 Kings 16: 28);
Jehoshaphat	(1 Kings 22: 50; 2 Chron 21: 1);
Joram	(2 Kings 8: 24);
Joash of Judah	(2 Kings 12: 21);
Jehoash or Joash of Israel	(2 Kings 13: 13; 14: 16);
Jotham	(2 Kings 15: 38; 2 Chron 27: 9);
Ahaz	(2 Kings 16: 20; 2 Chron 28: 27);
Manasseh	(2 Kings 21: 18; 2 Chron 33: 20).

The distinction between these lists is not a difference of kingdoms; for kings of both kingdoms appear indiscriminately in them all. The omission of "and they buried him" or "and he was buried" from the first list is probably due to the absence of any tradition or mention of the burial place in the records accessible to the writer; and its presence in the second and third lists beside "he slept with his fathers" confirms the suggestion that the two expressions have different connotations. Further, although the writers say of two of

them that "he slept with his fathers," neither was in fact
buried with them (Ahaz, Manasseh); and they say of four
others that "he slept with his fathers and was buried with
his fathers" (Rehoboam, Asa, Jehoshaphat, Joram), again
keeping the two expressions distinct. Clearly therefore "he
slept with his fathers" is not the same thing as "he was buried
with his fathers.' If, too, "he slept with his fathers" had
meant that he slept ever after in the same grave as they, it
must have followed the statement that "he was buried with
his fathers," as he will already have been buried.

Since then "he slept with his fathers" cannot connote being
committed to or lying in the grave of his fathers, it must
describe the manner of the person's death; and here the important point is that "he died" and "he slept with his fathers"
nowhere occur together except in the one case of Ahab (1
Kings 22: 35, 37, 40).

The next point which needs to be taken into consideration
is that "he died" is said only of kings who are described as
meeting a violent or unnatural death. Such were Tibni, who
presumably perished suppressing a revolt, Azariah of Israel
who died of injuries received in falling out of a window,
Jehoahaz who was taken captive to Egypt where presumably
he died (possibly from the consequences of his capture and
imprisonment, although nothing is said of the manner of his
death), Jehoram who died of a disease sent as a punishment
for his sins, Ahab and Josiah who were killed on or in flight
from the battlefield; two others, Amaziah and Amon, were
murdered and buried in Jerusalem (2 Kings 14: 20; 21: 26).

The suggestion may therefore be made that "he slept with
his fathers" means "he died in common with, *i.e.*, like his
fathers"; and the preposition used in this expression often
has this force, as describing the common lot of mankind.[1]
It will not, however, mean simply that "he went the way of

[1]   *Ibid.*, p. 146. *Cf.* Francis Brown with the cooperation of Samuel
Rolles Driver & Charles Briggs, *A Hebrew and English Lexicon of
the Old Testament* (Oxford 1906), pp. 767-768 (s.v. עם e).

all flesh"; [1] for that can be said in a sense of all men, whether
they meet violent or peaceful ends. Rather will it have been
restricted to any and every king of whom the text does not
say that "he died," *i.e.*, who did not meet a violent or unnatural end, in the language of these writers; in other words,
it means that any king of whom "he slept with his fathers"
is said died in his bed or met a natural end as his forefathers
(or a majority of them) may be assumed normally to have
done. In such cases the grave would generally but not always
necessarily be known. If however a king had met a violent
or unnatural death, when the notice said simply that "he
died," the burial place might well not be known; for in such
cases the body might have been buried secretly or by night
or have been left unburied, when no tradition of its burial
place would be likely to have been preserved.

If this explanation of "he died" and 'he slept with his
fathers" respectively is accepted, only one exception to the
general rule can be found. The Massoretic text as it stands
says in the case of Ahab that "he died" (because he had died
of wounds received in battle) and adds as an afterthought
that "he slept with his fathers" (1 Kings 22: 35, 37, 40). In
fact, Ahab is the only king to whom both formulae are
applied; and, since *ex hypothesi* they contradict one another,
the text at once falls under suspicion. This is confirmed by
the fact that "so Ahab slept with his fathers; and Ahaziah
reigned in his stead" is not found in one uncial manuscript
of the LXX and is omitted by the Chronicler (2 Chron 18: 34).
The obvious conclusion is that it must have been added by
some one anxious to bring the notice of Ahab's death into
line, as he supposed, with those of the deaths of other kings
but ignorant of the precise connotation of the expression
which he was interpolating into the text.

The rule observed by the biblical authors was applied only
in the case of the kings of Israel and Judah; for "he died"
was used of foreign kings, *e.g.*, Hazael and Nahash, whose

[1] Heidel, *op. cit.*, p. 144.

deaths were not described presumably because nothing was known of them (2 Kings 13: 24; 1 Chron 19: 1), and of ordinary people whether they died a natural death like Elisha (2 Kings 13: 20) or an unnatural death like Uzza (1 Chron 13: 10). Further, the Chronicler is not always consistent; he says of David that "he died," although he died in his bed (1 Chron 29: 28), and of Asa, who died of a disease, that "he slept with his fathers and died in the one and fortieth year of his reign," possibly because he wished to introduce the date (1 Chron 13: 10). However, *exceptio approbat regulam*, which may be accepted as defining the original connotations of these two expressions, whatever misuse of them may afterwards have crept in after the Exile.

A similar distinction between natural and unnatural or violent death was drawn by the draftsman of the Babylonian Code of Ḥammu-rabi; he uses "he died" for an unnatural death with only one exception and "he went to his fate" with unbroken regularity for a natural death. [1]

Quite different is the import of "he was gathered to his people" or "his fathers (אבותיו or נאסף אל־עמיו)" or simply "he was gathered in (נאסף)."

Taken superficially, these expressions might well refer to collecting a man's bones into a grave, specifically into the ancestral grave of his family; for the verb is used once or twice of collecting bones for interment (2 Sam 21: 13) and of disposing of a body in the grave (2 Kings 22: 20; 2 Chron 34: 28). This interpretation is indeed possible when the expression stands in isolation, *e.g.*, when God tells Aaron that "he shall be gathered unto his people" (Num 20: 24) and Moses is warned "thou also shalt be gathered unto thy people, as Aaron thy brother was gathered" (Num 27: 13; *cf.* 31: 2) and when the historian records that "all that generation were gathered unto their fathers" (Judges 2: 10); but it cannot be maintained when the attendant circumstances are considered.

[1]   Godfrey Rolles Driver and John Charles Miles, *Babylonian Laws* (Oxford 1952 and 1955; 2 vols), vol. ii, pp. 154, 206.

The person concerned is most commonly said to have died before being "gathered to his fathers" or "his people." So Abraham "breathed his last and died (in a good old age) and was gathered to his people" (Gen 25: 8); Ishmael, Isaac and Jacob, each in turn "breathed his last breath (and died) and was gathered unto his people" (Gen 25: 17; 35: 29; 49: 33); and Moses was told "die... and be gathered unto thy people, as thy brother Aaron died... and was gathered unto his people" (Deut 32: 50). Clearly, therefore, dying is something which precedes being gathered to one's fathers.

However, although Isaac and Jacob were buried in the same grave as Abraham, sometimes like Jacob long after being gathered to one's fathers (Gen 49 : 29-50 : 13), Abraham was buried not in an ancestral grave but in a new one which he had purchased for the purpose (Gen 25: 9-10). Aaron died in the wilderness (Num 32: 39) and Moses was buried alone in Moab where "no man knoweth of his grave unto this day" (Deut 34: 6). Also, a burial notice may follow that about being gathered in or to one's fathers; so the Lord tells Josiah "I will gather thee to thy fathers and thou shalt be gathered to thy grave in peace" (2 Kings 22: 20; 2 Chron 34: 28) and Jeremiah declares that "the slain of the Lord... shall not be lamented neither gathered nor buried" (Jerem 25: 33). Clearly therefore being gathered to one's fathers is something which precedes burial in the grave. Equally clearly, therefore, it is different from being gathered into the grave, which follows it.

One of the Psalmists seems to make clear what the ancient Hebrews thought when a man was "gathered to his fathers"; for he says that, when a man dies, "his soul shall go to the generation of his fathers" (Ps 49: 19). In other words, firstly he expires; then his soul or spirit, *i.e.*, that part of him which is immortal, leaves this world and 'is gathered to his fathers' in the world below, where his ancestors already are; and lastly his body is consigned to a grave, commonly the ancestral grave, in the world above. The expressions here discussed, however, say nothing of his condition in the after-world but leave the reader to surmise what it may be from such information about his life on earth that he may have or from the context in which his death is described. [1]

In conclusion, then, breathing one's last breath and dying and being gathered to one's ancestors or one's people and being buried in the grave are four separate processes which must be kept distinct in attempting to discover Hebrew views on the subject of death.

This brief contribution to the understanding of the Hebrew scriptures is offered as a token of esteem and respect for the distinguished Jewish scholar to whom the present volume is dedicated

as one of those who are

חכמי שיח בספרתם ומושלים במשמרותם

---

[1] Heidel, *op. cit.*, p. 188.

JEWISH PARTICIPANTS IN THE POLISH INSURRECTION OF 1863

Thirty-Eight Newly Identified Names

By Abraham G. Duker

The College of Jewish Studies, Chicago

THE HISTORY of the participation of Jews in the liberal nationalistic and social reform movements of the various nations and peoples since the beginnings of the Emancipation should logically constitute an area of equal interest to researchers both in Jewish history and of the countries or movements concerned. However, because of various factors affecting the status of the Jewish people and its history, this area has been cultivated primarily by Jewish rather than general historians. Moreover, studies in this field have usually not been accorded proper recognition by the writers of the histories of the particular countries, nationalities, or ideologies involved. While research carried out by Jewish historians has been motivated by an understandable pride in achievements, the need for support from history in the Jews' struggle for emancipation or for the maintenance of equality have also played important roles. The extraordinary rise of antisemitism in the present century has contributed to the feeling that defense against it would be aided by the emphasis on Jewish contributions to western civilization and to the welfare of the countries concerned. The outpouring of books on the participation of the Jews in the armed forces of the First World War was, therefore, an understandable reaction to the antisemitic propaganda that began with the accusation of the *Dolchstoss* in Germany during that conflict and continued, following it, with the "plot of the Elders of Zion". The success of the propagandists brought to the fore thriving antisemitic schools in historiography. In

Germany this crowd was an important factor in the rise of Hitler to power and, therefore, also in the outbreak of World War II. In other countries, too, historians served as "Hitler's professors", sometimes without awareness of the ridiculousness of their role, as for instance, in Poland before the nazi assumption of power [1].

Antisemitic historians have utilized the participation of Jews in the patriotic, social reform, or revolutionary movements of the various countries, a natural precursor and consequence of Emancipation, as weapons against the Jews, the democratic and leftist movements, and sometimes even the Christian churches. This was achieved through a methodological application of the myth of the Jewish plot for world domination or at the very least the accusation of "Judaization" of Christian and native cultures through the assimilation and participation of Jews as well as of Jewish converts to Christianity and their descendants. Such writings were too often ignored by historians. Critiques and exposés of such theories by well-meaning scholars were not as frequent and as thorough as they might have been. Too many spokesmen for democratic and socialist movements did not want to identify their ideologies too closely with defense of the Jews, because of the rising popularity of antisemitism. Moreover, the idea that the Jewish problem should be solved through assimilation led to a lack of interest in Jewish history or in any view that might emphasize Jewish group survival or group culture [2]. We know enough now of the Jewish experience in

---

[1]   Max Weinreich's *Hitler's Professors: The Part of Scholarship in Germany's Crime Against the Jewish People* (New York 1946) is a most useful introduction to the German aspect of this problem and a reminder of the need of similar studies of other countries. A good example of the impact of the myth of the Protocols of the Elders of Zion on the thinking of a serious and respected sociologist is Florjan Znaniecki's little known *Upadek Cywilizacji Zachodniej. Szkic z Pogranicza Filozofji, Kultury i Socjologji* (The Decline of Western Civilization, A Sketch From the Border of Philosophy, Culture and Sociology) (Poznan 1921), 111 pp.

[2]   *Cf.* Edmund Silberner's הסוציאליזם המערבי ושאלת היהודים (Western Socialism and the Jewish Question) (Jerusalem 1955).

the Soviet Union to understand the brutality of a solution through assimilation in a "proletarian" society. Of course, communist propagandists operating within the Jewish community and appealing on the basis of Jewish interests have been involved in their own apologetics, emphasizing Jewish participation in the labor movement. They have often been thwarted by changes in the party line, which have condemned its very leaders, including a large proportion of Jews, as traitors.

There was a rise of interest in Jewish history in Poland between the two world wars. Most of it can be traced to the Jewish national revival. Much of it was centered in the Yiddish Scientific Institute. Despite the use of Yiddish and a social-materialistic approach to history, participation of the Jews in the country's life and irredentist movements was a matter of pride to Jewish historians. Such studies were also utilized as weapons against the ever-expanding antisemitism in academic and literary circles. True, they were not very effective, particularly since they evoked little interest on the part of the general Polish historians. Poland's predicament, due to her geographic location, social and national composition and economic situation, led to an alarming rise of antisemitism and, with it, to the growth of the antisemitic schools in historiography. Some historians sought to reconstruct a past in which the Jews figured as an evil factor in Polish history. Participation by Jews in movements on behalf of Polish freedom was interpreted as a part of a plot to ruin Poland. Jews were blamed for bringing about the eighteenth-century partitions. The insurrection of 1831 was interpreted as a masonic-Jewish plot to keep the Tsar's army away from the revolutionary movements in France and Belgium. Similarly, the uprising of 1863 was interpreted as an error perpetrated under the impact of Jews and converts. In line with nazi thinking, the acculturation and assimilation of the Jews in Poland was viewed by representatives of this extremist school as an anti-Christian and anti-Polish plot. Many

others whose nationalism was not extreme enough to be
racist viewed Jewish assimilation with disfavor [1].

The forthcoming celebration in 1963 of the centenary of
the January insurrection of 1863 brings to mind the tragic
death of the Jewish community in Poland. When the hundredth anniversary of the [November] insurrection of 1830-31
was observed, Dr. Schipper, a popular leader, martyr and
scholar, published a book on this subject [2]. Earlier in 1923,
on the occasion of the sixtieth anniversary of the 1863
insurrection, Dr. Gelber, a productive historian, published
a volume on the Jews. [3] The overwhelming majority of the
Polish Jews was brutally murdered by the nazis during
World War II. A different attitude of Polish intellectuals
to the Jewish problem would probably have saved many

[1]   Representative of the extremist school is Jędrzej Gieitych's
Tragizm Losów Polski (The Tragedy of Poland's Fate) (Pelplin 1937).
Cf. also an exposé of this approach in Alexander Bocheński, *Dzieje
Głupoty w Polsce. Pamflety Dziejopisarskie* (A History of Stupidy in
Poland. Historical Pasquinades) (Warsaw 1947), pp. 118-19. The
history of Polish antisemitism is still to be written.

[2]   Ignacy Schipper, *Żydzi Królestwa Polskiego w Dobie Powstania
Listopadowego* (Jews in the Kingdom of Poland in the Period of the
November Insurrection) (Warsaw 1932). Jacob Shatzky, ייִדן אין
1831 דעם פּוילישער אויפֿשטאַנד פֿון (Jews and the Polish Insurrection of
1831), היסטאָרישע שריפֿטן (Historical Writings) (Yivo), edited by
A. Tscherikower, vol. ii (Wilno 1937), pp. 355-89; Isaiah Warszawski,
"ייִדן אין קאָנגרעס פּוילן 1815-1831" (Jews in Congress Poland 1815-
1831); *ibid.*, p. 322-54; N. M. Gelber, "די ייִדן פֿראַגע אין פּוילן אין די יאָרן
1830-1815 (The Jewish Question in the Years 1815-1830),
בלעטער פֿאַר געשיכטע (Pages of History) (Warsaw), vol. i., nos. 3-4
(August-December 1948), pp. 41-105; and in Hebrew "שאלת היהודים
בפולין בשנות 1830-1815, *Ziyyon*, vols. xiii-xiv (1948-49), pp. 106-43;
idem, "היהודים ומרד הפולנים בשנות 1830-1815" (The Jews and the
Insurrection of the Poles in the Years 1830-31), *Mezudah* (London),
vol. vii (1954), 220-44.

[3]   N. M. Gelber, *Die Juden und der Polnische Aufstand 1863*
(Vienna and Leipzig 1923). This was followed by Jacob Shatzky's
critical review "ייִדן אין דעם פּוילישן אויפֿשטאַנד פֿון 1863" (Jews in
the Polish Insurrection of 1863), היסטאָרישע שריפֿטן (Historical
Writings) (Yivo), edited by A. Tscherikower, vol. i (Warsaw 1929),
col. 425-68. *Cf.* also Jacob Shatzky's געשיכטע פֿון ייִדן אין וואַרשע
(History of the Jews in Warsaw), 3 vols. (New York 1947-1953).

lives. Polish Jews also perished in Soviet labor camps. Here again it is to easy to trace the causes for such treatment to the psychopathic dictator. However, one cannot refrain from remarking that this drastic policy also stemmed, at least in part, from the communist line concerning the Jewish problem.

Very likely some studies will be published by the few remaining Jewish historians in Poland in 1963. Surely publications on this subject will also appear in Israel, the United States and possibly also in other countries. However, at present, the study of the participation of the Jews in the 1863 insurrection is a matter of adding to our knowledge of history and of setting the record straight. It no longer can serve as an instrument of apologetics. Of course, the problem of such participation is quite different so far as non-Jewish Polish historians are concerned. Interest of Polish historians in Poland and abroad on this subject will help to prove whether they care to include the history of Polish Jewry in the history of Poland.

The following list includes thirty-eight hitherto unknown names. Gelber listed 119, while Shatzky listed 100. [1] I have on hand a few additional names. However, I was not able to ascertain definitely whether these were names of Jews. I, therefore, omitted them. With the exception of two names, the list is culled from two Polish archives, [2] in which I

---

[1] *Cf.* Gelber, "Verzeichnis der Jüdischen Teilnehmer", note above, pp. 219-32; Shatzky, *ibid.*, cols. 453-60. Regrettably, neither list is fully documented.

[2] Battignoles Archives [Bat. Ms.], nos. 2600-2602, Correspondence of Comité de Patronage et de Placement pour les Refugiés Polonais, 1864-66; Rapperswyl Archives [Rap. Ms.], nos. 418-419, "Kwity i Prośby o Wsparcia z Funduszów Komitetu Franko-Polskiego, 1863-69" (Receipts and Applications for Aid of the Fund of the Franko-Polish Committee 1863-69); Rap. Ms. 2019, Papiery i Akta Delegacyi Galicyjskiej Ustanowionej do Rozdziału Funduszów Zebranych w Galicyi i w Wielkiem Księstwie Poznańskim, 1870-1885 (Papers and Acts of the Galician Delegation Established for the Disbursement of Funds collected in Galicia and in the Great Duchy of Poznanie, 1871-1885); Rap. Ms. 482, Chodźko's Correspondence; both collections were a part of the Polish National Library (Biblioteka

gathered material during my researches in Poland in the
1930's in connection with my studies on the Great Emigration
of 1830-31 and the Jewish Problem. [1] The list is a small
portion of the raw materials from which will arise Jewish
history's monument to Polish Jewry, a great community
which did not survive to truly celebrate the one thousandth
anniversary of its existence in the present decade.

Jewish Participants in the Polish Insurrection of 1863

1. BEREK, LYSIUS; "a Pole of the Mosaic religion", and
   father of three children; emigrated with his family. [2]
2. BERKOWICZ, SAMUEL; an "active fighter". [3]
3. BLUMENTHAL, BERNARD; son of a Warsaw bookseller.
   Born in March 1843, he was compromised through the
   revolt and came to Paris in June 1868. [4]
4. BRANDSTETER, ROBERT; an active fighter. [5]
5. CUKIER, CHIL (YEHIEL); liaison among various divisions;
   emigrated with his family. [6]
6. DZOBAS, ISRAEL; "an emigrant of 1863". [7]
7. ESTERMAN, JÒZEF (JOSEPH); a participant in the Insurrection, he requested aid to cover his transportation

Narodowa), located at the Military Library (Biblioteka Wojskowa)
in Warsaw. On the destruction of the collections, *cf.* Helena Więckows-
ka, *Listy Emigracyjne Joachima Lelewela* (Joachim Lelewel's Emigre
Letters) (Krakow 1948), vol. i, p. viii.

[1] For a partial list of my publications in the field, *cf.* my "The
Polish Democratic Society and the Jewish Problem, 1832-46,"
Jewish Social Studies, vol. xix, no. 4 (July-October 1957), 99-100, n. 1.

[2] Rap. Ms. 419. Received aid, 20 fr., March 30, 1866 and 5 fr.,
May 14, 1866. He suffered from a chest illness.

[3] *Ibid.* Received 10 fr., April 6, 1867. He lived under very difficult
conditions. A child of his died shortly before he applied for aid.

[4] *Ibid.*, to Chodźko. Received aid on June 19 and July 24, 1868,
5 fr. each time.

[5] *Ibid.* Received 20 fr. on July 28, 1864.

[6] *Ibid.* Received 5 fr. on March 4, 1868. He was recommended by
Antoni Skotnicki.

[7] Rap. Ms. 2019, March 30 [1871].

to London where, he stated, his existence would be assured. [1]

8. GOLDREICH, SAMUEL; supplied revolutionaries with weapons; emigrated with family, including five children. [2]

9. GOLDSTEIN, EDWARD; forced to leave Poland because of his participation in the arrangements for a patriotic prayer service in 1862; returned in 1863 to join the "Death Zouaves", was wounded, escaped from Königgraetz after a year and a half of imprisonment. From his meager savings he gathered in Paris a large collection of art objects, which he presented to the National Museum in Krakow in 1909. In recognition of this he was appointed its curator. He died in 1920. [3]

10. GUTTER, ELJASZ [ELIJAH]; fifty-three years old; was recommended by Ludwik Kròlikowski, as a participant in the Insurrection. [4]

11. HIRSZFELD, DANIEL; listed as the "well-known" emigrant of 1863; was recommended by Rupprecht and Rustejko. [5]

12. JAKÓBOWICZ, SIMON [-JAKOBOWITZ]; deported to Siberia for participation in the Insurrection. His wife Sara and three children sought refuge in France. [6]

13. JEKEL, STANISŁAW; identified as a Jew (*starozakonny*); jeweler; born in Warsaw in 1840. He participated in the Insurrection and emigrated in 1864. [7]

14. JOHELSON, DAWID; of Wilno, two months in Paris. He was "compromised with the Russian government together with his parents who were still being sought". [8]

---

[1] Bat. Ms. 2600, May 11, 1865.

[2] Rap. Ms., 419. Requested 150 fr. in order to open up a little store. Received 20 fr. on November 7, 1864.

[3] *Nowy Dziennik*, (Kraków), August 31, 1933. Clipping in my possession.

[4] Rap. Ms. 419. He received 10 fr. on November 22, 1866.

[5] Rap. Ms. 2019. March 30 [1871].

[6] Rap. Ms. 428. Application to Chodźko, September 4, 1866, January 14, 1867, another letter undated.

[7] Rap. Ms. 419. He received 10 fr. on May 9, 1869.

[8] Rap. Ms. 428. Letter to Chodźko, probably in his own hand writing, no date.

15. KAPLAN, ADAM [AARON]; born in Kremenpol; member of a "revolutionary committee." He was in touch with Sienkiewicz, a student at a music school, from whom he obtained revolutionary newspapers. This aroused the suspicion that he spread "revolutionary literature." Exiled from the Kingdom of Poland at the order of the Ministry of the Interior; returned to Poland in March 1866. [1]

16. KLUGMAN, CHAIM; his activity in the Insurrection was certified by General Różycki. He emigrated with family. [2]

17. KRAUSHAAR, RAFAŁ; wounded in one of the earliest skirmishes; [3] lauded by Kwiatkowski as "a learned Jew in real poverty." [4]

18. LEWIN, SALOMON. [5]

19. LEWINSKI, ISAAC. [6]

---

[1] M. S. Dayan; "היהודים בתנועת החפש של רוסיה" (Jews in Russian Liberation Movement), העולם (Haolam), vol. xxiii, no. 46, November 28, 1935, p. 731. He may have been Kaplan who, according to Shatzky ("1863", p. 458.) was sent to Archangelsk ("according to the memoirs of the oldest Polish Socialist Limanowski, read in manuscript form").

[2] On April 18, 1866, he wrote to Chodźko as follows: "Czynność moja w Czasu Powstania 63ᵍᵒ roku dobrze znana, prześladowany przez Moskala, byłem przemuszony majątek, familię i wszystko co my drogo było zostawić i ucieczką się uratować" (My activity during the Insurrection of the year 63 is well known, persecuted by the Muscovite, I was forced to leave my property, family and all that was dear to me and save myself by flight). The letter was signed "Chaim Klugman". He stated that he and his family had been getting along well until now, but he was forced to apply for relief. On September 7, 1866, he described himself as a "Pole, a father of a family from the last Emigration". The letter was signed Jan [-John] Klugman. A letter written after January 12, 1867 and signed "J. Klugman", was addressed to Mᵐᵉ Chodźko. He enclosed a copy of a letter by General Edmund Różycki: "Nous certifions par le présent que Mʳ Chaim Klugman par suite, du derniers événements en Pologne a été obligé de quitter sa patrie. Le General Edmound Ruzycki. Paris le 5 Nov 1865." All of Klugman's letters were written, it would appear, by public scribes, and were located in Rap. Ms. 428.

[3] Rap. Ms. 419. He received 20 fr. on December 30, 1863.

[4] Rap. Ms. 2019, March 13, 1871.

[5] Rap. Ms. 2019, List.

[6] Ibid.

20. LONDYNSKI, ABRAHAM; designated General Wysocki as a witness that he was utilized in various capacities by the National Government. [1]

21. MARCUS, SZYMON [-SIMON]; active in supplying the revolutionary army. Forty years old; knew German; sought a job in a candle factory. [2]

22. NOWITZKI, SIMON; Dr. Korabiewicz was a witness that he was "an aged cripple, seriously wounded in the January revolution". [3]

23. PARAJNIEWSKI, ABRAHAM. [4]

24. PARASOL, ABRAHAM; supplied arms to the Polish army and died in exile in Karlsruhe. His oldest son was sent to Siberia. His widow applied for aid for her three young children. [5]

25. PARASOL, son of Abraham Parasol. [6]

26. ROZENBAUM, JAKÒB; fought as a soldier and became a "cripple from wounds inflicted in the ranks in 1863". He "considered himself a Pole". [7]

27. ROSENBLUM, L. [8]

28. RUBINOWICZ, CHIMEL; was forced to escape together with his brother, Simon, because of persecutions. [9]

29. RUBINOWICZ, SZYMON [-SIMON]; see Rubinowicz, Chimel.

30. SADOWSKI, NATHAN; of Gombin (Gąbin); age 21; participated in the National Guard. [10]

---

[1] Rap. Ms. 419. Received 5 fr. and 10 fr., February 22, 1867, January 2, 1868.

[2] Bat. Ms. 2602. Undated registration card,

[3] Rap. Mr. 2019, March 30, 1871.

[4] Ibid. List.

[5] Rap. Ms. 419. Received November 29 and December 26, 1866, 10 and 5 fr.

[6] See Note 5.

[7] Rap. Ms. 428, to Chodźko, July 12, 1867, February, 22, 1868. He enclosed certificates by physician and landlord. He received 10 fr. on May 19, 1867.

[8] Rap. Ms. 2019, List.

[9] Rap. Ms. 419. The letter was signed in Yiddish. He and his brother received 5 fr. each on October 7, 1866 and July 9, 1866. He received 10 fr. on May 24, 1866.

[10] Rap. Ms. 2019, March 30, [1871].

31. SALINGER, ABEL; a fighter in 1863; suspected of spying for the Russians, but found innocent by a Court of Honor (probably in the Emigration). [1] Recommended by Leon Hollaenderski on February 7, 1864, as a Jew of Augustowo who deserved special consideration from the Poles. [2]

32. SCHMERKOWITZ, MOISE. [3]

33. SEGALOWICZ, AARON; of Tykocin; supplied the revolutionary army with food. [4]

34. SIMON (first name not known); was killed by the Russians in a skirmish near Włocławek in 1863. His wife Sara emigrated with their three children. [5]

35. SCHWEJDER, HAJA; of the gouvernement of Suwałki; supplied bread to the revolutionary army; was deserted by her husband who went to England [6].

36. STRAGOWSKI, MOJŻESZ [-MOSES]; served in the region of Kowno under Czarnoskalski. Five months in Paris; he specified in his application for aid in securing employment that he knew Hebrew, German and Russian well, and Polish and French fairly well. [7]

37. SZKLARSKI, JUDEL (JUDAH); participated in the Insurrection. A father of six children; heartily recommended by many Poles, [8] including General Różycki. [9]

38. SZMIDBERG; a lieutenant who addressed a meeting in London on March 1, 1865. [10]

---

[1]   Rap. Ms. 419. He received 20 fr. on February 12, 1864.

[2]   Rap. Ms. 428.

[3]   Rap. Ms. 2019, List.

[4]   *Ibid.*

[5]   Rap. Ms. 419. Received aid, November 23, 1866.

[6]   Rap. Ms. 2019.

[7]   Rap. Ms. 428.

[8]   Rap. Ms. 419. Received 20 fr. on March 30; 5 fr. on June 20, 1866 and 10 fr. on April 5, 1867.

[9]   Rap. Ms. 2019. March 30 [1871].

[10]   *Głos Wolny*, London, March 31, 1865, no. 63, pp. 257-58, where he is called *"starozakonny"*, a Jew.

CONCERNING EXPERIENCE AND REVELATION

By Morton S. Enslin

The Theological School of St. Lawrence University

In the preface to his *Leben Jesu*, H. E. G. Paulus, the stormy petrel of the theological world a century and a quarter ago and the man who provided the most complete analysis of the gospel stories from the angle of thoroughgoing rationalism, made a memorable remark: "It is nonetheless the task of the lover of history not to leave details inconceivable and therefore unbelievable without first trying to see whether they could be conceivable and thus all the more believable." Today rare would be the historian or biblical critic who would espouse either Paulus' methods or results, although many the preacher who, without in all probability ever having heard of the doughty Heidelberg professor of the yesteryears, trots out on occasion, as a modern "common-sense explanation" of this or that of the New Testament miracle stories, essentially the explanations which Paulus had with great ingenuity and detail set forth only to see them totter and crumble before the barrage leveled at them by the twenty-seven-year-old David Friedrich Strauss.

But this statement tucked away in the midst of a lengthy sentence-paragraph, in which Paulus urged that his "opinions concerning the miracles should not be taken as the chiee thing," was a challenge to his day — and might well be to oure too. It runs so counter to our inherited outlook on theology. It is scarcely an exaggeration to say that in every age the predominant verdict of orthodoxy has been: "The more mysterious, the more holy." Thus what in other spheres of interest would be regarded as problems challenging investigators to grapple with the enigma, without letting go until it blessed them with an explanation, too often in religion have been regarded as *"given's," "Thus saith the Lord's,"* which are not meant to be understood but are to be accepted on faith. Certainly in my boyhood the statement was a commonplace, "If we could understand God, we should be God." It seemed to me as a boy, it seems to me even clearer as a man, that there are enough problems and enigmas which remain such, struggle though we may, that it is unwise to rule oneself out of the race at the start by refusing to attempt to start. Nor is it, I think, fair to retort that this is simply flogging dead dogs; that that attitude may have been true of the past but that it is now quite outmoded. Certainly the emphasis in the point of view which we are being told today—and not in hushed whispers—is the only proper one for man, namely, that of the new orthodoxy, with its altogether-other and infinite God who is everything in contradistinction to poor, frail, finite man who is nothing, is precisely this. Our search for the secrets of life, even for God himself, is presumptuous, if not downright blasphemous. Man is not to quest; instead he is to remain passive until he be found, until the altogether-other God deigns to disclose to him what he could never discover for himself, and which it would be impious for him to attempt.

It is against this background, which I do not think I have unfairly burlesqued, that the word of Paulus appears to me of consequence for us today: "It is nonetheless the task of the lover of history not to leave details inconceivable and therefore unbelievable without first trying to see whether they could be conceivable and thus all the more believable." As I have studied the little section known to us of the story of man's sojourn on this tiny sphere, the one fact increasingly borne in on me has been the exact negation of this note so dominant in much present-day theological thought. And this negation is man's indomitable spirit. His head may be bloody, but it always remains unbowed. One Eden after another may be closed to him—and the history of the past has been rich in eviction notices, with Cherubim with "the flame of sword which turned every way" to prevent his return to the peaceful garden of the past. But he has not waited, either placidly or by necessity; instead he has hewn out new clearings from the forests, has reared new cities in the wilderness. And from these catastrophes he has learned most of his lessons. The fruits of these experiences, sometimes bitter, sometimes sweet, have—slightly to mix the figure—become his subsequent diet. And once they have become so established, it has not been long—his memory for origins is very brief—before he begins to hear them echoing back from the invisible cliffs of life in portentous tones which he identifies as the voice of God. Thus once again what day before yesterday he had thought to be a new and painful discovery he now is convinced is an ageless revelation from on high: As it is now it always has been. Thus I have not infrequently toyed with the idea that it would not be an impossible task to present a very good case that most theology is the result of the tough experiences of life which men have undergone, the disasters and the shipwrecks from which they have emerged with a new and greater confidence. The verdict of history seems often to be that man, a veritable Antaeus, has found his strength renewed each time he is flung to earth. For some this seeming fact of history will lead to renewed singing of William Cowper's lines,

> God moves in a mysterious way
> His wonders to perform.

With them I have no quarrel, for I too enjoy singing that hymn. My insistence is simply that what God says and does he has said and done through human lips and hands, as their possessors have struggled toward the far horizons. The Ten Commandments are hallowed by the portentous word: "Thus saith the Lord." But it seems clear beyond dispute that God's voice announcing them was not heard until they had become an established practice on at least one part of this little planet. This appears to me a veritable Ariadne thread running through the labyrinth of the past. I commend it to all who are interested in the history of doctrine. I believe that it would be a task not without profit to follow it in the case of most—not to say all—of the principal doctrines and dicta of both Jewish and Christian theology. I shall attempt it in a modest way, in the remaining paragraphs, in one tiny corner of the field long especially dear to me.

That there is a clear-cut and unmistakable opposition to wealth in the pages of the Synoptic Gospels few will deny. The form in which the famous Matthaean beatitudes appear: "Blessed are the poor in spirit: for theirs is the kingdom of heaven. . . . Blessed are they that hunger and thirst after righteousness: for they shall be filled," [1] can hardly be original. Rather the crisper and less sophisticated form in which they stand in Luke: "Blessed are ye poor: for yours is the kingdom of God. . . . Blessed are ye that hunger now: for ye shall be filled," [2] can scarcely fail to be the earlier and more primitive, quite regardless of the relation in which the completed gospels as known to us now stand. Thus, while in my own judgment Luke is later than Matthew and is heavily dependent upon it for those sections of double tradition commonly designated by the enticing letter Q, I see no slightest difficulty in the recognition that on occasion the later writer was familiar with and preferred a more primitive tradition of this logion or that.

So also the familiar parable of Dives and Lazarus [3] hits the same note. The teaching of the parable is tranparently clear despite the fact that subsequent labored exegesis has often tended to obscure it. There is no slightest indication that Lazarus was a good man, Dives a bad one, and that these facts determined their subsequent fates. Rather, Lazarus, was abjectly poor; Dives was rich. Because of this and this alone, each received his reward. Lazarus was instantly transplanted to a heaven of bliss, Dives to a hell of torment. This

[1]   Matt 5: 3, 6.
[2]   Luke 6: 20 f.
[3]   Luke 16: 19-31.

crystal-clear emphasis has often been obscured. The detail of the dogs licking Lazarus' sores—to any Oriental self-explanatory: here was but one more indication of the utter wretchedness of Lazarus, tormented by even the accursed village mongrels—has been unwarrantably romanticized in the light of our quite different attitude to dogs in the West: they were sympathetic and affectionate in contrast to the hardhearted mogul. Of course this is utterly mistaken, the reading as musical notes of what are but flyspecks on an ancient manuscript. The fates of the two are dependent solely on their lots in life. The wheel will turn. In terms of the Magnificat, which is the classic expression of this same note,

> He hath put down princes from their thrones,
> And hath exalted those of low degree.
> The hungry he hath filled with good things;
> And the rich he hath sent empty away. [1]

The same note is struck very loud and clear in the story of the Rich Ruler. [2] His quality of life may well have been good; there was one difficulty—"one thing thou lackest"—and it was, as Mark makes clear, all-important: he had property. This must be cast aside were he to become a disciple and able to enter the coming kingdom. This has been obscured in the later rewriting by Matthew who, in addition to such other alterations as the change of the initial reply, "Why callest thou me good? none is good save one, even God," to the query more appropriate and seemly in later Christian ears, "Why askest thou me concerning that which is good?" has substituted for the uncompromising "One thing thou lackest" the far easier "If thou wouldest be perfect." Thus what in the primitive account is a perfectly clear and undebatable prerequisite for every man if he is to hope for entrance into the kingdom has been toned down into an innocuous counsel of perfection. And on the basis of this it has seemed easy to rid

[1]   Luke 1: 52-54.
[2]   Mark 10: 17-31 = Matt 19: 16-30 = Luke 18: 18-30.

the story of its embarrassing demand. This was no general requirement; rather, in this particular case Jesus saw that wealth was for this man a hindrance—a special diagnosis which, of course, does not apply generally. Thus we may keep our modest bank accounts with unconcern. *They* do not hamper *us* as *his* wealth did *him*. And accordingly we can blissfully disregard an embarrassing teaching, while asserting in equally unqualified tones profound belief in both the teacher and the sacrosanctness of his revelation.

Surely the subsequent section in Mark lends little support to this bit of theological shadowboxing. The disciples do not appear to understand it as a special diagnosis for a special case: "Who then can be saved?" And Jesus' reported answer is equally unambiguous: It is utterly impossible for a rich man to be saved except by an actual miracle of God. It is easier for a camel to go through the eye of a sewing needle—an obvious impossibility not to be toned down or explained away by learned-sounding nonsense about a fancied narrow street in Jerusalem popularly known as Fat Man's Misery; or by the even more insipid and stupid substitution of *cable* for *camel* (as if that helped any!)—than for a man with wealth to be saved.

These several samples, and they are far from exhaustive, would seem amply to warrant my earlier statement that in the Synoptic Gospels there is a clear-cut and unmistakable opposition to wealth. I would go farther. It appears to me that this emphasis, which finds early reflection in the letters of Paul, is no later interpolation into the primitive accounts but a fair reflection of the attitude of Jesus himself. This latter fact has frequently been recognized, but often with quite unwarranted conclusions attached. It is not that Jesus approached his mission with clear-cut views in this regard, as modern socialists and social gospelers, with notions about sharing wealth, fondly believe. Rather, his attitude arose as the fruit of his own experience.

Firmly convinced as he was that the promises of God long

ago made to Israel were about to be realized; the kingdom long delayed, largely through Israel's sins, was now to be established; in a very literal sense, the present age was speedily to close and a new age to dawn with a new earth catastrophically to appear when the supernatural Son of Man should descend from heaven to mount the judgment throne—he had, as God's prophet, sounded his clarion call. Like an Amos or an Isaiah before him, he "knew" that he was God's prophet, chosen to announce the immediate dawn of the kingdom by sages long foretold. What had led him to this confidence that he was God's chosen herald of the new day is far more easily asked than answered. What led a Micaiah, an Amos, an Isaiah, a Jeremiah, a Paul, a Mohammed to essentially the same conclusion? In part, especially in view of the modern almost careless use and understanding of the word *prophet*, the answer may seem easy. But the dominant, overpowering, unsettling, and all-blinding confidence that in a very real sense he has been chosen, as other men have not, to be the divine mouthpiece; that when he speaks it is literally not he but God who is speaking, so that all opposition to his message is opposition to the express word of God himself—that is a problem which men wiser in the intricacies of the human brain than am I must attempt to explain.

That Jesus *was* so convinced would seem as certain as the causes which led him so to believe are obscure. The consequences are immense. The prophet knows that he is right, and does not argue for his message. He sounds it unequivocally as God's imperious herald; he does not argue for it. It is unfortunate that the crystal-clear κηρύσσειν, to "herald," to "proclaim as a herald"—the verb the evangelists regularly use—has been obscured for English readers by the misleading to "preach," which fails utterly to transfer that earlier, and central, note, and introduces, as faulty translation so often does, a new and utterly misleading element to the confusion of the later reader.

Apparently, unless the whole gospel account is hopelessly addled, this proclamation of the speedy dawn of the kingdom in its apocalyptic form was *good* news. This was one of the differences between the older form of prophecy of an Amos or a Jeremiah and the newer prophecy, apocalypticism. Much water had run under the bridge. The nation was down, prostrate; but this was not the end. God had promised, and God never fails. Actually, the very hellishness of the moment was the indication that the time of relief was at hand. Thus the diabolical act of an Antiochus Epiphanes was in a way the first blast on the heavenly *Posaune*. The time of relief was at hand. Thus, while the older prophets had been prophets of doom, scourging the people for their sins, warning them with the tragically ironic and mocking shriek, "The Day of the Lord," that certain doom was in store unless they repented forthwith and immediately, during the successive centuries all this had changed. One tragedy after another had come. All life's billows had passed over the prostrate people. But it was not, could not be, the last chapter. Wrong might seem forever on the throne, right forever on the scaffold—but, behind the shadows, God stood triumphant, keeping watch above his own. Sometime, when God in his omniscience knew the time had come, the promise would be fulfilled.

How, I see no way to guess, Jesus had become convinced that this cosmic moment had come, and that he, as God's chosen prophet, had been anointed to proclaim it. Of course all Israel would hearken: it was good news, glorious news: God's greatest gift to men was about to be bestowed. Of course all God's children would hearken joyfully and stretch forth their hands in happy prospect. All he need do was to sound the note. The nation would rejoice and accept.

But the nation neither rejoiced nor accepted. And from our seats two thousand years removed it seems small wonder. Those who were wealthy and in seats of power, who were responsible for the task of keeping the little heavily-loaded

Jewish ship of state on even keel, with Roman legions in the ever-near distance, with home rule fanatics ever trying to egg the nation into an outburst that would be suicide—to them this clarion call to await and welcome joyfully the impending cataclysm was anathema. To those in authority a preachment of axes laid at the roots of trees always comes too close to home, even though the heralded wielder of the ax be God himself. Thus the prophet found himself confronted, as has always been the case, with the amazing situation: what was so clear to him was obscured from those who heard. He knew that he was right. God had told him. What then could be holding them back, blinding their eyes to the one immensely valuable pearl of price, in comparison with which all other values were as nothing? On the other hand, many were hearing his word with joy. Those who found themselves in the mire might well welcome the turn of the wheel. Whichever way it turned, be it forward or back, could not but help to bring them up. Of course they heard him gladly. The teaching of the Magnificat was as acceptable to those of low degree as it was maddening to those of high.

The consequence? It does not appear to me of particular surprise. Convinced that he was right: it was God, not he, whose word it was; and also convinced that it was an immeasurable boon, the greatest blessing ever vouchsafed to men—why did the people act as they did? What was holding them back from accepting news which anyone who had half an eye with which to see must realize was incomparable in value? Whatever it was, be it good or bad in itself, it was bad if it led men to refuse this gift valuable beyond all compare. And the answer seemed obvious: it was the wealth and power of those in positions of prominence which led them to fear the change. It was the learning of the wise which blinded their eyes and deafened their ears to God's promised gift. Those who were poor, the outcasts and the wretched, were eagerly accepting the promised change. Was not the answer transparent? Of course then this wealth and power were evil since they blinded men's eyes and deafened their ears. Hence, "Blessed are ye poor" was obvious. The poor were hearkening, as the rich were not.

Thus it appears to me highly probable that this appraisal of wealth and position, which in the earliest days of the Christian movement made its appearance, was perfectly natural and inevitable in consequence of the situation itself. To see this appraisal as a divine verdict revealed from above and accepted as such *in vacuo* is far from realistic. Once established, once the movement was underway, of course this verdict from their crucified leader became increasingly part of their outlook, and speedily it came to be regarded as part of God's plan, which had been purposed in his mind from the very beginning to be revealed at the proper moment. To a religion which fondly believes itself to be one of revelation, all that *is* has been planned and revealed by God, not discovered by men in consequence of their experience with life.

Thus speedily it gains its theological accreditation: "For behold your calling, brethren, that not many wise after the flesh, not many mighty, not many noble, are called, but God chose the foolish things of the world, that he might put to shame them that are wise...." [1]

But this is not the end of the story. The movement which eventually came to realize itself and to be recognized by others as a new movement, a new religion, by the very nature of its mainspring drive—the impending collapse of life as it was then known and the birth of a new world—had been largely recruited from life's "little ones." But it did not stay so. As the years wore on, those who were wealthy and wise came gradually to be enrolled, in a manner which has been paralleled time without end in other groups and cults. And this, of course, had far-reaching consequences.

I have already hinted at some of them. The earlier words,

---

[1] I Cor 1: 26 ff.

"Blessed are ye poor" and "Blessed are ye hungry," are easily transformed by a few so natural touches of interpretation: it is the poor "in spirit," that is, those who "feel their spiritual needs," who are heirs of the kingdom; those who hunger and thirst "after righteousness" who are to be filled. And the uncompromising story of the Rich Ruler ceases to be an uncompromising challenge; rather it becomes a counsel of perfection—"if thou wouldest be perfect"—and soon the diagnosis of a special case which the reader is sure does not apply literally to him, for he does not need it as that poor misguided youth in the past so tragically did. The process can be seen everywhere at work: the unqualified word about divorce is softened down by the addition of the far from happy "saving for the cause of fornication"; [1] the flaming prohibition of anger against one's brother is softened by the innocuous and flaccid "without due cause." [2] We may at times find difficulty in isolating Jesus' words. One thing would seem very sure. He did not talk platitudes. What teacher—not to say prophet—ever did tolerate anger at one's brother "without due cause"? And thus men who would be shocked at the thought of transgressing any of the words of Jesus are spared from the even greater shock of attempting to observe them as he apparently had intended them.

This so natural process of softening down an earlier teaching which had arisen spontaneously from the situation then at hand, when it no longer fitted, is so clearly evidenced in two early Christian writings that I cannot forbear to cite them. The first is found in the second-century writing, the *Shepherd of Hermas*, usually included now among the so-called Apostolic Fathers. In the early days it was a Christian book which for many seems to have enjoyed a higher popularity than did some which are now safely bound in the canonical New Testament. It is included in that great fourth-century manuscript, *Codex Sinaiticus* (‎א), which with *Vaticanus*

---

[1] Matt 5: 32; cf. 19: 9.
[2] Matt 5: 22.

(B) is properly regarded as our greatest manuscript treasure. The passage is so explicit, as well as of such interest, that it may be quoted in full despite its prolixity:

When I was walking in the country I noticed an elm and a vine, and was considering them and their fruits, when the shepherd appeared to me and said: "What are considering in yourself about the elm and the vine?" "I am considering, sir," said I, "that they are very well suited to one another." "These two trees," said he, "are put as a type for the servants of God." "I should like," said I, "to know the type of the trees of which you speak." "You see," said he, "the vine and the elm?" "Yes, sir," said I, "I see them." "This vine," said he, "bears fruit but the elm is a sterile tree. But this vine, if it does not grow upon the elm, cannot bear much fruit, because it is spread on the ground, and the fruit which it bears, it bears rotten, when it is not hanging on the elm. When, therefore, the vine is attached to the elm, it bears fruit from itself and from the elm. You see then that the elm gives much fruit, not less than the vine, but rather more." "How, sir," said I, "does it bear more?" "Because," said he, "the vine, when it hangs on the elm, gives much beautiful fruit, but when it is lying on the ground, it bears but little fruit and rotten. This parable, therefore, applies to the servants of God, to the poor and the rich." "How, sir?" said I, "let me know." "Listen," said he. "The rich man has much wealth, but he is poor as touching the Lord, being busied about his riches, and his intercession and confession toward the Lord is very small, and that which he has is weak and small, and has no other power. But when the rich man rests upon the poor, and gives him what he needs, he believes that what he does to the poor man can find a reward with God, because the poor is rich in intercession and confession, and his intercession has great power with God. The rich man, therefore, helps the poor in all things without doubting. But the poor man, being helped by the rich, makes intercession to God, giving him thanks, for him who gave to him, and the rich man is still zealous for the poor man, that he fail not in his life, for he knows that the intercession of the poor is acceptable and rich toward the Lord. Therefore the two together complete the work, for the poor works in the intercession in which he is rich, which he received from the Lord: this he pays to the Lord who helps him. And the rich man likewise provides the poor, without hesitating, with the wealth which he received from the Lord; and this work is great and acceptable with God, because he has understanding in his wealth, and has wrought for the poor man from the gifts of the Lord, and fulfilled his ministry rightly. Among men, therefore, the elm appears as if it bore no fruit, and they do not know nor understand that if there is drought the elm which has water nourishes the vine, and the vine, having water continuously, gives double fruit, both for itself and for the elm. So also the poor, interceding with the Lord for the rich, complement their wealth, and again, the rich helping the poor with their necessities complement their prayers. Both, therefore, share in the righteous work. Therefore he who does these things shall not be deserted by God, but shall be inscribed in the books of the living. Blessed are they who are wealthy and understand that their riches are from the Lord, for he who understands this will also be able to do some good service. [1]

Lengthy comment upon this passage is unnecessary. The emphasis is quite different from that of the earlier days. No longer are the poor the only ones who hear and accept. By the time of Hermas the membership had come to include those of wealth and position. The accident of their coming had naturally resulted in a distinct modification of outlook, although traces of the earlier note remain in the constant refrain about the poor having the ear of God.

[1]   Hermas, *Sim.* II, 1-10.

The other treatment of the matter of wealth stems from Alexandria, from the pen of its most urbane Christian scholar, Clement. In what is probably a somewhat expanded sermon or popular lecture under the title, "Who is the Rich Man Who is Being Saved?" Clement grapples with the famous story in Mark 10. In this great cosmopolitan and cultural centre were many wise after the flesh, many mighty, many noble, many rich, and Clement was a zealous advocate for the Christian church. Much in the Christian heritage, especially its seeming contempt for brains and ability, not alone in the pages of the gospels but in the letters of Paul, was alien, if not disgusting, to the cultured and well-born; and in the best sense of the word Clement was the apostle to the genteel! In this sermon he grapples with the toughest of the problems, the Markan story of the Rich Ruler. And allegorical exegesis—that especial product of the Delta city, in no small measure due to its most enthusiastic purveyor, Philo—proved a wonderful tool for making a passage mean something quite different from what its original author had intended.

The superficial meaning of the story, said Clement, is, as is generally the case with the Saviour's utterances, especially the seemingly simpler ones, [1] far from the real meaning. The rich man who is being condemned is not the man who possesses wealth in gold and fields, but the man with a wealth of passions. Wealth in and of itself is not under the divine interdict, else God would indeed have been unjust to allow children to be born into the lap of luxury. [2] Nor could the Lord justly demand that we feed the hungry and perform those other duties, failure in doing which entails the woe of fire and the outer darkness. [3] Nor is poverty *per*

---

[1]   *Cf.* "For the sayings which appear to have been simplified by the Lord himself to his disciples are found even now, on account of the extraordinary degree of wisdom in them, to need not less but more attention than his dark and suggestive utterances"—Clement, *Quis Dives* 5.

[2]   *Quis Dives* 26.

[3]   *Quis Dives* 13.

se either a blessing or especially commendable. The abject beggar whose life is one constant but fruitless attempt to gain the necessaries of life has little time and less thought for rapt contemplation of God. And the man who thoughtlessly strips himself of his property in obedience to the seeming demand of the sacred text but who speedily regrets his deed and hankers for his now gone possessions is actually in a far sorrier state, for the wealth of greed and longing for his erstwhile riches both deafen his ears and blind his eyes to all else. And this damning wealth of passions can be the curse of poor and rich alike. It was this which caused consternation to the twelve disciples, with their anguished "Who then can be saved?" So far as property was concerned, they had abandoned the little which they had. Surely it would have been arrogant in the extreme had Peter meant by his "Lo, we have left all and followed thee" his pitiful little fishing smack and lines. [1] No, Peter and his fellows knew the meaning, knew that they still were freighted with the destructive wealth of passions which bring death when they are present. What the Lord was enjoining was to put aside, not the means of living, but the things, the appetites, which use these badly, in a word, the infirmities and passions of the soul. There are two kinds of poverty: [2] that which is blessed, which Matthew means when he says, "Blessed are the poor in spirit"; and that other sort, the lot of those who are truly miserable, being destitute of God, more destitute still of human possessions, and utterly unacquainted with God's righteousness. The man who is truly and nobly rich is he who is rich in virtues and able to use every fortune in a holy and faithful manner. The spurious rich man is he who is rich according to the flesh and has changed his life into outward possessions which are passing away and perishing, belonging now to one, now to another, and in the end to no one at all. Thus God's word is:

[1] *Quis Dives* 20.
[2] *Quis Dives* 17.

Detach yourself from the alien possessions that dwell in your soul, in order that you may become pure in heart and may see God, which in other words means, to enter the kingdom of heaven. And how are you to detach yourself from them? By selling them. What then? Are you to take riches for possessions, to make an exchange of one wealth for another by turning real estate into money? Not at all. But in place of that which formerly dwelt in the soul you long to save, bring in another kind of wealth that makes you divine and provides eternal life, namely, resolves that are fixed in accord with God's commandments [1].

So Clement continued. As sober exegesis this was, of course, nonsense, as allegorical exegesis so invariably is. This is not what the passage meant or the original speaker's intent. So far as good wholesome advice is concerned, in a day when the outlook on life had radically changed—no longer was the world to end on the morrow—it may well have been admirable and needed.

My object in this essay, which I am happy to be able to offer in appreciation and tribute to Dr. Neuman, a distinguished scholar and a generous friend, was not to attempt to answer the question as to whether a particular teaching was good or bad, either for its day or for ours. My aim was a quite different one, simply to suggest, by this theme as a convenient example, that much of what we have come to treasure as theology or Torah or divine decrees or decretals or revelations from on high has usually had a most mundane existence before being sanctified by a portentous off-stage voice: "Thus saith the Lord."

[1]   *Quis Dives* 19.

THE STORY OF ASCAMA I OF THE SPANISH AND PORTUGUESE JEWISH CONGREGATION OF LONDON WITH SPECIAL REFERENCE TO RESPONSA MATERIAL

By Isidore Epstein

Jews College, London

The story of the famous *Ascama* I of the Spanish and Portuguese Congregation of London forbidding its members to congregate for divine worship outside the Synagogue *Saar Asamaim* has been told at greater or lesser length by Picciotto, [1] Gaster, [2] Hyamson, [3] and Laski. [4] All these writers drew for their information on the rich store of archives of the Bevis Marks Synagogue (London). They did not, however, include in their field of research the contemporaneous Responsa literature which contains material supplementing in a number of details the story as told in their respective works.

The earliest reference to that *Ascama* in the Responsa is to be found in the *Sheelot u-Teshulot* of Zvi Hirsch Ashkenazi (1660-1718) No 38, which deals with the controversy at the beginning of the eighteenth century centering round the *Ascama*. Valuable material relating to the enforcement of the *Ascama* at the time of the establishment of the reform congregation in London is contained in the printed volume of the Responsa פרי עץ חיים of Abraham Belais (1773-1853) who, coming from the continent to London in 1840, was soon appointed *Rubi*, or teacher in the Sephardi School, and occa-

---

[1] James Piccioto, *Sketches of Anglo-Jewish History* (London 1875); 2nd edition, edited by I. Finestein (London 1956).

[2] Moses Gaster, *History of the Spanish and Portuguese Synagogue* (London 1901).

[3] Albert M. Hyamson, *Sephardim of England* (London 1951).

[4] Neville Laski, *The Laws and Charities of the Spanish and Portuguese Jews' Congregation* (London 1952).

sionally called on to sit on the Sephardi Beth Din to complete
the quorum of Dayanim. Even more valuable is the correspondence which passed between London and the continent
on the subject of the *Ascama*, in relation to the reform
movement and preserved in the Responsa of Mordecai Samuel
Ghirundi of Padua (1779-1852), entitled שו"ת קבוצת כסף, in
manuscript at Jews' College (Montefiore 164). [1] It is the object
of this article to present the relevant Responsa material in
the context of the story of the *Ascama*, discussing its terms
and purposes, as well as the conditions and circumstances
that led to the various revisions and amendments to which
it had been subjected from the time of its first promulgation
in 1664, until it was finally repealed in 1843, bringing the
story down to the year 1849, when those who had disregarded
the *Ascama* were absolved, as a result of successive steps
taken by the congregation, from the penalty of *herem* to
which they had been subjected in consequence of their action.

A preliminary of the account will involve a brief survey
of the origin of the present Anglo-Jewish community and
of the organization of congregational worship in its midst.
It all began about the year 1630 when a number of Marranos,
for the most part merchants of substance, fleeing from the
Spanish Inquisition, found refuge in England. For some
years living outwardly as Christians and even attending
Church services, they met secretly for occasional worship in
the home of Antonio Fernando Carvajal (*c.* 1590-1659), a
wealthy merchant who was their unofficial leader. In 1654
this new community of Crypto-Jews was joined by another
Marrano merchant, David Abarbanel Dormido (d. 1667),
who shortly after his arrival arranged a *minyan* at his home
for regular services. Under this dissembling veil of secrecy the
members of this community were able to live peaceably and
pursue undisturbed their affairs—occupational and commercial—and to prosper. But the outbreak of the war with Spain

---

[1] *See* H. Hirschfeld, *Descriptive Catalogue of the Hebrew MSS of
the Montefiore Library* (London 1904), pp. 46-47.

in March 1655 endangered the position of these Jews who were nominally Spanish subjects, and as such considered aliens. Faced with this critical situtation, they decided to throw off the mask together and to appeal for protection on the ground that they were *not* Spaniards but Jews. In pursuance of this policy a number of their representatives, which included such distinguished figures as those of Menasseh ben Israel (1604-1657), Dormido and Carvajal, submitted on the 24th of March 1656 a petition to Cromwell asking for a written assurance that they might be permitted to pray "without fear of molestation to our persons or estate " [1] The Protector, whilst not giving the written assurance, resolved to give the petitioners a verbal guarantee of security under which they might open a synagogue for public worship and enlarge their community by bringing into England more Sephardi merchants of good standing. [2] Armed with this guarantee, Carvajal and his friends acquired on December 19, 1656, in Creechurch Lane, a house, almost within a stone's throw of the present synagogue in Bevis Marks, which they converted into a synagogue and opened for public worship at the beginning of 1657 under the name of *Saar Asamaim* [3].

In 1663 on the 18th Heshwan a Mahamad (board), consisting of David Abarbanel, Dormido and Eliahu de Lima as Parnassim, and Mose Baruh Lousada as Gabbai, was elected with the special duty of preparing a Code of *Ascamot* (regulations) for the future governance of *Saar Asamaim*. This constitution, modelled mainly on that of the Amsterdam community from which the majority of the founders of the *Saar Asamaim* had come, was soon drawn up and adopted on *Shabbath*

[1] Dr. Cecil Roth, in a paper which he read on the occasion of the tercentenary celebrations of the Jewish Resettlement in England maintained that there was a *formal* favorable decision by the Counci of State on June 25,1656, on Menasseh ben Israel's petition, but that the page recording it had been deliberately torn out.

[2] *See Catalogue of Exhibition of Anglo-Jewish Art and History* (London 1956), No. 70.

[3] *See* L. D. Barnett, *Bevis Marks Records* (Oxford 1945), pp. 7 ff.

ha-gadol of 1664, when it was read out publicly from the *tebah* (reading desk) in the synagogue. [1] The first *Ascama* forbade under the penalty of *herem* the foundation of any other Sephardi congregation in the City of London and environs, or even an assembly for the purpose of worship of the persons, except on the occasion of a wedding or in a house of mourning, with the provisio, however, that at some future date, should circumstances demand it, the establishment of a second congregation might be authorized by the Mahamad.

The object of this *Ascama* as stated in the preamble was to ensure the maintenance and unity of the community. [1]

The enactment of the Conventicle Act in July 1664, which placed all but the members of the Established Church under disabilities, and imposed heavy penalties on the participants in any religious gatherings (apart from those of a household in which no more than five persons took part) not conducted in the form laid down in the Book of Common Prayer, brought the Jewish services within the proscription of that act. This led the three members of the Mahamad to appeal to King Charles II, and the result was the Royal Declaration of August 1664 declaring that the Jews "may promise themselves the effects of the same favour as formerly they have had, soe long as they demeane themselves peaceably and quietly with due obedience to His Majesties' Lawes, and without scandall to His Government." [2] This declaration, whilst promising

---

[1]   The *Ascamot*, 42 in number, were followed by 17 signatures to which was added later the signature of Haham Jacob Sasportas (1610-1698) on his arrival in England shortly after Passover of the same year.

[2]   The English text of *Ascama* I of the year 1664 was promulgated in Portuguese. As rendered by L. D. Barnett in his *El Libro de los Acuerdos* (Oxford 1931), p. 3, it reads as follows: "Considering how meet it is that we should endeavour to maintain this Kahal Kados Saar Asamaim, which God bless and increase, for His greater service, we in unanimity and harmony forbid that there be any other Congregation in this city of London, its districts, and environs, for reading prayers with Minyan, and that 10 persons meet for this purpose in any private house, except it be in the house of Bridegrooms and Abelim without separating themselves from the Congregation, (under)

royal favor and protection, implied, however, that the Crown looked upon the Elders and the Mahamad to enforce obedience to the Laws of the Realm and to the duties of civic life, and to maintain communal discipline and suppress disorderly conduct among the Jews.

Charged with this responsibility, the communal leaders proceeded in 1677 to revise the terms of the *Ascama* in which they perceived an effective instrument for exercising greater control over the members, as demanded by the new situation. A clear indication of the motive that prompted the revision of this *Ascama* appears already in the preamble. Its purpose is no longer as in the first version to maintain the unity of the congregation, but "to avoid causing scandal to the natives of this City as we are recommended by His Majesty (Charles II) whom God preserve." The greater effectiveness of this latter version as compared with that oι 1664 lay in the clause which vested the right to grant permission for the opening of another place of worship not as hitherto in the Mahamad, but in the hands of the *yehidim* (individual members) by means of a two-thirds majority given at a meeting of all the *yehidim* present. Furthermore, in order to impart even greater force to the *Ascama* it was (i) promulgated this time in the name of all the *yehidim* instead of that of the members of Mahamad only as was the case on the first occasion, and (ii) stipulated that a new synagogue shall remain always under the government of the synagogue *Saar Asamaim*. [2]

pain of Herem, following in this the Ascama which is observed in Amsterdam, unless in future times to come through circumstances that may happen it may be needful to divide ourselves as may be found fitting, whereof the disposition remains reserved for the Mahamad which shall be in office at the time, being united and harmonious and under a government as we are at present."

[1] *See* Barnett, *Bevis Marks Records I*, pp. 8-9.

[2] The text of the Ascama in the 1677 version, written also in Portuguese, is found in the Minutes of the Bevis Marks Synagogue: MS 129, p. 1 and reads as follows: "CONSIDERANDO quanto ymportante he Nossa uniao para nos conçervarnos sem cauzar — escandalo a os naturais desta Cidade, como somos recomendados de S. Mag/te — que Deos Gde — se acordou por todos os Yehidim deste

The *Ascama* was again revised in 1694, the motivation remaining the same, "the need to avoid causing scandal as we have been recommended by His Majesty King Charles II, of blessed memory," King Charles having died nine years earlier in 1685. In this latest version the prohibition of meeting elsewhere for divine worship was limited to within four miles [1] from the synagogue *Saar Asamaim*—a distance which covered the City of London and the suburbs —with the addition of the proviso: "That the Synagogue *Saar Asamaim* shall only serve for the Jews of our Portuguese and Spanish nation that are at present in this City and newly may come to it; and the Jews of other nations that may come

K.K. unanimes e conformos nao se consinta desta cidade de Londres e seue contornes mais que hūa so Esnoga e avendo pessoa ou pessoas de qualquer calidade que sejao que intentem separar esta uniaõ apartandose a rezar com Minian em qualquer lugar fora da Esnoga ainda que nao seja com titulo de fazerem outra yncurre desde logo em pena de Herem excepto em cazas de Noivos ou Abelim, e sera obriguado o Mahamad com ajuda de todo o Kaal aporemse contra os tais perturbadores por todas as vias e com todas as forças possiveis. E sendo cazo em algum tempo se reconheça ser forçozo repartirse naõ se fara scm preseder junta de todos os Yehidim cabesas de cazais, e nao se permitirá se naõ por os dous terços dos votos, hem entendido que fique sempre de baxo do governo desta Esnoga Sahar Asamaim".

[Considering how important is our union to preserve us without causing scandal to the natives of this city, as we are recommended by His Majesty whom God preserve, it was agreed by all the *yehidim* of this K.K. unanimously and in conformity, that there should not be allowed in this city of London and its suburbs more than one synagogue, and if a person or persons of any kind attempt to break up this union, separating themselves to pray with *minyan* in any place outside the synagogue—unless it be with no claim to make another— he incurs immediately the penalty of *herem*, except in houses of bridegrooms or mourners, and the Mahamad shall be obliged with the aid of all the Kahal to put themselves against such disturbers by all means and all the forces possible. And if it be the case at some time that it be recognized as necessary to separate, it shall not be done without a meeting of all the *yehidim* heads of families preceding it, and it shall not be permitted except by a two-thirds vote, it being well understood that it remains always under the government of this synagogue of *Sahar Asamaim*.]

[1] Laski, *op. cit.*, p. 6, note 139, ascribes the four miles limit to the year 1785. As seen it already appears as early as 1694.

shall be admitted to say prayers if it seems good to the gentle-men of the Mahamad." [1] This proviso is on the face of it but a re-affirmation of *Ascama* 2 adopted in 1664, [2] which likewise barred non-Sephardim from divine service at the *Saar Asamaim* except with the approval of the gentlemen of the *Saar Asamaim*. But the limiting clause of four miles, which allowed for the possibility of opening a place of worship outside the *Saar Asamaim* at which non-Sephardim could be admitted, made it necessary to incorporate the *Ascama* 2 in *Ascama* 1, so as to obviate the assumption that the new liberal policy adopted in regard to the attendance of non-Sephardim at Sephardi services held outside the four mile limit applied also to their non-qualified admission to the *Saar Asamaim*.

This comparatively liberal policy was forced upon the Mahamad by the influx of Ashkenazi Jews (*Tudescos*) whose numbers, as a result of the Glorious Revolution of 1688, had grown to such an extent that by 1692 they formed themselves into a separate community and opened a synagogue of their own in Duke's Place [3]. This rival synagogue imposed no restrictions on non-Ashkenazim whom on the contrary it admitted to full membership as *yehidim*. This open-door policy of the Ashkenazi congregation served to undermine the solidarity of the Sephardi community. Whenever a Sephardi member felt aggrieved for one reason or another with the Mahamad, he would break away from his mother community and join the Ashkenazim. The mumber of defec-tions grew to such an extent, particularly after 1704, probably in consequence of the controversy aroused by Haham David Nieto's famous sermon in that year on Divine Providence [4]

---

[1] These additions to the 1677 version of the *Ascama* are introduced in MS 129, p. 1 by the heading "Second Sequence".

[2] *See* Barnett, *El Libro de los Acuerdos*, p. 3.

[3] *See* Cecil Roth, *Archives of the United Synagogue* (London 1930), pp. 9 ff. and Barnett, *Bevis Marks Records I*, p. 31.

[4] This sermon was delivered on Sabbath *Parashat wa-yesheb*, 23 Kislew 5465 (1704).

that the Mahamad on the 1st of Ab 5465 (July 22,1705) sought to strengthen *Ascama* 1 by extending the penalties of the *herem* so that they should apply not only to the person or persons in prayers at any *minyan* outside the synagogue *Saar Asamaim*, which since 1701 was situated at Bevis Marks, but also to everyone who knows that some person or persons transgressed the *Ascama* and does not come and declare it, "such persons become at once declared subjects to this *Ascama* and to its penalties, so that all must separate from them and no one speak to them in any way or manner or business or any other matter." [1]

[1]   This version of the *Ascama* is described in MS. 129, p. 23 as the "Second Sequence to Ascama 1" and according to instructions when referred to was to be called "Ascama 44". Its full text in Portuguese reads as follows: "Havendo os senhores do Mahamad revisto a Escamah asima No. 1 e considerado quao necessario he para os hons fins que ella contem se observe, Legal e religiosamento ao pée da letra, Resolveraõ reteficala e fortificala, e para que nehum judeo argña ignorancia u fazerlhe acresentamento em companhia e com aprovaçao dos Sres adjuntos declarando que todo o judeo Espnanhol ou Portugues que rezida ou ao adiante rezider dentro desta cidade, ou nos limites ariba referidos rezar com miniaa em algun apozento ou caza fora deste santo lugar, inda que naõ seja a com titulo de fazer outra Esnoga (excepto em caza de noivos ou nos dias desemana e saliente Sabat en caza de lutozoa) incurre desde logo nas penas referidas com as mesmas forças e circunstanças que se fora nomeado, declarado e publicado nesta santa Caza. E na mesma pena incurrira todo aquelle que souber que qualquer pessoa ou peasoas transgridem esta Escamah e naõ vier e declarar e fazendo-o, ou sabendose proqualquer via, quem he, ou saõ que prevariquem este decreto, os taes ficaõ desde logo declarados incurridores desta Escamah e das penas della, para que todos se apartem delles, elhes naõ fale por nenhua via ou maneira, sobre negoçio, nem qualquer outra couza (*que e a declaracao da dita Escamah no. 1*) tudo encaminhado a nosa paz, uniaõ e conservaçao que o Senhor Deos se sirva conçedernos para sea Santo Serviço. Amen." [The Gentlemen of the Maamad having revised the *Ascamah No.* 1 above and having considered how necessary it is that it should be observed having regard to the good objects which it contains if it is observed: they resolved legally and religiously in the literal meaning to rectify and strengthen it, and so that no Jew should argue ignorance, make this addition to it in the company of, and with the approval of the Adjuntos, declaring that every Jew, Spanish or Portuguese, who resides or henceforth shall reside in this city or in the limits described

The additions to the *Ascama* made in 1694 and 1705 were finally incorporated in 1738 in the 1677 version which thus amended came to constitute the first *Ascama* as it appears in the first printed volume of the *Ascamot* which was published in 1785.

But all the measures adopted in order to strengthen the *Ascama* were of no avail. The frequency with which the *herem* was inflicted tended to reduce much of its effect. Furthermore, the Declaration of Indulgence of 1687, which meant religious freedom for all, rendered all too uncertain the position of the Mahamad in regard to their powers of pronouncing the *herem*. About six weeks before the outbreak of the Nieto controversy—June 12, 1705—the Attorney General, Sir Edward Northey, who had been asked whether the Mahamad could lawfully excommunicate for the infraction of any order of the Congregation, without fear of prosecution by the Crown, expressed doubt on the matter [1]. It was probably

above, (and) shall pray with *minyan* in some lodging or house outside this sacred place, even if it be not with (any) claim to form another Synagogue—except in the house of betrothed persons or in weekdays and outgoing Sabbath in the house of mourners—incurs at once the penalties described with the same forces and circumstances as shall be named declared and published in this Holy House.

And the same penalty shall incur everyone who knows that some person or persons transgress this *Ascama*, and do not come and declare it and if it be done and be known in any way who it is or they are who contravene this decree, such persons become at once declared subjects to this *Ascama* and to its penalties, so that all must separate from them and no one speak to them in any way or manner on business or any other matter (*which is the declaration of the said Ascama No. 1*) all directed towards our peace union and preservation, which may the Lord God be pleased to grant us for His Holy Service. Amen.]

[1]   The question addressed by the Mahamad to the Attorney General consisted of two parts: (i) their power of excommunication, and (ii) their right to refuse burial to transgressors. The question was accompanied by an English translation of the *Ascama* 1 in its 1694 version. Gaster, *op. cit.* p. 14 reproduces the full text of this version but does not tell us what the opinion of the Attorney General was. Hyamson, on the other hand (*op. cit.*, p. 92), reproduces the question but ignores the *Ascama* which, according to information supplied to me by Dr. Richard Barnett, was written on the back of the question. Hyamson's interpretation of the Attorney General's reply as being in support of the Mahamad is incorrect. A careful reading of the

in order to circumvent the difficulties of the situation, resulting from the reply of the Attorney General, that the Mahamad in the 1705 version of the *Ascama*, whilst retaining the penalties of the *herem*, studiously avoided the use of the term itself. But however this may be, the effect of all this was that a number of *yehidim* felt free to break away and join the Ashkenazim without being so much as rebuked by the Mahamad. There were nevertheless a number of individuals who, notwithstanding their desire to secede, felt sensitive about the *herem* and consequently appealed to Haham Zevi Ashkenazi, who was at the time in Altona, for his guidance on the matter. The question, as reproduced in the Responsa of Haham Zevi (No. 38) appears in two versions: first in Ladino (interspersed with Hebrew phrases), and them in a somewhat shortened form in Hebrew. The Ladino version, translated into English, reads as follows:

> A certain *Kahal Kadosh* [holy Congregation], which has an *Ascama* that its synagogue is solely for the Portuguese and Spanish Jews and which has ordained under the penalty of Herem that in such a City within five miles [1] of its boundaries should not be permitted to pray in a *minyan*, except in the house of a bridegroom or of mourners, has given as the reason that it was recommended by King Charles, peace be upon him. But as afterwards permission was granted by a law of the land for freedom of conscience to be tolerated [2], consequently the law enabled every synagogue to exist without fear of danger.
>
> The said *Kahal Kadosh* has another *Ascama* [that is the *Ascama* 2 already referred to above] that no Ashkenazi, Berber, Levantine or Italian to be admitted as a *Yahid*. Furthermore, if any of these were to attend this Synagogue, they were to be ignored and not to be called up to the Reading of the Law nor given any Mitzvah. The Ashkenazim who used to attend the said *Kahal Kadosh* separated themselves for the above reason and for some years now they have their own Synagogue separately, and no one from the said *Kahal Kadosh* has obstructed them.

somewhat tortuous language of the reply makes it clear that whilst the Attorney General considered it within the right of the Mahamad to refuse burial, he was doubtful whether they could excommunicate.

[1]   The five-miles limit is mentioned nowhere else as far as I have been able to investigate the sources.

[2]   *See* the reference to the Declaration of Indulgence above p. 9.

After this some Portuguese Yehidim for certain reasons [1] broke away from their *Kahal* and met and went to that of the Ashkenazim where they were admitted as *yehidim*. They were neither rebuked nor impeded by the Portuguese *Kahal* because of certains reasons [2] [probably the opinion of Northey]. Some other Portuguese and Spaniards have also taken their leave and have formally resolved not to return and worship to the said *Kahal Kadosh*.

So as to avoid any dissension that might ensue and having aversion to things which their conscience does not admit, it is asked whether after having taken their leave as *yehidim* those persons may congregate freely with the Ashkenazim in their Synagogues.

From Ashkenazi's reply it seems that the cause of the dissatisfaction of the seceders was the calling up to the Law of persons who were publicly desecrating the Sabbath and had non-Jewish wives.

In his reply Zevi Ashkenazi insists first of all that the *Ascama* of the congregation is binding on all the *yehidim*, and that none can separate himself without the consent of the majority of the community. Nor is it to the point to argue that the *Ascama* had originally been recommended by the King (Charles II) and that now under the new reign the same conditions no longer obtained; since there was no guarantee against the situation deteriorating, making the enforcement of the *Ascama* as essential as it was in earlier times. Nor is the fact that the community had not rebuked those who had earlier withdrawn to be taken as a precedent; because if the community had *then* agreed to *their* withdrawal, it does not agrre *now*. If on the other hand it had not agreed then, it was illegal.

The only reason which would justify the secession is the one motivated by religious principles such as those indicated

---

[1]   The reasons are given in the body of the responsum; *see* below.

[2]   The Ladino version has here inserted the Hebrew words אשר מפני כבוד הרבים ראוי לנו להשמיטן··· מפני כבוד אבינו שבשמים ותורתנו הקדושה. These words do not occur in the Hebrew version, but words to this effect appear there, and indeed more appropriately so, in explanation of the reasons why some Portuguese Jews broke away. It seems that the words in question have been misplaced in the Ladino version by the copyist.

above. "And if the spirit of purity informed some men in their zeal for the Lord of Hosts, and urged them to leave the Congregation so as not to acquiesce in evil, they deserve the blessing of God." "But," he concludes with a word of caution: "One cannot decide in any matter upon which there is contention without hearing both sides." He therefore demands "that anyone who wishes to act in accordance with his decision must first show his reply to the other party concerned, and warn it in the presence of two witnesses to submit the case before a Beth Din agreed upon, either in that City or any other City. But if the congregation is recalcitrant and refuses to appear before a Court, then leave is given to every person to withdraw himself from that Community."

Ashkenazi's reply seems to have had a deterrent effect, [1] the congregation having perhaps given way to the objection of the petitioners, and no more demands for secession were made until 1730, when a number of members left the *Saar Asamaim* and joined the Ashkenazi synagogue. Resolved to make an object lesson of the seceders, the Mahamad convened a general meeting of the *yehidim* on 16th Heshwan 5498 (1738) at which the *Ascama* I was once more ratified, and, in disregard of Northey's opinion, power was given to the Mahamad to inflict on the delinquent or delinquents pecuniary or other penalties. This *Ascama* also provided that in case of "impediments that might arise from any repairs in the Synagogue" the Mahamad should have the power "to order prayers to be said in any part of our building." [2]

In 1809 a meeting of the *yehidim* took place in which the

---

[1]   Gaster, *op. cit.*, p. 170. Where he deals with this dispute states that the question was put to Zvi Ashkenazi, but he does not give the source, which seems to be none other than this responsum. He further suggests, surprisingly enough, that "the answer of the Haham Zvi is not known." He is, however, correct in his assumption that it was of a deterrent character. *See* J. H. Zimmels, *Askenazim and Sephardim* (Oxford 1955), pp. 297-299.

[2]   See *Ascamot or Laws and Regulations of the Jewish Congregation entitled Saar Asamaim in London* (London 1831), p. 5.

prohibition against saying prayers with an unauthorised *minyan* was extended from four to six miles from the *Saar Asamaim* [1].

The Mahamad interpreted the *Ascama* in the most stringent possible sense, and did not hesitate to resort to the application of the *herem* for the slightest infraction of the *Ascama*, even when committed without any hostile intent against the congregation. An incident of this nature occurred in 1822 when the Mahamad inflicted the *herem* on a number of members of the congregation who, having met in a private house for the customary vigil observed on Shabuot night, had formed a *minyan* at the dawn of the day for prayers. Those who in the eyes of the Mahamad had incurred guilt were placed under the *herem*, and it was only after they had expressed their solemn contrition, and sought absolution from the Beth Din, that they were absolved from the *herem* and re-instated in their full rights as members of the congregation. [2]

The first attempt to establish a new synagogue was made at a meeting held on December 15,1839 at which the demand was made for the annulment of *Ascama* I. The demand was based on two considerations: (i) the convenience of members whose homes were situated in many parts of the City beyond walking distance of Bevis Marks, and (ii) the desire to introduce certain reforms in the services, in imitation of those adopted by the reform synagogues in Hamburg and other parts of Germany, including the abolition of the second day festivals. [3] An account of this attempt is given in Abraham Belais's *Peri Ez Hayyim*. [4] After reproducing the *Ascama* in its 1785 version, Belais writes:

---

[1]   *See* Hyamson, *op. cit.* p. 241.

[2]   *See* Gaster, *op. cit.*, pp. 169 ff. and Hyamson, *op. cit.*, pp. 235 ff.

[3]   For the history of the reform movement in England *see* Picciotto, *op. cit.*, ch. l-li; Gaster, *op. cit.*, pp. 191 ff.; Philipson, *Reform Movement in Judaism* (London 1907), pp. 129 ff; and Hyamson, *op. cit.*, pp. 273 ff.

[4]   Abraham Belais,   ספר פרי עץ חיים ועפריה דאברהם   (Livorno 5606), pp. 6 f.

Now in the year 5600 (1839/40), a number of notable and wealthy men among the *yehidim* living now far from the *Saar Asamaim* came forth asking for the remission of the *Ascama* on the ground that they were unable to come to the synagogue either on Sabbaths or Festivals. The congregation, however, refused their request. A number of meetings were held during the winter to consider the matter. At last the congregation declared itself ready to give them the necessary permission to open another synagogue nearer their homes, but on condition that it should be under the governance of the *Saar Asamaim*, and that all the proceedings and prayers should be in accordance with the usages and the order of service of the *Saar Asamaim* and that they should not act in any way contrary to the teachings of the rabbis. These men, however, refused to harken to the words of the congregation . . . because "the show of their countenance does witness against them" [Isa 3: 9] that they wish to alter and shorten the order of the prayers and the customs of Israel as they think fit. Indeed, their final attitude is indicative of their original intention, for their rejoinder to the congregation was: "We wish to have a synagogue according to our desire and to make additions and changes in the service as it seems good to us, nor do we wish to be under the governance of your synagogue or under the control of anyone else." Unfortunately nothing the Congregation could do or devise was of any avail with these men. And it came to pass on a certain day [continues Belais] that the Parnassim and the men of the Mahamad in office at that time sent for me and said to me that I should meet the two Dayanim, David Meldola and Abraham Haliva, in order "that you may tell us whether we may lawfully for the sake of peace annul the *Ascama*, or are bound to refuse permission to open a new synagogue for these people according to their own desire."

There then follows the reply of the three members of the Beth Din.

First they laid down the principle, which they support by reference to Joseph Karo and other authorities, that any *Ascama* enforced by *herem* can be remitted by the Beth Din at the request of the congregation.

The next point they proceed to discuss are the conditions under which such a request could be granted.

Considering the terms of the *Ascama* [they wrote] it is evident that its intention is to avoid any harm befalling the *Saar Asamaim* which is responsible for providing bread to the poor, the needy, orphans, widows and emissaries (from the Holy Land), as well as vagrants. For this reason it was stipulated that the approval of a two-thirds majority was essential . . . with all the *yehidim* being present at the meeting at which such an approval was given, so that one section should not benefit at the expense of another. From this it follows that if two-thirds of the congregation do agree to annul the *herem*, it is necessary for those who wish to establish a new synagogue to ensure that it should be under the governance of the *Saar Asamaim* and the control of its Parnassim, so that no harm befall the poor, and also that its management be like that of the *Saar Asamaim* so that no change be made therein in the liturgical usages ordained by our sages, nor any alteration which is against the law. If, however, they wish to introduce some innovation which is against the teachings of our sages, then even if the whole community give their approval the *Ascama* and *herem* remain in force, since it is in contradiction to the Torah and words of the sages.

To sum up [they conclude]: We, the undersigned members of the Beth Din, after examining all the works and opinions of authorities bearing on the subject, find that . . . if the congregation meets and two-thirds agree to annul the *Ascama* and allow these men to establish another synagogue, it is essential for the Parnassim and leaders of the congregation to see that no harm should ensue to the *Saar Asamaim* and that the donations and contributions of these people should be under the control of the *Saar Asamaim*, that they should not do in the new synagogue anything which is contrary to the Torah; that their usages and prayers shall be like those of the *minhag* of the *Saar Asamaim*; . . . and that they should not alter anything. Once the leaders of the congregation will ensure all this then the congregation shall repeal the *Ascama* and the *herem* attached thereto, and all will be in peace and harmony. Signed 21st Adar II, 5600 (1840): David Meldola, Abraham Belais and Abraham Haliva.

The advocates of the branch synagogue, however, refused to abide by these conditions and, determined to go their own way, proceeded to organize themselves, at a meeting held on April 15, 1840 and attended by 18 Sephardi and 6 Ashkenazi members, into an independent congregation, under the name of the West London Synagogue of British Jews. A committee was thereupon appointed to revise the prayer book, adapting it to the wants of the members of the new congregation. The first volume of this revised prayer book containing the daily and Sabbath services was published in August 1841. A few months after its appearance, Solomon Hirschel, the Chief

Rabbi of the Ashkenazim, and his three Dayanim—A. Levy, J. Levy and A. L. Barnett—joined Meldola and Haliva, the two members of the Sephardi Beth Din, in promulgating a "Caution," dated 9th Heshwan 5602 (October 24, 1841), against the use of the prayer book "because it is not in accordance with our Holy Law and whosoever will use it for the purpose of prayers will be accounted sinful." [1] This "Caution" was followed by a "Declaration" drawn up by Solomon Hirschel, and endorsed later by Meldola and Haliva as well as the three above-mentioned Dayanim of the Ashkenazi Beth Din, stating that "in accordance with the laws and statutes held sacred by the whole house of Israel, any person declaring that he or they reject and do not believe in the authority of the oral law cannot have any communion with Israelites in any religious rite or sacred act." Although drawn up on Ellul 24th, 5601 (September 9, 1841), the "Declaration" was not issued until about five months later on Thursday, January 20, 1842. This intervening delay was explained in a statement accompanying the "Declaration" to have been due "to the hope that there would be no necessity to give it publicity"; but "circumstances now require that it should not longer be withheld from the community." [2] The circumstances referred to were the imminent opening in Burton Street of the reform synagogue which had been fixed for a week later—Thursday, January 27. This declaration, which applied equally to the Ashkenazi as to the Sephardi members of the reform con-

[1] See Picciotto, op. cit., p. 379 (2nd ed., p. 374); Voice of Jacob, November 26, 1841; and Philipson, op. cit., p. 135. The Hebrew version of this "Caution" is preserved in the Allgemeine Zeitung des Judentums, 15 January 1842, where we also have the Hebrew names, otherwise unknown, of the three Ashkenazi Dayanim: J. Levy = Azriel ben David Halevi; A. Levy = Aaron ben Judah of Lissa; A. L. Barnett = Arieh ben Judah Leb Ben Issachar Baer of Korotschin. The first English name in full of J. Levy was Israel, as recorded in the approbation he gave to Belais' volume of Responsa in which he was joined by the two other Ashkenazi Dayanim.

[2] See Voice of Jacob, 4 February 1842, Jewish Chronicle, April 1845; Gaster, op. cit., p. 177; Philipson, op. cit., pp. 138-9; Hyamson, op. cit., p. 287.

gregation, was looked upon in many quarters, particularly among members of the reform congregation, as a *herem* (excommunication).[1] In point of fact, however, as a careful reading of the "Declaration" makes clear, it was nothing of the sort. Those who had joined the reform congregation were not subjected to the penalties of *herem*, which amounted to a virtual social ostracism, but were merely debarred from participating in a religious communion, many of whose basic principles they had rejected and spurned.

If one can speak of a *herem* having been imposed, it was in the action taken by the Elders of the Sephardi congregation against its seceding members—an action which in turn had been provoked by a letter which the latter had addressed to the Spanish and Portuguese congregation on January 12, 1842, asking that their names be struck off from the list of the members of the old congregation. In answer to this letter the Elders passed a resolution, which they forwarded to each of the seceders, and, which stated *inter alia* that

> according to the recorded opinion of our late Haham and his Beth Din, the *Ascama* No. 1 in its religious enactment applies to all Jews of the Spanish and Portuguese Community, whether Yehidim, congregantes or even strangers residing in the City, and that the withdrawal from a Yahid, with the contemplation of doing that which the enactments of the *Ascama* were intended to prohibit and prevent, will not exonerate the parties offending from the penalties of that *Ascama* or the governing body itself from enforcing them to the extent it may deem necessary while the *Ascama* remains the law of the Congregation [2].

Acting upon this resolution, the Mahamad on Saturday, Adar 24, 5602 (March 6, 1842) had the names of the seceders read out in the synagogue and issued an edict of excommunication against them together with a declaration of the penalties to which they had subjected themselves in consequence of their transgressions. These penalties involved "the forfeiture

[1] *Jewish Chronicle*, 4 April 1845.
[2] *Jewish Chronicle*, 18 April 1845. See also *Jewish Chronicle*, 4 April 1848.

of the rights and immunities of membership, vacation of their seats and in case of death in contumacy, ineligibility of burial in the *Carriera* [1] of the Cemetery and the accompanying rites." [2] They were also declared ineligigble to act in any religious office or to perform a Mizwah of any kind in the congregation. Nor was it permitted to accept from them any gift or offering during the time they remain under contumacy.

Scarcely had the *herem* been promulgated when an agitation was set on foot for the repeal of the *Ascama*. An account of the agitation, and the reason that prompted it, is given by Belais, who significantly enough was not a signatory to the joint-Ecclesiastical Declaration of 1841.

> When [writes Belais in his Responsa] [3] those who remained steadfast saw that the seceders persisted in their course to the great loss of income to the congregation . . . since those who had seceded were the more wealthy members of the *Saar Asamaim* and no poor man is now allowed by virtue of the *herem* to go and ask them for support, these people said, "How long will the *Ascama* and the *herem* be a snare unto us ? Come, let us see whether we cannot devise some ways and means of repealing the *Ascama* and the attached *herem* and make new regulations which should be to the advantage of the whole congregation and to the benefit of the *Saar Asamaim* and the poor and the needy of the congregation who depend on it, as well as for the religious benefit of some *yehidim* who are God-fearing but live far away from the synagogue and cannot walk to join the congregation in prayers ..
> Let us see therefore whether we cannot repeal the *Ascama*, which many have deliberately contravened. Surely God does not want this. Let us therefore make other regulations in its place.

Continuing his account, Belais tells us that

> when the *yehidim* first met to discuss the new demand, a number of members said: "Let us call in the Dayanim who signed the decision of the year 5600 (1840) and hear their opinion." And so two members of the Beth Din [Meldola and Haliva] went to the

---

[1]   "The *Carreira* is a row in the Bet Chaim. Burials are, save in the case of a Haham and certain other persons, consecutive in position irrespective of personal status", Laski, *op. cit.*, p. 34, Note 32.

[2]   *Voice of Jacob*, 18 March, 1842; Picciotto, *op. cit.*, pp. 381-382 (2nd ed., p. 376); Philipson, *op. cit.*, p. 140.

[3]   Belais, *op. cit.*, p. 7a-b.

meeting, but they did neither consult nor invite me to the meeting, although I was a signatory to the decision of 1840. These members of the Beth Din went and told the meeting that the *Ascama* could not be repealed without a two-thirds majority. This decision of theirs is, however, not sound, as any child who is neither wise nor foolish knows this to be the case since this is precisely what is written in the *Ascama*. Then a number of important individuals, who were concerned for the welfare of the congregation, fearing that we might not obtain a two-thirds majority (. . . since they knew that there were at the meeting certain members who for some specious reason did not wish to have the *Ascama* repealed), said, "We must need hold another meeting at which all the *yehidim* should be present and given an opportunity of voicing their opinion." During that week before the meeting of all the *yehidim*, a number of prominent *yehidim* came to me and said: "See what you can do for the sake of the zeal for the Lord of Hosts, so that the *Saar Asamaim* should not collapse and the poor of our people not perish. Girdle your loins like a warrior, and look into the works of rabbinic authorities in order to find some means to repeal the *Ascama* simply by the leaders of the congregation, without the need of a two-thirds majority, as we wish to make new regulations for the benefit of the congregation and the synagogue, and thereby remove the *herem* from the midst of Israel."

Belais then proceeds to argue that conditions had now so radically changed that the communal leaders on their own accord could repeal the *Ascama* without reference to the *yehidim*.

At the time of the enactment of the *Ascama* about 200 years ago [he writes] all members of the congregation dwelt in the neighbourhood of the Synagogue *Saar Asamaim*, nor was the congregation then as large as it is at present, and therefore it was insisted that a two-thirds majority was necessary so that none should withdraw and go to pray with another *kahal* or make a *minyan* in his own home. But with the process of years the members of the congregation have kept on increasing . . . (May they continue to increase and prosper). Some of them have become very rich, and find it unbecoming to live any longer in the City. They have therefore acquired houses outside the City with gardens and orchards. Some of them have furthermore removed their dwelling from their brethren of the house of Israel, not for the sake of pleasure but because of their health, in view of the unhealthy climate of the City itself.

Belais, however, realizes that the same argument was valid

when he attached his signature to the decision of 1840, and seeking to forestall such criticism he adds:

> Let it be known to anyone who, seeing this, my latter decision, will be wondering in which way has the situation changed from that of a few years ago, when I forbade the repeal of the *Ascama* until there was at least a two-thirds majority, whereas now I declare it permissible, with the approval of the majority of the leaders of the congregation only. To these [critics] I would reply that there is much difference between the conditions at the time when the first decision was given and those that obtain at present. ... At that time it was a matter of transgression, seeing that those who had seceded acted contrary to the teachings of our sages ..., therefore we insisted that there must be a two-thirds majority ..., but now the demand for the repeal of the *Ascama* is for the purpose of the performance of religious duties and for the welfare of the community; and furthermore the *yehidim* who wish to form another congregation agree that all the ordinances and regulations which they will introduce will be under the control of the Parnassim and leaders of the *Saar Asumaim*. This being the case the congregational leaders alone have the power to repeal the *Ascama*.

He further argues that the requirement of a two-thirds majority was merely a precautionary measure, and intended only for those times when the congregation was small and all members lived in the neighbourhood of the synagogue; and basing himself on the view of an eminent authority that in the case of an *Ascama* we do not follow its wording but rather the intention of those who drew it up, he argues that the very fact that the *Ascama* permits services to be held in the house of mourners and in the house of a bridegroom on the day of his wedding shows that the original framers of the *Ascama* were prepared to make concessions under conditions of hardship; and the same applies to those who live far from the synagogue.

Belais was evidently shifting his ground here, and all his attempts to justify his second decision do not stand examination. No wonder that Meldola in his letter to Ghirundi, which will be dealt with anon, speaks of Belais as a man who (quoting a rabbinic phrase) "overturned the dish upside down" and

changed his words in every detail. The congregational leaders,
however, paid heed to the opinion of the official Dayanim,
Meldola and Haliva, and referred the matter to the *yehidim*,
The *yehidim* met thereupon on several occasions to deliberate
on the question and at a meeting which took place on January
8, 1843, repealed the *Ascama* by a majority of more than three
to one. [1] No advantage, however, was taken of the decision
of the meeting, but it provided ground for an agitation to
remove the *herem* from the Sephardi members of the West
London Synagogue, and so early in January 1845 a resolution
was adopted by the *yehidim* that the Dayanim be instructed
to take into consideration how far the repeal of the *Ascama*
afforded a possibility for the re-admission of the members of
the Burton Street Synagogue to their rights and privileges
as Governors and Subscribers of the charitable institutions of
the *Saar Asamaim*. [2] The Beth Din being approached, however,

---

[1]   *See* Meldola's letter in Appendix, Document 1. וכן היה שנתקבצו
כל היחידים פורעי המם פעמים רבות ונשאו ונתנו בדבר… והסכימו ברוב
מנין דהיינו ב׳ שלישים … ויצא להם היתר ההסכמה כדין וכהלכה
According to a written communication to me by Dr. Richard Barnett,
"the *Ascama* was never exactly repealed, until 1906, if then!" *See
infra*, p. 34, n. 1). Evidently no record to this effect is traceable in the
minutes of the congregation, yet the above quoted statement from
Meldola makes it clear that there was a formal repeal. There is,
furthermore, the fact that whenever reference is made subsequently
to the *Ascama* it is spoken of as "repealed". It is, therefore, reasonable
to assume that there was a formal repeal and that this took place at
a *yehidim* meeting which was held (again, according to Dr. Barnett's
information) on January 8, 1843, at which the question of substituting
the *Ascama* 1 by an alternative was also discussed. It was to this
meeting that the *Voice of Jacob*, January 20, 1843, must have referred
when it reported that "at an aggregate meeting of all the members
of the Sephardi Congregation held last week, the needful modifications
[of the *Ascama*] were approved by a majority of more than 3 to 1.
The formal confirmation by another meeting is alone wanting to give
this effect." This formal confirmation, however, took long in coming,
and it was only as late as January 22, 1849, that the modifications
were confirmed by the *yehidim. See infra*, p. 31. The opinion may be
hazarded that as the repeal of the *Ascama* rested in the last analysis
on the decision of the Beth Din, no further confirmation was necessary.

[2]   *Jewish Chronicle*, February 7, 1845.

declared that "every person who had violated the *Ascama*
while still in force is in *herem*. The remission of the *herem* is
only for the future, but not retrospective." This declaration
was signed by David Meldola, Abraham Haliva and Abraham
Belais. [1]

The reply of the Beth Din did not still the agitation. In
November of the same year the Elders in meeting accordingly
resolved to appoint a committee to consult the rabbinic authorities, and others if deemed by them advisable, to ascertain
beyond question the state of the case, and should it appear that
the said parties are actually in *herem*, then to adopt such
measures as may be necessary to absolve them from the herem,
leaving in force all the other penalties which this body has
declared against them. Reference to this meeting is made by
Meldola in his letter to Ghirundi in which he tells us that in
the year 5606 three members of the committee came to see
him asking whether it was possible to remove the *herem* from
the seceders, and they put to the Beth Din a number of questions in writing whether those members who had withdrawn
from the *Saar Asamaim* before the repeal of the *Ascama* were
still in *herem*. Haliva thereupon turned to Isaac Walid in
Gibraltar, who merely confirmed the decision of the Beth
Din, namely that remission of the *herem* was not retrospective
and that there was no alternative but for every individual
to seek absolution for his offence from the Beth Din (dated
Sidra Wa-Yishlah [December 1845]). [2]

In the meanwhile, the campaign for the removal of the
herem from the seceders gathered increasing strength. A
determined move was made early in the year 1847 when at
a meeting of the *yehidim*, held on January 3, there was
presented a Memorial signed by fifty-seven members to
relieve the seceders from the *herem*. The resolution was passed

[1]   *See* Appendix, Document 1, and *Voice of Jacob*, February 14,
1845.

[2]   *Responsa* ויאמר יצחק (Livorno 5611 [1851/2]), *Yoreh Deah*,
no. 108).

at a first reading by 14 to 9, and confirmed on January 17 by 22 to 4. Subsequent to the meeting, H. de Castro and David Brandon laid before the Dayanim the resolution intended to be submitted to the Elders. Rabbi Meldola acting as spokesman said that the decision of the *yehidim* had made it a new case, and if the Elders passed such a resolution, he would give it his best consideration with the anxious desire to meet their views. [1] The next step, in conformity with constitutional procedure, was for the matter to be referred for the consideration of the Elders. A meeting of the Elders was held accordingly on February 28,1847, at which the resolution of the *yehidim* was presented, and after a debate the meeting passed by 15 to 3 a resolution declaring that the seceders be relieved from the *herem*, subject to the approbation of the gentlemen of the Beth Din, and requesting the Mahamad together with H. de Castro, the chairman of the Elders, and E. H. Lindo, the chairman of the *yehidim*, to confer with the Beth Din and obtain their sanction authorising the committee to comply, in the names and on behalf of the congregation, with any religious ceremony that might be required to give validity and effect to the said declaration. This was confirmed in March by 12 to 3. The resolution, however, expressly ordered that the absolution is from the *herem* incurred under the old *Ascama*, and it does not in any way affect the ecclesiastical censure recommended by the joint Beth Din of the various congregations. [2]

On Sunday, April 11, the Mahamad met to consider the decision of the Beth Din. At this meeting two documents were presented—one by Meldola and Haliva and another by Belais. The one signed by Meldola and Haliva stated that in their opinion no relief could be given from the *herem* except on the personal application of the seceders and on their declaring that they were prepared to return to their old congregation. As against this, the document submitted by

[1] *Jewish Chronicle*, May 28, 1847.
[2] *Jewish Chronicle*, April 16, 1847.

Belais set forth that a majority of 3 to 2 of the Board of Elders was sufficient to repeal a *herem* without even the concurrence of the Beth Din. The meeting declared in favor of Meldola and Haliva, they being the official Dayanim, and also a majority of 2 to 1. [1] In view of this divergence of opinion, Brandon proposed that Belais' decision should be submitted to the ecclesiastical authorities of Amsterdam and Leghorn, "to test the accuracy of these quotations and their applicability to the case in question." This proposal, however, casting as it would a reflection on the competence of the official Dayanim, was rejected by 17 to 2. [1] This attempt to override the local Beth Din, though defeated, obliged the Beth Din to seek the opinion of other authorities. Haliva accordingly addressed two letters to Walid in which he stated the arguments advanced by Belais and the quotations he used in support. Walid in his two replies to Haliva written from Tetuan, the first dated *Sidra Kedoshim* 5607 (May 1847) and the other the month of Ab 5607 (July/August) supported the decision of the Beth Din and contraverted one by one all the arguments of Belais. [2] Yet notwithstanding the concurrence of such an eminent authority as Walid with the decision of the Beth Din, Meldola felt very uneasy at the trend of things and accordingly turned to Ghirundi with a proposal which appeared to him the best way out for resolving the difficulties of the situation. [3] After reproducing the *Ascama* in its 1785 version and recounting briefly the story of the secession and the pronouncement of the *herem* on the seceders as well as the subsequent repeal of the *Ascama*, Meldola continues:

> Now in 1847 there arose many men among the *yehidim* saying that, since the *Ascama* had been repealed, it applies also to those who had transgressed it in 1842 and that the Beth Din is empowered without any request for absolution by the people concerned to remove the *herem*. Abraham Belais is now supporting them in this new decision. We two [Meldola and Haliva], however, stood

[1]   *Jewish Chronicle*, May 28, 1847.
[2]   *See* Walid, *op. cit.*, Nos. 106/107.
[3]   *See* Appendix, Document 1 [Montefiore No. 164, Responsum 605].

by our former opinion and replied that whilst we would do all
we could to bring about peace if only possible and make all
possible concessions, nevertheless the remission which took
place in 1843 does not cover those who seceded in 1842 as it is
not retrospective. All the arguments which Belais had used are
weak and are without any basis.

Meldola then proceeds to submit to Ghirundi his own
opinion. After a lengthy introduction declaring his own
unworthiness to decide on a matter of such import without
the support of greater authorities than himself, and condemning the reformers and showing that the seceders, having
violated the *Ascama*, had *ipso facto* incurred the penalty of
the *herem*, particularly since the *Ascama* had been ratified
with all the sanctions it involved in 1738, Meldola argues that
there must be a formal *hattarah* (remission), and asks Ghirundi
whether it is possible to absolve the persons concerned, even
if they did not wish to appear before the Beth Din, considering
that they are highly placed personages. In this case the
remission could be effected by any three people forming a
quorum as required by the law, provided they themselves
had not been present at the time when the *herem* had been
imposed and all that would be required was a proclamation in
the synagogue that the *herem* had been remitted; or whether
it is necessary that the persons concerned should formally seek
absolution either in person or through their representatives.
But in any event, Meldola emphasizes, the absolution would
be only as far as the transgression of the *Ascama* is concerned,
but the prohibition to join the seceders in religious services
must stand until they retract and repent of their sins. This
is dated 7 Ab 5607 (July 22nd 1847).

Ghirundi in his reply of 21 Elul [1] agrees with Meldola's
decision that the remission is not retrospective. He criticizes
Belais who, after having endorsed the first decision and having
agreed with Meldola and Haliva, had now changed his opinion
going so far as to permit people to join the seceders in prayers
in their "Church."

[1]   *See* Appendix, Document 2 [Montefiore No. 164, Responsum 606].

I know him [Belais] and all his past and we know who he is [1], and "in the place where there is a *hillul ha-Shem* no honor may be given even to a teacher". I am indeed astonished that he is not afraid to lend a hand to transgressors and to assume responsibility in such a matter as a terrible and awful *herem* which has been imposed by many great rabbinical authorities, Sasportas and others, as mentioned in your letter, pretending that he does not know that a public *herem* has a biblical warrant, according to all authorities. I am sure if you will induce many friends to speak to him he will incline his ears to the words of our sages, notify the transgressors, and tell them "All the words I said to you were sheer imagination on my part; I retract from my former opinion, so that it is forbidden to pray in the new synagogue, even according to the formularies fixed by the Men of the Great Assembly, until they go and ask remission from the Sephardi rabbinate and the leaders of the *Saar Asamaim.*

Ghirundi agrees with Meldola that the remission can take place, even if the transgressors did not come in person, by three ordinary laymen who were not present at the time when the *herem* was imposed, in order not to prevent them from repentance. He further advises Meldola to greet them with "words of peace and truth," saying to them all "You are our brethren," and to visit them and to receive them in his house, so as to inspire them with the desire to abide by the words of the sages, and to pray in accordance with the traditional usages of the *Saar Asamaim* and to observe the second days of the festivals, making it thus possible to join them in all sacred services.

Ghirundi submitted Meldola's letter, and his own reply to Rabbi Judah Pereira of Sarajevo, [2] who was on a mission at Padua, as well as to Arieh Ascoli of Rovigo, [3] who happened to be on a visit to Padua. Both these rabbis endorsed the decision of Meldola and Ghirundi, Pereira's reply being dated the 5th day of Sukkot 5608 (1847) and Ascoli's 22 Elul 5607 (1847). Meldola also addressed himself to Zvi Hirsch Chajes of Zolkiev through Ghirundi, with whom he was in frequent

---

[1]   On Belais' career *see* Hyamson, *op. cit.*, p. 208 and and *Jewish Encyclopedia, s.v.*

[2]   *See* Appendix, Document 3 [Montefiore No. 164, Responsum 607].

[3]   *See* Appendix, Document 4 [Montefiore No. 164, Responsum 608].

correspondence; and Ghirundi in transmitting to Chajes Meldola's letter attached to it his own reply. Chajes in turn sent off two replies to Ghirundi, one dated 8 Heshwan 5608 intended for Ghirundi himself, and another in Kislew of the same year which he asked him to transmit to Meldola, in both of which he concurred with the opinions of Meldola and Ghirundi. The reply to Ghirundi is in manuscript [2] and that to Meldola is incorporated in Chajes' volume of *Responsa*.[2] The two replies are similar.

Chajes, as stated, agrees with the opinion of Ghirundi and Meldola that the remission was not retrospective and that consequently a formal *hattarah* was still essential. He, however, does not concur with their view that any three laymen could constitute a Beth Din for the purpose. He points out that the ruling that the remission of a *herem* could be affected by a board of three laymen is only valid, according to a talmudic statement, where there are no scholars available, but not in such places "as the capital city of London where many scholars are to be found." Chajes further maintains that each individual transgressor of the *Ascama* must appear in person before the Beth Din and ask for absolution, since it was the Beth Din who, in the last analysis, was responsible for the proclamation of the *herem*. At the same time he maintains that this could be done in writing. He furthermore quotes authorities that it is customary not to consider those who had violated a communal *herem*-regulation as being in a state of excommunication, unless a proclamation to this effect has been made against them, and since the prohibition to have religious intercourse with the seceders was not on account of the contravention by them of the *Ascama*, but on account of the proclamation of the *herem* on 24 Adar, when their names were mentioned, and since they were not present at the synagogue at the time of the proclamation, there is no need for them to be present when the *herem* is removed. Still, Chajes continues, the sece-

---

[1] *See* Appendix, Document 5 [Montefiore No. 164, Responsum 609].
[2] שו״ת מהר״ץ (Zolkiew 1850), No. 46.

ders deserve to remain in excommunication because of their rejection of tradition, although this in itself would not have warranted a *herem*, in the first instance. At the same time he continues that even this could be overlooked and the *herem* be remitted for the sake of communal harmony and peace, as it is impossible to prevent people from having relations with them. Finally, Chajes concludes that it is permitted to remit the *herem* in their absence, but they should be informed that the Beth Din has decided to act in that manner. On 24 Kislev 5608 Ghirundi forwarded to Meldola Chajes' responsum, together with Pereira's endorsement.

At the same time a sympathiser with the seceders communicated with the rabbi of Leghorn seeking his opinion. There is every probability that the correspondent was Brandon himself who, refusing to take his defeat, stated in a letter which he addressed on May 20,1847 to the *yehidim*, who signed the Memorial against the *herem*, that, as the *yehidim* would meet again in November, he would in the interval endeavor to obtain opinions of those whom the Elders refused to approach. [1] The reply of the Leghorn rabbi—excerpts of the Hebrew original in English translation appeared in the *Jewish Chronicle* of November 5,1847—agreed with Belais that it was "in the power of the majority of the Mahamad to abolish an *Ascama* passed by a former board without consulting the ecclesiastical authorities." "This conclusion," the Leghorn rabbi wrote, "I have reached after consulting the authorities quoted by the rabbi in the minority." He further declared, "that the absolution having been passed by the majority of the Mahamad, it is their duty to carry it out without asking the parties who labour under the *Ascama* whether such abolition is convenient to them or not, or whether it is desired by them or not."

On January 2, 1848, a meeting of the *yehidim* was held at which David Brandon, armed with the reply of the Leghorn rabbi proposed a motion which was seconded by H. de Castro:

[1]   *Jewish Chronicle*, May 28, 1847.

"That all parties who may now be in *herem* for an infraction of the old *Ascama* of Kaal No. 1 shall no longer be considered as under that penalty."

To this resolution an amendment was proposed that the motion be *not put*. The result was 13 in favor, 18 opposed. The meeting then adjourned to Thursday, January 11, when several amendments were moved; the first, by Edward Foligno "That the meeting resolve to leave the said question to the decision of Dr. Adler, the Chief Rabbi of the German Congregation," was defeated by a majority of four. The second amendment which was moved by Solomon Almosnino consisted of two parts: (i) to the effect that the meeting is decidedly of the opinion and does hereby declare that the penalty of *herem* was never contemplated or intended so far as the declaration regarding the alterations in the services of the new synagogue were concerned, and that as far as the breach of the old *Ascama* of Kaal No. 1 is concerned, has never been inflicted on the parties by any act of the Elders; and (ii) as doubt exists in the mind of some *yehidim* whether religiously such a penalty is implied, the matter be submitted to Dr. Adler whose decision would be considered as a final settlement of the question. Almosnino's resolution was carried only by two votes—19 to 17, and the meeting adjourned to Tuesday, January 25, when a confirmation of Almosnino's motion was debated amid angry discussion. At that meeting a letter of the Beth Din was read which was not favorable to the resolution. A division took place resulting in the rejection of the resolution by 27 to 17. Thereupon de Castro gave notice of a motion similar to the one submitted by Brandon on January 2, which he had then seconded. [1] The debates were resumed at a meeting of the *yehidim* held on Sunday, February 20,1848 (16 Adar 5608) at which a letter was read by Belais approving de Castro's motion which read that "every person who may have incurred the penalty of *herem* by an infraction of the old *Ascama* of Kaal (resolution of the board) No. 1

[1]   *Jewish Chronicle*, January 20, 1848.

(now repealed) shall no longer be considered under that penalty, but subject to the same penalties and disqualifications as are in force against the members of the Burton Street place of worship under the declaration of the ecclesiastical authorities of the United Congregations." The motion was seconded by M. Picciotto who quoted in support copious extracts from the *Shulhan Aruk* and other authorities, presumably supplied to him by Belais. The reading of the extracts produced a sensation. Yet on a division the motion was carried only by a majority of one, 16 to 15. [1] The *yehidim* met again on March 5, for the purpose of confirming de Castro's resolution, and on division the resolution was defeated by a majority of 4—21 to 17. What is significant in the resolution were the words "that they now be relieved from any penalty *they may have* incurred." These underlined words are indicative of the considerable confusion that existed, as already a correspondent in the *Jewish Chronicle* pointed out, whether the seceders had been in *herem* by an act of the *yehidim*. One party contended that they were not, another, on the contrary; and a third that it was doubtful. To the writer himself, however, it was clear that the seceders had infringed a law (No. 1) and that the United Ecclesiastical Authorities had issued an excommunication against them. [2]

Undaunted in their efforts, the *yehidim* took up the matter again at a meeting held on Sunday, January 14, 1849 (20 Tebet 5609), when it was moved by De Castro "That this meeting... declares all persons who may have incurred penalties by an infraction of the repealed *Ascama* in reference to civil offences to the congregation are now relieved from such penalties, but that all ecclesiastical matters do continue as before to apply under and subject to ecclesiastical authorities." The motion was carried by a majority of 26 to 3. [3] Before however meeting again in order to confirm the motion,

[1] *Jewish Chronicle*, February 25, 1848.
[2] *Jewish Chronicle*, April 14, 1848.
[3] *Jewish Chronicle*, January 26, 1849.

as required by the laws of the congregation, the *yehidim*
resolved to adopt the report of the special committee appointed as far back as 9 January 1842 to frame proposals *in lieu*
of *Ascama* 1, which, as generally realized, was no longer in
consonance with the spirit of the time. This report, whilst
maintaining the gist of the prohibition of *Ascama* 1, as well
as its provision for the establishment of a branch synagogue,
on the approval of a two-thirds majority, did away with the
severe *herem* penalties, reducing the sanctions to matters of
pecuniary fines, exclusion from the membership of the congregation, and refusal of burial in the *Carreira* of the Cemetery,
while in contumacy. [1] Finally confirmed at the *yehidim's*
meeting of Monday, January 22, 1849 (28th Tebet 5609), the
adoption of this report cleared the way for the confirmation,
on the following Monday, January 29 (Shebat 6), of De Castro's
motion at the annual session of the *yehidim* by a majority of
21 to 4, with three abstentions. [2]

The Elders who had consistently opposed conciliation with
the seceders, sensing the strength of public opinion, were
anxious to take credit for these liberal measures, and hastily
convened a meeting for the preceding evening at which the
self-same motion was adopted by a majority of 15 to 7. [3]

Things were now moving rapidly. Three days later—
February (9 Shebat)—Meldola and Haliva, emboldened by
the concurrence of such authorities as Ghirundi, Chajes and
Pereira, issued a declaration in the form of a letter, written

---

[1] The *Ascama* in this modified form was subsequently embodied
in the 1850 printed edition of the Ascamot. The *Ascamot* were next
reprinted in 1906, but the first *Ascama* of that issue in the words of
Laski, *op. cit.*, p. 35, "is a pale and unsubstantial ghost of its sonorous,
majestic and miniatory predecessors. It mildly lays down that a
Synagogue intended to become an integral part of the Congregation
shall not be erected without the approval and consent of two-thirds
of the Yehidim present at a meeting called to consider such a proposal".
The dates of the *yehidim's* meetings of January 14 and January 22
to consider the report of the special committee I owe to Dr. Barnett.

[2] *Jewish Chronicle*, January 26, 1849.

[3] *Jewish Chronicle*, February 2, 1849.

in Hebrew and accompanied by a English translation, to de Castro, dealing with the *herem* as far as its application goes and the possiblity of its absolution.

> Having always been most anxious [so ran the first declaration] to establish peace and being actuated in all our proceddings by the Din, we are bound to pay attention to the wishes expressed by the majority of the *yehidim* and at the same time it is imperative for us to make an *hattarah*, and if the individuals do not wish to appear personally before the Dayanim, two respectable persons deputed by them amy on their behalf acknowledge their transgression of *Ascama* 1, now repealed, upon which we can prepare an *hattarah* allowing us hereafter to unite with them in society or speak with them, but in respect of דברים שבקדושה [sacred matters] unless they renounce the errors of their ways and mode of worship our decision must remain unaltered.

On March 5 (Adar 12), 14 of the seceding members gave the required authorization to de Castro and Guedalla, which they in turn submitted three days later on Friday, March 9 (Adar 15), to Meldola and Haliva, who readily granted the *hattarah* which was embodied in a declaration in English: "We hereby certify at the request of H. de Castro and H. Guedalla who this day appeared before us to make Attara on behalf of the following gentlemen. The same was done for the penalties of the Herem they were subject for their disregard of Kaal No. 1 Ascama and for *that only*, and the Herem be abolished accordingly." Then followed the fourteen names of the people who at their request were absolved from the *herem* and the signatures of David Meldola, Abraham Haliva and Joseph Elmaleh, a *Rubi* (a teacher), who was asked to make up a quorum instead of Belais whose attitude, as mentioned already had disqualified him in the eyes of his colleagues.

A few days later de Castro and Guedalla were able to inform their friends of the removal of the *herem* under which they had been laboring for their disregard of *Ascama* 1. [1] But this was not the end of the matter. The editoral in the *Jewish Chronicle* of March 23, 1849, welcoming the repeal of the *herem*, drew forth a protest from Rabbi Haliva against the

---

[1] *See* Gaster, *op. cit.*, pp. 178 and 180. Hyamson, *op. cit.*, pp. 292-3.

assumption of the journal that the repeal was complete;
whereas, so he asserted, it had been only partial. Thereupon
the *Jewish Chronicle* of April 27 reproduced a letter, written
by de Castro to Moses Mocatta a few hours after the *hattarah*
had been promulgated, showing that it was complete. The
letter reads as follows:

> "My dear Sir, I acknowledge with much peasure your letters
> addressed to myself and Mr. Guedalla containing the signatures
> of yourself and 13 other parties thereto; and according with our
> promise we placed ourselves in communication with the eccle-
> siastical authorities and we have the satisfaction to state that the
> Herem incurred by the disregard of *Ascama No.* 1 which was put
> in force against you has been *finally* and *fully* abolished this day
> against each and all the parties signing that letter (as far as As-
> cama No. 1 of Kaal) is concerned, in the presence of myself and
> Mr. H. Gudalla.
> Let us trust the good that will result *does not stop here*. I am
> etc. H. de Castro."

The *Jewish Chronicle* ascribed Rabbi Haliva's assertion to his
"want of acquaintance with the English language" a defect
which it had in the same context criticized as "having caused
much confusion and embarrassment recently." The editor of
the *Jewish Chronicle* evidently ignored, or perhaps was not
aware, of the fact that the letter to de Castro to which Haliva
was also a signatory and which formed the basis of the formal
hattarah was written in Hebrew of which the English version,
apart from some idiomatic expressions, was a faithful representation. What had rather determined Rabbi Haliva's attitude
seems to have been his interpretation of the phrase שבקדושה
דברים, "sacred matters," in regard to which the former decision
of the ecclesiastical authorities, as it was expressly stated, had,
remained unaltered. Did the phrase include also the acceptance of offerings and gifts to charitable institutions from
seceders? Rabbi Meldola, who we are told in the *Jewish
Chronicle* did not join Haliva in the protest, apparently held
that it did not. Haliva, on the other hand, held that it did.
Such in fact was precisely the question put to Meldola and
Haliva shortly after the promulgation of the *hattarah*. Their

reply, we are informed, was so involved that the committee appointed by the Elders to go into the matter had to report: "Your Committee regard that the answers given are not of that direct and straightforward character which they would have desired to present to you." [1] Nor could it be otherwise in view of the difference of opinion between Meldola and Haliva in the matter. [2] But, however this may be, the criticism in the *Jewish Chronicle* was soon to bear fruit. On April 29, 1849, a drastic proposal was put before the Elders that notice be given to terminate the services of Meldola, owing to his infirmities, and to Haliva owing to his lack of knowledge of the English language. This proposal, to the credit of the Elders, was defeated, but only to be followed by another attempt in December 1851, directed this time only at Haliva, to secure his retirement by offering him a miserable pension of £ 30 a year and one of £ 15 a year to his widow if she survived him. [1] The offer was naturally not accepted, and Haliva retained his office until he died in August 1853, [3] a few months after David Meldola who had passed on the previous April. [4] This aftermath of the repeal, as far as it affected Meldola and Haliva, had only served to embitter their lives, and it is no wonder that Meldola did not acknowledge Ghirundi's letters, and as late as Elul 1851 Ghirundi wrote to him expressing surprise at his silence. [5]

[1] Hyamson, *op. cit.*, p. 293. That charitable contributions were considered as "sacred matters" is indicated by the fact that according to a letter of Benjamin Elkin, one of the Ashkenazi leaders of the reform movement, which appeared in the *Jewish Chronicle*, April 18, 1845, members of the Burton Street Synagogue, including the *Ashkenazim*, were excluded from the charities in conformity with a resolution passed on April 20, 1842 (that is, after the repeal of the *Ascama* and the *herem*) and that since he had been a member of the new synagogue, he had not been applied to for any annual subscription to the Orphans Society.

[2] Hyamson, *op. cit.*, pp. 311-12.
[3] Hyamson, *op. cit.*, p. 312.
[4] *Hebrew Observer*, April 15, 1853.
[5] *See* Appendix, Document 6 [Montefiore No. 172. דובר שלום, by M. S. Ghirundi, Responsum 1776].

The battle was now over, and with it was buried, at least
in Anglo-Jewry, that formidable weapon—the *herem*—which
for centuries had enabled Jewish authorities to build up and
frame regulations for the governance and orderliness of
Jewish communal, social and religious life. That the *herem*
had become obnoxious to the new spirit of the age was an
opinion which no one ventured any longer to dispute. Yet
once the *herem* had been imposed, its remission in our particular case, in view of the reluctance of those involved to
submit themselves as penitents before the ecclesiastical
authorities, presented a difficult halakic problem, which
could be dealt with only on halakic principles and precedents.
It speaks well of Meldola's learning and halakic acumen that
he found within the framework of the halakah a satisfactory
solution, which received the approval of a number of rabbinical
authorities on the continent. In this connection it is well to
realize that those of the Sephardim who had joined the reform
congregation had incurred guilt for a double offence: one
which was of a purely communal character and described as
a "civil offence"—their withdrawal from the *Saar Asamaim*
in contravention of *Ascama* 1; another which was of a religious
character—their participation in religious services which were
contrary to Jewish law and tradition. The former concerned
only the Sephardi members and carried with it the heavy
penalties of the *herem*. The latter concerned equally the Ashkenazim and was the subject of the Declaration issued by the
joint Ecclesiastical Authorities. Whilst the *Ascama* 1 was
repealed and those who had transgressed it were relieved
from the penalties of the *herem*, the Declaration forbidding
religious communion with those who joined a congregation
which had rejected the authority of the oral law remained
unaltered; and, having in fact been explicitly re-affirmed in the
hattarah of 1849, [1] is from the standpoint of the halakah
considered binding, until such a time as it will be recalled by
the Ecclesiastical Authorities.

[1] *See* Gaster, *op. cit.*, pp. 177.

Appendix

Document 1: Letter of Meldola to Ghirundi, קבוצת כסף 605,
Montefiore MS. No. 164.

שו״ת מאת ידידי הרב הכולל מהר״ר דוד מילדולה מ״ץ בלונדרה·

בהיות שהק״ק ספרדים הי״ו שבעיר לונדרס יע״א יש להם הסכמה קדומה
משנת תכ״ד בעניז בית הכנסת שלהם הנקראת שער השמים שלא יוכל שום אדם
ספרדי גר או תושב להתפלל במניז או בבית כנסת אחרת חוץ בבית הכנסת
הנזכרת וזה נוסח ההסכמה הנ״ל·

אחרי התבוננות כמה הכריחו האחדות בינו להעמדתנו שלא לגרום חילול
ה׳ בין האומה בני העיר הזאת כאשר נצטוונו מרום מעלת המלך קארלוס הב׳
הסכימו כל היחידים בהק״ק כולם כאחד ובאגודה אחת שלא ינתן רשות בעיר
לונדרס ומגרשיה שתהיה בית הכנסת אחרת כי אם זאת של שער השמים ואם
יש איש אחד או אנשים מכל מדרגה שיהיה שגורמים להפרד האחדות הזה
ופורשים עצמם להתפלל במניז באיזה בית או חדר או באיזה מקום אחר
חוץ מבית הכנסת הקדושה הנ״ל הגם שלא תהיה ידועה ונזכרת בשם ב״ה
נלכדים מיד בעונש החרם מלבד החתן ביום חופתו והאבל בימי אבלו שיכולים
להתפלל במניז בתוך ביתם וכל יהודי ספרדי או פורטוגזי שלעת עתה מיושב
או עתיד יהיה בעיר הזאת או בתחומיה שאינו מקיים מה שנז״ל ילכד בעונש
חרם כמו שמפורש לעיל· וכמו כן עובר כל מי שיש לו ידיעה שיש עוברים על
זאת הסכמה ולא יבוא להגיד או שתבוא הידיעה באיזה אופן שתהיה מי הם
העוברים על הכתוב למעלה הרי הם בכלל העוברים על ההסכמה הזאת ומן
העונשים שלה כדי שכולם יבדלו מהם ולא ידברו עמהם בשום אופן שיהיה על
עסק משא ומתן או בכל דבר אחר· ומחויבים המעמד עם סיוע כל הק״ק לעמוד
מנגד כל העוברים בכל דרך ואופן שיהיה ואם באולי באיזה זמן מצד
ה ה כ ר ח מוכרח להבדל הקהל לא יעשה כי אם שיתווע דו כל היחידים והבעלי
בתים ולא יהיה ניתר להם כי אם ע״פי ש נ י ש ל י ש י ם מהקהל אך בתנאי שתהיה
תחת רשות והנהגת ב״ה של שער השמים הנ״ז אשר היא בעזר האל תהיה מיוחדת
ליהודים ספרדים ופורטוגזים בלבד שלעת עתה יושבים בעיר הזאת והבאים
לעתים· והיהודים מקהילות אחרות יתקבלו להתפלל לפי ראות אנשי המעמד
הכל מיוסד דרך השלום· וחתימי עלה הרב מהר״י ששפורטש בעל אהל יעקב
ואחריו שאר רבנים שישבו על כסא ההוראה דור דור וכ״ו של אותו העת
ויחידי׳ ועוד חדשוה בשנת התל״ז ועוד חדשו אותה בשנת התס״ד כדי לחזק
תועלת ב״ה שער השמים ומשנת התס״ד עד עכשיו שנת הת״ר לפי״ק שהם
קל״ז שנים אין פוצה פה ומצפצף·

ומעתה בשנת תר״ב קמו עמדו אנשים מיחידי וגדולי הקהילה ראשיה ומנהיגיה
ופרצו גדר ונתלוו עם אחרים ופתחו בית הכנסת הפך ההסכמה הנ״ל ועוד
זאת רעה שהיתה הפתיחה בהקריבם אש זרה אשר הביאו מן החדש חדשים
מקרוב בשנותם נוסח החפילות בכמה מקומות חסרו וגם קצרו ובטלו י״ט שני

ובשמעם ראשי וטובי העיר ומנהיגיה את הדבר הרע הזה כי היתה כזאת
בישראל נתאספו יחד פעמים רבות בבית וועדם לעמוד על הדבר והשתדלו
בכל עז ותעצומות לתוך השלום ולקרבם כדי להתרחק מזה מחלוקת כל מה
דאפשר בטרם תחיל שפיר גזרתם ופרסומי מלתא שעברו על ההסכמה הנ״ל,
כאשר ראו מעלת הזקנים והמעמד שהאריך הזמן ולא הועילו בכל השתדלותם
אחרי ימים נמנעו וגמרו לפרסם את הדבר בב״ה והכריזו גזרתם אשר גזרו בכ״ד
אדר תר״ב, וזה לשונם בלעז׳ ״מודיעים שבא לידיעת הוועד הכללי של הזקנים
שאחרי כל האזהרות ששלחו הם וגם ממעלת החכמים לא עלתה בידם מאומה
וכמה מיחידי הק״ק שסלקו עצמם מהיות יחידים פרצו גדר ההסכמה של הק״ק
וגם עשו נגד ה׳ ונגד דתנו, וכו׳ וכו׳: ונקבו א׳ לא׳ מהעוברים עליה בשמותם
ושלא יקברו וכו׳: אחר כל אלה הדברים הנה בשנת תר״ג קמו עמדו בוועד
היחידים (המתאספים מידי שנה בשנה) אנשים יראים ושלמים המבקשים להתיר
ההסכמה הנ״ל באמרם שהם שוכנים ודרים למרחוק הרבה ואינם יכולים לבא
בב״ה לא בשבתות וי״ט וגם רוצים להעביר החרם מעליה ולעשות תקנות
אחרות במקומה כי אין לך הכרח גדול מזה כתנאי ההסכמה הרוצים להתפלל
במנין בביתם· ושאלו את פינו לדבר הזה והשבנו להם שדת של תורה על פי
הדין אופן התרתה וכן היה שנתקבצו כל היחידים פורעי המס פעמים רבות
ונשאו ונתנו בדבר כאשר הורה לנו יוסף הננו רב תנא ופליג בחלק י״ד ס״א[1]
בש״ות מרן הורי וזקני הגאון מים רבים[1] והסכימו ברוב מנין דהיינו ב׳ שלישים
כאשר מפורש יוצא בהסכמה ויצא להם היתר ההסכמה כדין וכהלכה· עוד
בשנת תר״ו בוועד הזקנים הכללי נקבו ג׳ המיוחדים שבהם לראות אם יש
תרופה לפורשים להתירם מחרם שעברו וכו׳· ושאלו לנו איזה שאלות בכתב א׳
אם אילו האנשים שיצאו מקהילתנו בשנת תר״ב קודם התר ההסכמה עדיין
הם בחרם והיתה תשובתנו כי כל האיש עבר ההסכמה של קהלה בעודה
בתקפה נוהגת הרי הוא עדיין בחרם ובטול ההסכמה וכל התלוי שבטלו הקהל
אינו אלא רק להבא ולא לשעבר וכו׳ והיו חתומים בה אני דוד הוא הקטן,
ואברהם חלבאה, ואברהם בלעיש (הוא האיש אשר עתה הפך הקערה ושינה
את דיבור בכל פרט)· ויהי היום וי־הי בשנת תר״ז קמו מחדש ויצאו אנשים
מבין ועד היחידים ורובם אומרים שכיון שהותרה כעת ההסכמה הותרה גם
לאנשים שעברו עליה בש׳ תר״ב ויש כח ביד מעלת הראשים והזקנים להסיר
החרם מהפורשים וכו׳ ושאינו צריך לא פתח וכו׳ הם שגמרו הפה שעשה וכו׳
(ואברהם הוא העומד על ימינם בהוראותיו החדשים) גם לדבר הזה שאלו את
פינו ואנחנו שנינו בשם אלוקינו עמדנו בדבורנו והשבנו שנעשה כל מה שנוכל
לקרב השלום אם אפשר ולמצא כל הקולות שנוכל אך שבהתרת ההסכמה בש׳
תר״ג לא הותרה לאלו הפורשים בש׳ תר״ב כי ההתרה אינו אלא להבא וכו׳
ואותם סמוכות אשר הביא בזה ובשאר בפרטים הם רופפים, יצאו דחופים,
ואין להם על מה שיסמכו ואין בידינו כי אם להחזיק במעוז הדת ולהעמיד
משפטי התורה על תלם כי עץ חיים היא למחזיקים בה ומה׳ יבא עזרנו אכי״ר.

[1] רפאל בן אלעזר מילדולה (1685-1748).

תשובתי הקלה

הנה בשמים אלהי הרוחות אשר על כל דרכי איש עיניו פקוחות, יודע מחשבות
אדם כי מימי לא הלך לבי בגדולות, קטנטי מכל לעלות במעלות, ושהדי
במרומים כי לא להתפאר ולא לקנטר יצאתי, ולא לערוך שלחן במדבר באתי
לפני אנשים חכמים המה הישרים באמת ובתמים אשר חלק להם ה׳ בבינה,
ויראת ה׳ על פניהם רועי אמונה, הן הם הישרים בלבותם, לא באלה במטים
עקלקלותם, לכן אמרתי אלכה נא אחרי הקוצרים, כי מלתא כדנא אינה צריכה
לפנים ודבר שפתים ברוב דברים, אך ולמחסור ואני אנא אני בא להיות מקבץ
ועולה מספר אל ספר דברים שאין להם שעור כמה דנתון דברייתא ולהיות
כעובדים המתארים בלבושי אדוניהם לאסוף מלא חפניים להבהיל עיני ההמון
בהזכרת ספרים חוץ למקומם וענינם עד אשר ימלאון כעשר יריעות נייר
והעולה בידם וכמאמר החכם חמליין בעלם יאסוף אל ידו נצוץ השמש מלא
קמצו ובפתחו עמד מרעיד כי אינו רואה את כל מאומה בידו· ומכאן מודעה
כי אין מקומנו פה לכנס ולנגוע בקצהו בענין השנויים אשר עשו בעת החדש אשר
בדו מלבם כי מי זה ואיזה הוא יוכל להוסיף אפילו כקוצה של יוד מאת אשר
כבר הוכיחו אנשי חיל חכמי לבב גאוני וגדולי הדור נגד המחדשים בס׳ דברי,
הברית[1] וכאשר הזהרנו בהזהרתנו הנדפסת· אך עתה בשל עתה באתי רק בענין
הנוגע להסכמה הנ״ל כי אין עת לחשות לצאת לקראת נשק להחזיק בהוראה
כאשר הורנו מן השמים·

הנה מהר״י אדרבי בסימן ז״ן ע״ד הסכמה שכתוב בה כל העובר יהיה
בחרם ונידוי וכו׳ כתב וז״ל: ויש לדקדק אם יחייבו הרבים להבדיל ולהתרחק
מן העובר בדין מנודה ומוחרם וכו׳· וראיתי להר״ן דחרם שמטילין קודם מעשה
אינו אלא בסתם אבל כל שמפרש דהעובר יהיה דינו כדין מוחרם ומנודה ודאי
דחל הנידוי אף כאן שפירש בהסכמה שהעובר יהיה מוחרם ומנודה וכו׳ עכ״ל·
והר״ן בתשובה סי׳ ס״ה הביא אלו הדעות וראיותיהן וכו׳ ולבסוף העלה הר״ן
שכל חרם שמחרימים אף קודם מעשה אינו מדין קבלה אלא שהחרם שלהם חל
על העובר על תקנתם ולנהוג בו כדין מוחרם בב״ד וכן דעת הרמב״ן ז״ל, עד
כאן לשונו· וע׳ פי ג׳ עדים יקום דבר דהיינו הרמב״ן והר״ן ומר״י אדרבי
נקטין דהחרם חל אף קודם מעשה מעשה וחייבים לנהוג במוחרם דיני מנודה וא׳׳כ
בנד״ד דמפורש יוצא בהסכמה דכל העובר אינקורי לוגו[2] נלכד מיד בעונש
החרם אותם העברינים הם מנודים וצריך לנהוג בהם דיני המנודה וכו׳· ועוד
נוסף שסופר הקהל ע״פי גזר דין של וועד הכללי של הזקנים פרסם אותם וקרא
את שמותם א׳ לא׳ שפרצו ועברו ההסכמה של קהל No. 1 באופן שהסכמה כזו
בנד״ד אלים כחה שאפילו יבואו הקהל להתירה צריך התרה והעוברים עליה
צריכים התרה גמורה ממה שפסק מר״ן סי׳ רכ״ח ס״ן לשון מסופק בהסכמה

A collection of letters against reform, Altona אלה דברי הברית [1]
(1819).

נלכד מיד· = *Incurre logo* [2]

וכו׳ ורמ״א כתב וכן בשאר דברים וכו׳ באופן שאין לנו לזוז מלשון ההסכמה
שלנו ומאותה שעה והרגע שהתחילו להתפלל במנין כבר חל עליהם החרם כמו
שמפורש (אינקורי לוגו) נלכד מיד· ועוד שבאסיפת הקהל ט״ז חשון תל״ח
כתוב וז״ל גמרו לקיים ההסכמה ועוד הוסיפו וכו׳ והכונה שאין לזוז ממנה וכו׳
ולהחזיק במעוז ההסכמה הראשונה שכבר נלכד בחרם· ומה שהביא
החולק מפסק מרן סי׳ רכ״ח סעי׳ כ״ה נדרים וחרמים המטילים הקהל וכו׳
אינו ענין לנד״ד דשם מיירי ובא לאשמועינן שלא מקרי על דעת רבים שאין
להם התרה כלל אלא על דעתם בשאלת חרם אלא כשבאין להתיר אותן
החרמים וכו׳ אבל לעולם צריך שיתירו וכגון החרם שקבלו אחי יוסף כמו
שהביאו הפוסקים אבל אחד שעבר על ההסכמה מאין הרגלים שיהיה נפטר
בלא התרה כיון שההסכמה באותה שעה במקומה היתה עומדת: ומה שרצה
החולק לטעון שכיון שבעת הותרה הס לאילו הותרה הס להזכיר ואפילו הצבור
כשבאין להתיר לעצמן אינו אלא מכאן ולהבא אבל לא על מה שעבר כמו
שפסק בסעי׳ כ״ו והלכה למעשה הביאו רבני חברון בשו״ת מים רבים חלק
י״ד מי׳ ס״ב וכו׳ ומצאתי הון לי להנשר הגדול הרש״בץ בחלק א׳ בענין כ״ג
שם שמחלק בהסכמות בפרט החרם בלשון שהוא העתקת לשון הלעז וכו׳ עי״ש
א״כ מפורש יוצא בנד״ד ע״פי לשון ההסכמה שלנו שתיכף ומיד שעברו הרי
הם מוחרמים שהרי כתוב (אינקורי לוגי)· והבל יהמיון העוברים לחשוב
מחשבות שהחרם הותר להם· ומה שהביא החולק דחרמי צבור אינו צריך
וכו׳ אבל התרה צריך והלבוש שם כתב: אין נדרי צבור נתרים אלא מכאן
ולהבא ולא על מה שעבר כלומר דצריך תשובה על מה שעבר· ואם יאמר
האומר דאכתי יש מקום להצלת העבריינים מן החרם דפליגי אי חרם חל קודם
וכו׳ כבר העלו רובא דרובא דפוסקים ראשונים ואחרונים דחרם הוי דאורייתא
וספיקא לחומרא עיין בכנה״ג הגהת הר״בי ובשו״ת חנוך בית יהודה סי׳ ק״ב
ועוד כתב הרב מוהרח״ש סי׳ י״ח וי״ט דחרמי צבור הוו דאורייתא לכ״ע ויש
להחמיר וכו׳ וכמו שהעלה הר״ן בסי׳ ס״ב ותצא דינא דהתרא ודאי צריך אלא
דלא בעי לא פתח ולא חרטה שכתב התו׳ שבועות דף כ״ט ומה״ט ריק שורש
נ״א ע״ש·

איכו השתא עליכם אישים אקרא אשא עיני אל ההרים הרמים אולי יוכלון
למצא תרופה ומזור לעוברים ובפרט ליחידי קהילתנו הצועקים ואומרים הבה
לנו עזרה מצר שרוצים להסיר החרם מעל העוברים יען וביען אינם יכולים
לעמוד בדבר הזה כיון שמחמת הכרח הזמנים וקרוב דעת שמתקרבים עמהם
הם הולכים לבתיהם והם אינם רוצים שיהיו מכשול להם· אם יסכימו עמי בעלי
ההוראה דהינו להתיר החרם מעל העוברים אף אם אינם רוצים לבוא לפני
בית דין להתיר מפני הבושה היותם מגדולי ונכבדי ארץ והוא שיהיו ג׳ דודאי
לא היו במעמד ההסכמה ויתירו החרם מעל חמוחרמים העבריינים ויבערו הרע
מקרבם ובודאי דג׳ הדיוטות סגי כמ״ש התוספות בשבועות כ״ט ואי איתרמויי
איתרמי דיש איזה ת״ח אז הדבר יותר הגון דהחכם עוקר הנדר מעיקרו וסגי
גם לשעבר כמ״ש הרא״ש בתשובה כלל ז׳ ס״ד וז״ל חכם עוקר הנדר מעיקרו

וכשיתירו את החרם כאילו לא היה חרם לעולם ואין זה סותר למ״ש הרשב״א
בסי׳ תרצ׳ה דאין חרמי צבור נתרים למפרע וכו׳ וזה מיירי כשהצבור מתירין
לעצמם החרם אבל אם ת״ח אחר מתיר למוחרם לא גרע משאר התרות דהחכם
עוקר הנדר מעיקרו אף למפרע וכן יש לדייק מדברי הש״ך בס׳ רכ״ח עמ״ש
הש״ע דחרמי צבור וכו׳ כלומר אינו כשאר הנדרים וכו׳ נ״ל דהכא אינו עוקר
הנדר מעיקרו לפי שמתירים לעצמן הא אם יתיר החכם לאיזה מוחרם עוקר
הנדר מעיקרו וכו׳: ויכריזו בבה״כ הגדולה שהותר החרם הותר החרם ושום
אדם לא יהיה לבו נוקפו להיות נלכד בעונשו וסגי בהכי או דלמא בעינן שהם
ישאלו לעצמם או על ידי שליח לכם הגבורים משפט הברירה הדרך הנקל
להקל מעליהם את עוונם מה שיהיה יותר ראוי והגון לעשות ובטלה דעתי אצל
הגדולים ממני והריני מקבל עלי בראיות ברורות והיו למאורות ואיני אלא
כמזכיר מ״ש הרמ״א סוף סי׳ של״ד נהגו להקל מלמחות בעוברי עברה וכו׳
וכתב עליו הט״ז גדולה מזו וכו׳ דשמא ימנענו מלעשות תשובה כ״ש שבדורנו
וכו׳ ועתה אורי ישראל אורים גדולים לתשובתכם הנישאה אני מצפה להאיר
עינינו במאור תורתכם· ומכאן כי בהתרת חרם הסכמת הקהל להם אין ההתר
כ״א בזאת, אך לענין צרוף לכל דבר שבקדושה עודם באיסורם עומדים עד
אשר ישובו מעוונם ויבואו לפנינו ויחרטו על מה שעשו והאל בוחן לבות וכליות
יחיש את לב העוברים להיות מן השבים· אלה דברי דוד המתאבק בעפר רגלי
החכמים כו׳·ח ביום ז׳ לחדש אב שנת ודרשת והגידו לך אֵת דבּר לפ״ק המשפט
פה לונדון הבירה דוד בן כמו׳ הרר רפאל מילדולה ז״ל ס״ט העומד לשרת
בקודש בק״ק ספרדים יע״א·

Document 2: Letter of Ghirundi to Meldola קבוצת כסף 606,
Montefiore MS. No. 164.

לכבוד ידידי האלוף המרומם בחכמה בתבונה ובדעת הרב הכולל בן גדולי
ישראל כמהר״ר דוד מילדולה נר״ו יה״ל· עד בנין המקדש וההראלי·
קשר ברית אהבתו המתקיים מחדש בפסק דינו ועמו שבועה הביאני בעבותות
חדשות לקשר את נפשי מעדנות לשנות עולמים ומה הימים הראשונים ברצון
אף האחרונים כן אמור מעתה כי מכאן ולהבא יתד היא שלא תמוט בקשר אהבת
דוד ויהונתן אהבת התורה להעמידה על תלה כדין וכשורה ביראת ה׳ טהורה
עומדת לעד:
ראיתי בהשקפה לטובה את כל אשר שרטט וכתב בפסק דינו הבהיר על ענין
ההסכמה הידועה אשר קבלו עליהם יחידי סגולה מימי קדם קדמתה בגזרת
נח״ש שלא יוכל שום אדם לבנות בה״כ חדש בעיר לונדריש מלבד בית מקדש
הנקרא שער השמים וכו׳ ככתוב בשאלה· וארי נעשה שואל אם ההתרה שעשו
החכמים בהסכמת שני שלישים מהועד בשנת תר״ג לאנשים יראי ה׳
והחרדים אל דברו לבנות בה״כ אחרת (כי אין להם המקום בבה״כ הראשונה
או רחוקים ממנה) היא שייכה גם לעברינים אשר בלתי התרה חלפו תורות עברו

חוק הפרו ברית עולם לבנות להם בית תְּפָלָה ושלחו יד בנוסח התפלות שתקנו
להם אנשי כנה"ג ובטלו יום טוב שני וכו' לזה אשיב שיפה אמר חנ"ן מ"ר שיחיה
דוד בשתים ועלתה לו הלכה ברורה דאין התרה חלה לשעבר והעוברים
נלכדים בחרם כדפסק מרן י"ד סי' רכ"ח דין כ"ה וכ"ו ומטו לה משם
הרשב"א דאין נדרי צבור נתרים אלא מכאן ולהבא אבל לא לשעבר וכתב
מהר"שדם בח"מ סי' קנ"ג בשם מהר"ד ך שם שחל החרם על הדבר המוכתב
במפורש חל גם כן על הנוסף מאומד הדעת עש"ב באופן שהדין עם טוב העיר
כשפרסמו שם העברינים שבנו להם בית חדש להתפלל בו בלתי רשות והסכמת
שני שלישים מהועד כללי וטעמם ונמוקם עמם כי העברינים הללו נלכדו
בחרם ומיד שהתחילו ומה גם אחר שהתמידו להתפלל בבה"כ שלהם
אחר ההתרה כמש"כ הרב הפוסק והדין עמו גם במה שהשיג על החכם
המערער שעלה בדעתו להפוך בזכות העברינים אחר שגם הוא נמנה בבית
דין הצדק של הרב הפוסק לאסור עתה שינה בדיבורו ונהפך לאחר כאלישע
בן אבויה וקרו ליה יוסי שריא להתיר להתפלל בתוככי כנסיה שלא לשם שמים
כבית תְּפָלָה שלהם· ומה שעבר בדעת החולק להסתייע מפסק מרן סי' רכ"ח
דין כ"ה מלבד שהשיב לו הרב הפוסק בשם רבני חברון והרשב"ץ ואחריני
טובא אפשר להוסיף ולהזכיר לו מה שכתב הרשד"ם י"ד סי' קמ"ז וז"ל ק"ק
שהסכימו שלא יצא איש לבית הכנסת אחרת ויחיד עבר וטען טענה וכו' אין
בדבריו כלום עד כאן לשונו והשתא אתיא במכ"ש והיה אסור לבנות בה"כ
אחרת בלתי רשות שני שלישים מיחידי הועד של בה"כ הישנה והרב הפוסק
יכול לאמור לאותו החכם החולק כדאמר רבי שמעון בן יוחאי ליהודה בן גרים
אילמלא לא היית עמנו ולא נמנת עמנו יפה אתה אומר עכשיו שהיית עמנו ונמנת
עמנו יאמרו זונות מפרכסות זו את זו ת"ח לא כ"ש? ומכירו הייתי לשעבר
להחולק על האמת ואם זיינו עליו ספר יחוסו כאן במדינתנו וידענו מי הוא בעל
דברים· ובמקום שיש חלול השם אין חולקים כבוד· והנני מתפלא איך לא ירא
לנפשו לתת יד לפושעים ולהכנס בעובי הקורה של החרם חמור ונורא שהוטל
מכמה גדולי ישראל שהזכיר הרב הפוסק במכתבו הראשון על העובר על
ההסכמה ועושה עצמו כאילו אינו יודע דחרמי צבור הוי דאורייתא לכ"ע ויש
להחמיר· ומובטחני שאם מע'כת ירבה עליו רעים אוהביו יטה אזן לדברי
חכמים יראי שמים ויוקי אמורא עליה ויאמר לפני העברינים דברים שדרשתי
לפניכם טעות היה בדמיוני והנני חוזר מסברתי האחרונה וקים לי כסברתי
הראשונה באופן שאסור לכם להתפלל בבה"כ החדשה אפילו כנוסח אנשי
כנה"ג ככל קהל ועדה בישראל עד אשר תלכו לשאול התרה ממעלת רבני
הספרדים ומעלת שרי הועד של בה"כ שער השמים:

אמנם כדי שלא לנעל דלת דלת בפני השבים נאה ויאה סברת מע' הרב הפוסק
להסיר החרם מעל העוברים אף אם לא יבואו לפני בית דין לשאול התרה
מפני הבושה על ידי שלושה (אפילו הדיוטות) שלא נמצאו במעמד ההסכמה
וזה על פי הוראת הרמ"א והרב ט"ז (הזכירם לטובה הרב הפוסק נר"ו) כדי
שלא ימנעו לעשות תשובה כל שכן בדורנו שאין התורה חביבה כל כך חיובה

רמיא עלן למעבד כל טצדקי דאית בידנא לבטולי נדרי אסורי וחרמי דקיימו
עליהון דורות הראשונים כדי להסיר מדורות האחרונים חומר אסור החרם
ובפרט בנדון דידן לפתוח דרכי תשובה להאנשים המבקשים לחסות תחת צל
כנפי האמונה האמיתית ואיש על מקומו יבא בשלום ובמישור לשפוך שיחו לפני
ה' הקרוב לכל קוראיו לכל אשר יקראוהו באמת כפי נוסח התפלות אשר
קבלנו מרבותינו אנשי כנסת הגדולה ולא כפי דעת העוברים חדשים מקרוב
באו המבקשים לפרוק מעליהם עול תורה ומלכות שמים ולבטל יום טוב שני
ח"ו לא כאלה חלק יעקב· אמנם חובה עלינו לקדם פניהם בדברי שלום ואמת
באמור להם אחינו אתם, אחינו אתם, אחינו אתם, ולבקרם בביתם ולקבלם
בביתינו אולי ישובו לדברי חכמי האמת והצדק להתפלל כנוסח הקדום ולשמור
את יום טוב שני ואז יצטרפו לכל דבר שבקדושה כדברי דוד האחרונים מעלת
הרב הפוסק נר"ו דוד בכל דרכיו משכיל וה' עמו והלכה כמותו טעמו ונמוקו
עמו ויפה אמר חנ"ן לקרב את עם מרוחקים כשגם שלא יבואו לשאול התרה
בפני ב"ד אפילו ע"י ג' הדיוטות כמ"ש התוספות בשבועות דף כ"ט· והרי זה
דומה למאי דפסק הרב המופלא מוהר"י ששפורטש ז"ל (הוא בעל ההסכמה
הראשונה) בשו"ת אהל יעקב סי' י"ו וז"ל ואם ההסכמה שהסכימו שלא יוכל
שום יחיד להחלק לעשות בה"כ בבית אחר בלתי רשות והסכמת הקהל או רובו
יכולים ההחכמים יצ"ו בהסכמת בני קהילותם הרבים לבטלה וכו' אם כן
כשיסכימו רוב הקהילות לעשות יותר או פחות או לבטלה לגמרי יכולים הם
לבטל תקנתם כפי אשר יראה להם ואע"פ שק"ק ספרדים הם כעיר בפני
עצמה בעניינים אחרים בזה הם שוים לשאר הקהילות של בני העיר והולכים
אחר הרוב עד כאן לשון הרב ז"ל לעניינינו דון מינה ואוקי באתרין דהרב הגדול
מוהר"ר יעקב ששפורטש ז"ל הוא הראשון שחתם ההסכמה והתקנה שהושמה
בק"ק לונדריש לאסור לפתוח בה"כ אחרת ואיהו מארי דשמעתתא נמי מצא לה
פתח התר באופן המבואר בתשובתו הנזכרת והוא תנא רבא דמסייע לך
להסכים בכל תוקף עם מעלת הרב בכולל מוהר"ר דוד מילדולה והרב
הכולל מוהר"ר אברהם חלואה חבירו בתורה ויראת שמים שניהם כאחד טובים
משכילים יזהירו כזוהר הרקיע מצדיקי הרבים ככוכבים לעולם ועד·

נאם העומד על התורה ועל העבודה להכין אותה ולסעדה במשפט ובצדקה

בספר חוקה פה פאדובה כו"ח ביום אך טוב לחדש רחמים לסדר ולשנת למען
ישמעו ולמען ילמדו ויִרא את ה' אלוקכם ושמרו לעשות את כל דברי הַתּוֹרָה
הזאֹת לפרט גדול

הצ' מרדכי שמואל גירונדי ס"ט

Document 3: Approbation of Judah Pereira, קבוצת כסף 607,
Montefiore MS. No. 164.

כי אראה מראות אלהים והנה מלאכי אלוהים עליונים עולים למעלה מן
הארש ארש ערבה בדין עירובא ערב רב עלה משם לבנות עיר ערוכה בכל

ושמורה, הראשון אדם הרב הכולל בישראל להלל אין גומרים עליו את הלל
עד דוד הגדיל עצה הפליא תושיה פתח טוב פתח להאי פרשתא בכחו דהיתרא
רב שריא· ואחריו התמיך על ידו שני מקודש נהדר לו תואר ולו הדר ההוד לנו
הרב המובהק ונוגה לו ברק זהיר שם גירונדי נר״ו יאיר וזרח זרח רב זהיר
חמה ברה כיר״א והוא צוה לי הכי לשנות פרק זה בשימת עין עיני שכלי המעט
להיות כדל מסכים על הדין ועל האמת בשלום ובמשפט זאת חוקת התורה·
אי לזאת איני אלא מן המתמיהין משונה ביאה זו אחרי מי יצא מלך ישראל לא
מצינו מעולם גדול נתלה בקטן קטן קטני עבה כתותי מכתא שיעורא· זאת ועוד
כי לנעמי מודע דבחוסר אנן מחוסר ספרים ואין אומן בלא כלים[זכר׳ להיותי
הולך סובב מדלג על הערים גולה ומטולטל טילטול דגברא בשליחותייהו
דתקיפי מעוב״י¹ שאראי על דברי הבצרות לשכולות מרובות רבו משערות
מעלילות ברשע ברשעת הגויים האלה, גונדא דתועה נפיש שערא ולאיש אשר
אלה לו איך יעמוד בסוד קדושים ואלים תרשישים לדבר דבר לא חצי דבר
בנפש עצובה ורוח נשברה כלי הדיבר ניטל ממני ותסר דבורה· אך אמנם יען
דבורה הקל ממשיחא היא גופא עלי גזרה כן אשנה פרק זה בעמוד ואחזור
בעז״ה עליה בחזרתי אל תוך אהלי ויריעות משכונותי אהלה של תורה· והשתא
הכא סמכינן אחזקתא גדלה חזקתו של חבר כמני״ר שאינו יוצא מתחת ידו דבר
שאינו מתוקן ובריא עדיף כשמשא בטיהרא שיפה דן יפה גבר הורה· ואכן לשים
קנצי למילין לצד עילאה תוס׳ פרי כלפי ליא אלף עולות יעלה שלומו וטובתו
בהני ברכי דרבנן במותב רב חייא ורב חזנא ורב סמוכין מן התורה כתנ״ה·²
והתורה וכתנ״א³ הכו״ח פה עי״ת פדובה יע״א בה׳ לחג ה״ק הזה זמן שמחתנו
אם אתן שנת תרכ״ו לפי״ק הכ״ד איש צעיר המשתלת רב זעירה אפר
כירה יאודה פיריה ס״ט·

Document 4: Approbation of Aryeh Ascoli, קבוצת כסף 608, Montefiore MS. No. 164.

בהיותי פה העיר המהוללה פאדובה יע״א במדרש מנהל של הרבנים ומריה
דאתרא ה״ה מע׳ מורינו הרב מרדכי שמואל גירונדי נר״ו הראני את בית נכותו
ספרים נכבדים ויקרים ובתוכם שו״ת קבוצת כסף ה״ה פסקים על ענינים
שונים גלילי ידיו הקדושים ובהיות שצווני וזרזני בקריאתה זו היא הלילה תשובתו
הרמתה על ענין הבהכ״נ החדש שבנו בעיר לונדרוס מלבד בה״כ אחר של
הק״ק אחרי שיש להם הסכמה משנים קדמוניות בגזרת נחש שלא יוכלו להוסיף
בתי כנסיות אם לא מדעת שני־שלישי הועד הלא ארשו ארש ברזל ואין צורך
להוסיף בראיות על דבריו מי לא יודה שהרב הנ״ל הוא בקי בחדרי התורה
וידבר אמר מנופה בי״ג נפה ויהיו דברי אך למחסור יען מי שלמד בגמרא

¹ מעיר ואם בישראל·
² כתאות נפשו הטהורה·
³ וכתאות נפש אוהבו·

והפוסקים יודע היטב שהדין דין אמת ואני הצעיר מסכים עמו כיהודא ועוד
לקרא·

פה פאדובה ב״ך יברך לחדש רחמים שנת התר״ז הכ׳ אריה אסקולי העומד
על התורה ועל העבודה בק״ק רוויגו·

Document 5: Extracts from the Responsum of Chajes in
קבוצת כסף 609, Montefiore MS [1] No. 164.

יום ב׳ ח׳ מרחשון ה׳ יוסיף לו עושר וכבוד לפ״ק זאלקוא כבוד ידידי כנפשי
ומאדי ה״ה הרב הגדול המפורסם החכם השלם מוכתר בכתר שם טוב בתורה
ובירואה ובכל מידות שמנו חכמים מהולל בשער בת רבים לשם ולתהילה
כש״ת מו״ח מרדכי שמואל גרונדי האב״ד פאדווא יצ״ו

יקרתו הגיעני זה ערך עשרים יום ומפני הטרדות העמוסות על שכמי בימים
הקדושים לא יכולתי לשים עין עיוני על דבריו ועל דברי הרב מלונדון· ואולם
עתה באתי בקצרה ע״ד השאלה אשר ערך אל רו״מ בדין פרצות הגדרות
בעדת הספרדים אשר בלונדון הבירה···········

ומה שטען החולק [2] כיון דקי״״ל ביו״ד סי׳ רכ״ט דחרמי צבור אין צריכין
פתח וחרטה ה״ה דהקילו גם לענין זה דאין החוב מוטל על כל העם לנהוג עם
העוברים כמנודה, הנה עקם לנו את הישרות דהרי מפורש במקומו דרק סתח
וחרטה אין צריך אבל התרה עכ״פ בעינן וע׳ במשפט החרם להרמ״בן דמן
הדין גם חרמי צבור צריכין פתח וחרטה ועל ידי חכם דוקא, אבל כיון שכבר
נהגו בהתרה לבד י״״ל שע״ד המנהג הותנו כהאי דר׳ פנחס (שבת פ׳ כירה) כל
הנודרת ע״ד בעלה נודרת, ה״״נ כל המתקנים ע״ד הנהגת העם מתקנים עכ״״ל
ובנ״ד כיון דבשנת תר״ב לא היתה התרה להההסכמה אדרבא ראינו כי התאמצו
בכל עוז להשאיר אותה בתקפה בשיטא דכל חומר מוחרם על העוברים דהיכי
דהוכרז בפירוש כמו בענין שלפנינו אין כאן שום קולא מצד מנהג הקהלות
כלל··········

ומה דפשט להרב הפוסק דיש תקנה להתיר ע״י ג׳ הדיוטות ג״כ הנה נעלם
ממנו גמרא ערוכה (בכורות ל״ז ע״א) מובא בש״ע יו״ד ס׳ רכ״ח סע׳ א׳
דדוקא במקום דליכא מומחין סגי בג׳ הדיוטות ובעיר הבירה לונדון בלי ספק
נמצאו הרבה חכמים ובכה״ג אינו מועיל שאלה ע״י ג׳ הדיוטות: וע׳ שו״ת
חות יאיר ס׳ קכ״ט בארוכות לענין זה אע״ג דאמרינן (שבת פ׳ כירה דף [מ׳
ע״ב] קדושין דף נ״ט ע״ב) מי יימר דמזדקיק לי׳ חכם דאין החוב על החכמים
להיותם נדרשים לאלו אשר באים אליהם לשאול על נדרם, בכ״ז בנ״ד אשר
העם עוברים בכל רגע על איסור במה שמתערבים עם העוברים והולכים אל

---

[1] The extracts reproduced hereunder consist of material not covered
by the printed version of Chajes' reply to Meldola in his volume of
Responsa, 46.

[2] Abraham Belais.

בתיהם ומדברים עמהם ואין אפשרות לעמוד באיסור זה כבר מבואר ביו״ד
ס׳ רכ״ח סע׳ ט״ו ברמ״א דאע״פ שאין מתירין נדר של איסור בכ״ז אם יש
מכשול בנדר זה כגון שיש לחוש שיעבור בלי התרה ה״ז מתירין לכתחילה ומכ״ש
היכי דרבים עוברים בכל רגע על האיסור אזי גם נשאלין לכתחילה להתיר
החרם והחכם מצוה רבה עביד במה שמציל את העם במכשול עון.......... [1]

Document 6: Extracts from Letter of Ghirundi to Meldola in דובר שלום by Ghirundi, 1776, Montefiore MS No. 172.

אגרת שלומים שכתבתי על ידי אהרן מריני להרב דוד מילדולא מ״ץ
בלונדרש עם ספר קנאות, ומחברת ירושלים·

נהר יוצא מעדן מסיר הצער ומעדן הבשר נהר פלגיו ישמחו כל הקרוב
הקרוב אליו תוככי משכן שלו ומקבלו בסבר פנים יפות כנגיד ושר נהר דעה
והשכל דבריו ומשפט מכלכל, מעלת הרב החכם הכולל עניו כהלל הדר הוא
ידידי ואוהבי כמהור״ר דוד מילדולא, נר״ו..........

זאת תהי לי לעדה כי עודני עומד באהבתו בשגם כי האדון סגר עלי הדיבור
בארבע שנים והלאה ולא השיב לשתי אגרותי הארוכות שכתבתי לו אחת ביום
כ״א לחדש אלול התר״ז ואחרת ביום כ״א בחדש שבט התר״ח כללות ארבע
פסקי דינים לאשר ולקיים הוראת כת״ר על ענין ההסכמה הידועה אשר נהיית
במחנה קדשינו ולעשות סמוכין דרבנן לפסק דינו ולהורות כי יפה דן יפה הורה
לקרב את המרוחקים בהתרה גמורה לבא בקהל עדתו באהבה אחוה שלום
ורעות בתוך העדה כולם קדושים ויזכה להחזירם בתשובה לעבוד את ה׳
בקדושה ובטהרה..........

מובטחני שהאדון מצא בתוך אגרתי כא׳ כסלו תר״ח שני פסקים מהרבנים
מהור״ר צבי הירש חיות ומהור״ר יהודא פיריררה נ״י שהסכימו עם מעלת
כבוד תורתו בנידון ההסכמה הידועה ושם היה כמוסה אגרת מכתיבת יד קדוש
הרב זקנו מהור״ר יהודא מילדולא זלה״ה ולא ידעתי הטעם שהאדון לא כבדני
בתשובתו הרמתה בשגם שכתבתי לו שנית· על המצפה אעמודה לקבל בשרורותיו
הטובות ע״י הבי דוה״ר עם סיפור ארוך ממצב הקהלות ומצב כת החדשה
שצמחה בעירו ואם השלימו הקהילות זה אם זה ואם האפיקורסים שבו לדעת
האמת ולתקנות רבותינו, ועל הכל חפץ אני שישלח אלי סדר תפילות ומחזור
שהדפיסה הכת החדשה לומר בבה״כ שלה בספר חוקיה ומנהגיה שראיתי ביד
חכם אחד עובר ושב כאשר נדפסה בלונדון..........

מוהר״ץ הירש חיות פקד עלי לדרוש שלמו וטובתו וה׳ אלודי ישראל
יצליחהו בלימודיו ויזכהו לעמוד ולשרת הקודש ימים רבים ושנים ארכים
ולראות בנים סמוכים על שולחנו ולברך ברוך שהשמחה במעונו·

פאדובא עש״ק ראש חדש אלול, שוש אשיש בה׳

---

[1] For the rest of Chajes' arguments *see* his *Responsa*, 46.

HOME RITUALS AND THE SPANISH SYNAGOGUE

By Solomon B. Freehof

Rodef Shalom Temple, Pittsburgh

In honor of the seventieth birthday of Abraham A. Neuman, whose monumental history of the Jews of Spain will long be greatly valued, the author dedicates the following article on some aspects of the religio-cultural life of the Jews of Spain.

The well-known statement of Moses of Coucy concerning the observance of the mizwoth among Spanish Jews, has considerable religio-cultural implications. He says that in the year 4996 (1235) he was in Spain to "reprove the people" and that God gave him strength, so that as a result of his preaching "thousands and tens of thousands took upon themselves to observe the commandments of *tefillin, mezuzoth* and *zizith*." (*Semag*, Positive Commandments, end of § 3)

If, then, because of his preachments tens of thousands resolved henceforth to observe the commandments mentioned, then there were vast numbers of Jews in Spain who hitherto had not observed these commandments; and "tens of thousands" of those who did not hear him preach remained, for a time at least, non-observant.

Moses of Coucy is not the only witness to a widespread neglect of ritual observance in Spain. Jonah Gerondi, the Spanish moralist, was a contemporary of Moses of Coucy. He died in Toledo in 1263. In his books, *Shaare teshuba* and *Sefer ha-yirah*, he rebukes the people for the neglect of the commandments. While due to his moralistic purposes he may be somewhat overstressing the neglect, nevertheless he is frequently quite specific as to the commandments which are neglected. In *Shaare teshuba*, Chapter 3, §8 (all references are to the Mesivta edition, New York City, 1943) he says,

"You will see men mocking the commandment of washing the hands, and sit down to eat without blessing before the meal or after the meal." Chapter 3, §27: "There are many kinds of Sabbath works which some of the people are not careful about because they know nothing about them." Chapter 3, §76: "Some are not careful with making meat kosher by salting." In his *Sefer ha-yirah*, p. 8, he warns the people not to eat without a blessing and he adds: "If one is not able to recite the blessing, let him go to someone who knows in order to learn."

Joseph b. Todros Halevi, in his letters published in Kobak's *Jeshurun* (vol. viii, p. 37) attacks those who "treat holy things as profane and consider themselves free of prayer and *tefillin*." Isaac bar Sheshes (Responsa § 447) speaks of many who mock the rabbinical laws of *terefah*.

This neglect of commandments was not restricted to Spain. Moses of Coucy (*loc. cit.*) says, "And so it was in other lands." Meir of Rothenburg, in his Responsa (ed. Cermona §108) discusses with his correspondent the question of rebuking people who do not observe the commandment of *mezuzah* because they believe that only the man who actually owns a house is commanded to affix the *mezuzah*, but not one who merely rents a house or rooms. In the course of his responsum he cites a statement of Rabbenu Tam, "For the last ten years there has not been a *mezuzah* in the entire kingdom." Rabbenu Tam adds that this complete neglect should not be considered as constituting a valid *minhag*, but that people should be told that they *should* affix a *mezuzah*.

Also in his responsa (ed. Prague, Budapest, § 649) Meir speaks of those who do not put on *tefillin*, and he again quotes Rabbenu Tam who refers to those who mock the commandment of *tefillin* and ask scornfully:- "What do these straps avail?" In his responsa (ed. Lemberg, §223), Meir of Rothenburg quotes Judah b. Barzilai who refers to the neglect of *tefillin* in these words: "Even in the time of prayer most people (*ruba de-alma*) sin against this commandment."

Posnanski in his Preface (p. lxix) to the commentary of Eliezer of Beaugency on Ezekiel and the Minor Prophets, quotes Joseph Bechor Shor who denounces those Jews who say that to wear *tefillin* and to affix *mezuzoth* or to cover the blood after *shehitah*, are not actually commandments, but are only symbolic statements, as in the Song of Songs:- "Place me as a seal upon thy heart."

The fact that the neglect of these commandments was rife in France and Germany, as well as in Spain, indicates that this was not primarily due to philosophizing and allegorizing of the commandments. The neglect was present in lands where philosophizing hardly penetrated and is noticed as early as the time of the Tosafists. If the observance of the commandments had been well rooted in the lives of the people, it is hardly likely that the allegorizing of a few sophisticates would have effected so vast a neglect as the sources indicate.

As a matter of fact, the neglect of some of these commandments goes back at least to the time of the Geonim. The Gaon Joseph (*Ozar ha-Geonim* to Berakot, p. 41 §90) is asked whether a man who is not a great man (*gavra Rabba*) should be permitted to put on tefillin "since if he does put on *tefillin* it will appear to be false pride (*yohara*) inasmuch as the entire community does not put on *tefillin*." The Gaon answers, of course, that everybody should put on *tefillin*.

So too Sherira Gaon (*Ozar ha-Geonim*, Rosh Hashana, p. 28) is asked a similar question:- "Why do the majority of people scorn (*mezalzli*) the commandment?" He explains also that in Palestine, due to the many persecutions, the people have forgotten all about this commandment.

Michael Guttmann dealt with the questions of the neglect of the commandments in his pamphlet *Behinnat kiyyum ha-mizwoth* (Breslau, 1931), but he confines himself to the Greek (Alexandrian) period. Clearly there is need for a full study of this question going back to the *am ha-arez* of tannaitic times. Perhaps we have misjudged the significance of

this widespread non-observance. Except later in philosophi-
zing-allegorizing circles, it was not at all a *relapse* into neglect
of commandments which once had been fully observed;
rather, the fact was that full observance came later and was
the result of slow and persistent effort. The double connotation
of the word am *ha-arez* is significant. The word which at
first meant careless non-observance, "yokel," came to mean
an ignoramus. This surely hints that the growth in learning
and of observance went hand in hand; that just as the knowledge of rabbinic law slowly spread among wider and wider
circles, so did the observance of the commandments. The
latter was as great an achievement as the former. There has
been considerable investigation and writing of the ever-
widening circle of the learned, but almost none in the gradual
spread of the commandments.

This essay has for its purpose to gather some evidence of
the process of the spread of observance in Spain. There were
certain observances in Spain which were not found in the
rest of Europe. Some of these were learned from the Babylonian Gaonim and some seem to have originated in Spain.
These special observances seem to the writer to have been
motivated by the purpose of training the Jews of Spain to
observe commandments hitherto not widely observed. Other
methods of training were developed in other lands.

Morning Blessings

The Talmud in b. Berakoth 60b gives a series of short
blessings which are to be recited during the process of getting
up in the morning. When a man opens his eyes, he should
say, "Praised be Thou," etc. "Who openeth the eyes of the
blind." When he throws off the bedclothes, he says, "Praised
be Thou... "Who freest the bound." When he puts on his
garments, he says, "Praised be Thou...Who clothest the
naked," etc. These blessings are unmistakably provided
to be home ritual, to be recited at each successive stage of
the process of getting up in the morning by each individual.

These home blessings are now part of the regular prayerbook in the *birkoth ha-shahar*. How did they come into the public prayerbook when they properly belong at home? We have a clear statement as to how that happened in the great ligurgical responsum of the Gaon Amram. Early in his responsum he says that Gaon Natronai answered a question from the city of Lucena, Spain. He mentions that these various blessings are incumbent upon each individual as he rises from bed, but that it is the custom of all of Israel in Spain that the Reader in the synagogue recites them in behalf of those who do not know how to recite them. The report is given more fully in *Ha-manhig* of Ibn Yarchi, p. 7, section a. "Thus wrote Rav Amram that it is the custom of all the land of Spain in order to allow those who are not skilled to fulfill their duty, the cantor begins all the blessings with loud voice and they answer 'Amen' to each blessing." Clearly, then, the widespread custom to have these home personal blessing part of the public ritual originated in Spain, or, at least, we have no earlier reference to it with regard to any other country.

It may seem strange to us that the average Jew in Spain was not skilled enough in Hebrew to recite these simple blessings. This may well have been so; but it also must have been a fact that whatever the reason was, the rabbis were aware that these blessings which each man was obligated to recite at home were almost universally neglected and therefore to train the people into the habit of reciting them, the rabbinical authorities in Spain moved the blessings over to the synagogue and made them part of public worship. Thence it spread to other lands, and the original custom so clearly defined in the Talmud of reciting the blessings one by one at each stage of the process of getting up was never restored.

Kiddush in the Synagogue

The law (b. Pesahim 101a) is that *kiddush* should be made only in the place where the meal is eaten. However, the custom is now widespread that the *kiddush* is also recited by the cantor in synagogue. This is clearly a violation of the law of the Talmud. Rab Amram (see *Seder* of Amram, *ad. loc.*) says that *kiddush* is made in the synagogue for the sake of wayfarers who eat there. But Natronai says that we do so even though there are no wayfarers who eat there. He then explains how it can be that the wine is tasted by the congregation (which they should not do since *kiddush* should be at each man's home). He explains that the congregation is given some of the wine to place on their eyelids for the sake of healing. This is based upon the Talmud in Berakoth 43b where it is said that he who takes a haughty step loses a fraction of his eyesight; but one can restore it by means of the Friday night *kiddush*. The same responsum is given in *Ozar ha-Geonim*, Berakoth, p. 97, in the name of Natronai, and the Gaon Hai adds that they certainly *drank* the wine in the synagogue. Clearly this custom began or spread in Spain. Asher ben Yehiel (to Pesahim 101a at end), explaining how it happens that *kiddush* was instituted in the synagogue, uses virtually the same phrase which was used in explaining the Spanish custom of transferring the home morning blessings to the synagogue. He says, "Since there are people who do not know how to make *kiddush*, they establish the custom to make *kiddush* in the synagogue in order that they fulfill the duty of *kiddush* prescribed by the Torah." His son, Jacob ben Asher, in the *Tur, Orah hayyim* 269, says at the beginning of the section, "I wonder that this custom has spread," and ends the section by saying, "If I had the influence I would abolish it." Since the custom is justified by Natronai and is mentioned in the *Seder* of Amram, and since Jacob ben Asher wonders at it and would like to abolish it, it seems clear that the transference of the home ceremony of the *kiddush* on Friday night as a synagogue observance everywhere in Europe, had spread from Spain.

Unison Prayers

Asher ben Yehiel, having come from the Rhineland to Spain, frequently comments on Spanish customs, especially those of which he does not approve. In his responsa, section 4, §19, he objects to the custom of people joining with the cantor and singing the services in unison. Since it is the cantor's duty to fulfill the obligation of prayer for those members of the congregation who are not skilled in reading, it becomes the duty of the congregation, then, to listen intently to the cantor and say "Amen" after the blessings. If, however, they join in the singing with the cantor, there will not be a *minyan* of intent listeners. He ends up by saying that "those who sing along with the cantor seem to me to be acting in a light-minded way."

At all events, Asher ben Yehiel here refers to a custom which became established early in Spain, that the congregation joined in with the cantor in singing the services. This custom was referred to with admiration by Ashkenazic authorities in more recent times. Both Jacob Ettlinger and Jacob Emden, who were in Hamburg in the eighteenth to nineteenth centuries where they had opportunities to observe this Sephardi custom, refer to it approvingly. Jacob Emden in his *Siddur*, discussing the complicated customs of the Ashkenazim with regard to the selection of who shall be given the privilege of saying *Kaddish*, praises the custom of the Sephardim in that they all say it in unison and thus all disputes are removed. Jacob Ettlinger, in his responsa *Binyan Zion* (§122) refers to the custom of the Sephardim to recite in unison the entire service. He says, "For all the service of the Sephardim is in unison with equal voice without lagging behind or hurrying ahead. Therefore since they are accustomed to this unison recitation, they manage to be heard individually even though they are in harmony. Since we are not skilled, as they are in unison reading, it becomes ludicrous when we try it." He mentions this as a reason why we Ashkenazim should *not* institute the Sephardi custom. At all events, this congregational singing and recitation of both the *Kaddish* and the prayers is in consonance with the general Sephardi tradition of emphasizing the communal worship.

Cantor on the Bimah

The Sephardi custom is for the cantor to stand on the *tebah* (*bimah*) in the center of the synagogue to conduct the service. It is the Ashkenazic custom that only the Torah is recited from the central *bimah*, and the rest of the service recited by the cantor at the foot of the platform on which the Ark stands, thus fulfilling the implication of the verse, "Out of the depths I call unto the Lord." Abraham ibn Yarchi, in *Ha-manhig*, p. 19, refers to this difference of custom and explains it as follows: "It is a good custom in Spain that the cantor stands on the *tebah* (the *bimah*) in order that the entire congregation may hear the prayers, and thus he can fulfill the duty of prayer for those who are not skilled. If he did not do so, the majority of the congregation gathered there would not hear the prayers." Then Ibn Yarchi justifies this Spanish custom from the description in the Talmud (b. Sukkah 51b) of the synagogue in Alexandria where the leader stood on a platform in the center. At all events, it is clear that this custom too was derived from the fact that the public synagogue service itself was used as the prime method of training the people in worship.

Mourner Attending Synagogue

The Spanish emphasis upon the synagogue reflects itself even in the case of the mourner and his worship during *shibah*. Here, as in many of the other customs, there is some basis in Gaonic customs for a rather unusual observance in Spain. It is generally held that a mourner during *shibah* stays home during the whole week except on the Sabbath when he goes to the synagogue. Ibn Gayyat (*Shaarey Simhah*, vol.

ii, 51) quotes the Gaon Paltai to the effect that the mourner goes to the synagogue every day of the *shibah* if he does not or cannot have a *minyan* at home. Hai Gaon adds: "In Babylon everybody goes to the synagogue (everyday) except that in large cities most of them stay in their homes." Nachmanides reads this responsum more specifically to the effect that in Babylon *in the villages* they go to the synagogue every day; that is to say, in the villages where they cannot have *minyan* at home, mourners go daily to the synagogue during *shibah*.

This Babylonian village custom was carried over as a more general practice in Spain, and Ibn Gayyat says: "It is our custom from our ancient teachers to go to the synagogue (during *shibah*) and pray." So also Nachmanides in *Torath ha-Adam* (ed. Warsaw, 1840, p. 45a) quotes Ibn Gayyat as deciding that a mourner should go to the synagogue every day of *shibah*. These responsa and more are collected in *Ozar ha-Geonim*, Mashkin, p. 36. §94 ff., where there is also a quotation from *Shaareh Zedek* to the effect that in Babylon the mourners went to the synagogue every day but that are Palestine they did not do so. The law and its variations are discussed fully in *Tur, Yoreh Deah*, 393. Isaac bar Sheshes, in his responsa §158, says, that the custom varies in Spain; in Catalonia the mourners go to the synagogue only on the Sabbath, but in Saragossa they go every day to the synagogue; and, he adds, "Their custom should not be abolished."

Hanukkah Lights in the Synagogue

Abrahm ibn Yarchi, who was born and raised in the Provence, but who settled in Toledo in 1204, frequently notices the difference between his native customs and those which he met in Spain. In the *Ha-manhig*, p. 105, §148, he speaks of the duty of lighting the Hanukkah light in each house, so that the *mezuzah* should be at a man's right hand as he enters and the Hanukkah light (which they used to light at the door) should be at his left. Then he continues, "It seems

to me that there is no duty to light the Hanukkah lights
except at home where the man lives, and that the synagogue,
being free from a *mezuzah*, is also free from the Hanukkah
light unless, of course, the cantor lives there. "Nevertheless,"
he says, "the custom arose to have it in the synagogue since
the original miracle occurred in the Temple, and also since
the entire congregation gathers there." Abudraham, describing the customs of Spain (the new edition [Jerusalem
1959], p. 199) says that it is the duty of each individual to
light Hanukkah lights at the door of his house, with the
mezuzah on his right as he enters, and the Hanukkah light
on his left. Then he adds (p. 201) that the custom has been
established to have a Hanukkah light in the middle of the
synagogue and to light between *minha* and *maarib*, etc.
Thus, although all admit that the lights should be kindled
at home, it is clear that the custom of lighting the Hanukkah
lights in the synagogue arose in Spain.

Kapparoth

Apparently the slaughtering of a fowl as an atonement
for each member of the household was more a German custom
than a Spanish one. This can be seen from the responsum of
Solomon ben Aderet (volume i §395). He says that when he
found the custom had spread in his city (Barcelona), he
abolished it. "Nevertheless," he adds, "I heard from worthy
men from Germany who are with us in the school that all
the rabbis of their country follow the practice before the
Day of Atonement." Gaon Rab Sheshna is asked about the
custom (see *Ozar ha-Geonim*, Yoma, p. 62) and he says he
does not know the reason for the custom and then speculates
as to possible reasons for it. Then, giving the procedure, says
that the *shaliah* seizes the hen and places his hand upon its
head, etc., saying, "This one in place of this one." Jacob ben
Asher, who saw the procedure in Spain, makes the phrase
shaliah clearer and says the *shaliah zibbur* places his hand
upon the fowl and says, etc.

The Franco-German custom was that each householder performed this ceremony at home (*see*, for example, *Mahzor Vitry*, p. 373, at the beginning of the section on Yom Kippur). But the custom, when carried over into Spain, was moved over to the synagogue. Thus Abudraham, after saying that on the eve of the Day of Atonement "in some places it is the custom to slaughter the fowl for atonement," then quotes the same responsa of the Geonim and says also, "Thus it is the custom here; the cantor seizes the fowl and places his hand upon him and makes atonement and says, 'This one instead of this one, etc.'"

Congregational Sukkah

The Geonim Natronai and Hai (*Ozar ha-Geonim*, Sukkah, 33 ff.) say clearly that to fulfill the duty of *sukkah*, each must have a *sukkah* in his house; but that nevertheless it would be permissible to have a *sukkah* on the synagogue premises for the benefit of travellers (just as *kiddush* should be recited at home where the meal is eaten, yet is recited in the synagogue for the benefit of travellers). Therefore, if a *native* of the city makes use of a synagogue *sukkah*, it would not be a fulfillment of his duty. Then Hai Gaon says that there was a congregational *sukkah* in Bagdad.

Ibn Yarchi repeats most of these responsa in *Ha-manhig*, p. 64, and then adds, "Thus we learn from the responsum of Hai that the Spanish custom of a *sukkah* in the courtyard of the synagogue into which the members of the community come and sit, is not a proper fulfillment of the duty of the *sukkah*." In the recently published *Sefer ha-Miktam* by David bar Levi of Narbonne (ed. by Moses Blau [New York City 1959], on page 148) this Provençal scholar refers to the communal *sukkah* in Spain and mocks it as based upon an erroneous understanding of the law and, of course, as illegal. He refers to the statement in the Talmud, b. Sukkah 27b, according to which a man may fulfill his duty by borrowing another man's *sukkah*. Then the Talmud (based upon Leviticus

23: 42) says: "All Israel is able to sit in one *sukkah*." David bar Levi says, "This statement of the Talmud is misunderstood. In some places in Aragon they make a *sukkah* in the court of the synagogue and the entire congregation makes *kiddush* there and then they leave and go home and eat. This is surely," he continues, "an error of theirs." Thus again with regard to the *sukkah*, the tendency in Spain was to emphasize public communal observance, even though the law is clear that this should be a household ritual.

Congregational Seder

The twelfth-century Rhineland scholar, Eliezer ben Joel Ha-Levi (*Rabiah*, volume i, p. 179) reports that the custom in Spain and in Babylon was to have the *seder* in the synagogue. He says: "And in responsa I saw that even these days it is the custom in Spain and in Babylon that the cantor on Passover conducts the *seder* in the synagogue for the benefit of the ignorant who are unskilled in reciting the *hagadah*." Yet it is the consensus of opinion of the authorities that there should not even be *kiddush* in the synagogue on Passover evening because thus it would make five cups on Passover eve and there should be only four. There is no other reference to this statement of the *Rabiah* except a modern one in which Shemtob Gagin in *Keter Shemtob*, vol. iii, p. 106, praises this ancient custom and wishes that it still continued. There is no reason to doubt this reference of the Rhineland authority even though there is no parallel to it. It fits into the general mood of Spanish custom.

From these various indications it becomes fairly clear how the leaders of Spanish Jewry coped with the problem of building in the life of the people the habit of the fulfillment of the *mizwoth*. They used the public worship as a pedagogic instrument. Everywhere in Jewry it was chiefly the Torah reading in the synagogue which was the instrument of public instruction. Therefore it had to be read from the central *bimah* that all might hear, and emphasis was put upon close attention. But in Spain, not only the Torah reading but the entire service was read from the central *bimah* because the entire worship was used for the same pedagogic purpose. Hence also many rituals which should be fulfilled by the individual and in the home were carried over into the synagogue where they could be taught to the people until the custom of individual worship might become established. So it was with the simple blessings to be recited at home on arising, so it was with the *kiddush,* so it was with the joint recitation of the service, and so with the *sukkah,* with the *seder,* and so it was even in the case of mourners worshipping in the synagogue during *shibah.*

This method of using the public worship pedagogically was evidently not the one followed in the Rhineland. There the habit of the fulfillment of the commandments was inculcated not publicly but one might say privately and individually. Honored rabbis adopted strict observances in their own lives and their various observances were recorded by their disciples. Thus people were guided by their admiration of saints and scholars. There are no such books published by Spanish Jewry recording the individual scrupulous observances of famous rabbis as were written in the Rhineland. Generally when references are made to certain debatable customs, if the reference is to a Spanish scholar, it will be "So Rabbi So-and-So said," but if the reference is to an Ashkenazic scholar, it is more likely to be "So Rabbi So-and-So *did.*" In the Rhineland it was the piety in the personal life of the individual saint, in Spain it was the unison worship of the community which trained the people to the observance of the commandments.

SAMARITAN PROVERBS

By Theodor H. Gaster
Dropsie College and Fairleigh Dickinson University

THE FOLLOWING COLLECTION of proverbs current among
the Samaritans was made, in 1938, by Ab Ḥasdâ (Abul-
Ḥasan), son of the former high priest, Jacob ben Aaron (1840-
1918). It is contained in Cod. Gaster 2051, now in the John
Rylands Library at Manchester, England.

Most of the entries are simply clever translations of familiar
Arabic sayings, reproducing the characteristic assonance and
often also the plays on words. In the manuscript, the Arabic
original is actually given (in Samaritan characters) in an
adjoining column, and this usually accords with one or another of the forms registered in the standard compilations
of Freytag, [1] ʿAbbûd-Thilo, [2] Haefeli, [3] Bauer, [4] Socin, [5] Ben
Cheneb, [6] and Goitein. [7] Some, however — e.ǵ., No. 52 (which
is a quotation from Deuteronomy 13: 18); No. 68 (with its
mention of הכהנים בני לוי); No. 79 (with its reference to
הר ספרה, i.e., Mt. Gerizim); and Nos. 40, 93, 97 (where God
is called יהוה rather than אלה, as elsewhere)—would seem to
be of native Samaritan origin, and in such cases it is, of
course, the adjoining Arabic version that is the translation.
One proverb (No. 49) recurs in substantially the same form

[1] G. W. Freytag, *Arabum Proverbia* (Bonn 1838-43).
[2] S. ʿAbbûd and M. Thilo, 5000 *Sprichwörter aus Palästina* (Berlin
1933, 1937).
[3] L. Haefeli, *Spruchweisheit und Volksleben in Palästina* (Lucerne
1939).
[4] L. Bauer, „Sprichwörter und Rätsel," ch. 29 of his *Volksleben
im Lande der Bibel* (Leipzig 1903).
[5] A. Socin, *Arabische Sprichwörter und Redensarten* (Tübingen
1878).
[6] M. Ben Cheneb, *Proverbes arabes* (Paris 1905).
[7] S.D.F. Goitein, *Jemenica: Arabische Sprichwörter und Redensarten
aus Zentral-Jemen* (Leipzig 1934).

in Sirach 20: 31 (not in the Genizah Hebrew text); another (No. 27) is virtually identical with Proverbs 25: 17 (though the actual language differs); while a third (No. 38) reproduces Proverbs 21: 19 with a verbal variation. These parallels may, of course, be mere coincidences; in any case, the proverbs in question must have percolated to the Samaritans through secondary sources, for neither Sirach nor the biblical Book of Proverbs is known to them.

In transcribing the text I have subjoined to it cross-references to the aforementioned standard collections, though no claim is made that these are exhaustive.

The notes are designed simply to facilitate reading by those unfamiliar with Samaritan dialect and grammar. In the case of unusual words, I have duly cited the Arabic equivalent as it is given in the manuscript, and have occasionally added illustrative material from other Samaritan sources—principally, the Samaritan Targum to the Pentateuch, the writings of Marqeh (4th cent. C.E.), and the Liturgy. [1] I am indebted to Ab Ḥasdâ—my father's and then my own friend for many years—for supplying me (in private correspondence) with his explanations of some of the more obscure phrases. These have been incorporated in the notes.

It is a special pleasure to offer this study as a small tribute of esteem and appreciation to a scholar and friend who is himself no mean master of the דָּבָר דָּבָר עַל־אָפְנָיו.

---

[1] *Abbreviations*: Cowley = *The Samaritan Liturgy*, ed. A. E. Cowley. 2 vols. Oxford 1909. Marqeh = *Der Commentar Marqahs des Samaritaners* [extracts from the ספר פליאתה], ed. M. Heidenheim = *Bibliotheca Samaritana* III. Weimar 1896 (cited by the folio of the MS. as given in the margin). TS = *Das Samaritanische Targum zum Pentateuch*, ed. A. Brill, Frankfurt a. M. 1874-79.

(I am fully conscious of the inadequacies of Heidenheim's edition of Marqeh, but for many portions of the text it is the only published source available. Moreover, I have duly collated his readings with MSS. for my own forthcoming edition.)

Cod. Gaster 2051

1 לא תאמר לגנא גנא
ותעדף גנא

2 דחל מן לשנך
רב מן דחלתך מן סנך [1]

3 האיש דמדעו כשיר [2]
טב מן האיש העשיר

4 מן התהלך בדרך המלא [3]
עזרו בשתי החצרים [4] אלה

5 לא תלכד תרח [5] דלא תחכמו
ילא [6] יתך סתמו

6 מן יאמר לך אני במאהבתך מסתמך
לא תדעו אלא בעת לו תמך

7 הדר פני מן לטוב יאעיצך
בכל כוחך וחרוצך [7]

8 המות בארח העז הגדל
טב מן תאספו בשביל הדל

9 מה תעף קמס [8] ותנשא
אלא נפל על ארץ יבשה

3 Freytag 2287. *Cf.* Prov 28: 6
5 Freytag 2305
6 Freytag 1984

---

[1] Heb. שונאך.
[2] = Heb. ישר. In TS Deut. 32: 13, ישרון = כשיריה.
[3] "Integrity, perfection"; *cf.* No. 37.
[4] = Ar. دارين, i.e. this world and the next.
[5] = Aram. תרע; Heb. שער.
[6] Rt. לאה.
[7] "Assiduity, diligence," from rt. חרץ II. The Ar. equivalent is גהד.
[8] = קמץ, which renders עוף in TS Gen l: 20, 21, 26, etc.

10　הנפש אאט ¹ לכמוה
והקסמות תפל על מראוה ²

11　המים אשר איננו עצור
לו טטף ³ טטפה ינקר הצור

12　כל כלום יתאבד
אלא אלה וטוב העובד

13　מן יאהב לרעהו כמוהו
לא יוכל אחר ימכאו

14　מן ישמר מבטא שפתו
אתגלג ⁴ בין עמיתו

15　מן יתקרב לבלל אקרו ⁵
ילחט ⁶ הנגף מדל מישרו ⁷

16　מן יתפני לבצע עלמה
לא ישקח ⁸ נשמה ⁹

17　מן יבקש הרעות
לא ימצא לו בטח בכל הפאות

18　מן יקח השחד

10　Freytag 2688; Freytag 84; ʿAbbud 2707; Haefeli 579; Mak, *JAOS* 69 (1949), 224, No. 4.
11　Freytag 2487; Haefeli 549. Cf. *Gutta cavat lapidem non vi sed saepe cadendo.*
12　*Cf.* ʿAbbûd 2558

---

¹ = Heb. הַט.

² The Ar. equivalent is אשכאלאה.

³ = Heb. נטף. Cf. Cowley 848: ובזהב טטפנו וירד עלינו הטטף כמטר; Ben Hayyim, *Tarbiz*, vol. 4 (1939), 351. 17: טטף רד מן צדקון.

⁴ A common Sam. word for "praise"; *cf.* Kohut, *Aruch, s.v.*

⁵ = Heb. עיקרו, sensu "his stock."

⁶ = ילעט, from rt. לעט = לוט, "curse."

⁷ The Ar. equivalent of this proverb runs: מן תזוג מן עיר אצלה דק. בטעם ימחי יהוה; אלבין פלסה The second half is glossed by Ab Ḥasdâ; כל כספו.

⁸ = Aram. שכח, "find", as in TS Gen 3: 14; 37: 15; Deut 31: 17, etc.

⁹ "Tranquility, repose, enjoyment"; *cf.* Nos. 29, 65.

אִיקְרוּ [1] יכחד

19   המהרה מתגעלה

הקלמוס לשן היד ופעלה

20   לא תשים בידך קוטמה [2]

קדם תבלע דקדמה

21   מן סתם אזניו מן צעקות דיאנקו

ככן והוא לא ישמע צעקו

22   דילמד אנשים החסד ולא יעבדו

הוא הך עור בוצין מניר בידו

יזרח בו לבלעדו

והוא לא יעמי [3] מוקדו

23   אדרש [4] הגר

קדם החצר

והרחוט [5] קדם הדרך

24   שנים לא ישבעו

דרוש [6] חכמה ודרוש [6] עדפת מדלו

25   החל הקצף שגגה רמה

ואחריתו רחמה [7]

26   טוב הממלל דצדק בו אמורו בלשנו

20 Freytag 2028
21 Freytag 1319
23 Freytag i. 88; ʿAbbûd 3072; Haefeli 429; Socin 106; Goitein 536.— ʿAbbûd 3073; Haefeli 507
24 Haefeli 100; Socin 256
25 Freytag 138
26 Freytag 620

---

[1] = Aram. יקר, *i.e.*, "his honor, good repute."

[2] "Morsel;" *cf.* Syr. ܦܘܡܐ; Ar. قطم, *momordit.*

[3] = Aram. חמי, "see."

[4] Impv.

[5] "Companion".

[6] Partic. Qal.

[7] "(An act of) love."

ואתעויל [1] בו דשמרו באזנו

27 לא תסגי בהלכך לבית מאהבך
　　פן יתאבדך

28 למשלי הוי מסתכל
　　נשמת פגרך במעט המיכל
　　קח ממני מלים נהגות
　　נשמת הלב בחסר הדאגות

29 אן הוית תחפץ נשמת הלשן
אמעיט [2] מן הממלל אן הוה חדש או ישן

30 נצירות [3] האנוש
　　תוסיפו קדוש

31 רחם חברך
　　ירחמך מרך

32 מן לנפשו יקליץ [4]
　　איננו לטוב יאעיץ

33 הוי לצעירך עני בין אנשה
　　למען תהיה בזקנך מתנשא

34 צפור בידך הימינה
　　טוב מן עשרה על אילנה

35 לא תעבד ברחוקך או קרובך
　　במה לא תתריח [5] יעבדו בך

27 Prov. 25: 17. *Cf.* Aḥiqar ii. 74
28 Freytag 2341; Haefeli 751
33 Freytag 2800. *Cf.* Syr. Aḥiqar ii. 61
34 Freytag 2029; Mak, *JAOS* 69 (1939), 226, No. 21; Syr. Aḥiqar
　　ii. 49

---

[1] The Ar. rendering is קביחה; hence from rt. עול.
[2] Impv. Aph'el.
[3] "Piety, devotion, sincerity"; *cf.* Ben Hayyim, *Tarbiz*, vol. 4
(1939), 340, n. 38.
[4] = קלס; *cf.* TS Deut 32: 43.
[5] Rt. רחי = Aram. רעא = Heb. רצה.

36 אן אסתוללו הסוררים
אשתמדו היקירים ¹

37 האנש בלא מלא
כמטעמים בלא מלח

38 התשוב בארץ גזרה ²
טוב מן המושב את אשה סוררה

39 אהב את יהוה בכל מדלך
כי הוא הנתן לך

40 כבד אביך ואמך ומיסרך
יהיה יהוה מגן עזרך ³

41 החכום – – ינשק השוטר ידו
והסוכיל – – יסוד[ו] הנכר אבדו ⁴

42 הכין הרחוט ⁵
קדם לדרך תרחוט ⁶

43 לעשות מה צוך עבודך
אתפוגג ⁷ בכל מאדך

44 אן בטח לשן הצדיק בחצר השלטנה
לה הבסרה ברב עז והכוננה ⁸

36 Freytag 2980
37 Freytag 2957. *Cf.* also Greek and Syriac texts of Sirach 20.19, which, when combined, yield our proverb
38 *Cf.* Proverbs 21: 19

---

¹ "Men of honor, worth."
² *Cf.* Lev. 16: 22. ³ Cf. Deut 33: 29.
⁴ The Ar. equivalent of this line runs: יבחט אלעדו עלי אחלאכה.
Ab Ḥasdâ thus explained the proverb to me: חייב על השוטר, והוא
השופט על העם, ינשק יד כל איש נבון וחכם:– האיש הסוכיל יחפר
הנכרי על יסוד או אקר איקרו להבידו. ⁵ "Companion"; *cf.* No. 23.
⁶ Rt. רחט = רעט = Aram. רהט = Heb. רוץ.
⁷ The Ar. equivalent is אבצّר. Hence cp. Ar. أفوج, *festinavit.*
⁸ The Ar. equivalent of this proverb runs:
אן נטק לסאן אלעדל
פי דאר אלסלטאן
לה אלבשרה באעטם
אלעז ואלעמאר

45 השמר מן פרץ ¹ השליט ותאבד
   ולא תשטן מן אמר ועבד

46 מן יתגבר בחמסנו ²
   יתנגף בחמס ממנו ³

47 סבל רב החטא ממן תאהבו
   ולו הוה המתגן ואתו שלם
   מאהב בלא גנא מעט ממצאו
   ומדכר גנות המאהבים בלם ⁴

48 הסוכיל לא יתפורד מן סוכיליו
   בממצא הבצע מתזיאן ⁵ עליו

49 האנש דיסתיר כסלותו
   טב מן האנש דיסתיר חכמתו

50 לא תלך אלא על צוער
   והשאל לא תגער

51 כשלות האנש תסיר כף רגלו
   וכשלות הלשן תסיר מדלו

52 לא ידבק בידך מאומה מן החרם
   למען ישוב יהוה מחרון אפו ונתן לך הרחום

53 נשמת פגרך ורוחך ביראת אלהיך
   הלוך דרך אמונה יהיה תמיד אונח ⁶

47 *Cf.* Sirach 10: 6; 28: 2 (Greek); Test. Gad 6: 3-4; Proverbs 17: 19.
   — Haefeli 410.— Freytag 1657
49 *Cf.* Sirach 20: 31
51 *Cf.* Syr. Aḥiqar ii. 45; Sirach 5: 13*b*
52 Deuteronomy 13: 18

---

1 "Outburst (of anger)"; *cf.* No. 91.
2 = בחמסו (for the sake of the rhyme).
3 The Ar. equivalent is: יבתלו באטלם מנה.
4 The Ar. equivalent is מסתורה.
5 Rt. זין, "arm," *i.e.*, he takes up arms against it; *cf.* TS Deut
32: 26. The Ar. equivalent is עַאלב.
6 "Be at ease, in comfort"; a by-form of נוח. *Cf.* Cowley 540.14;
   זאת סוברו לחייה בתרי עלמה אנחות

54   לא תעשה בפנוסך ¹ ,אצוך,
מה לא תתריח יעשו האנשים בך

55   אן אהבת עדפת חדבך ²
טר מה אלה צוך

56   מן לא יצבה ³ ויגרש ⁴ ההול ⁵ מן לבבו
לא ישקח בטח לא בחוץ ולא במושבו

57   אתש ⁶ השן אטש כאבו

58   המות ייתי בפתע
והקבר ארון עמלותה ⁷

59   מהרו בצלות קדם ילך זבנותח ⁸
ובשובה קדם מותה

60   סטה ⁹ הבקע ¹⁰ על הרקע ¹¹
ושב פרח הכוס ¹² פרס ¹³
ואתרצצת ¹⁴ פסחות ¹⁵ החמורים

57   'Abbûd 377; Haefeli 762; Bauer 56
60   Haefeli 631

---

1   = Aram. בנס (Dan 2: 12); cf. TS Deut 32: 16, etc.
2   = חדוך = Heb. חדותך; cf. TS Gen 18: 12; 21: 6; Cowley 517.7, etc.
3   = Aram צבא, "wish"; cf. Marqeh 146b: הו דברא כד צבה.
4   For the construction, cp. TS Gen 24: 14; Num 23: 19; Uhlemann, *Institutiones Linguae Samaritanae* (Leipzig 1837), 228.
5   = Heb. הוללות, "folly"; cf. No. 83.
6   Impv. Qal, rt. נתש.
7   This may perhaps throw light on הלמות עמלים in Judges 5: 26.
8   = Heb. זמן.
9   "Departs"; cf. Marqeh 142a: עמי מלתה דמשפט ··· ולא תסטי מנה, and countless other passages.
10   "The stain"; cp Ar. بقع (v. Lane, *s.v.*).
11   "Garment". The word renders בגד in TS Gen. 27: 15; 37: 29; Exod. 28: 2, 4; 29: 4. Cf. also Marqeh 192ª: דאנון חבלו רקיע ארמלתה.
12   "Owl" (Lev 11: 17; Deut 14: 16).
13   "Bruised, wounded," *i. e.*, broken-winged.
14   The Ar. equivalent is ואתכאאֿתרת. Cp. Ar. راص?
15   "Lameness."

אמרתי מן חסר ממצא דיהרס ¹

61   שבק הרכיל ומה אמר

ועתק ² ביני ובינך מיתר

ומשיג ³ לא ינתק

62   מן בצעירו ישתדל

יצפר ⁴ אדון בעת גדל ⁵

63   מן יסגי מן הרדם

חלילה – – בכל מאום יתקדם ⁶

64   מן למדני אות אחד

הייתי לו עבד כי לבי יחד

65   נשמת הלב בחסר הדאג

ונשמת הלשן במעט הממלל ⁷

66   אן שבת ⁸ על הכסא

נשיאי מקוהך ⁹ לא תמעיסה ¹⁰

62   Freytag 2800
63   Freytag 2605
64   ʿAbbûd 4434; Haefeli 104
65   Cf. No. 28; cf. Haefeli 751

---

¹ The Ar. equivalent is אלסובאק (Haefeli 631 بتسابق). Hence, דיהרס means here "that overthrows his competitors, wins."

² "Make firm, enduring."

³ The Ar. equivalent is וצאל. I take the word to correspond to Heb. סוגה, סיג; cf. Marqeh 136ᵃ:

חייה לנטורי מצותה ומותה למי תרע (breaks through) סיגיו

⁴ "Turns out to be"; cf. Cowley 676 (= Heidenheim, *Sam Lit.*, 194, No. XCV): לו היינו טבים מה צפרנו דרסה לרגליה, and many other passages.   ⁵ Ms. גדלו. The correction is demanded by the rhyme.

⁶ "Is forestalled."

⁷ The rhyme suggests הלעג. Ab Ḥasdâ was evidently influenced by No. 29.   ⁸ ישבת =.

⁹ This word is not clear to me. The sense is obviously "the princes of thy court", so that derivation from rt. קוה = Ar. وق, Akkad. aqû is at least possible. (Definitely *not* מקומך in the MS.)

¹⁰ "Despise, abase, bring low" = מאס; cf. Marqeh 5ᵃ:

סניך עתידין ממעסים קמיך ולית בון תקומה

id., *apud* Cowley 20 מ: מי תהומה מעס ומי רקיעה תלא

(An Arabic مس, *vilipendit*, is registered by Castell.).

67　לא תדע צדיקך [1]

אלא בעת יהיה מן הלחץ אינקך [2]

68　אן אהבת בוצין איקרך לא יכבי

כבד בכל מאדך הכהנים בני לוי

69　החפי [3] מן הבינה והחכמה

לא פרקן [4] בינו ובין הבהמה

70　במהרה נחמה [5]

ובמאפק שלמה [6]

71　מבשל החמה [7] אכלו

72　לא תשנא אחד ואן פגת [8] לא ירענך

ולא תלך בצדיקות [1] אחד ואן פגת בו לא יועלנך

73　המדל [9] דמן החמס יגרע

ואן אתאסף ביד המלאה אוצפה [10]

74　רפא הדר׳ התאפק עליו [11]

רבות הלעג תחמול האימה

75　חרש ידיעין [12]

טב מן סוכיל מבטא

67　Freytag ii 175; Haefeli 412; Ben Cheneb 1252; Goitein 415
68　*Cf.* Sirach 7: 29
72　*Cf.* Freytag 554

---

[1] "Friend"; cp. Ar. صديق. *Cf.* the Sam. wedding-song, Ben Hayyim, *Tarbiz* 4 (1939), 355.4: וזבגם בחדו רב וצדיקה; *cf.* also צדיקות, "friendship," in No. 72.

[2] Rt. נקה *sensu* "deliver," as in Arabic.

[3] = Heb. חפה׳ חבא, "hide."

[4] "Difference."

[5] "Regret."

[6] "Amends"; cp. Heb. שְׁלֵם.

[7] "Hot meal."

[8] "Expect."

[9] "Property, possessions."

[10] = Heb. חְצפה.

[11] "Be patient with him."

[12] = Heb. יוֹדֵעַ.

76 תעבד עד תעגה

ולא תמך תבקשך וימנע

77 מן יזרע החסד בפנוס שכונו

בקצירו ישתמע שאונו

78 מן ידהה ¹ בלא גלל ²

אכן הבודן ³ על צלמו ⁴ מסתולל

79 הסערה בהר ספרה ⁵

אל האהלים תבקע

80 קח ממני מלים ושתאמה ⁶

רב העלג יאבד האימה

81 החטול ⁷ לא ינוס

מן החרוס ⁸

82 השתדל לעשות צדיקה

קדם תצפר עלמה ממך מפוקה

83 לבך מן ההול אמרק

ופני האנשים לא תרק

78 Freytag 1279

---

¹ The Ar. equivalent is צחך, "laugh." This may support Tur Sinai's conjecture of *ידההה, "plays," in Isa 11:8

ושעשע יונק על חר פתן ועל מאורת צפעוני ידו הדה

² "Cause"; cp. Heb. בגלל; Ar. أَجْل.

³ The parallel in Freytag 1729, as well as Ab Ḥasdâ's explanation:

מן יצחק בלי גלל תהי צחקותו מן קלות (חסר) חנוך טוב (היסר טוב) ועל פניו מאחר (או אטי או נחשל)

makes it clear that בודן means "boorishness, ill-breeding."

⁴ צלם in Sam. means "face."

⁵ I.e., Mt. Gerizim; cf. J. Montgomery, The Samaritans (Philadelphia 1907), 237 f.

⁶ "Consider, ponder, reflect, estimate," cf. Marqeh 183ᵃ: מן ידע; רביאנו לא משתאם; ibid, 198ᵃ: הך הו אי ישים מה הו; ʿAmram Darah, עבודה דעלמה מן ישום רביאנך: Cowley 31ל: apud Cowley 31 = Cowley; Durran IV = Cowley; ומדעה לא ישום; Pineḥas, apud Cowley 34ש: ונצען דלית משומנה :40. גלגות עקבאות נפלאותה שיאם אלהותך Heidenheim, Sam. Lit., 12.4: למען יראו וידעו וישימו .Cf. also Isa 41:20 דלית בון חדה משתאם.

⁷ = Heb. חתול, "cat."   ⁸ = הערוס = Ar. عرس, "dividing wall, fence."

84 שׂנס על ¹ מרכבך
ומהר לקראת מאהבך

85 חש הרע   ומנה אברח ²

86 מן אעצר ³   לא ייעצר ⁴

86 לעשות הטוב לא תדלס ⁵
ולא תהיה לאחיך לרע בלס ⁶

87 הכני ⁷ ישב בבטח
והרשע ראשו מטאטא ⁸

88 לא תצעיף ⁹   קדם תאסף ¹⁰
טב היתרון   באחרית לעם ישרון

89 אטע ¹¹ באשל לבך
היראה מן עבודך ורבך

90 אלך ¹² על טוב צרב ¹³

---

¹ שׂנס על = "hitch."

² Impv. Qal.

³ "Practises restraint".

⁴ "Come to harm, suffer hurt"; *cf.* TS Gen 3: 16 עצרון = עצבון;
ibid 6: 6 ויתעצב = אתעצר.

⁵ In TS Exod. 9: 7, 19 דלס renders סכל, and in TS Gen. 21: 23
it renders שקר. This is clearly the Greek δόλος and Latin *dolus* [cf.
Ar. دلس], but that meaning will not fit here. I therefore suggest that
our word be explained from Marqeh 10b:
ולא תדלס נביה זרז בעבדיך
and from Heidenheim, *Sam. Lit.*, No. XCVIII 18:
יוסף הפתור דמן זכותה לא דלס
This comports with the Ar. equivalent תמעק ("desist").

⁶ = בלש, "seek" (for the sake of the rhyme).

⁷ "The honest man."

⁸ Cp. Ar. طاطا "droop the head."

⁹ The Ar. equivalent is תתברע, "exalt thyself." But perhaps the
word really equates with Ar. ضعف, "be feeble (in spirit)," *i.e.*
"despair."

¹⁰ "Ere thou die."

¹¹ Imp. Qal.

¹² Imp. Qal.

¹³ Cp. Ar. ضرب, "be eager, bent on."

לא אחד לך יריב

91 מות הנער בעזה

כימי חתנו ¹ הלזה

92 לא תפרץ על מעט האקר ²

תחמסו ותחסר האיקר

93 אעבד ³ את יהוה בכל מאדך

בטובו יסעדך

94 לא תשקף מן חרך ⁴

אל אשת גרך

95 אכן המלשינים

ממללון ילחץ החשנים ⁵

96 אמר לו אה אבי עזבתי הרדם באצלחך

אמר לו אתנשם מן צאהך ⁶

97 האנשים דישימו מן מצות יהוה בלם ⁷

לא תדרש שלמם וטובותם כל ימיך לעולם

98 מאהב מדלה

מאהב מה לה

שנא מדלה

שנא מה לה

---

¹ Hebraice חתניו.

² "Stock."

³ Impv. Qal.

⁴ Cf. Cant 5 : 14.

⁵ The Ar. equivalent is אלצדור. But perhaps החשנים really means "those who keep silent" (from rt. חשה).

⁶ = Heb. צֵאתְךָ.

⁷ The Ar. equivalent is לגמא (cf. Ar. لجم; Eth. l-g-m, frenavit), taking the word as the Heb. בלם (Ps 32 : 9). Conceivably, however, the Sam. text (which here seems to be the original, in view of the use of יהוה rather than אלה, as elsewhere) should really run:

האנשים דימישו מן מצות יהוה בלם

when בל will be the common Sam. and Aram. word for "mind, heart." המיש בל will then be the direct opposite of the common Sam. and Syr. יהב בל, "apply the mind."

99 במה לשנה ממלל
לבה חשוב

100 לית עקה רמה
אלא ולה עקב [1]

101 הא מן הימים
ומה תוליד מן מעל [2]

102 במה דאנש עמל
ממרק [3] הוא אגרה

99 Freytag 2568
102 Freytag 2673.— Marqeh, *apud* Cowley, *Samar. Liturgy*, 19ב.

---

[1] "End."
[2] "Ah, for days and what mischief they may bring forth!" Note
the Arabizing 3rd. sg. fem. with masc. pl., as often in Sam.
[3] = Heb. שָׁלַם; *cf*. TS Gen 18: 21; Deut 32: 41.

THE PAPAL BULL *SICUT JUDEIS*

By Solomon Grayzel

Jewish Publication Society of America

1. Its Development

MOST OF THE POPES during the Middle Ages had occasion to issue formal statements about the position of the Jews and the practice of Judaism in the midst of Christian society. Such statements generally revolved about some issue of the moment, whether to protect Jews against a specific danger threatening them from Christians, or to repress their presumably expanding influence and activity which were considered a threat to Christianity, or to grant them privileges, or to rescind those already granted. Such letters, or Bulls, dispatched by various popes were addressed to secular rulers or to the clergy generally or particularly.

There was one such Bull which differed from these others in several important respects. For one thing, it was in the category of a statement of general policy, dealing with matters of faith and religious discipline and expressed in the form of a warning and exhortation addressed "To all faithful Christians." This is why it was sometimes called a *constitutio*, to distinguish it from letters conferring privileges or grants and from administrative orders. [1] As such, this Bull, which began with the words *Sicut Judeis*, was entered into the collection of Church formulations from which Canon Law was drawn. [2] Moreover, it appears to have been repeated more frequently than any other papal utterance concerning the Jews: being

---

[1] *See* Reginald L. Poole, *Lectures on the History of the Papal Chancery* (Cambridge 1915), pp. 40 f., 117 f. The term *constitutio* must not be confused with "constitution" as used currently.

[2] *Corpus Juris Canonici*, Decretalia Gregorii IX, Lib. V, tit. vi, c. ix., where it is headed "Constitutio pro Judeis."

used by six popes during the twelfth century (including Innocent III), by ten popes during the thirteenth, by four popes during the fourteenth (including an anti-pope), and by three during the fifteenth century. It is to be noted that it was used most frequently during the century of the papacy's greatest influence and that, as we shall see, it was subjected to increasing modification as time went on.[1]

The basic text of the Bull ran as follows:[1]

[1] For the text, in addition to the *Corpus Juris*, as above, *see* S. Grayzel, *The Church and the Jews in the 13th Century* [hereinafter to be referred to as C & J] (Philadelphia 1933), pp. 92-5, no. 5. Apart from additions and substantial modifications which will be discussed below, this text varied slightly in wording in every issue.

Sicut Judeis non debet esse licentia in synagogis suis ultra quam permissum est lege presumere, ita in his que eis concessa sunt nullum debent prejudicium sustinere.

Nos ergo licet in sua magis velint duritia perdurare quam prophetarum verba et suarum scripturarum arcana cognoscere, atque ad Christiane fidei et salutis notitiam pervenire, quia tamen defensionem nostram et auxilium postulant ex Christiane pietatis mansuetudine, predecessorum nostrorum felicis memorie . . . Romanorum pontificum vestigiis inherentes, ipsorum petitionem admittimus eisque protectionis nostre clypeum indulgemus.

Statuimus etiam ut nullus Christianus invitos vel nolentes eos ad baptismum per violentiam venire compellat, sed si eorum quilibet sponte ad Christianos fidei causa confugerit, postquam voluntas eius fuerit patefacta, Christianus absque aliqua efficiatur calumnia. Veram quippe Christianitatis fidem habere non creditur qui ad Christianorum baptisma non spontaneus sed invitus cognoscitur pervenire.

Nullus etiam Christianus eorum personas sine judicio potestatis terrae vulnerare aut occidere vel suas pecunias auferre presumat, aut bonas quas hactenus in ea qua habitant regione habuerint consuetudines immutare. Preterea in festivitatum suarum celebratione quisquam fustibus vel lapidibus eos ullatenus non perturbet, neque aliquis ab eis coacta servitia exigat nisi ea que ipsi preteritis facere temporibus consueverunt. Ad hec malorum hominum pravitati et avaritie obviantes decernimus ut nemo cemetarium Judeorum mutilare vel minuere audeat, sive obtentu pecunie corpora humata effodere.

Si quis autem decreti huius tenore cognito temere, quod absit, contraire tentaverit, honoris et officii sui periculum patiatur aut excommunicationis ultione plectatur, nisi presumptionem suam digna satisfactione correxit. Eos autem dumtaxat huius protectionis presidio volumus communiri qui nihil machinari presumpserint in subversionem fidei christiane.

Datum . . .

Even as the Jews ought not have the freedom to dare do in their synagogues more than the law permits them, so ought they not suffer curtailment of those [privileges] which have been conceded them.

This is why, although they prefer to persist in their obstinacy rather than acknowledge the words of the prophets and the eternal secrets of their own scriptures, thus arriving at an understanding of Christianity and salvation, nevertheless, in view of the fact that they have begged for our protection and our aid and in accordance with the clemency which Christian piety imposes, we, following in the footsteps of our predecessors of happy memory [1] . . ., grant their petition and offer them the shield of our protection.

We decree that no Christian shall use violence to force them into baptism while they are unwilling and refuse, but that [only] if anyone of them seeks refuge among the Christians of his own free will and by reason of faith, his willingness having become quite clear, shall he be made a Christian without subjecting himself to any opprobrium. For surely none can be believed to possess the true Christian faith if he is known to have come to Christian baptism unwillingly and even against his wishes.

Moreover, without the judgment of the authority of the land, no Christian shall presume to wound their persons, or kill them, or rob them of their money, or change the good customs which they have thus far enjoyed in the place of their habitation. Furthermore, while they celebrate their festivals, no one shall disturb them in any way by means of sticks and stones, nor exact forced service from any of them other than such as they have been accustomed to perform from ancient times. Opposing the wickedness and avarice of evil men in such matters, we decree that no one shall dare to desecrate or reduce a Jewish cemetery, or, with the object of extorting money, exhume bodies there interred.

Should anyone, being acquainted with the contents of this decree, nevertheless dare to act in defiance of it—which God forbid—he shall suffer loss of honor and office or be restrained by the penalty of excommunication, unless he make proper amends for his presumption. We desire, however, to place under the protection of this decree only those [Jews] who do not presume to plot against the Christian faith.

Given ——

The central ideas of this Bull were not new even at its first appearance, during the pontificate of Calixtus II (1119-

[1] At this point those predecessors were listed who were credited with the issuance of the Bull. Sometimes one or more names were overlooked.

1124). More than six hundred years earlier, Theodoric the Ostrogoth, basing himself on characteristic Roman respect for custom and precedent, expressed some of these ideas in a letter to the Jews of Genoa (ca. 500). [1] He said:

> Even as, when petitioned, we like to give due consent, in the same measure we dislike it when, because of our favor, laws are evaded, especially in such matters as we believe involve religious reverence . . . We therefore decree, by the authority of these presents, that you may erect a roof over the old walls of your synagogue, thus [in response] to your petition granting permission in so far as imperial regulations permit [2]; but no decorations of any kind may be added and there must be no overstepping the limits by extending the structure . . . We cannot command religious faith, for no one can be forced to believe who is unwilling to do so.

The great Pope Gregory I, toward the end of the sixth century, expressed himself to the same effect: [3] Jews were entitled to have a place "where they can observe their ceremonies unhindered"; and the pope added: "We forbid that the said Jews be unreasonably burdened and afflicted; they must, rather, be permitted to live in accordance with Roman Law. . ." Moreover, a few years later Pope Gregory began one of his letters with the very sentence which became the

---

[1]   Migne, *PL*, 69, col. 561; *cf.* James Parkes, *Conflict of the Church and the Synagogue* (London 1934), pp. 208 ff.

Sicut exorati justum cupimus praebere consensum, ita per nostra beneficia fraudes fieri legibus non amamus, in ea parte praecipue in que divinae reverentiae credimus interesse. . . . quapropter tegumen tantum vetustis parietibus superimponere synagogae vestrae praesenti vos auctoritate censemus, petitionibus vestris eatenus licentiam commodantes quatenus constituta divalia permiserunt. Nec aliquid ornatus fas sit adjicere, vel in ampliandis aedibus evagari. . . . Religionem imperare non possumus, quia nemo cogitur ut credat invitus.

[2]   For imperial Roman legislation on the subject of synagogue building see *Codex Theodosianus* 16. 8. 25 and 27. *Cf.* Parkes, *ibid.*, p. 182. *See also* Peter Browe, "Die Judengesetzgebung Justinians" in *Analecta Gregoriana*, vol. viii (Rome 1935).

[3]   September/October, 591: Jaffe 1157; *Monumenta Germaniae Historica (MGH)*, Regesta Gregorii I, Bk. II, no. 6—. . . *ubi praefati Hebraei . . . possint sine impedimento ceremonia celebrare. . . . Praedictos vero Hebraeos gravari vel affligi contra rationis ordinem prohibemus; sed sicut Romanis vivere legibus permittuntur . . .*

characteristic opening for the famous Bull here under discussion.[1] The Jews of Rome having submitted to the pope a complaint by their fellow Jews of Palermo, the pope urged the bishop of that diocese to make sure that justice was done to the Jews of his district. The prestige which Pope Gregory I enjoyed throughout the subsequent history of the Church thus fortified the principle of continuity which he asserted with regard to the Jewish position.

To the continuity of the regulations under which they lived and their right to unhindered worship, the Bull *Sicut Judeis* added a warning against attempts to convert the Jews by force. As we shall see below, the first issuance of the Bull in its developed form was probably connected with the outbreak of forced conversions incidental to the First Crusade. It was therefore necessary if the Jews were to be protected, for the Church to refute the argument that the persistence of Judaism or, as churchmen were likely to express it, "the stubbornness of the Jews," was contrary to God's will. Basing themselves on the strong condemnation of Jesus' opponents in the Gospel stories, the Church Fathers had minced no words when referring to the unwillingness of their Jewish contemporaries to give up Judaism.[2] "Blind" and "hard" were mild words used by Augustine.[3] On the other hand, it was Augustine himself who interpreted Psalm 59: 12 as a warning by Jesus not to kill the Jews, who are God's witnesses and whose lowly status and dispersion are punishment enough

---

[1]   To Bishop Victor of Palermo, in June, 598: Jaffe 1514; *MGH*, Reg. Greg. I, Bk. VIII, no. 25—Sicut Judaeis . . .. The same thought, using more or less the same words, is expressed in another letter of Gregory dealing with the same subject: *see* Jaffe 1562; *MGH*, *ibid.*, Bk. IX, no. 38: . . . *quia sicut illis quidquam in synagogis suis facere . . . ultra quam lege decretum est non debet esse licentia, ita eis contra justitiam et aequitatem nec praejudicium nec aliquod debet inferri dispendium.*

[2]   *See*, for example, Marcel Simon, *Verus Israel* (Paris 1948), especially chapter viii, "L'antisemitisme chrétien."

[3]   *See* Bernhard Blumenkranz, *Die Judenpredigt Augustins* (Basel 1946), pp. 186 ff.

for their sins. [1] How then was their conversion to be attained?
Tertullian, in the second century, when the Christian Church
was still subject to persecution, had argued that religion
must be accepted freely or not at all. [2] Similarly Lactantius,
a century later, asserted that nothing was essentially more
voluntary than religion. [3] Theodoric's letter cited above
reflected the same sentiment. Pope Gregory I insisted on
several occasions that the proper way to seek the conversion
of Jews was not by force or threats but by mildness and
persuasion. [4] He berated a bishop of Naples for interfering
with the Jews in the observance of their holidays, since such
interference not only fails to bring them nearer to conversion
but also violates ancient usage. [5]

---

[1] *De civitate Dei* 18, 46. In KJ the verse reads: "Slay them not,
lest My people forget; scatter them by Thy power and bring them
down, O Lord our shield." *Cf.* Blumenkranz, *op. cit.*, p. 208.

[2] Migne, *PL* 69, quoted in the note to col. 561: *Non est religionis
cogere religionem, quae sponte suscipi debet.*

[3] *Ibid. Religio christiana imperari non potest. Defendenda est religio
non occidendo, sed monendo; non saevitis, sed patientia . . . Nihil tam
voluntariam quam religio.*

[4] *MGH, ibid.,* Bk. I, no. 34; Jaffe 1104; March 16, 591, to the
Bishop of Terrason in southern France: *Hos enim qui a Christiana
religione discordant mansuetudine, benignitate, admonendo, suadendo ad
unitatem fidei necesse est congregare.* Again, in June of the same year,
he wrote to another bishop warning him that converts by force were
likely to revert to their old religion and become more devoted to it
than ever: *MGH, ibid.,* Bk. I, no. 45; Jaffe 1115: *. . . ad pristinam
superstitionem remeans inde deterius moritur unde renatus esse videbatur.*
Cf. *ibid.,* Bk. IX, no. 195; Jaffe 1722, where Pope Gregory says that
overzealous clerics must be made to understand that *magis utenda est
ut trahatur ab eis velle, non ut ducantur inviti,* which is an almost
verbal precursor of the statement in the Bull *Sicut Judeis.*

[5] *MGH, ibid.,* Bk. XIII, no. 15; Jaffe 1879; November, 602, to
the Bishop of Naples: *Qui sincera intentione extraneos ad christianam
religionem, ad fidem cupiunt rectam adducere, blandimentis debent, non
asperitatibus studere . . . Itaque fraternitas tua eos monitis quidem,
prout potuerit, Deo adjuvante ad convertendum accendat et de suis illos
sollemnibus inquietari denuo non permittat, sed omnes festivitates
feriasque suas, sicut hactenus tam ipsi quam parentes eorum per longa
colentes retro tempora tenuerunt, liberam habeant observandi celebrandique
licentiam.*

Pope Gregory's repeated warnings indicate how difficult it was to restrain an aroused mob and overzealous churchmen. He himself on one important occasion was not altogether consistent in upholding the objections to conversion by force and under threat. [1] His triumphant letter to King Reccared, hailing the entry of the Visigothic kingdom into the Catholic fold, speaks of the attempt of the Jews to bribe the king to leave them alone, but has not a word of criticism about the element of compulsion in the situation. Evidently even the saintly Pope Gregory was not ready to include destitution and exile in his definition of force. On the whole, the idea that conversion should be the result of peaceful efforts remained alive during the early Middle Ages. Popes Gregory IV (828-44) and Leo VII (936-9) expressed themselves to the same effect. [2] Pope Alexander II (1061-73), in a letter to the bishops of Spain in connection with the Reconquest, [3] quoted Gregory I's view that conversion should be achieved by peaceful methods, that the Jews must not be killed, and that synagogues should not be destroyed.

It is thus clear that a substantial part of the Bull *Sicut Judeis* had a long history by the time of its first issuance about the year 1120. The prohibition of physical violence

[1]   *MGH, ibid.,* Bk. IX, no. 228; Jaffe 1757; August, 599.

[2]   Migne, *PL*, 132, col. 1083; Aronius, *Regesten zur Geschichte der Juden im fränkischen und deutschen Reiche bis zum Jahre* 1273 (Berlin 1902), no. 125; *cf.* Salo W. Baron, *A Social and Religious History of the Jews* (2nd ed., New York and Philadelphia 1957), vol. iv, p. 6.

[3]   Migne, *PL* 146, p. 1386; Mansi, *Sacrorum Conciliorum Amplissima Collectio,* XIX, col. 964; Jaffe 4528, addressed to all the bishops of Spain: *Sic etiam beatus Gregorius . . . prohibuit, impium esse denuntians eos delere velle qui Dei misericordia servati sunt, ut, patria libertateque amissa . . . per terrarum orbis plagas dispersi vivant . . . Quemdam etiam epsicopum synagogam eorum destruere volentem prohibuit.* In a letter to the Prince of Benevento, Alexander II, echoing Gregory I (*cf.* Browe, *Judenmission,* pp. 231 f.) made the interesting remark: *Dominus noster Iesus Christus nullum legitur ad sui servitium violenter coegisse, sed humili exhortatione, reservata unicuique proprii arbitrii libertate, quoscumque ad vitam predestinavit aeternam non iudicando, sed proprium sanguinem fundendo ab errore revocasse.* S. Loewenfeld, *Epistolae pontificum romanorum ineditae* (Leipzig 1885), p. 52, no. 105.

directed against the adherents of Judaism and of physical force in the effort to convert them antedated the Bull by many centuries. The other gross forms of attack and persecution—such as pelting Jews and their synagogues with stones and the desecration of cemeteries—had certainly not been unknown before the twelfth century, [1] but had now become characteristic enough or local Christian-Jewish relations for the popes to take note of them. [2] It was not sufficient to make general statements about not changing the "good customs" that had obtained; specific examples had to be listed.

2. *Its Promulgation*

The relationship of this Bull to the Jews of Europe is a matter of great interest. It is reasonable to assume that the situation which called the Bull forth was the disastrous result of the First Crusade which so radically changed the status of the Jews. [3] Murder, pillage and forced conversions accompanied the march of the crusaders across central Europe. Although the reversion to Judaism on the part of forced converts was permitted by the civil authorities, on the assumption that with the passing of the storm everything would return to normal, the zeal aroused by the preaching of the crusade belied any such prospect. The General Peace, proclaimed for the Empire in 1103, for the first time classed the Jews with those who were in need of special protection. [4] Civil protection, moreover, was hardly enough in a situation created by an excess of religious emotionalism, and an appeal

[1] *Cf.* Bernhard Blumenkranz, *Juifs et Chrétiens dans le monde occidental*: 430-1096 (Paris 1960), esp. pp. 97 ff.

[2] For such occurrences in Rome, *see* the description of the turbulence in that city in Vogelstein u. Rieger, *Geschichte der Juden in Rom* (Berlin 1896), vol. i, pp. 218-21.

[3] Guido Kisch, *Forschungen zur Rechts- und Sozialgeschichte der Juden in Deutschland während des Mittelalters* (Zurich 1955), pp. 17 f.

[4] Guido Kisch, *The Jews in Medieval Germany* (Chicago 1949), p. 109; James Parkes, *The Jews in the Medieval Community* (London 1938), p. 106; Aronius, no. 314a, p. 141.

to the pope must have suggested itself soon after the events
of 1095-6. Pope Urban II had remained strangely silent in
the face of the ugly events which he had been instrumental
in arousing. The anti-pope Clement III was decidedly unsym-
pathetic and had even protested against the reversion of the
forced converts. [1] At the same time, the unsettled conditions
both in the Empire and in Rome which the popes of the
legitimate succession faced made an appeal to them impossible. [2] Peaceful conditions for the papacy did not return
until several years after the election of Pope Calixtus II in
1119. The Jews of the Empire then had an opportunity to
elicit a general statement of papal protection.

The above order of events constitutes a plausible theory, [3]
but unfortunately there is no way of proving its truth. No
actual copy of Calixtus' Bull is in existence; knowledge of
its issuance is based on the mention of Calixtus as the first
among the predecessors of the many popes [4] who are credited
with it. One cannot tell, therefore, whether Pope Calixtus
gave any indication of the people to whom the Bull was
addressed or of the situation that caused its promulgation.
If its wording was the same as that given above, it gave no
hint of the ravages caused by the crusaders. Another view
seems to be more cogent, namely, that the Bull was asked
for and given to the Jews of Rome. The turbulence of the
city during the first quarter of the twelfth century made

---

[1]   Migne, *PL* 148, col. 841. Aronius, no. 204: . . . *quod inauditum
est et prorsus nefarium*. But the anti-pope had no word of regret for
the method by which the conversion had been obtained.

[2]   *Cf.* F. X. Seppelt, *Papstgeschichte* (Munich 1949), pp. 112 ff.

[3]   Simon Dubnow, *Weltgeschichte des jüdischen Volkes* (Berlin 1926),
vol. iv, p. 407, takes the view that the Bull was issued for the benefit
of the Jews in general. Most others who dealt with the subject of the
Bull *Sicut Judeis* made the same assumption: *cf.* Peter Browe, *Die
Judenmission im Mittelalter und die Päpste* (Miscellanea Historiae
Pontificiae, vol. vi, Rome 1942), pp. 235 f. Aronius, no. 313a inclines
to connect its first issuance with events in France.

[4]   The first Bull extant is that credited to Pope Alexander III
(1159-81).

the need for such special protection obvious; [1] and subsequent popes repeated the Bull as an act of grace to their own Jewish subjects. One may assume that the Bull's extension to other Jewish communities came during the reigns of Calixtus' successors, perhaps during the time of later councils and crusades. [2]

The second pope to issue the Bull was Eugenius III (1145-53). During his reign the Second Crusade was in progress and the Jews of various parts of Europe were suffering in consequence. This pope would certainly have heeded their plea had the Jews turned to him for protection, since Bernard of Clairvaux, the most venerated Churchman of that day, had come out strongly in defense of the harrassed Jews. Yet Eugenius' Bull—assuming that it also did not differ from the *Sicut Judeis* issued by his successors—in no way reflects a situation like that of the attacks by crusaders. He, too, one must assume, granted the Bull to his Jewish subjects in the city of Rome who hailed him upon his entry into the city. [4]

There is no record of the next two popes issuing the Bull, perhaps because their relations with the city of Rome were not sufficiently peaceful. Alexander III, however, did issue it some time during his comparatively long reign of twenty-one years (1159-81). [5] For the first time one may assume that other Jews, besides those of Rome, were concerned with the

---

[1] Vogelstein und Rieger, *ibid.*, pp. 219 ff. Baron, *op. cit.*, p. 7 f. and n. 3 on pp. 235 f., while agreeing that it was given at the request of the Roman Jews, connects it with fears concerning possible enactments at the approaching First Lateran Council in 1123. If so, it would seem to indicate that the Jews of Rome were acting in behalf of all the Jews of Europe.

[2] Walter Holtzmann, "Zur päpstlichen Gesetzgebung über die Juden im 12ten Jahrhundert" in *Festschrift Guido Kisch* (Stuttgart 1955), p. 221 n. 3, points out that non-Roman recepients of the Bull are first mentioned in connection with the Bull issued by Pope Alexander III.

[3] Aronius, nos. 242-249.

[4] Vogelstein u. Rieger, *op. cit.*, p. 223.

[5] Jaffe 13973; Aronius, no. 313a.

document. A Jew by the name of Yehiel, scion of an important scholarly family, served Pope Alexander as financial advisor, and he may well have sensed the threat of hostile legislation emerging from the forthcoming Third Lateran Council. He may have acted as intermediary for Jewish communities who felt insecure and prevailed upon the pope to dispatch the Bull *Sicut Judeis*, originally given to the Jews of Rome, to such other places as France and England. [1]

It may be assumed therefore that, while the Jewish community of Rome continued to play the dominant role in obtaining the re-issuance of the Bull *Sicut Judeis* as soon as possible after the accession of a new pope, knowledge of the Bull had penetrated beyond Italy and that, by the latter part of the twelfth century, the Jews of the rest of Europe saw in it a statement that could be turned into a ready defense. The Church, too, now recognized it as more than an act of grace on the part of a pope after his ceremonious entry into the city. Of the three popes who followed Alexander III— Lucius III (1181-5), Urban III (1185-7) and Gregory VIII (1187)—only the first spent a few months in Rome, and these were troubled ones; they had no chance to issue the Bull. But Clement III (1187-91) did issue it and his Bull was preserved as a guide to Canon Law. [2] It was also issued by his successor, Coelestine III (1191-98), [3] and thereafter by almost every pope practically to the end of the thirteenth century: Innocent III, [4] on September 15, 1199, in the second year of his reign; Honorius III, [5] on November 7, 1217, in

---

[1]   Vogelstein u. Rieger, *op. cit.*, p. 225. Holtzmann, *loc. cit.*, mentions the archbishops of Reims and of Canterbury among those to whom the Bull was addressed. Baron, *op. cit.*, p. 238 n. 9, doubts the connection with the approaching meeting of the Third Lateran Council. This does not invalidate the possibility of Yehiel's intervention with the pope in behalf of the more distant Jewish communities.

[2]   Jaffe 16577; Aronius, no. 334; *see* p. 1, n. 2 above.

[3]   Aronius, no. 344. He, like his predecessor, is mentioned in the *Sicut Judeis* of Innocent III.

[4]   Potthast 834; *C & J*, pp. 92 ff., no. 5.

[5]   Potthast 5616; *C & J*, pp. 144 f., no 35.

his second year; Gregory IX, [1] on May 3, 1235, in his ninth
year, perhaps because his hold on the city of Rome was not
really secure till that year; [2] Innocent IV, [3] on October 22,
1246, and again on July 9, 1247, in his fourth and fifth years;
Alexander IV, [4] on September 22, 1255, in his first year;
Urban IV, [5] April 26, 1262, in his first year; none by Clement
IV (1265-68); [6] Gregory X, [7] October 7, 1272, and possibly
again on September 10, 1274, in his first and third years;
none by the three following popes who died within months
after their election; Nicholas III, [8] on August 2, 1278, in his
first year; Martin IV, [9] on August 2, 1281, in his first year;
Honorius IV (1285-7) and Nicholas IV (1288-92), dates
unknown. [10]

[1] Potthast 9893; C & J, pp. 218 f., no. 81.
[2] Cf. Seppelt, op. cit., p. 142.
[3] Potthast 12315; M. Stern, Päpstliche Bullen über die Blutbeschuldigung, pp. 14 ff.; C & J, pp. 260 ff. and 274 f., nos. 111 and
118. Cf. G. Bondy and F. Dworsky, Zur Geschichte der Juden in
Böhmen, Mähren und Schlesien von 906 bis 1620 (Prague 1906), vol. i,
pp. 25 ff.
[4] Fidel Fita, España Ebrea (Madrid 1890), part II, p. 87, drawn
from Boletin de la Real Academia de la Historia, 36-7 (1900), pp. 16-18.
[5] N. Ferorelli, Gli Ebrei nell' Italia meridionale (Turin 1915), p. 53;
Vatican Archives, Armarium II, 38, fol. 22r-24v.
[6] The existence of such a document has as yet not been indicated.
For Pope Clement III's attitude toward the Jews, see S. Grayzel,
"Jewish References in a Thirteenth-Century Formulary," JQR,
vol. xlvi (1955), 58.
[7] Bondy and Dworsky, op. cit., no. 27; Stern, Päpstliche Bullen,
pp. 18-22; idem, Urkundliche Beiträge, pp. 5-7; L. Ennen, Geschichte
der Stadt Köln (Cologne 1863), p. 64.
[8] B. and G. Lagumina, Codice diplomatico dei Giudei di Sicilia
(Palermo 1884-1909), vol. i, pp. 119 ff., no. 82.
[9] Ibid., pp. 117 f., no. 81.
[10] Vatican Archives, Armarium XXXI, 72, fol. 307v., gives a
Sicut Judeis in which the last two predecessors mentioned are Nicholas
and Honorius, thus indicating that Honorius IV issued the Bull and
that this was a copy of the document prepared for Nicholas IV who
was Honorius IV's immediate predecessor. Nicholas IV is also mentioned as the last in the series of predecessors in the Bull issued by
Clement VI: Regesta Vaticana 187, fol. 21r.; cf. Reynaldus, ad a.
1348, 33. See p. 22, n. 2 below.

There were no further renewals of the Bull until 1348.
One reason for this, during the rest of the final decade of
the thirteenth century, may have been the personalities
of the two men who occupied the Papal Throne: the non-
politically-minded Coelestine V, who soon resigned, and the
highly politically-minded Boniface VIII. The latter may have
refused to issue the Bull because of the growing influence
of the Inquisition, which found it an annoying limitation on
the inquisitors' desire to extend their jurisdiction over the
Jews. Pope Boniface may not even have been asked to renew
it because the Jews of Rome were in no position to approach
the pope. [1]

It is clear from the above—from the dates of issuance and
from the fact that copies of the Bull are found in various
parts of Europe—that the Jewish community of Rome had
in some way made itself responsible for obtaining the Bull
and for paying the fees involved. Other Jewish communities
could thereupon obtain copies from the Papal Chancery on
payment of a separate fee, but without going to the trouble
and expense of making the initial approach, [2] certainly more
difficult for non-residents of the city. The procedure was
facilitated by the wording of the Bull's address which generally
was the simple formula *Universis Christifidelibus* (To All
Faithful Chirstians), or some modification of it, rather than
to the Christians of any specific city or region. Nor did the
thirteenth-century Bull indicate the Jewish community that
had asked for protection. This may also explain in part why
two of the popes enumerated above are credited with two
issues of the *Sicut Judeis*, though in each case one of the
issues contains additional protection.

[1] On the condition of the Roman Jews during the last decade of
the 13th century, *see* Vogelstein u. Rieger, *op. cit.*, pp. 252-8.

[2] For a brief reference to fees *see* R. L. Poole, *The Papal Chancery*
(Cambridge 1915), p. 134. On expenses incurred in the process of
asking for papal protection *see* Grayzel, *JQR*, vol. xlvi (1955), 64.

3. *Its Expansion*

The popes, for their part, looked upon the Bull *Sicut Judœis* as a statement of general Church policy. Pope Innocent III emphasized this attitude by adding a prefatory statement to the *Sicut Judeis* which he granted early in his reign. Always desirous of acting in accordance with neatly regulated theological principles, he saw in this Bull, not only the limits within which Jewish life was to be lived, but also the bounds of his own authority respecting the "Jewish perversion of faith" (*perfidia Judeorum*). He consequently felt that he must explain his issuance of the Bull, and he set the tone for it by harking back to Augustine. [1] His introductory statement read as follows: [2]

> Although the Jewish distortion of the faith is deserving of thorough condemnation, nevertheless, because the truth of our own faith is proved through them, they must not be severely oppressed by the faithful. So the prophet says, "Thou shalt not kill them, lest in time they forget Thy Law"; or, more clearly put: Thou shalt not destroy the Jews completely so that the Christians may not possibly forget Thy Law which, though they themselves fail to understand it, they display in their books for those who do understand.

Pursuing the same thought of the Church Father, Innocent III, in a letter to Philip-Augustus of France, eloquently urged the repression of the Jews, but he began by restating the old principle that their dispersion and subjection are pleasing to God. [3] In fact, apart from the Bull *Sicut Judeis*, Pope Innocent III issued no communication favorable to the

---

[1] *See above*, p. 6, n. 1.

[2] *C & J*, pp. 92 f. — *Licet peridia Judeorum sit multipliciter reprobanda, quia tamen per eos fides nostra veraciter comprabatur, non sunt a fidelibus graviter opprimendi; dicente propheta: Ne occideris eos ne quando obliviscantur legis tue," ac si diceretur appertius: Ne deleveris omnino Judeos, ne forte Christiani legis tue valeant oblivisci, quam ipsi non intelligentes, in libris suis intelligentibus representant.*

[3] Potthast 2373, January 16, 1205; *C & J*, p. 104: *Etsi non displiceat Domino, sed ei potius sit acceptum ut sub catholicis regibus et principibus Christianis vivat et serviat dispersio Judeorum ... vehementer tamen oculos divine majestatis offendunt ...*

Jews; nevertheless, he who had ordered the extermination of the Albigenses warned crusaders and other Christians against doing the Jews physical harm. [1]

With few exceptions, other popes who issued the Bull did, when requested, extend additional protection by means of letters directed to princes and Churchmen in various parts of Europe where persecution of the Jews was rampant. But what is especially interesting in this connection is the fact that such protection was also extended by means of additions to the *Sicut Judeis*. This happened on three occasions in the thirteenth century and more frequently thereafter. If, therefore, one assumes that by the thirteenth century this Bull was meant to define Church policy, the additions to it must have been looked upon by those who made them as elaborations of that policy.

Before discussing the three additions, it may be helpful to cite instances when separate Bulls were issued on a subject which later became the substance of an addition to the *Sicut Judeis*. We have seen that in 1235 Pope Gregory IX granted the Jews a *Sicut Judeis* Bull. It appears to have afforded insufficient protection to the Jews of France and England who then found themselves in dire straits. A year later, Pope Gregory IX therefore responded to their plea and issued a more direct warning to their persecutors, thereby gaining the reputation of having been bribed by the Jews. [2] Graetz connects these two Bulls with a ritual murder accusation at Lauda. [3] Such a connection with the ritual murder libel was made by next pope, Innocent IV, who had also granted a *Sicut Judeis*. He, too, like his predecessor, speaks with horror about the cruelties perpetrated against the Jews by men who were obviously more interested in gain than in truth. [4]

[1]   Potthast 5257; *C & J*, p. 142, no. 32.
[2]   *C & J*, pp. 218 f., no. 81 and n. 2; and *ibid.*, pp. 226 ff., Potthast 10243.
[3]   Graetz, *Geschichte*, vol. vii, p. 92 and n. 4 at end of the volume.
[4]   Pope Innocent IV had issued his *Sicut Judeis* in October 1246. The following May he sent a series of letters concerning the ritual

No wonder that Pope Innocent IV thereupon decided to add the prohibition of the ritual murder charge to the list of those actions against the Jews prohibited by Church policy. On July 9, 1247, he granted a second *Sicut Judeis* in which the following was added immediately before the final penalty clause: [1]

> ... exhume bodies there interred. Nor shall anyone accuse them of using human blood in their religious rites; for they are instructed in the Old Testament against the use of blood of any kind, not to speak of human blood. Since, however, at Fulda and elsewhere many Jews have been killed on account of this suspicion, we, by the authority of these presents, strictly forbid the recurrence of this charge in the future. If anyone ...

The next addition was made by Pope Gregory X. Innocent's warning had done no good; cases of ritual murder accusation multiplied during the long interregnum in the Empire and spread to countries on its periphery. [2] Gregory X's statement on the subject was therefore longer and more detailed, so that the Bull itself appears almost like an introduction to the refutation of the charge which resulted in such barbarities. Moreover, even where the accused Jews were brought to trial, the judicial hearings were a farce, since a number of Christians were always on hand to testify against them. It was necessary, therefore, to re-assert the existing judicial

---

murder charge: to the Archbishop of Vienne, on May 28, 1247: *C & J*, pp. 262, no. 113 and 114; to the King of Navarre and Count of Champagne, June 12 and July 6, 1247; *ibid.*, nos. 115 and 117; to the Archbishops and Bishops of Germany, July 5, 1247: *ibid.*, no. 116.

[1]   *C & J*, pp. 274, no. 118: ... *corpora humata effodere, nec aliquis eis obiciat quod in ritu suo humano utantur sanguine, cum tamen in veteri testamento preceptum sit eis, ut de humano sanguine taceamus, quod quolibet sanguine non utantur; cum apud Fuldam et in pluribus aliis locis propter huiusmodi suspicionem multi Judei sint occisi; quod auctoritate presentium ne deinceps fiat districtius inhibemus. Si quid autem* ...

[2]   Graetz, *Geschichte*, vol. vii, p. 148, calls them an almost annual occurrence. Boleslav of Poland prohibited the libel in 1264: *cf.* Aron Eisenstein, *Die Stellung der Juden in Polen im 13ten und 14ten Jahrhundert* (1934), pp. 34 ff. On the possibility, if not the likelihood, of Pope Clement IV crediting the libel, *see* Grayzel, "Formulary etc.", *JQR*, vol. xlvi (1955), 58 ff.

procedure in which a mixed group of witnesses was required to condemn a Jew for murder. [1] This, too, was introduced into an expanded *Sicut Judeis*. The new material was introduced immediately after the prohibition against changing the old customs: [2]

> . . . from ancient times. Furthermore, we decree that the testimony of Christians shall not avail against Jews unless a Jew is among the Christian witnesses, since Jews [alone] cannot act as witnesses against Christians. For it happens from time to time that Christian children are lost and the enemies of the Jews thereupon accuse them of having stealthily kidnapped and murdered these Christian children and of having performed a sacrifice of their hearts and blood. Or the parents of the children, or other Christians who are enemies of the Jews, secretly hide these children so as to be able to accuse the Jews; and, in order to be able to extort sums of money from them as a means of purchasing freedom from torture, they make the totally false assertion that the Jews were the ones who had secretly and stealthily kidnapped the

---

[1] *Cf.* Kisch, *The Jews in Medieval Germany*, pp. 260 ff.

[2] Stern, *Blutbeschuldigung*, pp. 18-23; *idem*, *Urkundliche Beiträge*, pp. 5-7; Bondy and Dworsky, vol. 1, pp. 32-4, no. 27.

. . . temporibus consueverunt. Statuimus etiam ut testimonium Christianorum contra Judeos non valeat nisi sit Judeus aliquis inter eos Christianos ad testimonium perhibendum, cum Judei non possint contra Christianos testimonium perhibere; quia contigit interdum quod aliqui Christiani perdunt eorum pueros Christianos et impingitur in Judeos ipsos per inimicos eorum ut pueros ipsos Christianos furtim subtrahant et occidant, et quod de corde et sanguine sacrificent eorundem, ac patres eorundem puerorum vel Christiani alii Judeorum ipsorum emuli clam abscondunt ipsos pueros, ut possint Judeos ipsos offendere et pro eorum vexationibus redimendis possint a Judeis ipsis extorquere aliquam pecunie quantitatem, asserantque falsissime quod Judei ipsi pueros ipsos clam et furtim subtraxerunt et occiderunt et quod Judei ex corde et sanguine eorum sacrificent puerorum; cum lex eorum hoc precise inhibeat et expresse quod non sacrificent, non comedant sanguinem neque bibant, nec etiam comedant de carnibus animalium habentium ungues scissas; et hoc per Judeos ad Christianam fidem conversos in nostra curia pluries probatum; hac occasione huiusmodi Judei plurimi pluries contra iustitiam capti fuerunt et detenti. Statuimus quod Christiani in casu huiusmodi contra Judeos audiri non debeant, et mandamus quod Judei capti huiusmodi occasione frivola a carcere liberentur nec deinceps huiusmodi occasione frivola capiantur, nisi forte, quod non credimus, in flagrante crimine caperentur. Statuimus ut nullus Christianus novitatem aliquam exerceat in eosdem, sed in statu serventur et forma in qua fuerunt predecessorum nostrorum temporibus hactenus ab antiquo . . .

children and killed them and had sacrificed their hearts and blood. Since their Law clearly and explicitly prohibits them from sacrificing, eating and drinking blood, or tasting it even from animals of cloven hoof—as has been repeatedly proved before our court through Jewish converts to our faith—the frequent arrest and imprisonment of such Jews has been contrary to justice. We ordain that Christians must not be heard against Jews in such cases, and we order that the Jews arrested on this empty charge be freed from prison and that the Jews be not hereafter arrested on the basis of this empty charge, unless, perchance— which we do not believe likely—they are caught red-handed. We ordain that no Christian shall introduce any innovation with respect to them, but that they shall remain in the position and status which has been theirs from the days of our predecessors in times gone by till our own day...

A situation of still another kind, though also connected with witnesses and the judicial process, was the subject of an addition to *Sicut Judeis* by Pope Martin IV in 1281. The zeal of the inquisitors in ferreting out heresy made them try to extend their operations to Jews. They justified their going outside the confines of Christianity in a number of ways: a hostile Christian might accuse his Jewish neighbor or creditor of sacrilege or blasphemy or ritual murder; or a Jewsih convert to Christianity might be found to have continued his contacts with memebers of his Jewish family, thus laying them open to the charge of trying to lure him back into the Jewsih fold. The latter charge became especially frequent during the second half of the thirteenth century as a result of the many ritual murder libels and the ensuing riots with their inevitable forced conversions. A number of papal pronouncements bear on the subject of safeguarding the Christianity of the converts. [1] But Pope Martin IV was also convinced that this

---

[1] The Bull *Turbato corde* was repeatedly issued at the request of inquisitors in various parts of Europe: Clement IV, 1267, Potthast 20095, I. H. Sbaralea, *Bullarium Franciscanum* (Rome, 1759-68), III, 127; Gregory X, 1274, Potthast 20798, Th. Ripoll, *Bullarium FF. Praedicatorum* (Rome, 1729-40), I, 517; Martin IV, 1281, Bibliothèque Nationale, Fond Doat 37, fol. 193 ff., *cf. REJ*, III, p. 218, no. 53; Nicholas IV, 1288, Potthast 22795, E. Langlois, *Les Registres de Nicholas IV*, p. 62, no. 322, *REJ*, III, p. 220, no. 66; again in 1290, Potthast 23391, *Registres*, p. 511, no. 3186. An extract from a Bull

situation, like the charge of ritual murder, encouraged false accusations and false testimony, especially since the usual procedure was to force confession out of the accused rather than make the accuser prove his charge. His addition to the *Sicut Judeis*, therefore, attempted to make such accusations more risky; it also made it possible for a convert to move about with greater freedom, provided he had nothing to do with his former family.

Pope Martin's addition was inserted just ahead of the penal clause, and read as follows: [1]

> ... exhume bodies there interred. We also desire and decree that no inquisitor of the evil of heresy, or anyone else whatever his office, shall exert compulsion on the said Jews or on anyone of them on any man's petition; but that he who accuses them must give and submit to the court a guarentee [of trustworthiness] similarly secure. If the crime of which the Jew is accused is not proved, the accuser shall be subject to the same penalty to which the accused was bound and it shall be inflicted on him. And if a baptized Jew has converse with some other Jew whom he does not recognize, he shall not be held for punishment. If anyone ...

None of these three additions to the Bull *Sicut Judeis* during the thirteenth century acquired the force of Church policy either to the extent of being repeated by subsequent popes or of being included in the *Corpus Juris Canonici*. In fact, the one concerned with the inclusion of a Jew among the witnesses testifying against another Jew in a criminal case

bearing on the same subject, which may have been a repetition of *Turbato Corde* issued by Pope Boniface VIII, found its way into the *Corpus Juris Canonici*, Decretalium lib. V, tit. II, c. xiii. *Cf.* Browe, *Judenmission*, pp. 258 f. Note that this Bull by Martin IV was issued only a few months before the *Sicut Judeis* under discussion.

[1] Lagumina, *op. cit.*, pp. 117 f., no. 81: ... *corpora humata effodere. Volumus etiam et mandamus quod nullus inquisitor heretice pravitatis vel aliquis alter cuiuscumque dignitatis existat ad petitionem alicuius non teneatur cogere predictos Judeos vel eorum alterum, sed ille qui eos accusaverit det et prestet ydoneam fidejussoriam causionem curie; sed si legitime non probaverit delictum de quo accusatus est [sic] quod accusator teneatur ad illam penam sicut accusatus est teneretur et auferatur eidem. Et si aliquis Judeus baptizatus haberet aliquam familiaritatem cum aliquo alio Judeo et non cognosceretur [sic] quod non teneatur ad penam aliquam. Si quis autem ...*

was tacitly contradicted in a pronouncement of the Council of Vienne which was included in the *Corpus*. [1] What these additions point up is that the situation of the Jews by the end of the thirteenth century was—as we shall indicate below—beyond any aid from the vague generalizations contained in the Bull *Sicut Judeis*. Its granting had become a formality; and the long and specific additions to it, like that of Gregory X on the ritual murder libel, even went contrary to its nature as a *constitutio*. When the Jews of any part of Europe cast about for help from the imminent danger stemming in part from religious fanaticism, they would turn to the pope for a statement bearing on the specific problem which faced them. They frequently elicited such a statement, [2] quite apart from the Bull *Sicut Judeis*. When the Jews asked the protection of their secular ruler, they would submit a copy of the *Sicut Judeis*, sometimes one issued long before, but generally accompanied with a more specific papal protest against their persecution. [3] There were popes who, as far as

[1]   The oecumenical Council of Vienne was held from October 1311 to May 1312. The decision was included in the Clementinarum lib. II, tit. VIII, c. 1.

[2]   Every pope who reigned for any length of time during the second half of the 13th century, with the exception of Clement IV, and most of those of the 14th century as well, had occasion to issue protective pronouncements for the Jews.

[3]   The Jews would submit the documents for inspection by the local authorities, who would then incorporate these documents in an edict of their own. For example, Rudolph of Hapsburg, in 1275, acknowledged and ratified the Bull *Sicut Judeis* as issued by Pope Gregory X, with its long addition on the subject of ritual murder, as well as the Bull *Lachrymabilem Judeorum* which had been issued by Pope Innocent IV in 1247 and which bore on the same subject; *cf.* Stern, *Blutbeschuldigung*, p. 13 and the references there cited. A similar *Vidimus* is mentioned in Bondy and Dworsky, *op. cit.*, pp. 35-6. The same volume cites an earlier instance, in no. 25, pp. 23-8, where King Premysl-Ottakar II of Bohemia acknowledges seeing and ratifies the *Sicut Judeis* of Innocent IV and the same pope's Bull *Obviare non credimus*, directing the Bishop of Würzburg to oppose the mistreatment of the Jews in his diocese (September 25, 1253: *C & J*, pp. 292 ff., no. 132). On the other hand, King Martin and Queen Maria of Sicily, on June 28, 1392, acknowledged and ratified

is known, did not issue a *Sicut Judeis*, yet offered protection on a definite issue. Pope Boniface VIII, for example, one of the very few popes in the thirteenth century without a *Sicut Judeis* to his credit, responded to the request of the Jews of Rome for protection against the inquisitors who, claiming that every Jew was "powerful" and therefore in a position to intimidate witnesses, refused to let accused Jews see the names of the people who had testified against them, thus interfering with their defense. [1]

4. *Its Decline*

It is quite possible that, had the popes' residence in Rome remained uninterrupted, they would have continued issuing the official Bull of protection as part of the formality of their accession. But the prolonged absence of the popes from Rome during the so-called Babylonish Captivity broke the custom. At the same time, the Jews outside of Rome had learned that there was no advantage in obtaining the Bull's confirmation. There is hardly a trace of the wording of *Sicut Judeis* in the protective pronouncements of the first two popes (John XXII and Benedict XII) permanently resident in Avignon. [2] Its first reaffirmation in full was made by Pope

the *Sicut Judeis* of Pope Nicholas III of 1278, with no other Bull appended: Lagumina, *op. cit.*, no. LXXXII.

[1] *Exhibita nobis*, June 13, 1299, for the Jews of Rome and the same on July 7, 1299, for the Jews of the Comtat Venaissin: Digard, Faucon, Thomas et Fawtier, *Les Registres de Boniface VIII*, vol. ii, cols. 412 and 488, nos. 3063 and 3215: ... *vos asserentes potentes, publicationem huiusmodi vobis aliquando facere denegant, sicque vobis ex hoc debite defensionis facultas subtrahitur* ...

[2] Pope John XXII had occasion to speak out for the protection of the Jews when he urged both the civil and ecclesiastical authorities to take strong measures against the participants in the Shepherds' Crusade in 1320: *cf.* S. Grayzel, "References to the Jews in the Correspondence of John XXII," *HUC Annual*, vol. xxiii (1950-1), part 2, pp. 47-52, nos. x-xiii. No. xiii contains the phrase *specia ius sunt in testimonium catholice fidei reservati*. Pope Benedict's efforts to protect Jewish life seem limited to the one instance in 1338 when the Jews of a number of towns in Bavaria were accused of ritual murder

Clement VI in 1348. [1] This was the year of the Black Death,
when the Jews, accused of poisoning the wells of drinking
water, were subjected to great cruelty and slaughter. Messengers came to Avignon from various parts of Europe and
pleaded for protection. But again it was felt, presumably both
by the Jews and by the pope, that the statement in *Sicut
Judeis* was hardly specific enough to meet the situation. A
second Bull was therefore issued a few months later, referring
back to the above Bull, repeating the substance of its usual
preamble, summarizing the rest and then continuing to refute
the charge of poisoning the drinking water and demanding
that the persecutions cease. Addressed to the higher clergy,
it began as follows: [2]

and desecration of the Host. The pope suspected that it was a plot
and that some of the clergy were involved. He asked Albert of Austria
to investigate. *Cf.* Raynaldus ad a. 1338 §18-20; J. M. Vidal, *Les
Registres de Benoit XII, Lettres closes et patentes*, p. 571 f., no. 1966.
    [1]   *Sicut Judeis*, July 4, 1348: Raynaldus as a. 1348 § 33; Reg. Vat.
187, fol. 21r.
    [2]   October 1, 1348: A. Lang, *Acta Salzburgo-Aquilajensia* (Graz
1903), vol. i, pp. 301-2; Reg. Vat. 187, fol. 20v-21r. Raynaldus,
u.s., combines the two Bulls.
    *Quamvis perfidiam Judeorum, qui in sua duritia perdurantes prophe-
tarum verba et suarum scripturarum archana cognoscere atque ad christiane fidei et salutis notitiam pervenire non curant, merito detestemur,
attendentes tamen quod Judei predicti ex eo sustinendi sunt quod Ysaya
propheta testante temporum reliquie salve fient, eis invocantibus defensionis nostre presidium et christiane mansuetudinem pietatis, nos, felicis
recordationis Calixti, Eugenii, Alexandri, Clementis, Celestini, Innocentii,
Gregorii, Nicolai, Honorii et Nicolai IV, Romanorum pontificum
predecessorum nostrorum vestigiis inherentes, protectionis nostre clipeum
duximus indulgendum; inter cetera statuentes: ut nullus Christianus
eorundem Judeorum personas sine judicio domini aut officialis terre vel
regionis in qua habitant vulnerare aut occidere vel suas illis pecunias
auferre sive ab eis coacta servitia exigere, nisi ea que ipsis temporibus
facere consueverunt preteritis presumeret ullomodo, et quod si quis
statuti huiusmodi tenore cognito contra illud ire temptaret, honoris et
officii sui periculum pateretur aut plecteretur excommunicationis
sententia, nisi presumptionem suam digna satisfactione corrigere
procuraret, prout in eisdem litteris plenius continetur.
    Nuper autem ad nostram fama publica . . .*
    Clement VI issued one other Bull on the subject of events connected
with the Black Death and mentioning the Jews. It was addressed to

Even though we properly scorn the Jewish perversion of the faith, because they, persisting in their stubbornness, refuse to understand the words of their own prophets and the mysteries of their own scriptures and so accept the Christian faith and the promise of salvation, nevertheless, we recognize that the said Jews are to be tolerated, since the Prophet Isaiah bore witness that in time to come their remnant would be saved. To them, therefore, invoking our protective guardianship and the kindliness of Christian piety, we, following in the footsteps of our predecessors of blessed memory, the Roman pontiffs Calixtus, Eugenius, Alexander, Clement, Celestinus, Innocent, Gregory, Nicholas, Honorius, and Nicholas IV, have caused the shield of our protection to be granted, decreeing, among other things, that: No Christian shall dare, for whatever reason, to wound or kill these Jews without the judgment of the lord or officers of the country or region which they inhabit, or carry off their property, or exact forced service from them excepting such as they have been accustomed to perform for them in time gone by. Whoever, knowing the contents of this decree, attempts to act to the contrary shall lay himself open to the loss of honors and office or be punished by excommunication, unless he takes care to correct his presumption by means of the proper amends—as is clearly stated in those same letters.

Recently widespread rumor has made us aware . . .

One may note that this summary of the Bull *Sicut Judeis* does not contain any direct reference to forced conversion or to interference with the synagogue. It may be that Pope Clement VI simply emphasized life, property and forced services because these were the earmarks of the persecutions of the day; nevertheless, the missing items are significant.

Another restatement of *Sicut Judeis* in its practically unmodified form was issued by Pope Urban V, in 1365. [1] It may have been asked for by the Jews of France who had

the Archbishop of Magdeburg and dealt specifically with the Flagellants, asking for their repression along with the laymen and the clerics who had joined them: *Inter solicitudines*, October 20, 1349: G. Schmidt, *Päpstliche Urkunden und Regesten* (Halle 1886), no. 172; Reg. Vat. 143, fol. 94v-96r.

. . . *considerantes quod, cum plerique ex ipsis seu adherentes eisdem sub pietatis colore ad impietatis opera laxantes crudeliter manus suas Judeorum, quos pietas Christiana recepit et sustinet, offendi eos aliquatenus non permittens . . .*

[1] June 7, 1365: Bull. Rom., vol. iii, part II, p. 327; Reg. Vat. 254, fol. 36r. On the position of the Jews of France *see* Parkes, *Community*, pp. 372 f.

but recently been readmitted to that country in restricted numbers. Thus, the Bull was issued, during the Babylonish Captivity, twice in its usual form and once in considerably modified form.

The return of the popes to Rome might have been expected to bring about a revival of the Bull's use at the beginning of a papal reign; but this did not happen. The Bull was not issued by Urban VI. There is evidence of its issuance by Pope Boniface IX (1389-1404), who showed his favor to the Jews on a number of occasions. [1] The Avignon pope Clement VII, on the other hand, issued the Bull twice. The first time, in 1379, [2] therefore soon after his accession, it was intended perhaps as a symbolic assertion of legitimacy, since it revived an ancient custom. It concerned the Jews of Avignon and, after the usual beginning, deviated to guarantee their safety and their peaceful possession of communal property. The anti-pope issued it a second time, in its usual wording, in 1393, [3] perhaps in connection with events in Spain where under existing circumstances it was bound to be meaningless. But the next two popes of the Roman succession, Innocent VII and Gregory XII, did not issue any *Sicut*

---

[1] Browe, *Judenmission*, p. 235, concludes that such a Bull was issued by basing himself on a calculation made by M. Kayserling, *Geschichte der Juden in Portugal* (Leipzig 1867), p. 38. The calculation does not appear convincing. It is in any case unnecessary, since Boniface IX appears among the predecessors enumerated by Eugenius IV in his Bull issued in 1432 as given in Neubauer's note in *JQR*, o.s., vol. ii (1890), 530, though omitted in Stern, *Beiträge*, p. 43, no. 34. Among Boniface IX's many favorable pronouncements were: for the Jews of Velletri, *Licet Judei*, July 12, 1401: Reg. Lat. 89, fol. 185v-186r; for the Jewish settlers in Calabria, *Etsi Judeorum*, June 26, 1403: Reg. Lat. 108, fol. 99r.-v.; for the Jews of Rome, guaranteeing their peaceful possession of property, *Religioni convenit*, in 1403: Vernet, "Le Pape Martin V et les Juifs," *Revue des Questions historiques*, vol. 51 (1892), no. 68.

[2] Konrad Eubel, "Zu dem Verhalten der Päpste gegen die Juden," *Römische Quartalschrift*, 13 (1899), p. 30, no. 2.

[3] *Ibid.*, 17 (1903), p. 184, no. 3.

Judeis, although the former ratified all the privileges that had been granted the Jews by his predecessors. [1]

By the time of Pope Martin V (elected in 1417), some two centuries of experience had shown that the basic regulations of the Bull *Sicut Judeis* were no longer relevant. The traditional idea that protecting the Jews was a matter of Christian piety could not be abandoned, but the areas of protection were now quite different. The Bull had long ceased to be a practical *constitutio* and had become just another papal pronouncement, subject to the vagaries of politics in an ecclesiastically turbulent age.

Once the Great Schism had been healed, it was but natural for the popes, Martin V and his successor Eugenius IV, to seek to re-establish the power and influence of the papacy. [2] Their vacillating attitude toward the Jews was a manifestation of the conflict between their innate sense of fairness and their desire to show unchallangeable zeal for the Church, between their attempt to retain the support of the princes and their desire not re-arouse the conciliar movement. Pope Martin appeared at first unfavorably disposed toward the Jews; but he soon changed his mind, under the urging of some civil authorities [3] who called his attention to the deteriorating condition of the Jews as a result of the activities of the preaching monks and the inquisitors. In the course of his reign, he issued a considerable number of pronouncements about the Jews. [4] Those between the years 1418 and 1422 were on the whole in their favor; and two of them bore unmistakable resemblance to the *Sicut Judeis*, commencing with the usual formula but then turning to matters of more immediate concern.

[1] Addressed: *Universis Judeis utriusque sexus ubilibet commorantibus: Quamvis potius*, August 1, 1406: Reg. Vat. 334, fol. 186v.

[2] *Cf.* L. Elliott Binns, *The Decline and Fall of the Medieval Papacy* (London 1934), pp. 202-4; Seppelt, *Papstgeschichte*, pp. 183 ff.

[3] Salomon Kahn, *Une Bulle inédite de Martin V* (Nimes, n.d.), p. 4. On the influence of King Sigismund *see* Max Simonsohn, *Die kirchliche Judengesetzgebung im Zeitalter der Reformkonzilien von Konstanz und Basel* (Breslau 1912), p. 20.

[4] Vernet, in the article cited above, lists 84 items.

The first of these, issued in Mantua in 1419, [1] was in behalf of the Jews of northern Italy. After stating that they must not be molested in their synagogues nor forced into baptism, it goes on to add that they must not be compelled to violate their Sabbaths and holidays, although they should not be allowed to work openly on Christian festivals; the wearing of the Jewish Badge should not be made harsher than it had been in their respective places of habitation; and they must be permitted to do business with Christians. The Bull ends on the usual note that it was intended for the protection of only those Jews who do not plot against Christianity.

Almost exactly four years later, [2] Pope Martin issued a

---

[1] Stern, *Beiträge*, no. 11; Raynaldus, ad a. 1419, § 2; Simonsohn, *op. cit.*, p. 23, gives the date as January 31; Vernet, *op. cit.*, p. 411, no. 9. The preamble also contains the phrase *quia imaginem Dei habent*. This *Sicut Judeis* was not as inclusive as the one given by Pope Martin at Constance, on February 12, 1418, *Quamvis potius*, addressed to the Jews of Germany and Savoy in response to their petition seconded by King Sigismund. The papal Bull approved a highly favorable list of privileges granted them by the papal vice-chamberlain Ludovicus Alamandi. See Stern, *op. cit.*, nos. 9, 10; Vernet, *op. cit.*, nos. 5, 6.

[2] Stern, *op. cit.*, no. 21; Vernet, *op. cit.*, no. 24; Raynaldus, ad a. 1422, § 36; dated February 20, 1422.

... *ipsorum Judeorum petitionem admittimus eisque nostre protectionis clypeum impertimur. Sane querelam quorundam Judeorum nuper accepimus, continentem quod nunnulli predicatores verbi Dei tam mendicantium quam ordinum aliorum ... Christianis inhibent ... ut fugiant et evitent consortia Judeorum ... propter quae nunnumquam inter eos et Christianos dissensiones et scandala oriuntur daturque materia ipsis Judeis ... in eorum perfidia perdurandi. ... plurimi Christiani, ut dictos Judeos redimi facere et eos bonis et substantiis spoliare ... possint, fictis occasionibus et coloribus asserunt ... Judeos ipsos venenum in fontibus iniecisse et suis azymis humanum sanguinem miscuisse .... Ex quibus occasionibus populi commoventur contra Judeos ipsos eosque caedunt et variis persecutionibus et molestiis afficiunt et affligunt. Nos igitur considerantes quod religioni convenit Christiane Judeis eo libentius ... oportunum prestare subsidium quo specialius sint in testimonium orthodoxe fidei reservati, eorum testante propheta tandem reliquie salve fient ... inhibemus ne de cetero talia vel similia contra Judeos ... ubilibet constitutos ... per quovis predicatores religiosos vel seculares ... populis predicare permittant; volentes, quod quilibet Christianus Judeos ipsos humana mansuetudine prosequatur nec eis in*

second *Sicut Judeis*, this time addressed to all Christians and applying to Jews everywhere. After the usual beginning and mentioning a number of the predecessors who had issued the Bull, he further motivates its issuance by pointing out that preachers to the Christians threaten with excommunication those who have any dealings with the Jews, even to the extent of making a fire for them or nursing their children, and that Christians stir up riots against the Jews by accusing them of poisoning wells, mixing blood with their matzot, and bringing calamities on mankind. Thus ill treated, Jews are discouraged from joining the Christian faith. The pope reminds the Christians that the Jews are preserved by God in order to provide testimony for the truth of Christianity and that the prophets had said that a remnant of them would be saved. He therefore goes on to forbid preachers to preach against them, to urge that they be treated with kindness, to permit them to have converse with Christians, to prohibit injuring their persons or property, to let them enjoy the privileges granted or to be granted them, to place them under civil or ordinary ecclesiastical (rather than inquisitorial) authority, so as not to subject them to exactions or molestations. Furthermore, lest the contents of this decree be kept from public knowledge, he orders that it be copied by the notary and be made known to all. The Bull, of course, contains the usual limitation to those Jews who do not plot against Christianity.

personis, rebus, aut bonis suis inferat iniuriam, molestiam vel offensamt sed sicut permissum est eis cum Christianis vicissim conversari, licea, etiam mutua commoda alterutrum suscipere. Quibus etiam Judeis de speciali gratia indulgemus ut omnibus et singulis privilegiis, gratiis et libertatibus et indultis quacumque auctoritate et per quousque et sub quacunque verborum forma concessis et in posterum concendendis ... uti valeant et gaudere; statuentes quod de cetero inquisitores heretice pravitatis nullam in eosdem Judeos ... auctoritatem valeant exercere seu ab eis quidquam exigere neque eos ad subeundum quiquod iudicium inquietare vel molestare presumant ... Illos autem Judeos ... volumus communiri ... qui nihil machinare presumpserint in subversionem fidei memorate. Verum quoniam difficile videtur presentes litteras singulis exhiberi, volumus quod huiusmodi ... transsumptum manu publici notarii in formam publicam redactum ... Nulli ergo ...

The issuance of so broad a privilege, on top of various other favorable pronouncements for the Jews—even of those of Spain—and other restrictions on the zealous preachers, [1] appears to have aroused a storm of protest. Within the year, Pope Martin rescinded the Bull and imposed restrictive regulations. [2] This hostile attitude prevailed, on the whole, till 1429 when it underwent another sudden change. At the beginning of that year, the pope issued a Bull of protection which outdid the *Sicut Judeis* of 1421 in the extent of protection and the number of privileges granted. [3]

There are two striking differences from the usual about this document. One is in the wording of the preamble. The Bull does not begin with the words *Sicut Judeis*, but with *Quamquam Judei*. It expresses the thought that, although the Jews choose to remain obdurate in their refusal to recognize the truth of Christianity, nonetheless the Church tolerates them as witnesses of Jesus and in the hope that Christian kindness will lead them to baptism. [4] The predecessors who granted protection by the usual Bull are mentioned, but not enumerated. The introductory words of *Sicut Judeis* occur somewhat later in the document, as a preface to the actual

---

[1] *Cf.* Stern, *op. cit.*, nos. 12, 16, 17; Vernet, *op. cit.*, nos. 19, 21, 22, 22b, 22c. On Martin's relieving the Jews of Spain from the restrictions imposed on them by the anti-pope Benedict XIII, see Stern, *op. cit.*, no. 18; Vernet, nos. 17, 18.

[2] For the pressure brought on the pope and for the rumors that became current that he had been bribed by the Jews, see Simonsohn, *op. cit.*, pp. 28-32. For the recall of the favorable Bull, see Stern, *op. cit.*, nos. 24, 25, 26; Vernet, *op. cit.*, nos. 28, 29, 32, 48, 48b.

[3] *Quamquam Judei*, February 13, 1429: Stern, *op. cit.*, no. 31; Vernet, *op. cit.*, no. 52.

[4] *Quamquam Judei, quos in diversis mundi partibus constitutos sacrosancta tolerat ecclesia in testimonium Jesu Christi, in sua velint duritia et caecitate perdurare, quam prophetarum verba et sanctarum scripturarum arcana cognoscere et ad Christianae fidei et salutis notitiam pervenire; quia tamen in suis necessitatibus nostra praesidia et favores interpellant, nos eis pietatis Christianae mansuetudinem et clementiam non intendimus denegare, ut huiusmodi pietate allecti suos recognoscant errores et suprema gratia illustrati tamquam ad verum, quod Christus est, lumen properent charitatis.*

grant of protection and privilege. [1] The second striking
difference between this Bull and *Sicut Judeis* is its use in
behalf, not of all Jews, but of the Jews of Italy. Perhaps this
accounts for its departure from the customary beginning,
namely, that *Sicut Judeis* as a formula had acquired the
tradition of universal application. One may speculate on the
possibility that the pope, having bound himself in 1421 not
to extend this privilege to the Jews of all lands, did not
consider it a breach of his promise nor an irritant to zealous
Churchmen in other lands to issue a Bull of protection to
the Jews of Italy so much more directly under his control.

The rest of the document follows pretty closely the *Sicut
Judeis* of 1421, the language being somewhat stronger. But
the few new items deserve mention. [2] Inquisitors are warned

[1] After describing the difficulties under which the Jews labor:
the hostile preaching, the scandalous accusations, and the riots which
these arouse—very much as in the case of the *Sicut Judeis* of 1421—
he continues:

*Nos considerantes rationi fore consonum quod sicut Judaeis licitum
non existit in suis synagogis ultra quam permissum est presumere, ita in
iis quae a jure concessa sunt ipsis nullum detur praeiudicium substinere,
quodque religioni convenit Christianae Judaeis eo libentius contra
ipsorum persecutores praestare praesidium quo speciales sunt in testimonium orthodoxae fidei reservati . . . in hoc etiam diversorum prae-
decessorum nostrorum Romanorum pontificum vestigiis inhaerendo,
huiusmodi supplicationibus inclinati . . .*

[2] *. . . nec non inquisitores commisum officium contra Judaeos ipsos,
nisi in debitis haeresis factoriam sapientibus, ac illa seu quodvis aliud
in fide catholica detrimentum et scandalum generandi aut fundationem
aliquam quovis modo exercere seu procedere . . . vel ad Christianorum
divina officia audienda invitos compellere . . . quod possint alia commoda
suscipere et quavis domus, terras et possessiones a Christianis emere
et conducere ab illis et locare et super omnibus praemissis et quibusvis
aliis rebus possint cum Christianis convenire . . . et eorum studia et
scholas frequentare et scientiam ediscere quae eisdem Hebraeis videbitur
et quas a Christianis docti erunt in terris, locis tamen Italiae et ad illos
mittere et sic, ut eis videbitur, suos filios ut scientiis imbuantur, hoc
tamen pacto quod non legantur libri neque scripturae catholicae fidei
contrariae, sed illae omnino reiiciantur et repellantur, et quod possint
manutenere eorum scholas et sinagogas et illas restaurare . . . et in omnibus
et singulis eorum causis, dissentionibus et controversiis super quavis
causa et negotio possint illas per viam compromissi aut alias per lauda,*

not to proceed against Jews unless they are found acting contrary to the interests of Christianity. Jews are not to be compelled to listen to a Christian religious service. They may buy and sell houses, land and goods, and carry on other business with Christians. They may send their sons to general schools to study and open schools of their own. They may settle their disputes in their own way, and any civil authorities who judge their lawsuits must be above suspicion of taking the law into their own hands. All this concludes with a rather strong penal clause, although it is stated, of course, that the whole applies to such Jews as do not plot against Christianity.

Not since the days of Gregory I had a pope issued a Bull in favor of the Jews so broad in its outlook or so opposed to the prevalent course of the relationships between the Synagogue and the Church. It was a courageous act for the pope thus to have set himself against the opinion-making preachers and the conciliar party among the Churchmen who, at the Council of Basel, acted to rescind all privileges granted the Jews. [1] Eugenius IV, Pope Martin's successor and apparently just as well disposed to the Jews, followed a more circumspect course. Early in February 1432 he issued a *Sicut Judeis* which harked back to the thirteenth-century model. [2] Following

et arbitria eorum concordare ... nec aliter quam aequum est eos inquietare, gravare, perturbare tam in causis civilibus et negotiis quam criminalibus, quodque illi ministrorum qui ab ipsis Hebraeis suspecti allegati fuerunt statim debeant eorum causas remittere superioribus locorum aut magistratibus supradictis ... quod pro rebellis reputabimus omnes hi qui huiusmodi nostrae constitutioni et voluntati contravenerint et contrafacient ... volentes tamen quod illi tantum Hebraei praesentibus et gratiis ... uti et frui possint qui iis non abutentur nec contra eos aliquando in contrarium machinabantur. Nulli ergo ... et si quis ...

[1]   For the Council of Basel, which met in July 1431 and therefore soon after Martin's death, *see* Simonsohn, *op. cit.*, pp. 37-45.

[2]   Stern, *Urkundliche Beiträge*, no. 34. Only the predecessors of the 13th century are mentioned.

... Ad hoc malorum hominum pravitati ... corpora iam humata, et quoniam iusta et aequa, postulantibus non est denegandus assensus. Statuimus ut in terris nobis et Romanae ecclesiae immediate subiectis omnes ordinarii provinciarum, terrarum et locorum iudices ecclesiastici seu temporales, in aliis vero ecclesiastici, tantum circa exactionem

the usual sequence of clauses, if not the exact wording, the Bull offers two novel additions toward the end. One refers to territory under papal government and orders that the collection from the Jews of taxes, subsidies and the like, be made through Jews designated by the Jews themselves. The second new statement, of general application, sets forth the principle that those who do not enjoy the freedom and privileges of a place should not be subjected to reprisals imposed on it, unless, of course, the Jews were the cause of the new burdens. This was not the only protective Bull issued by Pope Eugenius. He repeated several of the favorable clauses included in his predecessor's Bull of 1429, such as the prohibition against stirring up the populace by means of hostile sermons. [1] He even challenged the hostility of the Spanish clergy by coming to the defense of the hard pressed Jews of the Iberian Peninsula. [2] Yet such were the political conditions of the time, of which the pope had to be constantly aware, that he was compelled to change his attitude completely and in 1442 issued a Bull which was as hostile to the Jews as Pope Martin V's of 1429 had been favorable. [3] To be sure,

---

collectarum et onerum pro universitate seu ab universitate deputatos impositorum seu imponendorum exactione ad instantiam et requisitionem eorum Judaeorum, qui se ad eam rem deputatos per praefatam ipsorum universitatem ius dicere et obligatos ad solutionem praefatarum collectarum et onerum dumtaxat cogere et compellere debeant auctoritate praesentium iuris communis seu praefatorum locorum constitutionum vel consuetudinum et aliis remediis oportunis. Cum autem valde sit consonum aequitati ut qui commoda non sentiunt non debeant ipsis oneribus subiacere, decrevimus quod in quibus civitatibus, terris, et locis Judaei praefati civium privilegiis et immunitatibus non gaudeant, eisdem praefatos Judaeos ad represalias contra cives illarum civitatum, terrarum vel locorum quas incolunt institutas, nisi praefata represalia eorundem Judaeorum causa et contemplatione fuissent contra illas civitates, terras vel loca quas incolunt institutae, praefatos Judaeos non teneri nec eorundem vigorem conveniri debere. Illos autem Judaeos dumtacat ... Nulli ergo ...

[1] Stern, Beiträge, nos. 35, 38.
[2] Ibid., no. 40.
[3] Simonsohn, op. cit., pp. 50-4; Vogelstein u. Rieger, vol. ii, pp. 11 f.; Raynaldus ad a. 1442 § 15.

this Bull was directed to Castile and Leon, but the pope's attitude to Jews elsewhere became also considerably cooler than it had been. The pressures for a change of policy had apparently mounted.

There were, to be sure, letters of protection issued by various successors of Eugenius IV during the fifteenth century and more rarely in the centuries which followed. They were directed most often in favor of the Jews of Italy. Thus Nicholas V (1447-1455) showed evidences of vacillating just as his two predecessors had done. [1] So, too, Pope Pius II (1458-1464) harked back to some of the efforts of Martin V to make life easier for Italian Jews. [2] Pope Sixtus IV (1471-1484) made a valiant effort to halt the incitements against the Jews connected with the Simon of Trent ritual murder libel. [3] A century later, Pope Paul III (1534-1549) still went back to the privileges granted by Martin V to the Jews of Poland, Bohemia and Hungary. [4] These and other popes, sometimes in words and more often in spirit, recalled privileges and protective utterances ultimately derived from the Bull *Sicut Judeis*. The Bull itself, however, was not repeated. [5]

---

[1]   Stern, *Beiträge*, nos. 39, 40, 41, especially the last which repeats some of the items mentioned in the protective Bulls of his two predecessors on the subjects of preaching and conversion of minors. *See*, on the other hand, the harsh Bull surrendering to John of Capistrano: *Super gregem*, June 23, 1447, in U. Hüntermann, *Bullar. Franciscanum* (n.s.), vol. i, pp. 540-2, no. 1072; also the specific abrogation of Martin V's and Eugenius IV's privileges: March 1, 1451, in Raynaldus, ad a. 1451 § 5. *Cf.* Strack, *The Jews and Human Sacrifice*, p. 257.

[2]   *Humilibus supplicum*, July 27, 1459, A. Pezzana, *Storia della città di Parma* (Parma 1847), vol. iii, app. VII.

[3]   *Licet inter causas*, October 10, 1475, in Martene et Durand, *Amplissima Collectio*, vol. ii, cols. 1516 f.

[4]   Vernet in *RQH*, no. 84.

[5]   Cardinal Ganganelli, subsequently Pope Clement XIV, in his report on the ritual murder libels in Poland which he made to Pope Clement XIII (1758-1769), cited the *Sicut Judeis* of Innocent IV and the longer version of it issued by Gregory X. *See* Cecil Roth, *The Ritual Murder Libel and the Jew* (London 1935).

5. *Its Effectiveness*

We have seen the Bull *Sicut Judeis* grow from expressions of personal opinion on the part of theologians and popes into an organized statement of Church policy. As such it was used in the course of the twelfth and especially of the thirteenth centuries to define the relations between Jews and Christians. It began as the grant of a privilege to the Jews of Rome by the popes who were their direct sovereigns. Soon Jews elsewhere learned to use it to re-inforce their request for protection from the local authorities. It evidently helped the Jews greatly in times of distress, especially during the period when the popes were the undisputed masters of Church policy, the recognized guides of public morals, and the respected advisors, if not the suzerains, of emperors and kings. Even then the Bull did not stop all persecution, expulsion or forced conversion; but its effectiveness decreased as time went on, because of conditions inherent in the evolving situation of European society and economics, and because of the weaknesses inherent in the Bull itself.

The changes in the position of the Jews during the Middle Ages constitute too vast a subject for discussion here. [1] They became increasingly dependent on emperors, kings and the civil authorities of the towns. They became the pawns of political and economic policy. Their economic usefulness

---

[1]   The literature is too vast for citation at this point. Two basic books are: Otto Stobbe, *Die Juden in Deutschland während des Mittelalters* (Leipzig 1902), and J. E. Scherer, *Die Rechtsverhältnisse der Juden in den deutsch-österreichischen Ländern* (Leipzig 1901); *cf.* Herbert Fischer, *Die verfassungsgeschichtliche Stellung der Juden in den deutschen Städten während des 13ten Jahrhunderts* (Breslau 1951). Guido Kisch in his *The Jews in Medieval Germany* (Chicago 1949), sums up the subject from a new angle and gives the relevant literature. Much of it to the 13th century is presented in Baron, *A Social and Religious History of the Jews* (2nd ed., New York 1957), vol. iv. For the Iberian states, *see* F. Baer, *Studien zur Geschichte der Juden im Königreich Aragonien während des 13ten u. 14ten Jahrhunderts* (Berlin 1913), and his work on *The Jews in Christian Spain*, in Hebrew and in English.

had to be balanced against the political dangers of retaining them as a small but conspicuous minority of a different religious faith. To this was added the situation within the Church during the fourteenth and fifteenth centuries: the crying need for reforming the papacy and the growing power of the monastic orders, exercized through their preaching and exerted through the Inquisition. The religious as well as the secular clergy sought to maintain and extend their emotional hold on the population and could not, therefore, acquiesce in a policy of active toleration, such as the Bull originally implied, and pressed for its reduction to mere theoretical toleration. A theological doctrine calling for a *status quo* in human relations could hardly prevail against the turbulent forces of that day.

The Bull began by asserting that the Jews must continue living under established custom. Nevertheless, popes themselves modified the rules under which Jewish life was to be permitted. The introduction of the Badge was one such change. Innocent III prescribed it at the Fourth Lateran Council; but, aware that it was an innovation, he justified it on the basis of the biblical command of *tzitzit*. [1] This principle of visible separation grew into the prohibition of social contacts and eventually evolved into fixed ghettos. [2] Chan-

---

[1]   *C & J*, p. 308, no. 10: *cum et per Moysen hoc ipsum eis legatur injunctum.*

[2]   The prohibition for Jews to have Christian servants and nurses (*cf.* Gregory IX, *Sufficere debuerat*, March 5, 1233: *C & J*, p. 198, no. 69) was gradually broadened and intensified until a ghetto was adumbrated for Carpentras by Gregory XI (*Cum Judei*, September 7, 1376: *Reg. Vat.* 288, fol. 257), compelling the Jews to live separately as they had chosen to live prior to the Black Death. The development reached its culmination in the Bull *Etsi doctoribus gentium* by Anti-Pope Benedict XIII (May 11, 1415) which extended the prohibition to all contacts, economic as well as social, and practically called for a boycott to the death (*cf.* Simonsohn, *op. cit.*, pp. 3-16; Amador de los Rios, *Historia de los Judios de Espana y Portugal* [Madrid 1876], vol. ii, pp. 651 ff.). Gradually the restrictions of this frightful pronouncement became established, despite the objections to it on the part of many of the popes during the 15th century, as indicated above,

ges in the regulation of court procedure were another departure from established custom of which the Bull *Sicut Judeis*
spoke. [1] The condemnation of the Talmud, first ordered by
the Church in the thirteenth century, was certainly a clear
interference with the time-honored right of the Jews to
practice their religion as guaranteed by the Bull. [2] So, too,
was the increasing resort to conversionist sermons by per-
mitting monks to invade synagogues on the Sabbath. [3]

until it triumphed in terms of expulsion—total expulsion in the case
of Spain and partial expulsion to a ghetto in various places in Germany
and Italy.
    [1]   The Third Lateran Council ordered that a Christian must be
admitted to testify against a Jew (Decretalia Greg. IX, Lib. II,
tit. xx, c. 21; *C & J*, p. 297). By the time of Gregory X, the situation
had so far changed that the pope had to insist on the admissibility
of Jewish evidence (*see* p. 17, n. 2 above). Nicholas V, in one of his
repressive Bulls in which he returned to the attitude of the Anti-Pope
Benedict XIII (February 25, 1450: Stern, *Beiträge*, no. 46) forbids the
testimony of Jews against Christians. Calixtus III, on May 28, 1456,
prohibited Jews from testifying against Christians, but permitted
Christians to testify against Jews (*Si ad reprimendos: Bullar. Romanum,*
vol. iii, pt. 3, p. 76).
    [2]   Gregory IX, *Si vera*, June, 1939: *C & J*, nos 95-8; Innocent IV,
Ad instar, August 12, 1247: *ibid.*, no. 119 and note. See further for
the 13th century: Clement IV, *Dampnabili perfidia Judeorum*, July
15, 1267: Potthast 20081; Ripoll, *op. cit.*, vol. i, p. 487. Honorius IV,
Nimis in partibus, November 18, 1286: Potthast 22541; Raynaldus,
ad a. 1286 § 25. In the 14th century, the inquisitor Bernard Gui, in
1319, had all copies of the Talmud confiscated and burned in southern
France (Ph. Limborch, *Historia Inquisitionis* [Amsterdam 1692],
pp. 273 ff.). John XXII ordered its confiscation, on September 4,
1320, following the example of Clement IV: *Dudum felicis recordationis:*
G. Mollat, *Lettres communes de Jean XXII*, no. 12238; Grayzel,
HUC Annual, vol. xxiii, pt. 2, p. 54, no. xvi. For the condemnation by
the Anti-Pope Benedict XIII, *see* Simonsohn, *op. cit.*, pp. 4 f. Benedict
put the prohibition of the Talmud at the very head of his list. The
Reuchlin-Pfefferkorn controversy and the burning of the Talmud in
1553 are beyond our scope.
    [3]   Interference with Jews in their synagogue worship had developed
far beyond the attack with sticks and stones mentioned in the *Sicut
Judeis*. James of Aragon for a time permitted Paulus Christianus to
preach in synagogues (*cf.* Cecil Roth, "The Disputation of Barcelona,"
Harvard Theological Review, vol. xliii [1950], p. 140; Bzovius, *Hist.
Eccl.*, ad. a. 1263, no. 16). For similar permission by Louis IX of

Restrictions multiplied, while ancient customs were weakened.

An important example of the Bull's failure to make its point is the nice distinction which the Church drew between forced and voluntary conversion. The statement in the Bull is perfectly clear: baptism must be accepted willingly. Yet the meaning of the thought became doubtful early in the Middle Ages. Pope Leo VII, about the middle of the tenth century, for example, advised the Archbishop of Mainz to hold the threat of expulsion over the heads of the Jews. [1] The clergy at the time of the crusades may or may not have deplored the numerous forced conversions which resulted from those semi-religious movements, but they said nothing about their being invalid, and an anti-pope considered it unheard of for permission to be granted to these forced converts to return to their original faith. [2] The Church claimed that, baptism being a sacrament, it would be blasphemous to think that it could be disregarded. But this was not the difficulty; the real difficulty, as far as the Jews were concerned, was the narrowness of the interpretation of the term "forced." By the end of the thirteenth century, nothing short of death was considered sufficient objection to baptism. [3]

France, see U. Robert, REJ, III (1881), p. 216, no. 40. The repeated references by the popes of the 15th century to disturbances by preachers may refer to this attempt to impose conversionary sermons on the Jews. Nevertheless, Pope Nicholas V, on December 20, 1447, permitted the King of Sicily to compel the Jews to listen to such sermons four times a year: Raynaldus, ad a. 1447 § 22.

[1]   For this and other examples, see Browe, op. cit., pp. 142 f.

[2]   See p. 9, n. 1 above.

[3]   See the answer of Pope Nicholas III to a question addressed to him by some inquisitors of the Provence about Jews who claimed that they had been baptized in fear of death. They later wanted to return to Judaism and the inquisitors threw them into prison; but they still held their ground. The pope ruled that they were not absolute et precise coacti. Cf. Bibliothèque Nationale, Fond Doat 37, fol. 191 ff.; REJ, III, p. 217, no. 50. For a case in the early 14th century, see Grayzel, "The Confession of a Medieval Jewish Convert," in Historia Judaica, vol. xvii (1955), pp. 89-120. On the interpretation of forced baptism as illicit but not invalid, as set forth by Innocent III in 1201, see George LaPiana, "The Church and the Jews," Historia

The popes, to be sure, continued to plead against the use of force, but they never disqualified the results. They did not, in fact, go beyond a plea in their objections to this and to other violations of the Jewish status outlined in the Bull. The penal clause, [1] contained in this Bull as in practically all others, was rarely, if ever, enforced. No one, as far as one can tell, was actually removed from office or made to suffer excommunication for converting Jews by force or even for the tortures and murders to which they were subjected throughout the bleak years of the Middle Ages. [2]

The final source of weakness which made the *Sicut Judeis* all but inoperative was the statement toward its conclusion which limited its application to such Jews as plotted no injury to the Christian faith. It seems like a natural enough limitation for those days. In effect, however, it opened the doors wide to anyone who plotted against the Jews. With this as an excuse, on the basis of false accusations or exaggerations, any restriction or condemnation could be justified. The bitter invective levelled against the Jews in the Bulls imposing restrictions offers a sharp contrast to the mild and reasonable exhortations of the *Sicut Judeis*. [3]

What was left of the Bull *Sicut Judeis* on the eve of the Renaissance and the Reformation was the one basic principle: Thou shalt not kill them, lest my people forget.... It is a fact

---

Judaica, vol. ix (1949), pp. 129 f.; Browe, *op. cit.*, pp. 237 f.; *C & J*, pp. 100-103, no. 12.

[1] The clause which begins *Si quis autem* ...: "If anyone, being acquainted with the contents of this decree ..."

[2] Some of the minor nobility guilty of such murderous deeds were commanded to disgorge their ill-gotten gains (see *C & J*, pp. 264-7), and in the case of the Shepherds' Crusade, the miserable peasants were ordered destroyed partly because of their attacks on the Jews (*see* Grayzel, *HUC Annual*, vol. xxii, no. x and notes). On the other hand, such preachers of death and destruction as Vincent Ferrer and John Capistrano wielded great influence and were eventually canonized.

[3] Even so friendly a pope as Martin V spoke, in his restrictive Bull of 1425 (*Bull. Romanum*, vol. III, part 2, p. 453), of *enormitates et scelera detestabilia* which some Jews dare to commit.

that the papacy never abandoned this fundamental teaching, largely motivated by theology. The attitude soon to prevail was best exemplified by the anti-pope Benedict XIII, in his Bull of May 11, 1415.[1] After a long series of restrictions calculated to make life for Jews all but impossible, he concludes with an appeal, almost in the words of Gregory I, that the Jews must be attracted to Christianity with kindness and Christians must refrain from molesting them.[2] In this context, the words, which had been so eagerly sought after in the twelfth and thirteenth centuries, sound hollow, dead, a mockery of every hope of humane co-existence. Hardness and restriction eventually won the day everywhere during the Counter-Reformation.

One may conclude that it is an exaggeration to speak of the Bull *Sicut Judeis* as the papal pronouncement that protected the Jews during the Middle Ages. It may have done so in its early days when it still reflected the actual relationship between Christians and Jews. Later protection was the result rather of the general political and economic conditions which, even while undermining the Jewish position, guarded the Jews against total destruction. To the extent to which papal protection was effective, other pronouncements, more direct in their nature, played a greater role, especially those decrees which strengthened the hands of secular and religious princes. Probably the greatest protection offered by the Church was its constant reminder of human decencies and its reference to the Jewish poeple as an integral part of the Divine Plan. Christianity's unwillingness to surrender completely to its Greek heritage and its retention of its heritage from Judaism thus contributed to the survival of the Jewish people.

---

[1] *See* p. 34, n. 2 above.

[2] *Congruit autem religioni ac mansuetudini Christianae libenter contra injustas persecutiones humanum praestare subsidium ... plus enim blandimentis quam asperitatibus erga eos agendum est ... Mandamus ... quod tamen ipsos ultra ea quae in praedictis constitutionibus ... continentur gravari, molestari, seu in eorum personis offendi ... non permittant ...*

THE *YQTL-QTL* (*QTL-YQTL*) SEQUENCE OF IDENTICAL VERBS IN BIBLICAL HEBREW AND IN UGARITIC

By Moshe Held
Dropsie College

In certain poetic verses of the Hebrew Bible containing two hemistichs we find the same verb occurring in the "imperfect" [1] tense in one hemistich and in the "perfect" tense in the parallel one; [2] *e.g.*:

Ps 38: 12 אהבי ורעי מנגד נגעי יעמדו [3] וקרובי מרחק עמדו

"Those who love me, and my friends, stood back from my plague, and my intimates stood afar";

Ps 93: 3 [4] נשאו נהרות יהוה נשאו נהרות קולם ישאו נהרות דכים

"The floods lifted up, O Lord, the floods lifted up their voice, the floods lifted up their...";

Prov 11: 7 במות אדם רשע תאבד תקוה ותוחלת אונים אבדה

"When a wicked man dies, (his) expectation perishes; all hope of the evildoers perishes."

The same pattern occurs also with the *waw* (*wyqtl-qtl* or *qtl-wyqtl*) which, from the viewpoint of literary style, however,

---

[1] The terms "imperfect" and "perfect" are here used as a matter of convenience only. One should certainly prefer the more fitting designations *yqtl* and *qtl*.

[2] Note that in Ugaritic the order is normally *yqtl* in the first hemistich (= A) and *qtl* in the second (= B), since *yqtl* is the basic and more common tense in Ugaritic. In Hebrew the order may be reversed. This observation holds true of parallelism in general. Thus, Ugaritic tends to have a fixed pattern which is rarely, if ever, reversed, employing daily language in A while employing in B rare and poetic usages. Hebrew poetry, however, while generally following this pattern shows much more flexibility in such cases.

[3] *See* the note in *Biblia Hebraica*.

[4] The word דכים is a famous mystery; its relationship to Ugaritic *dkym* (I AB, 5: 2-3) is still not established.

does not seem to change the significance of the phenomenon
noted: [1]

Is 60: 16 [3] וינקת חלב גוים ושד [2] מלכים תינקי

"You will suck the milk of nations, suck the breast of kings";

Amos 7: 4 ותאכל את תהום רבה [4] ואכלה את החלק

"And it had devoured the great deep, devoured the plowland";

Ps 29: 10 יהוה למבול ישב [5] וישב יהוה מלך לעולם

"The Lord presided...; the Lord sat as king forever."

It should be noted at the outset that such a sequence of
yqtl-qtl (*qtl-yqtl*) or *wyqtl-qtl* (*qtl-wyqtl*) is acceptable not only
poetically but grammatically as well. What is involved is
the use of an "imperfect" form which in these cases is really
a preterit, well known in biblical Hebrew in such cases as
Num 23: 7; Is 51: 2; Hos 2: 15; Ps 44: 10 ff.; Job 3: 3, and
many others. [6] Surprisingly enough, modern biblical scholars
have been inclined to emend the Masoretic text of most of
these verses, especially those without the *waw*. The use of
the same verb in such a sequence would be, according to

---

[1]   *See* M. D. Cassuto, *Tarbiz*, vol. xiv (1942), 9; idem, *The Goddess
Anath* (Jerusalem 1953), p. 37.

[2]   For the vocalization *see* N. H. Tur-Sinai, *The Book of Job*
(Tel-Aviv 1954), pp. 114, 213, 219.

[3]   For the parallelism שד // חלב in biblical Hebrew and in Ugaritic
see M. Held, *Leshonenu*, vol. xviii (1953), 146.

[4]   For this expression *see* M. D. Cassuto, *Tarbiz*, vol. xiii (1942),
210; *The Goddess Anath*, p. 30.

[5]   למבול ישב is difficult. M. Lambert's emendation to למלך ישב
(*REJ*, 54 [1907], p. 268,, accepted by H. L. Ginsberg (*The Ugarit
Texts* [Jerusalem 1936], pp. 130 f.), is hardly convincing. For an
attempt to equate למבול ישב with לכסא ישב *see* J. N. Epstein, *Tarbiz*,
vol. xii (1941), 82. This suggestion would seem more attractive in
the light of Ps 9: 5; Job 36: 7. Cassuto rejects these interpretations,
finding in our verse a hint of an epic poem concerning the flood
(*The Book of Genesis*, vol. ii [Jerusalem 1949], p. 14); but this assumption
does not solve the inherent philological difficulty. It is possible that
מבול denotes the upper ocean (= המים אשר מעל לרקיע in Gen 1: 7),
as suggested by J. Begrich (*ZS*, vol. vi [1928], 135 ff.; Cf. W. F. Albright,
JBL, vol. lviii [1939], 98).

[6]   *See* G. Bergsträsser, *Hebräische Grammatik*, vol. ii (Leipzig 1929),
§ 7h.

them, incomprehensible and impossible to explain. [1] Thus, for example, they emend Ps 38: 12 to read מנגדי נגשו instead of מנגד נגעי יעמדו, [2] thereby eliminating the "imperfect" form יעמדו from our verse. Similarly, they suggest that we read in Ps 93: 3 נשאו instead of ישאו [3] and in Ps 29: 10 וַיֵּשֶׁב instead of וַיֵּשֶׁב [4].

Ugaritic poetry, however, shows clearly, as first noted by Cassuto, [5] that such emendations are gratuitous. From the poetry of Ras Shamra we learn that the aforementioned technique, claimed by modern scholars to be "tautological" [6] and "contrary to rule and usage," [7] was a common archaic literary device in Canaanite and hence, in view of the biblical passages just cited, in proto-West-Semitic. Note the following examples from Ugaritic poetry:

II AB, 6: 38-40   *'dbt bht[h b']l y'db* [8]   *hd* [9]   *'db* [*'db*]*t*

---

[1]   One can hardly find a modern biblical scholar who does not emend at least some of these verses.

[2]   C. A. Briggs, *The Book of Psalms*, vol. i (1906), p. 342; H. Gunkel, *Die Psalmen* (1926), p. 161, and others. T. K. Cheyne (*The Book of Psalms*, vol. i [1904], p. 169) "solves" the problem in his usual way by deleting וקרובי מרחק עמדו entirely.

[3]   H. Gunkel, *op. cit.*, p. 412; M. Buttenwieser, *The Psalms* (1938), pp. 340 f.

[4]   Briggs, *op. cit.*, p. 256; Gunkel, *op. cit.*, p. 126.

[5]   *Orientalia*, NS vol. vii (1938), 288 f.; *Tarbiz*, vol. xii, 171; ibid., vol. xiv, 9 f.; *The Goddess Anath*, pp. 37 f.

[6]   Briggs, *op. cit.*, p. 342.

[7]   Buttenwieser, *op. cit.*, p. 341.

[8]   For this root and its relationship to Hebrew עזב II *see* for the present M. D. Cassuto, J. N. *Epstein Festschrift* (Jerusalem 1950), pp. 5 f.; *The Book of Exodus* (Jerusalem 1951) p. 207. It is our conviction, however, that the root עזב II is attested in more biblical passages than have been hitherto noted. Thus, for example, the difficult expression עצור ועזוב (Dt 32: 36; 1 Kings 14 : 10; 21: 21; 2 Kings 9: 8; 14: 26) is probably to be vocalized עֹצֵר וְעֹזֵב or עָצוֹר וְעָזוֹב and rendered "ruler (*cf.* 1 Sam 9: 17) and caretaker" (*cf.* Ugaritic *'db* and Hebrew חבש in Is 3: 7).

[9]   *hd* (*hdd*), one of the epithets of the storm god, = Akk. *Addu* and Heb. and Aram. הדד (note that epithets normally occur in B whereas the given name occurs in A). This epithet of the storm god is the second element in the name of the Ugaritic king(s) *Nqmd* which, as

hklh[1] "Baal made preparations for his house; Haddu made preparations for his palace";

V AB, B: 38-41 (cf. *ibid.*, D: 86-88) [t]*ḥspn*[2] *mh wtrḥṣ* [t]*l šmm šmn arṣ*[3] *rbb*[4] *rkb ʿrpt*[5] *ṭl šmm tskh*[6] [*rbb*] *nskh kbkbm*[7] "She (Anath) drew some water and bathed: sky-dew fatness of earth, spray of the Rider of Clouds; dew that the heavens dripped, spray that the stars dripped";

we learn from the Akk. texts from Ugarit (J. Nougayrol, *Le Palais Royal D'Ugarit*, vol. iii (Paris 1955), p. 252; *ibid.*, p. 196, l. 9), should be vocalized *Niqmaddu* or *Naqamaddu*. The name is an "Ersatz-Name" (J. J. Stamm, *Die akkadische Namengebung* (1939), pp. 278 ff.), containing the elements *nqm* (= Heb. נקם "to avenge") and the divine name *Addu*.

[1] For the parallelism בית // היכל in biblical Hebrew and in Ugaritic *see* M. D. Cassuto, *Tarbiz*, vol. xiv, 6; *The Goddess Anath*, pp. 27, 77.

[2] The root *ḥsp* "ro draw, to scoop up (water, dew)" occurs also in I D: 51, 55, 199. It is probably to be connected with Akk. *esēpu(m)* (*CAD*, vol. iii, 330 f.) and Heb. חשף (Is 30: 14; Hag 2: 16). In C. H. Gordon, *Ugaritic Manual* (Rome 1955; hereinafter abbreviated *UM*), vol. iii, p. 241, no. 198, surprisingly enough, one finds Akk. *esēpu(m)* under Ugaritic *ʾsp* "to gather", while Heb. חשף is nowhere recorded. Following Al-Yasin (*The Lexical Relation* etc. [1952], p. 57) he prefers to compare our Ugaritic root with Arabic حسف (*UM*, vol. iii, 265, no. 650), which has nothing to do with Ugaritic *ḥsp*.

[3] *Cf.* Gen 27: 28, 39 where we should perhaps vocalize (וּ)מִשַּׁמְנֵי (*see* H. L. Ginsberg, *The Ugarit Texts*, p. 63).

[4] The restorations are fully corroborated by the parallel text, V AB, D: 86-88. For the parallelism טל//רביב in biblical Hebrew and in Ugaritic *see* M. D. Cassuto, *Tarbiz*, vol. xiv, 5 f.; *The Goddess Anath*, p. 79. The same parallelism, *ṭl*//*rbb* (!), occurs also in the now famous passage, I D: 44-45. However, Cassuto's interpretation of this passage (*Orientalia*, NS vol. viii [1939] 239; *Tarbiz*, vol. xii, p. 180; *ibid.*, vol. xiv, 6; *The Book of Genesis*, vol. ii p. 36) must be rejected. For the correct interpretation of the passage and its relation to 2 Sam 1: 21 *see* H. L. Ginsberg, *JBL* vol. lvii (1938), 209 ff.; *ibid.*, vol. lxii (1943), 111 f.; *Bib. Arch.*, vol. viii (1945), 56 f.

[5] *Cf.* Ps 68: 5 and *see* H. L. Ginsberg, *JBL*, vol. lxii, 112 f.

[6] *See* C. H. Gordon, *UM*, vol. iii, p. 297, no. 1253. Note, however, that Arabic نسيك given by Gordon as a cognate (following Al-Yasin, *op. cit.*, p. 79) has nothing to do with Ugaritic and Hebrew *nsk*.

[7] For the parallelism כוכבים // שמים in biblical Hebrew and in Ugaritic *see* M. Held, *Leshonenu*, vol. xviii, 147.

I* AB, 1: 16-17 *hm* [1] *brky* [2] *tkšd* [3] *rumm 'n kśd* [4] *aylt* [5] "Behold, (as) the buffaloes long for the water pool, (and) the hinds long for the spring";

I D: 114-115 *knp nšrm b'l ytbr b'l tbr diy hmt* [6] "The wings of the vultures may Baal break; may Baal break the pinions of them."

The observation mentioned above, namely that the verbal sequence of *yqtl-qtl* is accepted Ugaritic-Hebrew literary

---

[1] C. H. Gordon, *UM*, vol. iii, p. 259, no. 563. However, "if" or "or" does not fit the context, and one would prefer to equate *hm* with Hebrew הַן, הִנֵּה. See Ch. Virolleaud, *Syria*, vol. xv (1934), 311; H. L. Ginsberg, *The Ugarit Texts*, p. 22.

[2] The *y* in *brky* "pool" is unexplained, unless we take it to be a feminine ending.

[3] Note that in Ugaritic and in the Amarna Letters *t-* is often the preformative of the imperfect, third person plural, masculine.

[4] Despite the graphic difference (*š* and *ś*), both forms must be from the same root, as recognized by many scholars. C. H. Gordon (*UM*, vol. iii, p. 281, no. 975), by assuming that Ugaritic *š* always = *ḏ* (*UM*, vol. i, pp. 22 f.), is forced to emend our text, thus showing the weakness of his assumption. Note that most of the examples given in *UM*, vol. iii, pp. 257 f. are problematic and doubtful. Suffice it to say that wherever comparative Semitic grammar calls for a *ḏ* the Ugaritic scribes generally employ the phoneme *d*. For a more exact definition of this polyphony see H. L. Ginsberg, *The Legend of King Keret* (*BASOR* SS, 2-3, 1946), p. 49.

[5] *Cf.* Ps 42: 2. Our text shows clearly that the correct reading there is indeed תערג כאיל[ת] (haplography).

[6] *Cf. ibid.*, 128-129; 142-143; contrast *ibid.*, 118-119; 123; 132-133; 137. One is tempted to mention here also the description of the feast given by Baal to the "*šb'm bn aṯrt*" after having completed the building of his palace (II AB, 6: 47-54). According to Cassuto (*Orientalia*, NS vol. vii, 288 f.; cf. *Tarbiz*, vol. xiv, 9 f.; *The Goddess Anath*, p. 36) this passage should be read as follows: *špq ilm krm yšpq ilht ḥprt; špq ilm alpm yšpq ilht arḫt; špq ilm khtm yšpq ilht ksat; špq ilm rḥbt yn yšpq ilht dkrt yn*, thus obtaining a chain of *qtl-yqtl* (4 times). However, Cassuto's readings and interpretation, fluent and tempting as they are, seem quite doubtful when compared with the original publication in *Syria*, vol. xiii (1932), pl. xxvii. H. L. Ginsberg (*Tarbiz*, vol. v [1933], 91; *The Ugarit Texts*, p. 37), with due caution, reads this passage as follows: *špq ilm krm y[n] špq ilht ḥprt [yn]; špq ilm alpm y[n] špq ilht arḫt [yn]; špq ilm khtm y[n] špq ilht ksat [yn]; špq ilm rḥbt yn špq ilht dkrt [yn]*. For his translation see ANET[2] (Princeton 1955) p. 134.

style, may perhaps, with due caution, be used as a tool for textual criticism. According to our principle, we are not on firm ground in emending such "inelegant" [1] verses as Ps 29: 10; 38: 12; 93: 3, etc., in order to eliminate the verbal sequence of *yqtl-qtl*. On the contrary, one gains the impression that this technique may have been used more extensively in Hebrew poetry than is immediately apparent. A good case in point is Ps 26: 4-5, the Masoretic text of which reads as follows: לא ישבתי עם מתי שוא [2] ועם נעלמים [3] לא אבוא שנאתי קהל מרעים

ועם רשעים לא אשב

"I do not sit with faithless men, nor do I make common cause with rogues (!); I loathe the company of evildoers, and with reprobates I do not sit down."

The *qtl-yqtl* sequence ישבתי־אשב is here spread over two verses, and this may well have been the original reading. However, one is tempted to assume that a transposition of the verses would give a better and more archaic reading: [4]

לא ישבתי עם מתי שוא ועם רשעים לא אשב [5] שנאתי קהל מרעים ועם נעלמים

לא אבוא

We thus obtain the now familiar *qtl-yqtl* chain לא ישבתי־לא אשב as יעמדו־עמדו; נשאו־ישאו; Ugaritic *y'db-'db*; *ytbr—tbr*, etc. Such a transposition recommends itself even more when one bears in mind the use of בוא בקהל in biblical Hebrew; note, for example, Ez 38: 13 הלשלל שלל אתה בא, הלבז בז הקהלת קהלך "Is it that you came to despoil? Did you assemble your

---

[1] H. Gunkel, *Die Psalmen*, p. 161; B. Gemser, *Sprüche Salomos* (1937), p. 44.

[2] *Cf.* Job 11: 11; 22: 15. More prosaic is אנשי און (Job 34: 36).

[3] The Masoretic נעלמים is difficult, and many scholars emend our נעלמים to מעולים (Gunkel, *op. cit.*, p. 112, and others). One would expect, in parallelism to v. 5a, עוּלִים. *Cf.* Job 22: 15 מתי און //(!)‏ארח עַוָּלִם.

[4] Indeed, this phenomenon may be considered archaic already in Ugaritic. Note that the *yqtl-qtl* (*qtl-yqtl*) sequence is primarily attested in the Baal epic, rarely in Aqht, and never in evidence in Keret. This is hardly surprising in view of our observation in *JAOS*, vol. lxxix (1959), 171 f., n. 49.

[5] Note the alliteration in our transposed verse: ישבתי, שוא רשעים, אשב

host to carry off plunder?" *Cf.* also Gen 49:6; Dt 23:2, 3, 4, 9; Jud 21:8; 1 Kings 8:2-3 (= 2 Chr 5:3-4); Ez 23:24.

Turning now to Ps 29, labeled a poem of Phoenician origin by no less an authority than H. L. Ginsberg, [1] we note that the Masoretic text seems to be defective in many respects, a fact recognized by a majority of scholars. However, all suggested restorations seem to overlook a basic fact: the *qtl-(w)yqtl* sequence, characteristic of our chapter in its original archaic state, is still evident from verses 5 and 10 in the received text: שׁבר־וישׁבר (v. 5); ישׁב־וישׁב (v. 10). In the former verse the original vocalization is almost certainly not שׁבֵר (participle), but rather שׁבֵּר ("perfect")! It so happens that as far back as 1935, and with no reference to the *yqtl-yll* (*qtl-yqtl*) sequence, H. L. Ginsberg [2] independently proposed to supplement the obviously defective text of v. 7 [3] to read קול יהוה חצב להבות [ויחצב יהוה להבות] אש "The thunder [4] of the Lord strikes flames; [5] [the Lord strikes flames] of fire." In view of the evidence presented above and bearing in mind that our chapter is replete with Canaanite allusions, [6] this

---

[1] *The Ugarit Texts*, pp. 129 ff.; *ibid.*, p. 35 f.; *Atti del XIX Congr. Intern. degli Orient*, (1938), קיץ 173 ff.; *Bib. Arch.*, vol. VIII, 53 f.

[2] *The Ugarit Texts*, p. 131.

[3] The structure of v. 7 as compared with vv. 5, 8, 10 clearly reveals that something has been omitted in v. 7.

[4] קול in this verse, as in many other biblical verses (*e.g.*, Ex 19:16; 20:18; Is 30:30; Joel 2:11; 4:16; Amos 1:2; Ps 18:14 [= 2 Sam 22:14]; 46:7; Job 37:4), means "thunder" and not "voice". *Cf.* Ugaritic *ql* in II AB, 4-5:70-71; *ibid.*, 7:29-31.

[5] Since the passage is a description of thundering and lightning it seems plausible to take חצב here in the sense of "to kindle, to flash." *See* J. Barth, *Wurzeluntersuchungen* (1902), p. 22. *Cf.* Ugaritic *šrh larṣ brqm* in II AB, 4-5:70-71 = Job 37:3! (H. L. Ginsberg, *The Ugarit Texts*, p. 31; JBL, vol. lxii, 109 f.; *Bib. Arch*, vol. viii, 57).

[6] Note that בני אלים in v. 1 (otherwise attested only in Ps 89:7) = Ugaritic (*dr*) *bn il* (Gordon, *Text* 2:17, 25, 33; Text 107:2), *phr ilm* (Text 17:7), *mphrt bn il* (Text 2:17, 34; Text 107:3), *phr bn ilm* (II AB, 3:14). Furthermore, the localities in our chapter, לבנון and שׁרין (v. 6) as well as מדבר קדשׁ (v. 8) (not the Desert of Sinai!), are all in Syria (II AB, 8:18-19; 20-21; SS:65). Note also the enclitic *-m* in וירקיד־ם (v. 6) and *see* n. 4 above.

suggestion would seem to gain much in probability; the
vocalization חָצֵב ("perfect"; not חֹצֵב [participle]) should by
now be self-evident. Furthermore, it is plausible that this
same sequence should also be restored in verses 3 (קול יהוה הרעים
על המים [וירעם] יהוה על מים רבים) 8; [1] (קול יהוה החיל מדבר [וי]חל יהוה
מדבר קדש) and perhaps even in 9.

The phenomenon that we have discussed in some detail
may also prove to be of help in the textual criticism and interpretation of the Ugaritic texts themselves. We shall mention
only a few examples here. Surely, the original reading of
V AB, B: 40-41 must have been, following the *yqtl-qtl* pattern,
as follows: *ṭl šmm tskh [rbb] nskh* [2] *kbkbm* and not, as Virolleaud [3] and Gordon [4] are inclined to read, twice *tskh*. Similarly,
the original reading of I D: 114-115 must have been: *knp*
nšrm bʿl yṯbr bʿl ṯbr diy hmt, [5] and not, with Virolleaud, twice
yṯbr. [6] On the other hand, we believe that we are justified
in restoring II AB, 6: 18-21 to read: *y[l]k* [7] *llbnn wʿsh lšryn*
mhmd arzh h[lk l]bnn wʿsh šryn mhmd arzh [8] "They set out
to Lebanon and its trees, to Sirion (and) its choicest cedars;
they go to Lebanon and its trees, Sirion (and) its choicest
cedars."

Similarly, one is inclined to restore BH, 2: 49-51 to read:

[1] After having written these lines, we notice that our restoration,
arrived at independently, is very close to the one suggested by S.
Mowinckel, *Psalmenstudien*, vol. ii (1922), p. 47.

[2] That this reading is the only correct one is fully corroborated
by V AB, D: 87-88 *ṭl šmm [ts]kh rbb nskh kbkbm.*

[3] Ch. Virolleaud, *La Déesse ʿAnat* (Paris 1938), p. 26.

[4] *UM*, vol. iii, 297, no. 1253.

[5] For this correct reading *see* already F. Rosenthal, *Orientalia*
NS vol. viii, 229 f.

[6] Ch. Virolleaud, *La Légende Phénicienne de Danel* (Paris 1936),
pp. 158, 162, 163-164.

[7] C. H. Gordon (*UM*, vol. ii, 142b) restores l. 18 to read: *y[tl]k,*
leaving l. 20 unrestored. However, Virolleaud's plates (*Syria*, vol. xiii,
xxvii) show clearly the possibility of restoring *y[l]k* in l. 18 and
h[lk] in l. 20.

[8] *lbnn-šryn* is attested not only in Ps 29: 6 but also in a new OB
fragment from the Gilgamesh Epic. *See* T. Bauer, *JNES*, vol. xvi
(1957), 256, r. 13 *Sa-ri-a ù La-ab-na-na.*

kšbʿt lšbʿm aḫḫ ym[zah] [1] *wtmnt ltmnym šr* [2] *aḫyh mẓah* "His seventy-seven brothers reached him; the children of his eighty-eight brothers reached him."

Our pattern may sometimes be a useful tool for interpretation as well. Thus it seems to us that II AB, 3: 14-16 *štt* [xxx] [3] *btlḫny* [4] *qlt* [5] *bks ištynh* cannot be rendered, with Gaster, [6] Driver, [7] and others: "[Muck] is placed on my table; filth am I made to drink from my cup" (passive participle feminine from *šyt* "to place"), but rather should be translated: "I drink [derision] from my table; scorn from a cup do I drink"

[1] Ugaritic *mṣʾ-mẓʾ* does not mean "to find" but rather means "to reach" (contrast Gordon, *UM*, vol. iii, 290, no. 1145, and G. R. Driver, *Can. Myths and Legends* [Edinburgh 1956], p. 160). Note that *mṣʾ-mẓʾ* is an allograph to *mǵy*, and the latter never means anything but "to reach". The interdialectal distribution of "to reach" is as follows: Akk. *kašādu(m)*; Ugaritic *mǵy* (*mṣʾ-mẓʾ*); Heb. נגע and מצא (note Lev 5: 7 and 12: 8); Aram. מטא; Arab. بلغ.

[2] C. H. Gordon (*UM*, vol. iii, 330, no. 1885) renders *šr aḫyh* "his kinsmen", but offers no etymology. G. R. Driver, on the other hand, renders our phrase "the chiefs of his two brothers" (*Can. Myths and Legends*, p. 73), connecting our *šr* with Akk. *šarru(m)* and Heb. שר (*op. cit.*, p. 148), which is hardly convincing. Gordon's rendering is certainly more to the point since the context indicates that *šr aḫyh* denotes some kind of kinship. The word *šr* may be related to Babylonian *šerru(m)* (Assyrian *šarru*) "child".

[3] Something like Heb. בשת, Ugaritic *btt* (II AB, 3: 18-19; 21-22) is required by parallelism, but no attempt to restore the text seems warranted at present.

[4] Ugaritic *tlḫn* shows that the pre-Ugaritic etymologies suggested for Heb. שלחן are without any basis. Nevertheless Arab. سلخ "to strip off (hide)" and Aram.-Syr. שלחא "hide" are still given in Koehler-Baumgartner, *Lexicon* (1958), pp. 976 f., alongside Ugaritic *tlḫn*! The following interdialectical distributuion of "table" will suffice to show that שלחן is Canaanite and Canaanite only: Akk. *paššūru(m)*; Ugaritic *tlḫn*; Heb. שלחן; Aram. פתורא; Arab. مائدة.

[5] Ugaritic *qlt* is no doubt related to Heb. קלון. However, its relation to Akk. *gillatu(m)* (C. H. Gordon, *UM*, vol. iii, 319, No. 1683) is doubtful, since *gillatu(m)* in Akk. does not mean "shame" but rather "crime" (*CAD*, vol. v, 72). As a matter of fact, *gillatu(m)* denotes a higher degree of crime than *arnu(m)* (B. Landsberger, *OLZ*, vol. xxvi [1923], 73).

[6] *BASOR*, no. ci (1946), 24; *Thespis*, (New York 1950), p. 167.

[7] *Can. Myths and Legends*, p. 95.

(first person "perfect" from *šty* "to drink"). [1] This in turn shows that the restoration *pglt* [2] (= Hebrew פִּגּוּל) is excluded, since one may eat a "*pglt*" but not drink it; nor is such a restoration sustained by parallelism. Similarly, I*AB, 1: 16-17 *hm brky tkšd rumm 'n kśd aylt* cannot be rendered with Virolleaud, [3] Gordon, [4] and others: "Or the pools that the buffaloes crave, yea the spring of the craving of the hinds" (substantive with *t*-preformative and infinitive *Qal* respectively, or the like) but should rather be translated: "Behold, (as) the buffaloes long for the water pool, the hinds long for the spring" ("imperfect" third person plural masculine [5] and "perfect" third person plural feminine respectively).

Finally, it may not be out of place to note that our sequence may sometimes be helpful in vocalization where the Ugaritic consonantal script leaves us in doubt. Thus, we may assume that in I*AB, 6: 11-14 *apnk ltpn il dpid yrd lksi ytb* (= *yqtl*) [6] *lhdm* [7] *wlhdm ytb* (= *qtl*) *larṣ* [8] the first occurrence of *ytb* is "imperfect"-preterit whereas the second is "perfect," again exhibiting the *yqtl-qtl* sequence with its stylistic variation in form but identity in meaning.

We might add in passing that the same observations hold true of the active-passive sequence of identical verbs in biblical Hebrew and in Ugaritic, but the details of this sequence must be reserved for another occasion.

---

[1] W. F. Albright, *JPOS*, vol. xiv (1934), 119; M. D. Cassuto, *Tarbiz*, vol. xiv, 9; *The Goddess Anath*, p. 37; C. H. Gordon, *Ugaritic Lit.* (Rome 1949), p. 30; *UM*, vol. iii, 331, no. 1903.

[2] T. H. Gaster, *op. cit.*; *idem*, *Thespis*, p. 447; G. R. Driver, *op. cit.*

[3] *Syria*, vol. xv, 312.

[4] *Ugaritic Lit.*, p. 39.

[5] *See* above p. [5], n. 3.

[6] Since the preformative of *ytb* in the first person *Qal* "imperfect" is *a* (I AB, 3-4: 18; II D, 2: 12; II K, 6: 38, 53), the vocalization according to the Barth-Ginsberg Law (J. Barth, *ZDMG*, vol. xlviii [1894], 4 ff.; H. L. Ginsberg, *Tarbiz*, vol. iv [1932], 382; *The Ugarit Texts*, p. 63; *Orientalia*, NS vol. viii, 318 ff.) will be *yaṯibu*.

[7] For the parallelism הדם // כסא in biblical Hebrew *cf.* Is 66: 1.

[8] This is a sign of mourning for Baal's death. *Cf.* Is 47: 1.

NEW LIGHT ON THE EPOCH OF AKABIAH B. MAHALALEL

By SIDNEY B. HOENIG

Yeshiva University

THE PRECISE SETTING of the era in which Akabiah ben Mahalalel flourished has been the subject of dispute among scholars. Following Menahem ha-Meiri, [1] Z. Frankel, [2] Brüll, [3] I. H. Weiss [4] and others [5] regarded Akabiah as functioning in the generation after Shemaiah and Abtalion, *i.e.*, as a contemporary of Hillel (*ca.* 30 B.C.E.). Their contention rests on the fact that Akabiah is not called *Rabbi*, and hence must be dated before such a title was introduced. [6] The mishnaic record of the offer to Akabiah to become Ab Bet-Din [7] is also taken to indicate that this incident occurred either after Shammai's death or perhaps before Shammai's induction into the Great Sandedrin, when Menahem had resigned the position; [8] in the subsequent Hillelite dynasty an Ab Bet-Din does not function. [9] The reference to the *Azarah* [10] likewise is recognized as proof for Temple days, [11] as is also the notion that in the pre-Jabneh period an individual opinion could not be maintained in the face of a majority view; hence the mishnaic note that Akabiah was asked to retract. [12]

[1] *Bet ha-Behira* on Abot, Introduction, 39; ed. New York 1944.

[2] *Darke ha-mishnah*, 58.

[3] *Mebo*, vol. i, 49.

[4] *Dor dor we-dorshaw*, vol. i, 176

[5] *Seder ha-dorot*, 119; G. Alon, *Toledot ha-Yehudim*, vol. i, p. 123; Hyman, *Toledot Tannaim*, 987.

[6] *Cf.* S. Zeitlin, *The Pharisees and the Gospels* (New York 1938), p. 269.

[7] Eduyot 5. 6-7. *See below,* p. 7, n. 2.

[8] Hagigah 2.2. *See below,* p. 6, n. 8.

[9] Shabbat 15a. *See below,* p. 8, n. 8.

[10] Eduyot, *loc. cit. See below* p. 2, n. 1.

[11] *Ibid. See below,* p. 7, n. 3.

[12] *Ibid.* א״ר יהוד׳ חס ושלום שעקביא נתנדה שאין עזרה ננעלת בפני כל אדם מישראל בחכמה וביראת חטא כעקביא בן מהללאל

These various arguments, however, may be refuted on the
basis that a reference to Shemaiah and Abtalion [1] or to the
Azarah may be made even by teachers living after 70 C.E.
Likewise the lack of the title *Rabbi* is a commonplace even
among later teachers, for example, Ben Azzai and Ben Zoma.
Moreover, the disagreement by an individual with a majority
opinion is not limited to the years after 70 C.E.; it may have
been current even long before the Jabneh era, as shown, for
instance, in the retort to Jose ben Joezer, recorded in *Eduyoth*.[2]
The request for Akabiah's retraction, therefore, is not proof
of a date. The existence of a position of Ab Bet-Din may
also be seen in the reigns of Rabban Simon ben Gamaliel II, [3]
if not in the days of R. Eleazar ben Azariah. [4]

On the strength of the above views, Derenbourg, [5] Brüll [6]
(in a reconsideration of his own view point) and others, [7] as
well as Albeck [8] today, believe that Akabiah ben Mahalalel
lived in the time of R. Eleazar ben Azariah. The circumstances
of Akabiah's excommunication are seen to fit the age of
R. Eleazar ben Hyrcanus of Jabneh who also was excommunicated because of his views [9]. Akabiah's disagreement with
R.Akiba [10] as well as with Dose ben Hyrcanus [11] of that era,
and the fact that Akabiah's statement is recorded among the
testimonies of Mishnah *Eduyoth* determined in Jabneh, are
adduced to place Akabiah in the early part of the second
century C. E.

[1]   *Ibid.* אמרו לו מעשה ··· והשקוה שמעיה ואבטליון
[2]   *Eduyot* 8.4   וקראו לו יוסי שריא
[3]   Horayot 13 b. *See* S. B. Hoenig, *The Great Sanhedrin* (Philadelphia, 1953), p. 68.
[4]   Ber. 27 b; *cf.* Hoenig, *op. cit.*, 65.
[5]   *Essai*, p. 37.
[6]   *Mebo*, 271.
[7]   S. Mendelsohn, JE I, 320 ; H. Strack, *Introduction to Talmud
and Midrash* (Philadelphia 1931), p. 109.
[8]   *Mabo la-mishnah*, 220.
[9]   B.M. 59 b.
[10]   Negaim 1. 4.
[11]   *Ibid.*

These contentions also may be set aside. The institution of excommunication was not limited to the Jabneh period; it is recorded as an instrument earlier, in the period of Simon ben Shetah. [1] Moreover, references in *Eduyoth* go back to Joshua b. Perahiah and Jose ben Joezer. [2] Dose b. Hyrcanus and R. Akiba are indeed of the Jabneh era, but the tannaitic text does not demonstrate a direct retort to Akabiah. The Mishnah simply records opinions of different generations. [3]

It is here suggested that for a substantial proof of Akabiah's period one should turn to internal evidence in the tannaitic texts. An examination of the Mishnah *Eduyoth* recording the Akabiah incident reveals that it contains the word *Makom* (מקום) as an appellation of God. [4] A study of the time of the introduction of this term into Jewish usage may, therefore, throw light on Akabiah's identification and period.

The use of the term *Makom* is found often in tannaitic sources. Thus it is recorded in the name of R. Eleazar ben Azariah with reference to the forgiveness of sins. [5] Rabban Gamaliel II also uses the term in his explanation of the Passover ritual. [6] In this tannaitic period the usage of *Makom* by Rabban Johanan ben Zakkai seems to be the earliest, [7] though the ordinary mishnaic text of *Middoth* 5 : 4 includes the term also with reference to priestly practice in Temple days. [8] Other tannaitic references contain the appellation

---

[1] Ber. 19a   שלח לו שמעון בן שטח לחוני המעגל צריך אתה להתנדות
[2] Eduyot 8. 4.
[3] Negaim 1. 4.
[4] Eduyot 5. 7.
[5] Yoma 8. 9   את זו דרש רבי אלעזר בן עזריה מכל חטאתיכם לפני ה'
תטהרו עבירות שבין אדם למקום יום הכפורים מכפר *Cf.* Epstein, *Mabo le-nusah ha-mishnah,* 1306 concerning this Mishnah. For R. Elazar and Makom *see also* Tosefta Arakin 4.25 אמר ר' אלעזר בן עזריה אם לגבוה
אין אדם רשאי להחרים את נכסיו שחס המקום עליו וכו'.
[6] Pes. 10. 5   פסח על שום שפסח על בתי אבותינו במצרים.
See different recensions—Naples ed. הקב"ה instead of המקום.
[7] Tosefta B.K. 7. 10   רבן יוחנן בן זכאי אומר בוא וראה כמה חס המקום על כבוד הבריות.
[8] Middot 5. 4   ברוך המקום ברוך הוא שלא נמצא פסול בזרעו של אהרן.
See Tosafot Yom Tob *ad. loc.* explaining *makom* as *lishkat ha-gazit.*

Makom in midrashic context explaining biblical verses, [1] and
also as utilized by the later generations of Tannaim such as
R. Akiba, [2] R. Simon, [3] Rabbi Joshua b. Korha, [4] Ben Azzai, [5]
R. Meir, [6] and others. [7]. The talmudic explanation of *Makom*,
however, is amoraic. [8]

In specific analysis, the Hebrew appellation *Makom* is
equivalent to the Greek τόπος (place). Harry A. Wolfson
believes that "by the time of Philo the term 'place' as an
appellation of God . . . must have already been in common
usage in Palestinian Judaism".[9] Following A. Marmorstein [10]
he notes that "this Palestinian Jewish use of the term has
been taken to have either a Philonic or Persian origin but it is
undoubtedly of native Jewish origin".[11] He notes that in
Greek philosophy a "suggestion for the use of it does occur . . .
perhaps before the time of Philo".[12] He shows that Philo
gives a Jewish application of it in *De Somn* I, 11, 62ff. and in

---

[1]   במדה שאדם מודד בה מודדין לו' היא קשטה עצמה 7 .Sotah 1
לעבירה המקום ניולה.
כ' ה' אלהיכם ההולך עמכם' הם באין בנצחונו של בשר ודם Sotah 8. 1
ואתם באים בנצחונו של מקום.
[2]   חביבים ישראל שנקראו בנים למקום Abot 3. 14
Tos. Yoma 4. 14 ...כך אמר המקום מי גרם להם שיעשו להם אלהי זהב
[3]   ר"ש אומר הלוה ואינו משלם אחד הלוה מן האדם כלוה מן Abot 2. 9
המקום ברוך הוא
ר"ש אומר כשאתה מתפלל אל תעש תפלתך קבע אלא רחמים Abot 2. 13
ותחנונים לפני המקום ב"ה
[4]   Mekilta Yitro 1; Tos. Peah 1. 4. מחשבה טובה המקום מצרפה
עם המעשה
[5]   Songs of Songs Rabbah 3. 5 ואין שכחה לפני המקום
[6]   Sanh. 6. 5. ר"מ אומר ... א"כ המקום מצטער על דמם של רשעים
שנשפך
[7]   Tos. Sotah 3. 14 סיסרא לא נתגאה לפני המקום
Tos. Taanit 3. 1 בטוחים אנו שאין המקום מביא מבול לעולם
Tos. Niddah 2. 6 ...והמקום משמר עליו שנא' שומר פתאום ה'
[8]   Gen. Rabbah 68. 9; Pesikta Rabbati 21. ר' הונא בשם ר' אמ' מפני
מה מכנין שמו של הקב"ה וקוראין אותו מקום שהוא מקומו של עולם ואין
העולם מקומו. See also Ben Yehuda, Dictionary s.v. מקום p. 3272.
[9]   Philo I, 247.
[10]   *The Old Rabbinic Doctrine of God* (1927) vol. i, 92-93.
[11]   Philo I, 248.
[12]   *Ibid.*, 247.

his comment on Exodus 21: 13 ("I will give thee a place to
which he who has slain a man shall flee") : "For here," says
Philo, "he uses the word place not space . . . but figuratively
of God himself" (*Fug.* 14.75). [1]

Wolfson's study shows that Philo, perhaps from Greek
origin, uses *place* as a name of God, but there is no evidence
in his investigation of the counterpart of τόπος (place), *i.e.*,
the Hebrew appellation מקום being used in Palestine in the
predestruction era. The *Middoth* text referring to priestly
practice in Temple days actually does not have this phrase
in the authentic readings. [2] It is to be emphasized that we
find the term only in the tannaitic literature of the second
century C.E., and not before. [3] It is very possible that the
term was used in Greek thought in Alexandria in the first
century and then adopted into Hebraic usage after 70 C.E.
Two factors may have impelled this : a) The desire not to
use *Adonai-Kyrios* (Lord) which was adopted by Christians
for Jesus, [4] and b) the need to demonstrate that even without
the Temple, God was omnipresent. The fact, too, that the
term *Makom* is not found in any earlier statements before
those of Rabban Johanan ben Zakkai and R. Eleazar ben
Azariah shows that its usage is only from the Jabneh era
onwards.

With specific reference to Akabiah ben Mahalalel the
ordinary mishnaic text contains the work *Makom*, indicating
God. The reading in *Eduyoth* [5] is מוטב לי להקרא שוטה כל ימי
ולא לעשות שעה אחת רשע לפני המקום שלא יהו אומרים בשביל שררה חזר
בו. An examination of the Munich MSS, [6] however, shows that
the term is lacking there, though the word לפני remains.

---

[1]   *Ibid.*, 249.
[2]   *See* Munich MSS, vol. ii, p. 500 b.
[3]   *See* notes p. 3, from 5 on.
[4]   *See* S. Zeitlin *JQR* (1948), "Liturgy of the First Night of Passover," 443.
[5]   Eduyot 5. 7.
[6]   Munich MSS, vol. ii, p. 388 line 2.

The reading, therefore, could be מוטב לי להקרא שוטה כל ימי
ולא לעשות שעה אחת רשע לפני ". . . And I shall not be made
(designated), even for a moment, a wicked person, *to my
face . . .*" [1]

This reading indicates that the maxim of Akabiah is early ;
it supports the contention that Akabiah belonged to the
Second Temple era, before 70 C.E. But the question remains
—specifically, when? The fact that there was no position
of Ab Bet-Din during the early patriarchate of the sons of
Hillel, *i.e.*, from about 10 C.E. on, [2] and also that Akabiah
refers back directly to the actions of predecessors Shemaiah
and Abtalion, [3] sets the *terminus ad quem* and, therefore,
limits the time of Akabiah's activity to the period of Hillel,
when there was a change, the only one in historic perspective,
in the position of Ab Bet-Din. In the early epoch, *i.e.*, during
the period of the *Zugoth*, the Great Sanhedrin consisted of
two parties—strict constructionists and loose constructionists
in the interpretation of the Torah. [4] Apparently when Hillel
became *Nasi* after the incident with Bene Bathyra [5] he had
little opposition in the Sanhedrin. His attitude was one of
victory, as seen in his bold remark to Bene Bathyra, [6] and this
despite his personal characteristic of humility. [7] Hillel's
dominance throws light on the statement in Mishnah *Haggigah*
that "Hillel and Menahem did not disagree." [8] Thus Hillel
was paving the way for the abolition of the Ab Bet-Din
position. But such aspiration or desired situation could not
be effected by him immediately. However, when Menahem

---

[1] *E.g.*, "our confrontation" לא יהיה לך אלהים אחרים על פני in
the Decalogue Ex 20, 3. *cf.* Nahmanides *ad loc.*
[2] Shabbat 15a; *see* Hoenig, *op. cit.*, p. 63.
[3] Eduyot 5. 6.
[4] *See* Hoenig, *op. cit.* 47.
[5] Pesahim 66.
[6] *Ibid.*
[7] Shabbat 30b לעולם יהא אדם ענוותן כהלל
[8] Hagigah 2. 2 הלל ומנחם לא נחלקו *See* L. Ginzberg, *Law and Love*
(Philadelphia 1955), pp. 91, 100, 247 note 11.

left, [1] the propitious moment may have arrived. It was then that Akabiah was offered the position of Ab Bet-Din, [2] perhaps with the understanding that he too yield to Hillel, but he refused. Though it may be amazing, Akabiah felt that his opinions were not those of a minority ; hence his assertion that "I obtained my opinions from many and they heard from many; I stood fast in my tradition and they upheld their tradition . . ." [3] Akabiah was adamant in his refusal to retract his own opinion and consequently accept the offered position. Thereupon Shammai instead entered as Ab Bet-Din under the leadership (*nesiuth*) of Hillel. [4]

Shammai's acceptance of the opposition leadership, *i.e.*, of the strict-constructionists in the interpretation of the law, may in a sense have come with the agreement and understanding of subordination to Hillel. This may be deduced from the fact in only one rare instance is it recorded that Hillel was subordinated to Shammai, who had gained the upper hand. [5]

It is apparent that Shammai and his pupils ordinarily accepted the rule of Hillel in practice. This is evident in the record of a rare Temple incident, when the pupils of Shammai, in Hillel's presence in the Azarah, sought to negate his conduct; [6] only by a ruse did Hillel send them off. [7] Yet it is recorded that on that day the Shammaites prevailed over the Hillelites and sought to establish the Halakah in line

---

[1] Hillel and Menahem may have been together about 20 years. See *Zadokite Fragments*, Text A, ed. S. Zeitlin (Philadelphia 1952), p. 21.

[2] Eduyot 5. 6 אמרו לו עקביא חזור כך בארבעה דברים שהיית אומר ונעשך אב ב״ד לישראל

[3] *Ibid.* אני שמעתי מפי המרובים והם שמעו מפי המרובים אני עמדתי בשמועתי והם עמדו בשמועתן

[4] Hagigah 2. 2.

[5] Shabbat 17a ואותו היום היה הלל כפוף וישב לפני שמאי כאחד מן התלמידים

[6] *Cf.* Eduyot 1. 12.

[7] Bezah 20 a.

with their own opinion. [1] However, a pupil of Shammai, Baba ben Buta, recognizing that the Halakah was established according to the House of Hillel, acted according to that opinion [2] and aptly illustrated the strength of the Hillelite opinion without anyone demurring. The dominance of Hillel was thus retained. [3]

It is interesting to note that the *Azarah* incident does not mention Shammai; only his pupils are cited. [4] This may allude to the fact that Hillel outlived Shammai. [5] With Shammai's death apparently there was only sporadic opposition to the Hillelite dominance. In the Great Sanhedrin of the *Zugoth* a pragmatic approach [6] prevailed in dealing with the Law; usually a vote was taken to obtain direction for correct procedure and action. Hillel's view commonly prevailed; differences of opinion existed only later, in the academies or schools of thought where theoretical investigation prevailed and consequent disagreement occur' red, [7] but such academic argumentation did not affect the judicial decisions which still followed the dominant Hillelite view.

With Shammai's death the patriarchate was firmly and finally established in the Hillelite dynasty. [8] Thus, Akabiah's refusal, a generation earlier, to accept the position of Ab Bet-Din unwittingly led to the strengthening of the Hillelite dynasty and its dominance in the interpretation of the Halakah.

---

[1]   *Ibid.* אותו היום גברה ידם של בית שמאי על בית הלל ובקשו לקבוע הלכה כמותן

[2]   *Ibid.* יהודה בן בבא שהיה יודע שהלכה כבית הלל

[3]   *Ibid.* ואותו היום גברה ידן של בית הלל וקבעה הלכה כמותן ולא היה שם אדם שערר בדבר כלום

[4]   *Ibid.*

[5]   *See* Frankel, *Darke ha-mishnah*; contrarily Hyman, *Toledot Tannaim* s.v. שמאי p. 1119.

[6]   *Cf.* Ginzberg, *op. cit.*, 95.

[7]   *Ibid.*

[8]   Shabbat 15a הלל ושמעון גמליאל ושמעון נהגו נשיאותן בפני הבית מאה שנה

THE COMPOSITION AND TRANSMISSION OF AVERROES' *MA'AMAR BE-'EṢEM HA-GALGAL*

By Arthur Hyman

Dropsie College

Averroes, the majority of whose writings consists of commentaries on Aristotle's works, [1] was also the author of a number of independent treatises known variously as אגרת, מאמר, דבור, דרוש, שאלה (تعليق, مقالة, كلام, مسائل, مسئلة, مسألة; quaestio, quaesitum, sermo, tractatus, epistola). [2] Dealing with a variety of philosophical and theological topics, these treatises contain answers to inquiries addressed to Averroes or solutions to problems posed by him. In these treatises Averroes usually develops his own views on the subject or subjects under discussion and, when necessary, he refutes opinions which he holds to be erroneous.

The *Ma'amar be-'Eṣem ha-Galgal* (*Sermo De Substantia Orbis*) is a collection of such independent treatises which have as their common subject matter the nature and properties of the heavens. [3] The Arabic text of this collection is no longer extant, but the work has been preserved in a Hebrew and a Latin translation. [4] Made from the Arabic original, these translations are independent of each other. [5]

[1] For a description and listing of Averroes' commentaries, *see* H. A. Wolfson, "Plans for the Publication of a *Corpus Commentariorum Averrois in Aristotelem*," *Speculum*, vol. vi (1931), 412-427.

[2] The Arabic terms are not translated consistently into Hebrew and Latin.

[3] The contents of the work are discussed in Pierre Duhem, *Le Système du Monde*, vol. iv (Paris 1916), pp. 532-559.

[4] For a description of these translations *see* Moritz Steinschneider, *Die hebräischen Übersetzungen des Mittelalters* (Graz 1956), pp. 178-185, esp. pp. 182-185.

[5] The Latin translation from the Arabic was translated into Hebrew by Judah Romano (early fourteenth century). To his translation Romano appended a Hebrew commentary based almost exclusively on Latin works. *Cf.* Steinschneider, *op. cit.*, p. 183.

The Hebrew translation from the Arabic, which has been preserved in a number of complete and partial manuscripts, [1] is the work of an anonymous translator. [2] It has reached us in a recension made by Moses of Narbonne, [3] who is also the author of a commentary which accompanies the text in most manuscripts. [4] In Narboni's recension the work is divided into three treatises, the third of which, in turn, is divided into three chapters. [5]

[1] *See* Steinschneider, *ibid.*, p. 179 and p. 183. Steinschneider's listing is somewhat unclear, for one gains the impression that only the manuscripts listed on p. 183 contain all or part of the text. However, an examination of the catalogues and other available evidence show that some of the manuscripts listed on p. 179, but not listed again on p. 183 also contain all or part of the work. These manuscripts are: Steinschneider 6 (now owned by the Jewish Theological Seminary in New York), containing the whole work; Bl. 112, containing chapter five (according to the Latin); Mn. 36, containg chapters four and five (according to the Latin). I was unable to ascertain whether any of the other manuscripts listed on p. 179 and not listed again on p. 182 contain any part of the work.

[2] On the basis of the available Hebrew manuscripts and using a sample of the early printed Latin editions for purposes of comparison, I have prepared a critical edition of the anonymous Hebrew version, together with an English translation of the work, a commentary and an introduction. This work as well as Romano's Hebrew version and the Hebrew commentaries of Narboni and Romano will be published by the Medieval Academy of America as part of its Averroes series.

[3] Moses of Narbonne, as will be seen, is not the original editor of the collection.

[4] Narboni finished this commentary in 1349. Cf. Steinschneider, *Hebräische Übersetzungen*, p. 178.

[5] The first of these treatises carries the superscription "A Treatise by Averroes the Philosopher concerning the Substance of the Celestial Sphere" (מאמר לאבן רושד הפילוסוף בעצם הגלגל), and the second "The Philosopher [Averroes] also wrote a Letter concerning this Subject and it is the Following" (עוד כתב החכם אגרת אחת לזה והיא זאת). The third treatise carries no special superscription, but each of its component chapters is headed "First Chapter" (מאמר ראשון), "Second Chapter" (מאמר שני), and "Third Chapter" (מאמר שלישי) respectively.

In an introduction to the third treatise, Narboni summarizes each of the three component chapters. The first chapter, he writes, deals with Aristotle's view that the celestial body is not composite, the second chapter explains in what sense the celestial body is simple, and the third

The Latin translation from the Arabic, made between 1227 and 1231, [1] is probably the work of Michael Scot. [2] This version, usually called the Old Latin, has been preserved in a large number of manuscripts [3] and in a number of fifteenth- and sixteenth-century printed editions. [4] Most recently it appeared in an edition of Alvaro de Toledo's commentary on the work. [5] The Old Latin which lacks a portion of the text appearing in the anonymous Hebrew translation, is divided into five chapters. [6] In some of the sixteenth-century editions this missing portion appears as a sixth chapter in a Latin translation made by Abraham of Balmes from the anonymous Hebrew text. [7] These sixteenth-century editions also contain

chapter establishes that the celestial body is neither heavy nor light.

המאמר הראשון יחקר בו בסבת הדרוש האחד והוא אשר ביארו ארסטטן
בפועל בשמע הטבעי׳ ר״ל בשהגרם השמימיי בלתי מורכב׳ ר״ל שהצורה
נבדלת אינה תנאי במציאותו׳ והמאמר השני יתן בו סבת הדרוש השני׳ והוא
שהוא פשוט׳ רצוני שהגרם השמימיי אינו מורכב מחומר ונפש בו׳ ואם הוא
מחובר בצורה נבדלת .... והמאמר השלישי יתן בו הסבה בשהוא לא קל ולא
כבד והוא אשר ביארו ארסטטן בהשמים והעולם׃

[1] R. de Vaux, „La Première Entrée d'Averroës chez les Latins," *Revue des Sciences Philosophiques et Théologiques*, vol. xxii (1933), 193-245, *passim*.

[2] *Ibid.*, 222-223. Cf. Ernest Renan, *Averroès et l'Averroïsm*, 3rd ed. (Paris 1866), pp. 205 ff. and Steinschneider, *op. cit.*, p. 181 and p. 182, n 554. De Vaux agrees with Renan (Steinschneider) that Michael Scot is the probable translator. However, he rejects Renan's arguments and substitutes other ones of his own.

[3] Georges LaCombe in *Aristoteles Latinus*, Pars Posterior (Cambridge 1955), p. 1292 lists 79 extant manuscripts of the Old Latin. Professor Paul O. Kristeller of Columbia University was kind enough to bring to my attention a number of additional unlisted manuscripts. I hope to record these in my forthcoming edition.

[4] For a list of some of these editions, *cf.* Steinschneider, *op. cit.*, pp. 182-183. Among other editions of Aristotle's works containing the *De Substantia Orbis* are those of 1550-52, 1560 and 1573-76.

[5] Alvaro de Toledo, *Comentario al „De substantia orbis" de Averroes*, ed. P. Manuel Alonso (Madrid 1941).

[6] Alonso's text, which is the only one deviating from this scheme is divided into four treatises. A manuscripts dated 1243 shows that the division of the Old Latin into five chapters is already very early. *Cf.* R. de Vaux, *op. cit.*, 223-224.

[7] These two additional chapters are preceded by the remark: *Haec duo sequentia capita, ab Abramo de Balmes latinate donata, quan-*

a seventh chapter for which no underlying Arabic or Hebrew has been found so far.

Comparing the text of the anonymous Hebrew translation with that of the Latin, the following scheme emerges:

Hebrew Text	Latin Text
First Treatise	First Chapter
Second Treatise	Fifth Chapter
Third Treatise, First Chapter	Second Chapter
Third Treatise, Second Chapter, First Section	Third Chapter
Third Treatise, Second Chapter, Second Section	Sixth Chapter (appears only in some of the sixteenth-century editions)
Third Treatise, Third Chapter	Fourth Chapter
———	Seventh Chapter (appears only in some of the sixteenth-century editions)

An analysis of the work shows that the title *Ma'amar be-'Eṣem ha-Galgal* (*Sermo De Substantia Orbis*) applied originally only to the first treatise of the collection. [1] In time,

---

quam ab hoc tractatu separata esse videantur, cumiam ei finis sit impositus: quia tamen in eadem versantur re in qua et priora: ideo ipsa sextum et septimum tractatus huius capita constituimus.

[1] This is evident from the conclusion of the first treatise which reads: "and this treatise is called 'The Discourse concerning the Substance of the Celestial Sphere,'" (ונקרא המאמר הזה הדבור בעצם הגלגל); *vocetur igitur iste tractatus Sermo de substantia orbis*). Further, Averroes' own references to the work in *Long Commentary on Physics* 1, com. 60; 1, com. 79, and *Long Commentary on De Caelo* 2, com. 3 are all to the first treatise. For these references *cf.* M. Alonso, *Teología de Averroes* (Madrid-Granada, 1947), pp. 93-94. Moreover, Narboni in his introduction to the third treatise (*cf.* below, p. 5) writes: "... and it is especially fitting [to comment on the third treatise], inasmuch as we have already commented on Averroes' treatise *Concerning the Substance of the Celestial Sphere* [the first treatise]. For the following [third] treatise is in a certain sense part of his [Averroes'] treatise *Concerning the Substance of the Celestial Sphere*, so much so that we see earlier Latin writers calling these

other treatises by Averroes dealing with the celestial bodies were added to this treatise and the collection as a whole became known as *Ma'amar be-'Eṣem ha-Galgal*. However, so far no adequate account has been given of the original number of added treatises and of the history of transmission of the Hebrew text.

Most scholars, unfamiliar with the Hebrew version, assume that the collection is composed of five original treatises which they identify with the five chapters of the Old Latin translation. Steinschneider, however, taking into account that Narboni's text is composed of three treatises, maintains that the collection is composed of the original *Ma'amar be-'Eṣem ha-Galgal* (the first treatise) and two additional treatises by Averroes.[1] He identifies these three treatises with three works found in the Escurial list of Averroes' works, entitled respectively "A Treatise concerning the Celestial Body," "Another Treatise concerning the Celestial Body," and "Another Treatise concerning this Subject [the Celestial Body]." [2] Steinschneider finds support for his opinion that the work is composed of three original treatises in Narboni's introduction to the third treatise. In this introduction Narboni indicates that the text of the *Ma'amar be-'Eṣem ha-Galgal* which had reached him was composed of three treatises. [3] Stein-

treatises in their totality *Concerning the Substance of the Celestial Sphere*, [that is] *sustancia orbis*." ויותר ראוי אחר שכבר פירשנו מאמרו ... בעצם הגלגל· כי זה המאמר הוא חלק באפן מה ממאמרו בעצם הגלגל· עד שראינו חכמי הקדמונים מהרומיים יקראו אלו המאמרים בכללם בעצם הגלגל· שושטנסיאה אורביש·

[1] Steinschneider, *op. cit.*, p. 182 writes: „... wir werden in der That 3 Stücke nachweisen."

[2] In the Escurial list these titles are مقالة فى الجرم السماوى, مقالة اخرى فيه, and مقالة اخرى فى الجرم السماوى. *Cf.* Ernest Renan, *Averroès et l'Averroïsm*, p. 463, l. 16— p. 464, l. 2. P. M. Bouyges suggest that the Arabic original might be found in the Escurial. *Cf.* M. Bouyges, "Notes sur les philosophes Arabes connus des Latins au Moyen Age," *Mélanges de l'Université Saint-Joseph*, Beyrouth (VIII, 1) 1922, p. 30, n. 3.

[3] *See* the quotation from Narboni's commentary (p. 4, n. 1 end), in which the phrase "for the following treatise" (כי זה המאמר) refers to the third treatise in its totality.

schneider leaves the impression that the Old Latin, which is divided into five chapters, marks a later redaction of the text.

On the basis of a manuscript listed by Steinschneider, but of the relation of which to the *Ma'amar be-'Eṣem ha-Galgal* he was not aware, we are now in a position to determine the original parts of the collection and to describe the transmission of the Hebrew text more accurately. The evidence provided by this manuscript is supported by internal evidence taken from the content and structure of the *Ma'amar be-'Eṣem ha-Galgal.*

In some of the manuscripts of Solomon ibn Ayyub's Hebrew translation of Averroes' *Intermediate Commentary on the De Caelo* [1] there appears an appendix headed "In reply to the question mentioned at the end of the first treatise of this commentary [the *Intermediate Commentary on the De Caelo*] the philosopher Averroes answers . . . . " [2] An examination of this appendix shows that it is identical in content with the first section of the second chapter of the third treatise in Narboni's text (chapter three in the Latin). [3]

Though identical in content with the corresponding portion of Narboni's text of the *Ma'amar be-'Eṣem ha-Galgal,* this appendix has its own technical vocabulary [4] and its own

---

[1] *See* Steinschneider, *op. cit.,* pp. 128-129. For the Arabic original of the *Commentary,* cf. M. Bouyges, op. cit., 18-19.

[2] אמר החכם אבן רשד על השאלה אשר זכרה בסוף המאמר הראשון מזה
הביאור (השמים והעולם האמצעי).

This appendix does not appear in the Latin translation of the *Intermediate Commentary.*

[3] I am indebted to Professor Harry A. Wolfson of Harvard University for calling my attention to this appendix and for suggesting that it may correspond to a part of the *Ma'amar be-Eṣem ha-Galgal.* The manuscript that I had at my disposal is found in the Friedman collection at Harvard.

[4] This vocabulary will be recorded in my edition. A sample of the difference between the two Hebrew translations is provided by the following comparison of their respective beginnings and ends:

Narboni: אמר ב"ר שלמה שהתבאר מענין הגרמים השמימיים שהם מחוברים
ממניע ומתנועע ושהמניע בם בלתי גשם ··· וזאת השאלה לא עמדתי עליה אלא
אחר חקירה רבה וזמן בלתי מועט והוא מן המעלה והזכות באשר היא עד שמי

style of translation. Moreover, it contains passages which differ from the corresponding passages in Narboni's text, but which agree with their counterparts in the Latin translation. [1] From this evidence it follows that the appendix and the corresponding section of Narboni's text are two independent translations of the same underlying Arabic original. This makes it unlikely that the appendix was originally a part of Narboni's third treatise which was taken from this treatise and added as an appendix to the *Intermediate Commentary on the De Caelo*. Rather, a part of Narboni's third treatise was originally an appendix to the *Intermediate Commentary on the De Caelo*. [2] We may conclude, therefore, that Narboni's third treatise is a collection of earlier treatises rather than an independent treatise as Steinschneider, following Narboni, thought. Thus, there exists no need to identify the three treatises in Narboni's text with the three titles in the Escurial list of Averroes' works.

That Narboni's third treatise is not one original work but a collection of earlier independent treatises is supported by three additional considerations derived from the content and structure of the third treatise. Firstly, the contents of the component chapters of the third treatise overlap. This would have been unlikely had this treatise been one work originally. Secondly, each of the component chapters and sections of the third treatise has its own independent con-

שתבצר ממנו זאת השאלה הנה אי אפשר שיגיע לו השלמות האנושי כלל׃ והאל העוזר אין אדון זולתו ופי׳ המשכילים ימלא תהלתו׃ ית׳ וית׳ תמה השאלה׃ תהלה לאל המשיב לכל מושב׃
Ibn Ayyub: אחר שנתבאר מן הגשמים הרקיעיים שהם מחוברים ממניע ומתנועע ושהמניע בלתי גשם ... וזאת השאלה לא עמדתי עליה כי אם אחר עיון רבה חקירה וזמן בלתי מועט׃ והיה מן החשיבות והזכות כאשר היא עד שמי שנתעלמה ממנו זאת השאלה אי אפשר שיגיע לו השלמות האנושי כלל׃ והאל ידריכנו מדריכו לישרה ושלם המאמר׃ ושבח לאל׃

[1] These variants will be recorded in my edition.
[2] In the text which I had at my disposal the colophon listing Solomon ibn Ayyub as the translator precedes the appendix. But a careful examination of the terminology and the style of the appendix left no doubt that ibn Ayyub translated not only the *Intermediate Commentary*, but also the appendix.

clusion. This supports the view that these chapters and
sections were independent works originally. Finally, section
two of the second chapter of the third treatise [1] does not
appear in the Old Latin. This omission would have been
unlikely had this section formed part of a larger treatise.

A remark in Narbonis commentary provides an additional
clue concerning the transmission of the Hebrew text. Com-
menting on a question raised by Averroes toward the end of
the third treatise but not answered by him in that passage,
Narboni writes: "But as for Averroes statement resolving
the doubt which befalls people, we have transferred it to an
earlier place and we have combined it with the second chapter
[of the third treatise], since we saw in this arrangement a
more natural order." [2] From this remark it is clear that in the
text which reached Narboni, section two of the second chapter
of the third treatise (which contains the answer to the question
raised by Averroes) followed the third chapter of the third
treatise [3] and that Narboni changed this order. [4]

In summary, we have shown that the collection known as
Ma'amar be-'Eṣem ha-Galgal contains six originally independent treatises and we have identified three stages in the
transmission of the Hebrew text. Averroes wrote a treatise
entitled Ma'amar be-'Eṣem ha-Galgal which is identical with
the first treatise of the present collection. In time, five treatises by Averroes dealing with the celestial bodies were added
to this collection and four of these treatises were combined

---

[1] Chapter six in some of the sixteenthcentury Latin editions.
This chapter carries as place and date of its composition Morroco, 573
a. H. (1178). From what has been said it follows that this date applies
with certainty only to the present chapter not to the work as a whole.

[2] (ומה שאמר [אבן רושד] ש י ע ת ק ב כ א ן) מה שאמרו בהתרת הספק אשר
סופר [צ״ל סופק] על האנשים כבר העתקנוהו אנחנו לפני זה ודבקנוהו עם
המאמר השני· למה שראינו בו מן הסדור הטבעי· ואין צורך להשיב הנה מה
שכבר נאמר·

[3] The order of the third treatise in the text which reached Narboni
was: First Chapter; Second Chapter, First Section; Third Chapter;
Second Chapter, Second Section.

[4] Cf. above, p. 4.

into one. [1] This edition, composed of three treatises, was the one which reached Narboni. Narboni, in turn, rearranged the third of these treatises producing the text which has reached us. From these considerations it also becomes clear that the five chapters of the Old Latin translation correspond to five originally independent treatises.

This brief study provides one more illustration of how the careful study and comparison of texts sheds light on their history and on their transmission. Moreover, it offers an indication of the relevance of the Hebrew textual tradition to the study of medieval philosophy. It is presented here as a token of friendship and affection to President Abraham A. Neuman, whose researches have helped to clarify the role of the Hebraic strand in the fabric of medieval culture.

---

[1] It is impossible to determine whether the four works which make up Narboni's third treatise were combined before being added to the collection or afterwards.

ON BEING JEWISH TODAY

By HORACE M. KALLEN

New School for Social Research, New York

THE WORD "Jewish" is today extremely ambiguous or "ambivalent." Actually, "polyvalent" would be closer to the historic record. There are so many ways, among individuals and groups, of being Jewish today that many of them like to say to others, "I am a Jew; you are not." Or, "yes, you are a Jew, too, but it's you who are the kind of Jew who creates antisemitism." And so on, over a long range of diversifying antagonisms and conflicts within a context of identity claimed or denied.

Now, as the reader must know, the words "Jew," "Jewish" and their variants are words signifying what logicians call a class; they are collective, not singular, terms. They are ways of identifying individuals, alone or in groups. We feel, but are rarely conscious of the feeling, that individuals are all different, each one from all others; and that at bottom the differences are ultimate. We do not like to recognize this. The human mind prefers to unify, prefers to digest differences in identity. Identifications enable it to treat the diverse as if they were homogeneous; they simplify its problems of living on in a world not made for it; so all the arts and sciences and religions making up the cultures of mankind aim at identifications by force or by persuasion. They tend to forget that identifications are meaningless without the difference they strive to unify, without the multitudinous Many they work and fight and argue to turn into a single One.

So far as people are concerned, each individual is unique; he cannot be identified with any other individual unless the other one eats him up—as cannibals do when they crave the powers and form of their human meals. Cannibalism is one

of the earliest ways of turning the different into the same;
and we are all aware of the religious, political, economic and
cultural cannibalisms among the powerholders of the modern
world, even though we call them by other names—such as
imperialism, colonialism, communism, nazism, catholicism—
and Judaism as well. As live human beings struggling for
survival, we are unique, and governments of all sorts strive
by all the methods that their police power can invent to pin
down and "fix" this uniqueness. They use fingerprints, blood
types and their individual differentiae, footprints, postures,
ways of walking, standing, sitting, and so on. Mistaken identities happen—but the mistake is always somebody else's,
not one's own. If we had identical twins and our twin is
mistaken for us and we for our twin, neither the twin nor
we would mistake ourselves for one another. We are more
than reasonably sure of our own identity.

But when identification is carried beyond one's ever-
present feeling of personality, when it comes to labelling
that which we feel in terms of heredity, or religion, or occupation, or culture, or any other category, identification becomes
ambiguous and problematical. Suppose one is identified as a
"Jew"—how would other "Jews" regard the identification!
For example, would the Teitelbaum or Lubavitcher Judaic
communities in the Brownsville or Williamsburg sector of
New York City acknowledge members of differing denominations as Jews? Again, I do not doubt that many persons who
identify themselves as Jews not only concede but deprecate
the fact that the members of those fundamentalist enclaves
are entitled to the characterization "Jew," and sharply
distinguish themselves from them—even to the point of
refusing to live where they live and to accept them for neighbors. Others would accept them and live among them simply
because they are "Jews." They, or most of them, on the other
hand, would flee all contact with the rest of "Jewry," and
isolate themselves from it in self-containing ghettos. One
apparently is now being planned somewhere in New Jersey.

The deprecations and exclusions which both practice follow from one or another of certain wider divergences of doctrine and discipline. There are first of all those that establish the Jewishness of Jews on their commitment to some particular supernaturalist creed and code. Let us call such true believers Judaists. Among them there will be groups who refuse to accept the full import of the word "Jew." They will argue that this includes secular components, and violates Torah and its commandments. Further, there are those to whom the word "Jew" points first and foremost to secular and secularizing ideals and ideas; they will stand as Jews who refuse to be classified as Judaists.

One instance of the first group are the Judaists of *Meah Shearim* in Jerusalem. They refuse all identification with any person or association called Jews, by themselves or by others, if the latter differ in creed or code. They reject the State of Israel and all its works; they denounce and sabotage it, especially when as *Shomre Shabbos*, they are defending holy Sabbath from desecration, even while accepting the safety and the liberty of denunciation which the State provides. Their creed and code, and the ways and works which express and enact them, embody a mode of life, a set of attitudes and beliefs, of customs, folkways and mores which together compose a culture, more or less embattled, dependent on aid and comfort from believers in a like culture elsewhere— notably here in Williamsburg, U.S.A.

Instances of the second group are provided by a variety of associations of Jews such as the Zionist, the Bundist, the fraternal, the scholarly, the economic, the journalist, in their combinations and permutations. At least by contrast with the Judaists of *Meah Shearim* in Jerusalem, of Williamsburg or Brownville in New York, they do compose secular societies. Even as Judaists, they distinguish themselves into two classes, much as the Roman Catholics so distinguish themselves. The entirety of the Roman church divides, as the reader knows, into what they call the Teaching Church and the Believing

Church. The Teaching Church consists of the clergy in their order and hierarchy. They are the professionals, by training and vocation charged with safeguarding and advancing their creed and code, with authority to teach and impose it. They expect obedience and assistance from the Believing Church. This consists of the "laity," the adjuvant and passive non-professionals who pay the professionals for the ' spiritual" services they are believed to render, as they pay doctors and nurses, lawyers and policemen and judges, legislators and congressmen and governors and presidents; and as they pay for the construction and maintenance of places of service such as churches or hospitals or capitols and so on. We are perhaps not as aware as we might be that a similar division between professionals and laity obtains among Judaists of course, but among Jews no less. Professional Jews or Judaists are the men and the women whose vocation it is to keep going and spreading whatever attitudes, ways, works, and establishments that the words "Jew," "Jewish," "Judaism," "Jewishness," "Judaic," "Judaistic," or their surrogates, signify. The words denote the sources of livelihood of the professional Jew or Judaist. They signify what he makes his living from, but by no means necessarily how he lives or what he lives by, or in

Professional Jews include social workers as well as rabbis, cantors, morticians, *shohatim*, *mohalim*, sextons, *melamdim*, journalists, kosher food purveyors, and the like. What is "Jewish" in the Jewish community is first and last in their professional custody; it rises or falls, spreads or narrows, stays traditional or becomes "progressive" in virtue of how they think about it and how they act on what they think. Issues over *Who Is a Jew?*, debates over *The Jewish Question*, arise first and last among the professionals and spread from them to the laity. To realize and to understand the differences between the various Judaisms—hasidism, mitnagdism, orthodoxy, conservatism, reform, American-councilism, reconstructionism, and other denominational *isms*—we must needs study the controversies between professional Judaists.

This is not the case with controversies over Jewishness. To realize and understand those, we must begin by looking elsewhere; for at first there were no secular professionals; they appeared much later; they may rightly be appraised as a manifestation of modernity, and a consequence of the discomfort, unrest and disappointments created among believing Jews by teaching Judaists on such subjects as the Judaist creed and code and on their expression in ways of life; on modes of speech; on modes of instruction, on antisemitism; on the relation of Torah to "worldliness" and on similar themes. All of them signify ideas and skills wherewith the teaching Judaists created believing ones and kept the Judaist establishment with its institutions a going concern.

I say "created," because, however greatly we may dislike recognizing the fact, there are no "born" Jews or Judaists. Psychologically there are Jewish parents, but not Jewish offspring. A newly born infant is neither a Jew nor a member of any other communion or culture. It may grow into a member of any. It grows into a Jew or Judaist because its parents surround it with a cultural environment believed to be Jewish and so shape its growth and development that its personality becomes a configuration with this environment. If it had been similarly dependent on Chinese care and education in a Chinese culture, it would grow up into a Chinese in the modeling of its facial expression as well as the qualities of its personality. The condition is the same for the new births of all peoples—American or European or African or Asiatic. Recent history has only made it more conspicuous for the young of Jewish parents subjected to the Hitlerian or Stalinist sadistocracies. And the history of immigrants into our own country, Jewish and non-Jewish alike, and of their "Americanization," provides evidence of this human condition in another area of the human enterprise. Acculturation by contagion is an ongoing process everywhere. Caricaturists illustrate it when any of one culture draws a figure from another. A Russian caricature of Mr. Eisenhower, for example, will distort his features toward the Russian, as an American of Krushchev distorts his toward the American, without either making the subject unrecognizable or destroying his identity.

This identity has for its vital center a sort of funded mentality of beliefs, values, feelings, habits of perception and interpretation, that it has absorbed from the places where it lives and the persons with whom it speaks as it works and plays and worships and fights; it has for its functional lifespace other such formations which tend to recast and to blur the basic diversities of individuals and to mask what we know to be their irreducible, their indefeasible, individualities. Minutiae of language, of posture, of gesture, accent and rhythm, of hairdo and dress, of food preferences, and so on indefinitely, become intrinsic formations within the habits whence character builds itself and personality utters itself. Once established, each formation becomes an interest more and more able to resist change, and to absorb changes as well; to continue and to grow by diversifying.

Of course, this is the condition of individuality in all societies and all cultures, no less than the Jewish. Everywhere individuals grow up and grow older only as they change in order to preserve and confirm their identities. After long intervals of not seeing each other they meet and tell each other, "Well, you haven't changed: I'd know you anywhere"— as if it were a compliment and not an insult. For in the nature of things, to live is to change. I myself would rather ask of old friends I see for the first time in many years: "What difference have the years made in you? What changes are you conscious of and can account for? What's *new* with you?" Acknowledging their ongoing identities, recognizing their frames and features, I know that if they have been truly alive, they have changed—if not so much visibly, more than I can grasp, inwardly, invisibly. I know that the identity of each is not a fixed state of being but a sequent series of events, one component of which, perhaps dominant, perhaps recessive, is the orchestration of properties and functions that the word "Jewish" intends.

Now there are two ways of being Jewish or Judaistic. Let us call one automatic and involuntary. This is the way an infant gets to be Jewish. Infants are helpless. To survive they must have the care of grown-ups. We could quite correctly interpret the statement of our Declaration of Independence that all men are created equal as meaning that they are created equal in helplessness and utter dependence on the care of grown-ups. Without this care they would equally die. This care is perforce creative. Within obvious limits, it creates youth in the psychological and social, if not the bodily, image of its elders. A baby cannot help sucking up with its mother's milk Jewish modes of feeling and thinking and speaking and doing. It cannot help absorbing from the family scene one or another article of belief or disbelief, of friendly or unfriendly attitudes toward what is different in people and things. That which is labelled "Jewish" for the most part evokes a sense of "belongingness"; sometimes it evokes resistance to belongingness. The words "Yid," "Goy," "Jew," "Gentile," carry, as the reader well knows, emotional resonances which play a positive role in the overall dynamic of our personal histories.

The terms and the feelings that go with them are experienced in childhood and go over as habits in later life. And so long as the meanings of the word "Jew" or its surrogates are not confronted by significant alternatives between which a child finds it must needs choose, it will grow up into a supernaturalistic Judaist or a secularistic Jew but will not know why or how. It will therefore, as is the custom, believe itself to be Jewish by birth; it will try to explain what it has become by "heredity," "destiny" and similar concepts. If its bringing-up has been, in one form or another, Judaist, it will come to Judaistic manhood at puberty, its parents and relatives will celebrate its *Bar Mitzvah,* and it may be entered as a member of the religious communion fully responsible for the discharge of its religious duties. At the same time, it will be continued as a non-responsible minor in all the other regions of living.

Of course, family income makes a difference. Among the poor, maturity and responsibility accrue to children when they get work certificates. Among the richer, they accrue at graduation from college, or later from professional schools. The world of today has brought about a tremendous social prolongation of infancy. Our modern world tends to keep its young under tutelage very much longer than the world of our grandfathers did, because it takes so very much longer to get trained into a doctor or a lawyer or an engineer or a business man, and it costs so much more.

Since growing up and growing older is a process of which the developing personality is mostly unaware, awareness of the process follows as a rule from confrontation of alternatives; from conflict, from shock, or from the chronic and acute challenges of the enterprises whereof growth composes itself. A Jew's or a Judaist's awareness of his group and his belonging to it is especially affected by one influence among the many which work powerfully toward the survival or extinction of Jews of all categories as Jews.

This influence is antisemitism. It is still a condition of our existence today that being Jewish handicaps an individual in the exercise of his powers. He cannot go as far as they would enable him to. It is of record that the generations of Jewish youth still find that they can advance freer and faster in the learned professions, including engineering and electronics, or for that matter in the industrial crafts, if they do not carry the label "Jew" along with them. The label handicaps them, even in communities untainted by the overt antisemitism of the east-European, near-eastern, Germanic or Slavic kinds. Thus, in our own country also, there is a constant social pressure toward de-Judaization—especially in fields where endeavor is competitive and the preparation required long and costly. The pressure is lower in the arts and sports, but there, too, it gives de-Judaization a favored position.

Now let the reader note well: being Jewish is today less of a handicap in the United States than anywhere else on the globe. But it is a handicap. In consequence, the record indicates, members of the learned professions, scholars and teachers in institutions of higher learning, intellectuals generally whatever their occupation, tend either simply and silently to fade out of associations with other Jews such as keep a person livingly Jewish, or to ignore or avert from Jewish responsibilities, or to suppress the identifying label "Jew." They would render themselves as indistinguishable as they can from their non-Jewish professional likes and neighbors. This is particularly noticeable in academic institutions, little less so in journalism or the literary and the graphic arts.

The tendency to dissociate oneself from the Jewish collectivity and to suppress as fully as possible the differentia of "being Jewish" is highly visible. That the suppression is so successful as the suppressors would like, does not follow. But they work at it, especially the literati, rationalizing their labors much as Pasternak rationalized conversion in *Dr. Zhivago*. An instance of success is exemplified by Alaska's Senator Ernest Gruening, who was able at long last to address a Jewish audience in the role and with the spirit of a Gentile-once-Jew who had disassociated himself from all Jews as Jews and could speak to and of them as "You people." The American-Jewish press commented sharply and sadly.

Jews purposing such disassociation can achieve it also in other ways than the honorable Senator from Alaska. One is the unconscious rejection of Jewish relations, of the Jewish collectivity with its creeds, its codes, its designs for living, its ceremonies, its habits of speech and thought—rejection of all that composes assemblages of individuals—however near together or however scattered—into a communion, a community or a people. Another is the intentional adherence to a different religion—conversion in thought or deed or both. In my own field this was the way taken by Bergson, by Scheler, and by Husserl: a way quite different from that of Sabbatai Zevi and other false messiahs. Still another is that imposed upon Baruch Spinoza. He had thought out, and expressed, conscientious alternatives to the Judaist creed and code prevailing in his community—differences which are the orthodoxy of many people who are acknowledgedly Jewish today. His community excommunicated him. Had they not done so, he would have continued a member of that community; and although excommunicated, he would not identify himself with any other. A still different mode of dissociation can be studied in the Jewish relations of Heinrich Heine and Benjamin Disraeli. Heine was baptized and never rejoined any Judaist communion. This did not detach him from the Jewish Idea nor did it affect his sense of belonging to the Jewish collectivity. Indeed, he became one of the spokesmen of the Hebraic cultural tradition to the secular world, as well as one of the creators of the classical liberalism of modern Europe; Matthew Arnold called him a soldier of humanity. If Heine gained nothing personal from baptism, Disraeli did. But he did not become an antisemite. On the contrary, he disclosed a somewhat blatant pride of ancestry and a Marrano-like sentiment for Hebraism. Dissociation by conversion as the price of personal survival is, of course, an old story among Jews, as Maimonides sadly was made aware, and as the appearance of Marranoism evidences. But the latter is only protective, not ambitious dissociation, a reaction to oppression, not an exploitation of liberty.

We must not leave out of account the dissociate who reunites himself with the Jewish collectivity. One instance is Ludwig Lewisohn who moved from Methodism into radicalism, humanism, Zionism, and at last into an orthodox Judaism. Another instance is secularist Louis Brandeis who added Zionism to his humanism. The reader can think of many others, like Sigmund Freud, like certain American Yiddi-

shists, many Bundists, and so on. They all exemplify the
possibility of reversing a widespread centrifugal trend in the
Jewish collectivity; reversing a behavior which indicated
that for many being a Jew today is a hardship and a burden
they strive to rid themselves of.

The trend I have just noted is a trend away from the entire
collectivity. But there are also mutual repulsions and conflicts within the collectivity which do not seek dissociation.
This follows from the indefeasible nature of the individual
as individual. We note a whole spectrum of separatisms
altogether Jewish. Some look spontaneous, like the Kabbalah
and its consequences or like the Haskalah movement or the
pre-Zionists' turn to Hebrew as a vehicle purely of literary
expression. This turn was taken in the eighteenth century.
In effect it converts a sacred tongue into a secular vernacular;
it serves to satisfy or to release from their frustrations numbers
of Jews of high intellectual capacity and literary power,
doubtful of Judaism, but unwilling or unable to find a way
out to self-expression in the languages of non-Jews. It happens
that the Jews are a people of many languages. Theirs has
been not only Hebrew, the sanctified language of the Bible
(once the vernacular of *am ha-arez*) nor vernacular Aramaic
which became the semi-sacred language of the Talmud; they
have added to these Ladino, Arabic, Yiddish, Spanish, English
as vernaculars of ongoing Jewish communities.

And yet, Yiddish seems to be following Hebrew toward
sanctification. In the minds of many Jews in many lands
where Yiddish is being displaced as the speech of the daily
life by the language of the country, a certain holiness accrues
to it as it recedes. Yiddishist parties form to preserve and
cherish and sanctify it, endowing it with virtues and powers
that were not apparent while it was still the language of the
daily life. How and why this happens depends on spiritual
and moral considerations which the language encodes, and on
what challenges them. Should the challenge in any way be
effective, should it necessitate a rival tongue for the uses of

the daily life, thus causing the encoding original to lapse into disuse, their cultivating this original becomes a sanctified occupation, the kind of priestly dedication it now seems to be for our Yiddishists and their World Jewish Culture Congress. Even communists of Jewish derivation so cherish Yiddish components of Jewish culture. Recently there was an article in *Yiddische Kultur* reporting on and condemning the suppression of all but the synagogal aspects of Yiddish cultural life by the Soviets. The author is Chaim Sloves, a Yiddishistic French communist. The magazine is a monthly published in New York by Communist YKUF, a culture association. All, whatever else they are committed to, work and fight to save their Yiddish from obsolescence and extinction. Doing this becomes a voluntarily chosen vocation and a source of livelihood. The chooser becomes a professional Jew and his Jewishness a secular profession in a secular field.

A divergent secularization, also with language as the conspicuous focus of interest, and with an entire cultural economy radiating from this focus, is the diversifying Zionist enterprise. This has been notably successful in bringing Hebrew back, even if through the synagogue, as an interest of the daily life of Jews everywhere, including places where Yiddish is receding. On the other hand, the militancy of Hebraicists against Yiddish in Palestine has been followed by a helpful pacifism in Israel, where Yiddish now gets all the free expression its pro-Soviet aficionados crave for it in the Soviets.

Incidentally, 1959 marked the hundredth anniversary of the birth of two major contributors to this secular component of the Jewish heritage. One, as is well known even by Khrushchev, is Sholem Aleichem; the other is Ben Yehuda. Ben Yehuda set himself a task far more difficult than Sholem Aleichem's. He had to endow the daily life with a new vernacular and eliminate the old, while Sholem Aleichem needed only to improve and beautify the old. Ben Yehuda worked at his chosen task with fanatical concentration; he took on the ways of a bigot. Sholem Aleichem undertook to make his people aware of themselves as they were, with their short-comings and merits. He worked at his task with sympathetic understanding and with laughter. Ben Yehuda created a dictionary for a new Hebrew-speaking generation. Sholem Aleichem created a literature worldwide in its appeal to all sorts and conditions of men in every variety of culture, even in the Soviets.

Now each of these heroes of the Jewish heritage signalizes a variation of it in a new direction, a phase of the continual formation in *Kelal Yisrael* of groups within groups, that differ from each other as Judaist denominations differ from each other, although perhaps not so intolerantly. It is likely, however, that they did show such intolerance in defending themselves as secularists against the Judaist intolerance of the Jew. And the record does show how bigoted could be the rivalry over Hebrew and Yiddish. But even this does not attain the intensity of *mitnagged* against *hasid* or orthodox against more liberal confessions. The Judaisms form a spectrum of Judaistic faiths, from the ultra-violet of the American Council for Judaism, to the infra-red of the Lubavitcher. The ultra-violet signifies a creed not particularly distinguishable from certain creeds called Christian. Without the Jewish label it could not be readily identified as Jewish. The infrared signifies a creed and a code of the *mizwoth* suffused with contingent superstitions, myths and symbols and compounded in a communion as complex as it is irrational, and as terribly important to its adherents as it is complex. Between, range denominations and sects distinguishable in the order of the complexity of their doctrines and disciplines; from Agudath Israel, through various configurations of orthodoxy, varieties of conservatism, denominations of reform, up to reconstructionism. In terms of tradition in modernity this last seems seminal. For as creed it is "Judaism without supernaturalism"; as code, it is *Shulhan Arukh* with secularist sanctions.

Everyone is very well aware that these spectral units of the Judaist aggregate do not fuse to form the one white light of Judaism. They are hardly good neighbors; nor always good allies in the common defense against critical phases of chronic antisemitism. Their professional leaders compete for the adherence of the Jewish "laity." They confront the "laity" with alternatives whose formation and clash transpose the condition of being a Jew today from an involuntary to a voluntary one. The choice is now to be one kind of Jew or another kind of Jew or not to be a Jew at all. Not alone youth is called upon to choose; all ages and generations are invited, and condemned for preferring any to any other by the beneficiaries of the unchosen. The condemnation is the more vigorous when the choice is Jewishness over Judaism, the secular as against the "religious" heritage. It is held not quite as blameworthy as the *shemad* for the sake of safety and opportunity that Pasternak points up, but almost. A scion of the *Yiddishe Gass* with a value-system expressed by the *Jewish Daily Forward* might move with it from its rebellion against Judaist supernaturalism, its cultivation of anti-supernaturalism and antireligion (such as used to advertise Yom Kippur-balls on *Kol Nidre* night) to its toleration, even its sympathetic understanding, of all that, and to its concern for Israel.

The turn from rejection to toleration, to appreciation, to defense, is a turn accomplished voluntarily, and in the context of the American Idea and the Jewish social and cultural heritage. By and large, such a turn characterizes almost all those groups which together compose the Jewish collectivity.

Not that their divergences fail of vital importance. Nothing could be more important for Jews in the United States than how and why the American Jewish collectivity is different from that held captive in the Soviets. For obviously, to the question of being a Jew today no general answer is possible because the *what* and *how* and *why* of being a Jew have dynamic relationships to the Jew's social environment and the faith by which that struggles to live on. What the answer shall be depends greatly on where, among whom, a Jew strives to continue as Jew. In the communist-dominated countries? In Moslem lands? In Germany? In Great Britain? In our United States?

Those among whom Jews would live as Jews affect the nature of their Jewishness. Their influence joins, to the spontaneous inner Jewish divergences, non-Jewish diversifications which express their own working and fighting faiths, their own cultures. Their influence tends fundamentally to affect the form and content of the Jew's struggle for the existence which is but prolongation of this struggle. The environment can liberate his powers, diversify the content of his Jewish being and strengthen its communal form. It can also arrest alteration and compel him to mark time. Or it can dilute and weaken his powers, dissipate the content of his Jewish being, and liquidate or break into fragments its communal form. The Jewish identity which confronts its non-Jewish milieu contronts either a cooperator, a competitor, an indifferent, or an enemy; sometimes confronts them all together.

And in free societies, the same holds of its Jewish milieu. There, too, an individual has to choose his way of being a Jew.

He has to choose—in some lands freely, in others under coercion and penalty. Considering a career, how would continuing as this kind of Jew and not that affect it? What design for living as Jew is most compatible with success in it? How will the designs one rejects influence one's own being and one's occupational destiny? How, indeed, would one fare if he ceased to be a Jew altogether? Answers to such questions are all choices. They commit him who answers to fighting the inescapable competitor; to ignoring or tolerating him, or to cooperating with him. As a rule, the answerer would like to convert the Jew who differs from him to his own faith and add him to his own communion. He has to convince the differer that being a Jew in his way is more advantageous as well as more excellent than being a Jew in any other way.

Should he fail—and he does—what is his alternative? I believe that it is a simple one and indispensable to the survival of the Jewish culture-complex. It follows, I think, from the fact that the differences which distinguish Jews from one another and which they condemn and fight about, are indifferent to the antisemite. All Jews look alike to the latter and are alike unworthy and alike to be penalized for being Jews. To free themselves from the penalties they merit, they must free themselves of their Jewishness; they should commit—and Pasternak, not to say many, agrees—a kind of spiritual suicide as Jews; they should convert to Christianity or to communism or some other *ism* but they should not continue as Jews. *Per contra* Louis Brandeis and many others urged that the self-respecting, the honorable thing is not to surrender or abandon Jewishness but to put an end to the antisemitism which penalizes being a Jew. They urged that it is just as natural, just as right, just as good for oneself and for one's society to be a Jew as to be a participant in any other of the world's faiths and cultures.

But the Judaist denominations, the Jewish organizations and brotherhoods raise the issue, *What kind of Jew*? Since there is obviously more than one kind, each different from the others, how are they to live and to grow, together with each other? How can they learn, in a world to so many of whose different cults and cultures antisemitism is intrinsic, to accept its import for the Jewish being and to confront it with pride and courage, and without illusion? How can they learn to make their ways freely in the non-Jewish world of the arts, the sciences, the professions or business and maintain their integrity as Jews?

The answer is a fighting faith in freedom which all sorts and conditions of Jews must need share with one another— and with free men and free societies everywhere. It is this faith, which the American Idea expresses, and America's pluralistic culture struggles so painfully to incarnate, that experience shows to be the first condition for success. It requires recognizing that different individuals and associations of individuals have an unalienable right to their differences and to equal liberty in expressing and realizing them. It requires understanding the different, appreciating them, working out such ways of living and acting together with them that the free union of all will assure to each that safety and freedom to live and to grow which, as our Declaration of Independence avers, it is entitled to by "the laws of nature and of nature's God."

Antisemitism often imposes alliances for "defense" which on occasion subordinates the struggles for place and preference between competing organizations of Jewish interest to the common purpose. Such alliances have not evinced any positive ideal of the Jewish being that could move any one confronted with the choice: *To be or not to be a Jew*, to prefer to be one. Nor do the Judaist organizations which enter into these alliances disclose today any more attractive competitive alternatives. They somehow do not orchestrate with the significant characteristics of Today.

It is in this respect that the secular organizations of Jewish interest could take advantage of a highly preferential position—a preferential position because they are more realistically attuned to the *modern* world. I underscore the word *modern*. I do not mean by it the contemporary. Most of what exists in 1960, however contemporary, is not modern. Very little of what is contemporary is modern. A great deal of it is mediaeval or pre-mediaeval. It exists in conflict with the works and findings of science and with the attitudes and methods of science. Its spirit and activities are authoritarian, not democratic. In most regions of the contemporary world people keep warning each other about their difference: *I am right, you are wrong. When you are in power, it is your duty to protect and support me, because I am right. When I am in power, it is my duty to suppress, to crush, to enslave you, or, if expedient, to destroy you, because you are wrong.* This is what the Christian world has said to the Jews through millenia; what the Christian and Moslem denominations have said to one another; what white suprematists say to the darker peoples; what Nazi racists say to Jews and others who are different from them; what communists say to non-communists.

When any invokes the rule of equal liberty, the principle of democracy, the retort comes: *Those are your principles, not mine. They require you to permit me the equal liberty which my principle requires me to deny you whenever I can.*

And "those-" are the principles of faith, thought and work which distinguish the modern from the contemporary. Modernity is signalized by belief in the parity of the different, in equal right for the different—for different associations as well as different individuals—to "life, liberty and the pursuit of happiness." Modernity grounds the moral claim to this parity on its natural and social sciences. It is by their light, as well as by the light of the democratic faith, that it sees being a Jew as no less natural and good and useful than being anything else; sees that Jewish mankind possesses the same indefeasible title to live on, to develop and fulfill itself without penalty and without privilege, even such privilege as the claim to be God's chosen people implies.

But Jewish mankind consists of all the divergent denominations, sects, movements, associations and so on, that Jewish individuals form for diverse and conflicting purposes and keep going by diverse and incompatible means. They are Jewish together, and none can be completely Jewish without knowing, appreciating, understanding and constantly communicating with all the others. They can be completely Jewish only by way of an orchestration of their diversities. And the orchestration must needs be such that it will take full account of what is dynamically new in the world of today, not the survivals of the world of yesterday or the day before yesterday. It must achieve modernity, not continue as only contemporary; that is, the cultural composition it shapes up must needs include democracy, science and technics in its harmonies.

Viewing the record, it has seemed to me that vital changes in the Jewish being which began as a shifting of its supernaturalist postulate from the centre to the periphery of Jewish culture, and of its secular beliefs and ways from the periphery to the centre, make more vital, more viable configurations with modernity than the much ballyhooed "return to religion." It has seemed to me that the transvaluations signalized by Sholem Aleichem, by Ben Yehudah, by Yehuda Leib Peretz and their Yiddish and Hebrew epigons are closer to the life, the labor, and the aspirational heritage of the Jewish *am ha-arez*, whatever his land, than those of their Judaistic competitors, with their abstract, diluted and thinned-out doctrines and compulsive rites. From the matrix which those protagonists shared came a number of secular conceptions of what it means to be a Jew today. The foremost European spokesman for what all of them share was Simon Dubnow: so far as Zionist Jews setting their destiny as Jews not in Israel are concerned, he seems to me to speak for them, too. Organizations like the Farband, like the Arbeiter Ring, like the rather combative and disputatious Bund, like the Labor Zionists, diverge as they may from one another, impress me as together nearer to what we must mean by modernity, and to possess a greater potentiality of survival as Jews within modernity.

True, in our own country they evince a curious sort of holdover of the fear of the painless liquidation of their Jewishness by modernity—i.e., of assimilation—that possessed so many of the *Kibbutzim* builders of the early *aliyoth* to Palestine. An example of the ambivalence is the project Circle City endorsed by the Arbeiter Ring. This is a design for an all-Yiddish cultural community of five hundred families freely developing both the secular and the religious modes of Jewish life and expression with a synagogue, a library, a museum of folk art, a school and a children's camp. The language of work and play is to be Yiddish, and living life as American Jews is to be supported by earning a living in some form of small manufacture, such as needlework, printing, making ballpoint pens, or truck or chicken farming and the like. The design sees Circle City as self-supporting and self-contained. It does not comprehend as it should an expanding and fertile free trade of thoughts and things with the entire American environment. It does not comprehend the school as organized to equip the community's children with the knowledge and skills to live on as Jews and Americans in an economy founded on science and constituted by technology. The design, Utopian or not, is nevertheless a testimony to the principle of equal liberty; accepting it is a free choice; executing it is the launching of a free enterprise, historically one more in the variety of such communities to which American democracy gives equal opportunity and equal protection under the laws.

It is a design that denominations of Judaists are perhaps already emulating. But for them it would be a design of self-isolation, of collective flight from modernity, not the free cultivation of a full Jewish life orchestrated to modernity. The design signifies a local concentration of what the Arbeiter Ring works at in diffusion among its seventy thousand members. Whether it succeeds or not, it signalizes a conception of being Jewish which has come to be more tolerant and inclusive as the generations of American Jews changed from immigrant to native. It offers the modern American Jewish youth, as I have noted in more than one center named for Sholem Aleichem, or for Yehudah Leib Peretz, an opportunity for personal commitment and Jewish loyalty more consistent than other forms of Jewish grouping with the doctrines and disciplines of modernity. It presents a more reliable and fruitful way of being Jewish today.

I do not dispute that the aspiration it expresses is Utopian. What, that is excellent in the human struggle to go struggling, is not Utopian, not a design for the future to make the present over into? The American Idea is such a design. The image of Israel is such a design. All such designs take account of the indefeasible individuality of individuals and of the no less indefeasible condition that the humanity they grow up into is shaped and nourished by the cultural heritage they begin their lives in; that it is advanced or retarded by the freedom or lack of it, for cultural exchange with communions and communities different from their own. All recognize that their indefeasible cultural diversities can live and prosper in the modern world only as they absorb and identify with their own cultural singularity the knowledge which is science and the know-how which is technology. The Universal Declaration of Human Rights is a global expression of all this and its seminal idea is the idea of the right to be different and the equality of the different in rights and liberties.

Somehow, there seems to be little awareness of this global expression among the non-secular organizations of mankind, and less commitment. Each seems to cherish its own cannibalistic, imperialist and colonial intention. And our Judaists are no exception. Perhaps such of us who feel ourselves Jews as well as, or rather than, Judaists, owe them the service of making clear to them that their survival depends far more than they think on acknowledging the equal right to live and grow of those who do not accept their creeds and codes, and on cooperating with them so that all may be striving together for the more satisfying attainment of their separate ends. Such a mission calls for a vision based on adequate knowledge and a will guided by that knowledge and committed freely, without reservation, to cherish and advance the Jewish heritage, to live on as Jew accepting the penalty laid upon being a Jew so long as it is laid, with courage and without illusion, and with the joy that comes with such courage and disillusion. This joy is the authentic *Simhath Torah* of the modern world. Men experience it, Jewish men experience it, Jewish men experience it, as they commit themselves to the values which identify them, not so much to the point of dying for them as to the condition of gladly living on for their sake in sorrow and suffering. [1]

---

[1]   This essay is based on an address before the National Conference of Jewish Communal Service, June 1, 1959, under the auspices of the Jewish Labor Committee and the Workmen's Circle.

S. BAER'S UNPUBLISHED TARGUM ONKELOS TEXT

By ABRAHAM I. KATSH

New York University

AMONG THE MANY microfilms of Hebrew MSS. which I brought from the USSR[1] is an unpublished Targum study by S. Baer, the Aramaic scholar. This MS., which is in the Baron David Günzburg collection in Moscow, attempts to restore a correct text of Onkelos on the basis of biblical Aramaic grammar and other early sources.

Isaac b. Aryeh Joseph Dov, known as Dr. Seligman (or Sekel) Baer (1825-97) was a leading scholar in the fields of Bible, Masorah, Targumim, grammar and liturgy. At first he followed the more conservative methods of Wolf Heidenheim, but later he turned to the more modern scientific principles of biblical studies of the nineteenth century.

Baer was soon recognized by biblical scholars as the leading expert on the Masoretic biblical texts. His editions of the greater part of the Masoretic biblical books, which he edited in collaboration with Franz Delitzsch, became the standard text for the biblical students in the universities and theological seminaries. It retained its authority, in spite of Christian David Ginsburg's[2] severe criticism of Baer, until the appearance of Kittel's critical edition in 1905-6.

In the Jewish world, Baer became famous for his publication of the תקון הסופר והקורא[3] and especially for his critical and annotated text of the prayerbook סדר עבודת ישראל עם באור

---

[1] *See* Abraham I. Katsh, *Catalogue of Hebrew Manuscripts Preserved in the USSR*, Part I (1957), pp. 1-62 and *Ginze Russiyah*, Part ii (New York 1958), pp. 138.

[2] *See* his introduction to the *Massoretico-Critical Edition of the Hebrew Bible* (London 1897).

[3] A correct guide for the בעל קורא and for the professional scribe of the ס״ת.

הנקרא יכין לשון.[1] In the notes to the prayerbook, Baer explains his reasons for selecting the respective variant readings and gives the sources of the various prayers.

What his Bible edition was for the biblical student, his prayer book became for the liturgical scholar. Up to the present time it has been the authoritative and standard text for the scientific study of Hebrew liturgy. [2] Baer's edition is not primarily a text for the ritual use in the synagogue, but rather a handbook for the liturgical scholar and teacher.

Baer's interest in the Targumim seems to have been started at a very early stage of his life. Already in 1852 he published an extensive study concerning the relation of *Targum Yerushalmi* to *Onkelos*. In this study [3] he endeavors to prove by a number of striking examples that the *Targum Yerushalmi* is an explanatory extension of *Targum Onkelos* and in many places it merely elaborates on difficult and unclear renderings of the text. This penetrating study shows that already at the age of twenty-seven Baer was well acquainted with the intricate problems of the Targum, its Aramaic philological peculiarities and sources.

In the sixth decade of the nineteenth century a great interest in the Targumim developed among the leading biblical scholars in Germany. It culminated in the formation of a group of Aramaic scholars for the purpose of editing a standard critical text of *Targum Onkelos*, based on manuscripts and reliable early printed editions. The leading members of the group were Professor Hermann Brockhaus, Dr. Anger, Dr. Roediger—all editors of the *Zeitschrift der Deutschen Morgenländischen Gesellschaft*.

M. Steinschneider was invited to draft a preliminary bibliographical plan for this edition. An outline was published in the form of a letter to Brockhaus in the *Zeitschrift*. [4] It

---

[1]   First published in Roedelheim in 1868.
[2]   A recent edition appeared by Schocken Publication House.
[3]   "Geist des Jeruschalmi (Pseudo-Jonathan)" in *MGWJ*, vol. i (1852), 235 ff.
[4]   Vol. xii (1858), p. 170.

seems that this attempt, like many other similar literary undertakings, failed to materialize.

It was at this time that Baer singlehandedly undertook the task of restoring a correct critical text of *Targum Onkelos*. In his unpublished introduction, which we present here in the original Hebrew, Baer outlined in great detail his methods of approach and the sources he used as evidence for his emendations and changes in the printed *Onkelos* text. His basic sources were the Aramaic parts of Daniel and Ezra which he utilized according to the grammatical principles of the Aramaic languages. In addition, he selected eight early and modern printed editions [1] from which he drew his readings. He stated that he also turned for evidence to the Targum quotations of early Bible commentators such as Rashi, Ibn Ezra, Nahmanides, and Bahya b. Asher. He also used the Aramaic lexicographical works of Nathan ben Yehiel [2] and Elijah Levita [3] as well as manuscript material of which he could avail himself.

Baer's variants from the present printed text are many and daring. Not only in vocalization, which are to be found nearly in every line, but even in the consonantal text itself he boldly introduces changes in spelling and grammatical form.

Scholars of his time could not accept such a sudden and drastic change. His method of comparing *Onkelos* with the biblical Aramaic, as Buxtorf had done earlier in his edition of the *Biblia Hebraica Rabbinica*, [4] was sharply criticized by various scholars who maintained that idioms in these Aramaic sources are widely separated in time and place and no comparative analogies could be made. [5]

---

[1]   מדפוסים שונים, ישנים וחדשים.
[2]   For his study Baer used the *Aruk*, Venice edition, 1531.
[3]   *Meturgeman* ; *Tishbi* (Isna 1541).
[4]   Basel 1618-19.
[5]   *See* A. Berliner, *Targum Onkelos* (Berlin 1884), vol. ii, pp. 189-196.

The Manuscript

The Günzburg MS. contains, in addition to the introduction, the complete Targum texts of Genesis and Exodus and a few leaves of stray notes to the other books of the Pentateuch. The upper part of the page occupies the Targum text, vocalized, accented (*teamim*) and masoretically arranged in open (*pethuhoth*) and closed (*sethumoth*) sections marked by letters *pe* and *samek* respectively. [1]

The lower part of the page contains explanatory notes which are of a twofold nature : (1) Philological explanation for the suggested reading and quoting a supporting source, and (2) Comments on a certain unusual rendering of the Targum or on its other characteristics, supporting it occasionally by a *Midrash, Targum Yerushalmi* or by a medieval biblical authority.

The Targum text is written in a very neat and clear square script, and the arrangement looks like a printed page. The text of the notes is written by the author himself, in a small cursive Ashkenazic hand; the headings quoted in the notes are in small square vocalized script. The whole MS. contains 241 pages.

The location and identification of this MS. could be considered to some extent as a rediscovery. The only person known to have mentioned it was Dr. A. Berliner who, while working on his *Targum Onkelos* edition in the early eighties of the last century, states that he borrowed this MS. from Baer and made some use of the notes. [2]

It appears that after the death of the author in 1897, the MS. came to the library of Baron Günzburg in Paris. The Günzburg collection was removed in 1910 to Russia. As Günzburg's bookplate shows the MS. was registered under number 854. The noted Russian-French Hebrew scholar and bibliographer, Senior Sachs (1816-1892), who was custodian

---

[1]   The *teamim* and *pethuhoth* and *sethumoth* sections are not found in our Targum texts.

[2]   *See* Berliner, *Targum* . . . vol. ii, p. 196.

and librarian of the Baron Horace Günzburg collection in
Paris, did not recognize its author, and in his short description
of his unpublished catalogue of the Günzburg collection, [1]
conjectures that this is a work of the German liturgical and
biblical scholar, Wolf B. Heidenheim (1757-1832). He evidently did not read its introduction which begins with the words
אומר בן אריה and the date of 1852 given at the end which is
twenty years after the death of Heidenheim. An important
clue to my identification of the MS. was the reference in the
introduction to the author's article in the *Monatsschrift*. [2]

Besides its value as to how the Targum should be grammatically read, the vast amount of material cited in the notes
should also serve as an important source of information for
scholars who work on a critical text of *Targum Onkelos*.
In addition, the philological discussion and commentaries
could be of great help to the understanding of the deeper
meaning of the Targum and its interpretation.

The Specimen

As a specimen of Baer's Targum text, a portion of the first
chapter of Genesis is presented here in facsimile. It contains
the complete vocalized text and his notes.

In order to furnish the reader with a perspective view of
the textual relation between Baer's projected Targum-Text
and that of the Sabbionetta edition (1557), on which Berliner
based his Targum text, a parallel comparative table of three
columns has been arranged.

Col. 1 Baer's text.

Col. 2 Sabbionetta text (1557) as reprinted by Berliner.

Col. 3 A selection of readings from early sources, manuscripts and printed editions which support Baer's
text.

It should be noted that only consonantal variants were

---

[1] Sachs describes the MS. in these words : קובץ תתנ"ד• תרגום
אונקלוס עם נקודות וטעמים ופירוש כנראה מהרווה.

[2] *MGWJ* (March 1852).

.: בראשית א ב :.

וַהֲוָה כֵן וַעֲבַד יְיָ יָת־חַיַת אַרְעָא לִזְנָהּ וְיָת־בְּעִירָא לִזְנָהּ וְיָת כָּל־רַחֲשָׁא
דִי־אַרְעָא לִזְנַגְהִי וַחֲזָא יְיָ אֲרֵי־טָב : וַאֲמַר יְיָ נַעֲבֵד אֲנָשָׁא בְּצַלְמָנָא כִּדְמוּתַנָא
וְיִשְׁלְטוּן בְּנוּנֵי יַמָּא וּבְעוֹפָא דִי־שְׁמַיָא וּבִבְעִירָא וּבְכָל־אַרְעָא וּבְכָל־
רַחֲשָׁא דִי־רָחֵשׁ עַל־אַרְעָא : וּבְרָא יְיָ יָת־אָדָם בְּצַלְמֵהּ בְּצֶלֶם אֱלֹהִים
בְּרָא יָתֵהּ דְּכַר וְנֻקְבָא בְּרָא יָתְהוֹן : וּבָרֵךְ יָתְהוֹן יְיָ וַאֲמַר לְהוֹן יְיָ פּוּשׁוּ וּסְגוֹ
וּמְלוֹ יָת־אַרְעָא וּתְקֵפוּ עֲלַהּ וּשְׁלוּטוּ בְּנוּנֵי יַמָּא וּבְעוֹפָא דִי־שְׁמַיָא וּבְכָל־
חַיְתָא דִי־רָחֲשָׁא עַל־אַרְעָא : וַאֲמַר יְיָ הָא יְהָבִית לְכוֹן יָת־כָּל־עִשְׂבָּא דְבַר־
זַרְעֵהּ דִי־בַר־זַרְעֵהּ מִזְדְרַע לְכוֹן יְהֵי לְמֵיכַל : וּלְכָל־חַיַת אַרְעָא
וּלְכָל־עוֹפָא דִי־שְׁמַיָא וּלְכֹל דִי־רָחֵשׁ עַל־אַרְעָא דִי בֵהּ נַפְשָׁא חַיְתָא
יָת־כָּל־יְרוֹק עִשְׂבָּא לְמֵיכַל וַהֲוָה כֵן : וַחֲזָא יְיָ יָת־כָּל־דִּי עֲבַד וְהָא
טָקֵין לַחֲדָא וַהֲוָה רְמַשׁ וַהֲוָה צְפַר יוֹמָא שְׁתִיתָאָה :
   ס

ב וְאִשְׁתַּכְלָלוּ שְׁמַיָא וְאַרְעָא וְכָל־חֵילֵיהוֹן : וְשֵׁיצִי יְיָ בְּיוֹמָא שְׁבִיעָאָה עֲבִידְתֵּהּ
דִי עֲבַד וְנָח בְּיוֹמָא שְׁבִיעָאָה מִן־כָּל־עֲבִידְתֵּהּ דִי עֲבַד : וּבָרֵךְ יְיָ יָת־יוֹמָא
שְׁבִיעָאָה וְקַדֵּשׁ יָתֵהּ אֲרֵי בֵהּ נָח מִן־כָּל־עֲבִידְתֵּהּ דִי־בְרָא יְיָ לְמֶעְבַּד : פ
אִלֵּין תּוֹלְדָת שְׁמַיָא וְאַרְעָא כַּד־אִתְבְּרִיוּ בְּיוֹמָא דִי־עֲבַד יְיָ אֱלֹהִים אַרְעָא
וּשְׁמַיָא : וְכֹל אִילָנֵי חַקְלָא עַד־לָא הֲוָה בְאַרְעָא וְכָל־עִשְׂבָּא דִי־חַקְלָא
עַד־לָא צְמַח אֲרֵי לָא־אַחֵת מִטְרָא יְיָ אֱלֹהִים עַל־אַרְעָא וֶאֱנָשׁ לֵית
לְמִפְלַח יָת־אַדְמְתָא : וַעֲנָנָא הֲוָה סָלֵיק מִן־אַרְעָא וּמַשְׁקֵי יָת כָּל־אַנְפֵּי
אַדְמְתָא : וּבְרָא יְיָ אֱלֹהִים יָת־אָדָם עַפְרָא מִן־אַדְמְתָא וּנְפַח בְּאַנְפּוֹהִי
נִשְׁמְתָא דִי־חַיִּין וַהֲוָת בַּאֲדָם לְרוּחַ מְמַלְּלָא : וּנְצַב יְיָ אֱלֹהִים גִּנְּתָא
בְּעֵדֶן מִן־לְקַדְמִין וְאַשְׁרֵי תַמָּן יָת־אָדָם דִי בְרָא : וְצַמַח יְיָ אֱלֹהִים

ּ: בְּרֵאשִׁית א :ּ

א בְּקַדְמִין בְּרָא יְיָ יָת שְׁמַיָּא וְיָת אַרְעָא: וְאַרְעָא הֲוַת צָדְיָא וְרֵיקַנְיָא וַחֲשׁוֹכָא
עַל־אַפֵּי תְהוֹמָא וְרוּחָא מִן קֳדָם יְיָ מְנַשְּׁבָא עַל־אַפֵּי מַיָּא: וַאֲמַר יְיָ
יְהֵא נְהוֹרָא וַהֲוָה נְהוֹרָא: וַחֲזָא יְיָ יָת נְהוֹרָא אֲרֵי־טָב וְאַפְרֵישׁ יְיָ בֵּין נְהוֹרָא
5. וּבֵין חֲשׁוֹכָא: וּקְרָא יְיָ לִנְהוֹרָא יְמָמָא וְלַחֲשׁוֹכָא קְרָא לֵילְיָא וַהֲוָה רְמַשׁ
וַהֲוָה צְפַר יוֹם חָד: ס
וַאֲמַר יְיָ יְהֵא רְקִיעָא בִּמְצִיעוּת מַיָּא וִיהֵא מַפְרֵישׁ בֵּין מַיָּא לְמַיָּא: וַעֲבַד יְיָ יָת־רְקִיעָא וְאַפְרֵישׁ בֵּין מַיָּא דִי מִלְּרַע לִרְקִיעָא וּבֵין מַיָּא דִי מֵעַל לִרְקִיעָא
וַהֲוָה כֵן: וּקְרָא יְיָ לִרְקִיעָא שְׁמַיָּא וַהֲוָה רְמַשׁ וַהֲוָה צְפַר יוֹם תִּנְיָן: ס
וַאֲמַר יְיָ יִתְכַּנְּשׁוּן מַיָּא מִן־תְּחוֹת שְׁמַיָּא לַאֲתַר חַד וְתִתְחֲזֵי יַבֶּשְׁתָּא וַהֲוָה כֵן:
10. וּקְרָא יְיָ לְיַבֶּשְׁתָּא אַרְעָא וּלְבֵית־כְּנִישׁוּת מַיָּא קְרָא יַמְמֵי וַחֲזָא יְיָ אֲרֵי־טָב:
וַאֲמַר יְיָ תַּדְאֵת אַרְעָא דִּתְאָה עִסְבָּא דְּבַר זַרְעֵהּ מִזְדְּרַע אִילָן פֵּירִין עָבֵד
פֵּירִין לִזְנֵהּ דִּי בַר־זַרְעֵהּ בֵּהּ עַל־אַרְעָא וַהֲוָה כֵן: וְאַפֵּיקַת אַרְעָא דִּתְאָה
עִסְבָּא דִּי בַר־זַרְעֵהּ מִזְדְּרַע לִזְנוֹהִי וְאִילָן עָבֵד פֵּירִין דִּי בַר־זַרְעֵהּ בֵּהּ לִזְנֵהִי
וַחֲזָא יְיָ אֲרֵי־טָב: וַהֲוָה רְמַשׁ וַהֲוָה צְפַר יוֹם תְּלִיתַי: ס
15. וַאֲמַר יְיָ יְהוֹן נְהוֹרִין בִּרְקִיעָא דִּי־שְׁמַיָּא לְאַפְרָשָׁא בֵּין יְמָמָא וּבֵין לֵילְיָא וִיהוֹן
לְאָתִין וּלְזִמְנִין וּלְמִמְנָא בְּהוֹן יוֹמִין וּשְׁנִין: וִיהוֹן לִנְהוֹרִין בִּרְקִיעָא דִי־שְׁמַיָּא
לְאַנְהָרָא עַל־אַרְעָא וַהֲוָה כֵן: וַעֲבַד יְיָ יָת־תְּרֵין נְהוֹרַיָּא רַבְרְבַיָּא תְּ־
נְהוֹרָא רַבָּא לְמִשְׁלַט בִּימָמָא וְיָת־נְהוֹרָא זְעֵירָא לְמִשְׁלַט בְּלֵילְיָא וְיָת
כּוֹכְבַיָּא: וִיהַב יָתְהוֹן יְיָ בִּרְקִיעָא דִי־שְׁמַיָּא לְאַנְהָרָא עַל־אַרְעָא: וּלְמִשְׁלַט
בִּימָמָא וּבְלֵילְיָא וּלְאַפְרָשָׁא בֵּין נְהוֹרָא וּבֵין חֲשׁוֹכָא וַחֲזָא יְיָ אֲרֵי־טָב: וַהֲוָה
רְמַשׁ וַהֲוָה צְפַר יוֹם רְבִיעָי: ס
20. וַאֲמַר יְיָ יִרְחֲשׁוּן מַיָּא רְחֵשׁ נַפְשָׁא חַיְתָא וְעוֹפָא יְפָרַח עַל־אַרְעָא עַל־אַפֵּי
רְקִיעָא דִי־שְׁמַיָּא: וּבְרָא יְיָ יָת־תַּנִּינַיָּא רַבְרְבַיָּא וְיָת כָּל־נַפְשָׁא חַיְתָא וְדִי־
רָחֲשָׁא דִּי רַחֵישׁוּ מַיָּא לִזְנֵיהוֹן וְיָת כָּל־עוֹפָא דִי־פָרַח לִזְנוֹהִי וַחֲזָא יְיָ אֲרֵי־
טָב: וּבָרֵיךְ יָתְהוֹן יְיָ לְמֵימַר פּוּשׁוּ וּסְגוֹ וּמְלוֹ יָת־מַיָּא בְּיַמְמַיָּא וְעוֹפָא
יִסְגֵּי בְאַרְעָא: וַהֲוָה רְמַשׁ וַהֲוָה צְפַר יוֹם חֲמִישָׁי: ס
וַאֲמַר יְיָ תַּפֵּיק אַרְעָא נַפְשָׁא חַיְתָא לִזְנַהּ בְּעִיר וּרְחֵשׁ וְחַיְתָא אַרְעָא לִזְנַהּ

[footnotes — illegible]

Gen. 1:1-24.

considered in the Table, disregarding the differences in vocalization. Vowel variants between these two texts occur nearly in every line and would be too numerous for reproduction in this brief Table. Repetitions of same variants were omitted, and plene or defective spellings (*male we-hasser*) were disregarded.

Explanation of Abbreviated Sources in the Table

The following abbreviations of early MSS. and printed editions were used in the third column of the Table. [1]

A. *Manuscripts*

1). MS.B.M. 71: Manuscript No. 71 (Add. 9400) of Margoliouth' *Catalogue of Hebrew MSS.*, British Museum, London. It contains the Pentateuch with Targum in alternate verses with Tiberian vocalization. Written in Franco-Ashkenazic hand, it includes a spurious colophon with a date of 1076. For further details see *Catalogue* . . . and C. D. Ginsburg's *Introduction* . . . p. 540 (No. 13) ff.

2). MS.B.M. 183: Manuscript No. 183 (Oriental 2228-30) of Margoliouth' *Catalogue of Hebrew MSS.*, British Museum, London. It contains the Pentateuch with Tiberian vocalization; Targum with Yemenite superlinear vocalization; Saadia's Judeo-Arabic translation and Rashi's commentary in three volumes. Written by a Yemenite scribe in Yemen date Sel. 1966 (1655). For further details see *Catalogue* . . .

B. *Printed Books*

3). Bible, Ixar, 1490: Pentateuch with Targum and Rashi printed in Ixar (Aragon, Spain) by the printer Eliezer Alantasi, 1490. Hebrew text and Targum both unvocalized. For further information *see* Steinschneider, *C.B.*, No. 8 and Ginsburg's *Introduction* p. 831 ff.

4). Bible Lisbon, 1491: Pentateuch with Targum, both with vowels and accents (Teamim) and Rashi's commentary, printed by Eliezer Toledano in Lisbon, Portugal, in 1491 (*See* Steinschneider, *C.B.*, Nl 10).

[1] Part of these documentary sources is based on Alexander Sperber's critical apparatus of Genesis in his recent excellent edition of *The Bible in Aramaic*, vol. i, (Leiden, 1959).

5). BR 1:   *The First Biblical Rabbinica*—Contains the
                             complete Bible, Targumim and many com-
                             mentaries. Edited by Felix Pratensis and
                             printed by Daniel Bomberg (Venice 1517)
                             (St., C.B., No. 28).
6). BR 6:   *The Sixth Biblia Rabbinica*—Revised and
                             edited by J. Buxdorf, the Elder, and printed
                             in Basel 1618-19 (St., *C.B.*, No. 423).

It is my hope that the rediscovery of this MS. and the presentation
here of Baer's novel and scholarly treatment of the Targum will add
greatly to the understanding of the biblical text.

BAER'S INTRODUCTION

יתברך העליון ויתפאר היוצר אשר חנני דעה

אומר בן אריה המחבר, זחלתי ואירא לדבר כי אין בי רוח
לגבר, ולא בינה לי לספר· אכן החכמה איננה בשמים· רובצת
היא בין המשפתים, ולכל אשר יטה לה אזנים, נדרשת היא
ותפקח עינים· ואני אכון לבי לשמים ואפתח לאומֶר השפתים,
הנה שמתי לתרגום האונקלוס העינים, אונקלוס הגר אשר קבל
מר' אליעזר ור' יהושע גדולי הכנפים ותרגם על פיהם ללשון
ארמית המים החיים למען יהיה לסעד לקרובי עץ חיים·
ותרגום הזה כמות שנדפס עתה בספרינו עליו תרד דמעה
עינינו ודוי עליו לבנו, כי נשחת הודו בשגגת המעתיקים ונרפש
מעינו הטהור על ידי סכלות המדפיסים הם קלקלו את תואר
טובו והורידו את הוד יפיפיתו עד שאין לנו כעת גם שורה
אחת שלא ישרצו בה טעיות בנקודות וחסרות ויתרות, מי ימנה
אותם ככוכבי שמים לרוב, וכלם מחסרון ידיעת המעתיקים
והמגיהים באו אשר טיב ל' ארמית לא ידעו, והיה זה מוסיף
וזה מחסיר וזה מחליף ונדו גם נעו ישגו וטעו·
זאת ראיתי ובתמהתי פה פציתי הכי לשבר הזה אין תרופה
ואין רפואה להחזיר עטרת תרגום זה ליושנה ולהדרו
כמראשונה?

ונדבתי את לבי ולגודל מלאכה זו קרבתי לברר וללבן את
לשונו מכל סגים ולגשת לזיקוקו פעם ופעמים וטורח ההג[ה]ה
לעמוס על שכמים עד שיצא זך וטהור כזהר השמים·

ואתה קורא נעים אמנה כבר ראו עיניך בהמליץ [1] ספרי
אשר על דברי מליצות התורה [כתבתי] את התרגום אונקלוס
כמו שהצבבתיהו על צד המקרא איך הוא מוגה ומטוהר ומתוכן [2]
אכן שם במילין על אודותיו לא הרחקתי על כללי מה ומה
הגהתי כי בעת לחשות אין לדבר יען כי שם התרגום רק לטפל
בא ולהבנת דברי ביאורי ואמרתי נצפין דברי לעת הכושר,
ועת הזאת עתה באה כי עזרני הבורא ובאתי עד הלום להניח
את כל התרגום שלם על כל התורה מבראשית [עד] לעיני כל
ישראל ומנוקה מכל מכשול ומועמד על עמדו הראשון·

ואתה דע את דרכי שהלכתי בזאת מלאכתי ובתקונים
שתקנתי ואען ואודיע לכל כי במלאכת ההגהה ותקון הזה לא
יכלתי להסמך על שום ספר מהדפוס או מכ״י כי אין אחד
שמצאתי כהוגן וכדאי ללכת בדרכו ולהגיה על פיו כי כל
הספרים לא נשארו בלי מעל ובכלם שבושים בזה מעט ובזה
יותר· וע״כ בחרתי דרך אחר ודרכתי בשבילי הכתובים
הארמיים שהם בספרים דניאל ועזרא והם היו לי למורים
ולמוליכים וישרתי על פיהם מסלות התרגום ובמלין שלא
נמצאו בכתובים ההם הלכתי אחרי כללי לשון ארמית
האמתיות והברורויות· ולהעמדת הגרסאות המשונות בדפוסים
שלא באו בספר כבספר הנחתי לפני ח' ספרים מדפוסים
שונים ישנים וחדשים וערכתי ספר מול ספר למצוא ככה הנוסחה
הנכונה· גם לא הנחתי את ספר הערוך ומתורגמן ותשבי· וזאת
לדעת כי כל גרסאות הערוך שהזכרתי שאבתי מן הערוך
דפוס ויניציא שנת רצ״א·

[1] The MS. of the המליץ as well as other of Baer's MSS. are in the Günzburg collection.
[2] So in the MS.

ובמקומות שכבר סללו המסלה גדולי המפרשים רש"י
וראב"ע ורמב"ן ובחיי וחבריהם אז בדרכיהם דרכתי· ולזאת
יעדתי בספרי מקום מיוחד בכל דף למטה ושם הגבלתי כל
התיבות מצד כתיבתם בנקודות וגרסאות וגם ביארתי שם כל
דברי אונקלוס לידע ולהודיע למה ועל מה תרגם ככה ולא
ככה· וכדי להבין את כל דברתי ששם הצעתי אציג הנה ראשי
כללי ל' ארמית אשר בם תשתנה מל' עברית והם...[1]

והוא העוזר והמושיע עליו תודתי שקרבני לעבודתו והאיר
עיני בתורתי וגם חזקני בבריאות גופי לעבוד את עבודה קשה
זו לכבוד שמו הגדול והנורא כן גם עד זקנה ושיבה אל תעזבני
ובדרך אמת ינחני· ותהי ראשית מלאכתי בהגהת ת"א ביום
ג', י"ז כסלו תר"ט לפ"ק (12 Dez. 1848) השלמתי את ת"א על ס'
בראשית ביום ג' ח' אלול ת"רט לפ"ק (21 Aug. 1849) והשלמתי
את ס' שמות ביום ב' י"ב שבט תרי"ב לפ"ק (2 Fcbr. 1852)·

תרגום אונקלוס [2] כמו שהוא עתה בספרינו מעורב הוא
מראשו ועד סופו מנוסחאות שהיו לפנים בת' הירושלמי',
והמעתיקים באו ולקחו נוסחאות מת' ירושלמי זה ושמו להם
יד בתרגום אונקלוס ואת נוסחאות אונקלוס העמידו בירושלמי·
ועד נאמן על זה דברי מלבד מה שהוכחתי במקומות רבים
בראיות נאמנות הוא הרמב"ן לבמדבר כ"ד, א' שכתב ז"ל:
רש"י כתב וישת אל המדבר פניו כתרגומו כי היה הרב מתרגם
בו ושוי למדברא דעבדו ביה בני ישראל עגלא אנפוהי ואין
כן בנוסחאות מדוקדקות מתרגומו של אונקלוס אבל הוא כתוב
בקצתן שהוגה בהן מן התרגום הירושלמי עכ"ל·
הנה תראה ברור כי יד המעתיקים חלו ביה בתרגום אונקלוס
ושנו את תוארו הראשון ואיננו עוד היום טהור בנוסחותיו

---

[1] It appears that the author intended to add the "Rules of the Aramaic language" at a later date. They are not in the MS.

[2] The material from here on, appears in the MS. on a different page but belongs to the Introduction.

כמקדם· והנה תרגום הירושלמי הזה הוא מקור נאמן לברר על
ידו את נוסחאה האמתי של אונקלוס כי כל מגמת תרגום
הירושלמי היתה להרחיב את תרגום אונקלום ולפרש כל
דבריו ביתר ביאור· וזאת נתאמת לי מראיות רבות עצומות
וברורות, ובכל יום מתחדשים לי עדים לסברתי זו אשר
חדשתיה· והא לך קצת מהראיות, ערוך שני תרגומים הנאמרים
בפסוקים שמות ל״ב, כ״ט אל ה׳· ועיין גם מה שכתבתי
בתרגום בראשית כ״ה, ג· ועוד שם פסוק כ״ז· ועוד שם ל״ז,
ל״ה ול״ט כ״ב· ויקרא י״ח, ה· ועוד עדות נאמנה בשמות
א, ט״ו גם במדבר כ״ג, א· לתרגום הירושלמי וַאֲמַר והוא אין
לו המשך כלל בפסוק אבל האמת יורה דרכו שהוא ראש
תרגום אונקלוס של פסוק המתחיל וַאֲמַר, ומועמד בירושלמי
לציון ראש הפסוק· וכן שמות י״ד, ל׳ מלת וּפָרֶק מתרגום
אונקלוס היא אשר אחזה הירושלמי ופירשה ע״י משיזיב· ועוד
עדות נאמנה בדברים ח׳, י״ח שתרג׳ אונקלוס יהב לך עצה
והוא ל׳ חוזק וכח משרש עוץ והנה בעל ת׳ ירושלמי בא גם
הכא לפרש מלה זרה ותרגמה במלת מִלְכָא כי חשב
שהוא מל׳ יעץ אבל טעה בסברתו כי מלת עצה זו משרש עוץ
היא ול׳ כוח היא ולא לשון עצה· אבל נשמע ונלמד מתרגום
המוטעה זה שהיה התרגום אונקלוס מונח לפני בעל תרגום
ירושלמי והוא סמך עליו כל תרגומו כי אם לא יהיה כן איך
תבא מלת מִלְכָא למלת כֹחַ של פסוק העברי?

והנה אף כי בעת בעל ת׳ ירושלמי היה התרגום של אונקלוס
עוד יותר מוגה ויותר נקי ממחלת שגיאות הסופרים מ״מ ראה
זה מצאתי אשר כבר בזמן ההוא נפלו שבושים במקומות אחדים
כגון מה שנמצא בשמות ל״ב, ל· אסק קֳדָם ה׳, איננו לשון
לומר כך וצ״ל לְקֳדָם ה׳, מ״מ שבוש זה כבר עמד בעת בעל

תרגום ירושלמי כי הוא הרגיש בקושי לשון זה וחשב ותקנו
באמרו אסק וַאֲצַלִי קדם ה'·

אונקלוס במקומות שראה דעות חז"ל רבות ומחולקות עמד
ברחב שכלו והרכיב דעות רבות כמו בראשית מ"ח, כ"ב·
שמות א', ח'·

בעל תרגום ירושלמי במקומות שמצא ‖את אונקלוס עוזב
פירושי חז"ל לדרוך דרך אחרת בא הוא ועזב דרך אונקלוס
וכתב דעת חז"ל וזה כדי לתת לפנינו כל מדרשי חז"ל כגון
בראשית מ', כ', מ"ח, כ"ב, שמות ב', י"ב·

את דברי אלה סברתי על תרגום ירושלמי ותרגו' אומקלוס
כתבתים ברחבה בל' אשכנז והפיצותים במכתב עתי של
החכם פראָנקעל בשנת תרי"ב (1852).[1]

TABLE OF VARIANTS

Sources Supporting Ms.D.	Sab. 1557 (Ed.Berliner)	Ms.D.	
MS.B.M. 183; Cod. De-Rossi, Parma, 7	פָּרֵישׁ	חסר	I, 2
BR 6-7	עַלאַנְפֵּי (twice)	עַלאַנְפֵּי	
Dan, 7: 1	וַחֲזָא	וַחֲזָה	4
	וְאַפְרֵישׁ	וְאַפְרֵשׁ	
Pol. Complut.	יְמָמָא	יוֹמָא	5
	רְקִיעָא	רְקִיעַ	6
	מַפְרֵישׁ	מַפְרֵשׁ	
BR 6	דְּמִןלְרַע	דִּי מִןלְרַע	7
Ibid. Dan. 6: 3	דְּמֵיעַל	דִּי עֵלָא	
MS.B.M. 183	תִּינְיָן	תִּנְיָן	8
	מִתְּחוֹת	מִןתְּחוֹת	9
BR 6-7; (See Berliner, note)	לְאַתְרָא	לַאֲתַר	
	וְתִתְחֲזִי	וְתִתְחֲזָא	
	וַחֲזָא	וַחֲזָה	10

[1] *See MGWJ* (1852), 235 ff.

Sources Supporting B	Sabioneta 1557 (Ed.Berliner)	Ms.B.	
	תַּדְאֵית	תַּדְאֵת	11
	דִּיתְאָה	דִּתְאָא	
BR 6-7	עִיסְבָּא	עֲשׂבָּא	
(twice)	דִּיבַּר־זַרְעֵהּ	דְּבַר זַרְעֵיהּ	
BR 6	פֵּירִין	פֵּרִין	
	וְאַפֵּיקַת	וְהַנְפְּקַת	12
	יְמָמָא	יוֹמָא	14
	דִשְׁמַיָּא	דִּי־שְׁמַיָּא	
	וּלְמִימְנֵי	וּלְמִמְנֵא	
	בִּימָמָּא	בְּיוֹמָא	16
	וְעוֹפָא	וְעוֹף	20
	אַפֵּי	אַנְפֵּי	
	דְּרַחְשָׁא	דִּי־רָחֲשָׁא	21
Bible, Ixar 1490	דְּאַרְחִישׁ	דִּידְחֲשׁוּ	
	דְּפַרַח	דִּי־פְּרַח	
	וּבְרִיךְ	וּבָרֵךְ	22
	לְמֵימָר	לְמֵאמַר	
Dan 2: 31	וּסְגוֹ	וּשְׂגוֹ	
	יִסְגֵּי	יִשְׂגֵּא	
MS.B.M. 71, Bible, Ixar 1490; BR 1; BR 6	וְחֵיַת	וְחֵיוַת	24-25
MS. BM. 183	רְיחֲשָׁא	רַחֲשָׁא	
	נַעֲבֵּיד	נֶעְבַּד	26
MS. BM. 183. BR 6	אֵינָשָׁא	אֲנָשָׁא	
	וְנוּקְבָּא	וְנֻקְבָּא	27
	וּסְגוֹ	וּשְׂגוֹ	28
	יְהָבִית	יָהֲבֵת	29
See verses 24-25 in this ch.	חַיַת	חַיוַת	30
	לְמֵיכָל	לְמֵאכַל	
Bible (Lisbon 1491)	שָׁתִיתִי	שָׁתִיתָאָה	31

THE MESSIANIC IDEA IN QUMRAN [1]

By William Sanford LaSor

Fuller Theological Seminary, Pasadena, California

THERE ARE THREE possible philosophies of history: the pessimistic, that sees man in a tragic rôle, unable to solve the problems of life, hence doomed ultimately, whether as a race or as a civilization, to failure; second, the optimistic, that sees man in a heroic rôle, struggling often against great odds, but at last triumphant in establishing his own Golden Age; and third, the apocalyptic, that sees man in need of divine intervention if he is to fulfil the destiny for which he was created.

Not all men are apocalyptists. As a matter of fact, the apocalyptist is often looked upon as a strange figure, out of touch with our modern, scientific world. There are those, indeed, who would seem to consign the apocalyptists to the lunatic fringe of humanity.

It was about half way along the road to the doctorate at Dropsie College that I was therefore thrilled to hear the president of that institution in a public assembly give voice to quite the same hope that I myself have. Referring to the two great miracles that had already taken place, namely, the recovery of the language of the Torah as a living language, and the establishment of the State of Israel, President Neuman went on to ask—and I trust that in quoting only by memory I have not misrepresented him—, "Is it too much to hope that we may see in our lifetime the third and greatest miracle: the coming of Messiah?"

---

[1] I am indebted for valuable criticisms and suggestions to Professor George Eldon Ladd, my colleague at Fuller Theological Seminary, and to my former student, Dr. Robert B. Laurin, of California Baptist Theological Seminary.

It therefore gives me great pleasure to present this study to my teacher and friend, Abraham A. Neuman.

I

That the Qumrân Community was an apocalyptic [1] group is beyond question. It believed that it was living in the end of days and that the Messiah [2] was about to come. It looked upon the world as beyond hope of recovery. Even the religious leaders at Jerusalem were sons of Belial. Our problem is not here, but in the area of clarification and definition. Did the Qumrân Community look for the kind of messiah that we have in mind when we use the term—and just what do *we* have in mind? Was the Qumrân messianic concept that of a Davidic king? a suffering Servant of the Lord? a Son of Man? Was the idea developed out of the Hebrew Bible or did it come from some other source—Zoroastrianism perhaps?

Much has already been written on the subject, and we are indebted to all who have undertaken to discuss the subject for gradual clarification. Helpful surveys of the discussion can be found in an article by Raymond E. Brown [3] and in the two volumes by Millar Burrows. [4]

It is beyond my expectation in this study to present a final solution, but rather to attempt a clarification of the problem or problems, and to suggest a point or two for further study.

II

The Hebrew word מָשִׁיחַ from which we get our English word "messiah," is morphologically an "Aramaic-type" passive

---

[1] This word, like "messianic," "eschatological," and similar terms, is variously defined, and accordingly my statement may be challenged. For the moment I am using it in a broad, undefined sense, as I have in my introduction; the term "eschatological" would be better.

[2] Again I use a term that needs to be defined more precisely.

[3] "The Messianism of Qumrân," *CBQ*, vol. xix (1957), 53-82.

[4] *The Dead Sea Scrolls* (New York 1955), 220-222; 260-272; 330-331; *More Light on the Dead Sea Scrolls* (New York 1958), 297-352.

participle [1] from the verb מָשׁוֹחַ "to anoint." It can therefore be either a noun "the anointed one" or an adjective "anointed." The word "messiah" in English has come to have several shades of meaning, ranging from the vague "any kind of deliverer" to the technical "Davidic king of the messianic age." Part of our present problem is due to the fact that we have carried back into the Qumranic use of the term the variety of meaning found in our own use of "messiah." [2]

The word משיח occurs thirty-nine times in the Hebrew Bible, but never in the sense of "the Messiah" as a *terminus technicus*, indicating the Davidic King. [3] The word is used twice with reference to the patriarchs. [4] Four times the word is used of the priests, always adjectivally, "the anointed priest." [5] Usually the term is used with reference to the king. [6] In one or two instances, the word may be used of the people. [7] In one quite remarkable passage the ex-

---

[1] *Cf.* H. Bauer and P. Leander, *Grammatik des Biblisch-aramäischen* (Halle am Saale 1927), § 33*h*, and C. Brockelmann, *Grundriss der vergleichenden Grammatik der semitischen Sprachen* (Berlin 1908), § 138c.

[2] Even the difference between "messiah" and "Messiah" in English is important. Burrows seems to dismiss this by saying, "It is surprising that the use of a capital letter makes all that difference" (*More Light on the Dead Sea Scrolls*, p. 297); to which I would good-naturedly reply that a man whose name is Millar Burrows should be quite aware of the difference a capital letter makes.

[3] Some find the technical usage in Dan 9: 25, but the definite article is missing, and the context opposes this sense.

[4] Ps 105: 15; 1 Chron 16: 22; the word "prophets" is used, but the context clearly indicates the patriarchs.

[5] Lev 4: 3, 5, 16; 6: 15.

[6] Of Saul: 1 Sam 12: 3, 5; 24: 6 (*MT* 7) twice, 10 (*MT* 11); 26: 9, 11, 16, 23; 2 Sam 1: 14, 16. Of David: 2 Sam 19: 21 (*MT* 22); 23: 1; perhaps 22: 51 and Ps 18: 51. Of the kingly office in general: 1 Sam 2: 10, 35; 2 Sam 22: 51 and Ps 18: 51 (unless referring to David); 2 Chron 6: 42 (perhaps referring to Solomon specifically); Lam 4: 20; Ps 2: 2; 20: 6 (*MT* 7); 84: 9 (*MT* 10); 89: 38 (*MT* 39), 51 (*MT* 52); 132:10, 17. Of Eliab the brother of David as a possible king; 1 Sam 16: 6.

[7] In Ps 28: 8 *RSV* emends למו to לעמו and gets "his people" to parallel "his anointed." It is possible, however, to translate עז־למו as "strength is His" (the Lord's), in which case "His anointed"

pression "His anointed" is used of the Persian king Cyrus. [1]

Once the word is used in its most ordinary sense, "the shield of Saul [was] not anointed with oil." [2] The remaining two passages refer to an "anointed one" in Daniel. [3]

This hasty survey makes it clear that the term "messiah" is not a technical term in the Hebrew Bible. The terms "Messiah of Israel" and "the Messiah" do not occur. Terms such as "the anointed of the Lord," "His anointed," and "My anointed," refer to the kingly office in general or one of the kings in particular, including Cyrus, and may include the people. It was not until late in the days of the Second Temple that the term took on a technical meaning, possibly in Enoch 48: 10; 52: 4, and certainly in Psalms of Solomon 17: 36; 18: 8. By the time of the rabbinic literature, "the Messiah" was an accepted title. Likewise in the New Testament, the Greek equivalent "the Christ" (or just "Christ") was an accepted title.

Both Jewish and Christian writers began to exploit the Hebrew Bible and find numerous "messianic" passages. These were often taken out of context, in a proof-text methodology which has resulted in much confusion. [4] As a result, it is today almost impossible to read the word "messiah" without carrying back into it two thousand years of Jewish or Christian theology.

With the discovery of the Dead Sea Scrolls (or better, the Qumrân Literature), the term "messiah" has received considerable attention, chiefly because these materials help to

would probably refer to the kingly office. In Hab 3: 13 the parallel seems to support the use of "Thy anointed" with reference to "Thy people." The word את could however be translated "with" in which case God is portrayed as going forth with His anointed (the king) for the salvation of His people. Cassuto, ספר תרי עשר *in loc.*, seems to prefer this when he uses ולמלכו to discuss משיחך.

[1]   Isa 45: 1.
[2]   2 Sam 1: 21.
[3]   Dan 9: 25-26.
[4]   For a good corrective article, *cf.* R. E. Murphy, "Notes on Old Testament Messianism and Apologetics," *CBQ* vol. xix, (1957), 5-15.

fill the gap in our knowledge of the development of ideas in Judaism. As we have already noted, however, there has been the same tendency to carry back our ideas and read them into the Qumrân texts.

III

The failure to find the term "Messiah" as a *terminus technicus* should not, however, lead us to the conclusion that there is no messianic idea in the Hebrew Bible. The development in Judaism and Christianity, and in Qumranism as well, came from the stimulus of the Hebrew Bible or Old Testament.

There have been a number of valuable studies on the development of the messianic idea in Israel that make it unnecessary for me to go into details in this study. Two longer works that deserve mention are those by Klausner [1] and Mowinckel. [2] To these should be added two shorter works by Ringgren [3] and O'Doherty, [4] if only to help correct the individual viewpoints of the various writers.

Several writers have raised a needed protest against the lack of precision in terminology. Vriezen asks for distinction between the "specifically messianic expectations and the expectations of salvation in general." [5] Even more explicit is Coppens, who distinguishes three perspectives in Israel's hope: the *soteriological* (the constant hope for the Lord's redemptive activity in the various phases of history), the *eschatological* (the hope of a final intervention by which the

[1] J. Klausner, *The Messianic Idea in Israel from Its Beginning to the Completion of the Mishnah* (tr. from 3d Heb. ed. by W. S. Stinespring; New York 1955), 543 pp.

[2] S. Mowinckel, *He That Cometh* (tr. from Norwegian by G. W. Anderson; New York 1954), 528 pp.

[3] H. Ringgren, *The Messiah in the Old Testament* (*Studies in Biblical Theology*, 18; London 1956), 71 pp.

[4] E. O'Doherty, "The Organic Development of Messianic Revelation," *CBQ*, vol. xix (1957), 16-25.

[5] Th. C. Vriezen, *An Outline of Old Testament Theology* (Wageningen 1958), p. 352.

kingdom is established), and the *messianic* (the expectation of a specific person, the Anointed of the Lord, who is to serve as the ideal King). [1] It should be obvious that the eschatological and the messianic can and often do overlap; it should also be obvious that it is possible to have an eschatological hope without any Messiah. Mowinckel reminds us that "in a whole series of religious writings which speak of the future hope, the Messiah does not appear." [2] There is therefore a lack of precision, it seems to me, to say with Klausner that the origin of "both the impersonal Messianic expectation and the personal Messiah" is to be found in Moses, [3] or with McKenzie that "Messianism in Israel in its earliest form appears in the patriarchal promises and the Sinai covenant." [4] Having thus ventured to criticize others, I shall now attempt to sketch the development of the messianic idea in the Hebrew Bible.

1. It can be accepted as axiomatic, I think, that there was always a soteriological hope in Israel, implicit in the faith that God has entered into a covenant with Israel, whether at Sinai or through the patriarchs. Indeed, this hope has been traced back to the Garden of Eden by the biblical writers. The theocratic idea expressed in the Samuel story [5] suggests that God was to be the ideal king.

2. With the rise of the Israelite monarchy, the elements of this basic faith were explicitly attached to the king. He was "the anointed" (*cf.* 1 Kings 19: 16); he could on occasion perform priestly functions (*cf.* 2 Sam 24: 25); but more than that, he occupied an office that rated sacred titles, so that he

---

[1]   J. Coppens in *L'Attente du Messie* (Paris 1954), 35-38.
[2]   Mowinckel, *op. cit.*, p. 280. He lists several writings which seem to have neither the eschatological nor the messianic hope. A. B. Davidson long ago pointed out the same fact in Hastings' *Dictionary of the Bible* (New York 1899), vol. i 735.
[3]   Klausner, *op. cit.*, p. 18.
[4]   J. L. McKenzie, "Royal Messianism," *CBQ*, vol. xix (1957), 46.
[5]   1 Sam 8: 4-22.

could be addressed as "God" [1] and God's "son." [2] This much, at least, we can accept of "Royal Messianism." [3] At the same time, experience was piling up the evidence that the king was a human being, and as such he could become in varying degrees wicked and corrupt.

3. The next step seems to have been the expression of a hope that God's soteriological purpose would someday be fulfilled by the establishment of a holy kingdom with a holy king. But here the picture becomes increasingly complex. Isaiah saw the holiness of the Lord acting in judgment upon Israel, reducing the nation to a tenth, and then still at work until only the stump remained of what had once been a great tree (Isa 6: 1-13). From that stump was to come forth a shoot upon whom the Spirit of the Lord would rest, and he would bring in the Golden Age (Isa 11: 1-10). He was to be the Davidic king who would have an endless reign (Isa 9: 6-7). Klausner finds a pattern in the eighth-century prophets: "Sin brings punishment, punishment brings repentance, which in turn brings the Days of the Messiah." [4] But should this hope be termed "messianic" at this stage? Elements of messianism are present, but the term "Messiah," let us note, does not yet appear. At the same time, these passages doubtless helped to define the term "Messiah" at a later stage. Should the hope be termed "eschatological"? That depends on our definition of eschatology. [5] Is the

---

[1] *Cf.* Ps 45: 6 (*MT* 7). The expression כסאך אלהים עולם ועד can be translated "Thy throne is God for ever and ever," as well as "Thy throne, O God, is for ever and ever." I fail to see, however, how *RSV* can translate "thy divine throne...." The author of the Epistle to Hebrews saw in it a prophetic reference to the Son, *cf.* Heb. 1: 8.

[2] *Cf.* Ps 2: 7. Again, the author of Hebrews saw a prophetic reference to the Son, *cf.* Heb 1: 5.

[3] For a cautious approach to the subject, avoiding the excesses of those who import myth and cult into the discussion at every opportunity, *cf.* J. L. McKenzie, *art. cit.*, *CBQ*, vol. xix (1957), 25-52.

[4] Klausner, *op. cit.*, p. 38; *cf.* also p. 58.

[5] For a good discussion, *cf.* Th. C. Vriezen, "Prophecy and Eschatology," *VT* Supplement 1 (1953), 199-229. Vriezen defends the use of the word in a wider sense, p. 202.

eschaton the goal within history, or is it something beyond history? To the latter, the term "apocalyptic" is sometimes applied, and in contrast with it the term "prophetic" is used. [1] But does Hebrew thought divide between "history" and "beyond history"? The various strands of this problem, it seems to me, are not unravelled in the Hebrew Bible.

4. Hope in the ultimate success of the Davidic line is not abandoned. Zerubbabel was of the house of David, and his part, while not entirely clear, is integral with the promises of the prophets of the Second Temple (*cf.* Hag 1: 14; Zech 4: 6-10). The people Israel is likewise an essential part of the hope. With all of their prophecies of judgment and doom, the prophets never at any time suggest that Israel is to be replaced by some other nation as God's elect. Israel—whether by that term we understand the nation, or the remnant, or the ideal Israelite—is the Servant of the Lord. When at last the knowledge of the Lord covers the earth, it is because the Torah goes forth from Zion; likewise it is to Jerusalem that the nations of the earth come for instruction. [2] To this development of the prophetic hope we should probably give the name *messianic*. In the post-biblical writings the title "Messiah" is applied solely to the Davidic king who rules over this Golden Age.

5. At the same time, the idea of an irruption of special divine activity into history is also part of the prophetic message. Prior to the preaching of Amos the expression "the Day of the Lord" was in use, and Amos made it clear that this was to be a day of judgment. As late as the time of Malachi the fires of judgment are associated with the day of

[1] For a thought-provoling discussion, *see* G. E. Ladd, "Why Not Prophetic-Apocalyptic?" *JBL*, vol. lxxvi (1957), 192-200.

[2] Klausner claims that Christianity has attempted to remove the political and nationalistic part of the hope (*op. cit.*, p. 10). While I readily admit that this is to a large degree true, I have attempted in my unpublished Th. M. thesis, "The Exegetical Basis of Premillennialism" (Princeton Theological Seminary, 1943), to show that both the ancient Chiliasts and some modern exegetes of substantial ability have insisted upon retaining these elements in Christian interpretation.

His coming. In Daniel, the "stone cut from a mountain by no human hand" destroys the kingdoms of this world and the Kingdom of God is set up (Dan 2: 44-55) and one "like a son of man" comes with the clouds of heaven (Dan 7: 13). We might call this the *eschatological* hope. However, I would prefer to use the word *apocalyptic* for this development, and include both *messianic* and *apocalyptic* under the larger term *eschatological*. [1]

6. Although Christianity synthesized these ideas in the doctrine of the Incarnation together with that of the "Second Coming," Judaism maintained a distinction. This resulted in elaboration of the concept of the Messiah. In some writings, Messiah ben Joseph appears alongside the Davidic Messiah; in one writing a Messiah of the Levitical line appears. It resulted in considerable Son of Man literature. And it led to the distinction between "this world" and "the world to come"—although the distinction is not always as neat as our logical minds would like. [2]

IV

The Qumrân Community looked upon itself as living in the end of the age. The literature of Qumrân uses terms such as "the last days" (1QpHab 9: 7), "the final end" (1QpHab 7: 7, 13), "the final phase of the end" (1QpHab 7: 2), "the time of God's wrath" (CD 1: 2), "the season of visitation" (1QS 4: 18-19), "the generation of the visitation" (4QpHos^b 1: 10), "the last generation" (1QpHab 2: 7; 7: 2; 4QpHos^b 1: 11 restored), etc. Since this gives the modern scholar an opportunity to study the views of an eschatological sect from

[1] I would also prefer to remove the distinction between *historical* and *supra-historical* and hold that the activity of God that results in the establishment of the messianic age will occur, at least in its earlier stages, within history on this earth.

[2] Klausner, for example, contends that "the World to Come" can only refer to the messianic age when there are no references to the resurrection of the dead, Paradise and Gehenna, and the New World; *op. cit.*, p. 414. The developments I have mentioned are discussed in detail in Klausner.

its own literature, there has been much interest in the subject, and many valuable articles have been published. On many points there is substantial agreement; but several points still need clarification. For one thing, What kind of messiah was expected? Was the sect *messianic* or *apocalyptic* (as I have distinguished the terms, above)—or perhaps both? Did it look for one messiah, or two (or even three)—or none at all?

Milik finds "three Messianic persons" [1] in the Qumrân Literature. He supports his position as follows: (1) the language of 1QS 9:11, "until the advent of the prophet and the messiahs of Aaron and Israel," requires three persons; (2) two messiahs, obviously the Messiah of Aaron (or priestly Messiah) and the Messiah of Israel (or the Royal Messiah) are found in the Rule of the Congregation (1QSa or 1Q28a); (3) the *florilegium* of quotations in 4Q Testimonia, namely Deuteronomy 18:18ff., Numbers 24:15-17, and Deuteronomy 33:8-11, refer respectively to the Prophet, the Star of Jacob, and the blessing on Levi, which indicates belief in three messianic persons.

Milik's view is less attractive when studied in detail than when taken as a whole. For example, the first of these three "Messianic persons" is *the Prophet*. Milik alters his term a page later to "eschatological figures"—a decided improvement in my opinion—, and then goes on to point out that the prophet "seems scarcely to be mentioned elsewhere in the Qumrân texts and little further can be said about his functions and person." Milik reluctantly concludes that he is only a precursor of the Messiah, "the Elijah *redivivus* of Mal. 3.23." [2]

Milik, let us remember, has supported his identification of the Prophet as an "eschatological figure" by reference to Deuteronomy 18:18. This is an important passage and

---

[1] J. T. Milik, *Ten Years of Discovery in the Wilderness of Judah* (London 1959), p. 125; similarly, K. G. Kuhn, "Die beiden Messias Aarons und Israels," *NTS*, vol. 1 (1955), 178.

[2] Milik, *Ten Years of Discovery*, p. 126. I had suggested that the text was dealing with forerunners in my *Amazing Dead Sea Scrolls* (Chicago 1956), p. 155.

obviously left a strong impression on the popular mind. Rabbinic literature clearly distinguishes between an eschatological Moses and an eschatological Elijah. [1] Each of these is distinguished from the Messiah in the interrogation of John the Baptist recorded in the Fourth Gospel, which Wieder correctly relates to Deuteronomy 18: 18. [2] Moreover, the work of this "Prophet" should obviously have to do with the teaching of the Law, according to the context in Deuteronomy. This feature of the faith and practice of the Qumrân Community is so marked that considerable literature has appeared on the "Teacher of Righteousness" and the "Law Interpreter" in the Scrolls. [3] But Milik would have us believe that the eschatological prophet is scarcely mentioned in the Qumrân texts, while the priestly Messiah (the Messiah of Aaron) took over the title Teacher of Righteousness, "as he took over that of the Messiah of Israel," his functions including "the proclamation of the eschatological law." [4] I find it difficult to follow Milik here. Further, while recognizing that the messianic belief of the Qumranians is otherwise homogeneous and clear, Milik says it is rather disconcerting in the Damascus Document. However, there is sufficient material in the Habbakuk Commentary on the Teacher of Righteousness to indicate that he was a priest; hence the functions of the Teacher are not different in their eschatological setting (the Damascus Document) than in their historical

[1] In Deut. Rab., iii, end, Rabbi Jochanan ben Zakkai quotes God's promise to Moses, "when I bring Elijah the prophet unto them the two of you shall come together."

[2] John 1: 21; cf. N. Wieder, "The 'Law Interpreter' of the Sect of the Dead Sea Scrolls: The Second Moses," *JJS*, vol. iv (1953), 170.

[3] *See* my *Bibliography of the Dead Sea Scrolls* 1948-1957 (*Fuller Library Bulletin*, Fall, 1958), Nos. 3821-3871. M. Burrows, *More Light on the Dead Sea Scrolls*, 325-341, contains a splendid survey of the discussion.

[4] Milik, *op. cit.*, p. 126. He uses CD 14: 19 in his argument, where the singular form, "Messiah of Aaron and Israel" is supported by the fragment of 4QD^b; this is a *non sequitur*.

setting (the Habakkuk Commentary). Liver has felt the force of the problem arising from the attempt to identify the Teacher of Righteousness and the Interpreter of the Law with the Messiah of Aaron, and suggests that the relationship requires a fresh treatment. [1] I agree; only I would go beyond Liver to include the Messiah of Aaron which he has accepted without question.

Having reached an *impasse* with the first of the eschatological figures, we move on to the other two, "the Messiahs of Aaron and Israel."

The expression itself calls for a few observations. It is found only in the Manual of Discipline, only once, and not in the oldest exemplar of this composition. [2] The singular form of the expression, "the Messiah (anointed) of Aaron and Israel" is found in the Damascus Document three times and probably a fourth. [3] In addition the expressions "his anointed one" (CD 2: 12) and "the holy anointed one" (CD 6: 1) are found in the same document. There was much discussion about these readings when the Damascus Document was first published in 1910, [4] and with the discovery of the Qumrân Literature the subject was reopened with a new zeal. It was almost unanimously agreed that the Damascus Document should be emended to harmonize with the passage in the Manual of Discipline. [5] However, when a fragment of the

---

[1] J. Liver, "The Doctrine of the Two Messiahs in Sectarian Literature in the Time of the Second Commonwealth," *HTR*, vol. lii (1959), 161.

[2] In 1 QS 9: 11; 4 QSᵉ has the text of 1 QS 9:12 immediately after 8: 16; *cf*. Milik, *Ten Years of Discovery*, p. 123.

[3] CD 19: 10; 20: 1; 12: 23-24; restored in 14: 19. The reading is also suggested in CD 13: 21, but no part of the expression remains in the text.

[4] Then known as the Zadokite Fragments. For bibliography, *see* L. Rost, *Die Damaskusschrift* (Berlin 1933); H. H. Rowley, *The Zadokite Fragments and the Dead Sea Scrolls* (Oxford 1952); and my *Bibliography of the Dead Sea Scrolls* 1948-1957, Nos. 2650-2667.

[5] K. G. Kuhn, for example, said, "All instances where the word *mashiah* occurs in CD, it originally had a plural form," "The Two Messiahs of Aaron and Israel" in K. Stendahl, ed., *The Scrolls and the New Testament* (New York 1957), p. 60.

Damascus Document containing the passage of CD 14: 19
was found in Cave Four, and the reading was clearly in the
singular, Milik readily admitted that it was no longer possible
to look upon the passage in the Damascus Document from
Cairo as a medieval correction. [1] In my opinion, all of the
passages in the Damascus Document are affected by the
discovery of 4QS^e: if one was not emended, the theory that
all had been emended falls to the ground. [2]

We are then left with the single use of the expression in
the Manual of Discipline. On the basis of syntax I raised the
question whether the phrase "the Messiahs of Aaron and
Israel" could mean "the Messiah of Aaron and the Messiah
of Israel." [3] It was pointed out to me [4] that I had drawn my
evidence entirely from biblical Hebrew and Qumrân Hebrew
might observe different rules of syntax. Millar Burrows dealt
a serious blow to my argument when he pointed out that
the Manual of Discipline contains the expression, "the spirits
of truth and error" (1QS 3: 18f.), and said, "Surely this does
not imply that truth and error together form a unit, to which
both spirits belong!" [5] Now I must admit in all candor that
the context certainly appears to support Professor Burrows.
Yet I am forced to point out that "truth and error" can indeed
form a thought-unit, just as surely as do "good and evil"—and
the latter expression is found after a single *nomen regens* in
the phrase "knowers of good and evil" (Gen 3: 5). In my
opinion, it would be entirely possible to translate the passage
in the Manual of Discipline, "He created man to have dominion
over the world and made for him two spirits... they are

[1] Milik, *Ten Years of Discovery*, p. 125, n. 3. Liver, however, is
still assuming that the medieval copy (CD) contains scribal errors
or emendations; see *art. cit., HTR* vol. lii, 152.

[2] This substantiates my observation in "The Messiahs of Aaron
and Israel,'" *VT* vol. vi (1956), 428. There I also pointed out that
emendation of במשיחו הקודש in CD 6: 1 is not necessary, since a
similar construction is now found in 1Q30 1: 2.

[3] *Ibid.*, 425-429.

[4] First of all, I believe, in correspondence with Professor Ullendorff.

[5] M. Burrows, *More Light on the Dead Sea Scrolls*, 299.

the spirits of [the moral category of] truth and error." How-
ver, I am unwilling to press the point further concerning the
"messiahs of Aaron and Israel," since the syntactical question
should admittedly be studied at length in Qumrân usage.
At present I am interested in discovering whether the "Messiah
of Aaron" is indeed a messiah, and if so, what kind.

The expression "the Messiah of Aaron," so far as I can
discover, is not found in the Qumrân writings, other than
in the compound expression, "the Messiahs of Aaron and
Israel." Liver makes a point of "the precise definition of the
term 'Anointed of Aaron' (משיח מאהרון)," [1] but fails to document his reference, and I am unable to find it or any other
reference to it. [2] It is commonly agreed that this "Messiah
of Aaron" is the priestly messiah found in the Testament
of the Twelve Patriarchs. In my survey of the development
of the messianic idea, above, I did not go into the details of
the intertestamental period for two principal reasons: (1)
the relative date of much of this literature with reference to
Qumrân Literature is problematic; (2) the complexities would
only serve to obscure our attempt to work toward clarification.
The date of the Testaments is much in dispute; there are
undoubtedly post-Christian additions, and in the minds of
some, [3] the entire work is post-Christian. Since fragments of
the Testaments seem to be among the Qumrân finds, [4] a close
relationship between the Testaments and the Qumrân Community has been suggested. It is even possible that the Qumrân Community produced the Testaments, without the later
additions of course.

---

[1]   J. Liver, art. cit., HTR, vol. lii, 154.
[2]   The expression משיח מאהרון ומישראל occurs in CD 20: 1 but I
cannot see any justification for severing the last word from the rest
of the phrase.
[3]   Cf. M. de Jonge, The Testaments of the Twelve Patriarchs (Assen
1953), 171 pp.
[4]   Cf. Milik, Ten Years of Discovery, pp. 34-35. I say "seem" only
because there is still the possibility that nothing more than source-
material for the Testaments has been found.

In the Testaments of the Twelve Patriarchs, the Messiah is descended from Levi, and not, according to Charles, from Judah. [1] The references that Charles uses to support his view are not all pertinent, and Beasley-Murray comes to the conclusion that both a priestly messiah and a Davidic Messiah are found in the Testaments, the latter subordinate to the former. [2] Liver has summarized the material in a handy table. [3] According to the *Jewish Encyclopaedia*,[4] "The sole mission of the messiah will be the regeneration of mankind, and his kingdom will be one of justice and salvation for the whole world."

Since there is no reference to the priestly Messiah *per se* in the Qumrân Literature, it is necessary for us to study the material that concerns the Chief Priest. In the War Scroll there is a reference to "the Chief Priest and his lieutenant" (1QM 2: 1). There follows a list of other "chiefs" who do not appear to be eschatological figures. Further on in the scroll a war is described, thought by many to be eschatological, in which the anointed priests [*sic*] perform priestly functions— but there is nothing "messianic." [5] Still later, at the deliverance of the people, the priests are praying—but it is Michael who delivers the people (1QM 15: 4-5; 17: 6).

In the fragments known as The Order of the Congregation (1QSa or 1Q28a) and The Benedictions (1QSb or 1Q28b), the Priest again appears as an important figure. The passages are extremely significant, but unfortunately they are damaged

---

[1] R. H. Charles, *Apocrypha and Pseudepigrapha of the Old Testament* (Oxford 1913), vol. ii, p. 294.

[2] *Cf.* G. R. Beasley-Murray, "The Two Messiahs in the Testaments of the Twelve Patriarchs," *JTS*, vol. xlviii (1947), 5-9. The study has been brought up to date to include the Qumrân material in II. H. Rowley, *Jewish Apocalyptic and the Dead Sea Scrolls* (London 1957), esp. pp. 11-13.

[3] J. Liver, *art. cit.*, *HTR*, vol. lii, 178, n. 91.

[4] M. Buttenwieser, "Messiah," *JE*, vol. viii, 509.

[5] Liver, however, does make a point when he cites rabbinical tradition that the oil of anointing was hidden away until the end of days; *cf. art. cit.*, *HTR*, vol. lii, 153.

considerably. [1] In the first, two principal persons are present at a meal which may be eschatological or simply ritual. [2] One figure is the Chief Priest, who is nowhere called "messiah" in the text. [3] The other figure is specifically called the "Messiah (or anointed) of Israel," a title which does not occur in the Hebrew Bible. Twice in the course of the meal the Chief Priest acts first, and after him, if the restorations are correct, [4] the "anointed of Israel" acts. The Chief Priest admittedly has the place of prominence. But this is slender evidence on which to build a doctrine of two Messiahs. Even more slender, in my opinion, is the support proferred on the basis of the problematic "if God begets the Messiah" (1QSa 2: 11-12). [5]

The text of The Benedictions (1QSb) is even more fragmentary than 1QSa. One line of argument rests upon the location of the benediction for the "Prince of the Congregation" after that for the High Priest and the priests. It is not clear, however, that this implies relative prominence, or that it has any

---

[1] *See* Plates XXIII-XXV in D. Barthélemy and J. T. Milik, *Discoveries in the Judean Desert* (Oxford 1955), Vol. 1.

[2] The heading (1 QSa 1: 1) refers to "the end of days," but the close says, "This statute they shall do for every meal when at least ten men shall assemble" (1 QSa 2: 21-22). F. M. Cross thinks it is a liturgical anticipation of the Messianic banquet; *cf. The Ancient Library of Qumran and Modern Biblical Studies* (New York 1958), 53. Burrows raises an objection, "How the presence of the Messiah of Israel is to be explained on that basis it is difficult to see"—*More Light on the Dead Sea Scrolls*, 300. There is one quite obvious answer: the "anointed of Israel" may not have been the "Messiah of Israel."

[3] If Yadin's restoration is correct, the Chief Priest is called "the anointed priest"; *cf.* Y. Yadin, "A Crucial Passage in the Dead Sea Scrolls," *JBL*, vol. lxxviii (1959) 238-241.

[4] I have discussed this in detail in my unpublished Th. D. dissertation, "A Preliminary Reconstruction of Judaism in the Time of the Second Temple in the Light of the Published Qumrân Materials" (University of Southern California, Los Angeles, 1956), pp. 265-274, and in briefer form in *Amazing Dead Sea Scrolls*, pp. 157-162.

[5] Yadin's restoration in *JBL*, vol. lxxviii (1959), 240-241 disposes of this. Those familiar with the infra-red photos of the text, however, assure us that יוליד is clearly read.

messianic significance. Even more damaging to the argument is the fact that the expression, "the High Priest," does not actually occur in the text except in Milik's restoration.

Other references, such as those concerning the "Teacher of Righteousness," and the "Interpreter of the Law," cannot properly be used in the discussion of the "Messiah of Aaron" until there is much more clarification of the proposed identifications.

I find it difficult, then, to accept the position that "the anointed of Aaron"—if indeed there is any such person in the Qumrân texts—was a priestly messiah such as the one described in the Testaments of the Twelve Patriarchs. That the Qumrân Community favored the priestly or Zadokite line is beyond question. That the priests and the Chief Priest have prominent rôles in the Qumrân Literature is admitted. But to call the Chief Priest "Messiah" would mean a further watering down of the term, only one short step removed from calling all of the Qumranian sons of Zadok who lived in the last days "messiahs."

There remains, then, the "Messiah of Israel." This expression, unlike the expression "Messiah of Aaron," does occur in Qumrân Literature (1QSa 2: 20 and partially restored in 2: 14), as do the expressions, "the Messiah," and "the Messiah of Aaron and Israel."

Since we have been freed from the pressure to emend the text six times in the Damascus Document by the discovery of the fragment of 4QD^b, discussed above, it is reasonable, I think, to study these passages as relevant to a single messiah. Turning to them, we quickly note that in four of them (CD 19: 10; 20: 1; 12: 23-24; 14: 19) the expression is only that of a limiting factor of the contemporary period: "until the messiah of Aaron and Israel arises." In one of these (CD 19: 10) a detail of this eschatological event is included: "they that withdraw shall be given to the sword when the Messiah of Aaron and Israel comes." When the word משיח occurs independently in the Damascus Document (CD 2: 12;

6: 1), it does not seem to have any eschatological reference.

The "Messiah" or "Messiah of Israel" is mentioned in the Order of the Congregation three times: המשיח (2: 12), [1] מש[י]ח ישראל (2: 14), and משיח ישראל (2: 27). We have already discussed this passage, above. If it is a sacramental liturgy, then, of course, we can build little messianic doctrine upon it. If it looks forward to the eschatological banquet, then the reference is to the Messiah. The difficult and much-discussed passage, "when [God] shall beget (?) the Messiah" (1QSa 2: 11-12), may have reference to Psalm 2: 7, but this whole discussion needs restudy in the light of Yadin's article. [2] The word "messiah" probably occurs in 1Q30 1: 2 [מ]שיח הקודש, in a small fragment which yields little sense. Other forms of the word are found in the War Scroll in two places: "The oil of anointing" (1 QM 9: 8), which refers to the priests, and "Thy anointed ones, the seers of testimonies" (1 QM 11: 7), which seems to refer to prophetic figures. Neither passage contributes to our study. The word does not occur in the Habakkuk Commentary or the Thanksgiving Hymns.

One passage remains, unless I have failed to locate all occurrences of משיח in the published texts, and it is quite important. The document was originally identified as a Commentary on Genesis (4QpGen 49), but now is generally recognized as Patriarchal Blessings (4QPatrBles). [3] Commencing with the words from Genesis 49: 10, it continues, "until the messiah of righteousness, the scion of David shall come, for to him and to his seed has been given the royal covenant of his people unto the generations of eternity." There can be no doubt that we have here a clear messianic passage, and that it relates the Messiah to the Davidic house.

In addition to the texts containing the word "messiah," there is other significant material. Milik used as one support

---

[1] Unless we accept Yadin's restoration of [הכוהן] המשיה cf. note 3, p. 16, above.

[2] Art. cit., JBL, vol. lxxviii, 238 ff.

[3] Cf. J. M. Allegro, "Further Messianic References in Qumran Literature," JBL, vol. lxx (1956), 174-176.

for his "three messianic persons" the *florilegium* of quotations
in 4QTest, discussed above. The quotation which in his
opinion applied to the Messiah of Israel was Numbers 24: 15-
17, the familiar Star-and-Sceptre passage. This passage is
also used in the Damascus Document in a curious bit of
exegesis typical of Qumrân in which "the Tabernacle of
David" is mentioned, and "the Sceptre" is identified as "the
prince of all the congregation" (CD 7: 18). This is messianic
language, and it is related to David.

The reference to the "prince of all the congregation" turns
our attention to the Benedictions, where the "prince of the
Congregation" is mentioned (1 QSᵇ 5: 20). The context
applies to this prince the language of Isaiah 11: 1-5, which
again suggests that a messianic person is intended. Milik
further supports the case for a Davidic Messiah by a reference
to a Commentary on a Psalm, where the title "of David" is
interpreted by the citation of Isaiah 11: 1-5. [1]

Several other references seem certainly to refer to the
Davidic Messiah. One, identified as 4Q Florilegium, is chiefly
concerned with the House of David, the establishment of the
royal throne, and says explicitly, "He is the scion of David,
the one arising with the Interpreter of the Law." [2] Another
document identified as a Commentary on Isaiah (4QpIsaᵃ)
speaks of the "[scion of] David, who will arise at the en[d of
days]" along with war with the Kittim, ruling over the
g[entile]s, a reference to Magog, and going up from the Plain
of Acco to fight. [3] The fragmentary character of the text,
unfortunately, makes it of little use for other than corrobo-
rative evidence.

[1] In *Discoveries in the Judean Desert*, vol. i, p. 129. I have not seen
the Commentary referred to.

[2] *Cf.* J. M. Allegro, *art. cit.*, *JBL*, vol. lxxv, 177. Allegro says that
this certainly identifies the Interpreter of the Law with the Messiah
of Aaron. J. Silberman offers a correction to Allegro's translation in
JBL, vol. lxxviii (1959), 159, and suggests that it is a midrash
on 2 Sam 7: 11f.

[3] Allegro, *art. cit.*, 176-182.

In the Thanksgiving Hymns there is a passage (1QH 3: 5-18) that has been discussed frequently in connection with the messianic age. Licht says it is a vision of the end of days; that this is the only time in the *Hodayot* that the messiah is mentioned, and one of the few times in the scrolls; that nothing is said of the messiah's personality. Licht is of the opinion that the messiah is only a symbol of materialization of the ideal community. [1] One further fact could have been mentioned: the word "messiah" does not occur in the psalm. In fact, the only "messianic" symbol I find in the psalm is the expression "wonderful counsellor," as in Isaiah 9: 5. The hymn seems to be simply the expression of intense feeling. [2] If there is a messianic reference in this passage, it is certainly insufficient as a basis for messianic doctrine.

Since the War Scroll is generally taken to be the portrayal of an eschatological war, [3] it is remarkable that we find in it no mention of the Messiah. A passage in the twelfth column has sometimes been taken as messianic in view of a paean of praise to "the man of glory" (1 QM 12: 6-18). It seems more likely that God is the One being addressed. But even if the passage is viewed as messianic it contributes little to our study of Qumrân messianism.

Some word should be included concerning the Suffering Servant in the Scrolls. To me, the discussion has been rather unconvincing. Bruce has given a very careful survey, and although several times he has been willing to go further than I would with the evidence, he concludes only that the Community itself is viewed as fulfilling the rôle of the Servant. [4]

---

[1]　*Cf.* J. Licht, מגילת ההודיות (Jerusalem 1957), pp. 76-78.

[2]　Morton Smith says, "The prophet here is following that Old Testament tradition which compares the anguish of prophecy to that of a woman in travail."—"What is Implied by the Variety of Messianic Figures?" *JBL*, vol. lxxviii (1959), 66-67.

[3]　*Cf.* J. van der Ploeg, *Le Rouleau de la Guerre* (Leiden 1959), p. 25.

[4]　F. F. Bruce, *Biblical Exegesis in the Qumran Texts* (Grand Rapids 1959), p. 51. Bruce is willing to apply the expression Servant of the Lord to the priestly Messiah as a representative of the whole righteous community.

Similarly, discussions of the "eschatological Man" are to me unconvincing, and the methodology at times approaches "proof-text" technique. [1]

V

In this study, "conclusions" are premature. There are, however, certain observations that can be made.

1. The Qumrân Community did have an eschatological viewpoint and a messianic viewpoint. As far as it had developed, it was in keeping with the outlines laid down in the Hebrew Bible. The Messiah was of the line of David, and several messianic prophecies were applied to him. Even the name used by the Community, "the sons of Zadok," might possibly indicate that they chose to think of themselves in the line of the priest who supported David (2 Sam 15: 24-29; I Kings 1: 7-8).

2. There was a strong emphasis upon the priestly office, perhaps influenced by Ezekiel 40-48, where we also find the prominence of the Zadokite line (cf. 48: 11). The Community thought of itself as a community of priests or sons of Zadok. The Chief Priest is prominent at several points in the literature, including a sacramental or messianic meal. To speak of "two Messiahs" or a "Messiah of Aaron" is, however, in my opinion, not justified by the evidence. The Chief Priest performs no messianic function as commonly defined. He is present in two possibly eschatological passages: in the Order of the Congregation and in the battle described in the War Scroll. In neither case is he called a "messiah," and there is no textual indication that he had newly appeared. The "coming" of the Messiah, whenever it is mentioned, applies to the Davidic person with one possible exception, namely 1QS 9: 11, "the Messiahs (or anointed ones) of Aaron and Israel," where the "Messiah of Aaron" is commonly understood. I have previous-

---

1 Cf. G. Vermès, *Discovery in the Judean Desert* (Paris 1956), pp. 220-222; W. H. Brownlee, "The Servant of the Lord in the Qumrân Scrolls, II," *BASOR*, 135 (October 1954); 36-38.

ly challenged this interpretation, and I find in the present study no reason to abandon that position. In fact, with discovery of the Damascus Document (4QD^b) supporting the singular reading, there seems to be less reason now to find two Messiahs in 1QS 9: 11.

3. The "Son of Man" or apocalyptic element is absent from the Qumrân literature. This is all the more striking in view of the fact that we have been inclined to associate the Qumrân movement not with "normative Judaism" but rather with "sectarian Judaism".[1] Normative Judaism is generally thought to have rejected the apocalyptic movements, and these have been relegated to the sectarians. Further, although many of the writings of the intertestamental period are found at Qumrân, those commonly designated "apocalyptic" are missing. This is particularly evident in the case of Enoch, where eleven manuscripts are represented in the Qumrân fragments, coming from Books I, III, IV, and V, but no part of Book II (the Similitudes), in which the Son of Man doctrine is set forth. [2] We can only conclude that the eschatology of Qumrân was messianic rather than apocalyptic.

4. The Zoroastrian influence on the ideas of Qumrân has frequently been mentioned. This influence is particularly to be found, we are told, in the concepts of dualism, angels, Satan, and, according to Mowinckel and others, the heavenly savior (or Son of Man). But this presents a contradiction, for there is no Son of Man concept in Qumrân thought. The matter of Zoroastrian influence on Qumranic theology must therefore be restudied.

---

[1] These terms are discussed in G. F. Moore, *Judaism* (Cambridge, Mass., 1927), vol. i, p. 3.

[2] J. Albertson shows by mathematical probability that there is little likelihood that Part II was in the Qumrân library; *cf.* "An Application of Mathematical Probability to Manuscript Discoveries," *JBL*, vol. lxxviii (1959), 133-141.

THE LITURGICAL USE OF PSALM 78:38

By Leon J. Liebreich

Hebrew Union College-Jewish Institute of Religion, New York

PSALM 78:38 (והוא רחום וגו'), which in gaonic times was singled out for inclusion in the liturgy, is to be found in the Ashkenazic rite in the miscellany of verses appended to הודו (I Chron 16:8-36); toward the end of the יהי כבוד miscellany of verses preceding אשרי;[1] in ובא לציון; and before ברכו of the evening service for weekdays.[2] Although Ps 78:38 (and Ps 20:10) mark the conclusion of the יהי כבוד miscellany of verses, there can be no doubt that these two verses were originally intended as an introduction to אשרי in the *Pesuke de-Zimra*.[3] For, one need only consult the Siddur of R. Saadiah Gaon to be impressed by the phenomenon of the inseparability of והוא רחום וגו' and אשרי. In this Siddur והוא רחום וגו' precedes אשרי and ובא לציון in the morning service for weekdays, as well as אשרי in the afternoon service for weekdays.[4] Nor is Siddur R. Saadiah unique in this respect. The Yemenite rite follows the same practice.[5] It is obvious, therefore, that Ps 78:38 is inextricably interwoven with אשרי.

The occurrence of Ps 78:38 before ברכו of the evening

---

[1] Consisting of Ps 145 preceded by Pss 84:5, 144:15 and followed by Ps 115:18.

[2] To these may be added the use of Ps 78:38 as the opening verse of *Tahanun* on Mondys and Thursdays.

[3] *Cf.* Yehiel Zimmels in *Rav Saadya Gaon*, ed. J. L. Fishman (Jerusalem 1943), p. 539.

[4] See *Siddur R. Saadiah Gaon*, ed. Davidson-Assaf-Joel (Jerusalem 1941), pp. 39 (*Shahrit*), 25 below and 41 (*Minhah*).

[5] See *Tiklal* (Jerusalem 1894), vol. i, 66b-67a and 85a; or *Tiklal* (*Shibat Ziyyon*), ed. Joseph Kapih (Jerusalem 1952), vol. i, pp. 45, 64. *See* Assaf's Introduction to *Siddur R. Saadiah*, p. 29. *Cf.* Maimonides, *Mishneh Torah, Hilkhot Tefillah*, IX. 9.

service for weekdays suggests that this biblical verse might just as appropriately be recited before the other ברכו of the liturgy, namely, before the ברכו of the *Yozer* service. As a matter of fact, traces are not wanting of the recital of והוא רחום before ברכו of the *Yozer* service. Among the Genizah fragments published by J. Mann [1] and S. Assaf [2] והוא רחום actually precedes ברכו of the *Yozer* service. Moreover, a vestige of this practice is contained in a responsum of R. Hai Gaon in *Sefer Temim Deim* which records a divergence of opinion to the effect: שהללו אומרים והוא רחום בברכת יוצר והללו אין אומרים. [3] The usage of Ps 78: 38 was, accordingly, not limited to ברכו of the evening service for weekdays. Precisely the same practice was in vogue before ברכו of the *Yozer* service.

Another point to be noted is that the recital of Ps 78: 38 before ברכו in both the evening and morning services was not always restricted to weekdays. There is sufficient evidence to prove that Sabbaths and festivals were no exception to the prescription requiring Ps 78: 38 before ברכו of the evening and morning services. Thus in Seder R. Amram Gaon's descriptions of the Sabbath eve service and the morning service for Passover והוא רחום introduces ברכו, [4] and in an Oxford MS. described by S. Assaf the evening service for Tabernacles commences with והוא רחום. [5] Besides, there is the testimony of Abudarham [6] who, apropos of the evening service for Sabbaths, records the Sefardi practice in no uncertain terms: ערבית נוהגין בכל המקומות בספרד לומר והוא רחום כשאר הימים.

---

[1] *HUCA*, vol. ii (1925), p. 273, on which *see* S. Assaf in *Sefer Dinaburg* (Jerusalem 1949), p. 120.

[2] Assaf, *op. cit.*, p. 119. *See also* Zimmels, *op. cit.*, p. 542.

[3] Cited by Zimmels, *op. cit.*, p. 539 and Assaf, *op. cit.*, p. 120.

[4] For Sabbath eve see *Seder R. Amram*, ed. Warsaw 1865, vol. i, 25a; *cf.* ed. Frumkin (Jerusalem 1912), vol. ii, p. 7, note 1 in the variant readings. For the morning service of Passover *see* ed. Frumkin, vol. ii, p. 227 above. As regards והוא רחום before ברכו of the Sabbath eve service *see* further Assaf, *Mi-Sifrut ha-Geonim* (Jerusalem 1933), p. 75, note 3.

[5] Assaf in *Sefer Dinaburg*, p. 128, note 3.

[6] *Abudarham ha-Shalem* (Jerusalem 1959), p. 144; *cf.* p. 137.

In view of such attestation, Shemtob Gaguine, [1] commentator
of the current Sefardi rite, deplores the fact that Sefardim
have abandoned this well-established usage in favor of the
custom prevalent in France and Provence, according to
which Ps 78: 38 is omitted before ברכו of the evening service
on Sabbaths and festivals. The Sefardi rite, however, as well
as the Yemenite, Persian and Italian rites, follow Seder R.
Amram in retaining והוא רחום prior to ברכו on the eve of the
Day of Atonement. [2] And in this connection it is noteworthy
that in the Yemenite and Persian rites והוא רחום also
introduces אשרי in the afternoon service for the Day of
Atonement. [3]

It is perfectly understandable why Ps 78: 38 was deemed
a fitting prelude to the evening and afternoon services of
the Day of Atonement. Containing, as this biblical verse
does, the words יכפר עון, it is inherently in consonance with
the character of the day which is one of divine pardon and
forgiveness of sins. [4] On the other hand, it is not readily
apparent why this verse should have been introduced into
other liturgical contexts whose principal theme is not that
of pardon and forgiveness.

Various attempts have been made to account for the
liturgical appropriateness of Ps 78: 38 as an introduction to
ברכו of the evening service for weekdays. The various medieval
explanations cited in the commentaries of Landshuth, [5] Baer, [6]

---

[1]   *Keter Shem Tob* (Kedainiai 1934), vols. i-ii, p. 164 below.
[2]   For the Sefardi rite *see* Moses Gaster's edition of *Seder ha
Tefillot ke-fi Minhag Sefardim*, vol. iii (London 1904), p. 16. For the
Yemenite rite see *Tiklal* (Jerusalem 1894), vol. ii, 84a or ed. Kapih,
vol. iii, p. 119. For the Persian rite *see* E. N. Adler in *JQR* (Old Series),
vol. x, p. 616. For the Italian rite see *Mahzor Kol ha-Shanah ke-fi
Minhag Italiani* (Livorno 1856), vol. ii, 69b. This practice is traceable
to *Seder R. Amram*, ed. Warsaw, vol. i, 47a; ed. Frumkin, vol. ii, p. 344.
[3]   *Tiklal* (Jerusalem 1894), vol. ii, 116a or ed. Kapih, vol. iii,
p. 184. For the Persian rite *see* E. N. Adler, *op. cit.*, p. 617.
[4]   So Gaguine, *op. cit.*, p. 191.
[5]   *Siddur Hegyon Leb* (Königsberg 1845), pp. 218-219.
[6]   *Seder Abodat Yisrael*, (Rödelheim 1868), pp. 163, 183.

Gordon, [1] and Gaguine [2] cannot be taken seriously. Being purely homiletical, they are unsatisfactory from a critical standpoint. Of modern scholars, two have dealt with the problem. Ismar Elbogen [3] gives the following reason for the insertion of והוא רחום (and other verses) before ברכו of the evening service for weekdays: "Von den verschiedenen dafür gegebenen Begründungen ist die einleuchtendste, dass die Zeit bis zum Eintritt der Nacht ausgefüllt werden und dass unserem Gebete wie den anderen einige Bibelverse vorausgehen sollten." Plausible as this statement appears, it fails to explain why Ps 78: 38 in particular was selected for the purpose. Yehiel Zimmels, [4] after a careful study of the pertinent data, arrives at this conclusion: משמעו של פסוק זה הוא כעין בקשת סליחה בכלל ונטילת רשות לגשת אל ד׳ בתפלה ובתחנונים, ואינו בא דוקא לכפר על עון מיוחד. This would explain why והוא רחום is the opening verse of *Tahanun* for Mondays and Thursdays. In the first paragraph of this section of the service the worshipper voices an appeal for divine forgiveness of any sins he may have committed. [5] Zimmels' explanation, however, fails to account for the use of והוא רחום before ברכו, where תחנונים and a plea for pardon of sins are only remotely present. [6]

It can be demonstrated that the key to an understanding of the liturgical appropriateness of Ps 78: 38 outside the context of the Day of Atonement liturgy is to be found not in the words יכפר עון which it contains, but in the words והוא רחום, and in these words only. On the basis of the various sources adduced above, it has been observed that Ps 78: 38

[1] In his commentary in *Siddur Ozar ha-Tefillot* (Wilna 1914), vol. i, p. 533; *see also* the *Ez Yosef* commentary on pp. 533-534.

[2] *Op. cit.*, pp. 163-166.

[3] *Der jüdische Gottesdienst in seiner geschichtlichen Entwicklung*, 3rd ed. (Frankfurt a.M. 1931), p. 100.

[4] *Op. cit.*, p. 541. The aggadic interpretation of Ps 78: 38 in *Taanit* 8a which Zimmels cites on that page has no relevance to the liturgical use of that Psalm verse.

[5] *Seder Abodat Yisrael*, ed. S. Baer, p. 112.

[6] Not before the sixth benediction of the weekday *Amidah* is there a prayer for pardon and forgiveness of sins.

occupies a position at the commencement of a service or a section thereof. Apart from its occurrence prior to אשרי of the afternoon service and prior to ברכו of the evening service for weekdays as well as Sabbaths and festivals, it is also placed in juxtaposition to two of the principal parts of the morning service; namely, to אשרי which, together with the last five Psalms of the Psalter, constitutes the core of the *Pesuke de-Zimra*,[1] and to ברכו of the *Yozer* service. Similarly, where אשרי introduces the Musaf service, והוא רחום is likewise made to precede it.[2]

What possible significance could have been attached to והוא רחום, the opening words of Ps 78: 38, which gave this verse the status of a suitable introduction to both the afternoon and evening services and to two units of the morning worship, the *Pesuke de-Zimra* and the *Yozer* service? To begin with, Ps 78: 38 happens not to contain the Tetragrammaton, though the pronoun והוא manifestly refers to God. It is the absence of the Tetragrammaton which qualified this Psalm verse as a most appropriate prelude to worship. For, in the course of his devotions the worshipper has occasion repeatedly to invoke the name YHWH. Hence, before uttering his prayers, whether in praise of YHWH or in supplication to Him, Ps 78: 38, commencing with והוא רחום, serves as a forceful reminder to the worshipper that the name YHWH is expressive of the loving and compassionate aspect of God's character. Other names of the Deity occur in the various prayers, but Ps 78: 38 aims to stress the loving and compassionate side of God's nature as against the opposite side of His nature, that of a stern, austere and severe judge. The post-biblical concept of ד׳ as descriptive of מדת הרחמים and אלהים of מדת הדין[3] must have tacitly been assumed as the basis for the selection of Ps 78: 38.

[1] *Massekhet Soferim* 17. 11, ed. Higger, pp. 309-310, designates this group of Psalms as ששת המזמורים של כל יום.
[2] So in the Yemenite rite before Musaf of Rosh Hodesh. *See* the rubric in *Tiklal*, ed. Kapih, vol. i, p. 211.
[3] On this concept *see* A. Marmorstein, *The Old Rabbinic Doctrine of God* (London 1927), pp. 43-53.

Another point worth noting in this connection is the fact that not only the expression בקשת רחמים, but also רחמים standing alone, is, apart from its basic meaning of "mercy, love", also a synonym for prayer. Jastrow registers two striking illustrations:[1] אל ימנע עצמו מן הרחמים, "man must not despair of mercy", which is equivalent to "man must not cease to pray"; and שלשה צריכים רחמים, "three things must be prayed for".[2] If, accordingly, רחמים is but another term for prayer, then Ps 78: 38 with its opening words והוא רחום must have been deemed a fitting overture to the symphony of prayer which is conceived as רחמים. By means of this verse a feeling of assurance and confidence was instilled in the worshipper that his plea for divine mercy during prayer would not be in vain, directed as it is to God who is full of compassion.

That the determining factor in the selection of Ps 78: 38 for the commencement of a service or a principal part thereof was, except in the Day of Atonement liturgy, the phrase והוא רחום, and not יכפר עון, is evident also from a survey of the *Yozer* service. Central to this part of the liturgy is the Reading of the *Shema*, preceded by two benedictions and followed by one. Interwoven with the first benediction is a general appeal to divine mercy with no reference whatsoever to the pardon of sins: אלהי עולם ברחמיך הרבים רחם עלינו. Similarly, in the second benediction preceding the *Shema* there is a plea for God's mercy not in connection with forgiveness of sins, but in connection with the theme of the benediction. Thus, the words "O our Father, merciful Father, ever compassionate, have mercy upon us" are followed directly by "O put it into our hearts to understand and to discern, to mark, learn, and teach, to heed, to do and to fulfil in love all the words of instruction in Thy Torah." As for the benediction following the *Shema*, though an appeal

---

[1] Jastrow, *A Dictionary of the Targumim etc.*, p. 1468.
[2] Jastrow, *ibid.*, also refers to *Mishnah Abot* 2: 18: אל תעש תפלתך קבע אלא רחמים.

to God's compassion is lacking in the Ashkenazic rite, it is
an integral part of this benediction in Siddur R. Saadiah
where we read: חוס ורחם עלינו ברחמיך הרבים כי אל רחום וחנון.
This reference to divine compassion, too, is in conjunction
with the theme of the benediction which is Israel's complete
redemption and total deliverance. [1] So much for the morning
service. As regards the evening service, the Ashkenazic rite
contains no reference to God's compassion in the benedictions
preceding and following the Reading of the *Shema*. Traces
are not wanting, however, of a plea for God's compassion
in the evening service as well. [2]

In the light of the foregoing observations it is clear that
an appeal to a loving and compassionate God can be independent of a plea for divine pardon of sins. Part of the very
pattern of the *Yozer* service as presently constituted is an
appeal to the love and compassion of God in direct connection
with the particular theme of a prayer, such as devotion to
Torah or the hope for Israel's complete redemption; in which
case, the suitability of Ps 78:38 as a prelude to the *Yozer*
service is greatly enhanced. Its opening phrase והוא רחום
conforms perfectly to the pattern of worship, an integral
element of which is the reliance of the worshipper upon divine
love and compassion.

To conclude this study, an analysis will now be made of
the miscellany of verses appended to הודו (I Chron 16: 8-36),
of which Ps 78: 38 is a part. [3] Elbogen has made the following
observation with regard to miscellanies of verses in general: [4]
"All diese Sammlungen von Bibelstellen haben gemeinsam,

---

[1] *See* N. Wieder in *Saadya Studies*, ed. E. I. J. Rosenthal (Manchester 1943), p. 275, in conjunction with *Siddur R. Saadiah*, p. 16,
lines 19-20.

[2] See *Seder R. Amram*, ed. Warsaw, vol. i, 19a above; ed.
Frumkin, vol. i, p. 382, note 9 in the variant readings.

[3] I have dealt elsewhere with the role of Ps 78: 38 in ובא לציון.
See my "An Analysis of *U-Ba le-Ziyyon* in the Liturgy", *HUCA*,
vol. xxi (1948) pp. 176-209.

[4] Elbogen, *op. cit.*, p. 273.

dass sie lose aneinandergereiht sind, ohne jeden gedanklichen Zusammenhang und ohne jeden Übergang, meist sind es nur äussere Kennzeichen, wie gemeinsame Worte, welche die Verbinding herstellen." And with particular reference to the miscellany of verses attached to הודו Elbogen states: [1] "…. הודו לד' I Chron 16: 8-35…. an den eine beträchtliche Anzahl Bibelverse angeschlossen wurde, die heute zum Teil planlos scheinen, aber einst sicher ebenfalls nach einem bestimmten Plane und Zusammenhange angeordnet waren." [2] Unless, therefore, the key to the selection of miscellaneous verses is discovered, the miscellany following הודו appears on the surface as nothing but a hodge-podge, quite planless, loosely arranged, and with no attempt at any sort of thought sequence.

In the course of our discussion of Ps 78: 38 it was pointed out that the recital of this verse was designed to underscore the divine attribute of love and mercy, reflected in the name YHWH, in contradistinction to the divine attribute of justice, underlying the word אלהים. Beneath the surface of the miscellany of verses attached to הודו [3] is the rabbinic concept of מדת הרחמים and מדת הדין as expressed respectively by the two names of the Deity, YHWH and *Elohim*. [4] With this in mind, let us examine this mosaic of Psalm verses. [5] It commences with Ps 99: 5, 9, two verses which serve as a call to laud and exalt the Lord. It is important to observe

---

[1] *Op. cit.*, p. 272.

[2] *Cf.* the comment on this miscellany of verses following הודו by Menahem Mendel Landa, *Wa-Yaas Abraham* (Lodz 1936), p. 194: אין סדר וחיבור לפסוקים הללו המלוקטים

[3] On the phenomenon of placing a group of verses from the Psalms after a passage from the Book of Chronicles, in this instance I Chron 16: 8-36, *see* my observation in *HUCA*, vol. xxi (1948), pp. 186-187.

[4] In another connection the writer has demonstrated how the talmudic הזכרת השם and מלכות in relation to a ברכה (*Berakot* 12a, 40b) have influenced the compilation of the *Pesuke de-Zimra*. See *PAAJR*, vol. xviii (1948-49), 255-267.

[5] Its form is identical in the Ashkenazic, Sefardi and Yemenite rites.

that they contain the words ה' אלהינו, since the (threefold) occurrence of these two words suggested to the compiler's mind that 'ה has reference to מדת הרחמים and אלהינו to מדת הדין. This is crystal-clear from the type of verses he next proceeded to select, namely, Pss 78: 38, 40: 12 and 25: 6 belonging to the category of מדת הרחמים and Pss 68:35, 36 and 94: 1, 2 belonging to the category of מדת הדין. Once again we observe that Ps 78: 38 in which the Tetragrammaton is lacking, but which opens with והוא רחום, serves to introduce Ps 40: 12 which contains אתה ה' לא תכלא רחמיך ממני and Ps 25: 6 which contains זכר רחמיך ה'. On the מדת הדין side, Ps 68: 35, 36, verses without the Tetragrammaton but with the threefold occurrence of אלהים, introduce Ps 94: 1, 2 which, though containing the Tetragrammaton, speak of the Lord as שופט הארץ. The insertion of Pss 68: 35, 36 and 94: 1, 2 leaves no doubt that מדת הדין was part of the plan in the arrangement of verses.

The verses selected up to this point summon the worshipper to laud God whose two outstanding attributes are compassion and justice. At this juncture a transition is effected to the petitionary part of the collection of verses. The God of love and justice possesses the power of granting help, protection and deliverance (Ps 3: 9: לה' הישועה; Ps 46: 8: משגב לנו). The worshipper, accordingly, turns to the Dispenser of help and deliverance in supplication for the attainment of these blessings (Ps 20: 10, 28: 9). The Psalm verse 84: 13 is introduced for the simple reason that, like Ps 46: 8 before it, it commences with ה' צבאות. [1] Not only is the worshipper aware of the divine capacity to render help and deliverance, but he is also full of trust that God will manifest that capacity to him by virtue of His love and compassion. This thought is conveyed in Pss 33: 20-22, 85: 8 and 44: 27. The appeal here is to God's חסד, a parallel to רחמים in the earlier verses of the miscellany (Pss 40: 12 and 25: 6).

[1]   Moreover, according to *Yerushalmi Berakhot* 8d, Pss 46: 8 and 84: 13 were favorite verses.

Pss 81: 11, 144: 15 and 13: 6, in the order given, constitute the conclusion of the collection of verses. Toward the close of his group of verses, it would appear that the compiler's purpose was to end as he began, that is, to insert two verses in which both 'ה and אלהים occur. Hence Ps 81: 11 with its אנכי ה' אלהיך and Ps 144: 15 with its העם שה' אלהיו.[1] The final verse (Ps 13: 6) repeats the worshipper's perfect trust in God's love and his joy in the bright prospect of help and deliverance.

That an element of artificiality inheres in the process of grouping together scattered biblical verses cannot be denied. Nevertheless, when some basic principle is applied, as in the case of the mosaic of verses joined to הודו, the resultant compilation yields sense despite its heterogeneity. In so far as Ps 78: 38 is concerned, the group of verses following הודו furnishes added proof of its use in a context with emphasis upon divine love and compassion, irrespective of pardon of sins.

---

[1]　The author of *Wa-Yaas Abraham* (*see* above, p. 8, note 2) is baffled by the insertion of Ps 81: 11 with its reference to God as Liberator of Israel from Egyptian bondage. On p. 195 he states: פסוק זה אין לו שייכות לכאן. But apart from its being a verse in which both YHWH and *Elohim* occur, this verse was most appropriate if it be recalled that הודו and its accompanying miscellany of verses were originally intended for Sabbath only. And the Sabbath, of course, is a זכר ליציאת מצרים. *See* my "Ha-Shabbat be-Siddur ha-Tefillah", in *Sefer Ha-Yobel shel Hadoar* (New York 1952), p. 259. The Yemenites to this day reserve the recitation of הודו with its miscellany of verses for Sabbaths. See *Tiklal* (Jerusalem 1894), vol. i, 118b-121a; or ed. Kapih, vol. i, pp. 136-138.

THE TRIBAL SYSTEM OF ISRAEL AND RELATED GROUPS IN THE PERIOD OF THE JUDGES *

By HARRY M. ORLINSKY

Hebrew Union College-Jewish Institute of Religion, New York

DURING THE PAST QUARTER of a century, largely due to the writings of Albrecht Alt and especially of Martin Noth in Europe, and, following them, of W. F. Albright on this side of the ocean, it has become all but axiomatic in the reconstruction of the period of the Judges in ancient Israel (Early Iron Age, about 1200-1000 B.C.E.) that the tribes of Israel constituted in that period an amphictyony, a confederacy of tribes established at and bound together by a central religious shrine.

In his well-known monograph on *Der Gott der Väter* (1929), Alt made passing reference to amphictyony in early Israel. [1] A year later Alt's outstanding disciple, Noth, published in

---

* The essence of this paper was read at the 166th meeting of the American Oriental Society, Baltimore, April 10, 1956.

[1] On p. 59 Alt speaks of the unanswered "Frage, welche Gruppe der Amphiktionen von Mamre den Kultus des Gottes Abrahams in das gemeinsame Heiligtum eingeführt hat . . ." The monograph constitutes Heft 48 (Dritte Folge, Heft 12) in the series *Beiträge zur Wissenschaft vom Alten und Neuen Testament* (*BWANT*); reprinted in A. Alt, *Kleine Schriften zur Geschichte des Volkes Israel* (= *KS*), 3 vols (München 1953 and 1959), vol. i, pp. 1-78. *See also* Alt, *Die Landnahme der Israeliten in Palästina* (Leipzig 1925; = *KS*, vol. i, pp. 89-125); *idem*, *Die Staatenbildung der Israeliten in Palästina* (Leipzig 1930; = *KS*, vol. ii, pp. 1-65); and the article, "Israel, politische Geschichte," in *Die Religion in Geschichte und Gegenwart*, ed. H. Gunkel and L. Zscharnack, vol. iii (1929), cols. 437 f. Alt owed this theory directly to Max Weber, noted sociologist; *cf.* his *Gesammelte Aufsätze zur Religionssoziologie*, vol. 3 (Tübingen 1921), pp. 86 ff.; or his *Ancient Judaism*, translated and edited by H. H. Gerth and D. Martindale (Glencoe, Ill., 1952), pp. 77 ff. Weber seems to have been the first to connect the Judges period, as distinct from the patriarchal period, with amphictyony.

considerable detail his reconstruction of *Das System der Zwölf Stämme Israels*, [1] which included amphictyonic data from the regions of Greece and Italy. A decade later, in his volumes *From the Stone Age to Christianity* (1940) and *Archaeology and the Religion of Israel* (1942), [2] Albright asserted his acceptance of this idea, and many scholars have followed suit. [3]

[1]   Heft 52 in *BWANT*; and *cf.* his *The History of Israel* (New York 1958), ch. iii, pp. 85 ff. In the older literature, inspired by Greek example, scholars such as H. Ewald (*Einleitung in die Geschichte des Volkes Israel*, [3] [Göttingen 1864], vol. i, "Die zwölf Söhne und Stämme Jaqob's," pp. 519 ff.; English translation by R. Martineau, *The History of Israel*, vol. i [1883], pp. 362-85), made much of the number 12 (and 6; and multiples of 12, *e.g.*, 24, 48) —as though this number or its multiples pointed to amphictyony; one could relate similarly most of the unrelated peoples of the world because of their common use of the twelve-month solar-system. Among those who followed Ewald—the patriarchal period alone was involved—were H. Gunkel, *Genesis* [3] (1910), p. 332 ("gewiss sehr plausibel"), who had recourse also to the work of E. Szanto, "Die griechischen Phylen," in *Sitzungsberichte der Wiener Akademie, phil.-hist. Klasse*, vol. CXLIV (1901), v. Abhandlung, pp. 40 ff. Apparently independently of Ewald, A. H. Sayce, "The Cuneiform Tablets of Tel El-Amarna, now Preserved in the Boulaq Museum," in *Proceedings of the Society of Biblical Archaeology*, vol. xi (1888-89), 326-413, had observed (p. 347), "In all probability the name of Hebron was derived from the 'confederacy' of the three or four nations (Hittites, Amorites, and Canaanites) who met around its great sanctuary, which accounts for the absence of the name in the Egyptian geographical lists."

[2]   P. 215 in the former, pp. 102-5, 108 in the latter. In the meantime, several other scholars had adopted amphictyony for Israel in the period of the Judges, *e.g.*, T. J. Meek, *Hebrew Origins* (New York 1936 and 1950), pp. 25 f., 116, and passim (*see* Index, s. "Confederacy") H. S. Nyberg, "Studien zum Religionskampf im A.T.," *Archiv für Religionswissenschaft*, vol. 35 (1938), p. 367; K. Möhlenbrink, "Die Landnahmesagen des Buches Josua," *ZAW*, vol. 15 (1938), 238-268.

[3]   *Cf.*, *e.g.*, Danell, *Studies in the Name Israel in the O.T.* (Upsala 1946), p. 46 (with reference to Noth); S. Mowinckel, *Zur Frage nach dokumentarischen Quellen in Josua* 13-19 (Oslo 1946) pp. 20 ff. (who argues for a pre-Davidic ten-tribe amphictyony); L. H. Grollenberg, *Atlas of the Bible* (New York 1956), 57b; B. W. Anderson, "The Place of Shechem in the Bible," *Bib. Arch.*, vol. 20, no. 1 (1957), 13 f. Especially is this true of Albright's students, *e.g.*, G. E. Wright (-F. V. Filson) in *Westminster Historial Atlas to the Bible* (Philadelphia 1945 and 1957), p. 44b and *Biblical Archaeology* (Philadelphia 1957), pp. 87 f. (although Wright does not seem to employ the term "amphic-

In *Ancient Israel* (Ithaca 1954), I wrote (pp. 58 f.), "Except for occasional brief emergency alliances, the Israelite tribes maintained complete autonomy during the Period of the Judges and recognized no central capital or shrine for all Israel . . ." Limitation of space prevented there elaborate defense of this anti-amphictyonic position; this article is meant to make good that lack.

The most important single source for our problem and period is still the book of Judges. In reading this book carefully, one is struck time and again by several outstanding facts, which together help to make up a pretty clear and consistent pattern of tribal affiliation—or the lack of it. The facts are these. The "Judges" (Hebrew *shōphetīm*) were individual men who exhibited unusual military or physical prowess in time of dire circumstances for their kinfolk, leading them in victory over threatening non-Israelite invaders or in overthrowing the yoke of an enemy. [1] Ehud of

tyony"); Jacob B. Myers, *The Book of Judges* (in *The Interpreter's Bible*, vol. ii, 1953), 685a; John Bright, *Early Israel in Recent History Writing* (= *Studies in Biblical Theology*, No. 19, London 1956), p. 84, "That the Israelite amphictyony with its Yahwistic faith was a going concern in the period of the Judges is, of course, beyond question . . ."; *A History of Israel* (Philadelphia 1959), pp. 142 ff. The only outspoken opponent of amphictyony in Israel was Yehezkel Kaufmann, whose reconstruction of Israel's early history precluded this structure; *cf.* his *Toledot ha-Emunah ha-Yisreelit* (Tel Aviv 1937-ff.), vol. iv, n. 60 on pp. 399 f.; or *cf.* pp. 256-8 of M. Greenberg's one-volume abridgment and translation entitled *The Religion of Israel* (Chicago 1960).

[1] It has now become a commonplace to attribute the quality of charisma to these "Judges"; it is doubtful that even Max Weber ever imagined to what extent this concept of his would be exploited by subsequent generations of scholars, so that, *e.g.*, Roger T. O'Callaghan, *Aram Naharaim* (*Analecta Orientalia* 26 [Rome 1948]), p. 122, following his mentor Albright (*From the Stone Age*, etc., p. 216), who followed Alt (especially his monograph on *Die Staatenbildung der Israeliten in Palästina*; *cf.* in n. 1, p. 1, above, = *KS*, vol. ii, pp. 1-65), who followed Weber (*see* his *Essays in Sociology*, translated, edited, and with an introduction by H. H. Gerth and C. Wright Mills [New York 1946], Index, s. "charisma" and "charismatic authority" (pp. 471 f.); *Ancient Judaism* (n. 1 above), Glossary and Index, s. "charisma," p. 465), would help explain the phenomenon in the Early Iron Age

the tribe of Benjamin, Shamgar ben Anath, and Jephthah the son of a prostitute are cases in point. These military chieftains, brought into being by foreign pressures—never in peaceful times by domestic, inner-Israelite need—were not associated with any shrines. [1] And none of them was an amphictyon. [2]

from its use in the New Testament over a millennium later. Actually, it is most doubtful that the concept was part of Israel's religious outlook in the period of the Judges. When a man such as Jephthah the bastard demonstrated military acumen, or when Ehud assassinated Eglon king of Moab, people turned to them for leadership. No one recognized "the direct outpouring of divine grace" in anyone prior to an act of military or similar significance. It clarifies nothing to introduce the concept and term "charisma" from postbiblical times and read it back into a period over one thousand years and many civilizations and social structures earlier.

[1]   It is idle to compare—as everyone has long been doing (*cf.*, *e.g.*, Albright, *From the Stone Age*. etc., 216)—our *shōpheṭ* with later Carthaginian *suf(f)ete(s)* (*see* the Glossary in Z. S. Harris, *A Grammar of the Phoenician Language* [New Haven 1936], p. 153) so far as function and meaning are concerned; they are about a thousand years apart in time, and the historical circumstances and social structures were different. There is no evidence in the book of Judges that these "Judges" had anything to do with legal adjudication, for then it would have been internal, inner-Israelite needs that brought them into being. It was throughout external, military circumstances that created "Judges," and their function was to deliver (*hōshīʿa*) from the enemy the Israelites who were affected; then they "judged" (*shaphetū*), *i.e.*, ruled as chieftains, those whom they had militarily delivered, *cf.*, *e.g.*, the use of *shāphaṭ* in the tribes' demand to Samuel (1 Sam 8: 5-6), *śīmāh/tenāh lānū melek le-shāphṭēnū*, "Set up for us (Give us) a king to rule us," with the climax being reached in vv. 19-20, where "The people refused to listen to Samuel and said, '. . . We too will be like the other nations: let our king rule us (*ū-shephāṭānū malkēnū*), going out at our head and fighting our battles.'" And the *mishpāṭ* of the king (vv. 9, 11 ff.) has, of course, nothing to do with legal adjudication but with ruling and taxing the people with absolute power; the people needed and wanted a military leader against their external enemies, not a legal arbiter for themselves. (On Samuel—and his two sons—as judge rather than seer/prophet [8: 1 ff.] as being due to later, Deuteronomic editorializing, *see* S. R. Driver, *An Introduction to the Literature of the O.T.* [1913 edition], pp. 175 ff. Otto Eissfeldt, *Einleitung in das A.T.*[2] [1956], pp. 323 ff., argues differently.)

It may be noted here that with all the confusion in his treatment of the *shōpheṭīm* and charisma, Weber yet asserted (*Ancient Judaism*, p. 86), ". . . politico-military decisions, not legal decisions or wisdom,

It is significant, further, that no amphictyonic league ever
met at a shrine to decide a course of action or to pick a
"Judge." [1] One will go through all twenty-one chapters of
the book of Judges and fail to find mention of Shiloh, or
Shechem, or Bethel, or Ramah, or Beth-shean, or Gilgal,
or any other shrine, at which a confederacy of two, or six,
or twelve, or any number of tribes met as an amphictyony. [2]
This is an outstanding anomalous phenomenon in the midst

were the specific function of charismatic *shofetim*." As to how and
when the term *shōphet* in the Bible came to mean "adjudicate, ad-
judge"—that is a separate problem to be solved.

[2]   Significantly, there is no term in the Bible for "amphictyon,"
any more than for "amphictyony" or "charisma." As for the term
nāśīʾ (*cf. e.g.*, Noth, *Das System*, etc., Exkurs III, "Gebrauch und
Bedeutung des Wortes *nāśīʾ*," pp. 151-162; whence, *e.g.*, Bright,
op. cit., p. 98), it is indeed noteworthy that nowhere in the book that
is alleged to have sprung from an emphictyonic society, viz, the book
of Judges, is the term *nāśīʾ* found. And if *wa-yehī/wat-tiṣlaḥ rūaḥ
ʾelōhīm/YHWH* (*e.g.*, Jud 3: 10 Othniel; 14: 6 Samson) is interpreted
as denoting "charisma" (*cf., e.g.*, Bright, *op. cit.*, p. 144), then not
only does charisma become the property of many unlikely people in
the Bible (*cf.* Mandelkern's *Concordance*, s. *ruᵘḥ*) but the persons
generally designated as amphictyons, viz., the *nesīʾīm*, are the very
ones into whom the *rūaḥ* of God was never said to have entered.

[1]   Let those who believe that twelfth eleventh century B.C.E.
Israel operated with the concept of charisma ponder over this fact:
why, if a *shōphet* was chosen because God's divine grace was recognized
in him, did not the people perform the formal choosing of the leader
at God's shrine? Incidentally, when God's "spirit" is said to have
come over a man, he proceeded to go into action as a deliverer of his
oppressed people (*e.g.*, Gideon, Jephthah, Samson, Saul); but nowhere
does the text say that the people made that man a leader because
they recognized in him something of the divine. It would seem that
"charisma" and "amphictyony" are among several other concepts of
nineteenth-early twentieth century sociology that require thoroughly
fresh study.

[2]   Numerous scholars have assumed or argued for amphictyonies
of varying numbers of tribes in different periods at different centers:
cf., e.g., H. H. Rowley, *From Joseph to Joshua*, etc. (London 1950;
The Schweich Lectures of the British Academy, 1948), pp. 125 ff.
and the notes *ibid*. Thus Möhlenbrink (pp. 246 ff., *see* p. 2, n. 2 above)
argues for a "Dreistämme-amphiktyonie" involving Benjamin,
Reuben, and Gad. But the data are too glaringly inadequate to be
overcome by scientific methodology, let alone by "scholarly guessing."

of an allegedly existing amphictyony, or of several smaller amphictyonies. [1] Thus Shechem is mentioned but once in the entire book of Judges, in chapter 9, and it would have gone unmentioned altogether had not its Israelite inhabitants set up there a shrine to the non-Israelite—or perhaps in this region and period, semi-Israelite— god Baal-berith, and had not Abimelech, one of the many offspring of Gideon, tried to become ruler of the area. Nothing amphictyonic appears in the entire chapter of fifty-seven verses. [2]

Again, in chapters 19-21, when some riffraff (*bene belīya'al* is the Hebrew term, 19: 22) in Benjaminite Gibeah raped and caused the death of a Levite's concubine, so that in the blood-feud that ensued the entire tribe of Benjamin was subjected to revenge and ostracization, it is to Mizpah that the avengers came to take counsel against the Benjaminites.

---

[1]　There is a serious methodological error (*cf.* most recently Bright, p. 94) in assuming the existence of an amphictyonic league almost whenever and wherever a biblical book records the existence of a shrine. Shechem, Shiloh, Bethel, Gilgal, Kadesh—all were shrines in the twelfth-eleventh centuries; what does that prove for amphictyony? All these sites were shrines in Canaanite, pre-Israelite times; did amphictyony obtain in Canaanite society? Note may also be made here of the attempt to prove amphictyony, in this case "centered about a sanctuary located at Shiloh," by the assertion that "archaeological evidence tends to support the biblical impression" and the footnote, "See Hans Kjaer, 'The Excavations of Shilo 1929,' *JPOS*, X (1929), 87-174" (Myers; *see* p. 2, n. 3 above). I fail to see how the dig at Shiloh demonstrates amphictyony.

[2]　Yet Shechem has frequently been identified as the shrine around which the Israelite emphictyony revolved (cf., *e.g.*, Noth, *The History of Israel*, pp. 91 ff.; Bright, *A History of Israel*, pp. 147 ff.). Small wonder that this viewpoint has had to be defended by assuming and asserting that there were originally many references to Shechem (or Shiloh, or Bethel, or Gilgal, or Kadesh, etc.) as an amphictyonic center and that they were suppressed or excised from the biblical text; cf., *e.g.*, Hans-Joachim Kraus, "Gilgal, ein Beitrag zur Kultusgeschichte Israels," *VT*, vol. i (1951), 181-199, where Gilgal as the central shrine of an amphictyony is discussed; or, more recently, J. Dus, "Gibeon—eine Kultstätte des Šmš und die Stadt des benjaminitischen Schicksals," *ibid.*, vol. x, (1960), 353-374. On the other hand, if there were no amphictyony, there was nothing amphictyonic to suppress or excise.

A parallel, or supplementary, version has it that on the way
to Gibeah—the geography here is not certain at all—the
Israelites stopped off at Bethel to inquire of God as to which
tribe should lead them in battle against Benjamin, and the
reply was: Judah. The incidental statement is made there
(20: 27) that "the Ark of the Covenant of the LORD was
stationed there in Bethel in those days"; even if this were
so, and Shiloh was bereft of the Ark at the time, it is significant that Mizpah, and not Bethel, or Shiloh, is where the
Israelite consultation took place. [1]

One final instance, though the book of Judges readily
supplies several more. When the very critical struggle for
existence had to be mounted against the Canaanite forces
under Sisera, neither the poetic nor the prose version of this
crucial event, in chapters 4-5 of Judges, makes mention of
any central shrine, any religious focus, to which the Israelite
tribes gathered for amphictyonic consideration. [2] And so it

[1]   Another unanswered question created by the "amphictyonists"
involves this very incident. On the one hand it is stated, "In all
probability the divine throne of the sacred ark formed the centre
of worship . . ." (Noth, *op. cit.*, p. 91; *cf.* Bright, p. 146, "The focal
point of the amphictyony throughout its history was the shrine housing
the Ark of the Covenant, the throne of the Invisible Yahweh...."),
and on the other (Noth, *op. cit.*, p. 94, n. 3), "The meeting place of
the tribes in this story was Mizpeh (Judges 20: 1 ff.), and the only
[*sic*] part that Bethel plays in it is as the site of the Ark." But—as the
Talmud would put it—*mim-mah nafshak* ("whichever position you
take"): if the Ark "made" the amphictyony, then why was Bethel
ignored; and if the Ark played no such role, then what "made" the
amphictyony?

[2]   There would seem to be no justification for the assertion, "It is
clear from the Song of Deborah (Jud ch. 5) that the amphictyony
was in full operation in the twelfth century" (Bright, *op. cit.*, p. 145;
or *cf.* p. 144 on "the call to arms . . ."). In what verse is the amphictyonic shrine mentioned? And where was the Ark?

As for the fact that those tribal groups that did not bother to come
to "the help of the Lord" were cursed (v. 23), how does this point to
amphictyony? At what shrine were they cursed? Bright's note to
this (p. 144, n. 37), ". . . The Hittite treaties discussed above required
the vassal to respond to the call to arms," has no bearing on the problem of amphictyony. Does this aspect of the Hittite treaties indicate
amphictyony among the Hittites?

should come as no surprise when an objective reading of the book of Judges gives expression, more than once, to the statement that the period of the Judges was one in which there was no central authority in the land, and when each Israelite group did whatever it wished, without recourse to any central authority, religious or political. The Hebrew expression is: בַּיָּמִים הָהֵם אֵין מֶלֶךְ בְּיִשְׂרָאֵל אִישׁ אֲשֶׁר בְּעֵינָיו יַעֲשֶׂה (17: 6; 21: 25; in 18: 1 only the first half of this expression is employed).

It is far from unlikely that this very situation obtained also in Transjordan, among the Ammonites, Moabites, and Edomites. It is true that prevailing opinion has it, largely since Alt's monograph appeared in 1930 on *Die Staatenbildung der Israeliten in Palästina*, that "the surrounding nations were all highly organized. Edomites, Moabites, and Ammonites all had kings who were much more than tribal emirs ..." (Albright, *From the Stone Age*, etc., p. 221). Yet the evidence for this opinion is scarcely evident.

So far as the book of Judges is concerned, a contrary picture is clearly portrayed. Thus in Chapter 3 we are told that "Eglon king of Moab ... gathered to himself the Ammonites and Amalek, and went and defeated Israel, and occupied the city of Palms. And the Israelites served Eglon king of Moab eighteen years" (vv. 12-14). One may well wonder how highly organized, let alone powerful, was the land of Moab and Ammon, not to mention the elusive Amalekites, if it took the combined efforts of these three to subdue a portion of Israel, and if less than two decades later this part of Israel, under Ehud, was able to evict the conquerors.

It is, furthermore, in this very period and general region that the Midianites were able to conquer a part of Israel for seven years (chapters 6-9), at the end of which period the Israelites of three tribes, Naphtali, Asher, and Manasseh, under the leadership of Gideon, drove out the Midianites from western Jordan, chased them across the Jordan into Ammonite territory, and destroyed the backbone of their organization forever. Regardless of how the details became embellished and garbled in the retelling of the event, and even if we do not include "the Amalekites and all the Qedemites" that the preserved Hebrew text mentions (6: 33; 7: 12; 8: 10), it is not quite a highly organized Ammonite government that manifests itself in these chapters; rather do we get a picture of a considerable territory, rather sparsely settled, over which no one group had control. It is these very Ammonites that Jephthah is able to reduce with the help of but a few of the Israelite tribes (chapter 11). Clearly, we must be dealing here with but relatively small and essentially independent groups of Ammonites, Midianites, Israelites, Moabites, and the like, each led by a local chieftain. There is no hint of anything highly organized, of anything amphictyonic, of any kind of centralized authority, of any central shrine, on either side of the Jordan.

This picture, as the book of Judges appears to reflect it, seems likewise to be the very one that chapter 36 in Genesis and the archaeological data of Transjordan point to. In verses 31-39 of this well-known chapter we are given a list of "kings who reigned in the land of Edom before any king of the Israelites reigned." The number of kings listed is eight, and in all instances but two the city of his origin is given. Significantly, in not one single instance is a ruler succeeded by his son or by anyone from his own town. Not one of the six cities mentioned (Dinhabah; Bozrah; Awith; Masrekah; Rehoboth-on-the-river; and Pau. Husham came from "the land of the Temanites," and Baal-hanan's city is not given) ever became known as a "great central shrine," not even the best known of them, Bozrah. And nothing dynastic, or anything approximating centralized rule of monarchy, can be derived from this passage. On the contrary, the picture of Edom given here, in the period prior to King Saul (or, rather, David and Solomon), is exactly that of Israel itself during the period of the Judges, prior to the rise of centralized authority under the monarchy—one of petty chieftains, local military leaders, some of the rulers not unlikely ruling contemporaneously in different regions of the land. The fact that the biblical text refers to Edom's chieftains as *melākīm* should not impel the reader to jump to the conclusion that "king" in the classical sense is meant, any more than biblical *shōphetīm* in the book of Judges means "judges" in the classical sense. [1]

Transjordan, as is well known, has been combed topographically very well by Nelson Glueck. [2] There are hardly any places of significance that remained untouched by him. The data compiled by him shed much light on the clear picture drawn in the Bible. Nothing that I have been able to determine would suggest a centrally organized government in any of the Transjordanian countries during the period of the Judges. I am aware that for Moab evidence was drawn from two extra-biblical sources, "the Balu'ah stela of the twelfth century and the Mesha Stone of the ninth . . ." [3]

The Mesha Stone, it is everywhere recognized, is of very considerable importance for conditions in Moab, but—and this is a very great "but"—for the ninth century. It is fine supplementary material for the biblical book of Kings; but its significance for our own problem in the twelfth and eleventh centuries, the period of Israel's "Judges," is all too little. It is like using the biblical book of Kings—in the absence of the book of Judges—to prove that Israel was a monarchy

[1]   G. E. Wright's recent observation (n. 5 on pp. 43 f. of his article on "Archaeology and Old Testament Studies," *JBL*, vol. 77 (1958), 39-51), referred to favorably by Bright (p. 135, n. 21), is pertinent here, ". . . the rare use of the term 'king' for God in Israel's earliest tradition should not necessarily be taken to mean that he was not presented in monarchical form . . . 'king' (*melek*) in that particular Palestinian environment meant the local princeling of a comparatively small city-state, one among many . . ."

[2]   *Cf., e.g., The Other Side of the Jordan* (New Haven 1940), chap. v, "Edom, Moab, Ammon, and Gilead," pp. 114 ff., based upon the kind of material incorporated in his *Explorations in Eastern Palestine* (vols. 14, 15, and 18-19 of the *Annual of the American Schools of Oriental Research*) and related publications.

[3]   Albright, *From the Stone Age*, etc., p. 221.

and had centralized government in the earliest phase of the Early Iron Age!

As for the Balu'ah stele, it may be that it is in orgin a twenty-third century or so B.C.E. product that was reused in the twelfth or eleventh century B.C.E. [1] The inscription on it, however, can no longer be read, the surface is worn so smooth. [2] As to how the Egyptianizing relief on the stone representing deities can point to centrally organized government in Moab, I do not know; surely similar reliefs carved on steles from other places in Syria, Phoenicia, and Palestine [3] do not indicate this political setup.

When we look back upon the nature of Israel's conquest of Canaan and the manner in which the Israelites worked out their *modus vivendi* after that, one may wonder how the concept of "amphictyony" occurred to anyone in the first place. There is nothing amphictyonic about the structure of Canaanite society before or during the period of Israel's Judges. The city-states of Phoenicia, of the Philistines in Canaan, of the Arameans north and east of Israel, did not constitute amphictyonies. There was nothing in this period in this area to influence Israel in this direction. [4]

Rather are we reminded of the Mari document cited by Albrecht Goetze [5] in which "one of the correspondents of

[1]   *Idem, Archaeology and the Religion of Israel* (Baltimore 1942), p. 189, n. 53.

[2]   Glueck, *The Other Side*, etc., p. 126, described the stele as follows, "One thinks also of the famous stele found at Baluah near the Wadi Mojib, assigned to the 12th century B.C., whose worn lines of inscription can unfortunately no longer be read (Fig. 66)."

[3]   *Cf.* Albright, *op. cit.*, p. 43.

[4]   Thus most recently Noth, *The History of Israel* (in dealing with "The Life of Ancient Israel in the Palestinian-Syrian World: I. The Self-Assertion of the Tribes in Palestine, § 12, Their Connections with the Earlier Inhabitants of the Land"), pp. 141 ff., makes mention *passim* of the "Canaanite city-state system." Or *cf.*, *e.g.*, Bright (pp. 109 f.), "Canaan was politically without identity ... Palestine was a patchwork of (petty) states, none of any great size ..."

[5]   On pp. 119 f. of his Presidential address, "Mesopotamian Laws and the Historian", *JAOS*, vol. 69 (1949), 115-120; the Mari Document had appeared in *Syria*, 19 (1938), 117 f.

the king of Mari writes his master . . . 'There is no king who is powerful on his own. Ten to fifteen kings follow after Hammurapi, the king of Babylon, a like number after Rim-Sin, the king of Larsa, a like number after Ibal-pi-el the king of Eshnunna, a like number after Amut-pi-el, the king of Qatanum, but after Yarim-lim, the king of Yamkhat, there follow twenty kings.' The[se] few lines describe admirably the political system before Hammurapi united Mesopotamia; it consisted chiefly of shifting coalitions of small kings and sheikhs . . . It was the same from the Persian Gulf to the Mediterranean and the borders of Palestine . . .'' Substitute David and Solomon, or Mesha, for Hammurabi, and the pattern in Israel and Moab, after consolidation of the conquest and cutting up of Canaan's land empire, is strikingly similar.

Interestingly, it may well be that the early Israelite conception of God provides additional proof that nothing amphictyonic obtained in their societal structure. Already in the patriarchal period the Deity was not localized. He accompanied the patriarchal household in its seminomadic wanderings, and made and renewed covenants with them in several different places. In the period of the Judges the Deity was worshiped in a large number of places. Shrines were plentifully scattered in virtually every populated site, and it is likely that but few persons had to cross tribal boundaries to offer up sacrifice and prayer to God. Amphictyony, a centralized shrine and cult, is scarcely part of this concept or need. And that must be one of the reasons why various rulers, most notably Josiah, failed to destroy the numerous independent shrines all over the country. None of Jerusalem —for a very long time—or Tirzah, or Bethel, or Samaria, or Shechem, or Shiloh, or any other capital or shrine, could achieve this kind of centralized authority. God could be, and always was, worshipped everywhere.

To sum up. Israel in the period of the Judges consisted of tribes and city-states that shared much in religious belief and practice and that spoke the same language; but their economic and geographical conditions, their disposition to commerce rather than to agriculture, the extent to which they were exposed to invasion and even conquest of varying might and duration—these were the factors that determined the actions of the tribes. The tribes and city-states came, or neglected to come, to each other's assistance insofar as they were, or were not, threatened seriously by the invading force. The concept and structure of amphictyony existed in Israel no more than it did in Transjordan or anywhere else in western Asia at the time.

[After completion of this study, there came to hand William W. Hallo's article on "A Sumerian Amphictyony," *Journal of Cuneiform Studies*, vol. xiv (October 1960), 88 ff. It would seem that the political structure of this phase of Ur III is to be compared with the Solomonic period in Israel, when (according to 1 Kings 4: 7-5: 8; *cf.*, e.g., J. A. Montgomery (-H. S. Gehman), *ICC on Kings* (1951), 119-128, with full bibliography) the national government imposed upon each of twelve *neṣîbîm* "governors" or the like) in turn monthly dues for the upkeep of the royal household (including probably the national religious center) in Jerusalem. The use of the number "twelve" here, or in Hallo's Sumerian data, or in the case of Esau's *'allufs* in Gen: 36, ought not, as such, call to mind the amphictyonic structure of Greece many centuries and epochs later, where the number "twelve" was only incidental to this structure (*cf.* n. 2 above). Perhaps the number "twelve" as such should now be studied as intensively as the more fortunate number "seven" has been, so as to be understood in its proper setting.]

THE SAADIA—DAVID BEN ZAKKAI CONTROVERSY: A STRUCTURAL ANALYSIS [1]

By ELLIS RIVKIN

Hebrew Union College-Jewish Institute of Religion, Cincinnati

THE HISTORIAN is dependent on sources. The sources, in turn, are dependent on the historian. The historian can reconstruct the past only through the materials that have survived from the past. These materials, however, cannot do the reconstructing. They are necessary for the reconstruction, they set limits to the reconstruction; but they themselves cannot absolve the historian from his function.

The historian interacts with his sources. He must determine their reliability and their value. He must decide on their relevance. He must judge the relative weight to be assigned to the data. An historical reconstruction is the outcome of this interplay between the mind of the historian and the data that are available.

The historian shoulders a great responsibility. His reconstructions become the history of the past as long as they remain unchallenged. The alternative to a reconstruction is another reconstruction. As long as this is not forthcoming, the past is conceived of as being that which has been reconstructed. The past, as *objective* past, may have been radically different from that which is posited by the historian. The

---

[1] For other illustrations of the use of this method, *see* the writer's "The Utilization of Non-Jewish Sources for the Reconstruction of Jewish History," *Jewish Quarterly Review*, vol. xlviii (1957-58), 183-203; "A Decisive Pattern in American Jewish History" in *Essays in American Jewish History* (Cincinnati, 1958), pp. 23-61; "Unitive and Divisive Factors in Judaism," *Civilisations*, vol. vii (1957), 43-57; "Modern Trends in Judaism" in *Modern Trends in World Religions*, ed. J. Kitagawa (La Salle, Ill., 1959), pp. 59-97; "The Writing of Jewish History," *The Reconstructionist*, vol. xxv, June 15, 1959, and June 26, 1959.

truth of this distinction is continually being driven home by the discovery of new facts which alter greatly previous historical reconstructions, and by the proliferation of novel reconstructions built on facts that are not new.

No simple way out of the dilemma has been discovered. That historians presuppose an objective past is evidenced by their relentless search for facts and their rejection of reconstructions that are the free creation of the historical imagination. The objective past, however, though presupposed, eludes the most strenuous efforts of the historian.

A major obstacle that frustrates these efforts is the peculiar rôle of the *fact*. On the one hand, the fact seems stubborn and irreducible. On the other hand, it is plastic and pliable. The stubbornness of a fact derives from the consequences of its denial; for such a denial carries with it the collapse of historical reconstruction as a rational enterprise. A fact is stubborn because it resists all rational efforts at its annihilation.

A fact is nonetheless plastic and pliable despite its seeming autonomy because few, if any, facts exist that are fully determined. The *totality* of interconnections that knit the facts together in the objective past is irretrievable. For the objective interconnections the historian posits interconnections that seem to be warranted by legitimate inferences from the facts. Since the facts may sustain a variety of divergent systems of interconnections supplied by the minds of historians, even the most stubborn facts may prove amenable to more than one conceptual model.

The historian, therefore, has a twofold task: (1) to ascertain the facts, and (2) to bind these facts together through his powers of conceptualization. The first of these tasks has been consciously pursued since the dawn of critical historical methods of source analysis. The second has, until very recently, manifested itself only in the practice of the historian. Whereas the historian approaches his sources with crucial questions that seek to pry forth the facts, he rarely works out a con-

ceptual model of all his presuppositions and assumptions as
to the nature of the historical continuum. He rarely asks of
his conceptual model the searching questions that he asks
of his documents. Yet the facts that he has extricated from
his documents will be interconnected, for the most part,
through the presuppositions of his model rather than through
interconnections that can be established with factual certainty.

The totality of the interconnections that represent the
objective past is not available. The historian nonetheless
assumes that such a past existed, and his discipline seeks to
make the past as objective as possible. Historians do not
freely create the past, for the records from the past set limits—
though elastic ones—to possible reconstruction. Their purposes would be achieved if the facts could be determined in
such a way that the interconnections that may be inferred
from them are no longer susceptible to alternative interconnections. Under such conditions, the facts could bear
only one interpretation, and no historian would be able to
challenge the inferences rationally.

In some instances this has indeed been achieved. No rational
historian, for example, would question the fact that Lincoln
lived in the nineteenth century and was intimately involved
in the struggles between the Union and the Confederacy.
This excludes as a rational possibility his having lived simultaneously in France in the eleventh century as the Duke of
Burgundy. The inferences that we draw from all the contra-
dictory documents of the Civil War can never bring these
facts into question. These facts are hemmed in by restraints
on possible interconnections. If we were to seek to bind Lincoln
to France of the eleventh century, we would be blocked by
the inferences that all rational minds would draw from the
documents.

The historian makes the past objective to the extent that
his mode of conceptualization interconnects the facts in
such a way that alternative interconnections are unavailable

for rational minds. He approaches objectivity to the extent that he reduces possible alternatives. To the extent that an historian seeks to know an objective past through rational procedures, this would seem to be his goal.

In this article I should like to apply a structural mode of conceptualization to make intelligible and coherent a severe controversy between Saadia, the gaon of Sura, and the exilarch David ben Zakkai. The elucidation of this specific struggle will be sought through its links to a wider complex of factors that not only generated the controversy, but which also severely limited the range of possible resolutions.

II

In the year 930 a shock reverberated throughout the Jewish communities sprawled over the vast world of Islam. Saadia Joseph al-Fayumi, the gaon of Sura, had challenged the authority of the exilarch David ben Zakkai by refusing to give official sanction to some documents involving the settlement of an inheritance. In refusing to sign, Saadia had charged the exilarch with transgressing the biblical command: "Thou shalt not show favoritism in judgment." This defiance of the exilarch had explosive consequences. The exilarch, supported by the gaon of Pumbedita, Kohen Zedek, hurled a ban of excommunication against Saadia, removed him from his office as gaon of Sura, and stripped him of all his rights, privileges and powers. The exilarch appointed a counter-gaon, Joseph ben Jacob. Saadia retaliated. He removed David ben Zakkai as exilarch, and set up in his stead a rival exilarch, the brother of David ben Zakkai, Hasan. The Jews of Babylonia were split into two warring camps as powerful elements came to the support of the rivals. [1]

The shock of the struggle must have stunned Jews everywhere. The Academy of Sura was an institution which had been venerated and respected for more than two hundred

[1] Cf. Henry Malter, Saadia Gaon: His Life and Works (Philadelphia, 1921), pp. 109-15.

years. Its decisions in matters of *halakah* were considered binding throughout the Jewish communities of the Islamic world. And the gaon, the titular head of this institution, was viewed as one of the three great dignitaries who ruled those loyal to rabbinic Judaism.

The two other dignitaries who shared with the gaon of Sura this worldwide distinction were the gaon of the Academy of Pumbedita and the exilarch. In the year of the Great Controversy it would have been difficult to determine whether the exilarch, the gaon of Pumbedita, or the gaon of Sura enjoyed pre-eminence. A generation earlier, there would have been no question that the prestige of the gaon of Sura outranked that of the gaon of Pumbedita; and as for the exilarch and the gaon of Sura, it would depend on the criteria one chose as to who outranked whom. In Babylonia the exilarch had prerogatives that elevated him slightly above the gaon of Sura. [1] In the rest of the Jewish world, the gaon of Sura probably was more greatly venerated, for he was the authoritative spokesman for the *halakah*, the law that regulated the lives of those who adhered to rabbinic Judaism.

In the tenth century, however, certain changes had occurred which pushed the gaon of Pumbedita to the fore. Indeed, it seemed that Sura might close down. [2] Though this did not occur, Pumbedita secured equality with Sura in the year 926 when it was agreed that unassigned income, that is, moneys and gifts that were sent to the Academies without specific designation, were henceforth to be divided equally. [3] Previously Sura had taken two-thirds. It thus may have been that in the year of the Great Controversy, the gaon of Pumbedita may have had prestige equivalent to that of the gaon

---

[1] Cf. *Seder Olam Zuta* in A. Neubauer, *Medieval Jewish Chronicles* (Oxford, 1895), vol. ii, pp. 78, 83; Louis Ginzberg, *Geonica* (New York, 1909), vol. i, pp. 37-55.

[2] Cf. *Seder Olam Zuta*, p. 80; *Iggereth Sherira Gaon*, ed. B. Lewin (Haifa, 1921), p. 117.

[3] *Seder Olam Zuta*, p. 78.

of Sura—though the name of Sura probably still carried with it an aura that Pumbedita lacked.

Saadia Joseph al-Fayumi, the gaon of Sura who launched the Great Controversy, was not just another gaon of Sura. His appointment just two years before, in 928, through the decisive efforts of the exilarch David ben Zakkai, had shattered all precedent. The office of gaon in the past had been restricted to members of a handful of aristocratic Jewish families of Iraq. Never had a foreigner been invested with this dignity. And yet Saadia, an Egyptian by birth, of no noble parentage, had been elevated to this prestige-laden position. [1]

Many Jews throughout the world must have been startled. Others were no doubt perplexed. All must have been surprised. Those who gave the appointment serious thought and had followed the events in Baghdad must have concluded that Saadia had been rewarded for distinguished service in the cause of the three great institutions of Jewry. He had displayed polemical skills of a high order in his onslaughts against the Karaites who had challenged the authority of exilarchs and geonim. But even more. He had been the most brilliant champion of the authority of the exilarchate and gaonate with respect to control over a vital nerve center of Judaism, the calendar. This authority had been challenged by a Palestinian scholar, Ben Meir. The latter had attempted to retrieve for Palestinian scholars control over the calendar. This effort met with determined opposition from the exilarch and the geonim. Saadia had thrown himself into the controversy and had propounded an ingenious argument. He claimed that the calendar which the exilarch and the geonim claimed as authoritative had actually been promulgated by Moses on Mount Sinai. Since the Palestinian scholars had never used any other calendar, Ben Meir was violating not only a Sinaitic ordinance but was also flying in the face of Palestinian pre-

[1]   Cf. *Iggereth*, p. 117.

cedent. [1] Such an audacious invention by Saadia must have earned for him the admiration of those whose cause he championed, that of the exilarch and geonim. When, therefore, Saadia, in an unprecendented move, was appointed by the exilarch David ben Zakkai as gaon of Sura, it appeared to be for his loyalty and his brilliant services to those in authority.

How astonishing, therefore, must have been the unleashing of the Great Controversy! Saadia had been gaon for scarcely two years when he defied his supporter and benefactor David ben Zakkai and charged him with transgressing the biblical injunction: "Thou shalt not show favoritism in judgment." And when this was followed by the excommunication of Saadia by David ben Zakkai, the exilarch, and by Kohen Zedek, the gaon of Pumbedita, and when a counter-gaon was appointed, the shock must have stunned Jews throughout the world. And when Saadia responded with excommunications of his own, and when he set up a rival exilarch, and when Babylonian Jewry was split into two warring factions, the shock must have been heightened. And when in the course of the struggle the serious charges of bribery, exploitation, and dishonesty were hurled by each faction against the other, the initial shock must have given way to bewilderment and disillusionment.

What set off this controversy? The contemporary documents are sparse and of little help. According to the exilarchic document of excommunication, Saadia had violated a solemn oath that he had given David ben Zakkai at the time of his appointment to the gaonate. Saadia had sworn that he would be loyal to the exilarch and would never set up a rival exilarch. Saadia had violated his oath and in doing so had shown his true self: a base alien, unworthy of the prestige and honor that a deceived exilarch had bestowed upon him. [2]

---

[1] *Cf.* Solomon Zeitlin, *Secular and Religious Leadership* (Philadelphia, 1943), pp. 97-99.

[2] The text of the excommunication of Saadia is in *Zikhron le-Rishonim*, ed. A. Harkavy (Berlin, 1891), vol. v., pp. 231-34.

According to the pro-Saadia account of Nathan ha-Babli, Saadia had refused to sign official papers, sent to him by the exilarch, involving the settlement of an estate. At first Saadia refused to give any reason for not signing, even after the documents had been signed by Kohen Zedek, the gaon of Pumbedita. Only after persistent questioning did he charge the exilarch with violating the biblical injunction: "Thou shalt not show favoritism in judgment." Saadia's refusal to sign despite every effort of the exilarch and of the exilarch's son to avert a clash set the Great Controversy in motion. [1]

Nathan ha-Babli informs us that Babylonian Jewry was split into two factions. Saadia was supported by the influential Bene Netira (the Sons of Netira) and the wealthy of Baghdad. Ranged against Saadia was Chalaf ibn Sarjado, a man of great wealth and learning who at the time occupied a seat in the First Row of the Academy of Pumbedita and who was ultimately to become gaon of Pumbedita. After the struggle had gone on for several years, an incident occurred which involved an illegal beating by the exilarch of a litigant who had sought Saadia as a judge in his case. The furor that broke out following this highhandedness was of such a nature that Bishr ben Aaron, an influential merchant banker, with the support of other men of wealth, demanded that the exilarch, David ben Zakkai, and Saadia bring the controversy to an end. This was achieved. A meeting was arranged in which the two antagonists embraced one another and resumed their friendship. [2] It is to be noted that Bishr ben Aaron was the father-in-law of Chalaf ibn Sarjado, Saadia's bitterest opponent.

Aside from the letter of excommunication and the pro-Saadia account of Nathan ha-Babli, the sources extant are fragmentary and give no detail as to the issues. The Letter of Sherirah Gaon merely indicates that the controversy took place. [3] Saadia's position, which apparently had been stated

[1] *Seder Olam Zuta*, pp. 80-81.
[2] *Ibid.*, pp. 81-82.
[3] *Iggereth*, pp. 117-18.

in a full section of his *Sefer ha-Galui*, is only alluded to in the extant introduction to this work. [1] The vituperative attack by Chalaf ibn Sarjado is preserved only in the form of excerpts that a Karaite copied from a longer work by Chalaf. [2]

The sources obviously are not the kind of sources that make for clarity. Scholars, therefore, have reconstructed the controversy on the basis of what is available, and they have sought for an explanation in a variety of assumptions as to what could have triggered off such a controversy. Three interpretations have been offered: (1) Saadia was an individual of flawless integrity. Rather than countenance injustice, he defied the exilarch and exposed him as unworthy of his office. [3] (2) Saadia and David ben Zakkai were both strong personalities and therefore it was impossible for them to avoid a showdown. [4] (3) Saadia was a champion of the principle that the scholar class should be supreme, while David ben Zakkai

---

[1]   *Zikhron le-Rishonim*, pp. 152-54.

[2]   *Ibid.*, pp. 225-31.

[3]   H. Malter, *Saadia Gaon*, p. 109: "[The litigation that brought about the rupture] must have been part of an established system of administrative abuses and perversions of justice, which a man of Saadia's integrity and love of right could not possibly countenance."

[4]   *Cf.* M. Auerbach, „Der Streit zwischen Saadja Gaon und dem Exilarchen David ben Sakkai," *Jüdische Studien Josef Wohlgemuth, zu seinem sechzigsten Geburtstage....gewidmet* (Frankfurt a. Main, 1928), p. 21, asserts flatly that Saadia could not have violated an oath: „Ausgeschlossen ist es aber, dass ein Mann wie Saadja auch nur sein Wort, geschweige einen Eid gebrochen hätte. Es handelt sich wohl um eine unverbindliche Unterredung, der David—vielleicht im guten Glauben-mehr Wert, als sie verdiente, zulegte." Auerbach thus *assumes* an integrity that compels him to reject the evidence that Saadia did take an oath. Salo W. Baron argues that Saadia "played what appears in retrospect to have been a political game designed to discredit both the exilarch and his colleague of Pumbedita." Nevertheless, the basic issues revolved around "the incompatibility of the two vigorous personalities and the fundamental divergence of their conceptions of Jewish leadership" ("Saadia's Communal Activities," *Saadia Anniversary Volume* [New York, 1943], pp. 64-65). Jacob Mann likewise stresses the personality factor ("Varia on the Geonic Period," *Tarbiz*, vol. v [1933-34], 162-63 [Hebrew]).

espoused the principle that the secular authority, the exilarch, be pre-eminent. [1]

Basically these three views involve three questionable assumptions:

(1) Since it is assumed that Saadia must have been an individual of flawless integrity, he had no alternative but to launch the controversy. Such an assumption, however, is questionable in view of (a) Saadia's rôle in the Ben Meir controversy over the calendar where he invented a non-existent Mosaic calendar; (b) the subsequent reconciliation with David ben Zakkai who, according to Saadia, had been guilty of perverting justice; (c) Saadia's failure to point out immediately to Kohen Zedek, the gaon of Pumbedita, the flaws in the documents. Instead, he had the documents sent off to Kohen Zedek for his signature, and only after the latter had signed them and only after persistent demands that he give a reason did he finally claim that they involved perversion of justice. Such behavior—and this is the version of a Saadia sympathizer—is susceptible to an interpretation that is not quite as favorable to Saadia's disinterested concern for justice.

(2) Two personalities in conflict with each other could stir up such antagonism that it split Jewry into two warring camps. This assumption is challenged by (a) the fact that this was but one controversy in a *series* of controversies that both *preceded* the Saadia-David ben Zakkai rift and *followed* it; (b) by the participation in this controversy of three major institutions and the most influential men of wealth in Baghdad. It is difficult to see how so intense a struggle could have burst forth unless Saadia's defiance gave the signal for the unleashing of powerful antagonistic forces.

(3) The assumption that a major principle was the crucial issue is likewise questionable. Why did this principle loom

---

[1] *Cf.* Zeitlin, *Secular and Religious Leadership*, p. 104; Baron, *op. cit.*, p. 65. Raphael Mahler recognizes that the controversy involved a struggle for power that transcended the personal interests of the individuals involved, but he does not elaborate. *Cf.* his *Karaimer* (New York, 1947), pp. 76-77 (Yiddish).

so large at this time and not a decade earlier? Why should
the mere *assertion* of primacy stir up such intense hatreds?
Had not rival principles of authority coexisted for long
periods of time without excommunications and the appointment of counter-geonim and counter-exilarchs? Are we to
believe that Chalaf ibn Sarjado of Pumbedita opposed Saadia
so bitterly because he wished to see the principle of secular
leadership triumph? The question, therefore, remains: What
forces made this particular moment an appropriate one to
join battle in so destructive a fashion?

III

Perhaps the Saadia—David ben Zakkai controversy can
be clarified if we widen the perspective. Instead of concentration on this controversy as *sui generis*, let us approach it as
one of a *series* of unusual, even traumatic, events that occurred
in the first five decades of the tenth century. Each of these
events in its way was disturbing to the Jews throughout the
Islamic world. Indeed, one shock followed another with
such rapidity that by mid-century, that which had once been
a source of astonishment had become the normal and expected.

Consider the following major convulsions that *preceded*
the Saadia—David ben Zakkai outburst:

(1) A struggle between the exilarch Mar Ukbah and the
gaon of Pumbedita over the question of who was entitled to
the revenues from Khorasan. The exilarch was not only
deposed from office, but was forced into exile. No exilarch
had ever been deposed before! This remarkable achievement
was largely the handiwork of the merchant-court bankers
Aaron ben Phineas and his son-in-law Netira. [1]

(2) A severe struggle over who should be the legitimate gaon
of Pumbedita. David ben Zakkai, the new exilarch, supported
Kohen Zedek. The wealthy merchant-court banker Aaron ben

---

[1] Cf. *Seder Olam Zuta*, pp. 78-79. For the chronology of the events
and for the identification of the participants, *see* Mann, *op. cit.*, 148-54.

Amram favored Mebasser. In this controversy Saadia appears for the first time in exilarchal-gaonic politics, and he is an effective ally of David ben Zakkai and Kohen Zedek. The Mebasser—Aaron ben Amram faction is in turn aided by the Palestinian scholar Ben Meir. This controversy was marked by reciprocal excommunications. [1]

(3) A schism over the calendar. The Palestinian Ben Meir claimed the right of Palestinian scholars to determine the calendar, and his calculations were seriously at odds with those of the Babylonian authorities. In this controversy, the warring factions in Babylonia made peace and David ben Zakkai, Kohen Zedek, Mebasser, Aaron ben Amram, and Saadia joined forces to defeat Ben Meir. Apparently Mebasser

[1] It is evident from the sources that (1) the struggle between the David ben Zakkai-Kohen Zedek-Saadia faction and that of Mebasser-Aaron ben Amram must have been a very serious one, for it revolved around the question who was the rightful gaon and was accompanied by excommunication:

בחזירתינו אל ארץ יש׳ ארץ מולדתנו צוינו בכל מדינה ומדינה ועיר ועיר
לחזנים והיו קוראים הפתיחים שלכם ומנדים שנאכם, ומיכן נטרו איבה עלינו,
ובי״י בטחנו ולא נבוש׃׃

Ben Meir's letter in H. Bornstein, *The Controversy Between Saadia Gaon and Ben Meir* (Warsaw, 1904), pp. 49-50, 93. (2) Ben Meir supported the Mebasser-Aaron ben Amram faction:

ובאילו הימים הגיעו אלינו כל האגרות אשר כתבם דאוד (האומר) בן זכאי
הינו הידוע אצלכם במעשיו הטובים ודרכיו התמימים הוא ובניו וכוהן והמתחרר
אליהם סעיד בן יוסף אלדלאצי אשר הוא דומה להם והם דומים לו׃

Ibid., p. 50 and *cf.* pp. 56, 90, 91.—Since Mebasser appointed Chalaf ibn Sarjado, the son-in-law of the banker Bishr ben Aaron, to the First Row in the Academy of Pumbedita—a sharp break with precedent—it is to be assumed that Mebasser must have had the support of Aaron ben Amram, the father of Bishr ben Aaron, in his struggle with Kohen Zedek, David ben Zakkai, and Saadia for the gaonate of Pumbedita (cf. *Iggereth*, p. 120). The fulsome praise that Ben Meir lavishes on Aaron ben Amram indicates that the latter must have been the decisive personality in the support of Mebasser's claims (*cf.* Ben Meir's letters, *op. cit.*, pp. 49-50). It seems likely that either Aaron ben Amram supported Mebasser because the latter had appointed Chalaf, Bishr's son-in-law, to the First Row of Pumbedita, or that Mebasser appointed Chalaf because Aaron ben Amram had supported Mebasser's claims against Kohen Zedek.

was recognized as titular gaon of Pumbedita until his death
when he was succeeded by Kohen Zedek. [1]

(4) Chalaf ibn Sarjado, the son-in-law of one of the sons
of the merchant-banker Aaron ben Amram, and himself of
merchant stock, was appointed to the First Row of the Academy
of Pumbedita. This was unprecedented, for such a position
was not only hereditary, but it had been held exclusively
by an aristocratic group of scholarly families. [2]

(5) Saadia, an Egyptian, was appointed to the post of
Aluf in the Academy of Pumbedita. This was as startling an
appointment as that of Chalaf, for Saadia was a foreigner and

[1] The factional struggles in Babylonia offered a precious opportunity for Ben Meir to assert Palestinian independence:

ומכלל כל הדברים הללו יש הרשות לחבורת ארץ יש׳ על חכמי בני הגולה·
ואין לבני הגולה רשות על בני ארץ יש׳... ולא נראתה ולא נשמעה מעולם לבני
הגולה להורות או לדון או להעמיד רשות להם את בני יש׳...

(Bornstein, p. 70).—Ben Meir's action forced the Babylonian factions
to reconcile their differences; for it endangered the very foundations
of exilarchal and gaonic hegemony. Thus Saadia insisted that on the
matter of the calendar the Babylonian authorities were unanimously
agreed that Ben Meir was wrong (ibid.):

ועל זאת נבהלו כל רבותינו חכמי הישיבות, כי כמוה לא נהיה מעולם להכריז
המועדים שלא כהלכה· על כן בחרדתם כתבו אל כל ישראל אשר בכל
המקומות להודיעם כי כלנו שוין בדבר הזה, ואין ביניגו חלוקה כל עיקר...
ועל כן כתבו בכל המקומות להודיע את ישראל, כי ראש הגולה... וגם ראשי
ישיבות... וכל האלופים וכל החכמים ותלמידיהם שוין בדבר הזה... ואין ביניגו
חלוקה, ואין פרץ ואין יוצאת ואין צוחה ברחבתינו·

An agreement was reached by the quarreling Babylonian factions
that Mebasser was to be recognized as the official gaon of Pumbedita
with the understanding that he would be succeeded by Kohen Zedek.
Cf. *Iggereth*, pp. 119-20:

והות פלוגתא בין רבנן דמתיבתא ודוד הנשיא· דרבנן דמתיבתא אכנפו וקריוה
למר רב מבשר כהנא גאון (בר׳) מר רב קימוי גאון ודוד הנשיא קרייה למר רב
כהן צדק כהנא ב(·)ן מר רב יוסף והוה פלוגתא ביניהון עד חדש אלול שנת
רל״ג

ועבדו שלמא דוד הנשיא עם מר רב מבשר גאון ויתיב רב מבשר גאון ורבנן
דיליה לבדם ומובחרים דרבנן הוו בהדיא ומר רב כהן צדק ורבנן דיליה לבדם·
בשנת רל״ז בכסלו שכיב מר רב מבשר גאון ואתו רבנן דיליה לית כהן צדק·

[2] *Iggereth*, p. 120.

foreigners had never been granted a seat in the Academies. [1]

(6) Pumbedita in 926 was given equality with Sura in the apportionment of unassigned incomes. [2]

(7) Sura was temporarily without a gaon and presumably was threatened with extinction! [3] This must have been terribly disturbing, for Sura had been the foremost Academy for several centuries. And subsequently, when David ben Zakkai appointed Saadia to the vacant post, there must have been much bewilderment.

When, therefore, Saadia turned against his former ally and benefactor David ben Zakkai and deposed him from the exilarchate and appointed in his stead a rival exilarch, this shock may have been the most severe, but it was by no means the first.

Nor was it the last. The reconciliation between Saadia and David ben Zakkai was followed, on the death of Saadia, by these events: (1) The Academy of Sura was closed. [4] (2) A serious quarrel broke out between Chalaf ibn Sarjado and Nehemiah for the office of gaon of Pumbedita, and Chalaf proved the stronger. [5] Thus Chalaf, the bitterest enemy of Saadia and one born of merchant stock, became the head of the Academy that survived.[6] (3) Chalaf as gaon of Pumbedita appointed to lucrative judgeships two of his former enemies who had been close associates of Saadia. (4) After the death of Chalaf a struggle took place between Nehemiah and Sherira for the gaonate. [7]

It is thus evident that the half-century during which the Saadia—David ben Zakkai controversy occurred was a period

[1] Cf. *Saadyana*, ed. Solomon Schechter (Cambridge, 1903), p. 15; Mann, *op. cit.*, p. 276.

[2] *Seder Olam Zuta*, p. 78.

[3] *Iggereth*, p. 117; *Seder Olam Zuta*, p. 80.

[4] *Iggereth*, p. 118.

[5] *Ibid.*, pp. 120-21.

[6] Cf. *Zikhron le-Rishonim*, p. 228.

[7] *Iggereth*, p. 121; *cf.* "Bodleian Geniza Fragments," ed. A. Cowley, *JQR* (o.s.), vol. xix (1907), 104-06.

marked by corrosive events. Not only did controversy follow controversy, but in the process the renowned Academy of Sura was deprived of its existence and the exilarchate shorn of its pre-eminence.

These convulsive years stand out markedly in one other respect. They contrast sharply with the centuries that prece· ded. For a period spanning more than two hundred years, the seventh through the ninth centuries, no such devastating controversies had occurred! [1] Indeed, the expansion and consolidation of Islam, first under the Ummayads and then particularly under the Abbassids, witnessed the flourishing of the exilarchate and the gaonate. Whereas in the seventh century the scholar class had been completely subordinated to the exilarch, the eighth century saw the rise to eminence of the Academy of Sura and the ninth century the development of the prominence of Pumbedita. At the end of the ninth century, *three* powerful, wealthy, and influential institutions flourished. Where there had been but one there were now three!

And another point. Not a single controversy is recorded involving the exilarch and the gaon of Sura *prior* to the tenth century. And only three controversies are recorded involving the exilarch and the gaonate of Pumbedita! [2] But—and this is to be underlined—not a single one of these controversies involved the extinction of either the exilarchate or the gaonate!

Yet in the space of fifty years in the tenth century an exilarch, Mar Ukbah, was deposed and exiled; geonim and counter-geonim, exilarchs and counter-exilarchs made their appearance; a world-renowned Academy was closed; and the exilarchate dwindled into relative insignificance. [3]

Surely, then, the David ben Zakkai—Saadia controversy was not the only upheaval that took place in this period, even though it was the most decisive and dramatic conflict of these turbulent years.

[1] Cf. *Iggereth*, *passim*; Ginzberg, *Geonica*, vol. i, pp. 14-16, 63.
[2] Ginzberg, *op. cit.*, pp. 16-22.
[3] Cf. *Seder Olam Zuta*, pp. 82-83.

IV

The problem of an adequate interpretation of the David ben Zakkai—Saadia controversy can best be solved if it is treated as part of the larger problem of the conflictual character of tenth-century events. This larger problem in turn must be approached through a structural method. This method makes a sharp distinction between two types of data: the structural and the verbal. By structural data I mean the kind of facts that are concrete and exclusive; by verbal data I mean words that do not necessarily convey information. The first kind of data precludes interchangeability, *i.e.*, if these concrete facts are true, they cannot be replaced by contradictories. Such contradictories would be non-factual. A concrete fact of this type would be an individual, such as Saadia, or an institution such as the exilarchate or gaonate. Evidence for Saadia's existence excludes the possibility of Saadia's having been Kohen Zedek. These two individuals are not interchangeable. Similarly a gaon of the tenth century is not interchangeable with an exilarch.

Verbal data, on the other hand, are not necessarily exclusive. They can be simultaneously invoked to justify contraries. They do not necessarily communicate information; indeed, they frequently impede and obscure such communication. They may be deceptive, though their assertion is meant to be taken seriously. Identical verbalizations may be asserted by the bitterest of enemies.

Verbal data, however, have an intimate connection with concrete individuals and institutions. Though they may not communicate information, they are nonetheless essential for the functioning of concrete entities. Indeed, verbal data have a relationship to individuals and institutions as means for achieving ends, through the use of effective and affective words. These words will tend to be prestige-laden and emotive, and they will have the power of arousing intense feelings in the listeners. The words that will be selected by an indivi-

dual or an institution will be those which have achieved status
and respectability. In any given society, the choice of verbalization cannot be accidental if certain goals are envisioned.
Since this is so, the words primarily convey to the historian
the verbal forms that the seeking of ends must utilize; they
do not necessarily reveal either the motivation or the goals.

The document that contains David ben Zakkai's excommunication of Saadia reveals data of both types. Of the
structural type, it confirms our previous knowledge of the
existence of certain concrete institutions, the exilarchate and
the gaonate, and certain concrete personalities. It likewise
points to the significant powers that these institutions enjoyed.
It indicates that the exilarch had been aware that the power
and the prestige of Sura might be used destructively against
the exilarch. For this reason he had imposed an oath on
Saadia binding him to unswerving loyalty. It furthermore
seeks to carry through certain concrete acts; the removal of
Saadia, his replacement by another gaon, and an effective ban
against Saadia and his allies. [1]

The rest of the document is largely made up of verbal data.

---

[1] The following data are concrete, for they deal with specific
powers and privileges that Saadia possessed as the gaon of Sura and
which the exilarch sought to block and nullify:

והסמכתי [עם ראשי הישיבות וא] ב בית דין ואלופים וחכמים [והחרימוהו
ונדוהו וה] עבירו אותו מגדולתו [והעבירוהו מתורת] חבר ונתפרסם קלוני···
הרי הוא מאוס הרי הוא ירוד הרי הוא מעובר הרי הוא כהדיוט לכל דבר אין
חוששין למינויו ואין למידין ממנו ואין משגיחין בכתבו ואין מקימין אצלו ולא
מעידין אותו וכל כתב שהוא יוצא בקיומו הרי הוא בטל וחותמו כחרש שבורה
וטבעתו ככלי אין חפץ בו אין ברכתו ברכה ולא נידויו נדוי הרי הוא ירוד
כאבותיו··· עתה נדו והחרימו תמיד עם כל מי שקורא את סעיד אלפיומי עוכר
ישראל בשם לוי שהיה נקרא בו תחלה וכל ההולך אל מושבו וכל הנשפט אצלו
וכל המחנה אתו בנדבה או במתנה וכל העוזרו בסתר או בגלוי וכל הכותב
אצלו שאלה או פסק דין או שטר או כתובה או גט וכל שקורא אגרתו או
שכותב לו תשובה בשמותא דישראל יהוי··· וכל בית הכנסת שתראה את כתב
עברה הזה יקראוהו ויעשו כאשר פירשנו ואל יסורו ימין ושמאל·

From David ben Zakkai's excommunication of Saadia in *Zikhron
le-Rishonim*, pp. 233-34.

The exilarch is taking action against Saadia only because Holy Scripture enjoins that righteousness triumph. He is removing Saadia only because he has betrayed the lofty principles that the exilarch and his scholarly associates exemplify. The exilarch and his supporters are the defenders of the exploited and the downtrodden. They are motivated only by the interests of all Israel and are themselves free of any base motives. [1]

If we were to assume that David ben Zakkai was motivated

---

[1]   Cf. *ibid.*, p. 231:

דעו כי [הקדוש ברוך הוא צ]דיק וישר ותמים כעינין שנ׳ הצור תמים פעלו וצוה
ישראל ללכת לפניו בתמימות שנ׳ תמים תהיה· ובזמן שאדם מהלך לפניו
בתמימות מושיבו בטח· ואם מעקש דרכיו ומכניס בעצמו גסות וגאוה ונשען
מבינתו ואומר קבלו דעתי הוא נכשל במעשיו ונודע לכל שהוא ככסף סיגים
מצפה על חרש ויתפרסם קלונו ותודע חרפתו שכך אמר שלמה הולך בתם ילך
בטח וג׳ ואמרו חכמים אין הקב״ה מ שלם רעה לרשע עד שמגלה עונותיו שלא
יאמרו כשר היה למה נענש…

This part of the excommunication consists of verbal data. Saadia could have used this entire section against David ben Zakkai without altering a word. These words do not communicate information either about the exilarch or about Saadia. Their use, however, does indicate that they served a purpose: the exilarch had to justify what he was doing by an appeal to elevated principles and appropriate sacred texts. In the subsequent parts of the excommunication, the exilarch compares Saadia to Jeroboam and the prophets of Baal; he denounces him for exploiting the people; he charges him with sowing dissension and with stirring up jealousy; he accuses him of homosexual practices. Is one, therefore, to assume that the exilarch was a paragon of virtue and a model of righteousness?

It is significant that David ben Zakkai had to explain to Jewry how Saadia, if he was so dastardly, came to hold such a high position. The exilarch, therefore, pictures himself as having been taken in by Saadia's dissembling and by his winning ways. He realizes that he should have known better than to have trusted a foreigner of base parentage. He, therefore, is appointing one who is truly worthy of so honored a position. Cf. *ibid.*, p. 232:

והיה מראה מעצמו ארחות יפ[ות ומדות טובות] וענוה ושפלות רוח ודרכי
[ישרים וגנב את לבבי] ואת לב אנשי ישראל כא[בשלום וכמה אנשים] נלכדו
במצודתו במכמרתו [והשתמש בעטרה שאינן] ראוי לה והנחלנוהו בכבו[ד שלא
ראה לא הוא ולא] אבותיו וכחזקת[ו גבה לב]ו עד להשחית והתחיל ללכת[
בגדולות ובנפלאות…

by personal ambition, this assumption could not be supported by any public pronouncement of the exilarch. Had he proclaimed in the letter of excommunication that he was removing Saadia because the latter stood in the way of his ambitions and had he refrained from the citing of biblical texts, his goals would have been frustrated by his own actions. No matter what his motives might have been, David ben Zakkai had no alternative but to present his case in the language of piety.

Similarly Saadia was constrained to use identical language. He could no more express raw motives of ambition than could the exilarch. Any claim that he made had to rest ultimately on the same type of religious text as that of his opponent. Irrespective of his motives, he would have to stride before the public in the armor of pious rectitude. [1]

The concrete data, however, are essentially different. The exilarch appointed a new gaon, a particular individual who could not be freely interchanged with Saadia. Similarly Saadia invested Hasan, the brother of David ben Zakkai, with the exilarchal office; Hasan was obviously not freely interchangeable with David ben Zakkai. When it came to concrete acts, these proved to be absolutely exclusive in character. Yet each concrete act was necessarily justified by the antagonists by an appeal to an identical vocabulary of religiosity.

The Jewish population for whom these words were formulated undoubtedly repeated them as they took sides. Armed with identical *words* from Holy Writ, the antagonists *concretely* demonstrated that, though these words may have been necessary, they served as the moral and religious justification and rationalization for whatever concrete *action* was being carried out.

---

[1] The extant sections of Saadia's *Sefer ha-Galui* are full of biblical verses extolling righteousness, justice and integrity—virtues which presumably were foreign to David ben Zakkai's character (*Zikhron le-rishonim*, pp. 150-92). According to the pro-Saadia account of Nathan ha-Babli, David ben Zakkai had trangressed the biblical injunction: "Thou shalt not show partiality in judgment" (cf. *Seder Olam Zuta*, p. 81).

This mode of analysis does not assert that all verbalizations are non-communicative, but it suggests that as conveyors of information they must be concrete and non-transferable. Frequently words that were communicative in one phase of history cease to be so once they have achieved emotional and institutional prestige. The word "democrat" in the eighteenth century was exclusively used to describe an individual who was sharply distinguishable from others; in our own day, it tells us next to nothing. Similarly, the words in the Bible may have been highly communicative in the early history of Israel, but virtually meaningless in the polemics of David ben Zakkai and Saadia.

In seeking a solution of the Saadia—David ben Zakkai controversy from the larger perspective of the corrosive events of the tenth century, one must analyze (1) the nature of the three institutions, the exilarchate, the gaonate of Sura, and the gaonate of Pumbedita, and (2) the role of certain influential merchant banking families. The controversies, the precedent-shattering acts, and the convulsions— all involved the interactions of exilarchs, geonim, and merchant bankers.

The exilarchate and the gaonate were institutions, *i.e.*, they were systems of interrelationships. That system of interrelationships which appears to us as the exilarchate is distinguishable from that system of interrelationships that reveals itself as the gaonate. The gaonate expressed itself in two distinct systems of interrelationships, the one manifesting itself as the gaonate of Sura, the other as that of Pumbedita. Each of these systems bound together individuals in a hierarchy of privileged relationships that set them apart from each other and from the rest of Jewry. The exilarchate and gaonate were complexes of privileges, the wielders of coercive powers, and the beneficiaries of economic surplus derived from a variety of taxes, fees, and gifts. Both institutions were so structured as to guarantee a self-perpetuating and oligarchic ruling class. Though these institutions may have been rivals, they enjoyed one feature in common: a privileged status. [1] Those individuals who were drawn together in each of these distinct patterns of authority and privilege had a stake in enhancing their privilege as against the other groupings of individuals. In addition, each institutional complex had a crucial interest in preserving its system of interrelationship intact against any threat to its existence.

As systems, the exilarchate and the gaonate functioned simultaneously as relatively independent complexes and as relatively interdependent. That which linked them together was the ultimate source of their authority: their dependence on the existence of a differentiated historical entity, the Jews, and of a differentiated outlook on reality, Judaism. Neither the exilarchate nor the gaonate was a function of the caliphate of Islam, though it had certain crucial connections with each of them. The exilarchate and gaonate would have ceased to exist if they had severed their relationships to the Jews, or if they had abandoned Judaism. Hence, the continued existence of these institutions required that their functional rôle to Jews and Judaism be maintained at all costs. They shared a veneration for the same sacred texts that underwrote their authority, however much they differed as to the quantitative allocation of authority to each institution.

These complexes of aristocratic and oligarchic privilege and power wielded authority by virtue of certain sacred texts that were believed to be endowed with divine sanction. The exilarch justified his regal splendor and his princely prerogatives by an appeal to the Davidic dynasty as a divinely ordained institution. His right to rule tied him to biblical writ. Were he to discard these sacred texts, he would be without privilege, without wealth, and without power. No matter what the problem, there were certain words he had to use and a divine authority that he had to invoke.

The gaonate was likewise wedded to a system of divine

[1]　For the structure of privilege, see *Seder Olam Zuta*, pp. 78, 83-88.

authority and to a collection of sacred texts. The geonim
exercised legislative, judicial, and coercive powers because
they claimed to be the heirs of those scholars whose legislation
had become binding on all Jews. This legislation was to be
found in the Mishnah and the Gemara. The geonim wielded
power, collected taxes, and judged their fellow Jews by virtue
of these writings that were deemed to have divine sanction.
If, therefore, they were to preserve their prerogatives, they
were constrained to utilize the vocabulary in which their
power was grounded.

Though these institutions may have been in rivalry, they
were not free of their umbilical relationship to the identical
system of sacred texts. In struggling with each other, the
exilarch reached into the same verbal arsenal as did the
geonim. These texts sustained the life of both institutions,
and only death could bring about a separation.

If, then, the exilarchate and the gaonate were interrelationships knitted together through the fibers of power, privilege,
and wealth, and if these institutions were dedicated to the
perpetuation of their privileged status, then it is evident
that any disintegration of the foundations that supported
these privileges would have a disastrous effect on the relationship of these institutions to each other. [1] The rivalry which

---

[1]   The exilarch as an hereditary prince wielded great authority
and surrounded his person with all the symbols of royalty (cf. *Seder
Olam Zuta*, pp. 83-84). The gaonate was aristocratic and oligarchic.
Even such influential positions as that of *resh kallah* were hereditary
and could be held by youngsters (*ibid.*, p. 87):

וכך היה מנהגם אם נפטר א׳ מראשי כלות ויש לו בן הממלא את מקומו יורש
מקום אביו ויושב בו ואפילו היה קטן בשנים· וכך מן החברים כשיפטר א׳ מהם
אם היה בנו ממלא את מקומו יושב בו ואין אחד מהם דולג על מפתן חבירו···

The seats in the academies were likewise hereditary and hierarchi-
cally structured. Merit did not entitle one to a more distinguished
seat (*ibid.*):

ואם יהיה א׳ מהם מן הז׳ שורות גדול בחכמה מן האחר אין מושיבין אותו במקומו
מפני שלא ירשה מאביו אבל מוסיפין לתת לו יותר מחוקו מפני חכמתו·

A handful of families monopolized the most important positions
of gaon, *ab beth-din*, and *resh kallah*. Cf. L. Ginzberg, *Geonica*, vol. i,

had been relatively benign, *i.e.*, a mere effort to extend the power, wealth, and prestige of one against the other, would become malignant, *i.e.*, a struggle for self-preservation even

pp. 6-14. That the geonim had no intention of relinquishing such prerogatives as tax exemption is unambiguously enunciated by Nahshon Gaon (874-882):

הכי חזינא שאף על פי שמשליכין המלך ושריו על ישראל זמיונות בלי חק
ומדחיקין ומכבידין עול על הצבור אסור ליקח מן הרבנים כלום·

Teshuboth ha-Geonim, ed. A. Harkavy (Berlin, 1887), responsum 537, p. 264. The exilarchs and the geonim wielded their authority through coercive measures. Thus the stringent *malkuth marduth* was imposed upon anyone who defied a rabbinical injunction. The victim was lashed until he either recognized the authority of the court or died under the blows:

ומלקות דאורייתא לא נהגא היום אלא מכת מרדות נהגא ומכת תורה ארבעים
חסר אחת, ומכת מרדות אינה כן אלא חובטין אותו עד שיקבל או עד
שתצא נפשו· וכל *Shaare Zedek* (Salonica, 1792), responsum 39, p. 91b
מקום שאי אפשר לקנוס כגו' חייט או אורג שהם עושים מלאכה לאחרים שאי
אפשר לקנוס לממון של אחינו ישראל קונסי' אותם בעצמם· משמתי' ליה
ומלקינ' ליה עד דמקביל עליה דינא·

Shaare Teshubah (Leipzig, 1858), responsum 216, p. 21; *cf.* Jacob Mann "The Responsa of the Babylonian Geonim," *JQR*, vol. x (1919-20), 335-65. — The decisive manner in which these dignitaries reacted to any threat to their privileges is illustrated by the following examples: (1) The exilarch Mar Ukbah was exiled when he sought to extend his jurisdiction at the expense of the gaonate of Pumbedita. (2) David ben Zakkai's resorting to the secular authorities to compel the Jews to show the respect that was due his son—an act in which the geonim acquiesced (cf. *Seder Olam Zuta*, pp. 78, 86). Apparently this was not at all unusual (*ibid.*, p. 86):

ואם יצא בנו של ראש גלות לכל מקום שירצה נושאין לו פנים ומכבדין אותו
ונותנין לו מנחה ואינם נמנעים בזה הדבר אבל עושין עמו כל א' וא' לפי כבודו
ולפי גדולתו· ואם לא ישאו לו פנים ולא יכבדוהו במתנותיהם שולח אביו פתיחות
וחמות·

The exilarchate and the gaonate were so *structured* that they could *function* only in an oligarchical fashion. To have functioned otherwise would have required so radical a restructurization as to deprive the word gaonate or exilarchate of meaning; *i.e.*, there would have emerged *new* structures which *functioned* differently. Hence the exilarchs and the geonim utilized verbalizations as means for strengthening their oligarchical functions, never to endanger them. The oligarchical and aristocratic nature of the gaonate and exilarchate is well documented in Raphael Mahler's *Karaimer*, pp. 68-88.

if this meant the annihilation of the rival institutions. If the revenues should precipitously decline, if previous sources of income and prestige were to dry up, if significant communities of Jews were to withdraw their loyalties, if, in a word, conditions became such that it was *impossible* for three institutions to wield the power or to accumulate the wealth or to enjoy the prestige to which they had become accustomed, then a destructive struggle for existence could scarcely be avoided.

This is precisely what occurred in the tenth century. It was during the first decades of the tenth century that the foundations which supported the exilarchate and the gaonate began to crumble.

However, before this process of disintegration can be analyzed fully, it is necessary to discuss two merchant-banking families of Baghdad. One of these is linked to the name of Aaron ben Amram; the other, to that of Joseph ben Phineas. Each of these served sometimes jointly, sometimes separately as the court bankers for the Caliph Muqtadir. They rendered various fiscal services, not the least important of which was the advancement of large sums of money for the payment of troops of the caliph. As security they were assigned the income from the taxes of the wealthy province of Ahwaz. Such a rôle clearly indicates that these merchant-bankers were not only extremely wealthy, but influential. [1]

Joseph ben Phineas had a son-in-law whose name was Netira and who was an active associate of Joseph. The influence that these two had with the caliph is indicated by the fact that they were instrumental in having the caliph send the exilarch Mar Ukbah into exile. [2] Netira had two sons,

---

[1] For the rôle of the bankers, *see* Walter Fischel, *Jews in the Economic and Political Life of Medieval Islam* (London, 1937), pp. 1-44; Jacob Mann, "Varia," pp. 154-67.

[2] Joseph ben Phineas and his son-in-law Netira insisted that the exilarch Mar Ukbah be exiled, even though the caliph was willing to reinstate him (*Seder Olam Zuta*, p. 79): וכיון ששב היה קשה הדבר על נטירא ועל יוסף בן פנחס ועל הנלוים עמהם· והיו מדברים עליו אל המלך עד שצוה המלך שיצא [מכל מלכותו] והגלה אותו פעם שנית·

Sahl and Isaac, who were ardent supporters of Saadia in the Great Controversy. [1]

The sons of Aaron ben Amram followed in their father's footsteps. One of these sons, Bishr, married off his daughter to Chalaf ibn Sarjado who was of a family of merchants, but at the same time a scholar. [2] It was this Chalaf who was appointed to the First Row of Pumbedita by Mebasser, the gaon of Pumbedita; it was he who ultimately became the gaon of Pumbedita.

It is also to be noted that Aaron ben Amram supported Mebasser in his struggle for the gaonate of Pumbedita against the claims of Kohen Zedek and his supporters David ben Zakkai and Saadia.[3] It was Aaron's son Bishr who intervened to bring the Great Controversy to an end. [4]

These banking families clearly played a prominent rôle in the struggles of the tenth century. What was this rôle and how did they come to play it? In the previous centuries merchant-bankers did not have a decisive voice in the affairs of the exilarchate and gaonate. This fact is underwritten by Sherira Gaon who takes pains to point out that Chalaf ibn Sarjado was from a family of merchants and not from the families of scholars. [5] Yet in the tenth century Joseph ben Phineas and Netira supported the Gaon Judah of Pumbedita in his struggle with the exilarch Mar Ukbah over the revenues of Khorasan, and they were responsible for having him exiled; Chalaf ibn Sarjado was appointed to the First Row of Pumbedita; the sons of Netira were influential supporters of Saadia against David ben Zakkai; Bishr ben Aaron imposed a reconciliation on Saadia and David.

Whence, then, the power wielded by these merchant-banking

---

[1] *Ibid.*, p. 80; *cf.* A. Harkavy, „Netira und seine Söhne...," *Festschrift für A. Berliner* (Frankfurt a.M., 1903), pp. 39-40 (Hebrew).
[2] *Seder Olam Zuta*, p. 82. For the identity of Bishr ben Aaron, see Fischel, *op. cit.*, p. 41, n. 1.
[3] *Cf.* n. above.
[4] *Seder Olam Zuta*, p. 82.
[5] *Iggereth*, p. 120.

families in the affairs of the exilarchate and gaonate? We must assume that they performed vital banking and political functions for these institutions. Through this rôle they came to have a decisive voice in the affairs of the gaonate and exilarchate.

The influential position enjoyed by these bankers in caliphal finances gave them powerful political leverage. The removal of the exilarch Mar Ukbah from an hereditary and venerable office is evidence enough of the weight that the bankers carried with the caliph. However, it is more than likely that this leverage was used because the bankers had financial ties to both the gaonate and exilarchate. If the revenues from Khorasan were diverted from Pumbedita to the exilarch, it is clear that the income of the gaon of Pumbedita would be reduced. Joseph ben Phineas and Netira presumably were threatened with grave losses if the exilarch successfully carried through his plan, and they did not hesitate to use every bit of their power to defeat his design.

In view of this incident and in view of the financial rôle that the bankers played at the court of the caliph, it is plausible to assume that these families were deeply involved in the fiscal operations of the gaonate and the exilarchate. Two crucial functions immediately suggest themselves: (1) The transmission of funds from Babylonia for the exilarch and from Babylonia and the communities throughout the world for the gaonate. (2) The advancement of large sums of money to the geonim and the exilarchs on the security of future income. [1]

---

[1] The sources that testify to the rôle of the banking families as transmitters of funds derive from the time of Nehemiah Gaon, *i.e.*, subsequent to the Great Controversy. As to their function as lenders of money to the exilarchs and the geonim, our sources are silent. Such a function, however, is to be assumed, if the power of these banking families over such powerful and independent institutions is to be accounted for. It would indeed be hazardous to assume that, whereas the caliph had to resort to these bankers to cope with his financial difficulties, the geonim and the exilarchs managed their revenues and expenditures with such skill that they needed no such help. It

Such functions, especially the latter, were fraught with significance. The gaonate and the exilarchate came to be dependent upon the banking families, and these in turn did not shrink from the implications of this relationship. Every event that involved the exilarchate and the gaonate in the first decades of the tenth century simultaneously involved the great banking families. Joseph ben Phineas and Netira force the expulsion of exilarch Mar Ukbah; Aaron ben Amram vigorously supports Mebasser for the gaonate of Pumbedita against Kohen Zedek; the merchant Chalaf ibn Sarjado is made an important dignitary in the Academy of Pumbedita; the Bene Netira support Saadia in the Great Controversy; the banker Bishr ben Aaron imposes a reconciliation on the rival factions; Chalaf ibn Sarjado becomes the Gaon of Pumbedita.

We are thus confronted with a complex problem. The banking families obviously play a significant rôle in the events that preceded and those that followed the Great Controversy. But why was the animosity so keen and the antagonism so bitter? Why were not these families simply assimilated into the previous pattern which had displayed rivalry but of a non-destructive kind? Why the destructive character of the involvement of these families in the gaonic and exilarchal affairs? The answer to these questions is to be sought in the nature of the economic and political problems that confronted the exilarchs, the geonim, and the merchant-banking families in the tenth century.

V

These problems were essentially insolvable. No matter what moves were made, disaster was inevitable. Between

would also be rash to assume that the banking families were disinterested in the financial affairs of the gaonate and the exilarchate or that they were unaware of the power that these institutions wielded. In view of our knowledge of the relationship of merchants and banking houses to medieval ecclesiastical institutions, it is hardly likely that Jewish merchants and bankers would become involved in exilarchal and gaonic politics for purely religious motives.

the years 900 and 1000, the economic and political foundations that had previously supported a regal exilarch and two wealthy, powerful, and influential academies crumbled. Confronted, in turn, with their own collapse, these institutions and the banking families associated with them turned on each other in a most destructive fashion. They cut each other down in so violent a manner that even the triumphant victor was a victim. They turned on each other with such hatred that thousands of their worshipful subjects turned in disgust and desperation to the Karaite heresy.

Between the years 900 and 1000, the following developments took place: (1) The fragmentation of the Abbassid empire and the emergence of independent caliphates and emirates. [1] (2) An equivalent fragmentation of the Jewries of the Abbassid realms and the appearance of independent autonomous centers in Egypt, North Africa, Spain and Italy. [2] (3) A shrinking of the total resources available for the support of the wealth, privilege, power and prestige of the ruling institutions in Baghdad. (4) The expansion of Karaism and the defection of large numbers of Jews from Rabbinism.

The problems were insurmountable. The collapse of the Abbassid empire could not be offset by anything that the exilarch, the geonim, or the bankers did or did not do. Yet this collapse unleashed forces whose *minimum* effects were bound to alter radically the existing institutions *irrespective of the policies they adopted*. It was absolutely impossible for the exilarchate and the gaonate to maintain their previous wealth, power, and prestige. In the face of the structural realities that they were powerless to prevent, the possibilities for coping with the situation were severely restricted: (1) The exilarchate and gaonate could renounce their claims to

[1]   *Cf.* Philip K. Hitti, *The History of the Arabs* (Princeton, 1943), pp. 450-83; William Muir, *The Caliphate: Its Rise, Decline, and Fall* (Edinburgh, 1924), pp. 566 f.

[2]   *Cf.* Simon Dubnow, *Weltgeschichte des jüdischen Volkes* (Berlin, 1926), vol. iii, pp. 479-510.

power, wealth, and prestige. (2) The dwindling of resources could be shared equally, *i.e.*, each institution could shrink its demands proportionately to the reduction in income. (3) The dwindling of the resources could be offset by increasing the demands on those Jews who still lived in areas under their control. (4) A struggle for survival between the institutions could take place. If the other institutions could either be eliminated or their share of the available resources drastically reduced, then perhaps the surviving institution could maintain its former position or at least some semblance thereof.

The controversies of the tenth century leave little doubt as to which of the alternatives was chosen. Each institution sought to preserve itself and in doing so reached out for whatever help was available. Alliances were made and just as quickly broken. For this reason the controversies could reveal no principled character. For this reason the verbal barrage was a façade which obscured the crucial issues.

An analysis of the events scarcely leaves room for any other interpretation:

(1) The Aaron ben Amram faction hurled excommunications against the David ben Zakkai-Kohen Zedek-Saadia alliance. The excommunications were reciprocated. Yet when Ben Meir attempted to utilize this factional struggle to assert Palestinian independence, the enemies became friends and united their forces against this threat to Babylonian hegemony. [1]

(2) During the first year of Saadia's gaonate, the Bene Aaron banking family appears to have been on good terms with Saadia. Indeed, Saadia informed his coreligionists in Egypt that the Bene Aaron and Netira could be of service to them at the caliphal court. [2] Yet in 930 Saadia threw down the gauntlet.

(3) Saadia was appointed gaon of Sura by David ben Zakkai.

[1] *Cf.* p. 12, n. 1, p. 13, n. 1.
[2] *Ginze Kedem*, ed. B. Lewin (Haifa, 1923), vol. ii, p. 35.

It may also be assumed that the Sons of Netira favored this appointment, in view of their subsequent devotion to Saadia. David ben Zakkai appointed Saadia as a reward for Saadia's loyalty to David and to Kohen Zedek in the struggle with Mebasser and Aaron ben Amram, and also for Saadia's brilliant polemics against Ben Meir and the Karaites. The tenseness of the situation among the ruling groups was such, however, that David ben Zakkai feared that once Saadia became Gaon of Sura he might be weaned away from the exilarch's cause. He, therefore, imposed upon him an oath that he would be loyal and never appoint a counter-exilarch. [1]

(4) In Saadia's first year in office there was peace. In 930, however, over some technicality which was presumably so trivial that Kohen Zedek, the gaon of Pumbedita, did not even notice it, Saadia declared war against his benefactor and removed him from his exilarchal throne. David ben Zakkai became enraged and countered with the removal of Saadia from his post. Babylonian Jewry divided into two warring camps, and no charge was too extreme to be levelled at an opponent. Saadia accused the exilarch of perverting justice; the exilarch accused Saadia of exploiting the people, of deception, and of violating a sacred oath.

Saadia was supported by the Bene Netira banking family and other wealthy families. David ben Zakkai was supported by Kohen Zedek, by Chalaf ibn Sarjado, and the latter by his father-in-law, the banker Bishr ben Aaron. [2] Chalaf was

---

[1] *Zikhron le-Rishonim*, p. 232.

[2] Cf. *Seder Olam Zuta*, p. 82. For the following reasons it is safe to assume that Bishr ben Aaron was opposed to Saadia: (1) Bishr is *not* mentioned by Nathan ha-Babli as one of Saadia's supporters. In view of the fact that Nathan attributes to Bishr the crucial rôle in settling the controversy, Nathan's failure to mention Bishr as one of Saadia's allies indicates that Bishr must have been aligned against Saadia. (2) Bishr's son-in-law Chalaf was Saadia's bitterest enemy. (3) Bishr took the initiative in bringing about a reconciliation. Since at the time the anti-Saadia faction was in power, only that individual most responsible for the exilarch's victory could have ordered David ben Zakkai to make peace.

particularly vituperative in his attack on Saadia and Saadia's associates. He charged him with using strong-arm tactics and of violating the Sabbath in seeking to bribe the state officials.[1] He accused Saadia of homosexual practices and insisted he could produce reliable witnesses who testified that Saadia had performed an homosexual act in the presence of the Torah; he also alleged that the youth of Nehardea wearied themselves in panting after Saadia as an object of their homosexual desires. [2] Chalaf heaped on Saadia's followers every sort of abuse. He bestowed upon one the name "Rat Face"; another he dubbed as "good for nothing but sexual intercourse." [3] If it is borne in mind that Chalaf was a respected dignitary who sat in the First Row of Pumbedita and that these serious charges and countercharges were being hurled by the distinguished spokesmen of religious institutions of renown, it is clear that this was no minor episode.

And yet how does it all end? Saadia and David ben Zakkai embrace one another at the command of Bishr ben Aaron, as though nothing had occurred! [4] And just a few years later Chalaf ibn Sarjado becomes the Gaon of Pumbedita [5] and appoints to the lucrative judgeship of Mosul none other than his former enemy "Rat Face"! [6]

(5) Though Pumbedita was triumphant and Sura was no more, peace was not completely restored. Chalaf ibn Sarjado

---

[1] *Zikhron le-Rishonim*, p. 227:

ויגרם הדבר להכות רבים מישראל בשבט השליטים בשבתות ובחדשים ויחלל הוא את השם גם את השבתות להביא משאות לפחות והסגנים ביום צאתו עם חסר אל דאר מוברך. Cf. also *ibid* , p. 226.

[2] *Ibid.*, p. 230.

ובעליית דרב אלבקר ראוך אנשים כשרים תחת הנערים עם כתבי הקדש אף נערי נהרדעא נלאו ממצוא לך.

[3] *Ibid.*, pp. 227, 228.
[4] *Seder Olam Zuta*, p. 82.
[5] *Ibid.*, p. 83; *Iggereth*, pp. 120-21.

[6] ניתחברו אליו זקן פסילות יומי בה אלי עמרון בן זלאלה ופני עכבר יומי בה אלי אפרים (בן) שטיא אלדי קד נצבה כלף בן סרגאדו דיאן אלמוצל.
Zikhron le-Rishonim, p. 227.

had to fight off Nehemiah for the post of Gaon, and then after Chalaf's death, Sherirah had a quarrel with the same Nehemiah. [1]

It is, therefore, clear that if an individual had pinned his faith on *any* of the outstanding personalities of his day, and if he had taken seriously the verbal clusters as conveyors of information, he would have found himself completely disoriented and hopelessly confused. He would either have had continuously to reshape his loyalties as the rogues, the perverts, and the scoundrels of one controversy were transformed into exemplars of official righteousness in the next; or he would have had to draw the conclusion that both the gaonate and the exilarchate were morally corrupt and spiritually bankrupt. The spokesmen for these institutions had publicly displayed their unworthiness to provide leadership, for in their quarrels they had betrayed every spiritual principle that they had officially advocated and which had justified their authority, privilege and wealth. It is little wonder, then, that the tenth century witnessed the spread of Karaism, which held out the hope of an integrity that was structural, *i.e.*, factual, rather than verbal. [2]

If, on the other hand, an individual living in the tenth century had analyzed these controversies structurally, paying little heed to the verbal jousting, he would have found the message of the pattern of events to be rather simple. Aware that the disintegration of the Abbassid caliphate inevitably carried with it the fragmentation of empire, and that it

[1]   *Iggereth*, p. 121; letter of Nehemiah Gaon in "Bodleian Geniza Fragments," ed. A. Cowley, *JQR* (o.s.), vol. xix (1907), 105-06.

[2]   Whereas in the ninth century Karaism was a comparatively small dissident movement, in the tenth century it not only gained a strong foothold in Palestine and Egypt, but also it produced scholars of such eminence as Solomon ben Jeruham, Yefet ben Ali, Sahl ben Mazliah, and Jacob Kirkasani. For the expansion of Karaism in the tenth century, *see* Raphael Mahler, *Karaimer*, pp. 271-360. It was not long, however, before Karaism was sustaining itself on its verbal resources and was demonstrating incongruence between structure and verbalization (*cf. ibid.*, pp. 361-90).

meant the sundering of the Jewish communities in North
Africa, Italy and Spain from dependence on the institutions
in Baghdad, he would have assumed that the dwindling
resources, caused by the loss of revenue from these now
independent communities, would be catastrophic for both
the gaonate and exilarchate. He would also have realized
that the banking families in their efforts to stave off disaster
would join the fray with all the wealth and influence that
they possessed. The shifting character of the allegiances
would have been a clear signal that the verbal barrage was
deceptive. He would have recognized that Ben Meir's calendar
reform was an attempt to take advantage of the factional
struggles in the interests of Palestinian independence. [1] He
would have carefully watched the banking families shifting
from co-operation to destructive rivalry.

When the Great Controversy broke out, he would have
been alert. He would have noted that the Bene Netira were
supporting Saadia and that Bishr ben Aaron was supporting
David ben Zakkai and Kohen Zedek. He would, therefore,
have assumed that the Bene Netira had used their influence
with Saadia to challenge David ben Zakkai's authority as
well as those who supported him. This was an appropriate time
for launching a controversy because the Bene Netira were

---

[1] The controversy between Ben Meir and the Babylonian authorities over the calendar is an excellent illustration of the difference
between structural and verbal data. As information, the controversy
reveals a simple message: (1) Ben Meir is saying: "Since your authority
is being undermined by your factional strife, this is an excellent time
to achieve independence for Palestine. I shall make use of all authoritative texts available to achieve this goal." (2) The geonim, the
exilarch and Saadia reply: "We will not abdicate our authority even
if you challenge us with chapter and verse. We have an arsenal of
texts at our disposal, and if necessary we can even insist that the
calendrical system that we use had its origin on Sinai." The message
is brief and concrete. The verbal façade, however, involved long
disquisitions on fine calendrical issues that obscured the real message.
That the chief antagonists understood the message is evident from
the fact that the verbal barrage proved completely ineffective: each
side refused to be convinced by the other.

apparently, at this time, very influential with the caliph, and, it may be assumed, in rivalry with the Bene Aaron. The Bene Netira were attempting through Saadia to consolidate all three institutions in such a way that their interests would be most effectively served. The Bene Aaron banking family under the leadership of Bishr ben Aaron and Chalaf ibn Sarjado fought strenuously to prevent the victory of their rivals. And they succeeded largely because the death of Caliph Muqtadir was apparently accompanied by the elimination of the influence of the Bene Netira at the court. The forces of Bishr ben Aaron were victorious, and Saadia was forced to retire. [1]

The meaning of the reconciliation would likewise have been clear to a tenth-century proponent of structural analysis. The intensity of the Great Controversy had had deleterious effects. Though Saadia may have been defeated, his supporters were still powerful, and large numbers were sympathetic to his cause. When, therefore, an incident occurred which threatened to unleash a new round of hostility, Bishr ben

[1] Unfortunately, the sources are very vague about the course of events and are especially unhelpful in communicating the data that we need. The reconstruction that I am proposing adopts the following line of reasoning: (1) Since Saadia started the Great Controversy, he must have been certain of powerful allies (the Bene Netira) and he must have chosen a time that would favor a victory for himself and his allies. (2) Since the Bene Netira supported Saadia, and the Bene Aaron supported David ben Zakkai, these two families must have been antagonistic to each other. Though they had previously co-operated, they were now rivals. This could only mean that the Bene Netira, temporarily at least, had gained ascendency at the caliphal court; hence this was a good time for Saadia to challenge the exilarch. (3) According to both the pro-Saadia account of Nathan the Babylonian and the anti-Saadia diatribes of Chalaf ibn Sarjado, the Saadia forces were very active in using their influence at the caliphal court. The caliph, however, refused to intercede. (4) Saadia and his allies were defeated only when the death of Caliph Muqtadir in 932 changed the power constellation at the court. The Bene Netira must have lost their favored status and the Bene Aaron elevated to the position of court bankers. For the sequence of events, cf. H. Malter, *Saadia*, pp. 115-18; Baron, *op. cit.*, pp. 65-69; Mann ,"Varia," pp. 163-165.

Aaron and other influential families stepped in and laid down the law: Saadia and David ben Zakkai would have to become reconciled in a public way, regardless of what they thought of each other. Saadia would return to Sura, but after his death Sura would be disbanded. In order to soften the blow, certain of Saadia's most loyal associates, such as "Rat Face," were to be given judgeships by the Gaon of Pumbedita. As for the exilarch, his independence would be curtailed, and he would have to content himself with a very reduced status. Pumbedita, however, would reign supreme and the incumbent of the office of gaon would be none other than Bishr's son-in-law Chalaf!

Thus not long after the Great Controversy came to an end it was apparent that the banking family of the Sons of Aaron had successfully installed one of their own as gaon of Pumbedita; they had closed the doors of Sura and eliminated the claims of its scholars to the dwindling revenues; they had shorn the exilarch of much of his regal glitter. It may be surmised that had the Bene Netira—Saadia faction won out the situation would have been much the same: Sura instead of Pumbedita; the Bene Netira instead of the Bene Aaron.

The Great Controversy was indeed a great controversy, but only partially because of the antagonists. It was the culmination of a series of struggles to offset the consequences of disintegration. It was the most violent because the outcome could no longer be compromise, but consolidation and annihilation. The proof is not in anything that was said but in the outcome: the collapse of renowned Sura, the impotence of the exilarch, and the desperate condition of Pumbedita. [1]

---

[1] The shattered state of affairs is summed up starkly by Chalaf ibn Sarjado in a letter written after his elevation to the gaonate of Pumbedita:

ובכל זאת המחלוקת שיש בישיבה נדכינו ושחנו עד עפר ואין לנו רשיות שבא
מהם לחם חוקנו כי חרבו ואשר נותרו הוצרכנו אנחנו לצאת אלהם אחר שהיו
גדולי הישיבה שופטים יוצאים ברשיותנו וגם הקרקעות שהיו לנו חרבו ואבדו
באותן השנים הרעות שעברו עלינו אפסו כספינו וקרקעתינו ונשתפכנו כאבני

Though triumphant, Pumbedita was threatened with poverty and was compelled to beg piteously for alms and recognition from Jewish communities that had once viewed her with veneration! [1]

The mighty institutions that had ruled a world were in shambles. The Great Controversy was the symptom of structural disintegration. Saadia and David ben Zakkai were protagonists in a life-and-death struggle for institutional survival, but unbeknownst to these titans was the grim truth that defeat awaited victor and vanquished alike. The exilarchate and the gaonate were cut down by forces that neither genius nor dedication nor verbal ingenuity could avert.

קדש בראש כל חצות ונתנו מחמדינו באוכל להשיב נפשנו ולא נשתייר לנו זולת
כתבי אבותינו ולא נתן אלהינו למוט רגלנו ותחס עינו עלינו משחתינו ויתן לנפשנו
לשלל ובכל הקורות אותנו ולא עזבנו ארחות אבותינו והגינו התורה מתוך דוחק·
"Bodleian Geniza Fragments," *JQR.* (o.s.), vol. xviii (1906), 402.
Cf. Nehemiah Gaon's plight in *ibid.*, vol. xix (1907), 105-06.

[1]   *Cf.* Sherira's plaint, *Saadyana, op. cit.*, pp. 118-21:

ומרוב הדוחק הן כבד עלינו הצער ורבצנו תחת משאינו ואין לאל ידינו ואין
בנו יכולת··· ומתוך דחק וצער כתבנו אליכם ודברים האלה ומרוב שיחנו
וכעסינו הרבינו בדברים עמכם··· כי ימנעון חוקי החכמ׳ יעזבון את התורה
ויתעסקון(?) במלאכות··· כי מאז החרישו אבותיכם התחילה הישי׳ לחסור
ועתה הנה הולכת וחסור ספו שנה על שנה··· ואם אמור תאמרון בלבבכם כי
תישארון אתם על מתכונתכם ולא יישחתון מדרשיכם והישיבה נשחתת··· ואיך
ישחת הראש וישלם הגוף ואחר הראש הגוף הולך···ולכו במנהג אבותיכם ובדרך
הוריכם והחזירו את הדבר לישנו והגידו לנו ספיקותיכם למען תראון את
התשיבות והתגובבו בם וגם יחזק לב הישיב׳ בראותם כי אתם פונים אליהם
ופוחדים למזוניהם···

THE ORDINARY JEW IN THE MIDDLE AGES:
A CONTRIBUTION TO HIS HISTORY

By Cecil Roth

Oxford University

It has been observed more than once, but even now is imperfectly realized, that as regards past generations—and especially the Middle Ages—Jewish historiography concerns itself almost exclusively with the upper classes on the one hand, and with the learned elements on the other: two segments which to a great extent overlapped, but were by no means identical. As regards secular history, our sources are the Chronicles, which devoted attention to the personalities and activities of those most in the public eye—that is, the rich—and the Records, which were mainly interested in those persons from whom revenue could be obtained and considered the poor only intermittently if at all. The Hebrew sources on the other hand deal mainly with the progress of scholarship and the vicissitudes of the leaders of the community. We lack therefore to a great extent the details of the life of the Jews of the lower class—humble, penurious, unlearned: the class which, in the general population, made up the vast majority. I wish in this paper, written to honor one of the most distinguished contemporary Jewish historians, to begin (though no more) to delineate the Ordinary Jew of the Middle Ages: more in the hope of drawing attention to the subject than of executing anything that approaches a complete portrait. Inevitably, my materials will be derived principally from those areas—England, in particular—of which I have the most detailed knowledge.

The preliminary problem presents itself: Did this Jewish proletariat, as we may provisionally call it, with all reserve in fact exist? Especially, did it exist among the Jewries of

northern Europe, with their high standard of learning and
their almost complete dependence on usury as the basis of
economic life? For these areas we have handed down to us a
generic picture of small groups of Jews, living in comfort
on the interest of their invested capital, and devoting the
whole of their very considerable leisure to the study of the
Talmud: this being, as I suggest, the economic explanation
of the phenomenon of the *Baale ha-Tosafoth* and their intense
intellectual activity even in remote villages and townships.
It is, however, self-evident, from a moment's consideration,
that this picture cannot be comprehensive. For round about
the wealthy householders who formed the mainstay of the
communities there must necessarily have been grouped large
numbers of subordinates and dependents—servants, teachers,
bakers, butchers, nurses, clerks and so on—who to some extent
constituted the household retinues of the well to-do and whose
economic and social status was far humbler. Not infrequently,
such persons are mentioned in the records specifically. But
there were others in addition, to whom the term "proletariat"
can apply somewhat more correctly. A very interesting
Exchequer Account in the Public Record Office, London
(E 101, W.R. 249/4), as yet unpublished, gives details of the
assets of (or it may be a levy on) the Jews of Lincoln in 1240.
In all, there are just over one hundred names, including
(non-dependent?) women but not children. This gives an
approximate conception of the total Jewish population of
the city at the time, which must have been in the region of
two hundred and fifty or three hundred souls all told. The
amounts specified vary largely, ranging up to sums like £ 17.
2s. 10d. in the name of Peitevin f. Elias and Floria, his
daughter. At the other end of the scale are amounts as low
as sixpence (obviously, *de minimis curat rex*!). This is followed
by a very interesting list, unique in my experience, of those
who had nothing (*De hiis qui Nichil habent*), comprising
twenty-three names (or, including two pairs of sisters,
twenty-five) out of our total. Unfortunately, we are not always

certain whether the persons specified were in fact paupers or the dependents of the well-to-do. The names include those of one *clericus* (clerk and copyist, I imagine, rather than scribe: "De Samuel clerico Jacobi filio Leonis") and one *famula*— whose mistress, however, with her husband, are also included among the moneyless. The list comprises, too, two sons, and two granddaughters, of a Rabbi ("Magister"). [1]

The English communities were no doubt smaller than the average in Europe in the Middle Ages, and in some places on the continent far larger numbers were reached. At Nuremberg, according to the lists given in the *Memorbuch*, not fewer than 628 persons perished in the massacre of 1298, suggesting a total community of at least one thousand (unless, as is unlikely, the carnage was utterly comprehensive). On what their economic life was based is not easily to be determined, but certainly they must have relied on something other than usury.

A point which has a very considerable bearing on the life of the ordinary Jew, and in particular of the ordinary Jewess, is the size of the average family. It is generally taken for granted that in former times the birth-rate among Jews as among their neighbors was very high. It does not appear to me that the sources substantiate this view. If I am not mistaken, few of the eminent Jewish scholars of the Middle Ages—Rashi, Rambam, and so on—are known to have had families which would have been considered of more than average number even today. Certainly, the high infantile death-rate has to be taken into account (we know generally of the surviving children only), but it was probably lower among the Jews with their high pediatric standards than among their neighbors, and in any case this would not explain the phenomenon in its entirety. [2] The medieval English rec-

[1] *See* Appendix to this article for the full text of this document, which I publish for the detailed light it throws on the composition of a medieval Jewish community.

[2] The family history of Nathan of Rome's four children was

ords, which took into account with meticulous attention every person who might be of profit to the royal treasury, comprise fairly exhaustive information regarding the heirs and families of all Jews who were above the status of paupers, and the picture they convey is most suggestive. The families of some outstanding personalities were very small: for example, the great financier of the twelfth century, Aaron of Lincoln, is, I think, recorded to have had only two sons, while Aaron of York, the thirteenth century "Presbyter Judeorum," had the same. In my book, *The Jews of Medieval Oxford*, which I tried to make as exhaustive as possible, the genealogical trees show three families of five (in one case all sons, in the others three sons and two daughters), the others all being smaller. Norwich, investigated by Dr. V. D. Lipman, presents much the same picture (three five-child families and one perhaps of six in the middle of the thirteenth century in a community of perhaps two hundred, with normal families of two or three children). Exceptional as it seems were the cases of Rabbis Moses of London and his son, Elijah Menahem of London, each of whom had six sons (but apparently no daughter): no other member of that mighty and well-documented rabbinic clan seems however to have had more than one or two children, so far as our information goes. When we come to Italy in the age of the Renaissance, the picture becomes still more clear. We have a list [2] of the Jewish refugees of various origins who received safeconducts from the King of Naples in 1492. Out of twenty persons mentioned, five seem to have been unmarried or unaccompanied; two had their wives, but no children; one family of six children is recorded, four of three children, four of two children, two with one child. One widow, with a daughter, is also recorded.

tragic. His eldest-born died at the age of one month: the second survived to the age of eight years, and the third to three; the fourth died before circumcision. But this record seems to have been wholly exceptional.

[2] N. Ferorelli, *Gli ebrei nell'Italia meridionale* (Turin 1915), p. 84.

At the time of the enquiry into the murderous attack on the
Jews of Asolo in North Italy in 1547, minute details were
recorded of all the local Jewish families. One has five children,
two have three, two two, and others only one. [1] Returning
to northern Europe; the comprehensive lists of martyrs in
the Rhineland cities which comprise the Nuremberg *Memorbuch* normally include children generically with their parents,
mentioning only "and his son" or "and his sons." But it is
probable that, in the case of large families, the number would
be specified, and here once again the impression is not given
of large families, many indeed being apparently childless.
The detailed list of Munich martyrs of 1185 specifies two
families of four children, one of three children, seven of two
children, one of a single child. At Münster in 1287, according
to the same source, we find two families of five children,
there of four children, four of three children, two of two
children, and two of a single child. Of course, we must take
into account the enormously high infantile death-rate of the
Middle Ages, as mentioned previously. However, were we
to double the figures given above, the size of the families
would not even begin to enter into the fabulous range which
is generally associated with this period in our ideas. [3]

I have touched here only superficially on a subject of the
greatest importance, which obviously deserves fuller and
more systematic treatment. [3]

A close inspection of the English records suggests a hitherto
unsuspected aspect of the social and economic history of the
Jews in northern Europe. As is well known, there were in

[1] M. Osimo, *Narrazione della strage compiuta nel 1547 contro gli
ebrei di Asolo* (Casale 1875).

[2] The only really large family I have traced in the Middle Ages is
that of the 15th-16th century Alsatian Rabbi Johanan Luria, who
speaks pathetically in his (unpublished) Pentateuchal commentary
of his 21 sons: from how many mothers is not indicated.

[3] The 19th century of course presented a different picture. In
Victorian England, for example, Sir Sidney Lee's grandmother was
one of 26 sisters.

medieval England something under thirty established Jewish communities, most of them to be sure very small. Compiling, however, an exhaustive list of places in England in which Jews are mentioned in the twelfth and thirteenth centuries, I have now reached a total of approximately two hundred, to which I am sporadically able to add fresh place-names as new sources of information are published. Many of the places in question are tiny villages, unknown except in the immediate neighborhood. The problem now suggests itself: How did the Jews of these isolated places live? It is out of the question that they could earn a livelihood there by the practice of usury, even though in some cases (but only in some) isolated transactions may be recorded in their names. We are driven to assume that they were engaged in petty trade, handicrafts, and even perhaps some sort of horticulture. Here, presumably, we have the type of the "assimilated" English Jew of the Middle Ages, living in close contact with his Christian neighbors, seldom seeing a fellow Jew, and, so far as we can judge, with no opportunity for any intellectual outlet such as was possible even in a small community. It is, perhaps, significant that at the end of the thirteenth century, when adverse conditions drove many English Jews to embrace Christianity, many of them are stated to derive from small places whose names are new to Anglo-Jewish historiography.

Another glimpse of the existence of a Jewish proletariat in medieval England results from the fact that, although our documentation is so considerable, there are many persons of whose existence we are made aware by only a single mention in the records. Had they been professional financiers, they could not have escaped more frequent mention, whether in the taxation-rolls or in connection with lawsuits or disputes or the enrollment of charters. Moreover, such casual mentions are preserved only by accident: a person whose name is mentioned once, perhaps in connection with a petty misdemeanor, might not have been known at all but for this. Hence these isolated records suggest the existence of large numbers of persons who were never even once mentioned in such sources. Once again, the problem arises: How did they earn a livelihood? To be sure, some of these isolated mentions are the result of an isolated financial transaction, usually of a small amount, but my impression is that these do not denote professional usurers. It is likely that a Christian of the lower classes would approach some humble Jew for a petty loan, knowing that Jews were supposed to lend money: and the latter might advance a sum out of his savings, or perhaps ask a communal magnate for financial assistance in order to permit him to carry out the transaction, which would be duly registered as prescribed by law. (The "Borsa communis judeorum" mentioned at Norwich in the thirteenth century might have been a regular institution which existed for this purpose.) This would not explain the major question, how the communal proletariat normally earned their living. So far as I am aware an answer to this question is available, so far as the Middle Ages are concerned, only as regards Sicily where, as we know from both Jewish and non-Jewish sources, the bulk of the Jews of the lower classes were steve-dores, dock-laborers, metal workers and so on, with the ignorance, vices, and pastimes of persons of that class. That there was any parallel to this in northern Europe is unproved. We find, however, in the *responsa* of Elijah Menahem of London an interesting picture of how pious Jews, in order to avoid even the conceivability of *shaatnez*, would drape linen cloth over a cloth and hold it out from them, so as to avoid its being in contact with the wool they were wearing on their bodies. Here apparently we have a picture, not reflected in the secular sources, of medieval English Jews engaging in the traditional Jewish occupation of cloth-peddling.

Another sidelight is provided by the description *le Chanteur* or *le Romanzur* which we find appended to the names of one or two thirteenth-century English Jews; the former designa-tion, being found in association with the latter in respect to the same person, does not therefore mean *hazzan*, or synagogue cantor, as might otherwise be imagined. Here, therefore, we seem to be confronted with the figure of a Jewish ballad-singer: and since it is pretty well out of the question that he can have earned his livelihood among his own coreligionists, his clientele must have been mainly Christian. We thus seem to have a glimpse of the itinerant Jewish ballad-singer: a figure who may perhaps help to explain in part not only the composition of romance ballads for Jewish marriages and festivities, such as those published by Blondheim, but also the percolation of non-Jewish influences of this type into Hebrew prosody.

Another aspect of activity is suggested by the title or description *bulistarius* or *le albelester*—i.e., the crossbowman—applied to some medieval English Jews. The Lateran Council had forbidden Christians the use of that awesome weapon—the atom bomb of the Middle Ages—which therefore for a while became the speciality of Albigenses and as it seems Jews, who in view of their acquired proficiency continued sometimes to be associated with it even after their conversion. [1] (The occasional obligation on the Anglo-Jewish communities to maintain the royal crossbowmen was probably a consequence of this.) I find in my English records for example Hameth Balistarius (1244), Joseph le Albelester who was killed (1276), and some others. Dr. Neuman speaks of Jews as crossbowmen in the medieval period also in Spain, but I do not know his authority. There are a few other instances of Jews in northern Europe who followed the profession of arms. (The occasional mass-levies in southern Europe, and the occasional mobilization of Jews to assist in the defense of cities, as at Worms in 1201, do not come into the same picture.) Again from English records I quote Benjamin le Chivaler (*Exchequer of the Jews,* ii. 280) and Bruno fil' Benedicti Militis (*Pipe Roll* 1192, p. 69). This links up with the

[1] I at one time imagined that the title *albelester* & c. denoted the crossbow-maker—a calling more in keeping with what we know of the Jewish tradition—but this now hardly seems to me to be tenable.

tale which emerges later in the Polish *responsa* of Jews serving in the local armies (*Responsa Manhir Enayim*, n. 43) or the account we are told of armed Jews streaming out from Venice and the environs in 1509 to participate in the capture and sack of Padua. One may assume that the persons in question belonged to the lower strata of Jewish society. One English document introduces us to trial by combat proposed though not carried out between two Jews, one of whom pays a fine "ne esset tonsus ad pugnandum" (*Memoranda Rolls*, I John, p. 69).

The degree of literacy among the medieval Jews, of northern Europe especially, was very high: especially if we consider that they lived among a population in which illiteracy was all but universal. Whether, however, learning was as generally spread as chroniclers and most historians would have us believe is nevertheless somewhat doubtful. In a lawsuit of 1219 (*Exchequer of the Jews*, i. 17) a litigant states that "when a Jew is able to write, he makes his starr of acquittance with his own hand"—implying that this was not invariably the case. Ability to write does not to be sure necessarily imply a very high standard of literacy. The originals of some of the Anglo-Jewish "Shetaroth" published by M. D. Davis in 1887/8, preserved among the Muniments of Westminster Abbey, are in a sprawling and painful hand, suggesting less than constant familiarity with the art of writing. The number of books found among the assets of medieval Jews, both in England and overseas, must not blind us to the fact that in a majority of cases no books at all are mentioned: though of course this can be evidence as much of poverty as of the absence of intellectual interests.

In a very beautiful and characteristic passage, Zeev Javez gave an idealized picture of the *Haside Ashkenaz*, with their deep learning and profound piety. Certainly, the medieval Jews were not infrequently arraigned before the courts of justice, but *ex hypothesi* this was readily ascribed to the fact that Jewish financiers were inevitably implicated, or believed to be implicated, in commercial misdemeanors; and that prejudice sometimes resulted in prosecutions on flimsy charges. In the records, however, we find cases which seem to be reasonably well-established, and are presented without any appearance of prejudice, of commonplace and sordid crimes of the ordinary type committed by Jews—theft, rape, assault, murder. In twelfth- and thirteenth-century England, for example, there are sober records of a brawl between Jewish and Christian women (*Patent Rolls*, 1278, pp. 287, 290), of a quarrel between Jewish women one of whom is said to have "eaten" the mouth and ears of another (*Select Pleas of Jewish Exchequer*, pp. 11-2), quite dispassionate accusations of murder not only of Gentiles but also of fellow Jews (Roth, *Jews of England*, p. 277) and even uxoricide (*Curia Regis Rolls*, v. 25b). As is to be expected, Italian Jewry later on reflected local standards in such matters, and here there is even recounted a case of a murderous assault committed by one Jew on another in a synagogue (Colon, *Responsa*). Later, the family even of a scholar such as Leon of Modena seems to have moved, according to the naive account which he gives in his autobiography, among the very dregs of Venetian society. The diary (in bad Italian, with a few words of execrable Hebrew) of a sixteenth-century Siennese Jew of the lower orders which I published some years ago reveals a hardly credible standard of superstition, quarrelling, and ignorance.

I do not wish to go into the question of sexual morality, but from every country there are evidences that it was far from perfect. It seems pretty certain that the journey to Palestine so superbly recorded by Meshullam of Volterra [1]

[1] The traveller mentions in his record that he went to Palestine in fulfillment of a vow made in time of stress. Now, we know that his name in the secular records was Bonaventura di Manuele di Volterra, of whom it is recorded (Marino Ciardini, I *banchieri ebrei in Firenze nel secolo xv* [Borgo S. Lorenzo 1907], p. 10) that in 1460 he was "condannato alla pena del fuoco e al pagamento di fiorini 2,000 d'oro larghi pel reato di violenza carnale comesso su la figlia di Francesco di Piero Dati."

was the sequel to his escape from a condemnation to death in Florence for a sexual offense. In Renaissance Italy, even homosexual offenses among Jews are recorded. A fourteenth-century Spanish document (Jean Régné, *Catalogue des Actes de Jaime I, Pedro III et Alfonso III rois d'Aragon concernant les Juifs*, 1213-1291 [Paris 1911(?)], n. 1153) introduces us to a Spanish Jew and his son who were accused of theft, infanticide, fornication, usury, perjury, fraud, and assault, not to mention physical violence in the synagogue. What is perhaps most amazing is the evidence for the existence, in Spain and Italy at least, of brothels in the Jewish quarter. We are far removed here from the idealistic picture of Jewish life conveyed by the *Sefer Hasidim* and echoed by some Jewish historians.

The pastimes of the Jewish proletariat did not differ wholly from those of their neighbors. We are told that "in the Land of the Isle the Jews are lenient in the matter of drinking strong drinks of the Gentiles and along with them": and drinking in medieval England was a serious business. Rabbis indeed expressed their objection to hunting on humanitarian grounds: but this does not prove that Jews did not indulge in it, of which we have proof not only among the lordly Florentine loan-bankers of the age of the Renaissance but also, repeatedly, in medieval England and Spain. The constant condemnations of gambling demonstrate how extremely widespread that vice was in almost every European country.

I am painfully aware that the picture I have given is partial blurred, and inadequate. I have only been able to sketch in outline one or two details of the picture. For the rest, my impressions of the life of the Jewish proletariat in the Middle Ages are blotchy and defective, even as regards those areas with which I am most familiar. This paper will, however, have fulfilled its purpose if it directs attention to an important aspect of Jewish history which hitherto has to a large extent been neglected.

Appendix

Public Record Office, London
Exchequer Accounts E. 101 Q.R. 249/4 m. l.
Rotulus de Nominibus Judeorum et Judearum
De Juda le fraunceis. viii. li. et xv. s. Linc.' et Summis (?) starrorum
    eorundem.
De Lemoy fil' Isaac Generis eius. v. s. et v. den.'
De Josceo Longe. xxiii. den.
De Elya Genere eius. vi. s. et iiij^or den.'
De Abrah de Kent. xvii. s. viij. d. et ob.'
De Benedicto fil' Isaac. xiii. s.
De Abrah Genere Jude. iii. et iii. den.'
De Deusaut le Fraunceis. vi. et ix. den.'
De Leon filio Salom' xii. li. et xiii. d. Item xl. s.
De Jacobo filio Leon' xix. s. et iiii^or. den.
De Garcie Episcopo. iiii^or. li. v. s. et ix. den.
De Benedicto filio eius. xv. s. ix. d. et ob.
De Salom' le Normaunt (?) iii. s. et iiii^or. d.
De Daniel Le Prestre. xij. s.
De Benedicto fil' Leonis. xix. s.
De Joye fil' Elye. ij. s.
De Jacobo Le Prestre et Pictauino fil' eius. xii. li.
De Abrah' fil' Jacob' vi. den.
De Samuel fil' Elye. xxx. s.
De Deulecrese fil' Bretun et Jucte matre sua. vii. m. iii. s. et iii. den.
De Abrah' filio Salom'. xxv. s.
De Deulecrese filio Abrah'. xviij. den.'
De Peituin (?) filio Manasseril et Sarr'. viii. li. v. s. et iiii^oo. den.
De Jose (?) filio Benedicti. xxviii. s. iii. d. et ob.
De Pucele matre sua. xv. s. et ob.
De Richera vidua. iii. s.
De Duce Judea sua. ix. s. et j. den.
De Mosse de Graham. lxxvi. s. et ob.
De Haume Croc. xxxvi. s. viij. d. et ob.
De Bungay filio Magistri. xij. den.
De Jose de Colecest' Lv. s. cum Samulina matre sua.
De Aaron filio Abrah'. xi. s. et vi. den.
De Beniamiy filio Magistri. xv. s. et viii. den.
De Mosse de Colecest'. iiii^or. s. et viii. den.
De Avigay aua sua v. sol.
De Peitivin filio Elye et Fluria filia sua xvii. li. ii. s. et x. den.
De Dyaie fil' eius Elye et Iuetta (?) fil' eius viij. li. et ix. s.
De Jacobo de Oxon' Genere eius. xxiii. den.
De Isaac filio Elye. viii. li. xvii. s. et xi. den.
De Benedicto filio Isaac. xxx. s. et x. d.
De Fluria (?) vidua. vii. s. vi. et ob.

De Mose Sarre (?) Lxxii. s. x. den. et ob cum Sarra (*corrected from Siluria* ?) filia sua
De Isaac filio Mossei xxii. s. et ix. den
De Elema (?) vidua. vii. s. et xi. den.
De Jose' Lefraunceis ix. s. et viii. den.
De Picteuin filio Josc' (?) xix s. et iiii^or. den. Item per j. aliud starr'.
 Lx. sol. de j. cir' continenti. C.s. sub nomine Johannis filii Ran'.
De Manassei filio Dauid. ii. s. et iii. den.
De Benedicto filio Bonleuenge. xiii. s. vi. den.
De Picteuin (?) de Hedun', xlii. s. vii. d. et ob.
De Henna filio Pucle (?) ix. s. et viii. den.
De Viues Genere Abrahe. xv. s. et iiii^or. den.
De Abr' de Colecest'. x. li. vi. s. et vi. d. cum Joia fil' sua.
De Deulecrese filio Matatie. xiii. s. et x. d. cum Bella filia sua.
De Josc' de Herford. iiii^or. s. v. den. & ob (*over two small erasures*).
De Samuel' filio Benlevenge (*Blank*)
De Thira matre Manasseri x. s.
De Manasser' filio Aaron de Bedeford'. iiij^or. s. et xi. den.'
De Deulecrese de Graham'. vj. li. et ix. den.
De Jose de Bungeie. vj. li. xv. s. et vii. den.
De Benedicto filio Ghere (?). xlix. s. et x. den.
De Judea uxore Magistri. xxxiii. s. et viii. d. cum Henecota filia sua
 et flauetta fibesta ¹ sua.
De Elya Deulecrese. xi. s. et xi. den.
De Manasser' filio Magistri Josc'. xxiii^or. j. s. et v. den.
De Saria vidua. v. s. viii. den. ob.
De Elya filio Magistri xxi. s. et vi. den.
De Vives filio Mossei xxix. s. et iii. den.
De Abr' filio Cher' fil' Mossei. viij. s. et xi. den. cum Auigay filia sua.
De Borre (?) filio Samuel'. xxii. s. et iii. den.
De Vives filio David'. vi. s. et viii. den.
De Bele assez filia Garcie. xxix. s. et j. den.
De Salom' de Stanford. v. s.
De Benedicto filio Benedicti. xxi. s.
De Bonefei filio Bonefei de Oxon. x. m.
De Bentyt (?) filio Pictauin. xxxv. s. et viii. den.
De hiis qui Nichil habent
De Gente Matre Sarre Nichil
De Hakin filio Deulesaut—nichil
De Viuone Nepos Leonis nichil
De Samuel clerico Jacobi filio Leonis Nichil
De Viuecoc (?) filio Garcie Nichil
De Isaac filio Benedicti Nichil
De Benedicto filio Bese Nichil
De Samps̄ filio Magistri Nichil
De feme uxore Aaron Nichil

¹ ? filesta.

De Manasser' filio Magistri Nichil
De Sarotte (? Sarcote) Nepote eius Nichil
De Benedicto Genero Peteuin Nichil
De Rosa uxore sua Nichil
De Joia famula sua Nichil
De Hamecot et Cokeral filiis Isaac Nichil
De Genta Matre Jose Lefraunceis Nichil
De Abrah' filio Mossei Nichil
De Aaron filio Peteuin filio Jose, nichil
De Massekin Peyteuin nichil
De Sarra matre Abr' de Colecest'. Nichil
De Avigai filia Deulecrose de Grahā Nichil
De Geina et Joie fil. Jose de Bungeie Nichil
De Gikelota et Mucele fil' Elje fil' Magistri Nichil

De Samel' de Gimesby. C. iiii. sol. et vi. den.
De Benedicto Genero pictaui clerico. xx. sol. et viii. den.
De Jacobo genero Samekini. xvi. sol.

RABBI ISAAC TAMA AND THE ORDER
OF THE HOLY SEPULCHRE

By Simon R. Schwarzfuchs

Ecole Pratique des Hautes Etudes, Paris

DURING the second part of the eighteenth century the economic condition of the French Sefardi communities had so
much improved that the *Sheluḥim*, the emissaries of the
Palestinian Yeshivot, and especially those of Ḥebron, again
learned the way of southern France. In 1758, Samuel Shalem
visited Avignon. The following year he was in Metz where
the Ashkenazi community enjoyed a special status and great
prosperity. In 1768, Issachar Abulafia called on the communities of Nice, Carpentras, and Avignon. In 1775, Jacob
Burla and Yakar ben Gershon were seen in Carpentras. The
justly famous Ḥida visited France in 1755, and twice in 1778.
On the eve of the French Revolution, in 1789, Raphael
Abraham Leb-Arieh was in Bordeaux. [1]

Another *Shaliaḥ*, Mordecai ben Isaac Tamah, seems to
have remained in Europe. He first went to Holland where,
in 1765, he published a Hebrew edition of Maimonides'
responsa which he himself had translated from the original
Arabic. [2] Later on he went to America, then to Bordeaux
where Ḥayyim Joseph Azulai met him in 1777. The following
year Azulai was told that Tamah had lost his faith, that he
was reading Voltaire's books, and was denying the essential
principles of Judaism. Much upset by this information,
Azulai concluded: "May God allow him to make full
penance." [3] No wonder then that Mordecai Tamah chose to
remain in France.

[1] Abraham Yaari, *Sheluḥe Yisrael* (Jerusalem 1951), pp. 512, 516,
542, 570, 590, 631.
[2] *Peer ha-dor* (Amsterdam 1765).
[3] Ḥayyim J. D. Azulai, *Maagal tob ha-shalem*, ed. Freiman (Jerusalem 1934), p. 122.

It seems that he even brought his family, or at least a son, from Palestine to Bordeaux. Three documents which have recently come into our possession seem to bear this out.

The first document may best be described as an identification paper. In 1776, Jacob Rodrigues-Pereire, the founder of the first school for the deaf-mute, had received letters patent from King Louis XVI for the "Spanish and Portuguese Jews, known as the Portuguese merchants and New Christians." All previous grants made to them were renewed; full religious freedom was granted. They were given the right to settle in any part of the kingdom and to trade throughout France. All Portuguese Jews then living in France and those who were to come afterward were asked to register their names with the judges of the city they had chosen for their residence. It would seem that this right of registration was delegated, subject to confirmation, to the representatives of the "Spanish and Portuguese nation." Very probably these representatives had copies of the letters patent printed and used them to issue certificates. Our copy has this manuscript note:

> We, David Silveyra, general sindic and agent of the Jewish Spanish and Portuguese nation, residing in Paris, rue Tiquetonne, commissioned in consequence of the King's orders, to watch over the fulfillment and the maintenance of our privileges mentioned hereupon, certify that Isaac Tamar, Rabbi, age 22, five foot one inch, dark hair, belongs to our nation and that as such he is a naturalized Frenchman. He has come to me with a King's passport dated 1782 June 10 in order to go from here to Constantinople via Germany on his private business. He has fulfilled all formalities prescribed in the regulations of October 15, 1777 in order to enjoy all the privileges and prerogatives which Frenchmen enjoy in Constantinople and in the lands of the Great Lord. In order to ascertain the present [certificate] I have sealed it with my seal in Paris on the fourteenth of June 1782. [1]

[1] French text:
Nous David Silveyra sindic général et agent de la nation juive Portugaise et Espagnole résidant à Paris rue Tiquetonne, chargé en conséquence des ordres du Roi de veiller à l'exécution et au maintient de nos privilèges mentionnés cy-dessus et des autres parts Certifie que le S. Isaac Tamar Rabin âgé de vingt deux ans taille cinq pieds un pouce cheveux noirs est de notre nation et comme tel il est natura-

As will be seen later, the names Tama, Tamah and Tamar were often confused. Our Tamar was called Isaac, according to the well-known Sefardi custom of giving one's son his grandfather's name, whether the latter be alive or dead. His father, therefore, was Mordecai ben Isaac Tamah. It should be added that apart from Mordecai and Isaac Tamah the name Tamah or Tamar is unknown among Bordeaux Portuguese Jews. [1]

Tamar probably changed his mind about his itinerary. For in our second document, which is his passport, we read as follows:

> From the King
>
> To all officers on land and on sea, to the commanders of our fleet and to all upon whom our rule extends, greetings. We want and order you to allow safe and free travel from Paris to Marseille, and therefrom to Constantinople and Palestine by sea, Isaac Tamard, a Portuguese, French-naturalized Jew. You will give him every assistance he may need, and will not let any trouble or hindrance befall him. We beg and request all governors, officers of military and civil justice, to extend him in case of need every favor and protection. Given in Versailles the eleventh of August 1782.
>
> Louis

(Seal of the King) [2]

lisé français lequel s'est présenté chez moi avec un passeport du Roi en datte du dix juin courant pour aller de cette ville à Constantinople en passant par l'Allemagne pour affaires qui le concernent, lequel a satisfait aux formalités prescrites par le règlement du 15 octobre 1777, pour jouir des privilèges et prérogatives dont les Français jouissent à Constantinople et dans tous les États du Grand Seigneur, et pour que foi y soit ajouté au présent j'y ai apposé mon cachet à Paris le quatorze du mois de juin mil sept cent quatre vingt deux.

D. Siveyra

[1] *See* the list of Jewish names on tombstones in the Sefardi French communities in Moïse Schwab, *Les inscriptions Hébraïques de la France* (Paris 1904), pp. 223-239.

[2] French text:
De Par Le Roy
A tous nos officiers de terre et de mer, aux commandants de nos vaisseaux et à tous ceux sur qui notre pouvoir s'étend, Salut! Nous voulons et vous mandons que vous laissiez sûrement et librement passer de Paris à Marseille, et de là à Constantinople et en Palestine par la voye de mer Isaac Tamard, Juif Portugais naturalisé françois

Certainly Tamar, now called Tamard, had asked for a change in his passport. One may well ask what he intended to do in Jerusalem. Our third document, which is rather extraordinary, will give the answer:

We, grand officers, governors and administrators of the royal archbrotherhood of knights, pilgrims and brothers of devotion of the Holy Sepulchre of Jerusalem, settled in Paris by Saint Louis, King of France, in 1234, transferred to the Grands Cordeliers by Louis X in 1316, confirmed by letters patent of different kings of France in 1338, 1365, 1665 and 1381, and by different papal bulls, especially protected by the Kings Louis XIV, Louis XV, and Louis XVI, now ruling, having heard the report of the honesty, ability and strictness in observance of Isaac Thamar, naturalized Frenchman, ordinarily residing in Jerusalem, have appointed and do now appoint said Isaac Thamar to examine, and to have examined and copied in our name and in the name of said archbrotherhood, all titles, bulls and statutes of said archbrotherhood and the order of the Knights of the Holy Sepulchre of Jerusalem instituted by Godfrey of Bouillon in 1099 which may be found in the archive of the Church of the Holy Sepulchre in Jerusalem, and especially the ordinances relating to the foundation, restoration, and statutes of said orders which were issued by Louis VII, King of France, during his sojourn in Jerusalem in 1149, with the list of Frenchmen who have been admitted as knights of said Order in Jerusalem since 1733 up to this day, to pay all dues which may be claimed during this study and for the copies, to have the latter verified by the Reverend Father warden of the Recollets monks, established in this church, to have the verified copies authenticated by the Consul of France; we give him every authorization and necessary power. We beg said Reverend Father warden and Recollets monks to have all confidence in him and to give him every help for his mission. Therefore we have given him the present letters signed by us and the secretary general of said royal archbrotherhood. In order to ascertain it, we have sealed it with the great seal of our said royal archbrotherhood. Given in Paris in our assembly, the first of August 1782.

(Great seal)   Seven signatures. [1]

et que vous lui donniez toute l'aide et l'assistance dont il pourra avoir besoin, sans souffrir qu'il lui soit fait aucun trouble, ni empêchement. Prions et requérons tous Gouverneurs, officiers militaires de justice et civils, de lui accorder aussi en cas de besoin toute faveur et protection. Donné à Versailles Le onze août mil sept cent quatre vingt deux.   Louis, Par le Roy

[1] French text:
Nous grands officiers, gouverneurs et administrateurs de l'archicon-

It would seem that Isaac Tamar had become an instrument in a well-known quarrel between important Christian orders. It is said that on the day Jerusalem fell to the Crusaders, on the 15th of August 1099, Godfrey of Bouillon established the "Ordre du Saint Sépulcre de Jérusalem," which was to be a noble order with a long tradition. In 1317, Louis I, Duke of Bourbon, established the "Confrérie du Saint Sépulcre de la rue Saint Denis" in Paris. In 1336, a group of Parisian burghers established another brotherhood, the "Confrérie du Saint-Sépulcre des Cordeliers." Later on the two orders were to merge and to become associated with the Recollets monks. Because of a confusion with the ancient "Ordre du Saint

rérie royalle des chevaliers, voiageurs et confrères de dévotion du S. Sépulcre de Jérusalem fixée à Paris par St Louis Roi de France l'an 1234, transportée aus Grands Cordeliers par Louis X l'an 1316, confirmée par les lettres patentes des différents Rois de France de 1328, 1335, 1365, et 1381 et par différentes bulles des Papes, spécialement protégée par les Rois Louis XIV, Louis XV et Louis XVI, actuellement régnant, sur le rapport qui nous a été fait de la probité, capacité et exactitude du Sr Isaac Thamar, naturalisé Français, résidant ordinairement à Jérusalem, avons commis et commettons ledit Sr Isaac Thamar pour requérir et faire faire pour nous et au nom de la ditte Archiconfrérie, la recherche et expédition de tous titres, bulles et statuts concernant la ditte Archiconfrérie et l'Ordre des chevaliers hospitaliers et militaires du St Sépulcre de Jerusalem institué par Godefroi de Bouillon l'an 1099 qui pourront se trouver dans la trésor des chartes de l'église du St Sépulcre de Jerusalem, et notamment des ordonnances de fondation, restauration et statuts du dit Ordre donné par Louis VII, Roi de France, pendant son séjour à Jerusalem en l'année 1149, ensemble la liste des Français qui ont été reçus chevaliers du dit ordre à Jerusalem depuis 1733 jusqu'à ce jour, de payer les droits qui pourront être dûs pour les dittes recherches d'expéditions, faire collationner les dittes expéditions par le révérend père Gardien des religieux recollets établis dans la ditte église, et faire légaliser les dittes copies collationnées par le Consul de France; lui donnons à cet effet tous pouvoirs et toute mission nécessaire. Prions lesdits révérend père gardien et religieux recolets de lui accorder toute confiance et toute protection pour le fait de laditte commission et à cet effet lui avons délivré les présentes lettres signées de nous et du secrétaire général de la ditte archiconfrérie royalle; et pour que foi y soit ajoutée, nous y avons fait apposer le grand scel de notre ditte archiconfrérie royalle. Donné à Paris en notre assemblée le premier aout mil sept cent quatre vingt deux.

Sépulcre de Jerusalem"—everyone was making use of the name Saint Sépulcre—the brotherhood received in 1762 the title of "Ordre royal et archiconfrérie des chevaliers, voyageurs et confréries de dévotion du Saint-Sépulcre de Jérusalem," which turned it into a noble order. The ancient "Ordre du Saint Sépulcre" immediately protested against this misappropriation, and on June 2, 1776 King Louis XVI forbade the brotherhood to use its new title. The brotherhood did not accept his decision. It maintained that it was a royal knightly order and that it had been misrepresented. It kept protesting from 1776 until 1790, and tried to prove its contention. [1] This is why it retained the services of Isaac Tamar, who was entrusted with the mission of recovering all relevant documents believed to be preserved in the Church of the Holy Sepulchre in Jerusalem. Thus the son of the *Shaliaḥ* of the Hebron Yeshivah was hired in order to re-establish the good name of Christian religious order.

We do not know the outcome of his mission but it would seem that Isaac Tamah, the rabbi ordinarily residing in Jerusalem, returned to France and played an important part in connection with the Sanhedrin assembled by Napoleon.

In the archives of the Consistoire Israélite de Paris still exists this letter addressed to the Minister of the Interior. It reads as follows:

Sir,

D. Tamar, secretary attached to the delegation of the Frenchmen professing the Hebrew religion of the Bouches du Rhone department, has the honor to tell your Excellency that he wishes to print a report of the works of the assembly, of its discussions, the speeches which have been and which will be delivered there. This would be done under the censorship of any censor your excellency may wish to appoint...   Paris, August 23, 1806 [2]

---

[1]   *See* Couret, *Notice historique sur l'Ordre du Saint Sépulcre de Jerusalem depuis son origine jusqu'à nos jours* (1099-1905 (Paris 1905), pp. 452-67, and Michel de Pierredon—who copies mostly Couret—, *L'ordre équestre du Saint Sépulcre de Jerusalem*. Son historique, son organisation, ses insignes et ses costumes (Paris 1928), pp. 41-56.

[2]   French text:
A son Excellence Monsieur le Ministre de l'Intérieur.

His request was granted. In 1808, he published the minutes of discussions of the Assembly of Notables and of the Great Sanhedrin. [1] His name is indicated on the title pages as Diogene Tama: he had recovered his father's name. Like many French Jews, he had exchanged his Jewish first name Isaac for another. Perhaps, like his father, he had read too much Voltaire and, like Diogenes, was still looking for the man he wanted to be—an honest man.

Monseigneur,

D. Tamar, Secrétaire attaché à la députation des François professant le culte hébraïque du département des Bouches du Rhône, a l'honneur d'exposer à votre excellence qu'il désire faire imprimer un recueil de travaux de l'assemblée, de ses délibérations, des discours qui y ont été et seront prononcés, le tout sous la censure de celui qu'il plairait à votre excellence de nommer.

Il ose à cet effet supplier votre excellence de bien vouloir lui accorder son agrément pour procéder à ce travail désiré par la nation juive, qui pleine de vénération pour le plus grand des monarques, attend avec confiance et respect le résultat de ses intentions bienfaisantes.

J'ai l'honneur d'être de votre Excellence, le très humble et très obéissant serviteur.

D. TAMAR

Paris, 23 Aôut 1806 rue Villedot no 12

[1] For a full bibliography of Tama's publications, *see* Zoza Szajkowski, "Judaica-Napoleonica—A bibliography of books, pamphlets and printed documents" in *Studies in Bibliography and Booklore*, vol. ii, no. 3 (Cincinnati 1956), pp. 113-114, nos. 61-67.

THE BEGINNINGS OF EAST-EUROPEAN JEWRY
IN LEGEND AND HISTORIOGRAPHY

By Bernard D. Weinryb

Dropsie College

Leopold Ranke's contention that history shows "what really happened" (*wie es eigentlich gewesen ist*) and the expectation that history was to become a pure scientific discipline has been undermined by a number of trends during the last century.

Historicism, for one, with emphasis on "the infinite variety of particular historical forms immersed in the passage of time" has been instrumental in the rise of relativism. Darwin, William James, Marx, Comte, Freud, and others have contributed to the realization of the existence of "a realm of secret, irrational powers, the presence of attitudes, interests, purposes and unconscious drives behind the façade of reason."

In the post-World War I years "conflicting perspectives and interpretations" spread, and "distrust between groups" was augmented. Merton says in such a situation of mistrust and conflicting perspectives one "no longer inquires into the content of beliefs and assertions to determine whether they are valid or not . . . but introduces an entirely new question"; namely, "How does it happen that these views are maintained?" These ideas of *Seinsverbundenheit* strengthened the "conclusion that emotive and irrational factors"—group belonging, class interests, social stereotypes, dogmas, myths, residues, as well as systems of belief, ideologies, illusions, situations within society, class structure—"permeated history and society." [1] Or, according to Karl Mannheim, in

---

[1] Hans Meyerhoff, *The Philosophy of History in our Time. An Anthology* (Garden City, N.Y. 1959); Karl Mannheim, *Ideology and Utopia* (New York, 1936); *idem, Essays on the Sociology of Knowledge*

certain areas of historical social knowledge any finding inevitably bears the imprint of the position and perspective of the discoverer.

The new understanding of sociological and psychological factors and the impact of social psychology upon historiography ripened a recognition among historians that both their own psychology and the currents of their particular age have been colored by trends in society. Thus, relative objectivity came to mean for the historian "subjecting his own (and other historians') mental processes to the same critical appraisal as he uses for the source data with which he works." [1]

Historians and philosophers such as Benedetto Croce, Raymond Aron, John Dewey, Carl L. Becker, Charles A. Beard,. and others, formulated the idea that "all history is contemporary history," or "history as thought"—which really is a construction of the historian's mind. While the discussion continues of what history is, what its nature, methods and goals are, and while some reject the idea of subjectivist-relativist historiography, [2] the necessity of identifying the sources of the historian's bias has been generally acknowledged. Efforts to explain historical works center around the question, "How did it happen that these views are (or were) maintained?" It became plausible that "the past appears for historical knowledge insofar as it has a

(New York, 1952); Social Science Research Council, *Theory and Practice in Historical Study* (Bulletin No. 54) (New York 1946); Robert K. Merton, "The Sociology of Knowledge" in G. Gurvitch & W. E. Moore, eds. *Twentieth Century Sociology* (New York 1945), p. 368; *idem, Social Theory and Social Structure* (Glencoe, Ill. 1949); Nathan Rotenstreich, *Between Past and Present* (New Haven, 1958).

 [1] Arthur M. Schlesinger, "History, Mistress and Handmaid" in *Essays on Research in the Social Sciences* (Washington D.C., 1931), p. 152.

 [2] Chester McArthur Destler, "Some Observations on Contemporary Historical Theory," *American Historical Review*, vol. lv (1950), 503-29; Arthur O. Lovejoy, "Present Standpoints and Past History," *Journal of Philosophy*, vol. xxxvi (1939), 477-89; Maurice Mandelbaum, "Arthur O. Lovejoy and the Theory of Historiography," *Journal of the History of Ideas*, vol. ix (October 1948), 412-23.

meaning for the present." Hence the given present, the social and political situation in which the historian finds himself and the climate of opinion of the society in which he lives, determine his selection of "facts" from the past and his attitudes toward them, or as one observer, Rotenstreich in *Between Past and Present*, said recently, "we treat historical works of research as data for subsequent historical research."

The two developments behind this are:

(a) The myths propounded by historians and other writers, and the images of the past which they created have often, insofar as they penetrated the minds of "people of action," become an inducement to further action supported by these myths and images and thus have "created history." Marx's dictum, for instance, that all history is history of the class struggle, became a contributing factor in the development of socialist and communist trends and, in consequence, of today's world situation and the east-west political struggle.

(b) At the same time, this very realization of the impact of myths lent impetus to the search for a more refined critical evaluation of documentary sources and historical works. If, as Carl L. Becker pointed out, the realization grew that our picture of an historical event is determined both by "the actual event itself insofar as we can know something about it," and "by our own present purposes, desires, prepossessions, and prejudices, all of which enter into the process of knowing it," it is not surprising that the "imagined picture" of past events as related by different historians would be questioned and many a myth dispelled.

> "Written . . . history"—reads one of the propositions adopted by the Committee on Historiography of the Social Science Research Council—"is to be best understood not only by analysis of its structure and documentation, but also by a study of the possible attitudes arising from the life and circumstances of the author." [1]

Approaches such as these open new vistas for the historian who aims to probe deeper in his search for truth. He may

[1]   *Theory and Practice of Historical Study*, p. 135.

lose something of his sense of security under the impact of the broadening field of inquiry, the more demanding standards of his technique, and the multiplication of sources and approaches. But he acquires a sharper critical approach which leads him to question some accepted views and many of the myths with which historiography abounds.

What is true for historiography holds also for the legends and traditions with which historians often have to deal. A critical sense and resort to conclusions derived from anthropology, sociology, psychology, and psychoanalysis have led to more realistic conceptions of legends and traditions.

Traditions, legends and myths of origin have baffled many an historian. Many have dismissed these as unworthy of consideration, regarding them as the offspring of fancy and ignorance, or as stories which in the course of time have lost any resemblance to the facts from which they sprang. Others seek to find traces of facts behind the myths and hence regard them as an historical source. Anthropology and in part also sociology, psychology and psychoanalysis have advanced various explanations and theories. Some hold that legend and myth have had a political and social purpose in justifying rites or social or moral rules, in consolidating a group of people more strongly and in increasing social and political control. [1] Others regard these legends and myths as fictitious explanations of religious rites or social usages. Still others consider them wishful thinking by which a group makes its origins conform with its present desires. Russian historiography, too, has developed similar approaches to legendary materials. [2]

One need not necessarily subscribe in full to all these theories. But a comparison of legends and traditions of many peoples inevitably leads to the conclusion that these are

[1] Bronislaw Malinowski, "Myth in Primitive Psychology", *Magic, Science and Religion and Other Essays* (Glencoe, Ill., 1948), pp. 79, 85, 92-98, 102.
[2] D. S. Likhatchev, "Epitcheskoye Vremia Russkich Bilin" in *Akademiku Borisu Dmitrievitchu Grekovu ko dniu Semidesyatiletiya* (Moscow 1952), pp. 56 ff.

creations of a comparatively later date and that their authors, even when unknown, sought to justify an existing situation or an anomalous status, to serve a ruler, to strengthen social control, religion, church, national feeling, or similar causes and institutions. The history of most peoples shows a tendency to push their beginnings back in time in order to create legendary figures and events to sanction a doctrine or establish a status.

I. *Legends and Traditions of Origin of East-European and Other Jewries.*

About forty years ago I. Berlin [1] drew attention to a number of parallel themes in stories about the origins of some Jewish families in Spain and Italy as well as about the admission of Jews into Spain and Poland "in order that there should be neither drought nor lack of rain". Jewish historical research has failed to follow up these parallels in legends and myths in various countries despite the fact that such parallels, with minor variants, exist.

Jews of Spain, France and Germany have, since the middle ages, maintained that they came to these countries after the destruction of the First Temple (586 B.C.E.). Similar traditions were found among Jews in Persia (Iran), Aden, Yemen, Caucasus, Buchara, China, Cochin, Crimea. The Jews of North Africa—Morocco, Algeria, Tunisia and Libya—trace their origin to the time of the Second Temple. Some documents indicate that at the time of the first Crusade (1096) and later, the Jews of Worms, Augsburg, Regensburg, Halle/ Saale, Ulm in Germany, as well as those in some French cities and in Spain, held that their forebears had lived in those places since the destruction of the First Temple or some time before the birth of Jesus. The Jews of Regensburg stated in 1477 that their ancestors learned about the cruci-fixion only from a letter they had received from Jerusalem. In some parts of Morocco a legend has it that the Jews are

---

[1] *Istoricheskiya Subdy Evreyskago Naroda na Teritorii Ruskogo Gosudarstva* (Petersburg 1919), pp. 49 ff; 65 ff.

descendants of the Children of Ephraim (son of Joseph) who came there after the destruction of the First Temple. The Jews of Bukhara, Georgia, Daghestan, Azerbijan, and Armenia, regard themselves as descendants of the Ten Tribes; some of the legends and traditions among Yemenite Jews purport to show that they are descendants of a group which revolted against Moses and was driven to Yemen. Another tradition in Bukhara has it that fifteen hundred years ago the ruler sent to Persia to ask for Jewish immigrants realizing that his "land is large and all I need is Jews." These Jews for a long time enjoyed full equality with the rest of the population, the first restrictive decrees being issued only about a thousand years later. [1] It seems that the Jews in Dagestan, Crimea and

[1] Itzhak Ben-Zevi, *The Exiled and the Redeemed* (Philadelphia 1957), pp. 17, 18, 23, 33, 66, 67; H. Z. Hirshberg, *Me-eretz mebo ha-shemesh* (Jerusalem 1957), pp. 72, 161, 168 ff; *ZGJD*, vol. iii (1931), p. 33; Aronius, *Regesten*, pp. 1-2; Siegbert Neufeld, *Die Halleschen Juden im Mittelalter* (Berlin 1915), pp. 13, 18; S. Dubnow, *Weltgeschichte des Jüdischen Volkes* (Berlin 1926), vol. iv, p. 54; Albert M. Hyamson, *A History of the Jews in England* (London 1908), pp. 1-3; H. J. Zimmels, "The Historical Background of the Midrasch Eleh Ezkerah" in *Semitic Studies in Memory of Immanuel Loew* (Budapest 1947), p. 337; שכל בני גליותנו צרפת וספרד שהוא גלות · · ·
ירושלים. . .ולדעתי לכך רוב השמד היום בצרפת ואלמניה לפי שהיו גלות
החל ולא ראו בשבר ירושלים · · · Quoted by D. Ginzberg in *Ha-kedem*,
vol. i, No. 3, p. 120:
· · · יהודים שגלו בחורבן הראשון · · · הגלות שהלך לספרד · · · לא רצו לצאת
מבתיהם באמרם שבנין בית שני היתה פקידה לבד · · ·אשר כתב הגמון קדמון
מאוד והעיד מיהודים שבטוליטולה לא יצאו משם בבנין הבית השני ולא נמצאו
במיתת המשיח · · ·
Gedalia ibn Yachya, *Shalsheleth ha-kabalah* (Amsterdam, 1697),
pp. 14b, 94b · · · בחורבן בית ראשון באו ונתישבו בק"ק וירמיז ואחר כלות
חזרו הגולים לירושלים ולא"י ואלה אשר היו בוירמיז לא חזרו·
I. Heilprin, *Seder ha-doroth* (Zhitomir 1867), vol. i, p. 139; A. Neubauer, *Anecdota Oxoniensia* (Oxford 1887), vol. i, part iv, p. 141; *see* also S. Eppenstein, *MGWJ*, vol. lxiii (1919), pp. 165 ff; Joseph Sanbury, writing *ca.* 1672, mentions a tradition that Jews were brought to Spain after the destruction of the First Temple and they, like other Jews, did not want to follow the call of Cyrus to return:
· · · לא רצו אלה לעלות אל ירושלים ונתישבו באלו הארצות ועליהם נתובא
עובדיה [20 :1] וגלות החל הזה אשר כנענים עד צרפת היא אלימניה
ואשקלונה ופרוביניציה ופראנציא וגלות ירושלים אשר בספרד היא איספאניא·

environment also had traditions of descent from the Ten Tribes or from those who were exiled at the time of the destruction of the First Temple. [1]

Some of these legends and other traditions about the origin of Jewish settlements and communities may or may not originally have had a kernel of truth, but today many, if not all, are apocryphal. One is even justified in assuming that all the traditions of descent from "Galuth Shomron" or from the diaspora of the time of the destruction of the First Temple (586 B.C.E.) center around the cycle of stories about the Ten Tribes. The later books of the Bible are connected with the time of the Second Temple, while Judaism as a way of life, as it became known throughout the middle ages and later, is a product of post-exilic and talmudic traditions. If Jews in a certain country really descended from a group which separated from the main body of Jewry before the Second Temple and the talmudic period, their religious and cultural patterns must have remained quite different. Yet there is no shred of evidence in any source whatsoever of such a situation in any of the afore-mentioned countries. Elements of such a condition are found only among the Falashas in Ethiopia, who may not be of Jewish stock at all. In addition, the fact itself that parallel themes recur in such diverse countries and parts of the world as Spain, Germany and Poland, northern Africa and Asiatic countries, indicates that the general trend to give origins the status of antiquity is motivated by minority situations faced by Jews in all these countries.

Even as early as talmudic and early post-talmudic times projections were made for the purpose of allegedly acquiring the status of antiquity. Palestine was held to be the first country in the world, Hebrew the earliest language and the

---

[1] *Cf.* A. Firkowitch, *Abne zikkaron* (Wilno 1872), pp. 64, 70, 84. It may well be that Firkowitch did not invent the traditions but rather made "inventions" to prove them. At any rate, there is independent knowledge of such traditions; *cf.* A. Harkavy, *Ha-yehudim u-sefath ha-slavim* (Wilno 1867), pp. 109-110.

Jews the first people on the globe. Again, the claims upon Palestine were based on the view that the country belonged to the forefathers of the Hebrews but was conquered by Kenaan. R. Yehudah Halevi in the middle ages resumed the argument of the antiquity of Hebrew holding it to have been the language of Adam. [1]

Jews of both the middle ages and modern times have used similar arguments of "antiquity" in other connections, too. This sort of reasoning originated throughout the world in widely separated sections. Whether one interprets myths along the Freudian line as vehicles for wish fulfillment, or regards them as expressions of the collective subconscious or as an attempt at justification by means of antiquity so as to meet contemporary needs, it is clear that various Jewish groups felt the necessity of justifying the existence of their enclave and of giving a legitimate reason for it. They tried to find a "usable past" for the present, sought to legitimize their presence by a long history, by more or less fictitious contributions to the welfare of the indigenous people, by affirming that they had been invited to settle among them. In some cases, as in Christian countries where Jews in the middle ages were accused of having participated in the killing of Jesus, fictitious history was invoked to prove their innocence and their settlement was pushed back to the pre-Christian times. It was also necessary for internal reasons to provide a newer settlement with the appearance of continuity, of being heir to an older established one. In other words, the parallels between the various legends and traditions among diverse Jewish groups indicate that all, or most, of them are expressions of similar purpose—to meet hazardous situations of a minority settlement within another group.

In summary we might say that in Jewish legend, traditions,

[1] Babli Taanith 10a; Ber. Rabbah 15, 4. Kuzari 3, 68; *cf.* also I. Heinemann, "Ha-mahloketh al ha-leumiyuth ba-agadah uba-philosophia shel yeme ha-benayim" *Sefer Dinaburg* (Jerusalem, 1949), pp. 134-136; J. L. Maimon in *Sefer yobel . . . S. K. Mirsky* (New York 1958), p. 333.

and early historical writings, at least insofar as diaspora history is concerned, a number of recurrent themes sometimes occur together, sometimes separately. These themes may be divided into the following categories:

1. The beginning of a Jewish settlement at a specific place or in a certain country usually "goes back" to an early period i.e., often to a time either preceding the historic dawn of the given country or people, or coinciding with it. In the western and Muslim countries this theme is sometimes extended to the point where the Jews there antedate the beginning of Christianity or Mohammedanism. [1]

2. The Jews are supposed to have been invited by the people or their rulers to settle in the country because of the advantages they would bring with them.

3. The Jews allegedly saved the country from drought, plague or some other calamity, or made some basic contribution to the general welfare.

4. At the beginning of the Jewish settlement in a particular country or generally in the remote past, the Jews were treated well and enjoyed equal rights with non-Jews; a worsening of their conditions occurred much later, usually in the more recent past. [2]

5. The first settlers or groups brought with them a direct tradition, or heritage, of an older Jewish center or centers. This gives them prestige and standing.

We know of three principal legends in the case of Poland which more or less belong to these types. There is the story of Abraham Prochownik who, although a Jew, was proclaimed Prince of Poland about the middle of the ninth century but

[1] This tendency to "push back the beginning" or to give the justification of antiquity is not a special characteristic of a minority group like the Jews. Medieval Christian chronicles usually start with the creation of the world and with Adam and Eve in order to prove that their culture is more ancient than that of the pagans.

[2] Non-Jews or antisemitic materials usually reverse the approach, "finding" the contemporary (real or wished for) discrimination against the Jews as existing "from the beginning" or as having come about early as a result of the Jews' own misbehavior or faulty characteristics.

who urged the election of a Pole in his stead. According to this story, the Poles were undecided about the choice of a successor to their prince who had just died. They resolved that their prince should be the first man entering the town the following morning. Abraham Prochownik was the first arrival and was duly proclaimed prince. He persuaded the Poles to select one of their own people instead. Thus the founder of the dynasty of Piast, a mythical person in Polish history, became a Polish prince.

Another legend relates the coming of Jews to Poland at the end of the ninth century, at the time of the second semimythical Polish Piast prince. At that time—so runs the legend—Jews in Germany were being persecuted; a delegation of five rabbis came from there to the Polish prince asking him for the right to settle; after a council meeting lasting three days, he granted the request. Another version has it that he granted them right of asylum on condition that their prayers would assure a timely rainfall. Thus, supposedly, the first larger group of Jewish immigrants came from Germany in 894, and later the prince granted the Jews the privilege of free immigration, communal autonomy and protection. [1]

An analysis of these two legends will show that they were "created" not earlier than the late middle ages. [2] The name "Prochownik", which appears in the first story, means gunpowder merchant or maker of gunpowder. This indicates that the legend could not have been created before the

[1] H. Sternberg, *Geschichte der Juden in Polen unter den Piasten und den Jagiellonen* (Leipzig 1878), pp. 4 ff, 7 ff; S. Dubnow, *History of the Jews in Russia and Poland*, vol. i (1916), p. 40; J. Lelewel, *Polska Wieków Średnich*, vol. ii.

[2] There seems to be no possibility of tracing the time when these legends first developed. So far as is known there is no record of them before the 19th century (some actually assume that they were created in the 19th century for apologetic purposes). The oldest known record is apparently that of the second legend which is published in 1801 (Anonymous, *Phylacterium oder Argenton und Philo im Schosse der wahren Glückseligkeit* (Berlin 1801), summarized in *Der Orient* X (1649), 143-144, 155-156, 159-160; *see* also Aron Eisenstein, *Die Stellung der Juden in Polen im XIII und XIV. Jht.* (Cieszyn 1935), p. 6.

thirteenth-fourteenth century when gunpowder first became known in Europe. The second story, of the five rabbis from Germany requesting refuge, is apparently of still more recent origin. All five names are Sephardi. [1] This may indicate that the story was created about the time of or after the expulsion of the Jews from Spain (1492) when some Spanish Jews did come to Poland.

A third legend which was still being handed down by word of mouth in the nineteenth-twentieth century, connects the beginning of Jewish settlement in Poland with the Spanish expulsion. It runs more or less as follows: When the Jews were expelled from Spain they moved toward the East. After long wanderings they rested and said (another version is that they found a note which dropped from the sky saying) *Poh lin* [Hebrew: Here stay overnight]. The country received its name (in German: Polen, similarly in Hebrew and Yiddish)[2] from this word.

Similarly, individual communities had traditions of their own which fall into one or more of the categories mentioned. Thus a town in Galicia boasts that the prophet Jeremiah was buried there, and Lublin in Poland where Jews are known to have lived since the end of the fifteenth century asserts that a pupil of the Tanna R. Meir (second century C.E.) was buried in its cemetery. This cemetery, however, is not older than the sixteenth century.

II. *Historiography*

Historians and other writers dealing with east-European Jewry were bound to add some myths of their own. They, too, like those who created the legends, were responding to the needs of their own times.

In the nineteenth century historiography became motivated

[1] Rabbis Hiskiya Sephardi, Akiba Estremaduri, Immanuel Ascaloni, Natanel Barceloni, and Levi Baccari. According to the rendering by Lelewel, the first and third were from Palestine and the fifth from India.

[2] *JJLG*, vol. v (1909), 147.

by the struggle for liberalism and progress and, in the case of
a minority like the Jews, by the striving for emancipation.
Historiography thus became subordinated to political criteria.
Apologetics, an attempt to depict Jews as useful, to emphasize
their high ethical or educational standards, whatever the
case may be, or their "birth right", is another aspect which
a minority group may be inclined to employ. Both an appeal
to antiquity (a "useful past") and "contribution to the country" could be invoked here. Minorities and small nations,
whose history is so badly neglected in general historical
works have also the tendency, probably to a greater degree
than larger nations, to hanker for status, to emphasize or
overemphasize their importance in the world. In historiography this manifests itself by attempts to overstate the link
in the group's past with worldwide or global historical events
(great wars, large-scale developments, trade, science, the
arts, literature, communications, etc.), by stressing „participation", and inflating minor facts out of proportion to their
true value and their historical perspective.

There was also a specific situation in eastern Europe which
made the historian more aware of problems of the origin of
its Jewry, and at the same time indicated a desirable solution.
At the beginning of the nineteenth century, east-European
Jewry constituted about a half of world Jewry or more.
Some Jewish—and also non-Jewish—historians and writers
were on the lookout for an explanation as to why this region
in which the legal-economic situation of the Jews seemed to
be the worst, harbored so many of them. Again, in Russia the
particular conditions seemed to require a claim for great
antiquity. Russian Jewry of the nineteenth century (the time
of development of Jewish historiography) comprised relative
newcomers to Russia. They were Polish Jews who came to
Russia as a result of the Polish partitions (1772-1795), and a
very *small* group which had arrived a few years earlier.

For centuries there had been hardly any Jews in Russia,
and these few, for the most part Polish Jews, who lived in the

regions ceded to Russia after the Kozak uprising of the mid-seventeenth century, were expelled on several occasions, the last time in 1742. This fact, that the Jews were newcomers in the country, was stressed during the nineteenth century in Russia by some of those who were opposed to granting them political and/or civil liberty. Another factor was that the secularized Russian-Jewish intelligentsia influenced by German-Jewish enlightenment and by other movements had a sort of disdain for Polish Jews. The Jews in Russia were eager to draw a line between themselves and Polish Jewry, regarding themselves as rather superior in many respects. All this made Jewish historians and other writers in eastern Europe sensitive to problems of "belongingness," past history, roots, and the like.

The trend toward extending origins back into the distant past may also have been accelerated by the existence of a similar tendency among the Slavic nations themselves. Poles, Ukrainians and Russians sought to compensate for their own inferiority feelings by belittling the West, or demanded status by virtue of "antiquity." Since their own preserved historical records are of a comparatively late provenance, they were — and still are — likely to use any sort of indication of this, even using Jewish sources for this purpose. [1] Modern Jewish historiography is both a child of general historiography in terms of approach, methods and attitudes and, at the same time, has been motivated by the needs of the

---

[1] Thus the king of "Gebalim" in Hasdai ibn Shapruth's letter (10th century) has been identified with a Slavic or Polish prince. P. Kokovtsov saw the "special" or "exclusive" value of the "Khazar document" which Schechter published in 1912 from the Geniza in the fact that it contains new details about the beginnings of Russian statehood (August Bielowski, *Monumenta Poloniae Historica* vol. i, (Lwów 1864) pp. 51-83; l. Modelski, *Król Gebalim w liście Chasdaja* (Lwów 1919); P. K. Kokovtsov, *Novyi Evreiski Dokyment o Khazarakh* ... [reprint] [St. Petersburg 1913] p. 1. In Soviet Russia, as well as in other Eastern European countries (Poland etc.) the tendency increased lately to push back to almost pre-historic times the formation of the Slavic peoples.

Jewish minority situation. It is, like historiography generally, based on ideas of enlightenment, progress, liberalism, nationalism, etc. In addition it shows some features which are characteristic for a minority group. In this it is often not unlike the Jewish legends and traditions.

1. Jewish historiography has the tendency to push back the period of settlement in a country to an early period.
2. It is likely to emphasize that Jews brought (and continue to bring) benefits and that they had been invited to that country or were there at the earliest period.
3. It is inclined to emphasize information showing that non-Jews fraternized with Jews in the distant past, and that the rulers of the country accorded them equal, or very similar, treatment; the worsening of the Jewish situation came, supposedly, much later.
4. It is likely to exaggerate the rôle of individual Jews or to over-estimate their number, often generalizing single cases (talking of "mass immigration" to eastern Europe in centuries when at most a few individuals may have been involved).
5. These tendencies are likely to influence both the historians' responsibility, or lack of it, toward source material, and their critical approach.

Hypotheses and Theories

The hypotheses about the origin of Jewry in eastern Europe propounded during a century and a half may be divided into two large groups:

1. *Northern Black Sea or Southern Russia theories.* Most of these hypotheses assume that this area, where the early Russian state was formed, is also the place where the Jews first settled in Slavic lands, and that they arrived either before, together with, or at the dawn of Slavic-Russian immigration. Theories range from the assumption that the Jews were descendants of early pre-Christian settlers in the Bosporus State, later augmented by conversion of

the Khazars, to ideas about early immigrants from Palestine, from Byzantium, Persia, and the survivors of Khazar
descendants. Thus the Jews in eastern Europe are assumed
to be either non-Semitic, semi-Semitic, or fully Semitic
in origin.

2. *Western theories*. These approaches regard the Jews in the
   Slavic countries as originating predominantly or solely in
   western Europe.

Each of the two groups of hypotheses may, in turn, be
subdivided into secondary hypotheses and theories.

1. The Black Sea-Southern Russia theories fall into the
   following six categories:

   a. Scythian theory. Around 600 B.C.E. Jews came directly
      from Palestine to Scythia, geographically located in the
      southeastern part of European Russia. Their numbers
      were later augmented both by new immigration and by
      proselytes.

   b. Jews came from Babylonia and Persia to southern
      parts of modern Russia before the common era (the
      Ten Tribes) or in the first centures C.E.

   c. Jews came to the Northern Black Sea region through
      Greece and Byzantium or from Palestine via Greece
      at the time of the Graeco-Roman Bosporus Kingdom
      or during the time of the Byzantine Empire when
      oppression of Jews arose there (seventh to tenth
      centuries C.E.)

   d. Somehow connected with the Black Sea theory is also
      the Caucasus hypothesis. It assumes that Jews lived in
      the Caucasus after the destruction of the First Temple
      (sixth Century B.C.E.) or even earlier since the exile of
      the Ten Tribes (the destruction of Samaria, 719 B.C.E.).

   e. Khazar theory. The Khazars—and the ethnic Jews who
      lived in the Black Sea region since the first century
      B.C.E. or immigrated later—formed the backbone of
      Jewry in eastern Europe. Later, after the destruction
      of the Khazar state, they spread out to form nuclei of

Jewish groups in the Slavic lands (and Hungary).
This Khazar theory has several nuances. Some regard
the Jews as descendants of the Turkish Khazar tribes,
while others think that they descended from the Slavs
who were under the suzerainty of the Khazar state and
thus became converted to Judaism (Gumplowicz). Still
others relate eastern European Jews to both the
Khazars and the ethnic Jews who lived in Khazaria.

f. Kenaan or "panslavic" theory. This hypothesis, too,
belongs to the Black Sea-Southern Russia group
although it somewhat transcends the Black Sea geographic borders and has some connection with at least
one of the western theories. This hypothesis may be
summarized as follows: Early Russian (or Polish) Jews,
whatever their origin, were part and parcel of the local
population, spoke their language (language of "Kenaan"
in Jewish sources), and followed their customs. Later
they were assimilated in the masses of German Jews
who immigrated to the Slavic lands, adopting and
modifying the German language into Yiddish and
neglecting their older culture.

2. The western theories may be divided into the following
groups:

a. Trade route hypothesis. An early trade route leading to
the east existed throughout the Slavic lands and particularly in areas linked with the northern Black Sea
shore. Jews participated in this trade and settled at an
early date along the route.

b. Western persecution theory. Jews immigrated from the
west, mainly from Germany and Bohemia, during the
twelfth-thirteenth centuries, a period of persecution in
Germany; small settlements made up of Jews from the
west may have originated earlier because of previous
persecutions (Crusades) or because they came on
business trips from west to east.

The division into different theories is, however, not always so clearcut. The afore-mentioned hypotheses and assumptions seldom stand alone. A few of them are often combined; *i.e.*, sometimes one or more of the Black Sea-Southern Russia theories are connected with the western theories in a sort of compromise. [1]

Development of the Theories and Approaches

The Scythian theory, which, incidentally, found little echo in historiography, is based on assumptions of the biblical-critical school and other authorities that biblical writings show some traces of knowledge of the Scythians. This indirect indication of some contact of Jews with the Scythians was coupled with an assumption (lacking any proof) of the antiquity of the Jewish settlement in southern and southwestern parts of the territory of the Russia of today.

Babylonian-Persian and Caucasus theories are based, on the one hand, on the general approach of S. D. Luzzatto that Jewish cultural and religious development in the west, including eastern Europe, derives from Babylonia. The assumption further maintains that at the time of the last Sassanians (fifth-sixth centuries C.E.) Jews emigrated from Babylonia to southern Russia because of oppression. On the other hand, A. Harkavy and with him S. Cassel and others identified Africa (אפריקי), which is mentioned in the Talmud, with Caucasus. According to these ideas Jews lived there after the destruction of the First Temple or even earlier.

The Bosporus and Byzantium theories take their clue from the fact that epitaphs attest to the existence of Jews in parts of the northern Black Sea shore during the first centuries

---

[1] The theories here are formulated on the basis of the approaches of most historians, summarized in part by Berlin, op. cit., pp. 52-58; J. Brutzkus, "Istoki Russkago Evreystva," *Evreyski Mir* (Paris 1939), pp. 17 ff; M. Balaban, "Kiedy i skąd przybyli Żydzi do Polski", *Miesięcznik żydowski*, vol. i, (Warsaw 1930), 1 ff; Ph. Friedmann, "Der Onhoib fun dem Yidishn Yishuv in Mizrakh-Europe", *Yiddisher Kemfer*, vol. xxxii, no. 900 (April 1951), 35-42.

C.E., and from information on persecution of Jews in the
Byzantine empire. The enforced Christianization decreed by
Heraclius (634), the baptism decree of 721-2 by Leo III, the
Isaurian, as well as the alleged expulsions (786-809) and later
persecutions (Romanos I, 919-44), brought many Jews, so
goes the argument, to the northern parts of the Black Sea-
southern Russia region. Graetz at first adhered to this theory
but later repudiated it, while Samuel Krauss and others
supported it. [1]

The western persecution theory was promulgated largely
by Jost and Graetz who regarded the fact that eastern
European Jews speak Yiddish, which developed from the
German language, as a reason for assuming that all or most
of them came from Germany to eastern Europe, including
southern Russia. This emigration is placed in the twelfth-
thirteenth centuries, a period of severe persecutions in Germany. At that time, it is maintained, a larger group of German
Jews emigrated to the east. [2]

The most widely influential of the theories were the trade
route theory (2.a), the Kenaan or "panslavic" theory (1.f),
and the Khazar theory (1.e) sometimes coupled with the Kenaan hypothesis (1.f) or with the above-mentioned trade route
hypothesis and/or with the Babylon-Persia and Byzantium
theories (1.b and c).

In the last quarter of the nineteenth century, with the
publication of Heyd's *Levantenhandel*, of Roscher's theory
about the role of the Jews in the middle ages, and of the
edition of ibn Khurdadbeh's text, [3] the rôle played by the

---

[1] H. Graetz, *Geschichte d. Juden*, vol. V¹ (1860), pp. 188-189;
vol. V² (1871), pp. 166-169; (quoted by Berlin p. 57) vol. V (1909)
pp. 172 ff.; S. Krauss in *Jewish Encyclopaedia*, vol. iii, pp. 450-456;
idem, Studien zur Byzantinisch-jüdischen Geschichte (Leipzig 1914)
and repeated later (*cf.* also Salo W. Baron, *A Social and Religious
History of the Jews*, vol. iii, 2nd ed. [New York 1957], pp. 196 ff.)

[2] H. Graetz, *op. cit.*, vol. vi, p. 69.

[3] W. Heyd, *Geschichte des Levantenhandels im Mittelalter*, vol. i-ii,
(Stuttgart 1879); W. Roscher, "Die Stellung der Juden im Mittelalter", *Zeitschrift f. d. Gesammte Staatswissenschaft*, vol. xxxi (1875),

Jews in medieval trade began to be emphasized. This became still more pronounced at the beginning of our own century, in the wake of the discussion surrounding Sombart's theories about the connection of the Jews with the growth of capitalism. Studies in economic history of the Jews began to appear frequently. The problem of their rôle in the formation of trade routes has been pointed out by non-Jews and Jews alike. On the basis of the slightest evidence, or even without any evidence, it was taken for granted, probably with the image of contemporary Jewry in mind, that Jews played a large rôle in this development. This led to the assumption that Jewish settlements sprang up along the routes. [1]

In connection with the Slavic countries, the statement made by ibn Khurdadbeh (*ca.* 846) about the routes of the Rhadanites and the information furnished by Ibraham ibn Yaqub on his journey to Prague (tenth century) gained weight. [2] "Sometimes also they take the route back of Rome (Rumiyah-Byzantium)," says ibn Khurdadbeh, "and crossing the country of the Slavs, proceed to Khamlij (Itil) the capital of the Khazars. They embark on the Caspian Sea then . . . from there to China." And Ibrahim ibn Yaqub, describing Prague, states that to that city "come from Cracow Russi and Slavs with wares" and from Hungary "Moslems, Jews and Turks" [3]—Hungarians in Greek and Arab sources of the

503-26 (English translation by S. Grayzel in *Historia Judaica*, vol. vi [1944], 13-26); Ibn Khurradadbah Abu al Qasin, *The Book of the Routes and the Kingdoms* (*Kitab al-Masalik wal-mamalik*)(French by M. J. de Goeje in *Bibliotheca Geographorum Arabicorum*, vol. vi [Leiden, 1889] [Earlier publication by Barbier de Maynard in *Journal Asiatique*, 1865]).

  [1] Ignaz Schipper, *Anfänge des Kapitalismus bei den abendländischen Juden im frühesten Mittelalter* (Wien & Leipzig 1907), p. 19; idem, *Di Wirtshaftsgeshichte fun di Yidn in Poilen beeisn Mitelalter* (Warsaw 1926) (Polish edition 1911), pp. 29 ff.

  [2] F. Westberg, "Ibrahim ibn-Jakubs Reisebericht über die Slawenländer aus dem Jahre 965", *Memoirs of the Russian Academy* 1899; new edition: T. Kowalski, *Relacja Ibrahima ibn Jakuba z podróży do Krajów Słowiańskich w przekazie al-Bekriego* (Kraków 1946).

  [3] Ibn Khordadbah passage quoted from translation in Robert

time. Schipper combines these two pieces of information with the mention in Hasdai ibn Shaprut's letter [1] to the Khazar king of two Jews at the embassy in Cordova from "the king of the Gebalim, who are the Saqlab" [2] (Slavic, sometimes other European peoples, in Arabic sources) and with some other scraps of information; he then depicts a widespread Jewish trade between east and west, passing through Poland and Russia, in the wake of which a settlement arose. The trade-route approach was further developed by Brutzkus. Following Schipper to a great extent, although disagreeing with him on some points, he depicts an extended Jewish trade reaching from Mayence and Regensburg through the Slavic lands to the east during the tenth to twelfth centuries. He further suggests that Jewish settlements sprang up along these trade routes. A responsum ascribed to R. Jehuda Hakohen, author of *Sefer ha-dinim* who, according to Zunz was active chiefly in the third quarter of the eleventh century (Horedezki puts him in the first half of the eleventh century), purportedly implies the existence of a Jewish community in Poland. [3] It has a reference to two boys (mentioned as שני

J. Lopez and Irving W. Raymond, *Medieval Trade in the Mediterranean World* (New York 1955), p. 32; Ibn Yakub's statement is according to Kowalski's edition (preceding note) translated by B. D. Weinryb, "Origins of East European Jewry", *Commentary*, vol. xxiv (December 1957), 515.

[1] D. M. Dunlop, *The History of the Jewish Khazars* (Princeton, N.J., 1954), p. 136.

[2] P. Kokovtsov, *Erveysko-Khazarskaya perepiska v X veke* (Leningrad 1932); Schipper, *Wirtschaftsgeschichte*, pp. 28 ff. and further elaborated in *idem, Kulturgeshichte fun di Yidn in Poilen beeisn Mittelalter* (Warsaw 1926), pp. 12 ff., *idem, Dzieje Handlu żydowskiego na Ziemiach Polskich* (Warsaw 1937), pp. 2 ff; recently A. Ashtor (*Koroth ha-yehudim bi-sefarad ha-muslimith* [Jerusalem 1960], pp. 134-146) argues that *saqlab* means here German, and by "King of Gebalim" is meant the Emperor Otto I of Germany who sent envoys to Spain.

[3] The responsum is reprinted in V. Aptowitzer, *Introductio ad Sefer Rabia* (Jerusalem 1938), p. 451; *Or zarua*, vol. i, no. 694 (Zhitomir 1862, p. 196); reprinted in Fr. Kupfer and T. Lewicki, *żródła Hebrays-kie do Dziejów Słowian i niektórych innych Ludów Środkowej i Wschod-

אחים יתומים קטנים and נערים) who were taken prisoner from the
town פרימוט at a time of war or attack שהיה) בעת החרום
בפלוני or בפלנו). Following an earlier suggestion by Tykocinski,
Brutzkus identified פרימוט with Przemysl in Galicia (Primut/
Primus/Przemysl), suggesting that here is an account of the
attack of the Russian Prince Yaroslav of Kiev upon the
Galician cities in 1031. Because of the mention of two Jewish
children, it has been concluded that a Jewish community
existed at that time in Przemysl, which lay on the trade
routes from west to east. These trade route approaches, with
either a cautious or a clear cut belief in the existence of a
settlement were largely accepted as factual in Jewish historiography, and belief in them has had some impact upon non-
Jewish historiography. [1]

The Kenaan hypothesis takes its name from the expression
"Kenaan" (Gen. 9: 18, 25, 27, and other sources) which came
to mean "serf". Some medieval Hebrew writings applied this
designation to Czech or other Slavic and non-Slavic peoples.
Benjamin of Tudelah uses the word when speaking about
Prague for Czech or, perhaps, generally Slavic peoples. [2]

niej Europy (Wroclaw-Warsaw 1956), p. 36; J. Brutzkus, "Di ershte
Yediyos vegn Yidn in Poilin," Yivo, *Historische Schriften*, vol. i
(Warsaw 1929), pp. 55, 72 (Ukrainian translation: Ukrainska Akademia
Nauk, Istorychna Sekcia *Naukovyi Zbirnik na rik*, 1927, vol. xxvi);
partially repeated in *ZGJD*, vol. iii (1929), 97-110 and Yivo, *Schriften
für Wirtschaft und Statistik*, vol. i (Berlin 1928), pp. 69-75; H. Tykocinski, *MGWJ*, vol. liii (1909), 350.

[1]   Balaban, *Mies. Żyd.*, *op. cit.*, p. 6 remarks only that it is hard to
say if the Rhadanites settled in Poland; R. Mahler, *Toledoth ha-
yehudim be-polin* (Merchavia 1946) pp. 20-21 (cautious indication);
B. Mark, *Di Geschichte fun Yidn in Poilen* (Warsaw 1957), pp. 174 ff.
(speaks of a "trade-colonization stream" and "a Rhadanite wave of
immigration"); The new official Polish history (T. Manteufel ed.,
Historia Polski, vol. i, 1 (Warsaw 1958) mentions "the existence of a
colony of Jewish traders in Przemyśl at the beginning of the eleventh
century."

[2]   Benjamin gives the following reason for the name Kenaan
". . . because the people . . . sell their sons and daughters as slaves
to all nations." This may be his own rationale for an expression
developed in imitation of Latin documents which, from the ninth

Isaac Ber Lebenson, writing in the 1820's, tells about a
tradition וזקנו ספרו לנו "that some generations before us the
Jews in these regions spoke only in this Russian (Ukrainian)
language." He goes on to relate, in the name of Tadeusz
Czacki (1765-1813), author of the first history of Jews in
Poland (*Rozprawa o Zydach* [Wilno 1807]), that the Jews were
praying in Polish and states that "this is evidence that their
language was Polish or Russian . . . and from this it followed
as a hypothesis that the first Jews who came to dwell here
originated not in Germany . . . but came from among those

century on used "Sclave" to mean both Slavonic people and people
in the condition of servitude (*cf.* also S. D. Goitein in *JSS*, vol. xvii
(1955), p. 10).

In eastern Europe, however, the expression Kenaan (or Canaan)
does not seem to have had any derogatory connotation. The son and
grandson of the richest Jew in Cracow, Lewko (died ca. 1395) were
named "Kenaan". *See* Majer Balaban, *Dzieje Żydów w Krakowie i na
Kazimierzu*, vol. i, (Cracow 1912), p. 10; Schipper, *Wirtschaftsgeschichte*
pp. 130 ff; *see also* S. Huberband in *Builetyn Żyd. Instytutu Histor.*
(Warsaw 1951), no. 2, pp. 20 ff. Earlier the expression is found in
Josipon; ··· הם הנקראים סקלבי ואומרי אחרים שהם מבני כנען ··,·; There
are also a number of Slavic glosses in the Commentaries of Rashi (1028-
1105), Joseph Kara (ca. 1060-1130), in the responsa of R. Isaac b.
Mose of Vienna (circa 1180-1255) and others which may be Czech or
also from other Slavic languages. Benjamin himself differentiates
between "Kenaan" and Russia or Russians. Some Hebrew sources
identify "Kenaan" with Germany, *e.g.*, Ibn Ezra, commentary to
Obadia 1: 20, or David Kimchi. In glosses of R. Gershom לשון כנען
is identified with German while, on the other hand, Saadia identifies
"Ashkenaz" with "Saqlab." Apparently based on these and similar
sources is Jacob Emden's statement (in a letter of 1772) that our
forefathers called German the language of the land of Kenaan:
ושפת ארץ כנען (כך היא מכונה אצל אבותינו הקדומים) אשכנזית ···.
P. Rieger, *MGWJ*, vol. lxxx (1936), 455-459; *idem*, *MGWJ*, vol. lxxxi
(1937), 299-301; S. Krauss, "Die hebr. Benennungen der modernen
Völker", *Jewish Studies in Memory of George A. Kohut* (New York
1935), pp. 398-399; L. Gruenhut and N. Adler, *Die Reisebeschreibungen
des R. Benjamin von Tudela*, vol. i (1904) pp. 137-138; L. Zunz,
Gesammelte Schriften, vol. iii (1876), pp. 82-83; M. Mendelssohn,
Gesammelte Schriften, vol. xvi (Berlin 1929), p. 158; *see also* Rosenthal,
Historia Judaica, vol. v (1943), p. 60. It seems that "Kenaan" in
Hebrew was a generic name similar to the Arabic *as-saqaliba* (also
as-Saqlab, Sasqlab, Greek *Sklaboi*) applied in the middle ages to Slavic
but also to non-Slavic peoples.

who lived around the river Volga, a thousand years ago and
had a Jewish king . . ." [1] Harkavy [2] further developed this
theory of Lebenson although pointing out that what he says
by the authority of Czacki is not to be found in the latter's
work. Harkavy's reasoning is based mainly on the existence
of Slavic (Kenaan) glosses in Rashi, the Bible Commentary
of R. Joseph Caro, the *Or zarua* of R. Yizhak b. Moses of
Vienna, and coins with Hebrew Slavic inscriptions, etc.
which were found in Poland. He also seeks support in the
Slavic names of Jews and in some statements that in the
seventeenth century Jews in certain regions spoke Russian,
and that there are manuscripts in Parma containing Polish
translations of biblical books written by Polish Jews who
lived at the beginning of the sixteenth century in Brescia and
Mantua. All this is to substantiate the view that the Jews in
southern Russia are descendants either of old Jewish settlers
in the Greek cities on the Black Sea coast, or of Jews who
came from Asia through the Caucasus. The Kenaan theory
was further supported by a letter, found in the Cairo Geniza,
which is supposed to have been written in Saloniki in the
eleventh century about a Jew from Russia who knew only
"the language of Kenaan." [3]

The most spectacular development was that of the Khazar
theory sometimes coupled with the Kenaan and trade-route

---

[1] *Sefer teudah be-yisrael*, 2nd ed. (Vilno 1855), p. 35.
[2] Albert Harkavy, *Ha-yehudim u-sefat ha-slavim* (first published
in Russian).
[3] ... היצרכנו הודיעכם עסק מ׳ פל׳ בן פל׳ שהוא מקהל רוסיאה ונתארח
אצלנו בקהל סלוניקי ... אינו יודע לא לשון הקודש ולא לשון יווני גם לא
ערבי כי אם שפת כנען מדברים אנשי ארץ מולדתו ...
J. Mann, *The Jews in Egypt and Palestine under the Fatimid
Caliphs*, vol. ii (Oxford 1922), p. 192; a collection of the "Kenaan"
glosses (and other pertinent material) has recently been published;
Fr. Kupfer and J. Lewicki, *op. cit.* More recently the "Kenaan"
theory led to the formulation of a new version—apparently taking
a clue from Harkavy—of a hypothesis of the existence of a "Kenaan"-
Jewish language in the Slavic lands (Max Weinriech, "Yiddish,
Knaanic, Slavic," *For Roman Jacobson* (Amsterdam 1956), pp. 622-
632; *see also* Marmorstein REJ, vol. lxxiii (1921), 92-97.

hypothesis. This theory underwent many transformations including falsifications on a grand scale. Either by reason of the glamor of a former Jewish state, the willing acceptance of a little-known historical incident which left few traces, or because the theory offered an *easy* solution to the problem of the numerical predominance of eastern European branches in Jewry, (Kutschera emphasizes this point), it became widespread.

In addition, Russian historiography was destined to serve as a support for this theory. The old Khazar state existed in the territory which later became Russia and had many encounters with the Russians which are reflected in the older Russian chronicles. C. M. Fraehn's statement at the beginning of the nineteenth century that Russian history is interwoven with Khazar history, became for a long time one of the main assumptions of Russian historiography .[1] So also was the connection between Jews and Khazars to become acceptable.

It seems that Tadeusz Czacki's work at the beginning of the nineteenth century was the first to give some adherence to the view about the Khazar origin of the Jews. Trying to answer the question whence did the Jews come to Poland, he first states that as a result of oppression they migrated to Poland from the west (Germany, Bohemia). He goes on to tell about the Khazars and the existence of Jews in Khazaria, concluding very cautiously "that through neighborly and commercial relations Jews could little by little penetrate and later settle in Poland." [2] Lebenson, as mentioned above, adopts this Khazar idea.

Strong impetus toward entrenching the Khazar theory came from falsifications connected with the name of the

---

[1] V. O. Kluchevski, *Kurs Russkoy Istorii*, vol. i (Petrograd 1918); V. A. Parchomenko, *U istokov Russkoy Gosudarstvennosti* (Leningrad 1924), pp. 13-41; M. J. Artamanov, *Ocherki drevneyshei Istorii Chazar* (Leningrad 1936); V. N. Tatishchev, *Istoriya Rosiyskaya*, vol. ii, pp. 211, 212 ff. and N. M. Karamzin, *Istoriya Gosudarstva Rossiyskaga*, vol. i-ii, *pass.*; S. M. Solovyev, *Istoriya Rossii*, vol. ii, p. 348; and many others.

[2] *Rozpravy, O Żydach* (Kracow 1860), pp. 88 ff.

official of a Karaite community in Russia, Abraham Firkovich (1785-1874). In the 1830's, with the blessing of Russian authorities, he undertook a search for the origin of the Karaites in Russia. His purpose was to convince the government of Nicolaus I (1825-1855) that the Karaites lived on the territory of Russia from times immemorial, to show that they had little in common with the other Jews and that, therefore, they should be treated better than most of the Russian Jews. He travelled through the Crimea and Caucasus hunting in cemeteries and searching in the synagogues for material on the Karaites; he then went to Egypt and Palestine to study and collect old Hebrew manuscripts.

Firkovich, who had earlier forged some documents for his own private purposes, [1] falsified or fabricated many epitaphs on gravestones, injected many a spurious passage into old Hebrew manuscripts, affixed incorrect dates, and made alterations in authentic manuscripts. He did this to prove that the Karaite Jews originated from the Ten Tribes or the exiles after the destruction of the First Temple. He contended that Jews with Tataric names—all alleged progenitors of the Karaites— lived in southern Russia from times immemorial or arrived early from Persia, and he insisted that the Karaites converted the Khazars to karaitic Judaism. [2] He also inflated

---

[1]   A. Kahana, "Two Letters from Abraham Firkovich", *HUCA* vol. iii (1926), 359-370. A letter from Firkovich published by E. Deinard (his authenticity may be doubtful) would indicate that the former had "planned his finds" before he started out on his mission (*Massa Krim* [Warsaw 1878], pp. 20-40).

[2]   The relation between Karaites and the Khazars became one of the tenets of leading Karaites. It was recently discussed by Ananiasz Zajaczkowski, a well known Turcologist at the Warsaw University and the head of the remnants of the Karaite community in Poland today (*Ze Studiów nad Zagadnieniem Chazarskim* [Cracow 1947]). S. Szyszman recently argued this point vigorously ("Les Khazars Problems et Controverses," *Revue de l'Histoires des Religions* [1957], 174-221 and "Die Karäer in Ostmitteleuropa", *Zeitschr. f. Ostforschung* vol. vi [1957], 24-54). The new edition of the *Great Soviet Encyclopaedia* (vol. xlvi [1957], 23) states bluntly that the Khazars were converted to the Karaite religion, and this is uncritically repeated in a new

the importance of the Khazars—the alleged followers of the Karaite religion—and made a fictitious extension of the boundaries of the Khazar kingdom.

These alleged discoveries led, in the 1840's, and later to a great controversy in Russia and abroad. Some scholars accepted them as genuine—later modifying their stand somewhat—while others denounced them as forgeries. [1]

The long trail of forgeries which Firkovich left and the controversies which they aroused, brought into focus the problem of Khazar-Jewish relations, making it, as it were, fashionable, and this problem has left its mark until today upon Jewish historiography. The belief in the Khazar origin of eastern European Jewry, in fact of Ashkenazic Jewry in general, was supported by non-Jewish, [2] and particularly by Jewish writers from a variety of viewpoints and it found its most ardent champions at the beginning of our own century.

Max Gumplowicz (1864-1897) held that the Khazars and their followers had for a time ruled Poland; and that they

publication of UNESCO (Harry J. Shapiro, *The Jewish People. A Biological History* (Paris 1960), p. 55). Another Soviet publication points out that "the Karaites constitute a separate nationality even though they are historically connected with the Jews . . ." and that "Soviet scholars assert . . . the Karaites are historically connected with the mediaeval Khazars." (S. A. Tokarev, *Etnografia Narodov SSSR* (Moscow 1958), pp. 210-211).

[1] The literature on the subject is profuse and an echo is heard in most periodicals of Semitics of the period. Here only a few of the main items: A. Pinner, *Prospectus der, der Odessaer Gesellschaft für Geschichte und Alterthümer gehörenden älteren Hebräischen und Rabbinischen Handschriften* (Odessa 1845); Simha Pinsker, *Likkute kadmonioth*; 1860; D. Chwolson, "Achtzehn Hebräische Grabinschriften aus der Krim" in *Memoires de l'Academie des Sciences de St. Petersbourg*, vol. ix, no. 7, 55, 26-28; idem, *Corpus Inscriptionum Hebraicarum* (St. Petersbourg 1882) (there is also a Russian edition); Ch. Kunik, "Tokhtamysh i Firkovitch", *Zap. Akad. Nauk* 1876, addition to vol. xxvii, no. 3; A. Harkavy, "Die altjüdische Denkmäler aus der Krim", *op. cit.*, serie XXIV, 1876; A. Harkavy und H. L. Strack, *Catalog der hebr. Bibelhandschriften d. kaiserlichen öffentlichen Bibliothek zu St. Petersburg*, I-II, 1875; *cf.* also Weinryb, *op. cit.*, p. 511.

[2] For instance, K. F. Neumann, *Die Völker des südlichen Russlands in ihrer gesch. Entwicklung* (Leipzig 1855).

had been the only ones who carried on trade in early Poland and became the progenitors of Polish Jewry. [1] Some place names in Poland are also supposed to bear witness to Khazar origins.

Hugo v. Kutschera quotes K. Neuman and advances the theory that the vast majority of the Jews (Ashkenazim) are the descendants of Finn-Turkic people of the Khazars ". . . which were converted to Judaism in large masses." Like Gumplowicz, he maintains that also others, "the neighboring peoples", were converted to Judaism. He bases his theory mainly on the following reasoning:

a) In the eleventh century "many Jewish communities existed in Russia." These were Khazars who had immigrated to Russia.
b) Place and regional names like Ghazaria are found up to the fifteenth century.
c) Germany did not have enough Jews in the middle ages to settle in the east.
d) Ashkenaz is identified in the Talmud with Asia, and Asia meant the region between the Black Sea and Causacus.
e) The Khazars who became converted to Judaism escaped, like some others, to the west before the onslaught of the Mongols (thirteenth century) and formed the backbone of Ashkenazic Jewry. [2]

Isaac Schipper seems to have been influenced by both Gumplowicz and Kutschera, [3] but re-emphasized a number of other points. For him the immigration of Khazar Jews is *proven* by place names, mostly of villages in Poland such as Kozary, Kozara, Kozarow, Kawiori (should be derived from Kabaroi, a Khazar tribe), Żydow (allegedly from *Żyd*, Jew

---

[1] *Początki religii żydovskiej w Polsce* (Warsaw 1903).
[2] Hugo v. Kutschera, *Die Chasaren, eine Historische Studie*, 2nd ed. (Vienna 1910) (1st ed. 1909 [?]).
[3] He argues against some of the former's ideas, but takes over other of his approaches; indication of Kutchera's influence may be assumed since Schipper quotes Kutschera in other works.

in Polish). This supposedly indicates an early Khazar-Jewish agricultural population in Poland.

The "proof" that the Khazar settlements as shown by place names were Jewish is based on the fact that Jewish cemeteries existed in Kawyory and Kawyor, names allegedly derived from Khabar or Kabaroi which supposedly designated a Jewish Khazar tribe.

Again, the interest in Khazar problems, evident among scholars in the inter-war years, and also the general yearning for statehood in Palestine gave rise to a further extension of the Khazar theory. Poliak [1] follows in the footsteps of Gumplowicz-Kutschera-Schipper and others, using place names, and "corrected" place names, as proof of the existence of Khazars in a particular region; he also uses them for the "Greater Khazaria" (if we may call it that) approach. He also emphasizes the existence of groups in southern Russia of Jewish origin; he concludes at the same time that Judaism was spreading among neighboring tribes, too. Poliak, however, goes beyond his predecessors on a number of points, as follows:

a) Khazaria was—or became—an essentially Jewish-dominated area with converts and their descendants playing a minor role, numerically and otherwise.

b) The Khazar state was not destroyed in the tenth century but continued to exist with some changes of its borders— to the middle of the thirteenth century; *i.e.*, the period of the Mongol invasion.

c) For centuries after that time original Jews, and apparently some converts, continued to migrate westward, forming the bulk of east-European Jewry, among whom traces of these migrants are to be found; such traces range supposedly from types with reddish hair to such attire as the traditional *shtreimel* (fur hat), and the use of the Yiddish language which Poliak asserts came from the Crimean Gothic language. He also tries through "a philological

[1] A. N. Poliak, *Khazaria. Toledoth mamlaka yehudit be-Eropa* (Tel-Aviv 1942/3); (2nd ed. 1943/44; 3rd ed. 1950/51).

trick" to turn Jewish family names into Turkish ones and to make the organization of the Polish small town originate in Khazaria.

d) For the purpose of proving these points Poliak employs data which he seeks to justify by argument and erudition. For our purpose they could be summarized as a restatement of the alleged facts mentioned above; viz.: the existence of Jews in the area from the time of the Scythians through the Greek-Roman Black Sea colonies and the immigration from the Caucasus, Armenia, Babylonia, Persia, and Byzantium.

Since the Russian epos (biliny) about the hero Ilia Muromets, who is also counted among the holy men of the Russian Church, tells about fighting and defeating a "Jewish hero" from the "Jewish land", it is concluded that the Russians regarded "Khazaria" as a Jewish country, not as a Khazar one. The missing link—the proof that these biliny referred to Khazaria at all during its supposedly later existence as a more or less purely Jewish state—is based on the following circuitous reasoning:

> If the original legend [on which the biliny are based] is a tradition about the struggle of Khazaria with the Danube Bulgars and the Russians in the ninth-tenth centuries, and if its crystallizations were made after the Christianization of these two peoples (ninth-tenth centuries), then this rendering must be of a considerably later time ... The event which caused a new rendering of this old legend was surely some war or a number of border skirmishes in the eleventh, twelfth or beginning of the thirteenth century (pp. 206-207).

Another proof of the continuing existence of Jews in Khazaria—and of their having held some political power—is the presence of Prince Zacharia from Taman (Tmutorokan) at the end of the fifteenth century. Though his family originated in Italy, argues Poliak, "the Genoese (in Kaffa-Theodosia) only brought in a new Jewish dynasty in place of another one which ceased to exist ... Anyway this heritage (of Jewish dynasties) shows that these princes could still find support in a large Jewish local population" (p. 271).

By such methods has the Khazar hypothesis, during the last century, become part and parcel of east-European Jewish historiography. [1] It has been constantly repeated up to the present day. [2] As a result a number of sub-hypotheses have grown up to serve political and other purposes. [3]

III. *Critical Evaluation*

Any evaluation of theories and hypotheses concern-

[1] Only a few refuted the hypothesis. The Polish-Jewish historian Majer Balaban (1877-1942) was first a protagonist of the theory but later refuted it. Professor Israel Halperin of the Hebrew University recognizes the myth in this hypothesis. (See now his "The Jews in Eastern Europe" in L. Finkelstein ed. *The Jews Their History Culture and Religion*, 3rd ed. New York 1960, I pp. 287-320.)

[2] S. Dubnow, *Dibre yeme am olam*, vol. iv (2nd ed. (Tel Aviv 1940), pp. 161 ff. (in connection with Russia); Baron, *op. cit.*, B. Mark, *op. cit.*, Ph. Friedman, *op. cit.*, and "The First Millenium of Jewish Settlement in the Ukraine and in the Adjacent Areas"; *The Annals of the Ukrainian Academy of Arts and Sciences in the U.S.*, vol. vii (1959), pp. 1483-1516; and others.

[3] E. Renan used the Khazar theory as proof that Jews were racially mixed (*Le judaisme comme race et comme religion* [1883]); more recently, in 1947, when the UN Special Committee on Palestine (UNSCOP) was debating the partition of Palestine, Sir Abdul Rahman of India, in opposing a Jewish state, maintained that today's Jews have no claim to Palestine since they are descendants of converts to Judaism. "Khazars of Eastern Europe, Turco-Finn by race, were converted to Judaism. Can their descendants possibly claim any rights simply because the ancestors of their co-religionists had once settled in Palestine?" A similar argument was advanced in October 1947 by Faris el Khouri, delegate of Syria before the UN Ad Hoc Committee on the Palestine Question. On the other hand, some Jews apparently regard the alleged Khazar origin as a mark of status (*yihus*) as, for example, the late Hebrew poet Zalman Shneur who constructed for himself a theory of his family origin from Sephardi Jews (because of the name שניאור which allegedly comes from Sephardi "senior" [according to Zunz שניאור appears at first in Worms, *Gesammelte Schriften*, vol. ii p. 35]) and from Khazars who came "westward from their land." This is confirmed by the crosseyed members of his family לפעמים היתה מפתיעה אותי עקמומית עינים פתאומית אצל בני משפחה ... והרי זה ברור כי מן הכוזרים היא באה עקמומית זו (quoted in *Hadoar* [March 19, 1959], 321).

ing the early settlement of Jews must take two directions:

1. Inquiry into the basis of the theories. Any hypothesis in history serves similar purposes as in social sciences. It suggests problems for inquiry, forms a device for the organization of data and invites further research to verify or refute it. It acts as a means of discovering interrelations between facts. But the hypothesis itself has to be corroborated by facts and source material.
2. Investigation into the existence of Jews in a certain country or countries which may verify or disprove a certain theory, making it credible or incredible.

1. Evaluation of hypothesis.

Most of the above-mentioned hypotheses have little if any factual basis. The facts, or the alleged facts, supporting them are generally either unreliable, originate from earlier or later periods without any indication that they existed in the periods for which they are quoted or are generally based on myth or hearsay. [1]

As previously stated, the Scythian theory (which once was held as least acceptable but has lately been revived to some extent by Poliak) is based on general arguments without any proof from sources to indicate that Jews lived in the region of the Scythians at the time of their conquest and later on, or if so, that they continued to live there. The Bosphorus theory faces the same problem of "unknown continuity". The information about some Jews in the Bosphorus region as evidenced by a few inscriptions of the first century and some others—mostly doubtful ones—of the third and fourth centuries does not sufficiently establish that they existed

---

[1] A thorough and detailed analysis of all the texts and materials connected with the various theories and hypotheses would necessitate book-length treatment. I hope to come back to such an extended analysis at a later date. Here only the main problems and approaches are treated.

there continuously until many centuries later. [1] Nor do the inscriptions published by Chwolson embracing the second to the eighteenth century indicate any such continuity. The documents originate from the Firkovich collection which, as Chwolson concedes, are full of falsifications. D. Chwolson, originally a staunch defender of Firkovich, admits that the latter had changed many dates and that everything which went through his hands is suspect. "I am in the situation of a lawyer", writes Chwolson, "who has to prove that not everything which is found in the house of a notorious thief is stolen goods." He believed that he was able to differentiate between real and falsified inscriptions. [2] Others, H. Strack and A. Harkavy, for example, maintain that all inscriptions from the Crimea before the thirteenth century are falsifications.

Similarly, Harkavy's assumption that Babylonian-Persian Jews came through the Caucasus to southern Russian regions, has little if any proof in source material even if we may assume that these Jews were living in the Caucasus. The only place in which immigration of Persian Jews is mentioned is an entry in Joseph Hacohen's *Emek ha-baka*, written in the middle of the sixteenth century, that Jews (in 690) fled from Persia and finally settled "in Russia, Germany and Switzerland, where they found many Jews". [3] But, naturally, a sixteenth

---

[1] *Regesty i Nadpisi*, vol. i (1899), pp. 3-4; B. Nadel, "Żydowskie dokumenty ze starożytnego nadczarnomorza," *Biuletyn żyd. Inst. Historycznego*, no. 27 (1958), 1-21; *idem*, "A wichtiger mekor zu der geshichte fun di yidn in mizrach-Europe in onheyb fun ferten yurhundert," *Bleter far Geshichte*, vol. xi (1958), 98-108; *idem*, O Starogreckich napisach dotyczących żydów z rejonu czarnego morza," *Biuletyn* etc., no. 33 (1960), 77-87; E. R. Goodenough, "The Bosporus Inscription to the Most High God," *JQR*, vol. xlvii (1957) 221-244; *see also* B. Nadel, *Yidn in Mizrach Europe*, (Warsaw 1960), pp. 22 ff.

[2] *Regesty i Nadpisi*, vol. i, 5-34; D. A. Chwolson, *Sbornik Evreiskich Nadpisei* (St. Petersburg 1884); *idem*, *Corpus Inscriptionum Hebraicarum* ... (St. Petersburg 1882) (*cf.* p. vii).

[3] ‏...ויגוסו יהודים רבים מארץ פרס...ויתהלכו מגוי אל גוי...‏
‏ויבואו ארצה רוסיאה וארץ אשכנז ושוייציאה וימצאו שם יהודים‏
‏רבים, אף כי בהאל העיר אשר נקבר שם מר זוטרא...‏
Emek ha-baka, ed. M. Letteris (Kracow 1895) p. 19. As a matter

century source is no proof for the seventh century. In addition, the entire account seems to belong to the category of legends constructed at a much later date for some specific purpose. This may be seen from the fact that the grave of Mar Sutra (fifth century) is placed in "Hal" (Halle/S or Hall, Schwaben) followed by names of people who lived in the thirteenth century, and the mention of "Russia" as the name of a country or territory, for such a designation does not appear before the ninth-tenth centuries. [1]

Similarly there is no basis for the assumption that Saadia Gaon's reference (about 929) to a Jew who went to Khazaria indicates emigration from Babylonia (as stated by Chwolson and others) or that "travels of Babylonian Jews to the country of the Khazars were frequent." The sentence at the end of Saadia's responsum has, as Harkavy pointed out, no relation

---

of fact, this sentence served S. D. Luzzatto in formulating his theory about the impact of Persian Jewry upon European Jewry. He also tries to see in this entry an explanation for the existence of a large eastern European Jewry and assumes, without any basis, that Joseph Hacohen used older chronicles. Another version apparently of the same story or legend is found in a manuscript of the 15-16 century. This puts the alleged emigration of Jews from Persia in the 8th century and has סטכוניה instead of שויציה and היילא instead of האל. האל or היילא may mean "Halle/S (Neufeld, op. cit., p. 33) or Hall in Schwaben (M. Wiener, Emek ha-baka, p. 149 note 15). Schipper's attempt to see in this story proof for the existence of Jews in eastern Europe in the 7-8th centuries (making a conjecture of סלבוניה instead of סטכוניה and האליטש (Halicz) instead of האל, היילא) is valueless. Not only is the "source" itself of a later date (7-800 years after the supposed migration), but it also confuses various periods and events or legends (Zunz characterizes it as "ein Buch, das ... gänzliche Unwissenheit der Geschichte verrät") Zunz, Literaturgeschichte der synagogalen Poesie (Berlin 1865), p. 625, 7; Neufeld, op. cit., pp. 33 ff.; Schipper, Kulturgeschichte, p. 12.

[1] The attempt made in Soviet Russia recently to construct an early Russian state in the 6th or 7th centuries does not change the fact that the term "Russian land" or Russia as a country name begins to appear only in the 9th-10th cent. (cf. B. A. Ribakov, "Drevnie Rusy," Sovetskaya Archeologiya, vol. xvii (1953), 23-104; Akademiya Nauk SSSR. Voprosy Formirovaniya Russkoy Narodnosti i Nazii (Moscow-Leningrad 1958), pp. 17 ff, 25; cf. also A. Vucinish in Speculum, vol. xxviii (1953), 324-334; Huberband, op. cit., pp. 27 ff.

to the subject therein; it may be a later addition, and Saadia himself shows that his knowledge about Khazaria and Khazars does not go beyond what he had learned from some tales by Arab writers. [1]

Views about the persecution of Jews in Byzantium and their subsequent emigration are somewhat different. Even though, as Joshua Starr points out, [2] there was no continuous persecution during the 300 years from Heraclus to Romanus, and the special Jewish tax is open to question, Arab writers report on such an emigration from Byzantium. Masudi in his *Muruj al-Dhahab* (*Meadows of Gold*), written in 943-947, states that some time after the conversion of the Khazar king to Judaism, "there joined him Jews from all the lands of Islam and from the country of the Greeks" because of the oppression by Romanus in 943-44. [3] The so-called Cambridge Document of the Genizah which may have been written in the tenth or twelfth centuries mentions Jewish immigration from Baghdad and Greece after the conversion (or reform) by the Khazars. [4] The value of the Cambridge Document is, however, greatly diminished by the problem of its reliability and questionable authorship. Thus there remains only Al-Massudi's statement about some Byzantine Jewish immigration (and from Islamic countries) to Khazaria. [5]

---

[1] The sentence: דהוה במדינתכן חד גברא דשמיה יצחק בר אברהם ונפק ליה לכזר. A Harkavy, *MGW J*, 1882, p. 170; *idem*, "R. Saadya Gaon al Davar Hakuzrim," *Semitic Studies in Memory of ... Alexander Kohut* (Berlin 1879), pp. 244, 246; Baron, *op, cit.*, vol. iii, p. 197; Schipper, *Kulturgeschichte*, p. 21; Poliak, *op. cit.*, p. 130.

[2] J. Starr, *The Jews in the Byzantine Empire 641-1204* (Athens 1939), pp. 8, 11.

[3] A later Arab writer (Dimashqi 1327) apparently uses Masudi but erroneously construes the oppression and emigration in the time of Harun al-Rashid 786-809, Dunlop, *op. cit.* pp. 89 ff; Starr, *op. cit.*, pp. 90 ff. J. Marquart, *Osteuropäische und ostasiatische Streifzüge*, (Leipzig 1903), p. 6.

[4] Schechter, *JQR*, vol. iii (1912-13), 181-210; Kokovtsov, *op. cit.*, pp. 33-36; and Dunlop, *op. cit.*, pp. 155 ff.

[5] Attempts to draw conclusions about early Babylonian-Persian immigration because traces of Babylonian-Persian ritual are found in

Both ambiguous and uncertain is the basis of the trade-routes theory. First of all, the existence of trade-routes going through Poland before the twelfth century is only vaguely indicated; [1] this may show that whatever travel was going on was only incidental and of minor importance. [2] Also ibn-Khurradadbeh's above-mentioned statement that the land route from the west goes behind (*halfa* in Arabic) Constantinople "crossing the country of the Slavs" to Itil, does not necessarily give us a right to conclude that there was a route running much farther to the north than the Black

---

Mahzor minhag Kaffa (Berlin, *op. cit.*, pp. 123 ff.) or because of statements to this effect by its compiler David Liakhno or Lechno, seem to be unfounded. The mahzor as compiled by Liakhno in the 18th century may at best reflect the situation around 1500 when it was supposedly compiled by R. Moshe from Kiev, who had come there as a refugee, but no earlier (there is no independent information that the Liakhno mahzor is the same as that of R. Moshe of 1500). Liakhno himself apparently had no sense of responsibility about relating historical facts correctly. He repeats stories from hearsay as historical truths. This is clearly seen in his chronicle *Debar sofatayim* where dates, facts, as well as stories about Jews in Poland are faulty. The editor of Liakhno's chronicle I. D. Markon who regards it as "a detailed and true description" seems to have equated hearsay (סיפורים ששמע מפי מושלים) with truth. *See* "Sefer debar sefatayim . . . David ben Rabi Eliezer Lechno," *Devir*, vol. ii (Berlin 1923), 244-273. S. Bernstein's attempt to identify a number of anonymous piyutim in the mahzor with Persian-Jewish authors is, therefore, baseless (I. Markon, "Maamar al odoth mahzor minhag Kaffa," *A. Harkavy Festschrift* [St. Petersburg 1908], pp. 449-469; S. Bernstein in *Sefer . . . S. K. Mirsky* (New York, 1958), pp. 453-468; Liakhno's introduction is reprinted in Deinard, *Massa Krim*, pp. 147-149.

[1]   K. Maleczynski, *Die ältesten Märkte in Polen und ihr Verhältnis zu der Kolonisierung nach dem deutschen Recht* (Breslau 1930), pp. 10 ff. and *pass.* (there is also a Polish edition).

[2]   This may also be the meaning of the information contained in the first Polish Chronicle of Gallus Anonymus (entries end in 1112; extant manuscripts originate from 14-15th century) that Poland lies out of the way of the trade routes, at the same time mentioning that merchants cross it on the way to Russia. The attempt of Polish (and Ukrainian) historians in the last decades to construct, often by implication (like Kupfer-Lewicki, *op. cit.*, pp. 46 ff.), a picture of an early much traveled west-east trade route is rather a result of a nationalistic tendency "to be in the middle of world events" than based on actual source material.

Sea coast. This excludes Poland and most of Kievan Russia. But in the main it is still questionable whether the statement bears any reference to Jews or Rhadanites. Before the paragraph dealing with the land routes, where the above mentioned passage is found the manuscripts of ibn Khurradadbeh have another paragraph dealing with the routes of the Russian or Slavic merchants. The next paragraph, about the land routes, begins with the word "their", followed by the words "land route" with no indication in the text to whom this pronoun refers. It may mean the Russian merchants, not the Jewish Rhadanites. [1]

Likewise, Ibrahim ibn Yaqub's statement about Jews from Hungary coming to Prague has nothing to indicate that Jews travelled through Poland to Kiev and beyond. No better documented are the "extension" of the trade routes, dwelt on by Brutzkus and his followers. The scant information [2]

---

[1] Specialists are divided about this point. V. Minorsky (*Hudud Al-alam ... The Regions of the World* [London 1937] p. 429) asserts that the last paragraph concerns Russian merchants. V. V. Barthold, "Arabskiye Izvestiya o Rusach" *Sovetskoye Vostokovedeniye*, vol. i [Moscow-Leningrad 1940] *pass.*) reverses the order of the paragraphs, putting the one on land routes after the one dealing with Jewish Rhadanites ("their" would thus mean "of the Jews"). Lewicki, *op. cit.* (pp. 118-119) follows Barthold. *Cf.* also Marquart, *Streifzüge*, pp. 202-204, 350-353; Lopez and Raymond, *op, cit.*, p. 32, note 68.

[2] Quite valueless, of course, is Schipper's "supporting evidence" of trade by Jews of Poland with the East. He bases his assumption of such trade on the fact that Kalish Jews obliged themselves to pay for land for a cemetery with six pounds of pepper and other spices "and pepper they could only obtain by trade with the East" (*Wirtschaftsgeschichte*, p. 49). Not only was pepper (as well as other spices) regarded as a means of payment in the middle ages, but the Jewish privilege of 1367 provides for non-Jews to use pepper with which to pay fines for molesting Jewish synagogues. Brutzkus, too, quotes incorrectly (partly following Schipper) from some documents in order to prove his ideas about a large-scale trade with Mayence and Regensburg. Aronius no. 124 does not deal with "forbidding [for Jews] the trade in metal, cloth or spices and perfumes," but concerns the prohibition against touching the sign of the cross on the wares (*Zeichen des Kreuzes*). While Aronius no. 135, 158 do not show that "here [in Regensburg] an important Jewish Kehilla grew up fast"; each one of these documents deals with an *individual* Jew (the first document mentions land bought by a monastery from "a Jew Samuel" and the

about Jewish merchants going from (or via) Ratisbon (Regensburg) to Russia during the twelfth century for the purpose of trade tells us nothing about earlier centuries. Moreover it does not furnish a basis for identifying the *holke Russiya* which are mentioned in one or two Hebrew sources, with the *ruzari* of the general documents. The *ruzari* were Russians whose presence in Ratisbon made it necessary to build a Russian Church there. Nor is the identification of "Primut" with "Przemysl" in the responsum of R. Yehuda Hakohen of any significance. "Baploni" (or "Bapolnu" in the other version) does not necessarily mean Poland.[1] It may stand rather for an "unknown place" (במקום פלוני). It is also questionable if Przemysl would at that time have been called Poland. The whole region, known as "Grody Czerwienskie," seems to have been under Moravian, later Russian (Kiev), suzerainty during most of the tenth century. It belonged to Poland for a short time, again passing into the hands of Wladimir of Kiev in 981. In 1018 it was conquered by Boleslaus of Poland, and then reconquered by the Russians in 1031.[2] Equally unconvincing is the conjecture Primut < Primus < Przemyśl. Firstly, there are a number of other place names which could

---

second deals with "a Jew Abraham" who insulted the name of Christ (Brutzkus, op. cit., p. 62). Only in 1006-1028 is a Jewish quarter (*Juden-quartier*) in Regensburg mentioned (Aronius no. 150.) Nor is there any basis in the sources for Schipper's assertion (*Wirtschaftsgeschichte*, p. 47) that Benjamin of Tudelah and Petachya of Regensburg "definitely intended to inform Jewish merchants" [about the routes], that "Prague and Kiev are according to [their] report . . . the main centers in the Slavic countries of trade with the East," or that "Jewish traders from the West went mainly to Kiev." Similarly unfounded is the statement that Ibn Yakub got his information about the countries east of Prague "from Jewish traders who came to Prague from Eastern Asia" (*Kulturgeschichte*, pp. 15, 40, 42).

[1]   The concept of Poland as a country and state (and application of the name Polonia to it) seem not to appear before the beginning of the 11th century ("Bolonia" in Arabic may be still younger). For Ibrahim ibn-Yakob the concept is unknown; he calls it "the realm of Mieszko"; and also Benjamin of Tudela does not know it while Petachya mentions "Polin"; see also Huberband, op. cit., pp. 37 ff.

[2]   Manteufel, *Historia, op. cit.*, pp. 112,168, 174-5.

be written in Hebrew as פרימוט or the conjecture of Brutzkus (Primut<Primus<Przemysl) could be applied to them. There is a Pruem (Germany), a Premuda in Yugoslavia, and there are in Czechia a Přemyšl, Premysl, Prenet and Primda (Pfrimt, Phrimede, Pfrient). In addition, according to some newer research, Przemysl was not involved in any Russian-Polish struggles until the middle of the eleventh century. [1] And above all, the fact that two young boys were found there does not by any means prove the existence of a Jewish community. The terms ילד, קטן and נער in Hebrew in those days meant young men rather than children. [2]

Of still less import is the Kenaan hypothesis. It apparently arose from Lebenson's note which is no more than a repetition of hearsay based supposedly on Czacki, but has no basis in Czacki's book. Czacki had asserted that he had consulted Slavic manuscripts of a Bible Commentary; these, however, never existed.[3] One could continue the hypothesis was based on the existence of Kenaan glosses which, for the most part, are neither Russian nor Polish but Czech, and which could not have been inserted by the authors but by copyists several centuries later. [4] In addition, most of the Kenaan (Slavic)

[1] St. M. Kuczynski, "O wyprawie Wlodzimierza I ku Lachom w zwiazku z poczatkiem państwa Polskiego" *Sprawozdania Wroclaws-kiego Towarzystwa Nauk*, vol. iv (1949), 114-122; *cf.* also *idem, ibid.,* vol. v (1950), 106-114. The place names are noted in Antonin Profus, *Mistni Imena v Cechach* (Prague 1951), pp. 467, 479-481.

[2] Ephraim E. Urbach, *Baale ha-tosafoth* (Jerusalem 1955), pp. 407-408; *Or zarua,* iv, *ab zara* no. 202. These meanings are also found in the Bible (Dan. I: 4, Eccl. 4: 13, Chr. II 22; 1-2).

[3] Harkavy, *Hayehudim* etc., pp. 14-17. Poliak, *op. cit.,* p. 17. Nevertheless Grätz and Zunz repeat that Jews in Poland, Lithuania, or Russia spoke Slavonic until the 13th century (Graetz, *Geschichte,* vol. ix (1866), pp. 71-72; L. Zunz, *Die Ritus der synagogalen Poesie* (Berlin 1859), p. 73; *JQR,* vol. iv, 703.

[4] The printed Rashi text has many additions which are missing in the manuscripts. These again are a few centuries younger than Rashi; the same is true of the Caro commentaries. *Cf.* A. Freiman, *MGWJ* vol. lxxx, 433; A. Berliner, *Beiträge zur Geschichte der Rashi Commentare,* p. 30; A. Geiger, *ZDMG,* 1862, 299; S. Eidelberg, *Yivo Bleter,* vol. xli (1957/58), 358.

glosses concern "realia" for which there were no known Hebrew equivalents. The copyist, who lived much later than the authors (extant copies are younger by a few hundred years), usually prepared the manuscript for use in study or teaching and often made marginal notes explaining a word in current speech. But this furnishes us with little information about the author's, or even the copyist's, alleged Slavic vernacular just as the use of Slavic expressions written in Hebrew letters in the minute books of Jewish communities during the sixteenth to eighteenth centuries [1] do not attest to the spoken language of the secretary. We know for a certainty that they spoke Yiddish.

The only document which may seem to prove something in this direction would be the letter from the Genizah, which Mann assigns to the eleventh century, about a Jew from Russia who knew only *leshon Kenaan*. It is not, however, a transcript of a real letter but a form, [2] or a model prepared by a scribe. Such form letters may have been prepared on themes related to real events or may have been a product of the imagination of the scribe. But even if it is either a copy or a draft of a genuine document, it leaves a number of problems unsolved which diminishes its importance. The time the letter was written may fall in the eleventh century but may equally well be in the twelfth-thirteenth century. [3] Another point is that we cannot be sure that a Slavic language is meant by the term *leshon Kenaan*. As we have seen, German, too, is at times mentioned in this way. And finally, given all the positive possibilities that we have a genuine copy, and that the person

[1]   *See*, for instance B. D. Weinryb, *Texts and Studies in the Communal History of Polish Jewry* (New York 1950), pp. 53, 70-71, 162, 182, 188, 229, 242-3 and *pass.*; I. Halperin, *Pinkas waad arba arazoth* (Jerusalem 1945) pp. 531-555 and *pass.*

[2]   *Cf.* also Marmorstein, *REJ*, vol. lxxiii (1921), 92-97; Starr, *op. cit.*, pp. 171-172.

[3]   This writer is indebted for analysis of the handwriting to Prof. S. D. Goitein who is preparing a corpus of all the Geniza manuscripts. According to Prof. Goitein the ductus of the script is found in the 11-12th century but also in documents from the 13th century.

could speak only a Slavic language, a single Jew may have been the exception rather than the rule. [1]

The Khazar hypothesis is not rendered more plausible because one writer copies it uncritically from another.

Discounting the general considerations of Gumplowicz and Kutschera [2] which are merely unfounded speculations, one finds nothing on which to base the theory. The so-called proof which Schipper-Brutzkus-Poliak and others offer amounts to a recital of place names; the mention of Khazars here and there, with no specification that they were Jews; the so-called Hasdai-King Joseph correspondence; Firkovich's falsifications; and some of Poliak's speculations.

Place names, utilized by some historians as guides to settlement history, are of little, if any, value when they stand alone without any supporting evidence. To realize the worthlessness of such a method one need only consider the many Romes and Berlins in the United States which were scarcely original settlements of Italians or Germans, respectively, or Cairo, Ill., and Cairo, N.Y., or Moscow, Idaho, and St. Petersburg, Fla., Petersburg, Va., or Russia, Ohio, none of which has any connection with the settlement of Egyptians or Russians; there are scores of similar place names. In the case of place names indicating some connection with Khazars there is a special situation which invalidates any possible value for our purpose. Khazaria comprised a conglomeration of nationalities—Turks, Moslems, Slavs, Finns and other groups—

---

[1] In the responsa of modern times we sometimes find a witness's testimony in a Slavic language because he could not speak Yiddish, but this surely does not reveal anything about the Jewish group as a whole (*cf.* also S. Dubnow, "Razgovornyj yazik i narodnaia literatura polsko-litovskich Yevreev v. XVI i pervoy polovine XVII v.," *Evreyskaya Starina*, vol. i (1909), 7-41).

[2] Schipper himself showed some of the weaknesses of Gumplowicz's approach. Harkavy demonstrated (*Evreyskaya Starina*, vol. iii (1910), 632-635) that Kutschera was unfamiliar with the source material, ending his criticism with the words (which the angel allegedly said to the Khazar King in his dream) **כונתך רצויה אבל מעשיך אינם רצויים** (your intentions are acceptable but not your works).

ruled by a minority of a Judaized group. The fact that Jews were a minority is attested by almost all sources. Among these is Ibn Rusta, writing about 903, who says: "Their supreme ruler is a Jew and likewise . . . those of the generals and the chief men who follow his way of thinking. The rest of them have a religion like the religion of the Turks." Astakhari says, about 932: "The smallest group is the Jews, most of them being Muslims and Christians though the King and Court are Jews." Again, Massudi, writing between 943 and 947, states: "The predominating element in this country are the Muslims," and he adds that "in the Khazar capital there are seven judges, two for the Jews, two for the Muslims, two for the Christians, one for the Pagans."

Similar statements are found in other sources. This indicates that the Jews formed a small minority in Khazaria. [1]

There were also troops in Byzantium and elsewhere who were of Khazar origin but were hardly Jews. The general of the Kiev prince "Ivanko Zakharyich, the Khazar", [2] and many others apparently had nothing to do with Jews. Again, for the period following the Russian attack on Khazaria (965 or thereabouts) a number of Arabic sources refer to the conversion of the Khazars to the Moslem religion either as a condition for military aid from a Moslem ruler or for other reasons. [3]

There is, on the other hand, some information indentifying Khazaria and Khazars with Christianity. It is reported that

[1]   English translation Dunlop, *op. cit.*, pp. 91, 104, 108, 114, 207; *cf.* Lewicki, *Arabskie*, pp. 30, 67, 83; only ibn Fadlan says "the Khazars and their king are all Jews" but the "all" (*kulluhum* in Yaqut) is being regarded as an exaggeration or an interpolation.

[2]   Dunlop, *ibid.*, p. 253; Minorsky, *Oriens*, vol. xi (1958), 142. It should be mentioned that in Russian there is also a fowl called Kazarka (Branta) and any name, of person or place, may also originate from the name of the bird (cf. *Bolshaya Sov. Encyklopedia*, vol. xlvi (1957), s.v.

[3]   Muquaddasi writing *ca.* 985; Ibn Miskaway d. 1030; Ibn-Al-Attir d. 1234; Dimashqi d. 1327 (quoted by Dunlop 244 ff). Arabic sources also mention an earlier conversion of Khazars to the Muslim religion in connection with their defeat by Muslims in 737.

the Greek Emperor, together with the Russians, defeated the Khazars and their ruler Georgius Tzul (1016). Dunlop and some others think that the name of Georgius points to a Christian. The prince Sancherib who is mentioned after the account of Tzulos is regarded as a non-Jew. [1] Travellers of the thirteenth century maintain that the Khazars of Crimea and region—they call them "Ghazars"—were Christians. Friar John of Pian de Carpini, who travelled in 1245-1247, counts the Khazars (Ghazars) among the Christians. Another version has it still more clearly, *Gazaros qui sunt Christiani*, and states only that "the Brutaches are said to be Jews." A monk named William of Rubruck (Guillaume de Raysbroeck) who was in the area a few years later mentions Jews only in connection with the Caucasus and Persia, while he says that the Latins call the Crimea "Gazaria", and that the Greeks call it "Cassaria" without any indication of the existence there of Jewish Khazars. [2] Russian sources, too, identify Khazars as members of the Christian Church, and some south-Russian chronicles identify them with Slavs generally. [3]

This whole situation is still further confused by the fact that in documents from the twelfth to the fifteenth century, or even later, the Crimea and neighboring area are called Ghazaria with no relation to the existence of Khazars there at that time. [4] Poliak's conclusion regarding the existence of

[1] Dunlop, *ibid.*, p. 252; *see also* Minorsky, *Oriens*, vol. xi, 141 (the latter maintains that the prince Sancherib of upper Media "has no connection with the Tzanars or Khazars").

[2] M. Komroff, *Contemporaries of Marco Polo* (New York 1928), pp. 22, 36, 54, 81, William W. Rockhill, *The Journey of William of Rubruck to the Eastern Parts of the World* 1253-1255 . . . (London, Halkyut Society, 1900), pp. 12, 36, 42, 44 ff., 264; C. Raymond Bezaley, ed., *The Texts and Versions of John de Plano Carpini and William de Rubruquis* (London 1903) pp. 87, 122, 144, 185, and *pass.*; A. A. Vasiliev, *The Goths in the Crimea* (Cambridge, Mass., 1936), p. 164.

[3] Berlin, *op. cit.*, pp. 84, 95; Weinryb, *op. cit.*, p. 514.

[4] In the same way as, for instance, an Indian name of place or region in America (Minnesota or even Indiana) has no relation to Indians living there today.

Khazars or Jewish Khazars on the basis of the name of the
region is entirely arbitrary. [1] Even if place names did sometimes indicate a settlement or former settlement of Khazars,
we are still far from being able to identify it as a *Jewish*
settlement. Schipper attempts to identify the alleged Khazar
settlements on the ground that in two cases we have information of "Kawiory" which—according to Gumplowicz—should
be derived from "Kabar" or "Kabaroi", a branch of the
Khazars, and because the given documents identify them
with a Jewish cemetery. The truth is, however, as Balaban
points out, that this bears no relation to "Kabar" but means
simply a cemetery. [2] Poliak's attempts to "Judaize" the
later Khazar state, or assumed Khazar state, are based on
assumptions which have no basis in fact.

The Russian epos depicting the hero Ilya fighting Jews
makes no mention of Khazars or Khazar Jews, nor was its
rendering formulated at the time of the existence of any

[1] Poliak, *op. cit.*, pp. 242 ff. The Genoese office which dealt with
the Caffa colonies was called "Officium Gazariae" and the Genoese
called their colonies "empire of Gazaria" and the ruler of Gothia
(Theodoro) was known as "prince of Khazaria". Some sources seem
also, beginning with the 12th century, to confuse Khazars and
Cumans (*see also* Minorsky, *Oriens*, vol. xi, p. 142; *see* the writings
mentioned p. 42, note 2 and Vasiliev, *op. cit.*, pp. 134, 171, 178, 195;
M. Malowist, *Kaffa Kolonia Genueuska na Krymie i problem wschodni
w latach 1453-1475* (Warsaw 1947), p. 26.

[2] Balaban, *Mies. Żyd.*, vol. i, p. 11. However his contention that
"Kawior" comes form "Kirchhof" is not plausible; it is rather a
transcription of "Kever" or "Kevarim". (Schipper also derived the
hellenized expression "Kabaroi" from the Hebrew *haberim*, *Żydzi w
Polsce Odrodzonej*, vol. i, p. 14). In Magdeburg (ca. 1300), too, a
Jewish cemetery appears as "Kefer" "Judenkever" (MGWJ, XIV,
244-5). Poliak's argument for "Kabar" because only two places
were called "Kaviory" (p. 226) is valueless. In the 13-14th centuries
there were only a few Jews in Poland and, therefore, only very few
Jewish cemeteries. Also Schipper's contention that place names of
"Żidowo", "Żidów" in the 13th century should indicate the existence
of Jewish villages is nullified by the same author's statement that
in the 11th-15th centuries many "Christians in high positions" had
names like Żyd, Żydek, Żydowski, Żydówka, Judaeus, and only one
recorded case was concerned with a baptized Jew (*Kulturgeschichte*,
p. 37; *Wirtschaftsgeschichte*, p. 41).

"latter-day" Khazaria. According to Russian research the image of Ilya Murometz as a fighter for Russia took shape in the eleventh to thirteenth centuries, undergoing changes as late as the sixteenth and seventeenth centuries, and the extant rendering dates from the eighteenth and nineteenth centuries. The "Jew" there is no more than another foe of the Russians or Christians with whom the hero fought. [1] Before any conclusion from such a "source" can even be thought of, proof of the time of the rendering must be secured.

Poliak's account about the Jewish Khazars of Saraqhshin, which is identified with Saqsin, at first defeating the Mongols (1223) and thus "assuring the freedom of the Russians for a few years", [2] is entirely unfounded. Not only does all information about Saqsin [3] from the twelfth century and beyond apparently lack any connection with Khazars, and still less with Jewish Khazars, [4] but Poliak's construction of a Jewish prince has already been discredited long ago. Thus Poliak's conclusion about the tradition of Jewish princes in Taman and a large Jewish population there is valueless.

Zacharia Ghisolfi, Prince of Taman and vassal of Kaffa, which was founded about 1266 as a Genoese colony, was a descendant of an Italian Catholic noble family which, since the end of the thirteenth century, had been active in the

---

[1] Akademia Nauk SSSR, *Russkoye Narodnoye poeticheskoye tvorchestvo*, vol. i, (Moscow-Leningrad 1953), pp. 228, 339, 420-421; *Bolshaya Sovejtskaya Enziklopediya* s.v.

[2] Poliak, *op. cit.*, p. 239 and *pass.*

[3] *See* Dunlop, *op. cit.*, pp. 248-249 and notes 66-73.

[4] Poliak's explanation that Plano Carpini's "Saxi" means Saqsin (*ibid.*, p. 240) is either a mistake or otherwise of no avail for our purpose. Plano Carpini himself mentions Sassi among a multitude of other groups conquered by the Mongols. In the statement of Benedict Polonus whose travelogue is preserved in that of Carpini, Sassi or Saxi is identified with the Goths "who are Christians." The story about resistance concerns a city "Orna" or "Ornas" which was inhabited by Christians and Moslems and "Ghazars who were Christians" and was under Moslem rule (Rockhill, *op. cit.*, p. 36; Bezaley, *op. cit.*, pp. 87, 122; *see also* Vasiliev, *op. cit.*, pp. 164-165).

Black Sea and surrounding area. One of his forefathers, Biscarello Ghisolfi—"civis januensis" (Genoese citizen)—was also active around 1300 in the diplomatic service of the Mongol rulers in Persia and was several times sent as envoy to the Pope and the Christian kings of France and England. Zacharia's father and predecessor as Prince of Taman had married a local woman, a Cherkessian. Some years after Kaffa had been conquered by the Turks in 1475, the main city of Taman, Martega, also fell into the hands of the Turks (1482). Having lost his principality Ghisolfi tried to return to Genoa but was overtaken on the way by the ruler of Moldavia. He then attempted to work on two fronts. He turned to the Bank of St. George in Genoa, the protector since 1453 of the Kaffa colonies, asking for a considerable sum of money. He also was negotiating with the Russian prince (or tsar) Ivan Vassilyevich III of Moscow about moving there, and about other matters. Our information runs up to about 1500. Ivan Vassilyevich was interested in drawing Mengli-Girey, the Tartar Khan, protector and friend of Ghisolfi, to his side in his political maneuvers against Poland. He worked with the help of a Jewish agent in Kaffa called Choza Kokos [1] and apparently one Zacharia or Scaria. When the correspondence of Ivan III of Moscow with his agents and with Ghisolfi was published, the editor, finding the words "Zaccaria or Scaria the Jew" (*Zhidovin*) in one of the documents, inserted the word Jew (*Zhid*) in his headings to the documents about Zacharia Ghisolfi. This gave rise to the legend about "the Jewish Prince Zacharia of Taman". [2] The baselessness of this myth became clear a long time ago through publications of relevant documents. [3]

[1] A "Cocus filius Isaac" is found among the representatives of the Jewish group in Kaffa in 1455 (*Evreyskaya Starina*, vol. v (1912), 68-69).

[2] *Jewish Encyclopedia*, vol. vi, p. 107; I. M. Barats, *Sobraniye Trudov* ... vol. i, no. 2 (Paris 1927), 438.

[3] *Atti della Societa Ligure di Storia Patria*, VI; F. Brun, *Chernomorye. Sbornik izsledovanii po istoricheskoy geografii*, vols. i, ii (Odessa 1877, 1880); J. Brutzkus, "Zacharia Kniaz Tamanski," *Evreyskaya Starina*, vol. x (1918), 132-143; Vasilyev, *op. cit.*, pp. 206 ff; Berthold

These show clearly the origin of the Ghisolfi family as
Genoese Catholics. In truth, Zacharia Ghisolfi is not even
designated as a Jew in the text of the documents, but chiefly
as either an Italian (*Fryazin*) or Cherkess, because of his
mother. Another publication of some of the documents about
Ghisolfi by another editor who did not put in the heading
"Jew" shows no "Jewish traces". [1] The false "Judaization"
of Ghisolfi because of his biblical proper name [2] served Poliak
as a basis on which to Judaize Taman and a latter-day
Khazaria.

The Hasdai Ibn Shaprut-King Joseph correspondence which
Schipper regards as genuine while Poliak labels it apocryphal
literature though he quotes the letters profusely, proves
nothing as long as its authenticity cannot be established.
All research notwithstanding, the origin of the letters is still
obscure and they may be of much later provenance. It has
been suggested more recently that the Hasdai letter is connected with the cycle of tales about the Ten Tribes. [3] The genuine-
ness of the King Joseph letter, in both the short and the long

Spuler, *Die Mongolen in Iran*, 2nd ed. (Berlin 1955), pp. 219,
229-231; C. Roth (*The History of the Jews of Italy* [Philadelphia 1946],
p. 135) pointed out that this legend is improbable because of the
exclusion of Jews from Genoa.

[1] The documents were published in *Sbornik Imperatorskago
Russkago Istoricheskago Obshchestva* vol. xli (Petersburg 1884), 8,
12, 40-41, 50, 71-73, 77, 114, 30 (reprinted-shortened in *Regestry i
Nadpisi*, vol. i, pp. 77-84, 88, 92); the second publication is *Zapiski
Odesskago Imperatorskago Obshchestva Istorii i Drevnostey* vol. v,
(Odessa 1863), pp. 275 ff. *See also* Malowist, *op. cit.*, pp. 54-55, 277 ff.
290-292, 337 ff.

[2] In Kaffa and that area other non-Jewish Zaccarias were also
active as, in the middle ages, biblical names are generally not a rarity
among Christians. *See* Lopez and Raymond, *op. cit.*, Index; G. I.
Bratianu, *Recherches sur la Commerce Genois dans la Mer Noire en
XIII Siecle* (Paris 1929), pp. 39, 188, 225. There were an Isaac Prince
of Gotia (15th cent.), a David Emperor of Trebizond, a Daniel Metropolitan of Gotia, Bishops Israel (7th cent. Caucasus), Aaron (11th
cent. Cracow), Abraham (10th cent. Freising), Isaia (11th cent.
Kiev) and so on.

[3] *See* I. Halperin, "Hakuzarim weha-shvatim ha-genuzim b'igereth
Hasdai . . . el Melek Kuzar," *Zion*, vol. xviii (1953), 80-82.

versions, is rendered doubtful also because it shows no trace of the dual system of the Khazar kingship although some indication of it is found in the Hebrew Cambridge document. And this duality is an established fact. In other words, the author of the King Joseph letter, who probably came from Europe, was not even familiar with the government system in Khazaria. Similarly valueless are Firkovich's inscriptions until it can be proven by independent information that they are all genuine as to content and correct as to dates.

A number of other statements which Poliak makes are likewise unfounded or inaccurate [1] or based on legends and tales which travellers inserted in the descriptions of the journeys. [2] His theories about the Gothic origin of Yiddish, the prevalence of red-headed Jews in the Ukraine, the origin of the *Shtetel* from Khazaria, or the influence of the Golden Orde upon the Privilege of Boleslaus of Kalish (1264) are mere phantasies. [3] Not only did Crimean Gotia encompass an area too small to influence a large Jewish population, but recorded words of their Gothic language of the fifteenth century show it to be so different from Yiddish that probably no philologist could concur to the possibility of so great a change in language in a comparatively short time. Red-headed Jews are to be found not only in the Ukraine but also in Galicia, Hungary, Poland, and even North Africa. [4]

[1] For instance that Petachya of Regensburg called Saragsin "meshekh" (p. 72), even though Harkavy thought so, or that he travelled on the Dniepr southwards (p. 78), or the statement which Balaban supposedly made (p. 91). None of this is found in the respective sources (*see* also Dunlop, *op. cit.*, p. 248; Minorsky, *op. cit.*, p. 129).

[2] Petachyah's story about the "messengers of the kings of meshekh and magog" is embedded in the ten-tribes cycle and story about his eating manna etc.

[3] Some of the criticism is to be found in Friedman, *Yivo Bleter*, vol. xxxvi, (1952), 294-300; Landau, *Kiryath Sefer*, vol. xxi, (1944-45) 19-24; Aeshcoly, *Moznayim*, vol. xviii (1944), 298-304, 375-383; *see* also Zajaczkowski, *op. cit.*, pp. 18-19, 38-39, 42, about the theories of Brutzkus.

[4] Fishberg gives the following percentages: Ukraine 3.95%; Galicia 4.17%; Poland 3.50%; Hungary 5.0%; North Africa 2.6%

If there is any value in using anthropological or physiological data for determining the origin of a group, then bloodcounts are the best method since they are apparently unaffected by environment. Comparing the frequencies of A and B blood groups, one finds "a remarkable uniformity of the Ashkenazim as a whole (B frequencies being lower) vis-à-vis other Jewish groups." In fact, B frequencies among east-European Jews—Lithuania, Poland and Ukraine—range from 12.43 to 13.00 against 18.50 of Iranian Jews, 20.79 of Jews from Iraq, 25.93 of Krimchaks, 20.62 of Jews from Bukhara, and 20.23 of the Karaites. More recent research in a genetically determined blood abnormality known as thalasemia and evidenced in a lowering of the glutatione content of the blood, and of anemia under certain conditions, seems also to indicate a cardinal difference between east-European-Ashkenazic and Sephardi-Oriental Jewry. The investigations conducted during the last years in Israel indicate "that most acquired hemolytic anemias . . . and all causes of thalasemia show . . . a well-defined ethnographic distribution." Ashkenazic Jews are not afflicted by these blood sicknesses, while sixty per cent of Jews from Kurdistan, and some twenty per cent of those from Iraq and Iran, five per cent of Karaites and Turkish Jews, and twenty per cent of North African Jews are affected.[1]

These blood differences between east-European and Ashkenazic Jews and those of Oriental and Mediterranean countries may probably serve to disprove any ideas about

---

(*Zeitschrift fur Demographie und Statistik d. Juden* vol. iii (1907); no. 11, p. 8; Ernst Schwarz, "Die Krimgoten", *Saeculum*, vol. iv (1953), 163 ff., see also *idem, Goten, Nordgermanen, Angelsachsen* (Bern and Munich 1951), *pass.*

[1] A. E. Mourat, "The Blood Groups of the Jews," *The Jewish Journal of Sociology*, vol. i (1959), 155-175; A. Szeinberg, C. Szeba and others, "Studies on Erythocytes in Cases with Past History of Favism and Drug-Induced Acute Hemolytic Anemia," *Blood*, vol. xii (1957), 603 ff.; *idem*, "Selective Occurrence of Glutatione Instability in Red Blood Corpuscles of the Various Jewish Tribes," *Blood*, vol. xiii, 1043-53; *idem*, "Hemolytic Trait in non-Ashkenazic Jews . . ." Reprint, *Quarterly Review of Harefua*, (1959).

Babylonian-Persian or Khazar ancestry of east-European Jewry.

2. Factual Information About Jewish Khazars and Jews in Eastern Europe.

Although an *argumentum e silentio* has an inherent weakness, nevertheless the fact that Jewish sources after the tenth and eleventh centuries, as well as non-Jewish sources dealing with Jews, have so little to say about either Jewish Khazars or about Jews in eastern Europe in the middle ages may show that the Khazars had slight impact upon Jewry, [1] and that Jewish settlements hardly existed in eastern Europe in those times.

a) To begin with, the information about Jewish Khazars is so meager in Jewish sources [2] that for a long time the whole conversion of the Khazars was thought to have been a myth. Apart from a few doubtful instances, the whole so-called heritage of information amounts to a mere, hazy mention of them by Saadya Gaon in the east and by Abraham Ibn-Daud and Yehuda ben Barzilay in the west. Ibn-Daud, writing apologetically (about 1160) against the Karaites states that "King Joseph sent a letter to Hasdai . . . telling him that he is a rabbanite . . . and we saw in Tolede /some/ of their grandchildren who were learned men and they informed us that the remnants /of the Khazars (ושאריתם)/are rabbanites." Yehudah al-Barceloni writing between 1090 and 1105 gives an

---

[1]   Poliak's attempt to find a justification in rationalizing that the Byzantines were anxious to avoid letting Khazaria be in contact with Europe is unfounded.

[2]   Discounting here the much discussed correspondence between Chasdai-King Joseph, Schechter's Khazar document, the few letters published by Neubauer, Kaufmann and Mann which are unclear and doubtful as to provenance, authorship, and partly even meaning. Neubauer, *JQR*, vol. ix (1896), 26-29; Mann, *ha-tekufa*, vol. xxiii (1924), 253-259; *idem*, *Tarbiz*, vol. iv, (1933), 391 ff; D. Kaufmann, *Gesammelte Schriften*, vol. ii (Frankfort/M., 1901), pp. 190-202; Krauss, *Tarbiz*, vol. iii, 423 ff., Starr, *op. cit.*, 203-206.

abstract of King Joseph's letter. It seems, however, that his knowledge of the whole Khazar matter, like that of his contemporaries, was so vague that he apologizes for writing on the subject. He says that he is not sure whether they were really converted, and whether the text of the letter is genuine or falsified, or has additions, etc. [1]

Neither the two Jewish travellers of the twelfth century, Benjamin of Tudela and Petachya of Regensburg, [2] nor the few others who visited eastern Europe in that epoch, [3] mention anything about the existence of Jewish Khazars. The non-Jewish sources of the thirteenth century, Plano Carpini, William de Rubruquis and Arab writers describing the visit of the Egyptian Sultan to Crimea in 1263 [4]) also lack any reference to them. Nor do preserved names of Jews in eastern Europe [5] from the thirteenth to the

---

[1] Neubauer, *Anecdota Oxon.*, pp. 78-79; S. Assaf, *Jeshurun* September-October 1924, pp. 115 ff. (the extant copy is from the 16th century); see also *idem, Zion*, vol. vii (1941-42), 48-50. Kokovtsov, *op. cit.*, pp. 127-134; R. Yehuda Halevi in his introduction to Kuzari (mid-12th century) mentions the conversion.

[2] Among the countries from which merchants came to Constantinople and Alexandria Benjamin mentions also Khazaria (not that he saw Khazars there as Dunlop mistakenly interprets pp. 220, 230) But the country name (Khazaria) remained for the region centuries after the downfall of the state. Petachya mentions ארץ כוריא several times, again without indicating the existence of Khazars or Jewish Khazars; about the messengers of the Kings of "Meshekh" which he supposedly met in Bagdad, see above p. 47, note 2.

[3] Kupfer-Lewicki, *op. cit., pass.* There is a little more interest to be found among Karaites, probably because of their greater reliance on early Arab writers. *See* now also Zvi Ankori, *Karaites in Byzantium* (New York 1959), pp. 67 ff.

[4] They say the country is inhabited by Tartars, Russians and Alans (Vasiliev, *op. cit.*, p. 172; *see* there another description of the same period).

[5] The inscriptions on tombstones in the Crimea are here excluded because of their doubtful provenance (Firkovich collection). In Kaffa most of the names of the representatives of the Jewish community in 1455 seem to be of Oriental, Italian, or Greek origin (*Evreiskaya Starina*, vol. v [1912], 68-69.)

fifteenth centuries indicate any Khazar, Turco-Finnish or other eastern provenance. [1]

b) A somewhat similar situation is generally found in connection with Jews in eastern Europe. Conjectures and speculation about the early existence of Jews and their continued existence into later centuries find no independent support in source material. Alleged evidence drawn from the story about the religious debate that took place before the conversion of Prince Vladimir of Kiev (tenth century), or from the existence of a bishop of supposedly Jewish extraction— Luka Zhidyata—in Novgorod (eleventh century), or from the apologetic writings of the Metropolitan Illarion (eleventh century), have long been discounted as valueless.[2] Also unreliable is the story about Theodosius, the abbot of

[1] Jewish names recorded in Poland during the 14th century (58 names) are of Hebrew, German, and Slavic origin (or Slavic translation); in the 15th century: Poland: among 83 names 3 (3.6%) are Greek; Southern Poland (in Hebrew sources usually called "Russia") among 78 names, 3 Greek and one possibly of Turkish provenance. The Greek names are such as were already early found in the west (like Alexander, Kalonymos); the single "Turkish" may be a misspelling by the non-Jewish writer. The recorded names of over 200 Jews in Silesia in the years 1330-1360 are either of German provenance or Slavic translations of names of German provenance. Of 66 Jews in Breslau (same period) whose origin is recorded, the great majority came from the neighborhood of the city or from Bohemia and Germany, two from other parts of Poland, and three from Russia (may mean Galicia). (Schipper, *Kulturgeschichte*, pp. 252-256, 283-292; M. Brann, *Geschichte der Juden in Schlesien*, vol. ii (Breslau 1897) (Jahresbericht des Jüdisch-Theologischen Seminars), *Anhang* III pp. xv-lxvii.

[2] The text of the story of prince Vladimir's conversion contains a passage about Palestine being in the hands of Christians which applies to the end of the 11th and the 12th cent. The theme of religious dispute is found also a century earlier in connection with the conversion of the Bulgarian prince. Zhidyata (in some copies called Zhiryata) can be derived from a non-Jewish name. Some maintain that the writings are not at all of Ilarion himself, and there is no indication that his discussion is turned against living Jews; it may rather be a theoretical Christian attack upon Judaism in immitation of the Byzantine writings. (Berlin, *op. cit.*, pp. 135, 139, 140, 142; Barats, *op. cit.*, pp. 464 ff., 826 ff., 841, 860; I. V. Galant, *Voskhod*, vol. xvii (August 1897), 63; Akademiya Nauk SSSR, *Chudozhestvennaya proza Kievskoy Rusi XI-XIII v.* (Moscow 1957), pp. 77, 303.

a monastery in Kiev (1057-1074), who visited Jews for
religious discussions. This is no more than a didactic
legend. And again, the information in the Russian chronicles about a pogrom of Jews in Kiev in 1113 and the
mention of a Jewish street or Jewish gates in Kiev in
1146 and 1151 cannot be entirely acceptable without other
support. The preserved copies of the Russian chronicles,
made in the fourteenth to the eighteenth centuries, consist
of various layers, and have many interpolations [1]. In fact,
nothing about Jews appears in Russian legislation until
the second half of the sixteenth century when the right
of Polish Jews to come to Russia for business purposes
became a problem. [2]

Likewise doubtful are some stories connected with
Poland. [3] The fact is that neither Benjamin of Tudela
who travelled between 1165 and 1173, nor Petachya of
Regensburg (*ca.* 1175-1190) have anything to say about
Jews in eastern Europe. [4] Benjamin, who reported on
Jews in European and Asiatic countries, has nothing
to record about Jews east of Prague, although
he mentions the inclement Russian winter and lists a
number of the animals found in Russia. Petachya, who
definitely passed through Poland and southern Russia,
reports only that "in the land of Kadar [Crimea or there-
abouts] there are no [Rabbanite] Jews, only *minim*,"

---

[1] M. D. Priselkov, *Istoriya Russkago Letopisania XI-XV v.*
(Leningrad 1940), pp. 11, 13, 27.
[2] Galant, *op. cit.*, p. 61.
[3] *See* Weinryb, *Commentary op. cit.* 515 ff. The letter published by
Mann (*Texts and Studies*, vol. i (1931) p. 50) which speaks of Jews
from Russia could probably, like the one mentioned above, be from
the 12-13th century.
[4] The rationalizations offered by some historians for this silence
(that the existence of Jews there was widely known and therefore not
recorded by travellers, or that the travelogues are incomplete) are
rather exercises in avoiding to face the issue. Did not Benjamin record
better known settlements? Or how did it happen that the information
about the *same* area should be incomplete in *both* travelogues?

meaning apparently Karaites. He goes on to tell that these [Karaite] Jews explained that they didn't know about [orthodox] Jewish teachings, because their forefathers had not instructed them, and that they had never heard of the Talmud. [1] The only plausible explanation as to why neither of these travellers says anything about Jews in eastern Europe is that they met none there, that few if any Jewish settlements existed there. The non-Jewish travellers of the thirteenth century are also silent on this subject. Individual Jews may have resided here and there at that time. A Jew is mentioned as the owner or farmer of a village in western Poland (Silesia) about 1150 (or 1200), and two more Jews around 1200 are also mentioned. Apparently the silver coins (bracteates) inscribed with Hebrew letters [2] originated from the same period, the end of the twelfth and the beginning of the thirteenth century. If one is to believe the Polish chronicler, Vincent Kadlubek, Bishop of Cracow, King Mieszko III, 1173-1209, the same whose name is mentioned on some of the coins, imposed heavy fines upon Christians who molested Jews.

We have some information from Russia, or Galicia and Kiev, which in Jewish sources are usually identified as Russia, about a few Jews from there who arrived in western Europe and about some Jews who travelled from the west to those regions. [3] The situation of Jewish settlements

---

[1]   *Massaoth Rabbi Benjamin* (The Itinerary of Benjamin of Tudela) ed. by M. N. Adler (Oxford 1907); *Sibbub Rabbi Petachja* (The Travels of Rabbi Petachja (London 1858).

[2]   These coins are not necessarily coins minted by Jewish minters for the state. Private individuals may have at times received mintage rights (*see* for instance, responsum no. 903 of R. Meir b. Baruk (Prague 1608) reprinted in Kupfer-Lewicki, *op. cit.*, pp. 38-39. Coins with Hebrew inscriptions also originated in Germany (Saxony 1180-1212, Würzburg 1207-1227 [Aronius no. 389, 425] while, on the other hand, there were Ukrainian coins in Poland (11th century).

[3]   R. Moshe from Kiev (12th cent.) who was in contact with R. Shmuel b. Ali in Babylonia; Isaak from Chernigov (12th-13th cent.). A Benjamin from Vladimir (Volhynia?) 12th cent. in Cologne; Isaac b. Asher Halevi (ריב״א) 11th-12th cent.; Eliezer b. Nathan

in Poland and Russia and Hungary, around the beginning
of the thirteenth century, with a *terminus ad quem* of
1217, the year in which R. Yehuda He-Hasid died, can
be gauged from an exchange of letters between R. Yehuda
He-Hasid and R. Eliezer b. Isaac of Bohemia from Prague
(born *ca.* 1150). The latter, writing to R. Yehuda
He-Hasid, speaks about "most places" in Poland, Russia and Hungary
where there are no learned people . *''.* because of need [1]
so that they hire themselves a person, whomever they
find, who serves for them as a cantor, [2] a judge, and
teacher for their children, and they promise him all these
/gifts/. . . . If you prevent them from giving the gifts to
the cantor, these Jews would remain without Torah,
without prayer, and without a judge." He goes on to say,
"Even if you will now retreat from your decision, I am
afraid that they have heard your first words, and the
damage has been done." [3] This letter seems to indicate
that the settlements were new and small and still had
not grown into communities. It may also show that religiously these small Jewish settlements lay within the

(ראבן) 12th cent. (?) Joel b. Isaac, 12th cent., Isaac Durbalo, 12th cent.;
Eliezer b. Isaac 12th cent., *Sefer Raban* (Prague 1610) f. 8 ff. Aptovitzer, *op. cit.*, p. 465; *Makhzor Vitry* (ed. Hurwitz 1923), p. 243;
Or Zarua iv *abodah zarah* par. 118, 128 reprinted in Kupfer-Lewicki,
op. cit. pp. 98, 128-29, 139, 152, 158. (The editors usually try to
retrodate the documents for apologetic reasons); Zunz, *Synagogale
Poesie des Mittelalters*, p. 251; *idem, Gesammelte Schriften*, vol. iii,
pp. 82-83; *MGWJ*, vol. xxxix, p. 511; vol. xl, p. 134. A. M.
Hyamson, *op. cit.*, pp. 32, 113; Aronius, no. 304.

[1] מתוך דוחקם, שאין שם לומדי תורה מתוך דוחקם may mean economic difficulties or other stresses.

[2] Such a cantor was apparently ר' קלונימוס בר' (or 'ור) שבתי החזן
in Hungary who made a decision in connection with two Regensburg
Jews travelling from Russia, brought in *Shibbole ha-lekket* of Zidkiyah
b. Abraham, 13th cent. (ed. Buber, p. 47). The attempt to identify
(Kupfer-Lewicki pp. 61 ff.) our Kalonymos with Kalonymos b.
Sabbatai b. Moshe of Rome (*Encyclopedia Judaica*, vol. ix, p. 846) is
rather connected with the general tendency of retrodating the
documents.

[3] Responsa R. Meir b. Baruk (ed. Lwow) no. 112; Isaac b. Mose
of Vienna, *Or zarua*, vol. i, no. 113; Urbach, *op. cit.*, pp. 183-184.

sphere of influence of western Jews, assuming that a decision of a German rabbi could become so important for them.

More information in both Jewish and non-Jewish sources for Poland and partially also for Russia or Galicia is forthcoming from the middle and second half of the thirteenth century which seems to indicate some sort of group settlement, tiny groups to be sure, and mostly of western provenance, [1] during that and the following centuries.

In summary, all factual information about Jews in the Slavic lands during the later centuries of the middle ages, and the consistent lack of information for earlier centuries [2] may also be regarded as decisive, and contradicts the speculations about mass immigration from Babylonia, Persia, Caucasus, Byzantium, or Khazaria, even though some individuals may have come from those parts.

In Conclusion

What does all this add up to? Our analysis has shown that most of the theories about the origin of east-European Jewry succumb to searching criticism in the absence of factual information. Authors developed a kind of speculative game without a shred of evidence and often also without knowledge of background or understanding of the documents themselves. Most of these authors asserted crude hypotheses which they

[1] *See* Weinryb, *op. cit.*, pp. 516 ff; Berlin, *op. cit.*, p. 176; M. M. Litinsky, *Sefer koroth Podolia we-kadmoniyoth ha-yehudim sham*, vol. i (Odessa 1895), p. 20.

[2] As already stated, Russian legislation during the middle ages does not mention Jews until the 16th century. In Polish sources information on Jews is very scarce (Eisenstein, *op. cit.*, p. 132 f). A recent comprehensive search in Polish archives failed to disclose anything new belonging to the period prior to the 15th century (private communication of Prof. B. Mark, director of the Jewish Historical Institute in Warsaw). Of the Jewish authors, R. Isaac of Vienna was the one nearest to the Slavic lands. Yet among about 500 entries to an index to his *Or zarua* (first 3 volumes) there are only very few concerning Poland and Russia (Poland 2, Russia 2, and 3 doubtful entries).

bolstered uncritically with haphazard, third-hand documentation or with speculations. Often an hypothesis of this kind, printed in a publication, gained an air of authenticity and was quoted elsewhere, either by the same author or by someone else, as a fact. Most of the theories and hypotheses concerning the beginnings of east-European Jewry are no more than fiction.

Written history is doomed to be fragmentary because of the incompleteness of records. Events are only partially observed, only a part of what is observed is recorded, and only a part of what is recorded is preserved. Imagination is a most valuable asset to an historian; it may help him to fill in some of the inevitable gaps or to formulate some theories and hypotheses. But the rôle of theory and hypothesis in historiography is no different from their rôle in some other sciences. They are *devices* for exploring data. But, like imagination, they must be tested against the data and can be accepted only after their validity is proven by facts. In the cases we have been considering, they were based on a flimsy foundation. Instead of trying to ascertain the facts, the writers projected what they thought they should have been. The result is a record of what might have happened. Like the anonymous authors of the legends and myths, they invented artificial constructions responding to needs, real or imagined, of their time. Most of the theories and hypotheses may reflect the climate of opinion of the authors and their times, but are of little, if any, value to the understanding of the history of the Jews in eastern Europe.

The true beginnings of east-European Jewry resulted from a number of historical developments, with differences between Russia and Poland. In the former, or in the areas which later became Russia, or to which Russia spread, there were in existence at different times, perhaps even before the common era, some Jewish settlements which later disappeared in one way or another. Any remnants which remained until the middle ages were wiped out by the Mongol invasion in the thirteenth century. Most of the Jews who came later from Poland were expelled in 1742. There was little if any continuance between the various settlements, and surely not between all predecessor settlements and the settlement which became known as Russian Jewry. The latter is a result of the Polish partitions beginning with 1772, and a minor immigration of a few years earlier. Some small Jewish sects like the Karaites and the Tats may or may not have existed from earlier times.

Polish Jewry, from which Russian Jewry originated, does not antecede the twelfth century, except perhaps, in the form of some sporadic individuals, with a real settlement starting only in the thirteenth century and coming mainly from the west (Bohemia, Germany). Immigration during the subsequent centuries proceeded at a *very* slow pace. At the end of the fifteenth century, the population of Polish-Lithuanian Jewry was about 10,000 and 15,000. We have evidence that they were neither descendants of Khazars nor of any eastern Jewish group, although a few individual survivors and their children may have been among them, as some Sephardi Jews came either directly from Spain or via Turkey, while a few others came from the Genoese Kaffa Colony.

ADDENDA

It is also a mistake to attempt to identify with Poland the expression "Polia" (פוליא) mentioned once in the 12th and again at the beginning of the 13th century. In the first source Abraham Ibn Daud, writing about 1160, apologetically against the Karaites. elucidates the countries and regions where rabbanite Judaism is prevailing. From the context it is clear that Polia is understood to mean Apulia on the Italian Peninsula on the western shore of the Adraitic where Benjamin of Tudela found a few hundred Jews; it is counted there together with "the island of Sicily and Lombardy."

‎... וכל ארץ תוגרמה ואשכנז וצרפת וכל ארץ פוליא ומגינסיא
‎ואי סקיליאה וארץ לומברדיה ...

The other source is found in a responsum sent to R. Eliezer
ben R. Yoel Halevi (*ca.* 1140-1225) in Cologne from Moyence
concerning a woman from Verona (Italy) whose husband had
drowned. At the end of the responsum the Cologne rabbis
are asked to return the answer through one Ismael from
Verona so that it will arrive "before R. Yehuda the brother
of the deserted woman from Verona will come here [to
Moyence?] since he went to Polia on business." There is
no call to construe this as meaning that Yehuda went to
Poland. The sentence may simply indicate that "he went
to Polia"—in Italy, meaning either Pola lying on the Adriatic
sea across from Venice, or Apulia down on the Italian peninsula. He may have been traveling between Italy and Germany
for business purposes.[1] The more so that there is apparently
no Hebrew source of those centuries calling Poland "Polia",
while in the 11-12th century appear "malkhut Pola" and
"Erets Polia" as meaning places in Italy or Italy itself. [2]

[1]   Abraham Ibn Daud, "Sefer ha-Kabalah" in Ad. Neubauer, *op.
cit.*, p. 79; Aptovitzer, *Introductio ad Sefer Rabiah*, pp. 430, 432, 452,
484, *see also* p. 456, no. 133 where business relations between Jews in
Italy and Germany are indicated; Kupfer-Lewicki, *op. cit.*, pp. 168-172.
[2]   A. M. Haberman, *Sefer gezeroth Ashkenaz we-Zarefath* (Jerusalem
1946), pp. 26, 132, 248.

    I am indebted to the Social Science Research Council and the
L. Littauer Foundation for grants in support of studies in the history
of eastern European Jewry of which this is a part. Responsibility for
the views and conclusions of the study, however, rests with me alone.

THE COLONIAL JEWISH PEDDLER *

By Maxwell Whiteman

Dropsie College

In 1655 three New Amsterdam Jews, Abraham de Lucena, Salvador Dandrada, and Jacob Cohen, requested permission of the Dutch authorities to trade and travel on that high road of commerce the South River, as the Delaware River was once known, but their request was stubbornly refused by Peter Suyvesant. Although they were permitted to send two representatives to dispose of the stock which they had already shipped, they were not allowed to barter or trade their goods as they had hoped. This incident, a *cause célèbre* in American Jewish history, is probably the first instance of peddling by Jews in the mercantile economy of seventeenth-century America. The Dutch restrictions against the Jews engaged in retail trade explain the absence of similar peddling expeditions. [1] When later the ban was lifted, it became possible for Jacob Lucena to travel along the banks of the Hudson River, trading with the white settlers and the Indians. The pursuit of peddling was Lucena's apprenticeship in a business which he began shortly after his arrival in Dutch New Amsterdam in 1656. After the English had conquered the Dutch in 1664 and subsequently lifted other restrictions, Lucena became a full-fledged tradesman. [2]

---

* This is part of a larger study on the social and economic history of the Jewish peddler in America.

[1] Samuel Oppenheim, "The Early History of the Jews in New York, 1654-1664," *Publications of the American Jewish Historical Society* [=*PAJHS*] vol. xviii (1909), pp. 27-28; Edwin Wolf 2nd and Maxwell Whiteman, *The History of the Jews of Philadelphia from Colonial Times to the Age of Jackson* [=WW] (Philadelphia 1957), pp. 10-11.

[2] Jacob Rader Marcus, *Early American Jewry* (Philadelphia 1951), vol. i, pp. 35-36.

The economic conditions of the colonial peddler differed
greatly from the conditions that confronted the tens of
thousands of Jews who became peddlers during the nineteenth
century. There were no brilliant successes among the colonial
peddlers, none who rose from rags to riches, no Gimbel or
Guggenheim, no Straus or Seligman, but only those who
stepped up a rung or two on the ladder of success. The Jewish
peddler in the colonies was more than a pack carrier. Often
he was a sutler, an Indian trader, a drayman, a mule-driver
and an itinerant of many occupations. When he sold his
wares travelling on foot, or with a horse and cart, he differed
little from his nineteenth-century counterpart and, if good
fortune persisted, he climbed further up the ladder to become
a shopkeeper and perhaps a merchant. Colonial sutling was a
branch of peddling. Sutlers like Manuel Josephson [1] specialized
in supplying English troops at the isolated forts with the
seemingly insignificant items so vital to daily life. The Indian
trade involved another phase of peddling, and many of the
Indian traders had to become licensed peddlers. In each age
the peddler experienced the same hazards and failures of
their itinerant occupation, although the records of the colonial
peddlers that reveal these problems are as scarce as those of
the nineteenth century are overwhelming in number.

The Jewish peddler at the end of the seventeenth century
and in the first half of the eighteenth century is an elusive
figure, but there were enough peddlers generally to be of
concern to the colonies. In Massachusetts the wandering
peddler required more than a license to sell his goods: he had
to furnish a bond of assurance that he would not become a
dependent. The Jew, in addition to these restrictions, was
classed as an unwelcome stranger. [2] Rhode Island with a
religious climate a bit warmer to its Jewish merchants did not

---

[1] *Ibid.*, pp. 76-79.
[2] Leon Hühner, "The Jews of New England... *Prior to* 1800,"
PAJHS, vol. xi (1903), p. 77; Marcus, *op. cit.*, p. 103; but neither
of these works specifically mentions peddlers.

lure Jewish peddlers to its coast. [1] In Connecticut in 1659 "David the Jew" was fined for peddling to children in the absence of their parents. [2] By 1670 Jacob Lucena of New York had extended his trade to Hartford, but the subsequent history of Jewish activity in colonial Connecticut makes no mention of Jews specifically engaged in this trade. [3] Before the Jew inherited the mantle of the bony, sharp-trading New Englander, the Yankee peddler, or before he converted the countryside into a center of peddling, a war for independence was to be fought and a revolution, perhaps no less great, in the manufacture, sale and distribution of retail goods was to take place. New York and Pennsylvania became the active centers for Jewish peddlers, once they were properly licensed.

Pennsylvania required a license by 1730, [4] and in 1738 New York had a sufficient number of peddlers who had to be legally restrained from selling their goods. [5] Furthermore, each colony had its own restrictions on what could or could not be sold. Some encouraged the sale of domestic manufactures, some banned imported goods, and others forbade the products and manufactures of neighboring colonies. Behind much of this legislation, requiring the purchase of costly licenses and imposing other discouraging restrictions, stood a strong merchant class that had come into power in New England, New York, and Pennsylvania. The city peddler had become a competitor of the very merchant from whom he bought his goods, and the merchant used his influence

---

[1] David C. Adelman, "Notes," in, *Rhode Island Jewish Historical Notes* vol. 1 (1955), pp. 230-231 where the status of all peddlers in Rhode Island is described.

[2] William B. Weeden, *Economic and Social History of New England* 1620-1789, (Boston 1894), vol i, p. 200.

[3] Jacob Rader Marcus, "Light on Early Connecticut Jewry," *American Jewish Archives*, vol. i (1949), p. 3 ff.

[4] Richardson Wright, *Hawkers & Walkers in Early America* (Philadelphia 1927), p. 90.

[5] *Ibid.*, p. 233.

to introduce laws that would prevent the peddler from selling these goods within the city limits. [1]

The introduction of such legislation was related to the rapid growth of the colonial city as an economic center. The frontier towns and hamlets were dependent upon the city and its resources, and it was from the city to the new settlements that the peddler trudged with his bulging wallet of goods strapped to his shoulders. Those who travelled on horse or by cart, offered a larger variety of colonial merchandise than the cotton goods, cloths, notions and trinkets sold by the foot peddler. Heavier items, cutlery, small tools and other hardware weighed down the round topped carts whose big wheels sloshed through the muddy New York and Pennsylvania roads. For a supply of these goods the Jew was just as dependent on a reliable source as was the Yankee. At least one account records that in 1750 Benjamin Goldsmith, "A Jew Pedlor," obtained credit from Daniel Gomez [2] in the fabulous sum of £ 40.15.10. Gomez belonged to an outstanding family of New York Jewish merchants, and his ledger indicates similar transactions with other tradesmen or peddlers. [3] Since 1717 the Gomezes had operated an Indian trading post not far from Newburgh, New York and a full variety of colonial goods could be purchased from them. [4]

Although the Jewish peddler was by no means as common in this period as the Yankee, he was already being drawn into the same comic and anecdotal literature which had begun to envelope the Yankee. An account of a "Jew Pedlar" in a New York journal of 1753 [5] was, with the substitution of a word, the Yankee himself.

[1] Victor S. Clark, *History of Manufactures in the United States, 1607-1860* (Washington, D.C., 1916), pp. 69, 117; Wright, *op. cit.*, p. 89.

[2] "Gomez Ledger," *PAJHS*, vol. xxvii (1920), p. 246.

[3] *Ibid.*, p. 247 for reference to Abraham de Lyon "gone to Canastoga."

[4] Leon Hühner, "Daniel Gomez, A Pioneer Merchant of Early New York," *PAJHS*, vol. xli (1951), pp. 107-125.

[5] *Pennsylvania Gazette*, March 13, 1753.

"We have an account from the Country of the following comical affair, which lately happen'd, viz. A Jew Pedlar went into a House where he offered his goods for sale, but the good Man being out, and all his Family, except his Wife, who told the Pedlar that she could not buy any Thing, for her Husband had got the Key of the Money: The Pedlar then finding that the Woman was entirely alone, offer'd to make her a Present of a Piece of Calicoe upon Condition of her giving up her Charms to him: The Bait was very alluring, for the Thoughts of sporting with a young Man, and having a new Gown in the Bargain, made her readily yield to his Desires; he accordingly gave her the Calicoe, and after taking a Repast in the Banquet of Love, went about his Business; but had not gone far before he met with her Husband, and having some knowledge of him said, 'Sir, I have sold your Wife a very cheap Piece of Calicoe, and on six Months Credit,' with that the poor man stood amaz'd, and said, 'I wonder at my wife's ill Conduct in running me in Debt, when she knows that I have a considerable Sum of Money to pay in a few Months Time, and can't tell how to make it up.' He then persuaded the Pedlar to go back and take his piece of Calicoe, which he readily consented to, and when they came to the House, he ordered his Wife to give the Pedlar his Calicoe again, which she did after privately concealing a Coal of Fire in it; the Pedlar took his Calicoe and put it in his Pack (which was a Wallet slung across his Shoulders) so march'd off, pleas'd with the Thoughts of his Success; but for his sweet Meat he soon found sour Sauce; he not suspecting the Cheat, jogg'd along till he met with a Countryman, who seeing his Pack on Fire (and which was just then ready to blaze) cry'd, 'Hay, Friend, from whence came you?' '*from Hell*,' replied the Pedlar; 'so I perceive,' says the Countryman, 'by the Flames at your Back.' The Pedlar then look'd behind him, and to his great Surprize found all his Goods on Fire, which made him stamp and rave like a mad Man, and curse his Folly in cuckolding the poor Man."

In the course of this decade the Jewish peddler emerged as a specific figure in the colonial economy. The opening of the West in the 1750's demanded mobile merchants with ready goods to go to the Pennsylvania outposts, and the French and Indian War invited adventure and trade at the forts and stations in and about Albany, New York. The French and Indian War was to the New York peddler what the Pennsylvania outposts were to the Philadelphia peddler. Sutling and the Indian trade were easily stimulated. The sutler became involved in the marginal economy that was dependent on troops and the fortunes of war; on the other hand, the Indian trader, lured by the barter of furs and pelts for trinkets and hatchets, envisioned lucrative opportunities.

Colonial sutling attracted a number of Jews who, if they did not distinguish themselves by wealth, attained considerable prestige in the eighteenth-century Jewish community long after they surrendered the frontier post for city shopkeeping. Among these was Manuel Josephson, linguist, scholar, and synagogue president. Josephson was a sutler during the French and Indian War and witnessed the results of the Indian massacres at Fort Edward in 1757. [1] Jonas Phillips, in the years to come, was no less distinguished than Josephson. His first years in America were spent along the Hudson River, in supplying the military with groceries and dry goods that he carted from New York in exchange for furs when money was not available. [2] Later in life, when he settled in Philadelphia, his auction house became one of the very first peddlers' supply outlets in the country. [3] The comparative successes of Josephson and Phillips, about whom an extensive literature exists, dwarf the failures of those about whom few records have survived or whose destiny it was not to be remembered. The few contemporary notices that allude to peddling deal with the trade's occupational hazards, such as financial

---

[1]   WW, pp. 57, 82, 126, 397.
[2]   *Ibid.*, p. 62.
[3]   *Ibid.*, p. 184.

failure, disappearance, or murder on the highway. Levy Jacobs was among those whose fate remains unknown. He disappeared in the winter of 1759, and his partner, Mordiky Levy, advertised for him in vain in the New York press. Levy told the story of Jacobs who "left New York about five months ago, to go a peddling as far as Albany with a quantity of goods, and has not been heard of since." [1] Perhaps Jacobs fell victim to the marauding Indians or to the bitter winter of that year. No account of his return to New York has been found.

Others in the area of Dutchess and Ulster Counties encountered financial difficulties. They could not or would not pay for the merchandise which they had obtained on credit. Philip Samuel who was expelled from Boston in 1756, [2] possibly for peddling without a license, was being hunted in New York in 1760. [3] He, along with the partners Israel Joseph and Henry Mordicai, were publicly accused of absconding with merchandise of considerable value. [4] Before they could be apprehended the trio fled to Holland. [5]

The system of licensing of peddlers and hawkers in the colonies was carried over from England. Most of the colonies had their own system of licensing and established scales of rates or special fees for those who travelled on foot or by horse, or with a horse and cart. Since there was no reciprocal recognition among the colonies of peddlers' licenses, it is likely that the Connecticut Yankee who invaded New York State frequently did so without a license, as the New Yorker may have done when he went peddling in Pennsylvania. [6]

Although few records of colonial licenses have survived to

[1] *New York Gazette*, January 7 to January 28, 1760.

[2] Lee M. Friedman, "Early Jewish Residents in Massachusetts," *PAJHS*, vol. xxiii (1915), p. 83.

[3] *New York Gazette*, September 4, 1760.

[4] *Ibid.*, September 4; September 25, 1760.

[5] Philip L. White, *The Beekmans of New York* (New York 1956), pp. 649 ff.

[6] Wright, *op. cit.*, pp. 89-91.

indicate the total number of peddlers and the Jews among them for New York State, [1] the extant licenses in Pennsylvania provide an interesting description of licensing between 1762 and 1775. [2] The number of licensed peddlers in Pennsylvania for the year beginning with March, 1762 was indeed small. Only 19 licenses were issued, 16 for horse peddlers and 3 for foot peddlers, the cost being £ 1.11.0 for those who travelled by horse and a few shillings less for those went by foot. The cost of an annual license was almost as much as that of a marriage license and nearly equalled the cost of a tavern license. Jewish peddlers do not appear in these records until 1765 when Moses Abraham and Abraham Moses applied for a license to travel by horse. [3] In the six years that followed, all other licenses that were issued went to Irish or Scotch-Irish peddlers.

Of the eighteen licenses granted in 1771, only one was applied for by a Jew, Isaac Wolf, [4] who was later advised to begin business in a small way. [5] But in the peak year of 1772, when 49 licenses were recorded, 5 Jews were recipients, Joseph Solomon Cohen, [6] Michael Hart, [7] Benjamin and Isaac Wolf, [8] and Abraham Levy. [9] In 1773, 27 licenses were

[1]   No records of the licensing of peddlers in colonial New York have thus far been located.

[2]   *Licenses for Marriages, Taverns & Pedlars & c.* 1762-1775. Two vols., MSS, Historical Society of Pennsylvania. These records also include licenses for Bucks, Lancaster and York Counties in Pennsylvania and Kent County in Delaware. Not all of the licensees' names are supplied.

[3]   *Ibid.*, vol. 1, Moses Abraham and Abraham Moses, June 14, 1765.

[4]   *Ibid.*, vol. 2, Isaac Wolf, November 13, 1771.

[5]   M. Arthur Oles, "The Henry Joseph Collection of the Gratz Family Papers at the American Jewish Archives, A Survey of the Yiddish Material," in *Essays in American Jewish History* (Cincinnati 1958), p. 114.

[6]   *Licenses*, vol. 2, Joseph Solomon Cohen, March 6, 1772.

[7]   *Ibid.*, Michael Hart, April 23, 1772.

[8]   *Ibid.*, Benjamin and Isaac Wolf, August 7, and November 2, 1772.

[9]   *Ibid.*, Abraham Levy, December 8, 1772.

issued, but only 4 of these to Jews; renewals to Joseph Solomon Cohen and Abraham Levy, [1] and licenses to the 2 newcomers, Ephraim Abraham [2] and Jacob Isaiah Cohen, [3] who later became a successful and prosperous merchant. The following year 18 licenses were issued of which 4 went to Jews, three being renewals of the previous year. [4] In 1775, the last year for which there is a record, only one Jewish peddler appears among the 8 licensees, Lyon Nathan. [5]

Nathan, a former resident of Reading, Pennsylvania, moved to Philadelphia in 1770. [6] He was one of a small group of Jews who had emigrated from Germany after 1750 and settled in eastern Pennsylvania. [7] Unlike his fellow immigrants whose business careers show the evolution from peddling to shopkeeping, the sequence of Nathan's career was the opposite. He began as a shopkeeper, then became a peddler and an Indian trader. The six Indian traders registered as peddlers were, in addition to Nathan, Moses Abraham, Joseph Solomon Cohen, Benjamin Wolf, Abraham Levy and Ephraim Abraham [8] Their contribution to the development of the western trade was minor alongside the vast enterprises of David Franks, the Gratz brothers, or Joseph Simon. [9] It was from the Lancaster oldtimer Joseph Simon, or from Moses

[1] *Ibid.*, Joseph Solomon Cohen, May 10, 1773; Abraham Levy, November 30, 1773.

[2] *Ibid.*, Ephraim Abraham, June 1, 1773.

[3] *Ibid.*, Jacob Isaiah Cohen, May 12, 1773. For subsequent references to Cohen, *see* WW, pp. 70, 95-96, 133-134.

[4] *Licenses*, vol. 2. These were Joseph Solomon [Cohen], May 20; Isiah (sic) Cohen, October 6; Ephraim Abraham, October 6; Abraham Levi, December 8, 1774.

[5] *Ibid.*, Lyon Nathan, May 5, 1775.

[6] WW, p. 56.

[7] *Ibid.*, pp. 49, 56.

[8] *Ibid.*, p. 70 which is based on information in *Pennsylvania Archives*, 5th series, vol. 1, 374-379 where these men are recorded as Indian traders; however, in *Licenses*, they are described as peddlers. The dates in both source correspond to each other.

[9] William Vincent Byars, *B. and M. Gratz, Merchants in Philadelphia* (Jefferson City, Mo., 1916).

Heyman [1] who operated country stores in New Hanover
and Reading, that the peddlers, shopkeepers or Indian traders
obtained or sold their goods. A chain of country shops were
conducted in Goshenhoppen, New Goshenhoppen, Tulpe-
hocken, Womelsdorf, Hanover, New Hanover, Reading, York,
and Lancaster. [2] Their business was not always done for hard
cash or paper money. The German and Scotch-Irish settlers
had none of the first and very little of the other. Accordingly,
most of the trade was in exchange or barter for what was
known as "country pay." The calicos, woolen stockings, cutlery, hats, snuff and tobacco, which constituted some of the
peddlers' wares, were funneled from Philadelphia to the
frontier towns. In exchange, the peddlers, competing with
some of the shopkeepers, accepted deer and fox skins and
racoon furs, all of which were highly desirable commodities
that were shipped back to Philadelphia in payment for the
original goods purchased on credit. [3]

About this time the Jewish merchants of Philadelphia were
stunned by news that Jacob Isaacs and Emanuel Lyons had
become involved in an incident similar to that which confronted the New Yorkers in 1760. Unable to adjust themselves
to the ways of colonial society, these two peddlers, who had
already proved themselves unsuccessful at a number of other
occupations, absconded with a wagon load of goods in 1772.
Isaacs, who had come from Ireland, and Lyons, a bearded,

---

[1] *Pennsylvanische Berichte*, December 16, 1748 and February 16,
1749 for the advertisements of Moses Heyman's country store in
New Hanover, and January 16, 1755, July 24, 1758 and April 27,
1759 for his store in Reading, Pa.

[2] *Ibid.*, and WW, pp. 49, 56.

[3] *Pennsylvanische Berichte*, July 8, 1759, for an example of Benjamin Nathan's offer of barter, ,,Er nimmt an Bezahlung allerley was
die Leute haben, nehmlich Butter und Unschlicht &c." For type
and variety, describing 35 items of dry goods, hardware, agricultural
equipment, oils, food and trinkets *see Philadelphische Staatsbote*,
February 6, 1764 under Benjamin Nathan and Joseph Simon. For a
description of skins and furs see *Pennsylvanische Berichte*, January 16,
1755 under Moses Heyman.

German-speaking Hebrew teacher, were last seen driving their loaded cart in the direction of Lancaster. If they were ever apprehended, no record survives to tell the story. [1]

The absence of the Jewish peddler in New England was due chiefly to his being viewed as an undesirable stranger. In the South, with the exception of Georgia and South Carolina, Jews were made unwelcome by religious tests or by the restriction of their economic opportunities. [2] In addition, the geography of the South, with its swamps and plantations and its small, sparsely populated towns seperated by great distances, was not encouraging to a peddler seeking fresh communities in which to vend his goods. Perhaps for these reasons the literature of southern Jewish history is remarkably silent on the subject of Jewish peddlers. [3]

If the British Committee of Council for Plantation Affairs had acted on the petition of the chiefs of the Sephardi community of London, the "floating mass" of Jews "consisting of hucksters, hawkers, journeymen and others, either verging on pauperism or steeped hopelessly in the abyss" would have been the first body of Jewish settlers in South Carolina. The plan to transport London's underprivileged Jews to South Carolina was thwarted by inaction, and only because of this did the colony escape receiving a community of Jewish peddlers. [4] Instead, the first Jewish settlers who came to Charleston, while not affluent, did not depend on peddling as a means of earning a livelihood. Still, the venturesome nature of

[1]   WW, pp. 57-58 where the story is told in detail.
[2]   Abram Vossen Goodman, *American Overture, Jewish Rights in Colonial Times* (Philadelphia 1947), for an examination of these restrictions.
[3]   Barnett A. Elzas, *The Jews of South Carolina* (Philadelphia 1905); Charles Reznikoff and Uriah Z. Engelman, *The Jews of Charleston* (Philadelphia 1950) and Herbert T. Ezekiel and Gaston Lichtenstein, *The History of the Jews of Richmond from 1769 to 1917* (Richmond 1917) make no mention of the presence of peddlers in South Carolina or colonial Virginia. Marcus, *op. cit.*, vol. ii, pp. 400-401, dispenses with the colonial and eighteenth-century peddler in nine lines.
[4]   Elzas, *op. cit.*, p. 31.

colonial Jews makes it impossible to believe that an occasional peddling foray was not made. It is likely, for example, that the Pennsylvania peddler and Indian trader, Jacob I. Cohen, who joined Captain Lushington's militia company, [1] peddled his way to Charleston in time to join the American army.

As the American War for Independence became a certainty, the Jewish peddler is found again in his role of sutler. Among the new sutlers was Hyam Salomon. In the late Spring of 1776 Leonard Gansevoort informed General Philip J. Schuyler that Salomon was a man whose loyalty to the American cause was irreproachable, and he could be depended upon as one fit to sutle to the soldiers at Lake George. [2] When Salomon returned to New York City he was imprisoned by the occupying British for his sympathies with the colonies. Released in order to serve the Hessians as a commisary, Salomon worked in the guise of an American agent and, when discovered, was forced to flee for his life. [3] It is likely that he crossed paths with another sutler, Alexander Zunz, the Hessian Jew who followed the army of General William Howe. Zunz stayed in Philadelphia during the British occupation of the city and later moved with the British to New York. [4] Other Hessian sutlers operated in the South, and after the war Samuel Levy and Levy Solomons, who had come in with the British, settled permanently in Charleston, South Carolina. [5]

The American revolution brought to a close the minor role of the Jewish peddler just as it rescinded the legislation that limited his activity. Fifty years were to pass before the Jewish peddler seized the reins from the Yankee and began to penetrate into every nook and cranny of American territory with

[1]   *Ibid.*, p. 84.
[2]   Jacob Rader Marcus, *American Jewry—Documents, Eighteenth Century* (Cincinnati 1959), pp. 235-236.
[3]   Morris U. Schappes, *A Documentary History of the Jews in the United States*, 1654-1875 (New York 1952), pp. 52-53.
[4]   WW, p. 85.
[5]   Elzas, *op. cit.*, pp. 98-99.

his packs, bags, trunks and bulging wagons of goods. Meanwhile, the old legislation was replaced by new laws, in a sense no less restrictive, but based on the economic needs and changes of a vastly expanding nation. The Jewish peddler entered into the literature of America, the travel books of the Germans, and the frequently contemptuous observations of the British. He became the direct retailer to the nation and at one time constituted one third of the peddlers in the United States. Lauded as a forerunner of the department store he was actually the precursor of the five- and ten-cent store. The doors of the southern and of New England farmhouses were opened to him; he became a common sight in the Ohio Valley, and no stranger on a Mississippi River boat; he crossed the Plains, penetrated the passes of the Rockies, fought with the Indians, and buckled sacks of gold-dust to his belt. He was an integral part of American life.

EZRA STILES WRITES A HEBREW LETTER

By EDWIN WOLF 2nd

Librarian, The Library Company of Philadelphia

ON MARCH 8, 1773 the Reverend Ezra Stiles, the pastor of the Second Congregational Church of Newport, Rhode Island, wrote in his diary: "This Evening I went to the Synagogue it being the Eve of *Purim*. The Chuzan read thro' the Book of Esther. There I saw Rabbi Carigal I judge aet. 45. lately from the City of Hebron, the Cave of Macpelah in the Holy Land. ... He has the appearance of an ingenious & sensible Man." [1] Thereafter, Stiles saw much of Rabbi Karigal.

Stiles, educated at Yale, was one of the intellectual leaders of the British Colonies. Employed first as a tutor at his alma mater, he became friendly with Benjamin Franklin through a common interest in electrical experiment. Although he considered entering the active ministry, he studied law instead. His hesitation was due to an intellectual honesty which would not permit him to accept anything the truth of which he was not convinced of. Eventually, a patient study of the Holy Scriptures brought him to a firm belief in the truth of revelation, and in 1755 he accepted the pulpit at Newport. A linguist, with a knowledge of Hebrew, Arabic, Syriac and Armenian, a scientist, who made observations on the transits of Venus in 1761 and 1769, an antiquarian, who planned an ecclesiastical history of New England, and for a time the librarian of the Redwood Library, Stiles was generally recognized as the most learned man in New England. [2]

[1] Franklin Bowditch Dexter (ed.), *The Literary Diary of Ezra Stiles, D.D., LL.D.* (New York 1901), vol. i [hereafter refered to as *Diary*], p. 354.

[2] *Dictionary of American Biography* (New York 1936), vol. xviii, pp. 18-19. A detailed study of Stiles's connections with Jews, Judaism and Hebrew is in George Alexander Kohut, *Ezra Stiles and the Jews* (New York 1902).

Rabbi Isaac Karigal was one of the several Palestinian messengers who visited America during the eighteenth century. Much of what we know of him comes from Stiles's diary. Karigal, as he appeared in 1773, was "aet. 39 [this correction after Stiles had talked with him], a large Man, neat and well dressed in the Turkish Habit." He was well versed in "the Gemara, the 2 Talmuds (of which he preferred the Babylonish) the Changes of the Hebrew Language in different Ages &c." Curiously enough, his Arabic was not the equal of Stiles's. [1] Karigal was born in 1733 in Hebron, one of the holy cities and a center of mystical Judaism, and was certified a rabbi in 1750. Three years later he went to Europe, visiting London and most of the large cities on the continent. In 1762 he sailed to Curaçao where he spent two years as acting rabbi, and then returned to Amsterdam, crossed Europe and returned home to Hebron in the summer of 1764. From 1768 to 1771 he taught at the Beth ha-Midrash in London, and thence came once more to America, stopping for a year in Jamaica. In the summer of 1772 he arrived in Philadelphia, went on to New York and then to Newport. [2] On July 21, 1773, he sailed for Surinam, remained there for a while, and died in Barbados on May 17, 1777. [3]

An intellectually curious Stiles, already friendly with the Jews of Newport, was excited to meet a Palestinian Jew possessed of learning far beyond that of his American co-religionists. In the heritage of the New Englander was a strain of the messianic mysticism which underlay the permission granted by Cromwell for the re-entry of Jews into Puritan England. The hope for the coming of the millennium, set forth by Menasseh ben Israel as one of the reasons for

[1] *Diary*, p. 357.

[2] *Ibid.*, p. 395, where this information appears in the form of a "Memoir." Kohut, *op. cit.*, p. 155, corrects the date of his stay in Curaçao to 1762.

[3] E. M. Shilstone, *Monumental Descriptions in the Burial Ground of the Jewish Synagogue at Bridgetown, Barbados* (New York 1956), p. 100.

the English to admit Jews to their land, the glimmering belief that the Lost Tribes were to be found in America, and the sympathy which the Puritans felt for the Old Testament made the Jew in late seventeenth-century England an object of unusual interest. Judaism was then riddled with messianic hopes and plagued by the appearance of false messiahs, and the Hebraic mysticism which permeated non-Jewish circles stimulated an answering echo of Judaeo-Christian mysticism. If only the Jews could be brought to see the error of their ways, perhaps the age of the Messiah would begin. [1]

During the four and a half months Rabbi Karigal spent in Newport, Stiles met him in the synagogue, visited or was visited by him on twenty-five occasions. They had long theological, archaeological and linguistic discussions which seem to have delighted Stiles. [2] On July 14 he noted that he was "Writing a Hebrew Letter"; the next day he and the Rabbi discussed the coming of the Messiah; and on the following day the two scholars compared their editions of the *Zohar*. [3] On July 19 Stiles stated that he was finishing his "Hebrew Letter to the Rabbi," and in the afternoon "showed" it to him, because he had not had time to copy the eight pages. [4] Apparently, it was not finished when Karigal sailed two days later.

It is hardly to be supposed that Stiles, adept as he may have been in the Hebrew language, would have written a long

[1] Heinrich Graetz, *History of the Jews* (Philadelphia 1891-95), vol. v, pp. 18-50.

[2] *Diary*, pp. 354-399, *passim*.

[3] *Ibid.*, p. 398. On October 29, 1773, he recorded: "This day I received from London the *Zohar*, a Hebrew Folio Volume of 800 or 770 pages, Sultzbac Edit. 1684, and published at Nuremberg," *ibid.*, p. 298. Karigal's edition, he noted, was printed at Constantinople.

[4] *Ibid.*, p. 399. The "eight pages" were presumably not sent, and the letter was vastly expanded to its present form; or the English letter may have been finished, but only eight pages of the Hebrew. Could it be that when Stiles spoke of a "Hebrew" letter he meant the style and not the language?

and complicated treatise directly in Hebrew. Much more likely
would it have been for him to have first written his treatise
in English and then translated it into Hebrew. It took him
quite a while. In November, 1773, Stiles met another peri-
patetic rabbi, this time Tobiah bar Jehudah from near Cracow.
"We had much Conversation on the Zohar," he recorded in
his diary. [1] This was the stimulus he needed, for on December
3 he noted that he "Finished a Hebrew Letter of 22 pages
to R. Haijm Isaac Karigal." [2]

It is the original English text of this letter which follows.
Since Stiles mentions no other letter of such length, this
would seem to be the one he began writing just before Karigal
left Newport. [3] Written on 27 quarto pages in the autograph
of Stiles it is dated July 19, 1773. On April 28, 1814, Mathias
Lopez made a gift of it to the Library Company of Philadelphia.
Lopez came from Barbados, for an *Omer* chart he gave to
the library at the same time, bearing the name of Moses
Lopez, Junior, was written there. [4] It seems likely that Stiles
sent Karigal his English version as well as his Hebrew one,
and that it came into the hands of a member of the Lopez
family in Barbados after his death.

Not much need be said about Stiles's tractate. Its two
parts add little to our knowledge of the theology of the
period. It is, perhaps, surprising how imbued with cabbalistic
teachings they are. [5] However, the two-part tractate does

---

[1] *Ibid.*, p. 422.
[2] *Ibid.*, p. 423. Kohut, *op. cit.*, p. 133, in error, says "24" pages.
Stiles made another copy of the letter in Hebrew on December 30
which ran to 29 pages, *Diary*, p. 427.
[3] Abiel Holmes, *The Life of Ezra Stiles, DD., LL.D.* (Boston 1798),
pp. 169-170, says "One of the Doctor's Hebrew letters on the divinity
of the Messiah, and the glory of his kingdom, consisted of twenty-two
quarto pages." Since no other letter of this length to Karigal is
known, and since this describes the contents of the English letter, it
may be assumed that they are the same.
[4] Minute Books of the Library Company, vol. v, p. 86.
[5] Kohut, *op. cit.*, *passim*, speaks of Stiles's fascination with
cabbalistic literature.

constitute the earliest surviving example of an American attempt to write a talmudical essay.

THE TEXT OF THE LETTER

The least of the Disciples of JESUS, Ezra Stiles wisheth Satiety of Delights unto the illustrious and Venerable Hocham the Great Rabbi HAYM ISAAC KARIGAL; who daily & without ceasing lifteth up his Eyes unto the Things on high, and is enlightened with the Dew of Lights from Jehovah, and has been initiated into the secrets of Understanding and sublime Knowledge, and perfected in the hidden Mystery of the סוד at the mouth of the Masters of the Law, and by the Tradition of the wise Men of all Ages. Amidst the Darkness of the present Age, may the Lord shine upon thee, and lead thy Goings in the Path of Perfection; until thou shalt be laid up on high among the chosen Ones of Righteousness in the Crown of the Hosts, which crowd around the Throne of the Lord; and so be immersed in the mysterious סוד, to behold the Beauty of the Lord, and be swallowed up in the Splendor of his Glory. Amen.

Let the Thoughts & Meditations of my heart be acceptable upon the Messiah and the Greatness and Glory of his Kingdom. *All kings shall bow down to him, and all Nations shall serve him.* Ps. LXXII. 11.

Who is this great King of Glory? He is my Beloved and I am his. I will sing a Song unto my Beloved. How beautiful art thou, how pleasant for delights? But where is he to be found whom my soul loveth? Shall we seek him among the *Lilies*, among the Souls and pure Minds in the Garden of Eden? He is mighty and more exalted than the Multitude of the Princes of Hosts; and amidst the Ten Saphirots he hath reigned from Eternity, and shall reign over all the Sons of the Mighty, the Aralim and the Hasmalim, and over all the holy Beings; and unto him all the superior Powers bow down with one accord & all as one. Amen.

But who is this glorious King? He is the Son of Jehovah:
thus Jehovah said *thou art my son*—and also *kiss the son.*
Ps. ii. So *what is the name of his son?* Prov. xxx. As is the
name of the son of God, so is the name of the Messiah. There
are many sons of God which have been created, and these
are but as yesterday: but the Messiah is one son of God, and
he is the firstborn and beloved who never was created, for
he was with Jehovah before there were any other Beings in
the Universe, even from Eternity. Therefore the pure soul
of the Messiah is without any End to his Beginning or Original,
for there never was a time in which he was not to be
found the son of Jehovah. He is the Cohmah in the Saphirots, as it is said, *the Lord possessed me in the beginning of his Way,*
before his works of old. I was set up from everlasting, from the
beginning or ever the Earth was—Then I was by him as one
brought up with him: and I was daily his Delight, rejoycing
always before him. Prov. VIII.—Agreeable to this the prophet
says *Thou Bethlehem Epratah—out of thee shall he come forth*
unto me the Ruler, that is the Messiah, *in Israel, whose Goings*
forth have been from of old, from everlasting. Micah V. Jehovah
is the great סוד Mystery: and R. Becai said, *there are three*
Glories in the סוד. Also there are three degrees in Jehovah—
in the secret of the Degree, Cant. ii. 14. and each and all the
degrees in the Headship are one in the סוד, and there is no
End or Termination to their Unity or Headship. The Headship
of the Universe, or the Commencement of its Existence may
be run back into a סוף or End: to the Godhead there is no
סוף (it cannot be run back into a time when it was not) for
he is the Head, and to his Headship there is no Beginning.
The אין סוף of the ten Saphirots, or not to have a סוף End,
separates or distinguishes Jehovah and all that is essentially
in him, from the created Universe. There are three degrees
in Jehovah or the selfexistent Being, not as all Things are
in God, but as he is in Himself: and so if He is eternal, all
that is in his Essence, each Degree in him is also from Eternity.
R. Eleazar in the Zohar upon Leviticus, said, *the Mystery of*

the Elohim is this, there are three Degrees, and every one of these Degrees subsisteth by itself: and yet all of them are one, and combined together in one, nor can one be separated from the other. And again, *these are three degrees as they are all interwoven among themselves, and all are united one with another without Division*: as it is written, if you suffer me to arise & come to the Father—I have heard what is written in the Scripture I AM THAT I AM.

One of these three degrees is the *Mimra* or WORD of JEHO-VAH, and this is the pure soul of the Messiah. The Mimra of Jehovah was from Eternity, and so the soul of the Messiah is from Eternity.

The learned *Philo* of Alexandria, an Ambassador for the Jews, in his old age made his Apology for his people to the Roman Senate in the time of *Claudius Caesar*: but he wrote the most of his Books while a young man in the Time of *Augustus*, sixty years before the Destruction of the second Temple. This learned Man in his Treatise upon Abraham speaketh to this Effect: He that meditates upon God with deep attention will behold three Powers in the Unity; and will perceive a threefold Image of one Substance: the *Father* is called *Jah*, and he is between the *two Powers* nearest to him, and he is far the most antient of all Beings: of the two Powers, one is the Creator, and the other is the Ruler: and again, the middle God with his two Powers, gives forth to those who attentively contemplate him, a vision first of One and then of Three from his Unity. And *Philo* further says, that Abraham addressed the three Angels, not as three but as one Jehovah. And speaking upon the second of the three, he calls him by these Names, the WORD, the SON, and the first begotten of God. The Father of Beings caused to arise or shine forth his Son most antient even coeternal, and also called him his Firstborn. This Son beheld and knew all the Knowledge of the Father; and created & formed the Universe according to the Exemplar and Model which he saw in the Omniscience of the Father. God with his two supreme Powers,

as one Jehovah, giveth forth three appearances to the con-
templative Mind. The WORD is the firstborn of God—the
WORD is the eternal Resemblance of God. Again, the great
High Priest (the Messiah) is not Man, but the holy WORD,
in whom is no pollution. He is in truth the High Priest; he
is pure and in him is no sin being free from all Evil. To this
Effect *Philo.* Thus your eyes see how *Philo* describes three
Subsistencies in Jehovah; and the second of them he calls the
λογος και εικων και υιος Θεου, the WORD and IMAGE
and SON of God, and that this Son created the World. In
his own Words he says,—*Unto the One only selfexistent God
are two supreme & first powers,* GOODNESS *and* AUTHORITY:
*Goodness created the Universe: Authority is the diffused Energy
in the Rule and Administration of the Creation: a third which
is combined as a middle one between the other two, is the* WORD:
for by the WORD, *God is both good and governing. Of the two
Powers Government and Goodness, the Cherubin are the Symbols.*

Rabbi *Aba* said, the Spirit of the living God is one Spirit.—
R. *Simeon Ben Johaj* says in the Zohar on Genesis, *the Spirit
of the Elohim, that is the Spirit of the Messiah—the Spirit or
Soul of the Messiah is said to be in Jah, and the Spirit of the
Elohim is Shiloh.* Shiloh & Messiah are the same, and the
spirit of God is in him. This is a great Mystery. And this Spirit
is the pure Soul which is the WORD of God and the SON of
God. And thus the Messiah the Word is the Creator of the
World, as saith the Targum upon Isaiah XLV. 12 *I have made*
(Targum, by my *Word*) *the Earth & created Man upon it.* see
also Gen. I. 27. Wherefore altho' the Messiah was not himself
created, yet he created the Universe because he is the (Mimra)
Word of God, and Jehovah by his Word created the Earth &
the Heavens & all the hosts thereof.

Moreover the name Jehovah is the Messiah. *For thy Maker
is thy Husband, the Lord of Hosts is his Name, and thy Redeemer
&c* Isai. LIV. 5. Who is he that shall no more be called *Baali*
but *Ishi* to Israel? Hosea II. 17.—the Messiah, and he is
Jehovah—for *Jehovah shall reign over them on Mount Zion,*

Micah IV. 7. Messiah *Ishi* is the *Ishi* to his *Sister the Spouse* Cant. IV. 10. The Messiah is *the Man that is my Fellow saith Jehovah* Zech. XIII. 7. *And Jehovah shall be King over all the Earth: in that day there shall be one Jehovah and his Name one*, Zech. XIV. 9. The holy Name is in the Mimra, Word, which is Messiah according to the Targum of *Onkelos* and *Jerusalem* upon Gen. III-IX. 12.-XVII. 2.-xxviii. 21. - Levit. XXVI. 9. Deut. XX. 1. The WORD מימרא is not *Word* דבר Speech, if it is the Angel in whom the Name of Jehovah is: for Moses stood between the Word מימרא of the Lord and Israel, to relate the דבר *Word* Message of the Lord, as in the Targum on Deut. v. 5. In the Talmud Sanhedrin it is said, *What is the* [sic] *his Name of the King Messiah? R. Aba Son of Cohena said his Name is* JEHOVAH, *as it is said, and this shall be the name by which he shall be called* JEHOVAH OUR RIGHTEOUSNESS. *Upon which R. Levi said, o how happy the City whose name is as the name of its King, and the name of its King as the name of its God! happy the City whose name is as the name of its King, as it is written the name of the City from that day shall be* JEHOVAH IS THERE. When Shiloh shall come to the holy City, it will be found that *Jehovah is there*. Therefore the name of the King of Zion is Jehovah, and the sacred Name is thus *in this King*. The *Scripture calls the name of the Messiah the Lord our Righteousness because of his being the Mediator God, at whose hand we attain Righteousness for the Lord, and therefore he is called by the name Jehovah*. See Ikkarim Orat. 2. From all which it is proved that the holy Soul of the Messiah has existed from Eternity, one of the Three in the sublime Mystery of Jehovah.

As he created all, so to him belongs the Kingdom & Dominion over all the kings of this world, over all the angels in Heaven, and over all the Princes of the Princes of the Hosts throughout the Universe. *The Lord reigneth, he is cloathed with Majesty*, and the whole Creation bow before him. Hallelujah: Amen. Ps. XCI. 1 [actually Ps. XCIII: 1].

He sitteth the second among the three supreme Powers

in the Crown of the Kingdom: *Jehovah said unto my Lord, sit thou at my right hand.* Ps. CX. I. and from the days of old the Messiah (both the Lord & son of David) sat upon the Throne at the right hand of Jehovah, and with Jehovah he was the high & lofty one that inhabited Eternity. Isaiah saw him in the סוד the Secret of the sacred Three; and heard the Seraphim that stood & cried this unto that one to the other, saying *Holy, Holy, Holy, Lord of Hosts, the Earth is full of thy Glory,* Isai. VI. 3. He is the King of Glory. Jonathan Ben Uzziel thus interprets this passage—*Holy that is the Father, Holy this is the son, Holy this is the holy Ghost,* as was found in the copies of the Targums 300 years ago. R. Eleazar in Zohar on Deuteronomy, expounding upon Holy Holy Holy, says, *the Law was given by three holy Ones, by three Superiors, in three days, & resided in three Things the Tables and the Ark.* I am sensible that Jehovah is expounded by *three,* and by *four,* and by the Ten Saphirots, and by the Names Father, Mother, Son, Daughter, in the Zohar: all which is consistent Truth in the secret of the Mystery of God; and to all this there is a great & consistent Interpretation, as delivered in the Books of *Itzira* and *Zohar.* R. Bccai says upon Numb. VI. 24. *there are three Powers in Jehovah—every distinct power is like to each other and hath the same Name with it.* I understand with *Philo* and the Targums, that the Messiah is one of the three Holies in the glorious Mystery of God: and the Seraphin are incessantly crying to him Hallelujah. He is one of the *two anointed ones, that stand before Jehovah* and *of the two Olive Branches which thro' the two golden Pipes empty the golden Oyl out of themselves.* Zech. IV. 12. 14[actually Zech. IV: 14, 12].—pouring and diffusing forth the Influences of the Light, Love, Strength, and Greatness of Jehovah, to beautify the immense Universe: but concealed from our eyes, he stands the great High Priest before God in the heavens to make Intercession for the holy people on earth; as it is said Ps. CX. 4. The Lord said unto my Lord the Messiah—*thou art a Priest forever according to the order of Melchizedek.*

There was another high priest after the pattern of the priest
in heaven—one on Earth & one above; as *Philo* said in his
Life of Moses, *it was necessary that the priest who offered
Supplications unto the Eternal Father, should sollicit the advocacy
of the perfect & glorious Son of God towards the amnesty of
Sin.* And again saith Philo, *this Priest in the heavens is not
a Man, but the* WORD *of God.* Hence the Priest in the heavens
is the *Word*, the *Son* of God, and his Resemblance is as the
Resemblance of Jehovah, for the three powers in Jehovah,
they are Jehovah and the holy Name is in them. This is my
Opinion of the person of the glorious Messiah. Your opinion
of him is, that he is a great Angel above all Angels, and yet
not eternal, but that there was a Time when the Messiah was
not. In my Eyes he [is] infinitely greater & more glorious,
than he is in your Eyes. *Philo* does not make three Gods, for
Jehovah he is God and there is none besides him 1 Kings VIII.
60. Neither do we make three Gods, but three הויים persons
of Jehovah in a Unity, one of which הויים as I have said is
the pure soul of the Messiah. He reigned from Eternity, and
will reign over the Universe forever ages without End. From
the Throne of his Glory he sendeth forth the Influence of his
Goodness in the Paths of his Beneficence unto the minutest
of his Creatures. And *will God in very deed dwell upon Earth?
behold the Heavens & heaven of heavens cannot contain thee.*
2 Kings VIII. 27 [actually 1 Kings VIII. 27]. Yes verily, he will
dwell on Earth: very wonderful is this! Shiloh will come from
his place on high; the King of Glory will come & dwell with
us God manifest in the Flesh, to make known to the Children
of men his might and the glory & magnificence of his Kingdom; and so one of his Names is Emmanuel Isai. VII. 24 [actually
14]. Indeed he hath already been manifested sundry times since
the Creation to the men of his Treasury (whom he has selected
and associated into the closest communion with himself).
Appearances, if not in flesh, yet in bodily Resemblances, like
the appearances of angels, and thus he conversed with the
holy Patriarchs on Earth. He was the *angel of the Covenant*

which *led Joseph like a flock and inhabited the Cherubim*. Ps.
LXXX. I. He was with Adam & Eve in the Garden; he walked
with Enoch and Noah; he was Melchizedek (Zohar p. 120)
and dwelt at Salem, & blessed our great Father Abraham;
he was Jehovah-jirah, and one of the three angels, that in
the form of men visited the Tent of Abraham and eat the
Food of Sarah under the Tree in the Grove of Mamre; with
him Jacob wrestled; and it was he that wrought wonderfully
before Manoah and his Wife. And when concealed from the
Eyes of Man, he sendeth his prophets unto his people, and
poureth out upon them the holy spirit; as in the VIth. article
of the Creed R. Maimon saith, *God giveth the Influence of his
prophecy unto the men of his Choice and Glorification*.

Moses, David, Samuel, Isaiah and all the Prophets have
spoken and prophesied of three appearances of the Messiah
in a bodily Shape, in which visiting he should visit this World:
besides his luminous appearances at the Bush, and at Mt.
Sinai, and over the Mercy seat: one in the form of Angels;
one in flesh to atone for sin; and one with the Clouds of
Heaven. Lo I have spoken of the first or angelic Appearance
of the Messiah, it remains to speak of the other two. The
Alexandrine *Rabbi son of Joshua the son of Levi said, that he
had compared the Texts*, beholds his appearance with the Clouds
of Heaven, *or one like the Son of Man coming in the Clouds of
Heaven* Dan. VII. 13. *and poor and riding on an Ass* Zech.
IX. 9. that is, *if Israel are deserving* then the Messiah *will
come with the Clouds of Heaven; otherwise, poor and riding on
an Ass*. Talmud Sanh. II. Israel were not purified and deserving, as hitherto in the present Captivity, and therefore the
Messiah came *lowly* &c: but when they shall be purified,
he will come with the Clouds of heaven. And in this manner
were to be the two latter Appearances.

Expecting thou expectest the Messiah, and I also expect
him. However you know that all of us Christians believe,
that he came in the Time of the second Temple, which had
not been more glorious than the first, but for the Appearance

of the DESIRE of all Nations in it. The prophet Haggai saith
Chapt. II. 9. the Glory of this latter House shall be greater
than that of the former. He doth not say the *third* latter
House, but *this* latter House which Zorabbabel built in the
Time of Darius. Daniel prophesied, that within seventy Weeks
that is 490 years, Messiah shall come, *to finish Transgression,
and to make an End of sins, and to make Reconciliation for
Iniquity—and to seal the Vision—and Messiah shall be cut
off but not for himself.* At the latter End of the 490 years
Messiah must have come. From the going forth of the Com̄and-
ment to build Jerusalem unto the Destruction, of the City
and second Temple, was about 490 years. Then also ended
the 4000 years of Elias, who lived at Babylon, 200 years
before the days of Hillel the Great at Jerusalem. It is said
in Gemara Sanhedrin, *The opinion of the House of Elijah,
the World shall be six Thousand years,* 2000 *void,* 2000 *the
Law,* 2000 *the Days of Messiah.* (The Rabbins of the Talmud
have added, to his Words, *and for our many sins, there have
passed from them as many as have passed.*) *Elijah said to R.
Jehudah the Brother of R. Sala the pious, this World will not
endure less than Eighty five Jubilees, and in the last Jubilee
shall come the son of David.* The Chronology of the World
according to the Copy of the Law & the prophets in the
hands of Elijah and the Masorets after him, gives about 4000
years from the Creation to the Destruction of the second
House, and this is about 85 Jubilees of 49 years, or 4165
years. Since the Destruction of the 2d House, the Vision has
been no more. What Person ever came within the LXX Weeks,
which can be compared or resembled to Jesus of Nazareth
the son of Joseph? He was a prophet wonderful in Deeds,
Miracles and Doctrines; he came *just and having Salvation,
lowly & riding upon an ass, and upon a Colt the foal of an ass.*
Of whom did the prophet Zechariah speak c. XIII. 6. *What
are these Wounds in thy Hands? then he shall answer, these
with which I was wounded in the House of my Friends: Awake
my Sword against my Shepherd, against the Man that is my*

Fellow saith the Lord of Hosts: Who is the Man, the Fellow of Jehovah? *His Name shall be called Wonderful, Councillor, the mighty God, the everlasting Father, the Prince of Peace,* !sai. IX. 6. Jesus was anointed with power and with the holy Ghost without measure: *He bringeth good Tidings, that publisheth peace, that bringeth good Tidings of good, that publisheth salvation, that saith unto Zion, thy God reigneth.* Isai. 52. 7. He was *cut off*, as Daniel said & foretold— *he was wounded for our Transgressions, he was bruised for our Iniquities, the Chastisment of our Peace was upon him, and with his Stripes we are healed.* Isai. LIII. 5. Jesus the Son of Joseph was *cut off*, the Shepherd was smitten, and thereupon the 2d Temple was destroyed, and the sheep were scattered. The holy Nation, two Thirds of them were cut off in the Roman War, leaving only one Third as it is at this day, and these as [sic] passing thro' Fire, and tried & refined in a Furnace like the Trial of Gold. Zech. XIII. 8. 9.

From the beginning of the World to the Babylonish Captivity, the wise & holy Men were looking for a suffering Messiah. Ps. XL. Isai. LIII. and they understood the Sacrifices as a Symbol of the Sacrifice of the Messiah. But from Babylon to the Destruction of the 2d House, passing they passed over the *suffering*, and looked only to the *glorious* State of the Messiah. And yet there were in that period some holy persons of the House of *Shammai* and *Hillel*, and of the Fraternity of the *Essenes*, who spake of the Sufferings of the Messiah. There is to be found yet remaining in the Writings of your Rabbins a little a small Remnant like the Gleaning of the Vintange [sic]. R. *Aba* was one of the Sages of the Talmud. I have not his Words in his own Tongue; but he saith to this Meaning—The Light under the Throne of God is Messiah and his seed: God spake to Messiah and said to him, thy seed will by their Sons give or occasion thee great Trouble: and Messiah answered, lo I come to do thy Will o God; and so he consented to bear upon himself all their sins, as it is written in the Volume of Isaiah C. LIII. This account we have in *Pesikta* [sic], and in the Writtings of R. *Moses* the Preacher, and in the *Rabbots* (of R. Nachman 1500 years ago). R. Natronai asked what meaneth this, *We see not our signs, there is no more any Prophet, nor is there among us that knoweth how long*, Ps. Lxxxiv. 9 [actually Ps. lxxiv: 9]. R. Aha [sic] answered, this is spoken of that wicked Generation that would not believe the Signs & Miracles of our holy Messiah, but will say of him, that he doth those Things by Art Magic and that his signs are not the signs of the Messiah; and that as there is no prophet to set the Truth before them, if they do not see the proof of his Words, THEY WILL PUT HIM TO DEATH: wherefore the prophet saith, *o God, how long shall the adversary* &c. The same Thing is said, or the same sentiment is advanced in the Writings of your Rabbins upon the two Messiahs, *Ben Joseph* and *Ben David*, and upon the War of *Armillus—and the Messiah of Jehovah shall be slain; and Angels shall come & take him, and hide him with the Patriarchs. Imediately the Hearts of the Israelites shall be dissolved, and their strength shall be weakened: and they shall instantly flee to the Wilderness. And every one, whose heart is fixed in his Judgment (that he will not change his religion) shall return to the people of the World, saying is this the Redemption that we have been expecting. in which the Messiah is killed? And all who do not perceive the Redemption, will be disgusted with it, and return to the Nations of the World.—and Messiah Ben David shall go forth & with him Elias the prophet, and they shall raise to Life Messiah Ben Joseph at Jerusalem.* Thus we see from the Lights of the Rabbins how that Messiah the son of Joseph *shall be slain*, and that the *Messiah of God should be slain*, or according to Daniel Messiah shall be cut off. And in holy vision a *slain Messiah* is the *bruized God in the Secret of the Holy ones* Ps. lxxxix. 7. Jesus the son of Joseph & Mary was slain and cut off in the days of Caiaphas the high Priest; and God raised him from the dead, and He ascended to Heaven a bruised God in the סוד or Mystery. Of these Things there were 500 Witnesses, by whom he was seen after his

Resurrection from the dead. He was seen not only of his Friends, but his Enemies, who saw his Ascension and thereupon believed upon him, and with his Disciples testified these Things, so that thro' their Testimony 3000 Jews believed on him in one day; which number soon increased to 5000 Believers. R. *Becai* examined this Matter & its proofs with a diligent & deep Search, and viewed it all with the closest attention, and giveth it as his Opinion that Jesus of Nazareth arose from the dead, altho' he did not believe that he was the Messiah. Likewise *Pontius Pilate* testified his Resurrection in his Letter to *Tiberius Caesar*, written by his hand upon the Miracles, Death & Resurrection of Jesus the son of Joseph & King of the Jews, and sent to Caesar and the Roman Senate. If he arose from the dead, who can doubt but that he was a great prophet, and that his assertions are the Truth? Deut. XVIII. 15. He did indeed arise & ascend to Heaven, into the סוד or Mystery, and sat down on the Throne at the right hand of God Ps. cx. 1. being exalted to be a prince & a Savior to reconcile us to Jehovah, & to give to all that believe on him, & are united to him, Pardon and eternal Life.

You do not believe what I have said upon the Sufferings of the Messiah. However I believe with you the *glorious* appearance of the Prince of peace on earth, in the latter the future days. Shiloh will come the third time or in a third form, and to him shall be the gathering of the people. He shall come with the Clouds of Heaven (not again to be born of a Virgin) and shall reign in glory at Jerusalem, and all Nations shall serve him. And at that time the Saints shall know the happiness of the Men that believed on him in the time of their Lives. For *they, that are wise* (discerning) *shall shine as the brightness of the Firmament—and as the Stars forever & ever.*

A Meditation upon the Return of Israel to Zion, and upon the Glory of the Kingdom of the Messiah upon Earth.

The Desolation of the holy Land shall continue for 2300

Evening-Mornings or years, and then the Sanctuary shall
be cleansed, and the third Temple shall be built. Tobit XIV. 5.
*Afterward shall the Children of Israel return & seek the Ld
their God & David their King, & shall fear the Ld & his Goodness in the latter days* Hosea III. 5. *And I will settle you after
your old Estates* Ezek. XXXVI. 11. Amos IX. 14. All the XII
Tribes shall return from all Kingdoms & Lands, & shall go
up to Jerusalem, as it is said, *then shall the Children of Judah
& the Children of Israel be gathered together & appoint themselves one Head*. Hosea I. 11. They shall appoint to themselves
one head whose Name will be David, but not Messiah the
son of David. The prophet Ezekiel saith—*these Bones are the*
WHOLE *House of Israel*. The two Sticks are the Kingdoms of
Judah & Israel, & they shall become one Stick one Kingdom
in the Hand of the Lord, which hath never yet come to pass.
*Thus saith the Ld Gd. behold I will take the stick of Joseph,
which is in the hand of Ephraim, & the Tribes of Israel his
fellows, & will put them with him, even with the stick of Judah, &
make them One Stick, & they shall be one in mine hand—behold
I will take the Children of Israel from among the Heathen
whither they be gone, & I will gather them on every side, & bring
them into their own Land. And I will make them one nation
in the Land upon the Mountains of Israel, and one King shall
be to them all, and they shall be no more two Nations, neither
shall they be divided into Kingdoms any more at all*. Ezek.
XXXVII. Jer. XXX. *I will bring again the Captivity of Jacob,
and have Mercy upon the* WHOLE *house of Israel*. Ezek. XXXIX.
25. And upon the Restoration of the Children of Israel, they
shall inherit the holy Land, dividing it among the Tribes,
not according to the former Divisions, but according to the
plan of Ezekiel XLVIII Chapter. Between the Borders of
Judah & Benjamin shall be the holy Oblation to the Lord,
a Square of 25,000. The northern Division of which for the
Priests 10,000, and the Sanctuary or Temple shall stand in
the midst of it. The Division of the Levites 10,000 broad:
the remaining 5000 shall be a profane Place for the City &

Suburbs, and the City of Jerusalem shall be in the midst of
it upon Mt. Zion. Therefore the Sanctuary, or third Temple,
will not be again built upon Mount Moriah & within the
City as formerly; but at a Distance without the City 15,000
Cubits or Reeds to the north of the City. And yet, *thus saith
the Lord, I am returned to Jerusalem with Mercies; my house
shall be built in it—my Cities thro' prosperity shall yet be spread
abroad, and the Ld shall yet comfort Zion, & shall yet choose
Jerusalem.* Zech. I. 16. 17. This is a great Mystery, which I
cannot explain, unless it be spoken of the second House. At
that time the children of Israel shall increase to a great
Multitude, and the house of their fathers shall be multiplied
greatly, and it *shall be without number as the sand of the sea*
Hosea I. 10. And they shall be properous in Wealth & every
kind of good upon the Land of their Inheritance, and to
them shall be abundance of peace; as it is said, *a little one
shall become a thousand, & a small one a strong Nation—I will
make thee an eternal Excellency a Joy of many Generations*
Isai. LX. 15. 17. 22.

Then shall there be a Restoration of the holy Tongue, and
all people may speak Hebrew, which may then become the
universal Language for a thousand years, as it is said—*then
will I turn to the people a pure Language, that they may all
call upon the name of the Lord, to serve him with one Consent*
Zeph. III. 9. Then shall be a Re-establishment of the *Priesthood*,
of *Sacrifices*, and the holy Seasons, and of all the Service of
the Sanctuary, and a Revival of all the Statutes of the Law
of Moses. And this holy Service shall continue in the third
house three or four hundred years, until Shiloh shall come.
From the time of the taking away of the Taumid and daily
Sacrifice unto Messiah, shall be 1290 days or years and 1335
years, which make 2625 years (1290 + 1335 = 2625) Dan.
ult. And when there shall have passed from them 2300 Evening-Mornings or years (Dan. XII. and VIII. 14.) the Children
of Israel shall return and build the third House, inhabit the
Land, build houses & plant Vinyards, and *dwell every man*

under his own Vine & under his own figtree, and none shall make them afraid—Micah IV. 4. Isai. LXV. 21—for 325 years. And after this Time while the people of Israel dwell in Security, then Gog the chief Prince of Mesheah & Tubal, going up on the face of the Land of Israel, he shall go forth from his place out of the north countries and many people with him, a great Company & a mighty Army, and besiege the holy City in War. But fire shall fall from Heaven and destroy them.

After this, and at the end of 325 years, shall appear in the Clouds of Heaven in glorious Majesty the Messiah returning to his Kingdom on Earth. He shall come with Abraham, Isaac & Jacob, Enoch, Noah, Daniel, & Job and all the Saints of the first Resurection, and shall shine & reign before the Eyes of all Nations gloriously 1000 years. At his appearance Israel will know, that it is He, whom their fathers *pierced*; as they had also slain Isaiah and the other Prophets 1 Kings XIX. 11. so had they slain that great Prophet, of whom Moses spake, saying, *the Ld thy Gd will raise up unto thee a* PROPHET &c Deut. XVIII. 15. *And they shall look upon him whom they have pierced & they shall mourn for him as one mourneth for his only Son & shall be in Bitterness for him as one is in Bitterness for his first born,* Zech. XII. 10. This is the Mourning of Hadad-Rimon. After this Mourning, *the Ld Gd will wipe away Tears from off all faces, & the Rebuke of his pple shall be taken away from off all the Earth, for the Ld hath spoken it. And it shall be said in that day Lo this is our God, we have waited for him, & he will save us: this is* JEHOVAH, *we have waited for him, & we will be glad & rejoyce in his Salvation,* Isai. XXV. 8. 9. Then shall Israel be glorious, as it is said, *I will make you a name & a praise among all pple of the Earth, when I turn back your Captivity before your Eyes saith the Lord.* Zeph. ult. *And* JEHOVAH *shall reign over them in Mount Zion from henceforth even forever* Micah IV. 7, when the Saints shall be forever swallowed up in the Secret of Gd and in the hidden Mystery of the Most High. And unto him shall be the gathering of all nations, for *the Law shall go forth from*

Mt. Zion & the Word of the Ld from Jerusalem into all the Kms of the Earth, and *Jehovah shall be King over all the Earth, in that day Jehovah shall be one & his Name one. And it shall come to pass that everyone that is left of all the Nations which came up against Jerusalem shall ever go up from year to year to worship the* KING JEHOVAH SABAOT, *and to keep the Feast of Tabernacles,* Zech. XIV. 16. Blessed is the people whose God is JEHOVAH the Messiah. *Remember me, o Lord, with the favor that thou bearest unto thy people, o visit me with thy Salvation. That I may see the good of thy chosen, that I may rejoyce in the Gladness of thy Nation that I may glory with thine Inheritance.* Ps. CVI. 4.5.

On the appearance of the Messiah, all the Service of Moses shall cease and be taken away. There shall be no more *Atonement for Sin;* there shall be no more burnt offerings to the Lord for Sin, for SIN SHALL BE NO MORE; for all People shall be holy in the purified and holy Kingdom of the Messiah. Wherefore should there be SACRIFICES and burnt offerings to take away Sin, when there shall be Evil no more? And also *the Priesthood of the House of Aaron shall cease;* because the *Messiah shall be the high Priest* like unto Melchizedek, & he shall interceed with the Lord for his people; as it is said, *behold the Man, whose Name is the* BRANCH, *and he shall grow up out of his place, and he shall build the Temple of the Lord— & he shall bear the Glory, & shall sit & rule upon his Throne, and he shall be a* PRIEST *upon his Throne,* Zech. VI. 13 *And his Name shall be called Wonderful, Counsellor, the mighty Gd, the everlasting Father, the prince of peace.* Isai. IX. 6. And in the days of this *King* and *Priest* the holy Service shall be only Praise & Hallelujah. Amen.

The mosaic Law of Sacrifices has long passed away & is no longer observed in our days: for if the Priesthood be changed the Law is changed, as it is said by the prophet Jeremiah XXXI. 31. *behold the days come saith the Ld when I will make a* NEW COVENANT *with the House of Israel and the House of Judah,* NOT AS THE COVENANT *which I made with your Fathers in the day when I led them by the hand to bring them out of Egypt—I will put my Law within them, & will write it upon their Hearts—for all shall know me from the least to the greatest saith the Ld, for I will forgive their Iniquities & their sins will I remember no more.*

Thus your Eyes see a Change of the Law. The former Covenant & Law were given by the hand of Moses at Mt. Sinai. This passed away 1700 years ago: but you will restore the Service of Moses again in the 3d. Temple, altho' without the Command of the Lord. But this with all its Ordinances shall pass away, and a new Law & Covenant shall be given by the hand of the Messiah. He will not raise up a pure משנה only, but establish a new Covenant. In this new Law there will be no more the Ordinances of *Circumcision, Passover, Sacrifices of Sheep* & Oxen or the Blood of living Creatures, nor divers Purifications of the Flesh, for there will be no pollutions, neither any Statutes for men as Sinners, for they will be no more sinners. All men will be holy like the Angels of Light, & live the Life of Angels & superior spirits. And therefore the holy Service will no longer be regulated by the Statutes of Moses, but by the power of an endless Life. The Law of the Ld shall be in their hearts; all shall know the Lord, and this Knowledge is Life eternal. Circumcision is no more, but circumcised and uncircumcised will all be united as one in the Km of Messiah. With him will come & reign here, Adam, Abel, Enoch, Noah, Shem, Lot & Job, and all the proselytes of Righteousness, and all the holy & righteous persons of all gentile Nations & Ages, all which are not circumcised; yet they shall come & sit down together with Abraham and the Patriarchs and all the Sons of the Circumcision, in the Kingdom of the prince of peace and the Lord of the World. I believe that *Marriage & Childbearing* will be no more in the days of the Messiah, among the Children of the Resurrection; altho' both may continue with the Children of Flesh until the End of the Millennium. It must be your opinion that, when the Gentiles shall bow down before him, then Israel will comence Intermarriages with all Nations of the Earth, and so all their Children will become holy Seed. In a little time the Blood of Jacob will be diffused & spread among all people, and they shall become all of the seed & blood of Abraham, and thus *in him shall all the Families of the Earth be blessed* Gen. XII. 3. Now when this Thing shall come to pass, there must needs be an End of *Circumcision* & *Baptism*: for to what End, a Seal or sign or Mark to distinguish between the *holy* seed & *profane*, between the clean & unclean, when *all* flesh shall be holy? Where is it said that the Gentiles are to be circumcised in the Kingdom of the Messiah, who shall sprinkle clean Water upon you & upon us, for we shall all be clean Ezek. XXXVI. 25. You see, my Friend, that if Childbearing ceaseth, circumcision also ceaseth of course—if Chidbearing should continue, then the Blood will spread itself and sanctify the whole, and so there will be none for whose sake to separate; and therefore Circumcision & uncircumcision will be useless & as nothing in the Resurrection. Again, if there be no End to the accumulation of Posterity, in a little time the Increase of Mankind will be much greater than that there should be found World enough to contain them. Of Necessity then *Childbearing* and *Circumcision* must come to an End in the days of the Messiah. For the space of 300 years after the Return to Zion until the End of 2625 years, Parturition & Circumcision may continue, till the End of both at the Messiahs appearance in the Clouds of Heaven.

He will reign on Earth 1000 years & by a new Law & Institution. R. Eleazar in Midras Tehillim said, *the days of the Messiah will be* 1000 *years*. The Law of Moses cannot be compared with the Law of the Messiah, for the one shall surpass the other, *as much as Light excelleth Darkness*. The Law of this World or age is Vanity in comparison with the Law of the World to come, say the Rabbins: and further, in the World to come are no Sacrifices but those of Praise & Thankgiving, like the service of Angels & Aralim. These Things are asserted in the Books IKKARIM and JALKUT.

At that Time the Children of Israel shall be glorious in the Eyes of all Nations which came up against Jerusalem; who shall come up from year to year to worship the King the Ld of Hosts the Messiah and to keep the Feast of Tabernacles Zach. XIV. 16. Isai. LXVI. 23. And they shall know how the Ld is with you of a Truth—*he suffered no man to do them wrong, yea he reproved Kings for their sakes, saying toutch not mine anointed and do my prophets no harm* Ps. CV. 14. *For I will make you a name & a praise among all people of the Earth, when I turn back your Captivity before your Eyes saith the Lord* Zeph. ult. *I will gather all nations & Tonques & they shall come & see my Glory—all flesh shall come to worship before me saith the Lord* Isai. ult. At the period when all these Things shall be accomplished may the Lord remember me with the Favor of his people Ps. CVI. 4.

The Kingdom of the Messiah on Earth will not be eternal, but one Olam only of a 1000 years; and this is called נצח the VICTORY because all Evil will be then overcome, and there shall be only *Good & Peace* on Earth 1000 years, until the Conflagration of the World & until the Time of the new Heavens & new Earth.

We are informed of many wonderful Events that are to come to pass, such as the *Resurrection*, Day of *Judgment*, the *Conflagration*, & *Renovation* of the Earth &c: but as to the order of their succession we are ignorant, this being a secret. However we may indulge our speculations & offer our Thoughts without Offence. In your Opinion the Resurrection of the just will be in a little time perhaps about 40 years after the Coming of the Messiah; and that the wicked will not arise and stand in Judgment because they perish & are annihilated, according to the Sages of the Talmud, *the Resurrection of the dead will be of the righteous & not of the wicked.* I think the wicked will not come in the first Resurrection, but that they will arise in the second, as it is said *and some to Shame & everlasting Contempt.* Dan. XII. 3. The Sayings of the prophets cannot all of them be reconciled into Harmony, without admitting *two Resurrections*, and *after them a Conflagration*. The Saints are of the first Resurrection and shall come with the Messiah & live on Earth 1000 years, & reign with the King at Jerusalem. They shall come in spiritual Bodies, such as those in which the Angels appeared unto Jacob at Mahanaim, and to Gideon at Ophrah, and to David at the Threshing floor of Araunah: and therefore to them them [sic] there will be no *Sickness* nor *Death* nor *marriages* nor *childbearing*; then Sarah will be no more the Wife of Abraham; and the Woman who in this Life had been the Wife of two men or many Husbands, will be no more a Wife to them, neither shall the Husband of many Wives be any more the Husband of them. There will be no more Male and Female. The Sexes of the Silk-worm appear, not in the first Stage, but in their last Mutation; the Sexes in Man appear in the first State, but not again in the Change of the Resurrection, for all the Children of the Resurrection will be like the angels of Light. But they will reign with the prince of peace over all the Inhabitants of the Earth which shall not have seen Death, and yet however live without dying 1000 years, according to the years of the day of human Life before the flood—*for as the years of a Tree shall be the years of my people—and they shall build houses & plant Vinyards & eat the fruit thereof*—and their Children shall not die because Sons of 1000 years. Yet during the space of of [sic] 300 years after the Return of Israel and before the first Resurrection, Death shall reign. Men shall then die 100 years old, to which age all Children of the seed of Israel may usually live, as it is said—*Then shall there be no more an Infant of days, nor an old man that hath not fulfilled his days: for the Child shall die 100 years old, but the Sinner being 100 years old shall be accursed.* Isai. LXV. 20. However after the Resurrection there shall be no more Death (except at the Time of Gog Magog) but those who are born shall live unto the End: and at the time of the End all who are living in Flesh shall be changed without Death. Wherefore in the days of the Messiah the Children

may live 1000 years & not see Death. And so there may be
five or six Generations in the days of the Messiah. In all ages
& countries the number of males & females has been nearly
equal, and to a Woman four or five Children & no more.
If by the Law of all Nations every Man was to have four
Wives, there would be Wives for only one quarter of the men.
Or if an Imitation of Solomon was enjoyned, onely one Man
in 1000 would have Wives, & all the rest of the Multitude
of their Brethren none at all. But God in his Statutes has
comanded that there should be only one Woman to a man.
How small is the Number of Men that have many Wives &
from them many Children, as Ahab who had 70 Children.
And by means of one or many husbands Women cannot have
more than four or five Children apiece before the power of
Parturition ceaseth. To the Men before the Flood when the
day of Life was 1000 years there were not more Children,
than to those of the present day whose Life is but 70 years.

Years		Women
1000	.	Families
800	.	1600,000,000
600	.	800, — —
400	.	400, — —
200	.	200, — —
	.	100,000,000

They might begin to have Children at 100 or 200 years of age,
the other at 20; and yet neither the one nor the other have
above 4 or 5 Children apiece. From these principles we may
reason, & estimate the Number & Increase of Mankind in
the Millennium, that it will not exceed fourty times the
number now on Earth. In the beginning of the Millennium
let there be an hundred Million Families, 100,000,000, [1]

---

[1] There are indeed 150 million Families or 7 or 800 million Souls
on Earth. But the World can contain 100 times its present number
of Inhabitants.

and the Number of bearing Women the same: let there be five generations; the Age of parturition 150 or 200 years and the number of Children four or five apiece when they shall cease bearing. Thus the Increase of 1000 will not be above 30 or 40 times more than the present number of People in the World. And yet the World can contain many more than these without being filled, if all that are born should live to the End of the Millennium. They will live as in the Garden of Eden without Sickness, they shall no more suffer Fatigue & Toil or eat Bread with the Sweat of their Brow, for the Earth shall produce a Sufficiency & Abundance spontaneously. All people shall be holy from the least to the greatest, and shall go up to Zion from year to year to worship the King and to visit the Patriarchs & Children of the Resurrection. Abm Isaac & Jacob and the holy Elect shall dwell at Jerusalem with Messiah. Then also shall Abraham & the Saints, in *spiritual* bodies visit & travel among all Nations, in the Forms of Angels, to be conversant among the people of every province of the universal Kingdom; for they shall be sent forth from the presence of the King to carry the Law forth from Zion & the Word of the Ld from Jerusalem Micah iv. 2. And Mankind will rejoyce with Gladness & great Joy at these Interviews with them, with the greatest Attention learning of them the unseen Wonders of the upper World.

At the appearance of the Messiah, Satan & his angels will be bound in chains, no more to operate Evil among Men for 1000 years: as it is said, they *shall not hurt nor destroy in all my holy mountain, for the Earth shall be full of the Knowledge of the Lord as the Waters cover the Sea*, Isai. xi. 9. The nations shall rejoyce in every kind of Good, in the path of Perfection, and in the Light of the Countenance of the prince of Peace, even for many days, until the time of the End, and until the latter part of the Millennium. And then Satan will be loosed and break forth from his Imprisonment to go to & fro and walk up & down upon the Face of the Earth, to seduce a second time the Enemies of the King, even to stir up Gog &

Magog and those who shall be combined with them. Mankind
will imagine that they shall never fall again into Evil. But
to teach & make known unto the Children of Men, that their
Strength is Vanity & nothing without the strength & Influence of God, the *Lord will hold back the face of his Throne and
spread a Cloud upon it*, when upon Gods hiding and concealing
himself, the Saints are in Darkness, and we are involved in
evil. Thereupon Satan being lossed from Hell he will seduce
Men by guile. The Messiah the King of the World, is also the
King of the Universe: and during his Kingdom on Earth,
may from time to time go to heaven to visit his Kingdom on
high; when Satan shall go forth to deceive the nations in his
absence, and to encompass the holy City in War. The Prince
of Peace useth not Weapons of War, but Fire from Heaven
& from the Brightness of his Appearing, shall utterly destroy
them. For the King shall return from Heaven, and with him
an innumerable multitude of Angels that descend upon the
Chariot of the Clouds, and at his appearance Gog & his armies
shall be involved in Destruction. And then cometh the End,
the conclusion of the Millennium, for the Kingdom will not
be eternal on this Earth. Then the Saints which are alive on
Earth in fleshly Bodies will, in the Twinkling of an Eye, be
changed from their bodily cloathing to the Clothing of Light &
Glory, and will ascend from the Earth with the Saints of the
first Resurrection to meet the King & his Hosts aloft in the
Air. And at the same Instant will come on the second Resurrection, the Resurrection of all the wicked which sleep in
the dust who shall awake to Reproach. Then with the Horrors
of an amazing Desolation, the Earth with the third Temple
shall be burnt up in an awful & tremendous Conflagration.
As it is said in the Tradition of R. *Ketana* in the Talmud, the
World shall remain six thousand *years, and in the next thousandth shall it be destroyed*. So also St. *Barnabas* the christian
apostle who was also a Jew, said, *God finished the World in
six days & rested the seventh; Behold one day is as* 1000 *years.
He will accomplish all in six Thousd years, & rest the seventh*

thousand, when he shall judge the wicked, and change sun&moon & stars. R. Ketana said, *the seventh year is a year of Release & pardon, so the seventh Thousand year will be the season of Forgivness.* At this Time & at the End of the seventh Thousand year will be the day of Judgment, *when the Judgment shall sit and the Books shall be opened* (Dan. VII. 10.) to judge upon all the Seed of Adam, when *Gd will render to the good man according to his good deeds, and to the evil according to his Wickedness.* The wicked shall be punished & destroyed, being swallowed up in the Conflagration; but as to the righteous, the King shall carry them to heaven, & cause them to stand before the Throne & in the presence of JEHOVAH. Ps. XI. 6.7.

After the Conflagration shall be the NEW HEAVENS and NEW EARTH. And upon the new Earth there will be no Sea (which sheweth that the new Earth is to succede the Conflagration): and the Circle or Sphere of the Earth, shall have spread over it aloft the second sphere of the Firmament of Light, tho' the sun will no more shine between the Spheres. Then will appear the holy City of new Jerusalem, which God shall cause to descend out of Heaven; and it shall rest on Zion in the new Earth to receive the Saints there. It will be covered with a Cloud of Light, through which the Sun will not penetrate, neither will there be any more night there: but the Saints, Angels, Aralim Hasmalim, and all the Sons of the Mighty will walk & live forever with the King in the Splendor of his Glory: as it is said, *the Sun shall be no more thy Light by day, neither for Brightness shall the moon give Light unto thee; but the* LORD *shall be unto thee an everlasting Light, and thy Gd thy Glory. Thy Sun shall no more go down, neither shall thy moon withdraw itself, for the Lord shall be thine everlasting Light, and the Days of thy Mourning shall be ended.* Isai. LX. 19, 20. Some of the Learned are of the Opinion that This may be the everlasting Abode of the Saints; this is the glorious City which is not made with hands, for God shall build it; and there shall be no Temple in it—as it is said in the

Scriptures of the Christians, for *the Ld Gd almighty, and the Lamb are the Temple of it. And the City had no need of the Sun neither of the Moon to shine in it, for the* Glory of Gd did lighten it, and the Lamb is the Light thereof. Rev. XXI. 22. and Isai. LXVI. I. *Thus saith the Ld, the Heaven is my Throne.* Heaven & the Throne of Jehovah is this or that place and all places wherever he manifesteth his Glory, and lifteth the light of his countenance there upon his Saints, to give them to behold the BEAUTY of the Lord, and to perceive his Majesty & the Glory of his Kingdom. *But he is not far from every one of us,* for we live in him continually. If in his good pleasure he should open our Eyes, behold, we should see God & Heaven and the place all around us full of Angels and of an innumerable multitude of heavenly Hosts 2 Kings XVI. 17[?]. And so we should be ready to say with Jacob our Father—*How dreadful is this place! this is none other but the House* or Temple *of God, and this is the Gate of Heaven* Gen. XXVIII. 17. this is the new Temple or Sanctuary, & *Jehovah is there. Glory and Honor are in his presence, strength & Gladness are in his place* I Chron. XVI. 27. Thus the Inhabitants of the new Jerusalem dwell in HEAVEN; for the Ld will open their Eyes to behold themselves and the whole Universe ALL IN GOD, and within the Effulgence of his Glory. The Abodes of Angels & of the Intelligences of the spheres or Golgolim are in the palaces on high; they will with us be glorious & blessed in their going forth and returning WITHIN THE PRESENCE OF GOD. For the everlasting Residence of Men will be in the new Heavens & new Earth; and in them they shall approach & draw near to God after the manner of the angels of Light. And they shall go forth & return before God, and shall rejoyce in the Light of his Countenance forever & ever. In their Travels they will visit and behold all the Hosts of God, and the Orders of Beings in the glorious Golgolim or spheres, and the Abodes of the Universe, and thus return to their own Habitation at Jerusalem, in the midst of which shall be a Tree of Life for the healing of the Nations. Blessed are the Saints, for it will

be the Lot of their Inheritance to behold the Beauty of the
Lord, and to contemplate all his Works throughout the
imense Universe forever & ever ages without End. Then
they *that are wise shall shine as the Brightness of the Firmament
and as the Stars forever and ever*.

Many of these Things are to be found in the Writings of
the Hochamim or Wise Men of all the Antient Nations. And
thro' them, as thro' Streams from a fountain of Waters, they
have flowed down to us. All which is the Remnant or Relict
of the Knowledge which was comunicated by the Angels to
Noah, and has been preserved in the Writings of the *Chaldeans,
Egyptians, Greeks, Ismaelites* or Arabians: in the Books of
Enoch and *Abraham* and the twelve *Patriarchs*, the *Bahir,
Tikkunim, Zohar, Kaneh Binah*, and the *Rabbots* of R. Bar
Nachman: and in the Writings of *Hesiod, Plato, Zeno, Aelian,
Ovid, Virgil, Seneca, Cicero*, the *Sibbyls*, and the Disciples of
Amonius: *Menezius, Confucius, Zoroaster, Olamh Fodhla* and
the *Druids*; in the Traditions & Literature of *India, China &
Japan*, in the Institution of the *Lama*, and in the Cabbala
of all Peoples among whom Letters have been found. Much
of this antient Knowledge is gone to ruin, being swallowed
up and polluted in other streams which have issued from
corrupt fountains. But as Gold mixed with reprobate Silver,
or the Iron in the Image of Nebuchadnezzar, which mixeth
indeed but will not unite & cleave to the Clay; so a great
deal of this pure knowledge may be preserved among the
Traditions & in the Cabbala of the Nations—which all agree
with one accord in the Expectation of the King the DESIRE
of all Nations, the *Kingdom of Righteousness*, the *Conflagration*
and *Renovation*, and *Paradise* of this World in the Age to
come. And by the help of the fire of Moses & the Prophets, &
of men who have spoken by the prophetic Influence of God,
we may be able to separate from the Dross, the pure Gold
of Truth.

And thou, my honourable Friend, who hast *been very
pleasant unto me*, whose *Love to me is wonderful passing the*

Love of Women, may you come forth at that time and stand in thy Lot, and sit down with Abraham, Isaac & Jacob and all the Children of the Circumcision, and with Enoch, Noah, Daniel & Job and all the uncircumcised Saints, in the Kingdom of the Messiah. And to thy Wife, thy Son & thy Daughter may there be an Abundance of Mercy Rejoycing and Glory in the World to come. May thy Son be like Samuel sanctified to the Lord from the Womb. May God bless thy seed, that there may always be a Light unto thee in Israel. And when thou shalt send a Letter to thy Wife at Hebron in the holy Land, salute her & thy house in my name; for I love all thy Friends for thy Sake. And may thy Father & thy Mother rejoyce, when thou shalt be exalted and shine among the chosen Ones of Righteousness and among the Seraphim. Then may *thy Light break forth as the morning, and thine health—spring forth speedily, and thy Righteousness—go before thee, the Glory of the Lord be thy Rereward* [sic]. Isai. LVIII. 8. These are my Words, written at Newport Rhode Island in America, the 28th. day of the Month Tammuz, in the 5533d. year of the Creation. I am the least of the Disciples of JESUS of Nazareth.

EZRA STILES

July 19th. 1773.

SAADIA ON THE TRINITY
AND INCARNATION

By HARRY A. WOLFSON
Harvard University

IN HIS DISCUSSION of the Trinity, Saadia refers to two conceptions of it current among Christians. He describes them as the view "of the common people (عوام, עמי הארץ) among them" who "confess a Trinity which is conceived of only in corporeal terms" and "the elite (خواصّ חכמים) among them." [1] The expression "common people" as a description of one of the two contrasting views referred to by him does not give us an accurate idea of the view he had in mind. The exact meaning of the view which he had in mind here may be gathered from the work of his contemprary Yaḥyā ibn ʿAdi, a Christian apologist writing in Arabic. In that work, Yaḥyā tries to answer a certain Muslim critic of Christianity who argued that the Trinitarian formula "one substance (جوهر), three hypostases (اقانم)," supplemented by the Christian belief that each hypostasis is God, must logically mean a belief in three substances and hence threee Gods. [2] In answer, Yaḥyā draws a distinction between "what the ignorant (جهّال) among Christians imagine concerning the hypostases" and "what the most learned (علماء) among Christians and those versed in their doctrine say," ascribing

---

[1] *Emunot ve-Deʿot* II, 5, p. 86, 11. 5-7. Chapter references are to the Yozefov edition; page and line references are to the Arabic text edited by S. Landauer; English quotations are from Samuel Rosenblatt's translation, except where the discussion of the subject required a more literal translation of the text.

[2] Cf. *Petits Traités Apologétiques de Yaḥyā ben ʿAdi*. Texte arabe ... et traduit en français par Augustin Périer, Paris, 1920, p. 44, l. 5-p. 45, l. 2.

to the former the view that "the hypostases are essences of three subjects each of which differs from the other in virtue of its own self" and characterizing this view as being "only error and impiety, and one from which indeed it would have to follow that its exponents believed that the Creator is three substances and three Gods." [1] Now it can be shown, I believe, that by "the ignorant among Christians" Yaḥyā does not refer simply to mere uninformed people. He refers to that Christian sect known as the Tritheites, whose chief representatives were John Askusnages and John Philoponus, for the description of "the ignorant among Christians" as given by Yaḥyā corresponds exactly to the description of the Tritheites in Photius, which reads as follows: "Some of the more shameless, having taken nature (φύσιν) and hypostasis (ὑπόστασιν) and substance (οὐσίαν) to mean the same, did not shrink from affirming also that in the Holy Trinity there are three substances (οὐσίας), whence they teach, if not in word, yet at least in thought, that there are three Gods and three Divinities." [2] Like Yaḥyā's "ignorant among Christians," therefore, Saadia's "common people among them" is to be taken to refer to the Tritheites as represented by John Askusnages and John Philoponus. Accordingly, as we shall see, he couples these Christian Tritheites with the Dualists and criticizes both of them from a common principle. The Dualists he had in mind are the various followers of Zoroastrian Dualism, such as Manichaeans, Mazdakites, Bardaisanites, and Marcionites, who were known to the Muslims of the time of Saadia, and even after his time, and were to them still a subject of vital discussion. [3]

The common principle from which he criticizes the ditheism of the various forms of Zoroastrianism and the tritheism of

---

[1]   *Ibid.*, p. 45, ll. 2-8.

[2]   Photius, *Bibliotheca* 230 (PG 103, 1080 BC).

[3]   *Cf.* A. S. Halkin's note in his translation of Baghdādī's *Al-Farḳ bain al-Firāḳ*, p. 179, n. 2; *cf.* also *Ibn Ḥazm, al-Fiṣal, fi'l-Milal* (Cairo, 1317-27), I, pp. 34 ff.

the Christian sect is the belief in the unity of God in the sense
of numerical unity, as a denial of any form of polytheism.
This principle he establishes first by quoting, as he says,
"from the books of the prophets," [1] various verses which
affirm that God is one and there is no other God with Him [2]
and then supporting it by various arguments which he describes as being "by the way of speculation." [3] With this as an
established belief, he proceeds to discuss the view of the
Dualists, to whom he explicitly refers as the believers in
"two principles" (اصلين שני שרשים), [4] first refuting the arguments by which they support their view [5] and then refuting
their view itself. [6] But then he conjures up a straw-man who
raises two questions.

In one of the questions, he asks: "But in that case, what
is the meaning of these two names, Lord (*Adonay*) and God
(*Elohim*) that are constantly employed in the Bible with reference to God?" [7] This is quite evidently an attempt to show that
a sort of Dualism is implied in the Bible itself. It reflects a passage in which the rabbis of old suggest that the Dualists might
find an excuse for their belief in "two powers" (שתי רשויות) in
the names "Lord" and "God" which are used in the Bible. [8]

In the second question he asks: "But what is the meaning
of the statement in Scripture, 'And now the Lord God hath
sent me and His spirit'" (Isa 48:16). [9] This is not a question
raised from the point of view of Dualism; it is a question
raised from the point of view of the Trinity, for the very

---

[1] *Emunot ve-De'ot* II, 1, p. 80, ll. 6-7.
[2] *Ibid.*, p. 79, l. 15-p. 80, l. 6.
[3] *Ibid.*, p. 80, l. 7-p. 81, l. 2. So also in his Commentary on his
Arabic translation of Proverbs (9:13-18; 24:21-22; ed. Derenbourg,
pp. 53, 138), Saadia couples the Dualists and the Trinitarians in his
discussion.
[4] *Ibid.*, p. 81, l. 6.
[5] *Ibid.*, p. 81, l. 3-p. 82, l. 5.
[6] *Ibid.*, p. 82, ll. 5-14.
[7] *Ibid.* II, 3, p. 83, ll. 3-4.
[8] *Mekilta Baḥodesh* 5 (ed. Lauterbach, II, p. 231).
[9] *Emunot ve-De'ot* II, 3, p. 84, ll. 6-7.

same verse is quoted in an Arabic work by the Christian
Abucara as referring to the Chiristian Trinity. [1] It is to be
noted, however, that there is a difference between the Trinity
taken by Abucara to be referred to in the verse quoted by
him and the Trinity taken by Saadia's questioner to be
referred to in the same verse quoted by him. Abucara's
Trinity is not that of the Tritheites but rather that which he
ascribes to "the most learned among Christians," for Abucara
explicitly rejects Tritheism, of which, he says, "certain
unwise people" have accused the Christians. [2] The Trinity
of Saadia's hypothetical questioner is, as we have seen, the
Trinity of the Tritheites, inasmuch as his question is coupled
by Saadia with the Dualistic question and is answered by
the same principle of numerical unity. Quite evidently Saadia
has allowed himself to take the verse quoted by Abucara as
proof-text for his non-Tritheistic conception of the Trinity and
put it in the mouth of his fictitious questioner and make him
use it as proof-text for his Tritheistic conception of the Trinity.

Having disposed of the Trinitarian view of the "common
people" among the Christians, that is to say, the common
people who in their simple-mindedness, and perhaps unbe-
known to themselves, have a conception of the Trinity like
that of the professed Tritheites, Saadia takes up the Trinitarian view of "the elite" among them, who maintain that
their belief in the Trinity is based upon rational speculation
and subtle reasoning." [3] Not all those who were opposed to
Tritheism are taken up by Saadia. No mention is made by
him of such extreme opponents of Tritheism as the Sabellians
and Arians. The "elite" whom he speaks of are those who
represent the orthodox conception of the Trinity as approved
of by the Oecumenical Church Councils. The corresponding
"most learned among Christians" of Yaḥyā ibn 'Adī are

[1] Georg Graf, *Die arabischen Schriften des Theodor Abū Qurra*
III, 10 (1910), p. 153; VII, 15, pp. 193-194.
[2] *Ibid.*, III, 17, p. 149.
[3] *Emunot ve-De'ot* II, 5, p. 96, ll. 7-8.

more precisely described as "the learned Imams (الائمّة العلماء),
such as Dionysius [the Areopagite], Gregory [of Nazianzus
or of Nyssa], Basil the Great, John Chrysostomos," [1] on
whose Trinitarian view "all the three sects of Christians
agree," [2] by which three sects he means the Malkites, the
Nestorians, and the Jacobites. It is this orthodox conception
of the Trinity that Saadia undertakes to discuss. Now this
orthodox conception of the Trinity insisted upon the belief
in the unity of God. But it maintained that the unity of God
does not mean absolute unity but only relative unity, a
unity which may be conceived as consisting after a certain
manner of inseparable parts. In his discussion of this orthodox
conception of the Trinity, Saadia, therefore, tries to establish
first the principle that the unity of God means absolute
unity, that is, absolute simplicity, and then, from that principle, he proceeds to discuss the Trinity.

Preliminary to taking up Saadia's discussion of the subject,
I should like to make three general observations.

First, the unity of God in the sense of absolute unity or
absolute simplicity, with all its implications, was unknown
in Greek philosophy. In Greek philosophy, the unity and
simplicity of God went only so far as to deny of Him the
composition of matter and form. Nor could the conception
of unity in the sense of absolute simplicity be derived directly
from the biblical insistence upon the unity of God. The
unity of God insisted upon in Scripture means only numerical
unity. The conception of the unity of God in the sense of
absolute simplicity, with all its implications, was first introduced into philosophy and religion by Philo. He arrived at
that view by the rigid application of philosophic reasoning
to the biblical principle of the unlikeness of God to anything
else in the world. This I have explained in the chapter on
"The Unknowability of God and Divine Attributes" in
Philo, Vol. II, pp. 94-164.

[1] *Petits* (above p. 1, n. 2), p. 53, ll. 4-6.
[2] *Ibid.*, p. 54, l. 8-p. 55, l. 1.

Second, the Trinitarian controversies in Christianity turned on the question whether the unity of God should be conceived of as interpreted by Philo in the sense of absolute simplicity or whether it should be conceived of in one of thc various forms of relative unity enumerated by Aristotle. This I have explained in the chapters on "The Mystery of the Trinity" and "Heresies" in *The Philosophy of the Church Fathers*, Vol. I, pp. 305-365 and pp. 575-608.

Third, the controversies of divine attributes in Islam, which had arisen shortly after the Muslim conquest of Syria in the course of religious debates between Christians and Muslims, similarly turned on the question whether the unity of God should be conceived as interpreted by Christian orthodoxy in the sense of relative unity or whether it should be conceived of as interpreted by the heretical Sabellians and Arians in the sense of absolute simplicity. In these debates, we have reason to believe, the Christians represented the first person of the Trinity, the Father, as meaning "essence" or "existence" or "goodness," the second person, the Word or the Son, as meaning "life" or "knowledge," and the third person, the Holy Spirit, as meaning "knowledge" or "life" or "power". We may also assume that the Christian debaters tried to convince the Muslims that the second and third persons of the Trinity are nothing but the terms "knowing" and "powerful" or "knowing" and "living" or "living" and "knowing" or "living" and "powerful," by which God is described in the Koran and that there is nothing in the Koran against the Christian belief that the predication of God of either pair of these terms reflects the existence in God of real beings, or rather persons or hypostases, as they were called. The Muslims could find no flaw in the reasoning and no objection to the conclusion. They therefore accepted the view that in God there were real beings to correspond to certain terms predicated of God in the Koran. But then, when the Christian debaters continued to argue that these two persons of the Trinity, the second and the third, are

Gods like the first person, the Muslim balked and quoted
against them the Koranic verses, "say not three... God is
only one God" (4: 169) and "they surely are infidels who
say, God is the third of three, for there is no God but one
God" (5: 77). Thus there had arisen in Islam the belief,
which became the orthodox belief, that certain terms predicated of God in the Koran have, corresponding to them,
real beings in God, called attributes, which are coeternal with
God, but eternally inseparable from Him, and because they
were eternally inseparable from God and also because they
were not called Gods, the unity of God, so vehemently insisted
upon in the Koran, is preserved. The unity, however, like
the unity in Christian orthodoxy, was only a relative unity.

The establishment of this belief in the existence of real
attributes evoked opposition. This opposition was like the
Sabellian opposition in Christianity to the reality of the second
and third persons of the Trinity. It saw in the assumption
of real attributes, even though not called Gods, a violation
of the true unity of God, which, as laid down by Philo and
followed by Sabellianism, they regarded as absolute simplicity. Like Sabellianism in Christianity, therefore, which
declared the second and third persons of the Trinity to be
mere names of God designating His actions, this opposition
declared the terms predicated of God in the Koran to be only
names of God, designating His actions. In their interpretation
of terms predicated of God, these Muslim Antiattributists
thus arrived at a position first formulated by Philo. And
just as in Christianity, counterbalancing the Sabellian opponents to the orthodox conception of the Trinity there were
opponents whose conception of the Trinity degenerated into
Tritheism, so in Islam, counterbalancing these Antiattributis-
tic opponents to the orthodox conception of Attributes, there
were opponents with whom the belief in attributes degenerated
into a crude anthropomorphism. The name given to them
was "the Likeners" (المشبّهة), because they likened God to
other beings.

That this is how the problem of attributes had originated in Islam can be shown by arguments evidential, terminological, and contextual. To begin with, in Islam itself, the opponents of the reality of attributes argued that the orthodox conception of attributes is analogous to the Christian doctrine of the Trinity. Then, two Arabic terms used for what we call "attributes," namely, ṣifāt and maʿāniyy, are translations of two Greek terms, χαρακτηριστικά and πράγματα, which were part of the technical vocabulary of the Trinity. Finally, the terms upon which the earliest controversies over attributes centered correspond exactly to the terms by which the second and third persons of the Trinity were known to the Muslims. Thus in the reports of the earliest discussions of the problem of attributes, the controversies turn always either on the attributes "knowledge and power" or on the attributes "life and knowledge" or on a combination of these two pairs of attributes, namely, "knowledge, power, and life." All this I have explained in my papers on "The Muslim Attributes and the Christian Trinity," *Harvard Theological Review*, vol. 49 (1956), 1-18, and "Philosophical Implications of Divine Attributes in the Kalam," *Journal of the American Oriental Society*, vol. 70 (1950), 73-80.

This is what Saadia knew about the question as to whether the unity of God means only relative unity or absolute unity, when he was about to take up this problem preparatory to his criticism of the orthodox Christian doctrine of the Trinity. In Islam, he knew, it was involved in the problem as to the meaning of the terms "knowing" and "powerful" or "living" and "knowing" or all these three terms, "knowing, powerful, and living," when predicated of God. He naturally knew that among the Muslims there were three views on the problem and that the view which maintained that these three terms mean the existence of three real attributes in God was charged by its opponents to be analogous to the orthodox Christian doctrine that the second and third persons of the Trinity are real beings really distinct from each other. Finally, he knew that of the three persons of the Trinity the Father was described by the term "essence" or "existence" or "goodness," the Son by the term "life" or "knowledge", and the Holy Spirit by the term "knowledge" or "life" or "power."

With all this in the back of his mind, when, as a basis for his criticism of the Trinity, he wanted to establish the view that the unity of God is absolute unity, instead of attacking the problem directly, as did, for instance, his contemporary al-Muḳammaṣ, [1] he attacked it indirectly by discussing the meaning of the terms "living, powerful, and knowing," which are predicated of God in Scripture. [2] In the course of his discussion, he alludes to the three views current in Islam on the meaning of these three terms, without actually naming the sects sponsoring them. Having in mind, "the Likeners," to whom he refers as those who "compare God to His creatures" or as those who take every term predicated of God in Scripture "in its corporeal rather than in its metaphorical sense," [3] he establishes the unlikeness between God and any of His creatures as a scriptural principle. [4] Then, having in mind the Muslim Attributists' view that terms predicated of God reflect the existence in him of real beings called ṣifāt, "attributes," or maʿāniyy, "things" (πράγματα), he says: "Let no one imagine that in God there are different things (עינים معان)." [5] Having so briefly dismissed the view of the Attributists, he aligns himself with the Antiattributists and at great length he tries to show how the terms "living, powerful, knowing," when predicated of God, are "expalanations (פרושי شروح) of the term Creator." [6] These three terms, as we have seen, were the terms upon which the early controversies about attributes were centered.

Thus Saadia has established, indirectly, by rational argu-

---

[1] See *Perush Sefer Yeṣirah* by Judah ben Barzilai, p. 78. ll. 1-3.
[2] *Emunot ve-Deʿot* II, 1. p. 79, l. 19-p. 80, l. 4; II, 4, p. 54, ll. 14 ff.
[3] *Ibid.*, II, 1. p. 80, ll. 10-11.
[4] *Ibid.*, p. 79, ll. 13-14; p. 80, ll. 5-6.
[5] *Ibid.* II, 4, p. 85, ll. 6-7.
[6] *Ibid.*, ll. 17-18.

ments, that the unity of God does not mean only relative
or numerical unity: it means also absolute or internal unity,
that is, absolute simplicity. Having thus arrived by rational
arguments that unity means absolute unity he tries to find
scriptural proof-texts for it. He cites three verses, [1] of which
the first and the third are as follows: (1) "There is none else
beside Him" (Deut 4: 35); (3) "the Lord shall be one and
His name one" (Zech 14: 9). Of these two verses, the first
has been previously quoted by him as a scriptural proof-text
for numerical unity. [2] On what ground he quotes it now again
as scriptural proof-text for internal unity is not clear. Perhaps
on the basis of his own Arabic translation of the Pentateuch,
where this verse is translated by him to read, "There is no
other than He and there is none except Him", the verse was
taken by him to contain two kinds of denial: (1) a denial of
any other God; (2) a denial of anything else, eternal like
Him, within Him. [3] More certain it is that his third verse
has been taken by him to contain in its two parts affirmations
of two kinds of unity: the expression "the Lord shall be one"
was taken to mean numerical unity, and the expression "and
His name one" was taken to mean that "His name," that
is, name "Creator," is "one," because the terms "living,"
"powerful," and "knowing" are only, as he himself has said,
explanations of it.

As for the second of the three proof-texts, it is a quotation
in the Arabic text of his work of the original Hebrew of a
part of a verse in Job, here italicized, which in the Authorized
Version reads as follows: "Lo, these are parts of His ways:
but how a little portion is heard of Him?" (Job 26: 14). What

---

[1] *Ibid.* II, 4, p. 85, l. 21-p. 86, l. 2.

[2] *Ibid.* II, 2, p. 82, ll. 15-16.

[3] The Hebrew of Deut. 4: 39, אין עוד מבלעדו, is translated by
Saadia into Arabic: לא גירה ולא סואה, as if the Hebrew had read
אין עוד ואין מבלעדו, "there is no other than He and there is none
(or nothing) except Him". Elsewhere similar Hebrew expression
ואין עוד מבלעדי (Isa. 45: 21) is translated by Saadia simply by ולא
אלאה גירי. In Deut. 4: 39 there occurs only the expression אין עוד
which Saadia translates by לא סואה.

relevance this quoted part of the verse has here to his attempt
to show that the unity of God means internal unity is not
clear. Fortunately in this case, Saadia's Arabic version of the
Book of Job clears up the matter quite satisfactorily. His
Arabic version of this verse reads as follows: "Lo, these are
some of His descriptions (אוצאפה), but what thing thereof
(שי מן אלאמור) is heard of Him ?" Now the term *shay*, "thing,"
is used in the Kalam as synonymous with the term *ma'na*,
which I have shown to be a translation of the Greek πρᾶγμα,
as another word for *ṣifah*, "attribute." Thus al-Ash'arī is
quoted by Ibn Ḥazm as calling the attributes *ashyā'*, [1]
whereas Shahrastānī quotes the Ash'arites as calling them
ma'āniyy [2] The use of the term *shay* as the equivalent of
ma'na and *ṣifah* is also implied in al-Ash'arī's statement
that "'Abdallah ibn Kullāb used to call the *ma'āniyy* which
subsists in bodies accidents and he used to call them *ashyā'*
and he used to call them *ṣifāt*." [3] Saadia himself [4] and so
also Ibn Ḥazm [5] speak of the second and third persons of the
Trinity, which are regarded as analogous to the orthodox
Muslim attributes, as *shay'ani*, "two things," and Ibn Ḥazm
speaks of all the three persons of the Trinity as "three things
(*ashyā'*). [6] Accordingly, in quoting the verse of Job as proof-
text for the internal unity of God, Saadia takes that verse
to mean that none of "His descriptions," that is, none of
the terms which are predicated of God, is a "thing," that is,
a real attribute existing in God as something other than He.

Once he has established the absolute or internal unity,
that is, the absolute simplicity, of God, Saadia proceeds to
deal with the Trinity. "Hereupon," he begins, "I wish to say
that, with regard to this doctrine of the unity of God, the
Christians went astray and came to believe that there is in

[1]   *Al-Fiṣal fī al-Milal* IV, p. 207, l. 13.
[2]   *Nihāyat al-Ikdām* (ed. Guillaume, 1934), 181, l. 4.
[3]   *Makālāt al-Islāmīyīn* (ed. Ritter, 1929), p. 370, ll. 11-12.
[4]   *Emunot ve-De'ot* II, 5, pp. 86, l. 10.
[5]   Ibn Ḥszm, *Fiṣal* IV, p. 207, l. 22.
[6]   *Ibid.* I, p. 49, l. 1.

God an otherness (זולתות [זולתות]), which led them to make
Him three, thus deviating from the true belief in the unity
of God." [1] He therefore undertakes to refute them by rational
arguments, and, as he says, with the help of "Him who is
one in the true sense of the term unity." [2] And he is not going
to deal, he says, with the Tritheites, to whom he refers as
the "common people" among the Christians and whose use
of a scriptural proof-text for their view, as we have seen, he
has already refuted; nor, without telling us, is he dealing
with the heretical Sabellians, whom he does not even mention;
he is going to deal, he tells us, only with the view of the
authoritative representatives of orthodoxy. Reflecting the
opinion common among the Antiattributists that the view
of the orthodox Attributists is analogous to the orthodox
Christian Trinity, he speaks loosely of the three "hypostases"
as "attributes" and reproduces the reasoning by which they
claim to have arrived at "their belief in [the hypostases of]
the Trinity" as follows: "They arrived at these three attributes
(מדות, صفات) and adhered to them by asserting that only a
thing that is living and knowing can create and, because
they believed that the life and knowledge of that thing which
is the Creator are two things (شيئين, שני דברים) other than
His essence, these became for them three." [3] The three hypostases of the Trinity are thus represented by him to be
"essence" (ذات, עצם), "life" (حيوة, חיות), and "knowledge"
(علم, חכמה). The description of the first person as "essence"
and the description of the second and third persons as "life"
and "knowledge," are to be found, as we have seen, in the
various trinitarian formulae reproduced in Arabic works.

The arguments raised by Saadia against this orthodox
conception of the Trinity are two.

First, he argues in effect that the belief in the Trinity
involves a violation of the Law of Contradiction, for, on the

---

[1] *Emunot ve-De'ot* II, 5, p. 86, ll. 2-3.
[2] *Ibid.*, ll. 3-4.
[3] *Ibid.*, II, 5, p. 86, ll. 8-10.

one hand, the Christians insist that in God there is a numerical distinction between three persons and, on the other, they profess that God is immaterial. Having in mind the Aristotelian statement that 'all things that are many in number have matter,"[1] he phrases his argument as follows: "If [as they openly profess] they do not believe that God is a body, then their allegation that there exists in Him an otherness (غيرية, שנוי = זולתיות) to the extent that one attribute [*i.e.*, hypostasis] of His is not identical with any other attribute of His is equivalent to an allegation on their part that He is really corporeal, to which they only give expression by another term, for anything in which there is otherness is inevitably a body."[2]

It is to be noted here that this type of argument, phrased in various terms, has been discussed in Christian literature ever since the rise of the problem among the Church Fathers and it was a subject of disputation between Christians and Muslims during the time of Saadia. An analysis of the problem and of its solutions is to be found in my discussion of the mystery of the Trinity referred to above.

Second, he argues again in effect that, if the Christians believe that the existence of the second and third persons in the sense of the attributes of life and knowledge is compatible with the unity of God, why did they limit the persons to these two and did not add other persons to correspond to the attributes of power and hearing and seeing and the like.[3] A similar criticism of the doctrine of the Trinity is reported by ibn Ḥazm in the name of the Ashʿarites, who, as he was told by one of them, found fault with the Christians "because

[1]   *Metaph.* XII, 8, 1074a, 33-34.
[2]   *Emunot ve-Deʿot* II, 5, p. 86, ll. 13-16.
For the term שנוי in this passage the context requires זולתיות. The underlying Arabic term غيرية, as a translation of the Greek ἑτερότης means both "otherness" and "alteration". Judah ibn Tibbon took it here wrongly in the sense of "alteration". *See* Neumark, *op. cit.* (below p. 15, n. 6), p. 210. 4.
[3]   *Ibid.* II, 5, p. p. 87, ll. 11-19.

they assume that there coexist with God only two things
(شَيْئَيْن) and do not assume that there coexist with Him a
greater number of things,"[1] of which he mentions the
number "fifteen."[2]

Following this refutation, Saadia undertakes to refute
Christian interpretation of certain verses in the Hebrew
Bible as refering to the Trinity.[3] The number of such verses
quoted by him is six. Of these six verses, the four middle
ones, namely, Job 33: 4, Ps. 33/32: 6, Prov 8: 22, Gen 1: 26,
are, again, to be found so interpreted in Abucara's work.[4]
As for the other two verses, the sixth, "And the Lord appeared
unto him... and, lo, three men" (Gen 18: 1-2), it is taken
by some Church Fathers to refer to the persons of the Trinity;[5]
but I could not find any work where the first verse, "The
spirit of the Lord spoke by me and His word was upon my
tongue" (2 Sam 23: 2), was similarly used as a proof-text
for the Trinity. It is to be noted how careful Saadia is in
his choice of words. The four verses which he himself must
have seen used by Abucara as proof-texts for the Trinity he
introduces by such expressions as "I find some of them cite
as proof[6].... Also they say";[7] "I also found one of them
who interpreted";[8] "I have seen others who rely on... and
say."[9] The sixth verse, which he has not found in Abucara

---

[1] Ibn Ḥazm, Fiṣal IV, p. 207, ll. 22-23. Cf. answer to this kind of
objection by Elias of Nisibis in David Kaufmann, Gesammelte Schriften,
III (1915), p. 65.

[2] Ibid., l. 21.

[3] Ibid., II, 5-6, p. 88, l. 2-p. 90, l. 16.

[4] Op. cit., above p. 4, n. 1. The verses occur in Abucara as follows:
(2) Job 23: 4 in III, 10, p. 143;
(3) Ps. 33/32: 6 in VII, 16, p. 196;
(4) Prov. 8: 22 in III, 20, p. 153; VII, 14, p. 193;
(5) Gen. 1: 26 in III, 20, p. 153, VII, 16, pp. 195-196.

[5] Cf., e.g., Justin Martyr, Dialogus cum Tryphone Judaeo 56 and
126; Irenaeus, Adversus Haereses IV, 10, 1; Eusebius, Historia Eccle-
siastica I, 2, 7.

[6] Emunot ve-Deʿot II, 5, p. 88, l. 9.

[7] Ibid., l. 11.

[8] Ibid. III, 6, p. 89, ll. 9-10.

[9] Ibid., ll. 16-17.

but must have heard that it had been used by the Church Fathers, is introduced, by the words "Others conjecture... and say," [1] whereas the first, for which he evidently had no source at all, is introduced by the words "If they derive their proof from Scripture, as, for example, someone of them might assert." [2] In other words, he himself supplied the Christians with a proof-text only to refute it.

While his treatment of the Trinity Saadia, with the exception of an allusion to the Tritheites, does not contain a classification of the various sects in Christianity, such as may be found in Arabic works dealing with Christianity, [3] his treatment of Christology does contain a classification of views of the various sects. [4] He enumerates four sects, three of whom he describes as older and one as that which appeared only recently. [5] It would be futile to identify these four sects with any of the sects known to us from modern works on the history of Christian doctrine; attempts made by students of Saadia to identify these sects by that method have proved only confusing. [6] We must go to descriptions of Christian sects in Arabic sources for the identification of these four

[1]   *Ibid.* II, 6. p. 90, l. 1.2.
[2]   *Ibid.* II, 5, p. 87, l. 20-p. 88, l. 1.
[3]   *Cf.* Ibn Ḥazm, *Fiṣal* I, pp. 48 ff.; Shahrastānī, *Al-Milal waʾl-Niḥal* (ed. Cureton), pp. 171 ff.
[4]   *Emunot ve-Deʿot* II, 7, p. 90, l. 17-p. 91, l. 16.
[5]   *Ibid.*, p. 90, ll. 17-18.
[6]   Here are attempts to identify these four sects by the following authors: (1) Kaufmann, *Attributenlehre* (1877), pp. 50-51; Jacob Guttmann, *Die Religionsphilosophie des Saadia* (1882), pp. 108-113; Neumark, *Geschichte der jüdischen Philosophie des Mittelalters*, Zweiter Band 2 (1928), pp. 191-192; Ventura, *La Philosophie de Saadia Gaon* (1934), p. 184.
Kaufmann: (1) No identification; (2) Apollinaris; (3) Theodore of Mopsuestia; (4) Ebionites and Monarchians.
Guttmann: (1) Monarchianism and Sabellius; (2) Arianism; (3) Paul of Semosata; (4) [Spanish] Adoptionism.
Neumark: (1) Monophysites; (2) Dyophysites; (3) and (4) No identification.
Ventura: (1) Docetism of various Gnostic sects; (2) Chalcedonian Creed; (3) Roman Adoptionism; (4) Spanish Adoptionism.

sects enumerated by Saadia. Though the sources which we shall quote come from a time after Saadia, they undoubtedly reproduce Christological views as understood by Muslim writes at the time of Saadia.

The first sect is described by Saadia as that which believes that "both the body and the spirit of their Messiah are from the Creator." [1] Before we try to identify this sect, let us comment on the terms "body" and "spirit" which are used by Saadia in his description of the various views of these sects on Christology. These two terms, we take it, stand for what in Christological controversies is known as the contrast between the "humanity" (الناسوت, ἀνθρωπότης) and "divinity" (اللاهوت, θεότης) in Jesus, for it is the queston of the "humanity" and "divinity" in Jesus, and in the case of Apollinaris also the question of "soul" or of "rational soul" in Jesus, and not that of the "body" and "spirit" in him, that was the main point at issue in the Christological controversies. A similar use of the term "spirit," in the sense of "divinity," in contrast to "body," in the sense of "humanity," is implied in a passage in Shahrastānī, where, comparing two ways in which Christians explain the union of the Word with the body in Jesus, he reports that they either say that "it appears in it like the appearance of the spiritual in the corporeal" or they say that "the divinity puts on the humanity as a breastplate." [2] Taken in this sense, the statement that "both the body and the spirit of their Messiah are from God" means a denial of humanity or of a human nature in Jesus, and the sect thus described here by Saadia is to be identified with the Monophysites or, as they are known to the Muslims, the Jacobites. The Jacobites are described by the Muslims as believing that "the Word was transformed into flesh and blood, so that God became the Messiah and was manifest in his body, or rather He was himself the Messiah." [3] This

---

[1]   *Emunot ve-De'ot* II, 7, p. 90, l. 18.
[2]   Shahrastānī, *Milal*, p. 172, ll. 6-7.
[3]   *Ibid.*, p. 179, ll. 19-20; cf. Ibn Ḥazni,   *Fiṣal*, I, p. 49, l. 9.

is exactly what Saadia meant to say about the first sect, for
from his subsequent criticism of this sect it is clear that his
statement that "both the body and the spirit... are from
God" means that "some part of God became body and
spirit." [1]

The second sect is described by him as that which believes
that "his body was created but his spirit is from the Creator." [2]
This reflects exactly the following Muslim conception of the
Nestorians: "They maintain that Mary did not give birth
to God; she gave birth only to the man; and that God did
not beget the man; He begot only the God." [3] What Saadia
therefore means to say of the second sect is that they believed
that the humanity in Jesus was created, that is to say, was
given birth by Mary, but that the divinity in him was "from
the Creator," that is to say, was begotten by God.

The third sect is described by him as that which believes
that "both his body and his spirit were created but that
there was in him another spirit from the Creator." [4] This
formula, I take it, is made up of two formulations of the
Christology ascribed by Muslim writers to the Malkites, that
is, to those who followed the Decree of Chalcedon (451).
The first part of Saadia's formula, namely, "both his body
and his spirit were created," reflects exactly that formulation
of the Malkites' view which reads: "Mary bore the God and
the man." [5] The second part of Saadia's formula, namely,
"but there was in him another spirit from the Creator"
reflects that formulation of the Malkites' view which, after
stating that the Malkites believe that in Jesus there are two
natures, a human and a divine, adds that they believe also
"that the Messiah is a hypostasis (اقنوم) of the nature of
God only, and it is an uncompounded nature, being [un]derived

---

[1]   *Emunot ve-De'ot* II, 7, p. 91, ll. 5-6.
[2]   *Ibid.*, p. 90, l. 19
[3]   Ibn Ḥazm, *Fiṣal*, I, p. 49, ll. 6-7.
[4]   *Emunot ve-De'ot* II, 7, p. 90, ll. 19-20.
[5]   Ibn Ḥazm, *Fiṣal*, I, p. 49, l. 4.

from the two aforementioned natures." [1] This last statement, evidently, was taken by Saadia to mean, and perhaps that is exactly what it meant, that Jesus was born with two natures, a human and divine, and then another divine nature was added to it. If this is what the last statement meant, it was based upon a misunderstanding of the Chalcedonian Decree stating that "one and the same Christ" is "in two natures" and that these two natures are "in one person and one hypostasis," namely, "God the Word." [2] What the Creed means is that of the two natures in Jesus, the divine and the human, the divine nature, that is, the Word, is both a person and a nature, whereas the human nature is only a nature, and therefore it is the divine nature that constitutes the one person. [3]

Thus the first three sects mentioned by Saadia are the Jacobites, the Nestorians, and the Malkites, those whom Muslim historiographers describe as "their fundamental sects (عمدهم)" [4] or "their main sects." [5] These three sects, while differing in their Christological views, were all orthodox in their view on the Trinity, as is testified by Yaḥyā ibn 'Adī, who says that, with regard to the orthodox conception of the Trinity, "the three sects" are fully in agreement. [6] Ordinarily, in Muslim works dealing with Christianity, the Malkites are mentioned first, then come the Nestorians and the Jacobites, [7] and the Malkites are described by Mas'ūdī as "the

---

[1] *Al Ghazālī: Réfutation Excellente de la Divinité de Jésus Christ d'aprè les Évangiles*, Texte établi, traduit et commenté par Robert Chidiac (1939), p. 32, ll. 12-15 of the text, and cf. correction of reading on p. 87 of the introductory material.

[2] *See* Dnezinger et Bannwart, *Enchiridion Symbolorum* (1922), § 148.

[3] On the meaning of this, see the chapter on "The Mystery of the Incarnation", in my *Philosophy of the Church Fathers*, I, pp. 364-433.

[4] Ibn Ḥazm, *Fiṣal* I, p. 48, l. 22.

[5] Shahrastānī, *Milal*, p. 173, l. 11.

[6] *Petits* (above p. 1, n. 2), p. 55, l. 1 ff.

[7] *Cf.* Mas'ūdī, *Murūj al-Dhahab* (ed. Barbier de Meynard et Pavet de Courteille 1861-77), I, p. 200; *Al-Tanbīh wa'l-Ishrāf* (ed. de

pillars (عمد) and the pivot (قطب) of the Christians." [1] and by Ibn Ḥazm as "the most improtant of the three sects (اعظمها)." [2] Saadia, however, as will have been noticed, reverses the order, putting the Jacobites first and then the Nestorians and Malkites. The explanation, it seems to me, is that Saadia has arranged these sects in the order of his direct acquaintance with them. Born in Egypt, where he lived up to the age of twenty-three or thirty-three, he first bccame acquainted with the Jacobite view, for in Egypt the Jacobites were the dominant Christian sect. Then when he settled down in Irak he became acquainted with the Nestorian Christology, for in Irak the Nestorians were the dominant Christian sect. The Malkites who flourished mainly in Christian countries and in Muslim Spain always remained to him a far-off sect. He therefore puts them last. So also, it may be added, the work on the refutation of the divinity of Jesus, attributed to Ghazālī, [3] which was written in Egypt, [4] in its dealing with the Christologies of these three sects, similarly puts the Jacobites first.

The fourth sect is described by Saadia as that which "assign to him the position of prophet only, interpreting the sonship of which they apply to him just as we interpret the biblical expression 'Israel is my first-born son' (Exod. 4: 22), which is merely an expression of esteem and high regard, or as others (Muslims) interpret the description of Abraham as the 'friend' of God (Surah 4: 124)." [5] On the face of it, this description reflects the various heretical Christologies which shared in common the denial of the divinity of Jesus, such as the Christology of the followers of Paul of Samosata, which was known to the Muslims as the view that "Jesus

Goeje, 1894), p. 142, l. 11; p. 154, l. 4; *Ibn Ḥazm, Fiṣal* I, pp. 48, 49; Shahrastānī, *Milal*, pp. 173, 175, 176.
[1] Mas'ūdī, *Murūj*, I, p. 200.
[2] Ibn Ḥazm, *Fiṣal* I, p. 48, l. 23.
[3] *Op. cit.*, above p. 18, n. 1.
[4] *Ibid.*, pp. 25-35.
[5] *Emunot ve-De'ot* II, 7, p. 90, l. 21-p. 91, l. 2.

was the servant of God and His apostle like all the other prophets" [1] or that "he was an upright created servant"; [2] and as the Christology of the Arians, which was known to the Muslims as the view that 'Jesus was a created servant"; [3] and as the Christology of the Macedonians, which was known to the Muslims as the view that "Jesus was a created servant, a man, a prophet, an apostle of God like the rest of the prophets." [4] All these heretical Christologies may be described as reflecting the Ebionitic type of Christology, which was one of the three types of Christology that had existed in Christianity from the earliest time. [5] Ebionites as a sect or as a group of sects, it may be remarked, had disappeared before the rise of Islam and no longer existed at the time of Saadia. It is the common Christology of these three heretical sects that would thus seem to be reflected in Saadia's fourth sect. But there is the following question. Inasmuch as this type of Christology was known to the Muslims to have been shared by three sects and these sects were known to them to antedate the Nestorians and the Jacobites, why does Saadia designate those who followed this type of Christology as a single sect [6] and why does he describe them as a sect which appeared only recently?

The explanation which I should like to suggest is that, though the Christological view ascribed by Saadia to this fourth sect is exactly like that of the Samosatenians, Arians and Macedonians, it is not any of these sects that he has reference to here. His reference here is rather to an entirely new sect which we have reason to believe arose among Christians shortly before Saadia's birth in the same part of the Muslim world in which Saadia wrote his book. It happens

---

[1] Ibn Ḥazm, *Fiṣal* I, p. 48, ll. 13-14.
[2] Shahrastānī, *Milal*, p. 176, l. 12.
[3] Ibn Ḥazm, *Fiṣal* I, p. 48, l. 9.
[4] *Ibid.*, ll. 19-20.
[5] *Cf.* section on "Heresies with Regard to the Born Christ" in *The Philosophy of the Church Fathers*, I, pp. 587-606.
[6] *Emunot ve-Deʿot*, II, 7, p. 91, l. 3.

that the Koran, while rejecting the orthodox Christian type of Christology, upholds the Ebionitic type of Christology in such verses as "And they say, God hath a son. No!" (2: 110); "The Messiah, Jesus, son of Mary, is only an apostle of God" (4: 169); "The Messiah, son of Mary, is only an apostle" (5: 79). We know that debates between Christians and Muslims on this Christological view had been going on ever since their first encounter. We know that Christians as a minority group in Muslim countries were not entirely impervious to Muslim influence We know also that the Christian Arabic literature, through its discussions of all sides of the Christological problems, had kept alive among Christians in Muslim countries a knowledge of the Ebionitic type of Christology of the heretical Samosatenians, Arians, and Macedonians and also a knowledge of all the arguments in favor of it. What with all this, is it not possible that a certain group of Christians in Muslim countries, shortly before the time of Saadia, succumbed to Muslim influence and adopted a type of Christology that was more agreeable to their Muslim masters? That the Christology of this fourth sect was advanced in an effort to accommodate itself to the Muslim environment is indicated by the fact that one of the ways, mentioned by Saadia, whereby this sect tried to explain why, with their denial of the divinity of Jesus, they still continued to call him son of God, was by referring to the Muslims' explanation of the expression "Abraham, the friend of God," [1] which had come into use on the basis of the Koranic verse, "And God took Abraham for His friend" (4: 124). Elsewhere I have shown how at about the end of the eighth century, that is, somewhat over three quarters of a century before the birth of Saadia, under the impact of Islam, a modified conception of the Trinity appeared among a certain group of Nestorian Christians in Adiabene on the Tigris, [2] which is in that part

[1]   *Ibid.*, p. 91, l. 2.
[2]   *Cf.* my paper "An Unknown Splinter Group of Nestorians," *Revue des Études Augustiniennes*, 6 (1960), pp. 249-253.

of the Muslim world where Saadia's work was written. Here, on the basis of Saadia's description of the fourth sect, it can be further shown that probably the same group of Nestorians at the same time, again, under the impact of Islam, changed their own heretical conception of Christology for another heretical conception, which was akin to it. This assumption of the recrudescence among Nestorian Christians in Muslim lands, under the impact of Islam, of an old Christological view, well-known to them and quite akin to their own view, even though like their own view not considered orthodox, is a more likely explanation than the explanation, suggested by Guttmann, [1] that the Christology of Saadia's fourth sect was an importation of the Adoptionism which arose in the far-off Latin Christianity of Spain. In fact, Spanish Adoptionism itself arose partly under the influence of Oriental Christianity, for it arose under the influence of both Islam and Nestorianism, the latter of which by that time flourished only among Christians under Muslim rule, mainly in Mosul, Irak, and Persia.

Saadia's criticism of all these four Christologies is based upon principles which, he says, he has already discussed, or is about to discuss, in other parts of his work, and so we shall forgo the discussion of it here.

[1]   *Op. cit.* (above p. 15, n. 6), p. 112.

JOHANAN THE HIGH PRIEST'S ABROGATIONS AND DECREES

By Solomon Zeitlin

Dropsie College

It is stated in a Mishne (Maaser Sheni 5: 15) that "Johanan the High Priest removed the confession in connection with the tithe. He also abolished the Awakeners and the Knockers. Until his days, the hammer used to smite in Jerusalem. And in his days no one needed to inquire concerning *demoi*." [1]

יוחנן כהן גדול העביר הודיית המעשר אף ביטל את המעוררין ואת הנוקפין עד ימיו היה פטיש מכה בירושלים ובימיו אין אדם צריך לשאול על הדמאי

One must establish the text in order to understand the underlying reason for the abrogations by Johanan the High Priest, John Hyrcanus I. The text of the Mishne reads: העביר הודיית המעשר "He removed the confession in connection with the tithe." The text at the end reads: אין אדם צריך לשאול על הדמאי "No one needed to inquire concerning *demoi*." The text in a Baraita, however, reads as follows ביטל את הודוי וגזר על הדמאי "He abolished the confession (in connection with the tithe) and decreed on the demoi." [2] It will be shown in the course of the essay that this is the correct text.

The social and economic conditions prevailing at that period must be outlined to make intelligent the full import of John Hyrcanus' abrogations and decrees.

From the time of the Restoration to the period of John Hyrcanus, the Jewish community had undergone revolutionary changes in its social and economic structures. Judaea after the Restoration was a small, obscure country consisting of villages and one important city, Jerusalem. In the main, the inhabitants were divided into two classes: on the one hand priests and Levites engaged in the temple service, and on

[1] Maaser Sheni, 5.15; Sotah, 9.10. *Cf.* Yer. Demoi, 1.2
[2] Sotah 48a

the other landed folk, the *ame ha-arez*. [1] Priests and Levites received no monetary remuneration for their work in the temple other than a tithe from the crops of the landed folk, *ame ha-arez*, and gifts from the sacrifices brought to the temple. The Hebrew name for the priests' tithes was *Terumah*, for that of the Levites, *Maaseroth*. The priests received an additional *Terumah* over and above the regular tithe. To this tax which the farmers paid to the priests and Levites they also, during the Seleucid period and probably during the Ptolemaic rule over Judaea, had to give one-third of their crops and one-half of their fruit to the state. [2] These taxes were paid either with the products of the crop or with money equivalent. Hence the burden of taxation was indeed heavy on the farmers, the *ame ha-arez*. These taxes, paid by the farmers to the Seleucids, were retained by the state of Judaea when it gained its independence. Thus the farmer's tax burden was not relaxed in the time of John Hyrcanus I.

The life of the *ame ha-arez*, the farmer folk, was hard. They had to labor incessantly in the field from early morning until sunset to extract a mere living from the soil. They struggled constantly with inclement weather, suffered from destructive insects and, in some years, had to wage war against locusts. Water was often lacking and the heat intense. As long as the Jewish community consisted of two classes, the farmers supported the priests and the Levites in accordance with the biblical law. However, after the conquest of Judaea by the Ptolemies, a new social class emerged which did not engage in agriculture but in trade and manufacturing. Many Jews held high positions in the Ptolemaic court as tax collectors. They helped and encouraged the middle class of artisans and traders. Hence during the time of the Ptolemies there was a change in the social structure in Judaea. In addition to the existing two classes, there now emerged a third class, the traders.

[1] *Cf.* S. Zeitlin, "The 'Am Ha-arez,'" *JQR*, 1932, vol. xxiii, pp. 45-61.
[2] *Cf.* I Mac. 10. 29-33.

With the establishment of the Commonwealth this third class grew in prominence and power. Seafaring became an important factor after the conquest of Joppa by Simon, the Hasmonean. Now for the first time after the Restoration the Judaeans acquired a port, an outlet to the Mediterranean Sea. [1] The traders thereby gained a stronghold over the community. John Hyrcanus I was the first to engage mercenaries. [2] These were led by Jewish officers. A permanent army came into being in Judaea, and a corps of Jewish officers constituted a new social group.

Simon, the Hasmonean, and particularly his son, John Hyrcanus, conquered many cities which they colonized with Judaeans. John Hyrcanus undoubtedly followed the policy of the Seleucids who colonized newly conquered cities by settling Greeks in them. The land, however, belonged to the state. One may, therefore, assume that when John Hyrcanus conquered new territories and settled them with Judaeans, the land remained state property, and those who occupied the land were tenants. Some of them had the status of hereditary tenants; i.e., while the land belonged to the state, the colonists were entitled to live on these lands and their children had the right of occupancy by the law of inheritance. Another type of tenancy came into being. Men who had distinguished themselves in the wars, particularly the leaders of the military caste, received large tracts of conquered lands. This group did not cultivate the land but placed it in the hands of tenants who tilled it for a certain share in the produce, or who paid a fixed rental in kind.

According to the Pentateuch, the farmer had to bring the first fruit to the altar of the Lord and to make a confession while presenting this offering. The following words were included in the confession: "And now, behold, I brought the first of the fruit of the land which Thou, O Yahweh, hast given me." [3] Some of the farmers who brought the first fruit were only

[1] Cf. ibid. 14.34.   [2] Cf. Ant. 13.8, 4 (249).
[3] Deut 26: 10.

tenants, the land belonging to the state or the landowners, so the uttering of this phrase by them would have been false. Johanan the High Priest, therefore, abolished the confession.

John Hyrcanus also abolished the confession in connection with the *Maaser*. According to the Pentateuch, the man who brought the *Maaser* to Jerusalem in the third year had to confess, saying, "I have put away the hallowed things out of my house, and also have given them unto the Levites and to the stranger and to the orphan and to the widow according to all Thy commandments which Thou hast commanded: I have not transgressed any of Thy commandments, neither have I forgotten them." [1]

It will be recalled that before the establishment of the Second Commonwealth the Judaean society consisted primarily of two classes—the *ame ha-arez* and the priests and Levites. But later new classes emerged—artisans, traders, a military caste, and a working class who tilled the fields for the landowners. Many of the *ame ha-arez* resented the fact that they alone had to carry the burden of supporting the priests and the Levites, a burden which the urban population was not required to share. Many of the *ame ha-arez*, therefore, withheld the *Maaser*, the tithes, [2] and the priests and the Levites did not receive their due allotment. The truth is that the farmers refused to take into account the fact that when they gave their tithes they raised the prices for their grain to meet their tax obligation and, actually, the burden of taxation was distributed among the consumers as well as the farmers. Since the *ame ha-arez* were suspected of not giving the God-ordained tithe to the Levites and conceivably might perjure themselves in saying they "also have given them unto the Levites," John Hyrcanus ביטל את הודוי abolished the entire ceremony of confession for the *Maaser*. [3]

---

[1] *Ibid.* v. 13.

[2] Sotah 48. מקצתן מעשרין מקצתן אין מעשרין

[3] *Cf.* Yer. Demoi, 1.2 יוחנן כהן גדול העביר הודיית המעשר, העבירן שלא יתוודו.

The economic status of the Levites began to deteriorate. To improve their condition, John Hyrcanus גזר על הדמאי, decreed that those who purchased from the farmers should give the prescribed tithe to the Levites. [1] In order to avoid any adverse effect on commerce, the religious leaders limited this decree only to those who purchased produce from the *ame ha-arez* for personal consumption; but those who purchased for purposes of trade remained exempt. They also exempted those who purchased grain for the feeding of cattle from giving the tithe to the Levites. [2]

The word דמאי, generally interpreted to mean *doubt*, refers to produce upon which there was doubt as to whether the tithe had been taken from it. Elsewhere I have maintained that the word דמאי *demoi* has the connotation "common people," *ame ha-arez*, as the word δῆμος means "common people." [3] The word דמאי never occurs in the entire tannaitic literature in the sense of doubt, but only in reference to the produce of *ame ha-arez*. We may, therefore, say with certainty that the word *demoi* could not have the connotation of doubt.

The question may be raised that the decree of John Hyrcanus referred to the produce of the *ame ha-arez* while the text has it that he decreed on the *demoi*, the common people, produce not being mentioned in the decree. This is easily explainable on the basis of the short form of expression characteristic of the early tannaitic period. The following examples will suffice. According to the Talmud, Simon ben Shetah introduced a *Ketubah*, a writ, [4] but he really did not introduce a writ. What he did introduce was the formula that the groom should write a *Ketubah*, a writ, in which he pledged all his properties as security for the two hundred

---

[1] *Cf.* Sotah, 48 הלוקה פירות מעם הארץ מפריש.

[2] Tos. Demoi, 1.15 הלוקח לבהמה ולחיה ולעוף פטור מן הדמאי; *Cf.* also Mishne, *ibid.*, 1.3

[3] *Cf.* S. Zeitlin, *The History of the Second Jewish Commonwealth Prolegomena* 1933, pp. 69-70.

[4] שמעון בן שטח תיקן כתובה לאשה Shab. 14.

zuzim to be paid to his wife in case he should divorce her or
in the event of his death.[1] The *Takanah* of Simon ben Shetah
was to provide for the woman's economic security in the
event of divorce or the death of her husband. The main object
of the *Takanah* is not referred to.

Again, Hillel introduced the *Takanah* of *Prosbul*. [2] The
word *Prosbul* is borrowed from the Greek προς βουλῇ, before
the council (court). The substance of Hillel's *Takanah* of
Prosbul was that the creditor should write a declaration
(note) before the court. [3] The note, the principal object of
Hillel's *Takanah*, is not referred to. In a like manner the
produce of the *ame ha-arez* is not referred to in the decree
of John Hyrcanus; simply the word *demoi* is given. The use
of *Prosbul* and *Ketubah* as well as *demoi* shows the characteristic
manner of expression of the early tannaim.

The well-founded suspicion that many of the *ame ha-arez* did
not give the tithe gave rise to the *Haburah*, a new association
in Judaea. The *ame ha-arez*, the farmers, were suspected of
being personally unscrupulous both in relation to levitical
laws of purity and impurity and with regard to their products.
Consequently, many of the city dwellers, who were scrupulous
in their observance of the laws of levitical purity and the
laws of the tithe, would not partake of bread with them or
associate with them. This group was called *Haberim*, associates; *i.e.*, Jews who joined together. This association was
named *Haburah* in the early tannaitic literature.

The city dwellers, particularly the *Haberim*, were a cultured
group and laid great stress on the observance of the biblical
laws, particularly those with regard to levitical purity and
tithes. On the other hand, the *ame ha-arez*, the farmers, found
it impossible to develop the degree of culture and the
knowledge of the laws attained by the city folk. There was

----

[1] *Cf.* Yer. Ket. 8.11; B. *ibid.* ותיקן כל נכסיו אחראין לכתובה.

[2] הלל הזקן תיקן פרוזבל M. Sheb. 10.3. *Cf.* S. Zeitlin, "Prosbol,"
JQR 1947, pp. 341-62,

[3] שכל חוב שיש לי שאגבנו כל זמן שארצה.

a wide gap between these two groups. The observance of levitical purity and the giving of the required tithes affected the daily life of the people. Hence a *Haber*, who was scrupulous in the observance of these laws, could not partake of bread with an *am ha-arez* or associate with him. [1] Consequently tannaitic literature uses the term *Haberim* always in opposition to *ame ha-arez* but only in reference to the laws of agriculture and levitical purity.

Needless to say, the *am ha-arez*, the farmer, strongly resented the attitude of the *Haberim*. The *Haber* could not invite the *am ha-arez* to dine in his house—neither could he accept such an invitation from the *am ha-arez* to dine in his house. This resentment of the *ame ha-arez* developed into hatred towards the *Haberim*. On the other hand, the *Haberim* looked down upon the *ame ha-arez*, the farmer folk, as being the lower class in Judaean society. The antagonism between these two groups developed more and more and led to acrimonious social strife.

In time the term *ame ha-arez*, which originally meant farmer folk, came to be synonymous with "ignorance and immorality." It became an epithet of contempt and reproach for those who were ignorant, crude, immoral and who did not observe the Jewish laws. The word pagan, from the Latin *paganus*, originally also meant "countryman" but later became the appellation of the irreligious. Similarly the word "boor" or "hick" is occasionally applied not only to a farmer but to a rude and ill-bred person.

The word *Haber* later was applied to a learned man, a scholar. After the destruction of the Second Temple the term *Haber* was applied to a candidate of the *Bet Din*, Sanhedrin. [2]

The bitter feeling between the different social classes in Judaea derived from their economic difference and their

---

[1]   ואינו מתארח אצל עם הארץ Tos. Demoi, 2.

[2]   חבירים מהו ליכנס לקידוש החדש; אמר רבי הושעיה חבר הוינא
ואעלי אמר רב כהנא חבר הוינא Cf. Yer. Sanh. I.

social distinctions. Class conflict was unavoidable where such tension and antagonism flourished.

John Hyrcanus also abolished the "Awakeners" and the "Knockers." In the Talmud it is well explained that the Awakeners were the Levites who daily recited the following hymn in the temple:

> "Awake, why sleepest Thou, O Adonai?
>   Arouse Thyself, cast not off forever
> Wherefore hideth Thou Thy face
>   And forgettest our affliction and our oppression?
> For our soul is bowed down to the dust
>   Our belly cleaveth unto the earth
> Arise for our help and redeem us for Thy mercy's sake." [1]

The Levites sang daily in the temple during the wars against the Seleucids. They appealed to God to awake and redeem the people for His mercy's sake. They also recited the following hymn:

> "Nay, but for Thy sake are we killed all the day;
>   We are accounted as sheep for the slaughter." [2]

These appeals to God were superfluous after the great victories of the Hasmonean family and the establishment of the Jewish Commonwealth and the great military success of Hyrcanus which added large territories to Judaea. The Jews were no longer slaughtered as sheep and their souls were no longer bowed down to the dust. They were a courageous, victorious people who possessed dignity and pride. The abolishing of the awakeners was due to the confidence of John Hyrcanus in the stability of the Judaean State. The

---

[1] Ps 44: 24-27 עורה למה תישן אדני הקיצה אל תזנח לנצח למה
פניך תסתיר תשכח עניינו ולחצנו כי שחה לעפר נפשנו דבקה לארץ בטננו
קומה עזרתה לנו ופדנו למען חסדך
כי עליך הרגנו כל היום נחשבנו כצאן טבחה

[2] Ps 44: 23

hymns sung by the "Awakeners" were later incorporated in the Book of Psalms.

John Hyrcanus also abolished the "Knockers." The "Knockers" according to the Talmud are those who used to strike upon the calf between his horns. Johanan the High Priest said to them, "How long will you feed the altar with *nebelot*?" [1] The Babylonian Talmud renders the passage somewhat differently. "They used to knock him (the victim) as they do in idol worship. He [Johanan the High Priest] said 'How long will you feed the altar with *nebelot* (carrion)?'" How, asks the Talmud, could Johanan the High Priest say to them that they fed the altar with *nebelot* when the victim had been slaughtered? The answer was that Johanan said that they fed the altar with *terefot*, prohibited both for the altar and for human consumption. [2]

The talmudic explanation for the abolition of the "Knockers" by John Hyrcanus does not give the real historical reason. The explanation there is late. It seems that the "Knockers" were correlated with the "Awakeners." Prior to the time of Judah the Maccabeean the Temple had been defiled having been in the possession of Antiochus Epiphanes and his Jewish adherents. The religious followers of the Hasmoneans had no access to the temple. Appealing to God they *knocked with hammers* and recited a hymn, "Awake, why sleepeth Thou, O Adonai?" They cried that they were being killed daily for observing His laws. Even when the Temple was later rededicated by Judah, many Jews still

[1] Yer. Sotah, 9. את הנוקפין אותן שהיו מכין על גבי העגל בין קרניו
אמר להן יוחנן כהן גדול עד מתי אתם מאכילין את המזבח נבילות
[2] מאי נוקפין אמר רבי יהודה אמר שמואל שהיו מסרטין לעגל בין קרניו
כדי שיפול דם בעיניו אתא איהו בטיל .... שהיו חובטין אותו במקלות כדרך
שעושין אתו לפני ע״ז אמר להם עד מתי אתם מאכילין נבילות למזבח, נבילות
הא שחיט להו אלא טריפות .Cf. Tos., *ibid* עד מתי אתי אתם מאכילין את
המזבח טריפות
The text given in the Tosefta is based on the emendation in the Baby-lonian Talmud. *Cf.* also S. Lieberman, *Hellenism in Jewish Palestine*, 1950, pp. 139-143.

continued to recite prayers for victory, accompanying it by
knocking with hammers and reciting the hymn "Awake...."
John Hyrcanus abolished the "Awakeners," the Levites,
who sang in the temple the hymn, "Awake" and the "Knockers" who knocked with hammers beseeching God to awaken
and to help them to observe the laws of God and to overcome
their enemies.

This is the meaning of the words in the Mishne, "Until his
days/John Hyrcanus'/ the hammer used to strike in Jerusalem"; *i.e.*, by the Knockers. The Talmud explains that the
smiting of the hammer refers to the middle days of the Feasts--
Passover and Tabernacles [1]—and that John Hyrcanus forbade
any work which necessitated the wielding of the hammer on
the middle days of the feast. We may say with certainty
from internal evidence of the Talmud, Moed Katan, that
the knocking of the hammer, mentioned in this Mishne, had
no relation to kinds of labor which were forbidden on the
middle days of the feast. [2] The statement, "From his days
the hammer was not struck in Jerusalem," is an explanation
of the fact that the "Knockers" were abolished by John
Hyrcanus. Similarly the phrase, "and in his days none needed
to inquire about *demoi*" explains the decree of John Hyrcanus
that the consumer has to give the tithe.

The   original   text   of   the   Mishne   was   יוחנן כהן גדול ביטל
את הודוי וגזר על הדמאי ובימיו אין אדם צריך לשאול על הדמאי; אף הוא
ביטל את המעוררין ואת הנוקפין עד ימיו היה פטיש מכה בירושלים
Johanan the High Priest abolished the confession; *i.e.*, the
confession of the *ame ha-arez* when bringing the tithes. He
decreed *demoi*; *i.e.*, that the consumer had to give the tithe
to the Levites. In his days no one needed to inquire about
demoi; *i.e.*, since the *ame ha-arez* were not trusted in the
necessary tithe.[3] He also abolished the "Awakeners" and the

---

[1]   Sotah, 48. עד ימיו היה פטיש מכה בירושלים, בחולו של מועד
[2]   M. M. K. 1.10 הצינור והקורה ··· שנשברו מתקנן במועד, *Cf.* Talmud, *ibid.*, 11.
[3]   Yer. Sotah, 9 שהעמיד זוגות.

"Knockers," hence from his day on no hammer was smitten in Jerusalem.

The words עד ימיו היה פטיש מכה בירושלים "Until his days the hammer used to smite in Jerusalem," and the words ובימיו אין אדם צריך לשאול על הדמאי "In his days none needed to inquire on *demoi*" were grouped at the end of this Mishne by a later editor because of the similar words ובימיו and ימי.

The decrees and abrogations made by John Hyrcanus I reflect the political as well as the socio-economic conditions prevailing shortly after Judaea became an independent state.

TRANSLATION AND MISTRANSLATION
IN THE APOCALYPSE OF BARUCH

By FRANK ZIMMERMANN
Dropsie College

INTERTESTAMENTAL STUDY owes much to the pioneering
work of R. H. Charles. Of the Apocalypse of Baruch specifically, he prepared an excellent edition based on the Syriac
(London 1896), followed by the improved edition in the larger
Apocrypha and Pseudepigrapha, II, p. 470. Charles was the
first to prove conclusively that the Apocalypse was originally
written in Hebrew (cf. pp. lxiv f. of the 1896 edition). With
his blazing of the trail, one is able to follow through now
with further additions, explanations of difficult passages,
and restoration of readings that give new illumination to
the book. Through retroversion to the Hebrew, moreover,
we are now able to shed light on other features of Hebrew
style, for example, parallel stichoi, which have been hitherto
unremarked.

Thus, Charles pointed out some eight examples of paronomasia in the Hebrew. Further examination of the text in
the light of this discovery yields about a half dozen more
which he failed to notice. Thus for example, in 4: 3: "It
is not this building which is now built in your midst...." [1]
It is clear that the Hebrew original ran לא הבנין הזה הנבֹנה
ביניכם .... In 15: 8: "For this world is to them a trouble
and a weariness with much labor; and that accordingly
which is to come, a crown with great glory." [2] Probably
"world" and "labor" are played upon: עמל and עולם. The

---

[1] לא הוא הנא בנינא דהשא בנא בינתכון.

[2] הנא גיר עלמא איתוהי להון אגונא ועמלא בליאותא סגיאתא· והו הכיל
דעתיד כלילא בתושבחתא רבתא.

last part is not quite what Charles supposed עטרה בתפארת
רבה but rather פאר בתפארת רבה. For the purpose of the
paronomasia, פאר "headdress" may take over the significa-
tion of "glory." Comp. the verb פאר. 29: 6. "And those who
have hungered will rejoice: moreover, also, they will behold
marvels every day." [1] The Hebrew probably ran יראו נוראות.
35: 5: "But now our glorying has been made into dust, and
the desire of our soul into sand." [2] הפכה תפארתנו לאפר ותוחלת
נפשנו לחול 44: 10: "For that which runs now runs into
vanity, and that which prospers will quickly fall and be
humiliated." [3] הנבהל רץ להבל והמשכיל יפל וישפל or perhaps
והמשכיל יכשל וישפל. This fondness for paronomasia is
perhaps most fully documented in 51: 7: "But those who
have been saved by their works, and to whom the law has
now been a hope, and understanding an expectation, and
wisdom a confidence, to them wonders will appear in their
time..." [4] The passage probably ran:

ואלה אשד נושעו במעשיהם ואשר להם התורה לתקוה והתבונה לתוחלת והבינה
לבטחה להם יראו נוראות בעתם:

The author makes the same play in 29: 6: "They will behold
marvels every day." In 56: 6."...and She'ol to demand" is
obviously a play on words ושאול לשאול 85: 10: "For the
youth of the world is past" is clearly a word-play on עלומים
and עולם. The Apocalypse of IV Ezra has an intimate connection with our book, and in 14: 10 we have there exactly
the same phrase *quoniam saeculum perdidit iuventutem suam
et tempora appropinquant senescere.*

In a different category belong a number of readings
which indicate that the translator, the Greek translator most
likely whose version we do not possess, did not understand

[1] ותוב דין נחזון תדמרתא בכול יום.

[2] השא דין אתעבד עפרא שובהרן ורגתא דנפשן חלא.

[3] הו גיר דרהט השא לסריקותא הו רהט והו דמצלח בעמל נפל ומתחרך.

[4] אילין דין דאתפצין בעבדיהון נמוסא סברא וסכולתנותא סוכיא וחכמתא
הימנותא.

the Hebrew word in front of him. He confused Hebrew roots, wrongly identified words through their common meaning rather than through the more unusual meaning, made stock translations which give an off-the-road rendering, and misconstrued phrases because he did not perceive the drift of the sentence.

Thus for example in 3: 6-7 we have a passage which runs as follows: "Or, how shall one speak of Thy praises? or to whom shall that which is in Thy law be explained? Or shall the world return to its nature, and the age revert to primeval silence? and shall the multitude of souls be taken away, and the nature of man not again be named?" [1]

"The world return to its nature" is puzzling; moreover, the parallelism implies a circumstance of chaos and desolation in which the world would find itself at the beginning. Because the translator anticipated "nature of man" in the following verse (presumably ושם אדם לא יזכר עוד) he thought he saw the same thing in our present phrase. For sense, however, and for the appropriate parallel, the Hebrew probably ran ושבה הארץ לְשַׁמָּה which the translator misunderstood and associated with שֵׁם i.e. לִשְׁמָה.

13: 5-6 likewise contains a misreading: "Thou and those like thee may say to them (even) ye who have seen: 'This evil and (these) retributions which are coming upon you and your people (are sent) in this time that the nations may be perfectly chastened.' And then they will *expect*" [2] "Expect" ends rather abruptly. Expect what? It seems likely that the translator was at fault. Apparently, the underlying Greek read יֶחֱלוּ instead of יָחִילוּ. Translate: "Then they shall *quake*." Incidentally, in v. 11 following, the translation should not be: "But now, ye people and nations, ye are debtors because all this time ye have trodden down the earth, and

---

[1] הפךְ לה תצביתא לכינה ועלמא תוב אזל לשתקא
Observe that תצביתא is a Syriac mistranslation of χοσμος meaning 1) world 2) adornment.

[2] והידין נקוון

used the creation unrighteously," [1] but, as the Syriac suggests, the original text probably was in the Hebrew תְּחוּבוּ
or אַתֶּם חַיָּבִים "you will be *condemned*." Another mistranslation is found in 21:23: "Reprove therefore the angel of
death, and let Thy glory appear, and let the might of Thy
beauty be known..." "Beauty" is queer. [2] The word תפארה
was the problem word for the translator. He thought it
should be translated as "beauty," but it should have been
rendered as "glory." Then in 23:5 the translator confused
the word "creation" for "creature." The passage runs:
"Unless therefore the number aforesaid is fulfilled, the creature
will not live again... and Sheol will receive the dead." [3]
The word required in this context, however, is not "creature"
but "creation." The Hebrew בריאה can bear both meanings.
Very interesting in this connection is the fact that the same
mistranslation in IV Ezra 13:26 where the Son of Man (the
Messiah) is supposed to deliver "his creature," the correct
translation should be "creation." In 8:47 of the same book,
though our quotation begins at v. 46, the passage reads:
"Then he answered me and said, 'Things present are for
them that now be, and things to come for such as shall be
hereafter. For Thou comest far short that thou shouldst be
able to love my creature (*meam creaturam*) more than I'."
It is obvious that "creation" should be read. Exactly the
same mistake was made again in 5:45. Since it is acknowledged on all hands that there is an interrelation between
the two books, it is interesting though not surprising that
the same mistranslations should occur in both apocalypses.

   Chapter 27, in which God replies to the question as to how
long the trials will lengthen which presage the new world to
come, describes the twelve divisions of time which precede
the new dawn: commotions, slaying of great princes, death,

---

[1]   חיבין אנתון.
[2]   רבות יאיותך.
[3]   לא חיא בריתא.

desolation etc. The twelfth division will be chaos in the ming-
ling together of all those things aforesaid (v. 13). Vv. 14-15
continue: "For these parts of that time are reserved, and
will be mixed with one another and will minister one to
another. 15. For some will of themselves be of service, and
they will receive from others, and from themselves and others
they will be perfected..."[1] It seems quite probable that
we have an error in transmission. Because v. 15 started with
"will be of service," the translator in anticipation rendered
at the end of v. 14 "For these parts of that time... will
minister to one another." It can be only conceived with
difficulty how one part of time can minister to another part.
The *first* part of v. 14 "will be mixed with one another" gives
us the clue as to what took place. The Hebrew verb of v. 14
was most likely יערבו "will be mingled." We know of our author's
fondness for paronomasia and therefore we will not be wrong
to assume יעברו for the second half: "For these parts of
that time....*will pass* one to another. However, the translator read ויעבדו!

In one passage 44:15 a mistranslation is recognizable
almost at once. It is apparent that the translator was not
completely familiar with the nuances of ריב and רבב. The
text reads (v. 14): "These are they who have acquired for
themselves treasuries of wisdom.... and from mercy have
they not withdrawn... (v. 15). For to them will be given the
world to come, but the dwelling of the rest *who are many*
will be in the fire."[1] It is clear that the text demands the
dwelling of the rest who *contended, rebelled* will be in the fire.
The translator did not understand the phrase אשר רבו.

Then again in 48:4 as another instance: "Thou makest
known the multitude of the fire, and Thou weighest the light-
ness of the wind."[1] The "multitude of fire" of course is

---

[1] והוין מחלטן חדא חדא·····וחדא חדא משמשין.

[2] מעמרהון דין דשרכא דסגיאא בנורא הוא.

[3] סוגאא דנורא.

strange. It seems probable that the author originally intended "sparks of fire" (רביבי אש) which the translator misunderstood.

A puzzling syntactical construction is cleared up in 64: 3 when we retrovert to the Hebrew original: "And he (Manasseh) made an image with five faces: four of them looked to the four winds, and the fifth on the summit of the image as an adversary of the zeal of the Mighty One." [1] First of all, "zeal" is mistranslated. The Hebrew was undoubtedly קנאה and in the context here means "provocation to anger," Deut 32: 6, Ps 73: 58. Then the construction is an objective genetive, not subjective. Translate: "...a *satan* to provoke the Lord of Hosts." The Hebrew probably was שטן לקנאת יי׳ צבאות. Similarly, in 63: 1 we have "And the eight bright waters which thou hast seen, this is the rectitude and uprightness of Hezekiah king of Judah and his benignity (טיבותה) which came upon him." Charles regards the reading as wrong without attempting a solution. It seems quite likely that the "bounty, kindness" that is referred to is the fifteen years more of life than God vouchsafed to Hezekiah when he prayed for God's mercy. The original Hebrew was probably חַסְדוֹ which means the "kindness extended to him" by God, signalized here by the attention it receives from the author.

Finally a better translation secured through retroversion from the Hebrew is to be recognized in 69: 2. The passage with the correction reads as follows: "For the last waters which thou hast seen which were darker than all that were before them..... For the Most High made division from the beginning (*read*: made allotment from the beginning) because he alone knows what will befall." The translator did not get the complete sense of the passage and mistranslated חלק "divided" instead of "made allotment."

There are a few examples that presuppose slight changes

---

[1] איך דלוקבל טננה דחילתנא. Perhaps דלקובל is for the more usual דלוקבל "adversary."

in the Hebrew. Thus in 5: 3 we have a passage which runs:
"And thou wilt see with thine own eyes that the enemy will
not overthrow Zion, nor burn Jerusalem, but be subservient
to the Judge for a time." [1] It is quite clear from the preceding
verse what it is: "My judgment (God's), moreover, will
preserve its rights in its time," and since God is speaking,
the word "judge" is inappropriate in the context. It seems
probable that "judgment" should be read לְדִין for לַדַּין. It is
quite likely that the Syriac via the Greek lost in transmission
the idiomatic phrase which we can only guess at. Perhaps
יִשָׁמְעוּ לָדִין לְעִדָּן, "They will pay heed to the judgment for
a time."

In one passage, Baruch seeks an answer to the eternal
question as to how long will the wicked prosper, and how
long they will continue to enjoy themselves in their wickedness.
However the question is not quite put that way. The text
reads: (21: 19) "How long will that which is corruptible
remain, and how long will the time of mortals be prospered,
and until what time will those who transgress in the world
be polluted with much wickedness?" It is surely of no concern
to anyone as to why the wicked should be polluted, but rather
as the parallel clearly indicates: why do they live so long,
or prosper so long? I think that the text originally read
יְהוֹלֵלוּ, "live in a libertine fashion, live riotously" which
would suit our context very well. The translator read some
form חלל, "pollute."

In the same chapter, two verses later, there is a trace of a
doublet or gloss which, when removed, restores the correct
reading. The text reads: "And show to those who know not,
and let them see that it has befallen us and our city until
now according to the longsuffering of Thy power, because on
account of Thy name Thou hast called us a beloved people"
(31: 21). The Syriac renders אִיךְ נגירות רוחא דאוחדנך. One
reader apparently did not understand that the long-suffering

---

[1] אלא לדינא משמשין לזבנא.

and the forgiveness of God allowed the city's survival until now. It was not God's vindictiveness that caused the city's fall; rather his forbearance which permitted it to exist. A reader therefore glossed the text with "power" to annul "long-suffering." That is, he glossed the text with כוח as if questioning רוח. His gloss was then incorporated into the text. However, ארך רוח כוח, as the text would offer, is an impossible combination.

Faulty readings in the text, however, are not only due to confusions in the original text of the Hebrew. We must turn a critical glance on the other versions of the Greek and Syriac. In one instance at least a corrupt reading is to be attributed to the Greek. The passage reads from the Syriac (39: 5): "And after these things a fourth kingdom will arise, whose power will be harsh and evil far beyond those which were before it, and it will rule many times (וזבֹא סגינֹא) as the forests on the plain, and it will hold fast the times, and will exalt itself more than the cedars of Lebanon." It is obvious that the phrase "will rule many times" has something wrong with it. It is quite likely that κυρεία and καῖρος in one of the forms were confused with one another. Perhaps the Greek read κυριευσει κυρειας πολλης or κυριευσει κυρειαν πολλην. Our verse is not only an echo of Dan 11: 3 or 11: 5 but would be the precise usage of the Greek there. Translate therefore: "And it will rule over many dominions as the forests on the plain." Probably "trees" of the plain are meant actually. In 7: 2 where the Syriac has an impossible ואחדתוניהי "and you have seized it," we should read ורוחא אחדרתני, "And the Spirit returned me to the place where I had been standing before."

עתידה להתקיים· תם ונשלם שבח לבורא עולם· והארכתי
בזה לפני מזה בן מזה· נגש והוא נענה, כי יבין ויש מענה· [1]

[1] בין ההדפסה להגהה עלה בידי לזהות את ר' יוסף שלום אשר ענה על
אגרות אבנר· ר' שלמה אבן צרצה (סרסה) מביא בספרו ''מקור חיים'' על אבן
עזרא פרוש אחד בשמו· עיין מקור חיים על שמות ג· טו (מרגליות טובה,
אמסטרדם תפ'ב, מו· ב): אמר המחבר זהו לשון החכם ר' יוסף שלום בפרוש
זאת המימרא· הפרוש מכיל באור מתמטי ארוך ומסובך· משה שטיינשניידר
מונה את ר' יוסף שלום על סמך הפרוש הזה בין המתמטיקאים היהודיים של ימי
הביניים· עיין M. Steinschneider, "Die Mathematik bei den Juden",
Bibliotheca Mathematica (1898), 87,

כמו כן עלה בידי לזהות את החכם ר' חיים ישראל· זהו החכם ר' חיים
ישראל ב'ר יצחק הרופא מטולידה אשר העתיק את הספר ארגוזא של אבן
סינא מערבית לעברית· ר' חיים ישראל ידוע כמעתיק ספרים וכמחבר של
ספרים פילוסופיים· עיין עליו David Kaufmann, Gesammelte Schriften,
(Frankfurt a. M., 1908-1915), vol. iii, pp. 178, 475 ff.

וכו' [טו·יא] ואחר כן ביאר גבול מערב· יתחייב מאלו הפסוקים
שאדום בדרום ופלשתים בצפון· ועוד אפילו נודה לדבר
שאדום ופלשתים בדרום על כרחך צד דרום יחלק לפחות
לשני חלקים דרומית מזרחית ודרומית מערבית ואיפשר שיהיה
ארץ אדום בצד האחד ופלשתים בחלק האחר או ההפך ולא
יתחייב בעבור שיתוף השם של נגב שיהיה הארץ האחת שהיא
כפלשתים היא האחת אלא אם כן תהא גזירה שוה וכבר אמרו
חכמים ז"ל אין אדם דן גזירה שוה מעצמו אלא אם כן קבלה
מרבו ורבו מרבו עד הר סיני[1]· ומי שאין לו חלק ונחלה עם
זרע ישראל לא תדרוש ועוד שפירש אמר הכתוב כי צרפתה
היא מצדון לא מאדום כמו שאמר הכתוב· לך אל צרפתה
אשר לצדון [מ'א יז·ט] וכן שם ספרד לא נמצא בכתוב שהיא
מארץ אדום אלא אם היא ספרה והיא במזרח בואכה ספרה
הר הקדם [בראשית י·ל] ועוד שאפילו אודה לדברים שצרפת
וספרד הם שמות הערים הנזכרות לא מצינו בשום מקום
שישראל גלו לשם ואם תחשוב לגלות מיתתו של (אנטיוכס)
[אנטיפס] בן הורודוס שמת במאסר על ידי תבריגוס קיסר כל
זה אחר הורקנוס כמה שנים ואם כן נבואת עובדיה עתידה
להתקיים שאמר הגולים לצרפת ולספרד ירשו את ערי הנגב·
ואחר כך· ועלו מושיעים בהר ציון לשפוט את הר עשיו והיתה
לי"י המלוכה· וכל זה עדיין לא נתקיים כי לא מצינו אחר כך
שיצאו ישראל מתחת יד הרומיים וכמו כן לא מצינו שירשו את
ארץ הנגב ולא עלו לשפוט את הר עשו· והכתוב אמר· והיה
י"י למלך על כל הארץ ביום ההוא יהיה י"י אחד ושמו
אחד [זכריה יד·ט] ועדיין אנחנו רואים כל האומות מורדים
בזאת האמונה שלכם[2] ויתחייב מזה בהכרח שנבואת עובדיה

---

[1] פסחים פו·א·

[2] עיין בוכוח הרמב"ן, אוצר וכוחים ליהודה איזנשטיין (ניו־יורק תרפ"ח),
ע' 90· ע"ג במאמרי בסורא א (ירושלים־ניו־יורק תשי"ד), ע' 171·

של ארץ ישראל אבל צרפת וספרד הנזכרות באותו פסוק
הן בארץ שהיא מנגב לים האמצעי ומנגב לירושלים שנאמר
והיה לכם פאת נגב ממדבר צין על ידי אדום [במדבר לד· ג]
וכתב רבנו (משה) שלמה ז"ל כי לכך נקראת ארץ אדום תימן
לפי שהיה בדרומא של ארץ ישראל ומצינו צרפת בארץ
פלשתים וצידון מנגב לירושלים ושם ישב אליהו התשבי כאשר
נאמר לו קום לך צרפתה אשר בצידון ואומר· ויקם וילך
צרפתה [מ"א יז· ט-ו] וכן ספרד היא עיר סמוכה לים מארץ
אדום ושם מת(אנטיוכס) [אנטיפס] בן הורודוס במאסר על ידי
תבריאנוס קיסר כמו שכתוב בספר יוסף בן גריון ובסדר קבלה
עד כאן לשונך· דע כי במה שאמרתי למעלה יש תשובה לזאת
ולכן לא הבאתי במה שקדם מדברי ראיה על אבדן של אדום
מנבואת עובדיה אלא מנבואת ירמיה כדי שלא ישאר שום ספק
בענין אבל מכל מקום יש ויש להקשות· והתירוץ שתירצת
אינו כלום ויש להשיב על טענותיך אע"פ שאין צורך לבטל
דבר הבטול מעצמו· כי מה שהובאת לראיה שארץ אדום היא
בדרומה של ארץ ישראל ופלשתים גם כן וצרפת בארץ
פלשתים וצידון מנגב· ההפך יראה מן הכתובים כשבא
להגביל הארצות שלא כבשם אומר· ויהושע זקן בא בימים
והארץ נשארה הרבה מאד לרשתה זאת הארץ הנשארת כל
גלילות הפלשתים והגשורי מן השיחור אשר על פני מצרים ועד
גבול עקרון צפונה לכנעני תחשב חמשה סרני פלשתים העזתי
והאשדודי האשקלוני הגתי והעקרוני והעוים [יהושע יג· א-ג]
יראה מאלה הפסוקים שארץ פלשתים בצפון ארץ ישראל לפי
כשבא להגביל ארץ יהודה הנופל בגורלו אמר ויהי הגורל
למטה בני יהודה למשפחותם אל גבול מדבר צין נגבה מקצה
הימין ויהי להם גבול נגב מקצה ים המלח וכו' וגבול קדמה ים
המלח עד קצה הירדן וגבול צפון מלשון הים מקצה
הירדן [שם טו·א-ה], עד· ויצא הגבול אל כתף עקרון צפונה

לא יחסר ולא יוסיף שום דבר בתורה ולא בדברי חכמים ז"ל·
ועם כל זה בעבור שלא תתגאה בחכמתך אקבל בדרך קבלה
מה שאמרת בשמו ואומר אפילו אודה שהנביאים נבאו זאת
הנבואה על מלך הורקנוס שעתיד לכבוש את ארץ אדום
ולהכביד עולו עליהם לא יתחייב מזה שלא יהיה עוד מלחמה
אחרת ושולטנות בישראל על אומת אדום ושזאת הנבואה
הנאמרת בפסוק· ונתתי את נקמתי באדום ביד עמי ישראל·
היא עקירת אומת אדום מן העולם שראוי שיבוא המשיח אחריה
שלא תמצא שאמרו הנביא ולא תוכל לדקדקו משום פסוק·
לא בישר בזאת הנבואה שעתידין להמסר ביד ישראל עם היות
שם נבואות אחרות מעידים על מפלת אדום ועקירתן מן העולם
ואחת מהן נבואת ירמיה שאמר· והיתה אדום לשמה כל עובר
עליה ישום וישרוק על כל מכותיה כמהפכת סדום ועמורה
ושכניה אמר י"י לא ישב שם איש ולא יגור בה בן אדם [שם מט·
יז־יח] יתחייב מזאת כי זאת הנבואה היא אחרת חוץ מנבואת
ונתתי נקמתי באדום ביד עמי ישראל [יחזקאל כה· יד]
שאומרים בשם יוסף בן גריון ובשם ר' דוד קמחי לפי שבזמן
הורקנוס נשארו אדום על ארצם אלא שהיו למס עובד כפי מה
שאמרת בשמו שהיו נכנעים וכבושים תחת יד ישראל כי הכה
אותם המלך הורקנוס וימל אותם ויתן עליהם עבודת ירושלים
לשמור החומות ויתר העם היו למס עובד לבני יהודה· וזה יורה
שנשארו על ארצם ונבואת ירמיה תורה שלא ישאר שם בן אדם
כן יתחייב שנבואת ירמיה עתידה להתקיים ועל כן לא יהרוס
שום דבר מדעת חכמינו בהאמיננו דברי יוסף בן גריון ור' דוד
קמחי ז"ל·

ומה שאמרת ואין להקשות מפסוק וגלות החיל הזה לבני
ישראל אשר כנעניים עד צרפת וגלות ירושלים אשר בספרד
ירשו את ערי הנגב [עובדיה כ] לומר· שצרפת היא פרנסייא
והספרד היא אישפאנייא כי פרנסייא ואישפניא היו בצפונה

יהושע וכן כתוב׳ ולא הוריש (יהושע) [מנשה] את בית שאן
ובנותיה וישם את הכנעני למס והרש לא הורישם [שופטים א׳
כז־כח] לכך אמרו חכמים ז״ל וכשגברה ידם של בית חשמונאי
והגלו אותם משם ואותו היום עשאוהו שמחה כשנעקרה׳ בכך
הדמיון׳ ורוצה לומר׳ כמו אם נעקרה זאת הרשעה מן העולם
שנאמר עליהם׳ ועלו מושיעים בהר ציון לשפוט את הר עשיו
לפי שכתוב הכא בעקירת אומת הרשעה מן העולם׳ והיה י״י
למלך על כל הארץ [זכריה יד׳ט] וכתיב התם בעקירת
הכנעניים׳ י״י מלך עולם ועד אבדו גוים מארצו [תהלים י׳ טז]
ומלך מלך לגזירה שוה׳ שאלו היה כוונת החכם האומרו על
אדום ממש היה לו לומר עשאוהו שמחה שנעקרה אומת הרשעה
מן העולם שנאמר׳ ועלו מושיעים בהר ציון לשפוט׳ וישתוק׳
אלא ודאי להכי אמר אחרי כן׳ אבדו גוים מארצו׳ רמז לארץ
כנען הנקראת ארץ השם׳ על דרך׳ תמיד עיני י״י אלהיך בה
[דברים יא׳יב] ומלך מלך לגזירה שוה ואחרי כן יתמו חטאים
מן הארץ בה׳ ידיעה[1] רמז לארץ הידועה׳

ומה שאמרת בשם יוסף בן גוריון כי בני עשו היו נכנעים
וכבושים תחת יד ישראל כי הכה אותם המלך הורקנוס וימל
אותם ויתן עליהם עבודת ירושלים לשמור את החומות ויתר
העם היו למס לבני יהודה ואז התקיים מה שכתוב׳ ונתתי את
נקמתי באדום ביד עמי ישראל [יחזקאל כה׳יד] עד כאן
לשונך׳

דע כי חפשתי כל דברי יוסף בן גריון ולא מצאתי שאמר זה
הפסוק בשום ענין[2]׳ ואפילו אודה לך שאמרו׳ לא היה יוסף
בן גוריון נביא ולא חכם מחכמי התלמוד ואם לא נאמין לדבריו

[1] עיין Leo Prijs, *Die grammatikalische Terminologie des Abraham Ibn Esra* (Basel 1950), p. 45.
[2] רק החלק הראשון של המאמר נמצא ביוסיפון׳ חסרה שם הראיה מן הפסוק׳
עיין למעלה עמ׳ 8 הערה 5׳

ללכת רוצה לומר ללכת להתהלך זמן רב וכן צוה׃ לכו
התהלכו בכפל הלשון׃ ועל כן יתחייב מכל אלו הראיות
שאמרו חז״ל אמרו אמת שמדי ופרס אומה אחת ומלכות אחת
ואומת רומי מלכות אחת בפני עצמה הנרמזת בחיה הרביעית[1]׃

ומה שאמרת׃ ואין ראוי לומר שהרומיים הם אדום מטעם
שמלך עליהם איש שהיה מאדום כמו שאין קוראים לישראל
אדומיים או רומיים אעפ״י שמלך עליהם הורודוס שהיה
מאדום או מרומי כי אין העניינים הולכים אחר השמות אבל
צריך שיהיה השמות הולכים אחרי עצמות העניינים עד כאן
לשונך׃

דע כי אין זה הערך ערך אמיתי לפי שקונסטנטין הכריח
כל בני ארצו לאמונתו שבדא מלבו והכומר עמו[2] ולכן הוא
היה העיקר והשאר טפלה לו על כן נקראו בשמו ונמצא השם
הולך אחרי עצמימות הדבר אבל הורודוס שב לאמונתם של
ישראל ונתבטלה במיעוט על כן לא נקראו בשמו שהם העיקר
והוא טפל אליהם׃ ומה שאמרת ועוד שכתוב במגילת תענית בי״ו
בסיון גלו אנשי בית שאן ואנשי בקעתה אף הם היו יתד תקועה
לישראל בימי יוונים כלפי הערביים ומפני שלא נתחייבו גלות
בראשונה ולא הגלם יהושע בן נון ולא דוד וכשנתחייבו גלות
גברה ידם של בית חשמונאי והגלו אותם משם ואותו היום
עשאוהו שמחה כשנעקרה מלכות הרשעה מן העולם שנאמר
ועלו מושיעים בהר ציון לשפוט את הר עשיו והיתה לי״י
המלוכה [עובדיה כא] ואומר׃ י״י מלך עולם ועד אבדו גוים
מארצו [תהלים י׳טז] ואומר׃ יתמו חטאים מן הארץ ורשעים
עוד וגו׳ [שם קד׳ לה] עד כאן לשונך׃

דע כי בית שאן ובנותיה ובקעתה הם מארץ כנען ולא מארץ
אדום והדרים שם כנעניים ונשארו עם שאר מדינות שלא כבשם

---

[1] עיין שבועות ו׃ב: ותאכל כל ארעה [דניאל ז׳ כג] א״ר יוחנן זו רומי חייבת׃
[2] עיין במאמרי בתלפיות כנ״ל׃

עליה כאשר אמר בסוף ראה היוצאים אל ארץ צפון הניחו את
רוחי בארץ צפון [שם שם ח]׳ ועל כן צעק אליו כלומר ראה
כי שניהם על צפון בזמן אחד על כן לא תחשוב אותו לשתי
ממלכות ולפי זה העניין והראיות שהבאתי במה שקדם מדברי
ומפסוק הנאמר על בבל בסוף דברי הימים׳ והיו לי ולבני
לעבדים עד מלוך מלכות פרס [דהי״ב לו׳כ] ראיה שמלכות
מדי ופרס נחשבות למלכות אחת ואומה אחת ואחזור לענייני
ואומר׳ אחר שביאר ששני המרכבות האמורות בפרשה שהם
אחת ביאר לו גם כן שהמרכבה האחרונה שבה הסוסים ברודים
אמוצים שהיא נחלק לשתים· והוא אמרו והברודים יצאו אל
ארץ התימן [שם ו] ובזה רמז על מלך יון שהוא אחר פרס
ומדי וממשלתו נתפשט לארץ תימן שהיא הנגב· וכן היה שהרג
תלמי מלך מצרים ולכד כל ארץ מצרים וזה גם כן יורה מה
שאמרתי שמלך הנגב הוא מלך יון ומלך הצפון הוא מלך רומי
וכל זה בערך· ואחר שביאר שקצת המרכבה האחרונה יצא
לארץ תימן והגיד לנו שקצתה האחד יצא והלך בארץ׳ והוא
אמרו והאמוצים יצאו ויבקשו ללכת התהלך בארץ ויאמר
לכו והתהלכו בארץ ותתהלכנה בארץ [שם ו] רמז לו בזה
על מלכות רומי שהיא קצת מבני יון שעתיד להיות נבדל מיון
ולפי שלא תטעה בין צפון הנאמר במרכבה השניה [שם ו]
שהיא צפון האמתי ובין צפון המרכבה האחרונה לא פירש
מקום המרכבה האחרונה ועוד שממשלתו יתפשט במקומות
רבים משונות לפיכך לא יחד מקום ידוע למרכבה המורה על
מלכותו אלא אמר ללכת בארץ׳ וכן היה כי פעמים פשטה
מלכות רומי לדרום והיא ארץ מצרים ולפעמים לצד צפון
והיא בבל והוסיף עוד המלאך לבארו כי זאת המלכות תאריך
ימים על מלכותו משאר המלכיות והוא אמרו אחר מלת ״יוצא״
השוה למרכבות האחרות אמר מלות ״ויבקשו ללכת להתהלך
בארץ״ על שאר המרכבות וכפלו מלת ״להתהלך״ על מלת

על אויביו [יהיו] קיימ[ים] ושלא תרע לישראל עוד שום אומה
הראהו הב''ה והנה ארבע הקרנות שנאמר, ואשא עיני ואראה
והנה ארבע קרנות [שם ב·א] והשיבו המלאך אלה הקרנות
אשר זרו את יהודה ואת ישראל וירושלים [שם שם ב] וכל אלה
הקרנות ראשי אומות וממלכות והם ארבעה ועדיין עתיד
להיות קצת מהם והודיעו אחר כן ארבעה חרשים [שם שם ג]
שהם רמז שיבואו להחריב לאלו הארבעה שנאמר, ויבואו אלה
אשר זרו את יהודה להחריב אותם לידות את קרנות הגוים
הנושאים קרן אל ארץ יהודה לזרותה [שם ב·ד] אחר כך
הראהו בנין בית המקדש עד סוף כל הפרשה· ולפי שחשב
הנביא כי אלה הארבעה קרנות אשר זרו את יהודה שהם כללי
האומות וכי מדי ופרס כל אחד נחשב לאומה בפני עצמה וכי
יון גם כן היא אומה בפני עצמה ושלא נשארה אחריה אלא
אומה אחת להרע לישראל ושכבר עברו השלשה מהארבע
על כן הוצרך לקראו שניה ולהבינו שאין הדבר כמו שחשב
והראהו ד' מרכבות יוצאות מבין שני ההרים [זכריה ו· א] ורמז
לו באלו ארבע המרכבות שכללי האומות המושלות ממשל רב
ועשו רעה לישראל שאינם אלא ארבעה וביאר אחר כן גווני
הסוסים אשר בכל מרכבה ומרכבה כדי להודיעו מכל גוון
מהם אומה הרומזת אליה והיאך נחשב אותם· והוא אמרו
סוסים אדומים והשנית סוסים שחורים והשלישית סוסים לבנים
והרביעית סוסים ברודים אמוצים [שם שם ב] ואחר כך ביאר
ממשלת כל אחת ואחת והאדומים הם רמז למלכות בבל
ובעבור שכבר עבר ובוטל מן העולם לא הוצרך לפרש ענייני
מקומה ואחר כך ביאר עניני שאר המרכבות ואמר שהמרכבה
השנית והשלישית הרומזים על מדי ופרס שהם אחד והוא אמרו
אשר בה הסוסים השחורים יוצאים אל ארץ צפון והלבנים
הולכים אל אחריהם [שם שם ו] ורוצה לומר כי אלה השנים
מיני סוסים יוצאים אל מקום אחד והוא בבל וכי שניהם לחמו

א· ח] והוא רמז לשלשה המלכיות מן הארבע מלכיות אשר
ארבע מרכבות היו רמז אליהם על פי דברי חז״ל· וקודם
שיזכיר את המלכות הרביעית דבר לו המלאך דברים ניחומים
ואמר· שבתי לירושלים ברחמים ביתי יבנה בה [זכריה א· טז]
אבל אחר זה הזכיר את המלכות הרביעית במראה של ארבע
הקרנות [זכריה ב· א· ד] וכן במרכבות סוסים אדומים ברודים
אמוצים [שם ו·א] ונראה מזה כי עד אותו הזמן של זכריה הנביא
נגמר בנין בית המקדש שהיה בקרוב לתכלית מלכות פרס היו
שלש מלכיות מאותם הארבעה ועל כן היו מלכות מדי ופרס
נחשבות לשתי מלכיות מה· ומפני זה היתה מלכות יון היא
הרביעית ולא מלכות אדום עד כאן לשונך·

דע כי המראה הראשונה שראה איש רוכב על סוס אדום
ואחריו סוסים אדומים שרוקים ולבנים [זכריה א·ח] ראה דרך
פרט המלכים שמלכו ובמלכותם הרעו לישראל ושעתיד הב׳ה
לדון וליפרע לעמו מהם ואלה היו מלך בבל ומלך פרס ומלך
מדי ואלה הרעו לישראל ועבר הרעה בימי זכריה והודיעו
המלאך בזאת המראה שהב״ה דן אותם לפי מעשיהם שעשו
לישראל והוא לא הבין ושאל· מה אלה אדוני· והשיבו המלאך·
ואני אראך [שם א·ט] והשיב האיש העומד בין ההדסים כדי
שישמע זכריה ויבין אלה אשר שלח אדוני להתהלך בארץ
[שם א·׳] והרוכבים על הסוסים השיבוהו· התהלכנו בארץ
והנה כל הארץ יושבת ושוקטה [שם א·יא] ואז בקש המלאך או
הנביא שנקרא מלאך [1] רחמים על ישראל ואמר· י״י צבאות
עד מתי אתה לא תרחם את ירושלים ואת ערי יהודה אשר
זעמת זה שבעים שנה [שם א· יב] והשיב לו דברים ניחומים
ובשרו כי השם שקנא קנאת עמו וקוצף על כל הגוים ושעוד יבנה
ירושלים וערי ישראל וכל האמור בפרשה· ולפי שחשב הנביא
שאומת מדי ופרס שתי ממלכות וכי בנין זה הבית וקצף השם

---

[1] רוב המפרשים רואים במלאך ד׳ את האיש העומד בין ההדסים של פסוק י·

ושניהם המלכים לבבם למרע ועל שולחן אחד כזב ידברו
[שם יא· כז] כמו על יראתם שהוא אחד [1].

ומה שאמרת כי בסוף כל אותן המלכיות אמר׳ ובעת ההיא
יעמוד מיכאל השר הגדול העומד על בני עמך [שם יב· א]
וכשהזכיר אותם במראה השניה אמר שאחרי מלכות יון תהיה
הישועה לישראל כי יעמוד מיכאל השר הגדול ולא הכניס
ביניהם מלכות אחרת וכמו שנאמר׳ ועתה אשוב להלחם
עם שר פרס ואני יוצא והנה שר יון בא אבל אגיד לך את הרשום
בכתב אמת ואין אחד מתחזק עמי על אלה כי אם מיכאל שרכם
[שם י· כ-כא] וזה יורה שמלכות יון היתה האחרונה מאותן
המלכיות כי אין אחריה אלא מלכות ישראל אשר מיכאל
מתחזק להקימה עד כאן לשונך· דע כי לכל אומה ואומה שר
ידוע כמו שנאמר שר פרס שר יון מיכאל שרכם [שם י· כ-כא] וזה
השר עומד על כל פעם ופעם שיבוא שום רעה על עמו [2] וזה
המלאך שאמר דניאל כי עמד עמו· הוא היה הלוחם לא מיכאל
אלא שמיכאל עזרוהו שנאמר׳ והנה מיכאל בא לעזרני [דניאל
י·יג] כמו שעזר אותו הוא פעם אחרת שנאמר׳ ואני בשנה אחת
לדריוש עמדי למחזיק ולמעוז לי [שם יא· א] ר״ל שעזר אותו
על שר בבל כשמלך דריוש ואין זה העזר שמיכאל עוזר לאחרים
נקרא הקמתו של מיכאל אלא הקמת האחר· ואם היה הקמת
מיכאל היה האחר עוזר למיכאל לו לפיכך נשארה הקמת
מיכאל לסוף מלכות רומי· והראיה שהבאת מר׳ אברהם ן׳
עזרא סוף דבריו באותו ענין תשובתך על כן לא אביאנו בזאת
התשובה· ומה שאמרת וכן יתבאר בנבואת זכריה שבתחילה
ראה זכריה שלשה מיני סוסים אדומים שרוקים ולבנים [זכריה

1 כוונתו לנצרות הקאטולית־רומאית ולנצרות היוונית־ביזנטינית·

2 עיין חכמת בן סירא יז·יז (הוצאת מ·צ· סגל (ירושלים תשי״ג), עמ׳ קג):
לכל גוי הקים שר· ע׳׳ג תרגום יונתן על דברים לב·ח; George Foot Moore,
Judaism, vol. i, (Cambridge 1927), p. 227; L. Ginzberg, *Legends of
the Jews*, vol. v (Philadelphia, 1925), pp. 204-205.

עליה החיה השלישית והביא עניינים מתחילת מלכותם עד
שנבדלו מהם האומה המורה עליה החיה הרביעית וביאר
היאך כי ידוע הוא לאשר עינים להם לראות כי הרומיים הם
יונים כי כתים בן יון היה שנאמר׳ ובני יון אלישה ותרשיש כתים
ודודנים [בראשית י׳ד] והיו למלכות אחת ולאחר שמת
אלסכנדר נחלקו לשני ממלכות למלכות מקדוניא ולמלכות
רומי׳ ומלכות מקדוניא נקראת בזאת המראה מלכות הנגב
[דניאל י׳א ה׳ ו׳ ט׳ י׳א י׳ד׳ ט׳ו כה] וכן הוא מפורש במראה
השניה׳ וצפיר העזים הגדיל עד מאד ובעצמו נשברה הקרן
הגדולה ותעלינה חזות ארבע לארבע רוחות השמים ומן האחת
מהם יצא קרן אחת מצעירה והגדיל יתר אל הנגב [דניאל ח׳
ח־ט] ר״ל שיהיה מלכותו בצד נגב וכן היא ארץ הנקראת יון
דרומית וארץ רומי צפונית׳ ואין להקשות ממצרים שנקרא
נגב כי היא נגב הנגב ¹ וכן ארץ כוש נגב למצרים וכן ויעלו בנגב
[במדבר י׳ג כד] והיא ארץ ישראל שהיא צפונית למצרים ועל
כן אמר בזאת המראה הרביעית על מלכות יון׳ ובעמדו תשבר
מלכותו ותחץ לארבע רוחות השמים ולא לאחריתו ולא במשלו
אשר משל כי תנתש מלכותו ולאחרים מלבד אלה ויחזק מלך
הנגב [דניאל י׳א ד־ה] ר׳ל אעפ׳י שנתחלק מלכותו למלכיות
רבות ויחזק מלך הנגב וכן אמר במראה השניה ותגדל יתר אל
הנגב [שם ח׳ט] שזה נאמר על אנטיוכס ומלך הצפון נלחם
עמו שהוא מלכות היוצא ממנו מאומת יון שנחשב לאומה אחרת׳
ופסוק׳ ועמד על כנו נבזה [שם י׳א כא] נאמר על מלך רומי ²
שהוא מכונה באדום הנקרא בזאת הפרשה מלך הצפון לא על
מלך יון וזה הנרמז בחיה הרביעית׳ והראיה הגדולה שמלך
הנגב הוא מלך יון ומלך הצפון הוא מלך רומי מה שאמר

---

¹ רש׳י ואבן עזרא מבארים נגב כפרק ח, פסוק ט: מצרים׳
² עיין ברש׳י על אתר׳

התמיד ונהרג המשיח· ולפי שבזאת השבוע אירעו דברים רבים
משונים פתר אותה בפני עצמה והוא אמרו אחר כך· ואחרי
השבועים ששים שנים יכרת המשיח [שם ט·כו] וזה הוא אגריפס[1]
ואין לו והעיר והקדש ישחית עם נגיד הבא [שם שם שם] רוצה
לומר ואחרי זמן שיעברו השבועות ששים ושנים יכרת והיא
השבוע הנשאר ואלו ר״ל בסוף השבועים ששים ושנים היה
אומר מלת אחרי· ועוד היה לו לומר ושבועים ששים ושנים
תשוב ונבנתה רחוב וחרוץ ובצוק העתים ויכרת משיח והעיר
והקדש ישחית עם נגיד הבא אלא לכך הפסיק במלת ובצוק
העתים להפריש מן החשבון השבוע הנשארת ושבזאת השבוע
הנשארת יארעו דברים אחרים כאשר פירש בסוף וקצו בשטף
ועד קץ מלחמה נחרצת שוממות· ר״ל וקצו בשטף כי לקיצו
יבא אספסינוס באניות ותאריך המלחמה שנים רבות כאשר
אמר ועד קץ מלחמה שהיתה ירושלים נחרצת שוממות ור״ל
ולקץ לזמן וזה לפי סברת החכם ר׳ אברהם ן׳ עזרא ז״ל וזה
היה בשבוע האחרון· ולפי שאמר שהמלחמה תאריך ימים ואחר
כך יכרת המשיח ותחרב הבית ולא אמר כמה חשבון אלה
הימים חזר ופרט אותה ואמר· והגביר ברית לרבים שבוע אחד
[שם שם כח] רוצה לומר כי טיטוס ואספסינוס עשו ברית עם
ישראל עד שבוע שלם ובחצי השבוע יפרו הברית וילחמו חצי
השבוע עד שהשביתהו זבח ומנחה עד כלה ונחרצה·ובמראה
הרביעית פירש עניני החיה הרביעית וביאר שנתילדה מהחיה
הרביעית המורה עליה החיה השלישית· לפיכך התחיל וביאו׳
בזאת המראה מה שכבר נתבאר במראות השלשה שעברו·
ולפי שזאת המראה הרביעית המבארת עיקר עניני החיה
הרביעית ושזאת האומה המורה עליה החיה הרביעית נתיילדה
מהאומה המורה עליה החיה השלישית הוצרך להביא בתחילה
המראה הרביעית ענין המראה השניה המבארת ענין יון המורה

1 עיין ברש״י על דניאל ט· כו·

שיעמוד זמן רב או לעולם אלא דע כבר נגמר לפני השם
להחריבה׳ והודיעהו המלאך כי מתחילה נגזר חורבן הבית
אשר הוא מבקש בניינו עתה ושלא נשלמו עדיין שני גליות׳
האחד להבנות ירושלים העתידה ליחרב והוא שאמרו׳ שבועים
שבעים נחתך על עמך ועל עיר קדשך ולכלה הפשע ולהתם
חטאת ולכפר עון ולהביא צדק עולמים ולחתום חזון ונביא
ולמשוח קדש הקדשים [שם ט׳ כז] בזה הפסוק כלל רצון ישראל
וטובותם עד שיחרב הבית השני׳ כי מלות׳ לכלה פשע ולהתם
חטאת ולכפר עון כנוי לעונש׳ ולהביא צדק עולמים ולחתום
חזון ונביא כנוי הטובות׳ ורוצה לומר׳ לחתום חזון שהנביאים
נתבאו על הבית למשוח קדש קדשים[1] או יהיה פרוש ולחתום
חזון ונביא שיפסקו הנביאים׳ ולחתום משיח קדש קדשים ומלת
ולחתום מושכת עצמה ואחרת עמה׳ לפי סברת ר׳ אברהם ן׳
עזרא ז״ל ואחר שאמר השבועות דרך כלל החזירם דרך פרט
ואמר׳ ותדע תשכיל מן מוצא דבר [שם ט׳ כה] ר״ל לחרבות
ירושלים עד משיח נגיד שהוא כורש או זרובבל או הכהן הגדול
שבועים ושהם מ״ט שנה ושנה אחת לכורש הרי חמשים לגלות
שהם שבעים שנה למלכות בבל שהוא שנת הפקידה לא כמו
שחשב לפי מלאת לבבל שבעים שנה יבנה הבית אלא יפקדו
כמו שאמר׳ אפקוד אתכם [ירמיה כט׳ י] כאשר עשה כורש
אחר כן אמר׳ ושבועים ששים ושנים תשוב ונבנתה רחוב וחרוץ
ובצוק העתים [דניאל ט׳ כה] אמר כי זמן השנים שישב הבית
אחר הפקידה בלא בנין עם זמן שנים שישב בנויה שיהיה זמן
הכל׳ שבועים ששים ושנים׳ ולפי שכלל השנים שהם הבנין עם
שנות הבנין אמר ובצוק העתים ושבעה שהיו מזמן החורבן עד
משיח נגיד שהוא שנת הפקידה יהיה הכל תשעה וששים ונשארה
שבוע אחד להשלים השבעים שבועות והיא השבוע שבטל

---

[1] עיין באבן עזרא על דניאל ט׳כד: וטעם ולחתום חזון שכל הנביאים התנבאו
על דבר בית שני׳

כת׳ למה שאמר אחריה׳ וארו חיוא אחרי תנינא דמיא לדוב
ובסטר חד הקימת ותלת עילעין בפומה בין שינה [שם ז׳ ה]׳
ולא אמר בתר דנא כאשר אמר זה׳ לפי שהיה נפילתה סמוך
ובאחרות שהאריכו זמן גדול לזמן דניאל הוצרך לבאר
פרטיהם לפיכך במראה השנית התחיל לפרט ענין החיה
השנית הרומזת על מלכות פרס ולפי שלא נתחדש במלכותם
ענין זה שיעמוד זמן אלא ענין המן שהיה משלשה
עשר בניסן עד חולו של פסח שהם חמשה ימים לא יותר
כמו שכתוב במגלה.[1] על כן לא האריך וחזר לבאר ענין החיה
השלישית הרומז על מלכות יון׳ ובאר שלטן המלך הראשון
מיתתו ושולטנות הארבעה מלכים אחריו׳ והניח לבאר ענין
השלשה לפי שלא הרעו לישראל באותו זמן אלא יון אלא לבד׳
לפיכך באר כל הרעה שעשה לישראל׳ ומכל מקום אעפ״י
שלא ביארו המלאך עניינים הודיעו כי אלה הארבעה מלכים
היו מאומת יון׳ וכן אמר הכתוב ארבע מלכיות מגוי יעמודנה
ולא בכחו [שם ח׳ כב] ר״ל מגוי מאותו עם שאם היו מאומות
אחרות היה לו לשתוק ממלת ״מגוי״ ולומר ארבע מלכיות
יעמודנה ולא בכחו והודיעו גם שזאת [שזה] המלך המולך על
ארץ יון לא על רומי יתפשט מלכותו בנגב כי רומי היא צפונית
לארצו ואחרי שהשלים ממשלת אנטיוכס והרע שהרע לישראל
וכמה זמן יעמוד הרע ההוא ספק ולא זכר בכאן לא עמידת
מיכאל ולא שום דבר אחר׳ אחר כן במראה השלישית לא באר
שום דבר אלא היה מתפלל שיודיעהו דבר אחר שהיה נבוך
בה׳ והוא שאמר הנביא׳ כה אמר י״י כי לפי מלאת לבבל
שבעים שנה אפקוד אתכם [ירמיה כ׳ טי] והיה סובר כי כבר
עברו שבעים שנה ולא נגאלו והיה תמה כי נביא השם לא יכזב
והודיעוהו ביאור הענין שלא היה כמו שהוא חושב ואגב גררא
הודיעוהו׳ לא תחשוב כי זאת הבית אשר מבקש רחמים עליה

[1] עיין מגילה ט״ו א׳ ע״ג רש״י, שם, ד״ה יום טוב הראשון של פסח.

על מלכות רומי הנקראת מלך הצפון [1] לאחר שנבדלת ממלכות
יון לפי הראיות והטעמים שאמרתי מתחילת התשובה ועד עתה,
ואין צריך לכפול הדברים בלי תוספת על כן לא אשנה בהם.
אבל אגיד לך ראיה אחרת שלא זכרתיה לפי שזה מקומה והיא
זאת. דע כי דניאל ראה מראות האחת ומראה ארבע החיות
עד ומלתא בלבי נטריה [שם ז· כח] בשנת שלש למלכות בלשצר
[שם ח·א] והוא ענין האיל והצפיר עד ומראה הערב והבקר
אשר ראית אחת היא [שם ח·כו] והשלישית בשנת אחת לדריוש
בן אחשורוש מזרע מדי [שם ט·א] ומתחלת בתחלה יצא
דבר עד כלה ונחרצה תתך על שומם [שם ט·כג־כז] והרביעית
בשנת שלש לכורש מלך פרס [שם י·א] עד סוף הספר· ואין
להקשות מפסוק, ואני בשנה אחת לדריוש המדי [שם יא· א] כי
הוא מאמר גבריאל למה שנאמר, ואין איש מתחזק עמי על אלה
כי אם מיכאל שרכם [שם י·כא] שרוצה לומר ואין מתחזק עמי
לעזרני לנגד השרים העליונים כי אם מיכאל ואם עתה עזרני
ואם בשנה אחת לדריוש המדי עמדתי למחזיק ולמעוז לו [שם
יא· א] שעזרתיו [2]· ולפי שזאת החיה הרביעית היא הגדולה
והנמשכת לזמן רחוק והיא עיקר גלות ישראל הארוך והאפל
כשהראהו במראה הראשונה מראה הארבע חיות הרומזות על
הארבע מלכיות ביאר לו מיד פרטי הרביעית בדרך כלל·
ודע כי המראה הראשונה מאלו הארבעה מראות ראה אותה
בדרך כלל והשלשה האחרות הם פירוש זאת המראה הראשונה
ולפי שראה זאת המראה בימי בלשצר שהוא המלך האחרון
שמלך על מלכות בבל· והוא היה המין והאיש לא הוצרך
לפרט דבר מהחיה הראשונה כי אין שם דבר מחוכם ופתרונה

---

1   עיין אבן עזרא על דניאל יא· ה: מלך הצפון שהוא מלך ארם (ז״א רומי)·
על ארם־רומי עיין גטין יז:א; מדרש בראשית רבא סג:ז (הוצאת תיאודור־
אלבק, 686)·
2   עיין באבן עזרא על דניאל י·כא·

שהיא מלכות אנטיוכס מלך יון שהיא המלכות הפחות והקטן
מן הארבעה שהוא אחר אלסכנדר ואמר המלך הקטן יגדל
יתר אל הנגב שנאמר, ותגדל יתר אל הנגב ואל הצבי ותגדיל
עד צבא השמים ותפול ארצה מן הצבא ומן הכוכבים ותרמסם
ועד שר הצבא הגדיל וממנו הורם התמיד עד ערב בקר אלפים
ושלש מאות ונצדק קדש [דניאל ח. ט–ד] והם ימים ר״ל אלפים
ושלש מאות ערב ואלפים ושלש מאות בקר שהם הכל ששה
שנים וחצי שנה בקרוב שעמדו ישראל בצרה גדולה בימי
אנטיוכס[1] וכן כתוב בספר יון[2], אם כן מה שאמרת שאמר בחיה
הרביעית, ומילין לצד עילאה ימלל [שם ז. כה] הוא בעצמו
שאמר במראה השנית במלכות יון, ובאחרית מלכותם עד
ונפלאות ישחית [שם ח. כג] ובל האמור שם אינו אמת מהטעם
שאמרתי כי האחד מדבר על הרעה שיארע לישראל אנטיוכס
מלך יון והאחד מדבר על הרעה שיארע המלך העשירי המולך
באומה אשר החיה הרביעית מורה עליה ולא ראי זה
כראי זה.

ומה שאמרת, וכמו כן אמר במראה האחרונה לסוף מלכות
יון, ועמד על כנו נבזה ולא נתנו עליו הוד מלכות והחזיק
מלכות בחלקלקות [שם יט. כא] ואמר, וישוב ארצה ברכוש
גדול ולבבו על ברית קדש ועשה [שם יא. כח] וזרועים ממנו
יעמדו וחללו המקדש המעוז והסירו התמיד [שם יא. לא] כי
ענין והשחית עצומים הוא ענין ולקדישי עליונין יבלא וכן הוא
ענין, ולבבו על ברית קדש ועשה, וכן הוא ענין, וחללו המקדש
המעוז והסירו התמיד הוא ענין ויסבר להשניא זמנין ודת וזה
יורה שמלכות יון היא המלכות הרביעית אשר החיה הרביעית
מורה עליה עכ״ל.

דע שהפסוק, ועמד על כנו נבזה, עד, וחללו המקדש, ואמר

[1] עיין אבן עזרא על אתר.
[2] עיין באבן עזרא על דניאל ח.כה.

מלכים ¹ כמו שפירש וקרניא עשר מיניה מלכותא מלכין יקומון
ואחרן יקום אחריהון והוא ישנא מן קדמיא ותלתא מלכין
יהשפיל ומלין לצד עילאה ימלל ולקדישי עליונין יבלא ויסבר
להשניא זמנין ודת, וכל האמור שם, ומה שאמר, ובאחרית
מלכותם כהתם הפושעים [ח. כג] לאמר על אנטיוכס מלך יון
הבא שני לאלסכנדר שהוא המלך הראשון ². ואין להקשות
ממה שאמר, ובאחרית מלכותם שרוצה לומר אחרית כל
המלכים ושהיו שם קודם אנטיוכס מלכים רבים והוא היה
עשירי מאלסכנדר ³ לפי שזה הענין ובאחרית מלכותם וכו'
הנאמר במראה השנית הוא ביאור המשל שראה באיל וצפיר
העזים. וכן פירשו המלאך, כי האיל אשר ראית בעל הקרנים
מלכי מדי ופרס וצפיר העזים הגדיל עד מאד [שם ח.כ]
ובעצמו נשברה הקרן הגדולה הוא אלסכנדר כאשר אמר,
והקרן הגדולה אשר בין עיניו [שם ח.כא] הוא המלך הראשון,
ומה שראה ותעלינה חזות ארבע תחתיה לארבע רוחות השמים
[שם ח.ח] הוא מה שפירשו והנשברת ותעמודנה ארבע תחתיה
ארבע מלכויות מגוי יעמודנה ולא בכחו [שם ח.כב] ולפי שלא
צר לישראל בתחילת מלכות אלה אלא בסוף כי כן תמצא
שקודם לכך הרג תלמי מלך מצרים ובסוף מלכות אנטיוכס
הצר לישראל ובעבור זה אמר, ובאחרית מלכותם וגו' ועצם
כחו וגו' והשחית עצומים ועל שכלו והצליח מרמה בידו
ובשלוה ישחית רבים ועל שר שרים יעמוד ובאפס יד ישבר
ובמראה הערב והבוקר עד סוף הפרשה [ח.כג-כד] הוא
פירוש. ומן האחת מהם [שם ח.ט] שרוצה לומר האחת מן
הארבעה מלכים שמלכו אחר אלסכנדר יצא קרן אחת צעירה

¹ על העשרה מלכים עד אספסינוס, עיין ש.ברנפלד, מבוא ספרותי־
היסטורי לכתבי הקודש (ברלין, תרפ"ג), ב, רי"ח.
² עיין אבן עזרא על דניאל ח.כג.
³ עיין ברנפלד, שם, רי"ז.

ארבעה מלכים בארבע מקומות [1] והחיה הרביעית רמז
למלכות הרומיים הנקראים היום אדום, נמצא שהשנית היא
רמז למלכות מדי ופרס השולט אחר מפלת בבל.

ומה שאמרת, ועוד כי נאמר בחיה הרביעית, ואחרן יקום
אחריהון והוא ישנא מן קדמייא ותלת מלכין יהשפיל ומלין
לצד עילאה ימלל ולקדישי עליונין יבלא ויסבר להשניא זמנין
ודת [דניאל ז, כד–כה] וזה הענין בעצמו אמר על מלכות
יון והוא, ובאחרית מלכותם כהתם הפושעים יעמוד מלך עז
פנים ומבין חידות ועצם כחו ולא בכחהו ונפלאות ישחית
והצליח ועשה והשחית עצומיו ועם קדושים [שם ח.כג–כד]
וכמו כן אמר במראה האחרונה בסוף מלכות יון, ועמד על כנו
נבזה ולא נתנו עליו הוד מלכות והחזיק מלכות בחלקלקות
[שם יא. כא] ואמר, וישוב ארצו ברכוש גדול ולבבו על ברית
קדש ועשה וזרועים ממנו יעמודו וחללו המקדש המעוז והסירו
התמיד [שם יא. כח] כי ענין, והשחית עצומים ועם קדושים
[שם ח. כד] הוא ענין, ולקדישי עליונין יבלא [שם ז. כה] וכן
הוא ענין, ולבבו על ברית קדש ועשה [שם יא. כח] וכן ענין,
וחללו המקדש המעוז [שם שם], והסירו התמיד הוא ענין,
ויסבור להשניא זמנין ודת [שם ז, כה] והוא ענין, ולבבו על
ברית קדש ועשה, וזה יורה שמלכות יון היתה המלכות הרביעית
ואשר החיה הרביעית מורה עליה, עד כאן לשונך.

דע כי מה שנאמר בחיה הרביעית ומלין לצד עילאה ימלל
אינו הענין בעצמו מה שאמר בנבואה השנית, ובאחרית מלכותם
כהתם הפושעים יעמוד מלך עז פנים ונפלאות ישחית והצליח
ועשה והשחית עצומים ועם קדושים [שם ח.כג] כי מה שאמר
בחיה הרביעית, ומלין לצד עילאה ימלל וכל הענין האמור
שם מדבר המלך המולך על מלכות רומי הבא אחר עשרה

[1] עיין ברש"י על דניאל ז.ו; יוסיפון יד, הוצאת הומינר, סב.

ומפני שהוא גלוי ומפורסם וממקומו תדענו על כן לא אאריך
בו ומפני שהרגשת השיבוש השיבוש הקצרתי הלשון כדי להעלימו·
כי מה שאמר· ותלת עילעין בפומה בין שינה· וכן אמרין לה
קומי אכולי בשר שגיא [דניאל ז· ה] אינה רוצה לומר
שהצלעות הם רמז למנין המלכים שמושלים במקום החיה על
ארצה כי אילו היה כן היו לה קרנים כמספר המלכים או
אגפים כשאר החיות שהם דברים שהם חלק מגופיהם אבל אלו
העילעין שראה שהיה מכלה ומכרסם בין שהם דברים שהם
חוץ מגופה רמז לשעתידה זאת החיה להחריב מלכות בבל
שמלכו עליה שלשה מלכים לבד והם· נבוכדנאצר ואויל
מרודך ובלשאצר או נוכל לומר שלכד שלשה מדינות גדולות [1]
במלכות בבל שהם פאתי המלוכה דסברת ר' אברהם ז''ל ן'
עזרא[2]· ועוד כי אמר במראה השנית· האיל אשר ראית בעל
הקרנים מלכי מדי ופרס [דניאל ח·כ] ואם היו שתי ממלכות
שונות זו מזו למה ראה אותם בצורה אחת ואם הבין זה מפני
שהיו לזאת החיה שני קרנים ושאחת רומז למלכות פרס והשניה
למלכות מדי· כך יש לך לדון בחיות האחרות שהיו להם אגפים
או ראשים או קרנים ואין זה אמת· ולפי כל אלה הראיות
והטעמים תתחייב שאומת מדי ואומת פרס נחשבות למלכות
אחת על כן החיה המורה עליהם היא אחת ונשארו שלשה
חיות· אחת לבבל והיא הראשונה והשלישית ליון שהיו לה
ארבעה אגפים וארבע כנפים הרומזים על ארבע מלכיות
שהם בארבע הרוחות וכן היה שאחר אסכנדר מלכו מעמו

---

[1] עיין סדר עולם רבא, כח·

[2] עיין קדושין עד·א; ע'ג רש''י על דניאל ז· ה ,בשם ''רבותינו''·
חסר באבן עזרא הנדפס אבל נמצא בפרוש הקצר שלו על דניאל שנדפס ב
Miscellany of Hebrew Literature, vol. II (London), edited by A. Loewy.
חלק עברי, ע' 4: ואמר כי תלתא עילעין הן ג ארצות לא כבשן לא זה ולא זה
ושמותן הראן ונציבין ושחרזור·

המֹמלכה בימי אחשורוש של אסתר שמלך אחר כורש במלכות
פרס שהיא העיקר׳ וכן אמר במגלת אסתר׳ עשה משתה לכל
שריו ועבדיו חיל פרס ומדי הפרתמים [אסתר א׳ ג]׳ הקדים
פרס למדי שהוא העיקר׳ נמצאת אתה למד שעילם
המדינה היה ממלכות פרס ועל כן אמר ישעיה׳ עלי עילם
צורי מדי׳ כלומר׳ עלו על בבל׳ מלך עילם שהוא מלך פרס
ומלך מדי ואמר לשון "עלי" על מלך פרס לפי שהעליה
חשובה עליו שהוא היה העיקר ואמר לשון צורי למדי לפי
שהניח המלך כורש מלכות בבל לדריוש חותנו כלומר והתקיף
המושל על בבל הוא דריוש מלך מדי ועל כן אמר דניאל
בספרו׳ ודריוש מדאה קביל מלכותא [דניאל ו׳ א] ולא היה לו
למֹמר אלא ודריוש מדאה מלך על בבל אבל לשון קביל לפי
שאפילו לא היה מן הדין למלוך קבל המלכות מיד מי שנתנו
לו והוא חמיו׳ והראיה הגדולה שכורש מלך פרס לכד בבל
והוא היה העיקר מה שאמר בסוף דברי הימים׳ ויהיו לו ולבניו
לעבדים עד מלוך מלכות פרס ואם דריוש הוא לבדו לכד
בבל היה לו לומר עד מלוך מלכות מדי אלא ודאי שניהם צרו
על בבל ולכדהו׳ והניח כורש מלכות בבל לחתנו[1] כאשר
אמרתי והיה משועבד תחת יד כורש חמיו וכשמת דריוש חזרו
שלשת המלכיות לכורש ועוד יתבאר זה היטב בסוף התשובה
(כאשר) על ענין נבואת זכריה׳

ועוד הראיה שהבאת מן החיה השנית שאמר עליה׳ ותלת
עילעין בפומה בין שינה [דניאל ז׳ ה] ושאלה היו שלשה מלכים
בלי ספק עד כאן לשונך׳ על כרחך אפילו לדבריך אלו הג׳
יהיו למדי ואין זה אמת כי לא מצינו שמלך אחר דריוש כי אם
כורש הפרסי וזה דריוש היה המלך שמלך ראשונה אחר מפלת
בבל על מדי אם כן אנה הם השלשה ואם תדקדק חשבון ימי
הגלות עד הפקידה ואחר כך עד הגאולה תמצא הכל בנכון

[1]   עיין שם׳

יחיד׳ כדי שיהיו שתיהן נחשבות למלכות אחת אבל מצינו
מלכי מדי ופרס בלשון רבים ונזכר כל אחד בפני עצמו שנאמר
ודריוש מדאה קביל מלכותא [דניאל ו׳ א] וכן ניבא ישעיהו׳
הנני מעיר עליהם את מדי [ישעיה יג׳ יז] ואמר׳ עלי עילם צורי
מדי וכו׳ [שם כא׳ ב] ואמר הכתוב על מלכי פרס בשנת שלוש
לכורש מלך פרס [דניאל י׳ א] ושר מלכות פרס [שם י׳ יג] והנה
עוד שלשה מלכים עומדים לפרס [שם יא׳ ב] ועוד שאילו היו
מדי ופרס מלכות אחת היו הכתובים סותרין זה את זה כי אמ׳
בחיה השנית׳ ותלת עילעין בפומה בין שינה [דניאל ז׳ ה] ואלה
היו בלי ספק שלשה מלכים ונמצא בפרס ארבעה מלכים
ולמדי מלך אחד לכל הפחות הרי חמשה עילעין ועוד שנזכרו
לפרס ארבעה מלכים כמו שכתוב בחיה השלישית׳ וארבעה
ראשין לחיותא והנה זה ראיה עוד שמלכות פרס היא השלישית
מאותן ארבע מלכיות אשר החיה השלישית מורה עליהן עד
כאן לשונך׳ ואני תמה מאד על המתפאר בחכמתו היאך השיאו
רעיוניו לומר דברים כאלה ואומר כי מה שאמרו חז״ל׳ כי
החיה השנית רמז למלכות פרס ומדי אמרו אמת׳ כי אעפ״י
שהיו שני מלכים שתיהן נחשבות למלכות אחת ועל זה אמרו
בפתרון חלומו של בלשצר׳ פרס פריסת מלכותך ויהיבת
למדי ופרס [דניאל ה׳ כח] והם שתי מלכיות וכל האחד
חשוב בפני עצמו והיה בלשצר רואה מפלת האחד ואחר כך
שלטנות האחר היה לו לומר פריסת מלכותך ויהיבת למדי כי
הוא מלך בראשונה ואחר כך יגיד לו מפלת מדי ושולטנות פרס
אלא ודאי מלכות אחת היא ואעפ״י שהיו שם שני מלכים דריוש
המדי וכורש הפרסי וכורש היה חתנו של דריוש [1] ואפי׳ הכי
היה כבוש תחתיו ושניהם עלו על בלשצר לא דריוש לבדו׳
וכן העיר הנביא ישעיה ע״ה עלי עילם צורי מדי [ישעיה כא׳
ב] ועילם המדינה ראש מלכות פרס כי היא היתה ראש

---

[1] עיין אבן עזרא על דניאל ו׳ א׳

נבוכדנאצר וכורש וכבשו כל העולם לא נשתייר זכר לעמון
ולא למואב אלא לארצם׳ על כן יתחייב שיהיה פרוש הפסוק
כאשר הקדמתי׳

ועוד בעבור שהאומות לא יהיו נזכרים בשמותם בזמן דניאל
או אחרי זמנו כי הם מבולבלים אלו באלו ואיפשר שיהיה
בבלי וידור במצרים ואיפשר שיהיה מצרי וידור בבבל לקח
שם ארצם ולא שם ארצם בלבד הפרטי אלא הכללי מלך הנגב
ומלך הצפון ובפרט מלך פרס ויהיה מי שיהיה ומארץ שיהיה
וידור באותה הארץ נקרא על שם הארץ׳

ועוד אם היתה כוונת הפסוק על האומה למה אמר׳ וראשית
בני עמון׳ לפי שלשון "ראשית" אינו נופל על האומה שאם
רצונו לומר קצת יאמר וקצת מבני עמון אלא ודאי היה להם
ארץ ידועה בתחילה כשפשטה מלכותם על הארץ ואחר כך
לקחו ארץ אחרת׳ ויהיה פרוש הפסוק ככה זה המלך ימלט
מידו ארץ שהיה מאדום וממואב וראשית ארץ בני עמון׳ר״ל
הארץ שהיה מעמון תחילה׳ על דרך׳ ותהי ראשית ממלכתו
בבל וארך ואכד וכלנה [בראשית י׳]׳ ועוד לפי סברה
שאמרת כי נאמר על אומת אדום ומואב ובני עמון ממש היה
ראוי לאחר ביאת אותו הגואל שאתם מאמינים בו שישארו
אדום ועמון ומואב בזכרם הראשון כאשר יורה הכתוב וזה לא
שמענו ולא ראינו׳ והפך מזה אמר הנביא יחזקאל ע״ה על בני
עמון אמר׳ ונתתיך למורשה למען לא תזכור עוד בני
עמון בגוים [יחזקאל כה׳י]׳ וגם צפניה הנביא אמר׳ לכן כה
אמר חי אני נאום י״י צבאות אלהי ישראל כי מואב כסדום
תהיה ובני עמון כעמורה ממשק חרול ומכרה מלח ושממה עד
עולם שארית עמים יבזום ויתר גוים ינחלום [צפניה ב׳ט]׳ ומה
שאמרת כי חכמים ז״ל לקיים את סברתם חשבו את מדי ופרס
למלכות אתת ואין זה נראה מן הכתובים אלא בהפך׳ וזה שלא
נמצא בכל המקרא מלך מדי ופרס ולא מלך פרס ומדי בלשון

תוכר מאומה אחרת ונבדלת ממנה במדות ובחוקים׳ וכן תמצא
שאמר פורפיריוס במבוא שחיבר להגיון כשרצה לבאר ענין
הסוג׳ אמר׳ כי סוג הוא מה שהוא תחילת הדור או המוליד או
המקום כגון הרקול שנקראו הבאים אחריו וסרים אל חוקיו ואל
מדותיו כת ההרקולית אפי׳ היו זרים ואינם ממשפחתו [1] וכפי
זה הענין בעצמו היונים אדומים וכן נקראו המצרים והכושים
והארמיים והבבליים והפרסים ישמעאלים בעבור שהסכימה
דעתם על דעת מוחמד שהיה מזרע ישמעאל [2]׳ ומה שאמרת
כי המלאך אמר בדניאל כי מיד זאת החיה הד׳ עתידה
מלכות אדום להמלט לזמן הגאולה שנאמר׳ ואלה ימלטו
מידו אדום ומואב וראשית בני עמון [דניאל יא· מא]
ויתחייב מזה שמלכות אדום אינה אותה המלכות הרביעית׳
שמע תשובה· דע כי לא נאמר שהמלאך דבר על אדום וּמואב
ועמון ממש אלא על ארצם וכך הוא פירושו׳ ואלה ימלטו מידו
ארץ שהיה מאדום וארץ שהיה ממואב ומבני עמון [3]׳
והראיה שזכר מואב ועמון עם אדום׳ ומואב ועמון אינם נמצאים
בזה הזמן כי מזמן שמלך סנחריב ובלבל העולם [4] או משמלך

codicis Lipsiensis nunc primum edita.. cum codice Parisiensi Vin-
dobonensique qui vocatur Ketab Hada'at.. Michael Rosenstein
(Vratislaviae 1858).

[5] ספר ההתחלות לאבונצר נדפס בספר האסיף לצבי פיליפּאוומקי, לייפציג
1849· עיין שם, 47 ואילך·

[1] עיין בתרגום הצרפתי של המבוא של פורפיריוס ב Porphyre, Isagoge.
Traduction et notes par J. Tricot. Bibliothèque des textes philosophiques. (Paris 1947), p. 14. ע׳׳ג ·87 ואילך, 45 שם, ע׳׳ג שטיינשניידר,
רמב׳׳ם, באור מלות ההגיון, פרק י·

[2] עיין אבן עזרא על בראשית כז·מ· ע׳׳ג S. Krauss, Die hebräischen
Benennungen der modernen Völker, Jewish Studies in Memory of
George A. Kohut (New York 1935), p. 396.

[3] עיין באבן עזרא על אתר: הדרים במקום שהיו שם אדום ומואב וראשית
בני עמון·

[4] עיין משנה ידים ד·ד·

במה המוניכם תסיתום ובחכמת מה תשרתום ותהי לכם חזות
הכל כדברי הספר החתום ומה תפארת וכבוד יקנה׳ אשר
לבבו פונה׳ מהלכות בכל יום שונה׳ כי יבין ואין מענה׳

הנני משיב על כל שאלותיך אחת לאחת למצוא חשבון׳ כי
חכמים ז״ל אמרו׳ כי מלכות אדום היא המלכות הרביעית
מן הארבעה שהזכיר דניאל וכי לא יבוא משיח עד שתעקר
זאת מלכות אדום מן העולם ותמהת על זה לפי שלא נזכרה
באותם המלכיות מלכות אדום אבל הנזכרות היו כשדים ומדי
ופרס ויון עד כאן לשונך׳

הנני משיב על זה׳ דע בי מה שאמרו חכמים ז״ל הוא האמת
ואומת רומי (ה)נבדלת מאומת יון [1] כאשר אבאר בסוף בנבואת
זכריה ובמראה הד׳ היא הנקראת אדום׳ ואם לא נזכר אדום
בפרשה׳ כי דניאל לא כתב שום שם במראה הרביעית אלא
מלך הנגב ומלך הצפון כאשר אבאר לפנים ולאחר זמן כשמלך
קוסטנטין ועזב אמונת אבותיו והאמין באמונת השלוש על ידי
כומר אדומי או אם היה המלך עצמו אדומי כמו שאמרת אתה
בנוסח כתבך׳ מהזמן ההוא והלאה ותיחס כל האומה לאדום [2]
וכן הוא ראוי להתיחס לפי שכל הקהלה הסכימה דעתה על
דעת זה האיש׳ וכן תמצא שאמר אבנוצר [3] בספר הנקרא דעת
זה האיש [4] וכן תמצא שאמר התחלות הנמצאות [5] כי האומה

---

[1] נגד דעתו של אבן עזרא אשר רואה במלכות השלישית את מלכות יון וגם
את מלכות רומי׳ עיין אבן עזרא על דניאל ב׳׳מ: ומלכות ארם (ז׳א רומי) היא
מלכות יון׳

[2] עיין במאמרי בתלפיות כנ׳׳ל.

[3] זהו הפילוסוף הערבי אלפרבי (870—950)׳ עיין ,M. Steinschneider
Hebräische Übersetzungen (Berlin 1893), pp. 42ff. 290ff.

[4] זהו הספר אלעקל ואל מעקולאת או de intellectu et intellecto
(intelligibili) השם העברי של הספר זה בתרגומו של ידעיה הפניני הוא: ספר
השכל הנרצה הנהוג הידוע כתב הדעת׳ עיין שטיינשניידר, שם, 259׳ עיין
בהוצאה של הטכסט הזה בשם ספר השכל והמושכלות מאת מיכאל רוזנשטיין
Abû-Nassr Alfarabii de intellectu intellectisque commentario ad fidem

הארץ [תהלים קד· לה] וכן כתוב בספר בן גוריון, כי בני עשיו
היו נכנעים וכבושים תחת עול ישראל כי הכה אותם המלך
הורקנוס וימול אותם ויתן עליהם עבודת ירושלים לשמור את
החומות ויתר העם היו למס לבני יהודה[1] ואז התקיים מה
שכתוב, ונתתי את נקמתי באדום ביד עמי ישראל [יחזקאל כה·
יד] וכן כתב ר' דוד קמחי על פסוק זה כי איפשר שהיה בבית
שני שגברה יד ישראל על אדום והחריבום[2].

ואין להקשות מן פסוק, וגלות החל הזה לבני ישראל אשר
כנענים עד צרפת וגלות ירושלים אשר בספרד [עובדיה א· כ]
לומר שצרפת היא פרנסייא וכי ספרד היא אישפנייא כי פרנסייא
וכן אישפנייא בצפונה של ארץ ישראל והים האמצעי מפסיק
ביניהם, אבל צרפת וספרד הנזכרות באותו פסוק הם מארץ
אדום ופלשתים שהיא מנגב לים האמצעי ומנגב לירושלים
שנאמר, והיה לכם פאת נגב ממדבר צין על ידי אדום [במדבר
לד· ג] וכתב רש"י, כי לכך נקראת ארץ אדום תימן לפי שהיא
בדרומה של ארץ ישראל[3]· ומצינו צרפת בארץ פלשתים
וצידון מנגב לים ושם ישב אליהו התשבי כאשר נאמר לו, קום
לך צרפתה אשר בצידון [מ"א יז· ט] ואומר, ויקם וילך
צרפתה, וכן ספרד היא עיר סמוכה לים מארץ אדום ושם מת
אנטיפוס בן הורדוס במאסר על ידי טבריוס קיסר כמו שכתוב
בספר יוסף בן גוריון[4] ובסדר קבלה[5] ולא אאריך באלה
העניינים פן יכבד על המעיינים השמחים ללא דבר· לא לזרות
ולא להבר· כל איש חכם ומבין אל תהיו כסוס כפרד אין הבין

---

[1] עיין יוסיפון, כח, הוצאת הומינר, ירושלים תשט"ז, קח·

[2] דברי הרד"ק בנדפס הם: מזה נראה כי נבואה זו עתידה ואפשר גם כן
שהיתה בבית שני שגברה יד ישראל עליהם והחריבום וזה לא ידענו כי לא
נכתבו דברי בית שני בספר נבואות·

[3] עיין רש"י על ירמיה מט·ז· ע"ג רש"י על עובדיה יט; חבקוק ג·ג: תימן־
עשיו·

[4] יוסיפון סב· הוצאת הומינר, רכ"ו· ע"ג יוסיפוס, מלחמות ב·ט·ו (143)·

[5] בסדר הקבלה הנדפס אין זכר לזה·

אדומים שרוקים ולבנים [זכריה א· ח; ו·א] והוא רמז לשלש
המלכיות מן הארבע מלכיות אשר ארבע המרכבות היו רמז
עליהן על פי דברי החכמים ז"ל [1]· וקודם שיזכיר את המלכות
הרביעית דבר אליו המלאך דברים טובים דברים ניחומים
ואמר· שבתי לירושלים ברחמים ביתי יבנה [זכריה א· טז]
אבל אחר זה הזכיר את המלכות הרביעית במראה של ארבע
הקרנות וכן במרכבות סוסים אדומים ברודים אמוצים· ונראה
מזה כי עד אותו זמן של זכריה הנביא וגמר בנין בית המקדש
שהיה קרוב לתכלית מלכות פרס היו השלש מלכיות מאותן
הד'· ועל כן היו מלכות מדי ומלכות פרס נחשבות לשתי מלכיות
מהן· ומפני זה היתה מלכות יון היא הרביעית ולא מלכות
אדום·

ואין ראוי לומר שהרומיים הם אדום מטעם שמלך עליהם
איש שהיה מארץ אדום על פי דבריהם [2] כמו שאינן קוראים
את ישראל אדומים ולא רומיים אע"פ שמלך עליהם הורודוס
שהיה מאומת אדום או מארץ רומי כי אין הענינים הולכים אחרי
השמות אבל צריך שיהיו השמות הולכים אחרי עצמימות
העניינים· ועוד שכתוב במגלת תענית ביו בסיון [3] גלו אנשי בית
שאן ואנשי בקעתה אף הם היו יתד תקועה לישראל בימי יונים
כלפי הערביים מפני שלא נתחייבו גלות בראשונה ולא הגלם
יהושע בן נון ולא דוד וכשנתחייבו גלות גברה ידן של בית
חשמונאי והגלו אותם משם ואותו היום עשאוהו יום שמחה כשנעקרה
מלכות הרשעה מן העולם שנאמר [עובדיה א· כא] ועלו מושיעים בהר ציון
לשפוט את הר עשו [עובדיה א· כא] ואומר· י"י מלך עולם
ועד אבדו גוים מארצו [תהלים י· טז] ואומר· יתמו חטאים מן

---

[1] עיין ברש"י, מהרי"ק ורד"ק על אתר· ע"ג ילקוט שמעוני, ח"ב, רמז
תרע"ד·

[2] עיין תלפיות, שם, 140·

[3] הנוסחא בדפוס היא: בחמיסר ביה ובשתת עשר ביה· עיין *Hebrew Union*
College Annual, vols. viii-ix (1931-2), pp. 319, 328.

הפושעים יעמוד מלך עז פנים ומבין חידות ועצם כוחו ולא
בכחו ונפלאות ישחית והצליח והשחית עצומים ועם קדושים
[דניאל ח· כג־כד][1] וכמו כן אמר במראה האחרונה לסוף
מלכות יון· ועמד על כנו נבזה ולא נתנו עליו הוד מלכות והחזיק
מלכות בחלקלקות [דניאל יא· כא][2] ואמ' וישוב ארצו
ברכוש גדול ולבבו על ברית קדש ועשה ושב לארצו [שם שם
כח] וזרועים ממנו יעמדו וחללו המקדש המעוז והסירו התמיד
ונתנו השקוץ משומם [שם שם לא][3] כי ענין והשחית עצומים
ועם קדושים הוא ענין ולקדישי עליונין יבלא ‖וכן הוא
ולבבו על ברית קדש ועשה [שם יא· כח]· וזה יורה שמלכות
יון היתה המלכות הרביעית אשר החיה הרביעית מורה עליה[4]·
ועוד כי בסוף ספרו על אותן המלכיות אמר· ובעת ההיא
יעמוד מיכאל השר הגדול העומד על בני עמך [שם יב· א]·
וכשהזכיר אותן במראה השנית אמר שאחרי מלכות יון תהיה
הישועה לישראל כי יעמוד מיכאל השר הגדול ולא הכניס
ביניהן מלכות אחרת וכמו שנאמר· ועתה אשוב להלחם עם שר
מלכות פרס ואני יוצא והנה שר יון בא· אבל אגיד לך את
הרשום בכתב אמת ואין אחד מתחזק עמי על אלה כי אם
מיכאל שרכם [דניאל י·כ־כא]· וזה יורה שמלכות יון היתה
האחרונה שבאותן ארבע מלכיות כי אין אחריה אלא מלכות
ישראל אשר מיכאל מתחזק להקימה· וכן כתב ר' אברהם ן'
עזרא ז"ל שהישנים אשר לא הקיצו משנת האולת יחשבו
שהיהודים עכשיו בגלות אדום ואין הדבר כמו שחשבו אבל
רומי שהגלתנו היא מזרע כתים והיא מלכות יון בעצמה[5]· וכן
יתבאר בנבואת זכריה שבתחילה ראה זכריה שלשה מיני סוסים

[1] עפ"י רש"י המלך עז פנים הוא טיטוס· עפ"י אבן עזרא הוא אנטיוכס·

[2] רש"י מסב את הפסוק הזה על רומי·

[3] גם רש"י וגם אבן עזרא מסבים את הפסוק הזה על רומי·

[4] זאת היא גם דעת ר' חיים גלפפא (מאה י"ד)· עיין מבוא הערה 19·

[5] עיין אבן עזרא על בראשית כז·מ; עיין במאמרי בתלפיות י·א־ב, 142·

ואין זה נראה מן הכתובים אלא בהפך וזה שלא נמצא בכל
המקרא מלך מדי ופרס ולא מלך פרס ומדי בלשון יחיד כדי
שיהיו שתיהן נחשבות למלכות אחת מאותן הארבעה אבל
מצינו מלכי מדי ופרס בלשון רבים ונזכר כל אחד בפני עצמו׳
שנאמר׳ ודריוש מדאה קביל מלכותא [דניאל ו׳ יא] וכן ניבא
ישעיה באמרו׳ הנני מעיר עליהם את מדי [יג׳ יז] ואמר׳ עלי
עילם צורי מדי [כא׳ ב] ואמר׳ העיר י״י את מלכי מדי [ירמיה
נא׳ יא]׳ קדשו עליה גוים את מלכי מדי [ירמיה נא׳ כח]וכתיב
על מלכי פרס׳ בשנת שלש לכורש מלך פרס [דניאל י׳א]׳ ושר
מלכות פרס עומד לנגדי ואני נותרתי שם אצל מלכי פרס
[שם י׳יג] והנה עוד שלשה מלכים עומדים לפרס [שם יא׳ ב]׳
ועוד שאילו היו מדי ופרס מלכות אחת היו הכתובים סותרים
זה את זה כי אמרו בחיה השנית׳ ותלת עלעין בפומה בין שניה
[דניאל ז׳ ה] ואלה היו בלי ספק שלשה מלכים וכך פירש
רש״י [1] ונמצא לפרס ארבעה מלכים [2] ולמדי מלך אחד [3] ולכל
הפחות הרי חמשה עלעין׳ ועוד שנזכרו לפרס ארבעה מלכים
כמו שכתוב בחיה השלישית׳ וארבעה ראשין לחיות [דניאל
ז׳ ו] [4] והנה זו ראיה עוד שמלכות פרס היתה השלישית מאותן
ארבע מלכיות אשר החיה השלישית מורה עליה׳ ועוד כי נאמר
בחיה הרביעית׳ ואחרן יקום אחריהון והוא ישנה מן קדמיא
ותלתא מלכין יהשפל ומלין לצד עילאה ימלל ולקדישי
עליונין יבלא וי[ה]סבר להשניא זמנין ודת [דניאל ז׳ כד-כה]׳
וזה הענין בעצמו אמ׳ על מלכות יון׳ ובאחרית מלכותם כהתם

---

[1] ואני אומר תלת עלעין שלשה מלכים׳

[2] עפ״י התלמוד שלשה מלכים עמדו לפרס עד בנין הבית השני וסדרם היה:
כורש, אחשורוש ודריוש הפרסי׳ עיין מגילה יא־ב: סדר עולם רבא כח, הוצאת
בער ראטנער, 129׳ ע״ג רש״י על דניאל ז׳ ה׳ עיין חלק עברי, ע׳ פז׳
Hebrew Union College Annual, vol. xxi (1948).

[3] זהו דריוש המדאה׳ עיין דניאל ו׳א׳

[4] רש״י כותב שהארבעה ראשין הם ד׳ מושלין שחלק להם אלכסנדר מוקדון
במלכו את המלוכה׳

ישראל ובקנאת ירושלים עיר הקדש אשר היושבת שוממה
ובמאמר אדוני וגאוני החכם ר׳ חיים ישראל שצ״ו נערתי חצני
ואקום להשיב על דבריהם כפי אשר תשיג יד שכלי ומכלל
הדברים אשר אשיב עליהם אשיב על דברי מאישטרו אלפונשו
שהגיעו לידי בשלש אגרות ששאל לאנשים גדולים ממני
ולא רצו לענות אותו דבר׳ והוא ברוב חכמתו בעניין המשיח
החל ובביאתו גמר׳ וזה אשר אמר׃

זאת האגרת הראשונה

אבקש ממך ר׳ אבנר אב שרג׳א שתעיין במה שאמרו חכמי
התלמוד שמלכות אדום היא המלכות הרביעית מן הארבע
שהזכיר דניאל וכי לא יבוא המשיח עד שתעקר זאת מלכות
אדום שהיא הרביעית[1] כי זה תמה גדול׳ לפי שלא נזכרה באותו
המלכות מלכות אדום אבל הנזכרות שם בשמותם הם מלכות
כשדים ומלכות מדי ומלכות פרס ומלכות יון והזכיר כי מיד
זאת האחרונה שהיא הרביעית היתה עתידה מלכות אדום
להמלט לזמן הגאולה שנאמר׳ ואלה ימלטו מידו אדום ומואב
וראשית בני עמון [דניאל יא׳ מא] ויתחייב מזה שהמלכות אדום
אינה אותה הרביעית׳ ועוד כי לקיים את סברתם בכך חשבו
את מדי ופרס למלכות אחת וכי היא השנית מאותן הארבע
וכי מלכות יון היא השלישית מהן כדי שתשאר הרביעית אשר
קראוה מלכות אדום להעקר מן העולם קודם ביאת המשיח׳

---

[1] עיין מכילתא על שמות כ׃טו (הוצאת לויטערבאך ב, 268—269); מדרש
הגדול על בראשית ט׃יא (הוצאת מ׳ מרגליות, רנ׳׳ו, תרע׳׳ח); בראשית רבא
מד׃יז; פח׃ו (הוצאת תיאודור—אלבק, 439, 1084); תנחומא בובר, שמות, 80
ע׳ג מכילתא דרבי שמעון בן יוחאי, שמות כ׃ו (הוצאת האפמאן, 108)׃ כדאי
להזכיר שישנן נוסחאות שונות בנוגע למספר המלכיות: שש, מכילתא דרשב׳׳י,
188; שמונה, מדרש תהלים, ו, הוצאת בובר, 59׃ אבל עפ׳י כל הנוסחאות המלכות
האחרונה היא מלכות אדום שלאחריה יבוא משיח׳ ע׳ג L. Ginzberg, *Legends*
of the Jews, vol. v (Philadelphia 1925) p. 223.

תשובתו של ר' יוסף שלום היא ארוכה פי כמה מן האגרת
של אבנר. ר' יוסף שלום חוזר על טענות אבנר וסותר אותן
אחת אחת בפרטיות רבה. מתוך תשובתו המפורטת אנחנו
עומדים על ציודו המדעי ועל כשרונו הפולמוסי של "הצעיר
מצעירי התלמידים". אנחנו מוצאים אותו בקי בספרות
הפילוסופית והפרשנית של זמנו.

סתירת הזהויים המסורתיים של המלכות הרביעית עם
רומי ושל רומי עם אדום היתה בעיה תיאולוגית יסודית
באידיאולוגיה של ההמרה של אבנר והגנה על זהויים אלה
בעיה עקרונית בחזון הגאולה היהודי.

כתב יד פרמא מס' 533

את בקעי עיר דוד ראיתי כי רבו. ואמרו הבנים לבצר
החומה. וירדפו בחמה מתי שכל וחכמה. וידרכו ידם ולשונם
בכתיבה ובאמירה לסתור מי"י עצה. אשר מקדם לפניו גזורה
לכלה ונחרצה. ולהחפיא דברים אשר לא כן על עמו מי"י. ועל
נחלתו לבם הניאם. וי"י ישיב עליהם את אונם. ונבוני עמי לא
שתו לבם להשיב עליהם. כי עם תועי לבב הם. וכל אמרותיהם
גרועות וחרביהם מועדות. וכאשר רוח י"י באדם ידון. אין
כסות לאבדון. ומן החדר תבוא סופה צנוף יצנפם צנפה.
ולהם יהיה למוקש צנים פחים בדרך עקש. ובראותם אין
מביא להשיב על דבריהם. פערו פיהם לבלי חוק בארץ.
ולשונם תהלך בארץ. לבקש ארחות עקלקלות לפתות בני
תבל ולהדיחם ולהטותם ברוב לקחם. ועל כן אני הצעיר
מצעירי התלמידים יוסף שלום בקנאתי אשר קנאתי לאלהי

היא הקדמתו לתשובות המשובות. אבנר מתחיל את תשובותיו במשפט הבא:
"אמר מאיסטרו אלפונשו יישר כוחך לר' יוסף שלום אתה שלום וביתך שלום
וכל אשר לך שלום כי לא התרפית ביום צרה כבוד לתורה וללחום מלחמתה
ובמקום שאין איש השתדלת להיות איש והשבת לשאלותי תשובות, לשובב
נתיבות (כה"י קיח, א).

ישמעאל הופיעה בעולם במאה השביעית והיה צורך למצוא
מקום עבורה בחזון דניאל[1]· משום כך רואה הראב״ע במלכות
הרביעית של דניאל לא את רומי כ״א את מלכות ישמעאל[2]·
המלכות השלישית היא בעיניו גם יון וגם רומי· שהרי ״אנשי
רומי היו יוונים״[3]· הראב״ע הלך בזה אחרי המפרש הקראי יפת
בן עלי (מאה י)[4]· היו גם חכמים אשר זיהו את המלכות הרביעית
בדניאל עם יון ולא מצאו בדניאל שום רמז למלכות רומי· מאלה
ידוע לנו החכם ר׳ חיים גליפפא (מאה יד)· ר׳ יוסף אלבו·
בעל״ספר העקרים״ כותב שלפי דבריו של גליפפא צריכים
אנו לומר ״והרביעית למלכות היוונים״[5]· כמו כן היו כמה
מחכמי ישראל שלא הסכימו לזהוי של רומי עם אדום· בין
אלה נמנים רב סעדיה גאון והראב״ע[6]·

אבנר התנגד גם לזהוי של צרפת וספרד עם ארצות באירופה,
זהוי שנתקבל ע״י רוב חכמי ישראל בימי הביניים[7]· בהתנגדותו
לזהוי האחרון הוא מפרש פשטן·

מתוך אגרתו עומדים אנו על דרכי מחשבתו של מומר זה
שהן דומים לדרכי המחשבה של חכמי ישראל בדורו· וכבר
כתב עליו יהודה אריה די מודינא: ובכן לא ראיתי בין כולם
מהפך דברי אלהים חיים ומדרשי חז״ל למינו ורצונו בפנימיות
ודעת מזה אשר נראה שהיה פילוסוף הגיוני ותלמודי גדול
מאד״[8]·

[1] עיין אנציקלופדיה מקראית, שם·

[2] עיין אבן עזרא על דניאל ב· מ·

[3] עיין תלפיות שם, 142·

[4] עיין שם·

[5] ספר העקרים ד· מב (הוצאת הוזיק, כרך ד, חלק ב (פילאדלפיה, תש״ו),
418·

[6] עיין תלפיות, שם·

[7] עיין במאמרי Ashkenaz, Sefarad and Zarefat Historia Judaica,
vol. v (1943), 50 ff.

[8] בחינת הקבלה, שם· ע״ג· בער, תרביץ שם, 188, הערה 3· מעניינת ואופיינית

אגרת זאת דנה בעיקר בבעיות אלו: א· בזהוי של ארבע
המלכיות הנרמזות בחזון ארבע המלכיות של דניאל ובחזון
של ארבע הקרנות ומרכבות הסוסים בעלי הגוונים השונים
של זכריה· ב· בזהוי של רומי עם אדום· אבנר נוקט עמדה נגד
זהויים אלה שבהם קשור חזון הגאולה היהודי[1]· עפ״י חזון זה
תתגשם הגאולה בסוף הגלות הרביעית שהיא גלות רומי
(־אדום)· כבר בספרות האפוקריפית זוההתה המלכות הרביעית
עם רומי[2]· גם יוסיפוס כותב שדניאל חזה כי עתידה ירושלים
להיכבש ובית המקדש להיחרב ע״י הרומיים[3]· זיהוי זה חוזר
אחרי כן בספרות התלמודית והמדרשית ונתקבל על ידי רוב
חכמי ישראל בימי הביניים[4]· מתחילה לא התנגדו לזיהוי זה
אפילו חכמי הנוצרים, אולם אחרי כן בא מפנה והכנסיה
הנוצרית קבלה את זהויה של המלכות הרביעית עם יון, וקדם
להם הפילוסוף האלילי פורפיריוס (מאה ג לספירה)[5]· גם הזהוי
של אדום־רומי הוא מתקופה קדומה מאד[6] ועד זמנו של אב
הכנסיה הירונימוס (מאה ד) לא התנגדה לו הכנסיה הנוצרית
אליו ורק אחר כך קמה התנגדות חזקה לזיהוי זה· אף־על־
פי־כן עוד התיאולוג הנוצרי ריימונדוס מארטיני (מאה יג)
מקבל את מסורת היהודים שאדום בתנ״ך לפעמים משמעה־
רומי[7]· אבל רוב חכמי הנוצרים התנגדו לזיהוי זה מפני שידעו
שהוא מהווה חלק של החזון המשיחי היהודי· רוב חכמי
היהודים קבלו את הזהויים המסורתיים אבל לא כולם· מלכות

---

[1] אבנר טיפל בבעיות אלה גם בספרו ״מורה הצדק״· עיין *REJ*, vol. xviii,
(1889), p. 59.

[2] חזון עזרא (עזרא הרביעי) יב· יא (י־יא)·

[3] קדמוניות היהודים י· יא· ז (276)·

[4] עיין למטה עמ׳ 6, הערה 1·

[5] עיין ח·א· גינזברג, אנציקלופדיה מקראית, ב(ירושלים, תשי״ד), 688·

[6] עיין במחקרי בתלפיות ו· א־ב (ניו־יורק, תשי״ג), 129 ואילך·

[7] עיין שם, 150 ואילך·

פוליקאר אשר אבנר כינה בשם ''אגרת החרפות'' ותשובת
אבנר עליה בשם ''תשובות למחרף''[1] שלש אגרות וכוח של
אבנר אשר הוא שלח לאנשים שונים· אנשים אלה לא ענו על
אגרותיו של אבנר· אבל במקומם ענה עליהן אחד בשם ר'
יוסף שלום· אבנר הכניס אל תוך האוסף שלו את התשובות
הארוכות של ר' יוסף שלום וצרף אליהן תשובות עוד יותר
ארוכות בשם ''תשובות למשובות''· האנשים אשר אליהם שלח
אבנר את אגרותיו טרם זוהו· את האגרת הראשונה שלח אבנר
אל חכם בשם ר' אבנר; את האגרת השניה אל ר' משה
חזן·[2] בראש האגרת השלישית לא נזכר שום שם· כמו כן קשה
לזהות את ר' יוסף שלום· האחרון כותב על עצמו ''אני צעיר
מצעירי התלמידים··· ובמאמר אדוני ר' חיים ישראל שצ''ו''
ז'א שר' יוסף שלום כתב את התשובות עפ''י הורואתיו של ר'
חיים ישראל·

כל האוסף של כתבי אבנר ותשובותיהם של ידידים של אבנר
משלעבר עליהם נרכש בשנת שע''א (1611) ע''י יהודה אריה די
מודינא אשר כתב מבוא קצר בן שני עמודים לכה''י·[3] האוסף
נתגלגל אחרי כן לידי הביבליוגראף הנוצרי י·ב· די רוסי
ונמצא כעת בספרית פלטינא בפרמא·

לכבוד יובל השבעים של מורי ורבי פרופיסור אברהם
ניומאן נ''י שלרגליו ישבתי בדרופסי קוליג' ושמעתי לקח מפיו
בתולדות היהודים בספרד אני מדפיס את האגרת הראשונה
של אבנר ותשובת ר' יוסף שלום עליה·

<hr>

[1] עיין י· בער, תרביץ יא (ת''ש), 188 הערה 3, 190 ואילך·

[2] האם זה ר' משה נתן מטאריגה שבבספרדית שמו גם Azan ? הוא היה רב,
סוחר אמיד וגם משורר· י· בער, תולדות היהודים בספרד הנוצרית, מהדורה
שניה, (תל-אביב, תשי''ט), 243: חיים שירמאן, השירה העברית בספרד
ובפרובאנס (ירושלים-תל-אביב, תשי''ז), ב, 541·

[3] המבוא של מודינא נדפס בבחינת הקבלה הוצאת י· ש· ריגייו (גוריציאה,
1852, xiv-xiii.

מתוך "ספר אלפונסו"

מאת יהודה רוזנטאל
מדרשה ללמודי היהדות, שיקגו

מן הכתבים העבריים של אבנר מבורגוס (Maestro Alfonso
da Valladolid 1270–1350)[1], אותו המומר הפורה שתורותיו
האידיאולוגיות חתרו תחת יסודות יהדות ספרד והיו גורם
מכריע להתמוטטות חומותיה, ראו אור בדפוס רק קטעים
מעטים. עד היום הופיעו בדפוס קטעים מן הספרים הבאים:
"מורה הצדק"[2], "מנחת קנאות"[3] ו"תשובות למחרף"[4].
הקטע הנדפס של הספר האחרון הוא מתוך "ספר אלפונסו"
או כ"י פרמא·מס· 533[5]. כ"י זה שנעתק תחת פקוחו של
אבנר מכיל מלבד הספר "תשובת האפיקורס" ליצחק

---

[1] ידועים לנו שמותיהם של עשרה כתבים עבריים של אבנר והם: 1· פרוש
על פרושו של אבן עזרא על עשרת הדברות· 2· מורה הצדק אשר תורגם ע"י
אבנר לספרדית ונשתמר כולו רק בתרגום זה· חלק מן המקור העברי מובא
בספר "יסוד עולם" ליצחק הישראלי, סוף מאמר ד, ח"ב, הוצאת ברלין,
תר"ח, לו·א· 3· אגרת הגזירה· 4· תשובות למחרף· תשובות על ההתקפה נגדו
מאת יצחק פוליקאר· (קטע מן הספר הזה הדפיס י· בער בספר היובל לכבודו
של ג· שלום, ירושלים תשי"ח, קנ"ב ואילך)· 5· מנחת קנאות (עיין על ספר זה י·
בער, תרביץ שנה י"א (ת"ש), 188 ואילך)· 6· סוד הגמול (עיין בער, שם, 190)·
7· מגדל עוז (עיין בער, שם)· 8· תשובות על הספר מלחמות השם ליעקב בן
ראובן (עיין במאמר הביבליוגראפי שלי בארשת, שנה ב (תשי"ך), 139· 9· שלש
אגרות לאנשים שונים· 10· תשובות על התשובות של יוסף שלום· עיין
H. Graetz, *Geschichte der Juden*, vol. VII (Leipzig, n.d.), 445 f.
על תשובות חכמי ישראל על ספרי אבנר, עיין בארשת ב כנ"ל, ע' 147·

[2] עיין הערה 1·

[3] עיין שם·

[4] עיין שם·

[5] עיין בספריו *Mss. Codices hebraici Biblioth. I.B. De-Rossi*, Giovanni
Bernardo de Rossi, II (Parmae 1803), p. 73, no. 533. *Bibliotheca Anti
Christiana* (Parmae 1800), p. 101, no. 142.

בשיטה של ברייתא דנו״ב, שלאמיתו של דבר חולקת עליה׃

אולם בניגוד לגישת בעל הערוך ז״ל נראה שרש״י ז״ל
ביאר ברייתא בנו״א באופן אחר לגמרי. לפי שיטתו אין בין
צדוקים וביתוסים כלום. וזה לשונו (ב׳ סוכה מ״ג ע״ב)
״והכירו בהן ביתוסין. הרגישו תלמידי ביתוס והן צדוקים
ואינם מודים בערבה, שאינה מפורשת מן התורה״. הרי שלפי
רש״י ז״ל הביתוסים הם הם צדוקים. אלא שנעשו ״פרצה״
בפני עצמם כמובא באדר״נ נו״א לעיל. וכן משמע מפירושו
לב׳ חגיגה (י״ז ע״א) ד״ה ״אין כהן גדול״, וזו לשונו: ״שיבינו
הכל שאינו היום יו״ט מפני הצדוקין שהיו אומרים עצרת אחר
השבת״. והנה בכל מקום במשנתנו התייחסה דעה זו לביתוסים
(השווה מ׳ ר״ה פ״ב מ״א [לפי כל כתה״י] מנחות פ״י מ״ג
[ועי׳ בתויו״ט שם] וכן בתוספתא ר״ה פ״א הט״ו עמוד 210
ושם מנחות פ״י הכ״ג ע׳ 528, וכן בב׳ ר״ה כ״ב ע״ב, מנחות
ס״ה ע״א, גליון דמגילת תענית פ״א, הוצ׳ ליכטנשטיין, בספר
השנתי להיברו יונין קוליג׳ של סינסנטי, כרך ה׳ ע׳ 324. ואף
שאין ספק שזו היא ג״כ שיטת הצדוקים, מ״מ היה רש״י ז״ל
בוודאי נזהר מלייחס אותה דווקא להם, אם לא היה מזהה את
הביתוסים עמם. אלא שלשיטתו שתי הקבוצות הם חלקים מכת
אחת. ואולי זו היא ג״כ שיטת ר״ח שהעתיק שם בב׳ ר״ה כ״ב
ע״ב, ״ת״ר מה קלקול קלקלו המינין״ במקום ״מה קלקול
קלקלו הביתוסין״; משמע שלשיטתו אין חילוק בין צדוקים
לביתוסים. נראה שרש״י השתמש רק באדר״נ נו״א וביאר
כל הנאמר על הביתוסים והצדוקים לפי הנאמר שם מפורש,
וכמו שביארנו למעלה׃

שמעי׳ ואבטליון׳ ונתחלף שמו של שמעי׳ ביהושע בן פרחי׳׳
ראשונה׳ אנו מוצאים חילופים שונים בין יודה בן טבאי ויהושע
בן פרחי׳׳ ולא מצינו ככה בין שמעי׳ ויהושע בן פרחי׳׳
שנית׳ כנראה מהרבה מקומות׳ שימשו שמעי׳ ואבטליון כזוג
בהוראה והיו הרבה יותר קרובים זה לזה משאר הזוגות׳ והיה
לו להלל להזכיר את שניהם׳ ואז בוודאי לא היו מתחלפים
שמותיהם בשם יהושע בן פרחי׳׳ ועוד שבימי שמעי׳ ואבטליון
כנראה׳ לא היתה יד חכמי ישראל תקיפה במקדש׳ שהרי
מצינו שהלל מסר הקבלה מהם שפסח דוחה את השבת׳ ולא
היתה הלכה זו ידועה לכהני המקדש; ואם היו נוהגים לפי
שיטתם של שמעי׳ ואבטליון בוודאי לא היתה הבעיה מתעוררת
מעיקרא׳ אלא וודאי שמעי׳ ואבטליון׳ שהיו בני דורו של
הורדוס המלך׳ לא היה להם שום שלטון במקדש׃

לאידך גיסא יהוד׳ בן טבאי הוזמן מאלכסנדריה כאשר
מלכה שלמציון׳ ובוודאי היו הכהנים בני דורו נשמעים לו׃

לפי הדברים האלה׳ משמע שהלל בימי עלומיו הכיר את
יהוד׳ בן טבאי׳ זה אפשרי מאד׳ שהרי הלל האריך ימים הרבה׃
מכל האמור יוצא שמסורת הברייתא באדר״ן נו׳׳א מדוייקת׳
והמסורת באדר״ן נו׳׳ב נשתנתה לפי שיטתו של ר״ע׳ שאחזו
בה הרבה מחכמי א״י׳ והוקבעה כמסורת הבבלי׃

בערוך (ערך ביתוס) מובאת ברייתא זו לפי סגנונה בנו׳׳א׳
אולם כנראה השתמש בעל הערוך ז״ל ג׳׳כ בנו׳׳ב (או במקור
שש אב מנו׳׳ב) ולכן גרס הוא י׳׳ב׳ תלמידים היו לו לאנטיגנוס
איש סוכו ושמם צדוק וביתוס׳׳ וכן בסיפא דברייתא גורס
׳׳ויצאו מהם שנים משפחות רעות׳׳׳ כנראה ע״פ נו׳׳ב׳ וכן
ביאר הרשב״ם ז״ל בב״ב קט״ו ע״ב׳ ד״ה עם בת הבן׃
וכן פירש ג׳׳כ הרמב״ם ז״ל בביאורו למשנת אבות פ״א מ׳׳ג׃
ונראה שהרשב״ם ז״ל ואולי גם הרמב״ם ז״ל סמכו על המובא
בערוך׃ ע״י עובדה זו נתבארה ברייתא זו באדר״ן נו׳׳א

את יהושע בן פרחי׳ ששרפה בגדול (כלומר בבגדי זהב) א״ל
אנו ראינו ששרפה בלבן׳״ ברור שאין הכוונה שיהושע בן פרחי׳
בעצמו שרף את הפרה׳ זה לא יעלה על לב אדם׳ אלא שתחת
נשיאותו ובהדרכתו שימש כה״ג בן זמנו בבגדי זהב באותה
עבודה׳ כמבואר בתוס׳ מנחות כ״א ע״ב ד״ה שהכהנים׳
אולם תמוה מאד איך אפשר שהלל ובני דורו היו כבר בחיים
בזמנו של יהושע בן פרחי׳ ואף אם הלל עצמו האריך ימים
עד ק״כ שנה (כמבואר בסוף ספרי דברים) עדיין כמעט אי
אפשר שנולד לפני מותו של יהושע בן פרחי׳ ובודאי אין לומר
על בני דורו הפשוטים שגם הם ראו את העבודה הנעשית תחת
השגחתו של יהושע בן פרחי׳ אלא ודאי במסורה המקורית
נזכר כאן יהוד׳ בן טבאי׳ אולם מפני שלשיטת דבי ר״ע (שהיא
מר״מ) לא היה יהודה בן טבאי מעולם נשיא׳ הוכרחו לייחס
אותה עובדה ליהושע בן פרחי׳ וזהו שאמרו בספרי במדבר
ריש חוקת (פי׳ קכ״ג׳ ע׳ 151)׳ ״שאלו תלמידיו של ריב״ז
באילו כלים פרה נעשית אמר להם בבגדי זהב אמרו לו והרי
לימדתנו רבינו בבגדי לבן אמר להם אם מה שראו עיני ומה
ששרתו ידי שכחתי ק״ו למה שלמדתי וכו׳ וי״א הלל הזקן היה
אלא שלא היה יכול לומר מה ששרתו ידי״׳״ וכעין זה בתוספתא
פרה פ״ד (ע׳ ה״ז ע׳ 633)׳ ועי׳ בתוספתא ראשונים להגר״ש
ליברמן נ״י פרה שם (ח״ד ע׳ 226) שמוכח מן המו״מ בס״ז
שאמר הלל מה שאמר כשהיה חכם מפורסם׳ ומה שאמרו שלא
היה יכול הלל לומר ששרתו ידי׳ מפני שאירעה העובדה בימי
צעירותו׳ לפני שהיה בידו להורות׳ אמנם בודאי לפי שיטת
הספרי והתוספתא אמר הלל שראה פרה נעשית תחת הוראתו
של יוד׳ בן טבאי׳ ומסורת זו היא לפי השיטה שיהוד׳ בן טבאי
היה נשיא׳ בס״ז שנו יהושע בן פרחי׳ מפני שלפי שיטת השונים
אותה לא היה יהוד׳ בן טבאי נשיא מעולם׳

אין לומר שסיפר הלל על מאורע שאירע בימי רבותיו

מאורעות שנתקבלו על יודה בן טבאי׳ ליהושע בן פרחי׳.

כן ספרו בב׳ סנהדרין ק״ז ע״ב (הענין נשמט בד״ח ע״י הצנזורא׳ אולם עי׳ בדק׳ סופרים שם) שיהושע פן פרחי׳ ברח לאלכסנדריא׳ בוודאי אין מן הנמנע שבין יהושע בן פרחי׳ בין יודה בן טבאי יברחו למצרים׳ מפני חמת רודפיהם׳ אולם כיוון שבב׳ נמסר ששלח ליה שמעון בן שטח ליהושע בן פרחי׳ ״מיני ירושלים עיר הקודש ליכי אלכסנדריה של מצרים בעלי שרוי בתוכך״׳ וכמעט אותו הסגנון מובא בירו׳ בקשר ליודה בן טבאי׳ ברור שבעבודה אחת עסקינן׳ בירו׳ מסופר על יודה בן טבאי׳ ובב׳ על יהושע בן פרחי׳. אם כן נחלקו הבבלי והירו׳ ביחס לעובדה ההיסטורית׳ לפי הבבלי נעשה יוחנן כה״ג צדוקי׳ וברח יחושע בן פרחי׳ בן דורו׳ מפניו; ואף שנזכר שם בב׳ ינאי מלכא׳ נראה שההחליפו את יוחנן כה״ג בינאי מפני הנמסר בב׳ קידושין ס״ו ע״א׳ שרק בזמנו של ינאי נתהוותה המחלוקת בין מלכי החשמונאים וחכמי ישראל׳ לפי הירושלמי מעולם לא נעשה יוחנן צדוקי׳ ולכן לא היה לו ליהושע בן פרחי׳ שום נימוק לברוח למצרים׳

כן מסרו בבבלי את כל האמור באדר״ן על יודה בן טבאי שברח מן השררה׳ ואח״כ כשעלה לה סירב לרדת׳ על יהושע בן פרחי׳ (מנחות ק״ט ע״ב) בירו׳ פסחים פ״ו ה״א׳ ל״ג ע״א׳ מסופר כל זה על יהושע בן קבסי׳.

נראה שנשתנו הגרסאות מפני שלפי שיטת הרבה מרבותינו לא היה יודה בן טבאי נשיא מעולם׳ כמבואר בירו׳ חגיגה פ״ב ה״ב׳ ע״ז ע״ד׳ וכן ייחסו בירו׳ הנ״ל את כל המאורע ליהושע בן קבסיי׳ ולא ליהושע בן פרחי׳ כי לשיטת הירו׳ מעולם לא ברח יהושע לאלכסנדריה׳ אולם לפי הבבלי אפשר לייחס את כל המאורע ליהושע בן פרחי׳.

על פי הדברים הללו יש לבאר׳ כנראה׳ המובא בספרי זוטא יט׳ ג׳ (ע׳ 302) שאמר הלל על פרה אדומה׳ ״אני ראיתי

במלחמה (תוספתא סוטה י״ג ה׳ ע׳ 319; ירו׳ שם פ״ט הי״ד׳
כ״ד ע״ב; ב׳ שם ל״ג ע״א)· גם ריב״ז מזכיר את שם יוחנן
כה״ג בהוקרה (מ׳ ידים פ״ד מ״ו), אף שדברי ריב״ז שם
מכונים כנגד הצדוקים· לא היה מזכיר את יוחנן כה״ג לשבח·
אם לפי שיטתו נתהפך למין ואפיקורוס· א״כ נראה שבדורו
של ריב״ז עדיין גם חכמי ב״ה נטו להוקיר זכרונו של יוחנן
כה״ג·

מעניין שבב׳ (ברכות כ״ט ע״א) סיפרו ששימש יוחנן כה״ג
בכהונה גדולה שמונים שנה ולבסוף נעשה צדוקי· והביאו
את המאורע כהוכחה לדברי הלל· ״אל תאמן בעצמך עד
יום מותך״· אולם בירושלמי שבת פ״א ה״ו (ג׳ ע״ב) הביאו
עובדה אחרת לגמרי· בפירוש אותו הפתגם· ושנו: ״תמן תנינן
אל תאמן בעצמך עד יום מותך· מעשה בחסיד אחד שהיה
יושב ושונה אל תאמן בעצמך עד יום זקנותך· כגון אני· אתת
חדא רוחא ונסיתיה ושרי תהי ביה אמרה ליה לא תצוק רוח
אנא· אזיל ואשתוי לחבריך״· כנראה החליף סתמא דירושלמי
את המובא בב׳ מפני שלפי שיטת הירו׳ מעולם לא נעשה יוחנן
כה״ג צדוקי·

וזהו שנחלקו בירו׳ סוטה פ״ט הי״א (כ״ד ע״א) ביחס לו,
שלפי ר׳ יהושע בן לוי התקנות המיוחסות ליוחנן כה״ג מהן
לגנאי ומהן לשבח·

וכן גרסו גם בב׳ בברייתא (ב׳ קידושין ס״ו ע״א) העתיקה
הדנה על הפירוד בין חכמי ישראל למלכי בית חשמונאי·
ינאי המלך ולא יוחנן כה״ג כמובא על ידי יוסיפוס·

לפי תנא דברייתא בנו״ב אין ספק שיוחנן כה״ג הוא נעשה
צדוקי· כן מייחס אותו תנא את הפירוד בין חכמי ישראל
לצדוקים לדורם של תלמידי תלמידיו של אנטיגנוס· כלומר
לדורם של יהושע בן פרחי׳ ונתאי הארבלי; דורו של יוחנן
כה״ג· בהתאם לשיטה זו ייחסו במקורות שונים הרבה

כמובן גם אדר"ג נו"א הגיע לנו ע"י עורכים מבתי מדרש
של ב"ה, וגם הם הגיהו במקום שראו הכרח לזה, אמנם
הגהותיהם בנו"א מועטות, ולא שינו את הסגנון באופן יסודי;
ויש הבדל עיקרי בין השינויים הללו לשינויים שמקורם בתורת
ר"ע. כך נמצאים בנו"ב שרידים מתורת השמותים, שנמחה
זכרם, או שנשתנו בנו"א, נשתמרה בנו"ב ההלכה שקוראים
את שמע כאשר עולים למיטה, כשיטת ב"ש. אולם בנו"א אין
הדבר ברור כל כך. וזה לשון נו"א: "כיצד אדם בא ממלאכתו
אל יאמר אוכל קימעא ואשתה ואישן קימעא ואח"כ
אקרא קריאת שמע נמצא ישן כל הלילה ואינו קורא; אלא אדם
בא ממלאכתו בערב ילך לבית הכנסת או לבית המדרש
אם רגיל לקרות קורא אם רגיל לשנות שונה ואם לאו קורא
ק"ש ומתפלל וכל העובר על דברי חכמים חייב מיתה".
לא נתברר אם הוא צריך להיות שוכב בשעת ק"ש אם לאו.
אמנם בנו"ב הג' "מכאן אמרו חכמים עלה אדם למיטה יקרא
אם היה ת"ח יקרא את השמע בתחלה ואם רצה לשנות ישנה
וכל העובר על דברי חכמים הרי זה מתחייב בנפשו".

סיכום הדברים שבין נו"א בין נו"ב הגיעו לנו ע"י עורכים
מב"ה, אלא שנו"א עבר כנראה דרך תנאי דבי ר' ישמעאל,
ואולי עיקרו בבית מדרשו של ר' נתן, ולכן נקראת על שמו.
לאידך גיסא נו"ב הגיע לנו ע"י מסורת של דבי ר"ע.

מדברי האדר"ג נו"א אין להחליט בבירור אם נפרדו
החשמונאים מחכמי ישראל בימי יוחנן כהן גדול או בימי
צאצאיו, כלומר ינאי המלך. מפני החשיבות הגדולה שייחסו
לזכרונו של יוחנן כה"ג ומפני חיבתם למלכי בית חשמונאי
נזהרו הרבה חכמים מלזהות אותו כמייסד כת הצדוקים.

לפי שיטתם אירע הפירוד בין החשמונאים ובין חכמי ישראל
בימי ינאי המלך. בעלי שיטה זו לא דחו את המסורת שלפיה
שמע יוחנן כה"ג קול יוצא מבית קדשי הקדשים שנצחו בניו

ר״ע בשאר ברייתות שבחלק זה של נו״ב דאדר״נ׳ כן דוחה
תנא דאדר״נ נו״ב את דברי נו״א ביחס לקישוטי הנידה׳
בהתאם לשיטתו של ר״ע׳ בניגוד לנו״א שלפיו צריכה הנידה
לנוול עצמה כשיטת זקנים הראשונים בתו״כ סוף מצורע
(עי׳ שם׳ וב׳ שבת ס״ד ע״ב)׳ מוסר תנא דנו״ב רק איסור
קישוט׳ ומשמיט האזהרה לנוול עצמה׳ גם אינו מזכיר
האזהרה שבנו״א ״שלא יחבקנה׳ ולא ינשקנה׳ ולא ידבר עמה
דברים בטלים׳״׳ וגם קישוט זה׳ שהיא מוזהרת עליו לפי נו״ב׳
מבואר בצמצום ובדיוק: ״יכול שתתקשט מעילה ותישן אצלו
והיא נידה ת״ל לא תקרב״׳

כן במקום שלפי נו״א סוברים ב״ש שאין שונים אלא למי
שהוא ״חכם ועניו ובן אבות ועשיר״׳ מזכיר בנו״ב רק בני
אבות׳ לפי נו״ב (פרק ו׳ י״׳ ע״א) ניתנה רשות לריב״ז
ללכת ליבנה רק אחר שהבטיח לאספסיינוס שימלוך׳
ונתקיימה הבטחתו׳ כל זה מפני שנראה לתנא זה רחוק שהיה
ריב״ז באמת נחשב בין מצדדי רומי׳ אף שמוסר גם הוא שכתבו
עליו המרגלים שהוא מאוהבי הקיסר׳

לפי שיטת ר״ע׳ שריב״ז ביקש מאספסיינוס להעמיד בית
מדרש ביבנה רק אחר קיום הבטחתו למלכות׳ מובנת
תמיהתו של ר״ע על ריב״ז שלא הפציר בו באספסיינוס
שיסלח לבני ירושלים לגמרי על המרידה (ב׳ גיטין נ״ו ע״ב)׳
אם היה המו״מ קודם קיום ההבטחה׳ איך עלה על דעתו של
ר״ע שהיה ביכלתו של ריב״ז להעיז כל כך ולשאול
מאספסיינוס לעזוב את המלחמה׳

כן כולל תנא דנו״ב (ריש פ׳ כ״ג׳ כ״ד׳ ע״א) בקורת חריפה
נגד צאצאי הלל שהיו מחמירים לעצמם כב״ש ומקילים לכל
ישראל כב״ה (עי׳ ביצה פ״ב מ״ז)׳ כל זה חסר בנו״א׳ אולם
תנא דנו״ב ייחס שיטה זו לשמאי עצמו שאמר ״עשה תורתך
קבע״ והזהיר שלא להחמיר לעצמו ולהקל לכל ישראל׳

לעתיד לבוא היו אומרין כן · הלכו ופירשו להן ויצאו מהם שתי
משפחות צדוקים וביתוסים צדוקים וביתוסים לשם צדוק וביתוסים לשם
ביתוס״·

כאן מוטעם שצדוק וביתוס היו תלמידי אנטיגנוס· והכתות
נקראות על שמותיתם· נשמטה הבבא ״ותלמידיהם
לתלמידיהם״· לפי ברייתא זו לא מסרו התלמידים
לתלמידיהם פירושם של דברי אנטיגנוס ועל ידי כך הטעו
אותם· התלמידים הנבוכים הללו הם עצמם ביקרו את
רבותיהם· ואמרו להם· ״אילו הייתם יודעים וכו׳ ״·ועוד
נשמטה הקבלה של ״עולם אחר״ ותחיית המתים· ונזכרה
רק תחיית המתים· לפי ברייתא זו ״פירשו״ המעוררים·
כלומר שנעשו מינים· ונתרחקו לא מן התורה בלבד· אלא גם
מן הציבור· כאן נקראים הצדוקים והביתוסים לא ״פרצות״
אלא ״משפחות״·

כמו שחלק הראשון של אדר״נ נו״א מקורו בתורתם של
ב״ש· כך כנראה המקביל לו בנו״ב כולל תורתו של ר״ע·
כמובן לא שינו תלמידי ר״ע את סגנון החיבור בכל מקום
שחלקו עליו; אולם בהרבה ברייתות הגיהו לפי שיטתם הם·
כמו שיתבאר להלן·

לפי עורכי חלק זה של אדר״נ נו״ב· שהם מדבי ר״ע· אי
אפשר בשום אופן לקשר את הצדוקים עם צדוק הכהן· לשיטת
ר״ע אמונה בעוה״ב היא אחת מעקרי הדת· והדוחים אותה
אינם בכלל ישראל· ואיך אפשר שיקראו המינים הללו שיצאו
מכלל ישראל· על שם אב הכהונה· אלא ודאי היו לו
לאנטיגנוס שני תלמידים· ונקראו הכתות על שמותיהם·

הדגיש תנא זה עוד שאין להבדיל בין תחיית המתים ועולם
של הנשמות· שניהם אחד· לפי דבריו הצדוקים והביתוסים
דינם כמו שאר אפיקורסים ומינים·

נראה שהשינויים הללו מקבילים לשינויים שהכניסו תלמידי

עוד לפי מסורת האדר״נ כאן׳ אין חגי זכרי׳ ומלאכי נמנים
בין אנשי כנסת הגדולה׳ אלא קדמו לה (א׳ ע״ב)׳ כנראה
לפי שיטת המחברים׳ עזרא׳ המיסד את כנסת הגדולה׳ מאוחר
לזמנם של חגי זכרי׳ ומלאכי; אם כן בימי חיבור מסורת זו
עדין הכירו את העובדה ההסטורית שמלכות פרס שלטה
בא״י כמאתים שנה אחר זמנו של חגי׳ מסדר משנת אבות דחה
מסורת זו׳ והוא גורס ״ונביאים מסרוה לאכנה״ג״׳.

בחלק זה של האדר״נ מודגש עוד שהספרים משלי׳ שיר
השירים׳ וקהלת היו ״גנוזים״׳ שהעתיקו אותם אנשי חזקיהו׳
כלומר שהמתינו ולא רצו לכלול אותם בין כתבי הקודש׳
עד שבאו אנשי כנה״ג׳ ופירשו וקיבלו אותם. חולק אבא שאול
על הנאמר שם סתמא׳ ולפי שיטתו יש לבאר ״העתיקו״ לא
״שהמתינו״׳ אלא שפירשו׳ לפי שיטתו חזקי׳ וסיעתו עצמם
כללו את הספרים בין כתבי הקודש; וזו היא שיטתו של תנא
דברייתא בב׳ ב״ב ט״ו ע״א׳ המסורת שנשתמרה באדר״נ
נו״א מעידה על עתיקותו של חלק זה של הספר׳

הרי לפנינו ספר שנתחבר ע״י השמותים בימים קדמונים׳
לכל המאוחר סמוך לימי החרבן׳ החיבור הקדמון הזה כולל
ברייתא הדנה על התהוות הכתות׳ צדוקים וביתוסים׳ באופן
הסטורי׳ וכוללת תעודה רבת-ערך במקצוע זה׳

לעומת ברייתא זו מובאה באדר״נ נו״ב פ״י׳ י״ג ע״ב׳
ברייתא שניה החולקת על כל האמור למעלה׳ ברור שמקורה
העיקרי של ברייתא דאדר״נ נו״ב הוא הברייתא דנו״א הנ״ל׳
אלא כיון שבדברי אגדה עסקינן לא חדלו רבותינו מלהגיה
בה ולשנותה לפי הצורך׳ כדי להדגיש גנותם של הצדוקים׳

וזה לשון הברייתא לפי אדר״נ נו״ב: ״ב׳ תלמידים היו לו
צדוק וביתוס וכיון ששמעו את הדבר הזה שנו לתלמידיהם׳
ותלמידיהן אמרו דבר מפי רבן ולא אמרו פירושו׳ אמרו להן
אילו הייתם יודעים שתחיית המתים מתן שכרן של צדיקים

באדר״נ נו״ב (עי׳ להלן) ובב׳ גיטין נ״ו ע״א שלפי המסורות
ההן קבל ריב״ז רשות ללכת ליבנה רק אחר ההבטחה
לאספסיינוס.

עוד נמסרה בחיבור זה העובדה של יהוד׳ בן טבאי שרצו
להורידו מגדולתו׳ והוא סירב לרדת׳ אעפ״י שמתחילה סירב
ג״כ לקבל את משרתו (אדר״נ נ״א פ״י׳ כ״ב ע״א)׳ בב׳
מסופר כל זה על יהושע בן פרחי׳ נראה שלשיטת הבבלי
המתנגדים ליהושע בן פרחי׳ היו כהני בית חשמונאי׳ ואמר מה
שאמר כנגד יוחנן כה״ג׳ וכן לפי שיטת הבבלי הוכרח יהושע
בן פרחי׳ לנוס על נפשו לאלכסנדריא של מצרים (ע׳ ב׳
סנהדרין ק״ז ע״ב בדק׳ סוף׳; כל הענין נשמט מד״ח ע״פ
הצנזורא)׳ בניגוד לדברי הבבלי מסופר בירו׳ חגיגה פ״ב ה״ב
(ע״ז ע״ד) וכן שם סנהדרין פ״ו ה״ט (כ״ג ע״ג) שיהוד׳ בן
טבאי נס לאלכסנדריא׳ ועי׳ להלן׳ לפי האדר״נ כאן משמע
שאלה שהורידו את יהוד׳ בן טבאי היו חכמי ישראל עצמם׳
ונראה שהעלו את שמעון בן שטח במקומו׳ כמו שכבר
ביארתי במחברתי ״הפרושים ואכנ׳״הג״׳ ע׳ כ״א׳

עוד נמצאה בחיבור זה מסורת שלפיה המקום העקרי
ללימוד התורה היה עדין בירושלים׳ מסורת זו מובאה בקשר
לממזר שלא היו נותנים לו רשות לדור בעיר המקדש׳ הממזר
מצטער ואומר׳ אוי לי שגרם לי מזלי שלא להיות רשאי ליכנס
לירושלים׳ לולא כן הייתי לומד עם התלמידים בירושלים׳
מוכרח שכל זה נשנה או לפני החורבן או בשנים מיד אחר
החורבן׳ כאשר עדין היה טבעי לעלות לירושלים כמקום
העיקרי ללימוד התורה׳

עוד מסופר בסוף פרק י״ב (כ״ח ע״ב) על הכהן הגדול
שבדק אותו ריב״ז אם יודע הלכות טהרות; וכנראה היה הכהן
ההוא פינחס בן חבתא׳ כל הסיפור נמסר בדיוק׳ ונראה
שנתחבר על ידי בן זמן המאורע׳

בתורה׳ ואת מצותו הפר׳ זה המפר ברית בשר״׳ ונראה שלפי
מסורת הבבלי אין בין צדוקי לאפיקורוס ולא כלום; לכן
לא היה להם להבדיל בין צדוקי ואפיקורוס (וע׳ להלן)׳

הרי שנתקיימה מחלוקת אצל חכמי ב״ה עצמם ביחס
לעמדת כת הצדוקים׳ לפי שיטת תנא דבי ר׳ ישמעאל׳
שהשקפתו נמצאת בספרי במדבר׳ יש הבדל בין צדוקי
לאפיקורוס׳ אולם לשיטת דבי ר״ע׳ שהברייתא בבבלי
נשנית על פיהם׳ צדוקי הוא מין ואפיקורוס׳

כבר הבהרתי במקום אחר¹ שכל חלק זה מאדר״ן נו״א׳
הכולל בעיקרו מו״מ על פרק א׳ דמשנת אבות׳ מקורו בתורת
בית שמאי ונראה שנתחבר בעיקרו קרוב לזמן החורבן׳ עדין
נשתמרו בו ידיעות מדוייקות על המלחמה עם הרומאים׳
שאמרו המורדים ״׳כשם שיצאנו על שנים שלפניו [כלומר
שלפני אספסיינוס] והרגום כך נצא עליו ונהרגהו״׳ מסורת זו
תואמת לגמרי אל הנמסר על ידי יוסיפוס׳ שניצחו המורדים
את שרי הצבא הרומאים הראשונים׳ פלורוס וגאללוס (ע׳
תרגומו של הפרופ׳ יודה גולדין׳ ע׳ 182)׳ כן מבאר כאן שהיו
לאספסיינוס מרגלים בתוך ירושלים הכותבים על חצים
וזורקים ידיעות חוץ לחומה׳ הם הודיעו לאספסיינוס שריב״ז
הוא ״מאוהבי קיסר״׳ לפיכך מיד שבא ריב״ז לפני אספסיינוס
ניתנה לו רשות ללכת ליבנה׳ ולשנות שם׳ ולקבוע בה תפילה׳
המובא באדר״ן אח״כ׳ ״אמר לו רצונך שאומר לפניך דבר
אחד וכו׳ ״׳״ישבו מסופר המו״מ בין ריב״ז ואספסיינוס׳
שהודיעו שיעלה למלוכה׳ כנראה נוסף הוא על עיקר החיבור׳
ואף אם יעלה על לב איש שכל זה מעיקר החיבור עצמו׳
ברור מן הנאמר כאן׳ שכבר נתרצה אספסיינוס לתת לריב״ז
רשות ללכת ליבנה וליסד שם בית מדרש קודם שהבטיח הוא
לאספסיינוס שיעמידו אותו כקיסר׳ זה בניגוד אל הנמסר

---

¹ מבוא שלי למסכתות אבות ואדר״נ׳ ע׳ י״ח ואילך׳

ירושלים", כלומר המתנגדים לינאי למנות את יהוד' בן טבאי
לנשיאות בירושלים. כלומר שלמרות התנגדותו של המלך
ינאי, ישרת יהוד' בן טבאי כנשיא סנהדרין של העיר ירושלים.
אולם הוא ברח מפניהם לאלכסנדריא של מצרים (ירו' חגיגה
פ"ב ה"ב, ע"ז ע"ד). וזהו שסיפר הוא על עצמו (אדר"נ נו"ב
פרק כ', והשווה המקבילה בנו"א פרק י', כ"ב ע"א): "אמר
להם עד שלא נכנסתי לשררה הייתי בורח ממנה, כשנכנסתי
לשררה כל מי שהוא מבקש להוציאני (בתוכה) [מתוכה] אני
יורד עליו בקבקביות". כנראה נימוקו של יהוד' בן טבאי היה
שלא רצה להיכנס למחלוקת זו ולעורר מלחמת אחים.

כל דברי הברייתא מתאימים לגמרי אל העובדות
ההסטוריות, שנמסרו במקומות אחרים בדברי רז"ל וכן ע"י
יוסיפוס. וכן מתאים תיאורו של ביתוס בברייתא זו אל הידוע
מספרי יוסיפוס ומדברי רז"ל במקומות אחרים.

כאמור לפי תנא זה, אין הצדוקים נחשבים בעיקרם
כאפיקורסים ומינים. ונראה שכך היתה גישת הרבה מחכמי
ישראל בימי המקדש. הלא עובדה היא שהשביעו את הכהן
הגדול להקטיר הקטורת לפי שיטת הפרושים; ואף שחשדוהו
שהוא צדוקי הניחו לו לשרת בכהונה גדולה. לאמתו של דבר
עובדה היא שהפרה נעשתה ע"י צדוקי וכן הוקטרה קטורת
על ידי צדוקי ולא פסלו את הצדוקים מלהיות כהנים.

לאידך גיסא שנינו בספרי במדבר פי' קי"ב (ע' 121) "כי
דבר ד' בזה, זה צדוקי; ואת מצותו הפר, זה אפיקורוס".
כמעט אי אפשר לדמות שהאוחזים בשיטה זו יסכימו שכהן
גדול, הנחשד כצדוקי, יכהן במקדש. אלא כנראה דברי
הספרי הם לפי שיטת ב"ה, ודברי האדר"נ כאן הם בשיטת
ב"ש. (ועי' לקמן על השיטות השונות ביחס ליוחנן כה"ג).

בב' הובאה ברייתא זו בנוסח שונה, וזה לשונה "כי דבר ד'
בזה, זה אפיקורוס. ד"א כי דבר ד' בזה, זה המגלה פנים

אלקימוס הכהן הגדול׳ ונראה שיוסי בן יוחנן האריך ימים
אחריו׳ אחרי מותו של יוסי בן יוחנן ,עמדו בראש בתי מדרשיהם
של חכמי ישראל יהושע בן פרחי׳ ונתאי הארבלי׳ אם כן הם
בני דורו של שמעון חשמונאי ובנו יוחנן כה״ג׳ בסוף ימיו של
יוחנן כה״ג אירעה מחלוקת בינו ובין הפרושים כמסופר
בקדמוניות של יוסיפוס (ספר י״ג׳ י׳ה-ז)׳ [1]

בוודאי היו יהוד׳ בן טבאי ושמעון בן שטח עדין צעירים
באותם הימים׳ שהרי לא נכנסו לשררה עד יותר משלשים
שנה אחרי כן׳ כאשר מלכה שלמציון׳ אלמנתו של ינאי המלך׳
הנאמר עליהם שהם קיבלו מיהושע בן פרחי׳ ונתאי הארבלי
משמעו שהיו תלמידיהם בימי עלומיהם׳ כמו שהנאמר על יוחנן
בן זכאי שקבל מהלל ומשמאי׳ משמעו שהיה בין תלמידיו
הצעירים של הלל׳ והאריך ימים כנראה יותר מחמישים שנה
אחר מותו של הלל׳ אף שפרשו (לפי האמור כאן) בית
חשמונאי ״מן התורה״ בזמן ההוא׳ כלומר שהוציאו את חכמי
ישראל מן הסנהדרין הלאומי׳ עדין לא היו חכמי ישראל בשום
סכנה׳ מלחמת אחים בין הפרושים והצדוקים פרצה רק בימיו
של אלכסנדר ינאי׳ והוא רדף אותם כמסופר ע׳ יוסיפוס
(קדמוניות ספר י״ג׳ י׳א ׳ה)׳ באותו פרק זמן בקשו ״בני

---

[1] במו״מ המעניין של ישראל פרידלנדר הי״ד בנידון מאורע זה, ב-
J. Q. R. (שנת 1913–14, ע׳ 443 ואילך) משתדל להוכיח שפועל העובדה
היה ינאי המלך ולא יוחנן כה״ג, עיקר הוכחתו הוא שידוע מדברי יוסיפוס
עצמו שהוקירו הפרושים את יוחנן כה״ג עד יום מותו, וכן ייחסו לו כמעט כח
נבואה, כמו שהובא לעיל׳ אולם ברור שהכוונה בב׳ קידושין ס״ו ע״א היא
על יוחנן כהן גדול, שהרי אלעזר בן פועירה הנזכר שם כמסית את המלך
להתגרות בחכמי ישראל הוא כנראה אותו אלעזר בן פחורה שהיה מן הנוטלים
מעשר בזרוע (עי׳ ירו׳ סוטה פ״ט הי״א, כ״ד ע״א), והוא נתמנה ע״י יוחנן
כה״ג׳ בוודאי יש לקבל השערתו של ר׳׳א אבטוביצר שהיתה בידו של אביי
מסורת שינאי הנזכר בברייתא דלפנינו הוא באמת יוחנן כה״ג (השווה המו״מ
אצל ר׳׳א אבטוביצר, *Parteipolitik d. Hasmonäerzeit*, Vienna 1927, ע׳
200 ואילך)׳

באדר״נ נו״א (פרק ט׳, כ׳ ע״ב) ביחס אל משה׃ כאשר גינו
אותו אהרן ומרים שפרש מאשתו׃ ״לא היו דנין אותו בודאי
אלא בספק, ספק שדעתו גסה עליו ספק שאין דעתו גסה
עליו.״ וכן מובא בב׳ סוכה כ״א ע״א׃ שלא היו מביאין
דלתות כל עיקר [לתינוקות שנתגדלו להיות טהורים כל ימיהם,
כדי שיהיו ראוים למלאות המים לקדש בהם מי חטאת בטהרה
בלי שום פקפוק] ״שמפני שדעתו של תינוק גסה עליו שמא
יוציא ראשו או אחד מאיבריו ויטמא בקבר התהום.״ וכן בירו׳
ריש סנהדרין, ״שהגיס דעתו לדון יחידי, שאין דן יחידי אלא
אחד.״

משמע ש״דעתו גסה״ פירושו כמו שפירש רש״י ז״ל בסוכה
שם ״בטוח בעצמו״, ״כאילו הוא בעליה רחבה.״ אם כן
משמע מדברי התנא שלא היה ביתוס זה, גאותן או שהתני
מתפאר ברוב עשרו, וגם לא אציל ועדין, אלא נשתמש בכלי
כסף וזהב מפני שכך היא מסורת הצדוקים.

מדברי התנא כאן מוכח שאף על פי שנקראו ה״ביתוסים״
ע״ש ביתוס, הוא עצמו הלך בדרך הצדוקים. מהמעובדה
שככהן גדול התנהג ע״פ מדות הצדוקים, מוכח שהפרצה
שלהם נתהוותה קודם זמנו. רק בימיו נתהוותה פרצה שני׳ והיא
נקראת על שמו, מן הדברים הללו עצמם ברור שאין תנא זה
סובר שצדוק וביתוס היו בדור אחד.

מסורת היא ביד פרושים שהן מצערין וכו׳, פתגם
חריף זה בודאי מקורו בדברי פולמוס של הצדוקים נגד
הפרושים. ביתוס רצה להוציא מלבם של פרושים שיש עוה״ב.
לכן התנהג כמו שהתנהגו צדוקים בכללם, ליהנות עד כמה
שאפשר מהעוה״ז; ואף שלא הורגל בכך, הלך בעקבותיהם.

ע״פ הדברים הללו משמע שראשית צמיחת פרצת
הצדוקים היתה בימי תלמידיהם של יהושע בן פרחי׳ ונתאי
הארבלי. ידוע שיוסי בן יועזר מת על קידוש השם בימי

ועיי׳ במבוא למסכתות אבות ואדר״נ׳ ע׳ רי״ב והלאה׃ [1]
עמדו ופירשו מן התורה׃ לא נאמר כאן שנעשו מינים׃
נראה שלפי תנא קדמון זה אין לכנות את בעלי הכתות כמינים,
אלא שנתרחקו מן התורה והחכמיה וחדלו ללמוד אותה, ולקבל
אותה׃

ונפרצו מהם שתי פרצות׃ התנא מכנה את הכתות
כ״פרצות״, כלומר שני זרמים, בסגנון פרץ מים׃

צדוקים וביתוסין, צדוקים על שם צדוק, וביתוסים
על שם ביתוס׃ כיון שלא נזכרו לא צדוק ולא ביתוס
בברייתא זו לעיל׳ מוכרח שצדוק וביתוס הנאמרים כאן הם
אנשים מפורסמים ביותר, שאין צורך לזהותם׃ משמע שצדוק
הנאמר כאן הוא צדוק הכהן שכיהן בסוף ימי דויד ובימי
שלמה, ואליו התייחסו כל הכהנים הגדולים עד זמנו של
הורדוס (חוץ מאלה שהעמיד אנטיוכס הרשע)׃ ביתוס הוא
הכהן הגדול הידוע, שהעמידו הורדוס׃

יש להעיר שלא נאמר כאן ששתי הפרצות נתהוו בבת אחת;
רק שבמשך הזמנים יצאו שתי פרצות׃ האחת נקראה על שם
צדוק והשני׳ על שם ביתוס׃ על שם ביתוס׃ פירוש זה מוכרח כמבואר להלן׃

ביתוס היה משתמש בכלי כסף וכו׳׃ מעיר התנא על
ביתוס זה שלא היה מתחילתו רגיל והגון להשתמש בכלי כסף
וכלי זהב׃ הוא היה מהשכבות הנמוכות בעם, אלא שגידלו
הורדוס׃

לא היתה דעתו גסה עליו׃ הביטוי הזה מובא עוד הפעם

[1] אחר כתבי מה שכתבתי שם, מצאתי שכיוונתי שם במקצת דברי למה
שהעיר הג׳ באר שבע ז״ל, בתוס׳ לריש פרק חלק׃ והוא יסד דבריו על המובא
בס׳ העקרים של ר״י אלבו ז״ל מאמר ד׳ פ׳ ל״א׃ לפי דבריהם המונח ״עולם
הזה״ מתאר בספרות התלמודית כמה ״מדרגות״ של העתיד׃ יש ״עולם הבא״
שהוא עולם הנשמות, מיד אחר המות, כשיטתו של הרמב״ם ז״ל; ויש עולם הבא
שהוא לעתיד לבא אחר תחיית המתים, כשיטת הרמב״ן ז״ל׃ ועוד יש עולם
הבא שמשמעו ימות המשיח, עיי״ש׃

רבותינו לומר דבר זה״· [בכת״י ע הוגה רבותינו במקום
אבותינו· וכן בתו״י; אולם ברור שהג׳ העקרית כאן אבותינו·
כי מה לו למעתיק לכתוב אבותינו· שהוא סגנון מוזר בנידון
זה· במקום רבותינו הרגיל·] ברור שאלה שעמדו לא היו מן
התלמידים· אלא אנשים חוץ מחוגם הם שעמדו ודקדקו אחרי
התלמידים· ואמרו מה ראו אבותינו לומר דבר זה·

כנראה· שהמדקדקים הם צאצאי מחברי הפתגם· כלומר
צאצאי אנטיגנוס והמקורבים לו· ואולי גם יש להניח שבשמעון
הצדיק מדובר כאן· וצאצאיו הם החולקים על תלמידי
אנטיגנוס·

אילו היו יודעין אבותינו וכו׳· כלומר המבקרים הללו
הדגישו שמדברי אנטיגנוס יש לדייק שאין עולם אחר ואין
תחיית המתים· שאילו היו מאמינים בעולם הבא ובתחיית
המתים· לא היו מזהירים אותנו להיות כעבדים המשמשמים
את הרב שלא ע״מ לקבל פרס· האומרים דברים הללו הם
ממשפחות הכהנים הגדולים· וממשפחות המיוחסות הקרובות
להם· כמו שבוודאי היה אנטיגנוס איש סוכו· כבר ידועים דברי
יוסיפוס בנידון זה שהצדוקים היו מן המשפחות היותר נכבדות
בעם·

שיש עולם אחר ויש תחיית המתים; בברייתא זו עדין
ניכר הבדל גמור בין המונחים הללו· ״עולם אחר״ הוא עולם
הנשמות· שנכנסים אליו הצדיקים מיד אחר המות; ״תחיית
המתים״ היא לעתיד לבא· מפני שלפעמים נשתמשו במונח
עולם הבא גם על עולם של תחיית המתים· תקופות השתמשו
בו במקום שלא רצו להכריע בין ההשקפות השונות ואילו כאן
שנו ״עולם אחר״ בניגוד לעולם הזה· הצדוקים התווכחו בשני
הנושאים· והכחישו את עולם הבא של הנשמות וגם תחיית
המתים של הגופים· בזמן מאוחר נתערבבו שתי ההשקפות וגם
הוראות המונחים· ולא היו מבדילים ביניהם כמו במאמר זה·

צדוקים אומרים מסורת הוא ביד [צ״ל בית׳ כבכת״י ע] פרושים
שהן מצערין עצמן בעולם הזה ובעולם הבא אין להם כלום.״
יש להעיר על כך שבברייתא זו לא ניקבו תלמידיו של
אנטיגנוס בשמותיהם· אדרבא׳ לפי פשוטם של דברים יש
להסיק שעל כל פנים לא נקראו אותם ״שני תלמידים״ צדוק
וביתוס׳ ולא נקראו הכתות על שמותיהם· אלמלא היו באמת
צדוק וביתוס תלמידי אנטיגנוס ונקראו הכתות על שמותיהם׳
הרי עיקר חסר מן הספר·

עוד קשה על הביאור הרגיל בברייתא זו׳ הלא ידוע לנו
ממ׳ אבות ומאדר״נ עצמו׳ שגם יוסי בן יועזר וויוסי בן יוחנן
קבלו מאנטיגנוס׳ והיו תלמידיו· אם כן איך שנו בברייתא זו
״אנטיגנוס איש סוכו היו לו שני תלמידים״׳ אם רמזו בזה על
תלמידים אחרים· שאם כן היו לו ד׳ תלמידים· אלא וודאי שני
תלמידים הנזכרים כאן שלא זוהו הם יוסי בן יועזר וויוסי בן
יוחנן עצמם·

עכשיו עלינו לבאר דברי הברייתא׳ לפי הבבות שלה· התנא
מוסר שלאנטיגנוס היו שני תלמידים׳ והם הבאים אחריו׳
והיו שונין בדבריו· וגם שנו דבריו לתלמידיהם· כלומר
ליהושע בן פרחי׳ ונתאי הארבלי· ואותם תלמידים שנו
לתלמידיהם׳ וכנראה הם יהוד׳ בן טבאי ושמעון בן שטח·

עמדו ודקדקו אחריהן· ביאור המילים ודקדקו אחריהן
הוא שביקרו אותם׳ כמו שאנחנו מוצאים תכופות (עי׳ דוגמאות
במילונו של בן יהודה׳ ע׳ דקדק)· אי אפשר לבאר שדקדקו
אחרי דבריהם של רבותיהם׳ כי המונח ״דקדק אחריו״ יש
לו הבנה מסויימת· בכל מקום שמדקדקים אחרי איש הכוונה
שדנים אותו ומבקרים אותו·

וכן אין להניח שהתלמידים דקדקו אחרי רבותיהם׳ שלא
שייך בזה הביטוי עמדו· ולמה אמרו ״מה ראו אבותינו״׳
היה להם לומר ״מה ראיתם לומר דבר זה״׳ או ״מה ראו

מסורת עתיקה על ראשיתם של הצדוקים והביתוסים

מאת אליעזר ארי׳ פינקלשטין
בית המדרש לרבנים באמריקה

מפורסמת הברייתא באבות דר׳ נתן (נו״א פרק ה׳ הוצ׳
שכטר י״ג ע״ב) המתארת התהוותן של כתות הצדוקים
והביתוסים· אולם לא ה'עריכוה החוקרים החדשים כראוי·
ואדרבא· דחו אותה בשתי ידים· הנימוק לגישתם זו הוא·
כנראה· פירוש הברייתא לפי הערוך (ערך ביתוס) הרשב״ם·
והרמב״ם ז״ל· שלפיו נקראו הכתות ע״ש תלמידי אנטיגנוס·
צדוק וביתוס· נסתפקו החוקרים בידיעה זו· וביחוד אם בכלל
היו לו· לאנטיגנוס· תלמידים בשם צדוק וביתוס· להלן יבואר
שמקור פירוש זה הוא בברייתא החולקת על זו שלפנינו· ורש״י
ז״ל פירש ברייתא זו שלפנינו באופן אחר לגמרי· לכן יש
לעמוד עוד הפעם על ביאור הברייתא באדר״נ נו״א· לפי
הנאמר בה׳ ולפי ביאורו של רש״י ז״ל· וזו לשונה: ״אנטיגנוס
איש סוכו היו לו שני תלמידים שהיו שונין בדבריו והיו שונין
לתלמידים ותלמידים לתלמידים עמדו ודקדקו אחריהן ואמרו
מה ראו אבותינו לומר דבר זה אפשר שיעשה פועל
מלאכה כל היום ולא יטול שכרו ערבית· אלא אלו היו
יודעין אבותינו שיש עולם אחר ויש תחיית המתים לא היו
אומרים כך· עמדו ופירשו מן התורה ונפרצו מהם שתי פרצות
צדוקים וביתוסין· צדוקים על שום צדוק ביתוסי [צ״ל
ביתוסים] על שום ביתוס· והיו משתמשין [צ״ל ע״פ כת״י ע
ביתוס היה משתמש] בכלי כסף וכלי זהב כל ימיהם [צ״ל
ע״פ כת״י ע כל ימיו]· שלא [צ״ל ולא· כבכת״י ע] היתה
דעתן [דעתו· כבכת״י ע] גסה עליהם [עליו· בכת״י ע] אלא

לנו מתוכו פרטים שונים מקורות חייו של דלמדיגו; נודע לנו
על בעיות מדעיות שהעסיקו אותו בעת ששימש רופא הקהילה
בפראנקפורט דמיין, חיבור שכתב ועוד חיבור שפרסם בעת
ההיא – ואנו לא ידענו מזה ומזה; נגלו לנו מקצת מגעיו עם
רבים מחכמי דורו שאינם מישראל ועם ברוסציוס בפרט·
פרשת היחסים שביני לבין ברוסציוס, כפי שנגלתה כאן לפנינו,
עשויה לכאורה להוסיף על ההפלאה בדמותו של דלמדיגו,
שחוקרי היסטוריה וספרות התקשו כאחד להבינו· ברוסציוס
היה בנו של חקלאי ובן של בנו של טֶחָן בעיירה פולנית; הוא היה
לא רק פרופיסור באוניברסיטה קאתולית אלא גם כומר
קאתולי· דלמדיגו היה לא רק רופא אלא גם תלמיד-חכם
ורב, בנו של רב ובן בנו של רב בקנדיאה הרחוקה· לכאורה
היתה תהום כרויה ביניהם· אולם שניהם למדו בפאדובה
רפואה וחכמות אחרות; שניהם עשו את המתימטיקה
והאסטרונומיה הכרוכה בה מרכז עיונם, התעמקו במשנתם
של ראשונים ובמשנתם של אחרונים, נתנו דעתם על חידוש-יהם
המהפכניים ותהו על משמעותם; ועם זאת שניהם ראו עצמם
אנוסים שלא לגלות סוף דעתם אלא לצנועים או ברמז בלבד·
בשניהם נגעו רוחות הרנסאנס וההומאניזם, כשמסביבם שמרנות
וקנאות דתית· אין זאת אלא שרוחות אלה הן שקירבו רחוקים
והכשירו את הידידות האינטלקטואלית שנתרקמה בין שני
החכמים·

אבק מתימטי פורח אלא גילויים של החכמה האלוהית
השוכנת בך· הנה ביריד שעבר שלחתי לך מבוא לחיבור
יסודי בתחום המתימטיקה, שהדפסתיו בשפה העברית על
פי הזמנת איזה גביר[1], וביקשתיך מאוד ע״י המוסר לשלוח
לי התרת השאלה של פולידדאל[2] ···[3]; אכן אין לי ספק
שמיד לאחר נסיעתי[4], התרת את השאלה כאשר הבטחת,
ואילו לפי שעה, בוודאי מחמת רשלנותו של אותו יהודי,
לא ניתנה לי ההתרה המבוקשת···[5] כל המידות הטובות
שוכנות בך, אנושיות שכזאת, ענווה, אדיבות, עד כי אין
דומה לך· אם תשלח לי אפוא התרת הבעיה האמורה, אם
תודיעני מה חדש פרסמת או בדעתך לפרסם, אוסיף לעשות
לך שם בין החכמים, כפי שעשיתי עד עתה, אחלק עמך את
חיבורי יהיו אשר יהיו, אקדישם לך ואישבע בשמך· היה
בריא, איש יקר, למען תראה עצמה פולין כולה מהוללת
בשמך· היה בריא, עוד הפעם· עבדך המסור שלמה דל
מדיגו·

כתבתי במהירות לאין שיעור· אם נחוצים לכבודך אילו
ספרים שנדפסו באיטליה או באיזה מקום אחר, הודיעני נא
ואשלחם בלא דיחוי לעת היריד הבא[6]·

עד כאן מכתבו של דלמדיגו, המכתב הפרטי היחידי
שנשתמר ממנו, על כל כל פנים היחידי שלא נועד מלכתחילה
לרבים ושהגיע אלינו בלא ספק ככתבו וכלשונו· נתחוורו

---

[1] גם חיבור זה, אף כי נדפס, לדברי דלמדיגו, לא נודע לנו ממקור אחר·

[2] Polydedal.

[3] כאן כמה מלים אינן ניתנות לקריאה·

[4] מפולין·

[5] כאן חמש שורות שאינן ניתנות לקריאה, מחמת טחיבות·

[6] יש לשער שמכתב זה לא היה האחרון· לפי דברי המהדיר, מוזכר עוד
שמו של דלמדיגו ברשימה של ברוסציוס מיום 7 ביולי 1632 (כת״י הספריה
היאגיללונית 2363)·

מלפתוח בחליפת מכתבים אתך· אולם משעברתי, אחרי
מעגלי גורל שונים, לפראנקפורט, בה אני עוסק בחסד
אלוהים בריפוי חולים בשכר הוגן[1], נתחדשה התלהבותי·
את הזיק ללהבה הזאת ליבה אביר גרמני מסויים, שהוא
מלומד לא פחות מכפי שהוא למוד במלאכת הצבא, ואשר
נהנה בחוליו מעזרתי וטיפולי הרפואיים[2]· בעברו בצנעא
על כתבי, השגיח בשמך בקטלוג של המתמטיקאים
המהוללים אשר הכינותי לדפוס[3] ואמר כי אתה מוכר לו
היטב והחל לרומם את תהילתך בשבחים מופלאים· כמעט
ואין בכוחי להביע מה שמח לבי למשמע דבריו של האיש
הרציני והמכובד הזה· כי כן נודע לי מפיו על בריאותך,
דבר שביקשתיו לדעתו למעלה מכל, וגם על מצב
חקירותיך, מה הם העניינים החשובים שאתה עומד להיזקק
להם, ואילו מעשים מכובדים ומפוארים הנך מתכנן, ובאילו
שעשועים מהוללים בשדה הפילוסופיה כולה הנך מפעיל
את שקידתך, כיצד אתה מכונן יום יום ללא ליאות, ברוח
אמיצה ובגוף של הרקולס, את דרך חייך, ומעפיל לפסגות·

מי יתן לי אבר לעוף ולבוא אליך, למען יפול עלי נוגה
אורו של המשכיל באדם· מכיר אני אנשים, שמעתי, ראיתי,
והרי דבר אחד שאני מיטיב לדעתו יותר מכל, כי הנך אחד
האנשים המלומדים והעמוקים באמת, וכי רעיונותיך אינם

[1] דלמדיגו שימש בפפד״מ רופא הקהילה· לפי ההסכם שנחתם בי׳ אדר
שצ״א לחמש שנים, הורשה ליטול ״שכר טירחה ובטלה״ מן העשירים ״בדרך
השווה״, מן הבינונים – מה שיתנו לו ״אחד המרבה ואחד הממעיט״, ואילו מן
העניים לא הורשה ליטול שכר כל שהוא· ההסכם במלואו פורסם ע״י י·
ליבוביץ ב״הרפואה״, כרך מ״א, עמ׳ 65· בהוספה להסכם הנ״ל משנת שצ״ג
צויין: ״אם ירחיב ה׳ את גבולו בעושר ונכסים, יהיה מחוייב לשאת בעול המסים
כאחד מאיתנו״·
[2] בהסכם משנת שצ״א הותנה גם ״שלא יצא חוץ לעיר בלתי רשות ורצון
גבאי קהל יצ״ו, ואף אם שלח אליו שר או מושל יהיה מי שיהיה״·
[3] לא נודע ממקור אחר·

בעיתך האריתמטית בפני כל חכמי ההגיון והמתימטיקה
האיטלקיים, הצרפתיים, הספרדיים, הגרמנים, האנגליים,
הבלגיים, לכל – הריני אומר – המפורסמים ביותר והנודעים
לתהילה: לוילברורד סנליוס[1], לסיבראנד[2] הנהדר
והמופלא מאמסטרדם, לניקוליי מולר[3], לפיליפ
לאנדסברג[4], לאלברט גירארד[5], ליוסט בירגיוס[6], ליוהאנס
פאולהאבר[7], ליוהאנס קפלר[8], למטיוס[9], לגוליוס[10] ולאלף
אחרים, הגדולים שבחכמים, אולם אף אחד לא הצליח
להתירה· ואכן אין אני מצטער על עוזבי את פולין, שהיתה
לי למולדת שניה (שהרי בכל מקום מספקת לי אומנותי
אמצעים הוגנים למחיה), אלא בגלל זה שניטלה ממני
לחלוטין האפשרות ליהנות מפרי ההתרעות הנעימה ביותר
אתך· במשך כל חמש שנות ישיבתי בבלגיה[11] לא עלתה
בידי לפגוש מישהו מפולין שיכול היה להודיעני על אורח
חייך ומצב בריאותך, עד כדי כך שבאתי לכלל יאוש

---

[1] Willebrord Snellius van Roijen (1581-1626), מתמטיקן ופיסיקאי
הולאנדי·

[2] Sybrand

[3] Nicolai Mulerius 1564-1630) מתימטיקן פלאמי, הורה באוניברסיטה
של גרונינגן.

[4] Filip van Lansberge (1661-1632), הולאנד.

[5] Albert Grand מתימטיקן צרפתי, מת בהולאנד 1633.

[6] Jost [Justus] Byrgius (1552-1632), גרמניה.

[7] Johannes Faulhaber (1530-1635), גרמניה.

[8] Johannes Kepler (1571-1630) מלומד החצר בפראג, אחר כך – עד
1626 – פרופסור בלינץ.

[9] Adriaen Metius (1571-1635), הולאנד.

[10] Jakub Golius (1571-1635), הולאנד.

[11] היינו ארצות־השפלה, כמו שכתוב גם על מצבתו של דלמדיגו בפראג
(ליעבן, גלעד, 33): "גלילות אמסטרדם"· לפי זה עברו חמש שנים מן העת שעזב
דלמדיגו את פולין עד שנשתקע בפראנקפוורט דמיין· מעניין שלא הזכיר כאן
כלל את ישיבתו בהאמבורג־גליקשטאט, שהוזכרה גם במצבתו וגם בהקדמת
ספרו תעלומות חכמה (באזל שפ"ט), אין זאת אלא שישב שם זמן קצר בלבד·

איזה מכתב שלא הגיע לידינו, ועליו עונה ברוסציוס בהמשך
דבריו: "במה שנוגע לאותן השאלות המסובכות למדי
מדיאופאנטס, הרי אעיין בהן בחפץ־לב· יש אצלי בעיה
[מתימטית] לא אחת, אך עודני ממשיך כל הזמן לשומרן בלבי,
כי זכורה לי עצתו של הוראציוס, 'ינוחו בצנעא תשע שנים'·"·
ביתר אריכות – מתוך התעוררות עצמית ואולי אף כאן דרך
תגובה למכתבו של דלמדיגו – נזקק ברוסציוס לשאלה אם
אמנם הקדימו הסינים את היוונים בתגליות גיאומטריות
מסימות· לדעתו לא היו הסינים מסוגלים לכך, כי תרבותם
נחותה היתה משל האחרים· ראיה לדבר – ריבוי הסימנים
בא"ב הסיני, לעומת מיעוטם – עשרים וכמה אותיות בלבד –
בא"ב הלאטיני והעברי· בקשר לכך נגע גם בדברי אריסטו
על חלוקת כל הנמצא בעולם לשנים והבטיח לחזור ולדון
על כך עם דלמדיגו ביתר הרחבה בהזדמנות אחרת·

לבסוף ביקש מדלמדיגו למסור ד"ש לאחד החכמים
שבעירו, לשלוח לו, לברוסציוס, ספרים אחדים במתימטיקה,
ועוד ביקש את אהבתו של דלמדיגו: "אתה, אהבני להבא,
כפי שעשית עד עכשיו!"

ביריד האביב 1631 הוסיף דלמדיגו וכתב אל ברוסציוס,
כפי שיוצא ממכתב מאוחר יותר שלו· מכתב זה, מיום 5 ביוני
1631, המוסיף ומלמדנו לא רק על השתלשלות היחסים שבין שני
החכמים אלא גם על פרשת חייו ומעשיו של דלמדיגו
כשלעצמו, ניתן בזה במלואו[1]:

אישי הנאור והמלומד ביותר,

הצעתי, דוקטור חביב ביותר וגדול הפילוסופים, את

---

[1] מכתבו של דלמדיגו, כמכתבו הנ"ל של ברוסציוס, נכתב לאטינית ופורסם
בתרגום פולני· הנוסח העברי שלהלן הוא אפוא תרגום מן התרגום· ברוסציוס
רשם עליו אימתי ועל ידי מי קיבלו: Przez Jakuba Rzezuchowskiego
zięcia die 16 Iunii 1631.

מיום 24 בנובמבר 1630 אישר ברוסציוס את קבלת הדברים·
דרך ענווה או נימוס ציין שדלמדיגו הפריז בשבחו, מחמת
אהבתו אליו· ברוסציוס לא הסתפק בתכנית; לאחר שעיין בה,
נמשך לבו לראות גם את הספר עצמו ואמנם קיבל אותו "מן
האדון סיבאסטיאן"· סיבאסטיאן היה, כפי שציין ברוסציוס
במקום אחר, מוכר ספרים בקראקא, "איש צעיר ומלומד"[1]·
מהזכרתו בסתם ובשמו הפרטי בלבד, מסתבר שברוסציוס
ידע או הניח כי דלמדיגו הכיר בשעתו את האיש הזה או לפחות
ידע עליו· דרך אגב נמצאנו למדים מכאן דבר נוסף, שניתן
אז למצוא בקראקא ספר עברי אצל מוכר ספרים לא־יהודי·
עד עתה ידענו רק על מוכר ספרים יהודי שעסק במכירת
ספרים לאטיניים לאנשי האוניברסיטה, מוריה ותלמידיה[2]·

ברוסציוס נמנע מלהוציא משפט על הספר, כיוון שלא ידע
עברית[3] ולא עמד על תוכנו אלא על פי ציוריו הרבים· עם
זאת נתרשם כנראה ממראה עיניו, שכן עורר את דלמדיגו
להוציא את הספר גם בלאטינית: "עשה אפוא, יוסף שלי,
למען יפוצו 'מעינות'[4] כשרונך ויתפשטו במהרה־בקרוב לא
רק על פני פלשתינה אלא גם על פני לאטיום לאורכה
ולרוחבה, כי בדרך זו ימצא ספרך המלא וגדוש קהל
מעריצים לא קטן"·

נראה שנוסף לדפים שלח דלמדיגו לברוסציוס אחרי כן
היאגיללונית בקראקא· ואלה דברי ההקדשה: *Ad Praeclarissimum et ad*
miraculum Doctissimum Philosophum, Medicum, Mathematicum, ut
in universum dicam omniscium virum, Dominum Jo[hannem] Bros-
cium, Dominum meum colendissimum.

[1] ברוז׳ק, I, 417.
[2] Bartoszewicz, *op. cit.*, p. 98.
[3] אך בכתבו את קורות חייו של המלומד הפולני סטאניסלאב Grzepski
(1510-1524), שיבחו על ששקד מנעוריו על לימוד הלשונות היסודיות:
לאטינית, יוונית ועברית. ברוז׳ק, I, 195, 197.
[4] רומז לשם הספר: "ספר אילם המשלח מעינים··· ובו שתים עשרה עינות
מים" וכו׳·

נזדמן גם לקראקאו, מקום מושבו של ברוסציוס· אמנם רוב
הזמן הזה לא היה ברוסציוס במקומו· דלמדיגו הגיע לפולין
בשנת 1620 או בסמוך לכך לפני כן[1], ואילו ברוסציוס יצא בה
בשנה לפאדובה ושהה ארבע שנים – יולי 1620 עד יולי 1624 –
מחוץ לביתו[2]· מכאן שנפגשו פנים אל פנים רק לאחר שובו של
ברוסציוס מאיטליה וכמובן לפני יציאתו של דלמדיגו, בסמוך
לשנת 1625 או בראשיתה, מפולין[3]·

הקשרים שנתקשרו בין שני החכמים נפסקו עם יציאתו של
דלמדיגו, ולא נתחדשו אלא כעבור חמש שנים· בשנת 1629
הוציא דלמדיגו לאור, בבית דפוסו של מנשה בן ישראל
באמסטרדם, את "ספר אילם", שעיקרו דיון בבעיות
מתימטיות ואסטרונומיות[4]· בראשית השנה שלאחרייה עבר
לפראנקפורט דמיין[5], ומכאן חידש את הקשר הישן עם
ברוסציוס· יהודים מקראקא היו קשורים בקשרי מסחר עם
פראנקפורט דמיין ונמנו עם באי הירידים הגדולים שנתקיימו
בעיר זו פעמיים בשנה, באביב (ניסן) ובסתיו (תשרי)[6]· בידי
אחד הסוחרים האלה שלח דלמדיגו לברוסציוס שני דפים
מתוך ספרו הנ"ל, בהם תמונתו, תכניתו של הספר בשפה
הלאטינית וכן הקדשה מלאת הערצה לחכם הפולני, כתובה
בעצם כתב ידו, אף היא בשפה הלאטינית[7]· במכתב לדלמדיגו

זו, נוכח מכתבו של דלמדיגו עצמו להלן, לפיו כבר היה בשנת 1625
בארצות השפלה·

[1] באייר ש"ף כבר היה בליטא· ס' אילם, א'·

[2] ברוז'ק, I, 412.

[3] השווה להלן עמ' ז, הע' 11. דיאני (ברוז'ק, II, 32) הניחה משום מה
שהכירו זה את זה בפאדובה·

[4] השווה, I. Heilbronn. *Die mathematischen und naturwissenschaft-
lichen Anschaungen des Josef Salomo Delmedigo dargestellt nach
seinem Sefer Elim (Erlangen 1913).*

[5] H. Graetz, *Geschichte der Juden* X³, 149.

[6] Bartoszewic, *op. cit.*, pp. 88-89.

[7] שני הדפים נשתמרו, בכלל עזבונו של ברוסציוס, בספריית האוניברסיטה

ברוסציוס משתתף, יחד עם שופט היהודים, בחקירה חוזרת
של המעליל, אחר שהלה התוודה וחזר בו מדבריו· מסתבר
כי בשלב זה נעשתה החקירה כדין וכשורה, אף כי העדות
היתה עתה לזכותם של ישראל[1]· והנה יצא לאור לא מזמן
מבחר כתביו של ברוסציוס, דברים שנדפסו בשעתם ודברים
שלא נדפסו, ובכללם גם רשימות מיומנו האישי ומכתבים ממנו
ואליו[2]· לא נרשם ביומנו דבר של כלום בנוגע ליהודים, אף לא
בשנת העלילה; אותה שנה לא רשם בו בכלל שום דבר[3]·
בין המכתבים לעומת זאת מצויים שניים – משנות 1630–1631 –
שהוחלפו בין ברוסציוס לבין חכם יהודי בפראנקפורט דמיין,
הלא הוא יוסף שלמה דלמדיגו[4]·

כפי שיוצא מן המכתבים, הכירו שני החכמים זה את זה
מקודם, מזמן ישיבתו של דלמדיגו בפולין· כידוע שימש דלמדיגו
כמה שנים רופאו של הדוכס כרישטוף ראדזיביל, הפאלאטינוס
של וילנה ושר צבאה של הדוכסות הליטאית, מעוזם ומגינם
של הקאלוויינים והאריאנים· בשירותו – או גם שלא בשירותו –
ביקר דלמדיגו במקומות שונים במדינה הפולנית[5], ובוודאי

---

[1] באלאבאן, שם, עמ' 181.

[2] (להלן ברוז'ק). Jan Brożek. *Wybór pism*, vol. i-ii (Warszawa 1956).
הכרך הראשון נערך בידי ה· באריץ'; האחר בידי .J. Dianni

[3] עיי"ש כרך א' עמ' 422-421. לא נשתמרו רשימותיו משנות 1629-1619 –
(שם, 405).

[4] שם, עמ' 490-493, 485-487 על חליפת המכתבים העירני בטובו מר משה
מורגנשטרן, תל אביב· – עוד משפטים אחדים שיש להם נגיעה ליהודים שם
68, 396.

[5] ס' אילם ח': "…· כי ידעתי שכבודך כרוך תמיד אחרי הדוכוס הגדול
יר"ה"·· נדמה לי כי גם שהותו של דלמדיגו בליוווניה, שהיתה בדרך כלל נעולה
בפני יהודים, קשורה בשירותו, – במסע המלחמה לחבל זה בשנת 1622
בראשותו של כרישטוף ראדזיביל· אמנם לאחרונה ניסה ג· אלטר להוכיח כי
דלמדיגו עשה בליוווניה בשנת 1626 (G. Alter, ''Two renaissance astro-
nomers—David Gans, Joseph Delmedigo.'' *Rozpravy československé
akademie věd*; ročnik 68, 1958, sešit 11, p. 48). אך אין קיום להשערה

כאן לפעמים, בחוג צר של אנשי הרנסנס, גם קולו של יהודי מן
המקורבים למלכות¹, אך לא היה בכך כדי ליצור מגע רוחני
כל־שהוא בין חכמי האוניברסיטה לבין היהודים· המגע שנוצר
מתחילתה בינה לבינם, מגע מוחשי למדי, היה אחר לחלוטין·
בנייניה הראשון של האוניברסיטה הוקם משום־מה ברחוב
היהודים, וככל שגדלה ונתרחבה במשך הזמן, אנוסים היו
תושביו לנטוש בתיהם למענה, בתי מגוריהם ואף בתי תפילה
והקדשות ובית עלמין שלהם²· הסטודנטים היו נטפלים אל
היהודים ופוגעים בהם פגיעות קלות וחמורות, ואף מסים
ונתינות שנשתלמו להם, לסטודנטים, לא מנעו לחלוטין את
פגיעתם הרעה³· ואילו פרופיסורים שונים טרחו בחיבוריהם
המקצועיים ובחיבורים מיוחדים להוקיע את היהודים
ולהעליל עליהם עלילות ישנות וחדשות⁴· אופייני הדבר, כי
גם שמו של ברוסציוס לא הוזכר בתעודות עברה של קראקא
היהודית אלא בקשר לעלילה – גניבת לחם קודשם מבית־
יראה שבעיר (1635)· באחת המערכות של אותה עלילה נמצא

נעוריו (בשנות העשרים) באאוניברסיטה של ציריך .O. Bartel. *Jan*
מנכבדי העדה, Jan Trzeciecki, *Łaski*. Część I, Warszawa 1955, s. 90)
האוואנגלית בקראקא, נשתבח לאחר מותו (1544) שהיה "w żydowskim,
greckim i łacińskim językach biegły." (W. Węgierski, *Kronika zbioru*
העברית ewangelickiego krakowskiego, 1814, s. 7.- על התנועה ללימוד העברית
מחוץ לפולין וקשריה בהומאניזם וברפורמציה השווה ביחוד O. Kluge,
Die hebräische Sprachwissenschaft im Zeitalter des Humanismus,
ZGJD, vol. iii (1931), 81-97, 188-192; vol. iv (1932), 100-129.
¹ לפי ידיעה, שהובאה בשנת 1880 – ללא ציון המקור – בספרו של שויסקי
על הרנסאנס והרפורמציה בפולין, השתתף יהודי בשם Sul, ב־ Sodalitas
literraria vistulana שנתקיימה בקראקא זמן קצר בסוף המאה הט״ו·
השווה באלאבאן HŻK, I, 80-81, על פי שויסקי חוזרת הידיעה ונשנית
בספרי היסטוריה יהודיים ולא יהודיים·
² באלאבאן, שם, עמ' 31-32, 56-58.
³ שם, עמ' 177, 179, 180, 184.
⁴ K. Bartoszewicz, *Antisemityzm w literaturze polskiej XV-XVII
w.*, (Kraków 1914), pp. 123 ff.

בין ברוסציוס לדלמדיגו

מאת ישראל היילפרין
האוניברסיטה העברית

יאן ברוז׳ק המכונה ברוסציוס (1585–1652) נחשב אחד מגדולי
חכמיה של פולין בתקופה שלאחר קופרניקוס· הוא היה תוכן
ומתמטיקן והורה מקצועות אלה באוניברסיטה של קראקא,
הראשונה והגדולה באוניברסיטאות הפולניות· אוניברסיטה
זו, כמו שאר האוניברסיטאות רובן ככולן, נעולה היתה אז
בפני יהודים; צעירים יהודיים שביקשו ללמוד רפואה ומדעים
אחרים אנוסים היו לנדוד לפאדובה שבאיטליה[1]· אמנם
בהשפעת ההומניזם והריפורמציה הוחל גם באוניברסיטה של
קראקא בהוראת הלשון העברית[2]; אף נראה כי זמן־מה נשמע

[1] עיין J. Warchał, "Żydzi polscy na uniwersytecie padewskim."
Kwartalnik poświęcony badaniu przeszłości Żydów w Polsce I (1912),
zeszyt 2, p. 37 etc. ; ש· דובנוב, ״תלמידים יהודים באוניברסיטה שבפאדובה״,
ספר השנה ליהודי אמריקה, תרצ״א, 219–216· מאמרו של דובנוב אינו
למעשה אלא סיכום מאמרו הנ״ל של וארכאל· פרק־סיכום קצר על
האוניברסיטאות והיהודים כלול במאמר של Guido Kisch, "Universitäts-
geschichte und jüdische Familienforschung," *Jüdische Familien-
Forschung*, vol. X (1934), 566 etc. כוונתו להרחיב את הדיון על כך בספרו
על האוניברסיטה של פראג והיהודים (1935) לא נתקיימה·

[2] בשנות השלושים של המאה הט״ו (ואולי גם לפניהן), לאחר שהונהג בה,
בתחילת המאה לימוד היוונית· פרטים אצל מ. באלאבאן *Historja Żydów
w Krakowie* (להלן HŻK), כרך א, עמ׳ 524–526 ועיין גם H. Barycz
בקובץ *Kultura Staropolska*, הוצ׳ האקדמיה הפולנית, קראקא 1932, עמ 284
וכן בספרו *Alma mater jagiellonska* קראקא, 1958, עמ׳ 106· לאחר
זמן הופסקה שם הוראת העברית, מאימת הריפורמציה (K. Lempicki
בקובץ הנ״ל, עמ׳ 219-218)· ואמנם השפעת הרפורמציה על התעוררות
לימוד עברית ניכרת גם מקורות חייהם של אישיה· Walenty Krantwald,
מעסקני הריפורמציה בשליזיה, קנה לו ראשית דעת בלשון העברית בזמן
לימודיו (1516-1517) באוניברסיטה של קראקא (באריץ׳ בספרו הנ״ל, עמ׳
102); לאסקי, מראשי מנהיגיה של הרפורמציה בפולין, למד עברית בימי

תוכן הענינים בחלק העברי

PRINTED IN THE NETHERLANDS BY E. J. BRILL LEIDEN

מחקרים ומסות לכבוד

אברהם א. ניומן

נשיא מכללת דרופסי בפילדלפיה

העורכים

מאיר בן־חורין, דב ויינריב, שניאור זלמן צייטלין

א. י. בריל, ליידן
מטעם מכללת דרופסי בפילדלפיה
תשכ״ב

מחקרים ומסות לכבוד

אברהם א· ניומן